QUINLAN'S
ILLUSTRATED DIRECTORY OF
FILM COMEDY STARS

QUINLAN'S
ILLUSTRATED DIRECTORY OF
FILM COMEDY STARS

DAVID QUINLAN

b

B. T. Batsford Ltd, London

ISBN 0 7134 6149 7

Typeset by World Print Ltd, Hong Kong
and printed in Great Britain by
Butler and Tanner
for the Publishers

B. T. Batsford Ltd
4 Fitzhardinge Street
LONDON W1H 0AH

A CIP catalogue record for this book is available from
the British Library

To my wife
For her encouragement and understanding
(even though she hates Bob Hope and Danny Kaye)

Introduction

This is a biographical rather than a critical account of almost 300 of the most prominent or interesting comedy players in cinema history, from the 'golden' silence of the early 1900s to the rough-tongued, anarchic humour of films on the edge of the 21st century. Although a few personal opinions and assessments have crept in here and there, the primary object of the book is to inform and to entertain.

It began as a straightforward survey of comic stars from Charlie Chaplin to Eddie Murphy but, during the long months of its writing, I became fascinated with the work of other comedy figures less well covered in existing reference books. The attempt to chart the careers of, for example, such silent greats (and later character cameo comedians) as Chester Conklin, Hank Mann, Ford Sterling and Louise Fazenda grew into something of an obsession. And, if not all the facts or films ended up on paper, at least you will, I fancy, find more gathered together here than anywhere else.

I also discovered that there have been more comic leading lights in the movies than you could possibly imagine. Too many of these clowns and character players have been forgotten, and thus I hope to jog some pleasant memories of half-remembered names or faces.

My own earliest recollection of comedy stems, perhaps aptly, from a film called *The Good Humor Man*. Starring Jack Carson, it was written by a genius of comic visuals called Frank Tashlin. To a boy unfamiliar yet with even Chaplin, Keaton or Laurel and Hardy, it was one long laugh from start to finish. I never saw *The Good Humor Man* again, but entreated my parents to seek it out. When my father told me that, while away in the north of England, he had discovered the film playing at a local cinema, and taken a colleague who had literally fallen in the aisle laughing, I knew that someone, somewhere at least, also had a schoolboy sense of the ridiculous.

From that day to this, comedy stars have regularly occupied a large number of places in my lists of favourite movie people. Few chances are missed to renew acquaintance with Laurel and Hardy, the Marx Brothers, W.C. Fields, Bob Hope, Danny Kaye, Will Hay, Steve Martin or the early Woody Allen. Visual gags tend to make me laugh the loudest, but a good wisecrack can bring sudden laughter too, though originality has understandably become harder to seek out as the years have gone by.

Although I have endeavoured to include as many relevant entries as possible, a few minor 'funsters' have been left by the wayside. Britain, for instance, has produced a disproportionately large number of comedy people in relation to its overall film output, so some of the less interesting, especially the character players, have been eliminated to preserve a proper balance between Hollywood and British comedy stars.

A few of those players who may have had notable success on television, radio or on the stage, but have only made the odd film or two, have also been left out. If anyone's favourite is missing from the line-up that follows, please accept my apologies.

A word about the filmographies that follow the sketches of the artists' careers. These pursue the method established in my previous books on stars, directors and character players, in that the date that precedes a film or films should be the copyright date on the credits of the film. I've made a major effort to ensure accuracy in this department, although reliable information on the dates of some films remains hard to come by. An asterisk (*) before the title of a film in the filmography indicates that it is a 'short' of three reels (about 33 minutes) or less. Other symbols should be explained in the text, although a dagger (†) will more often than not indicate that the actor whose film this is directed it as well.

Whether you're 17 or 70, I hope that the pages that follow provide good browsing, information, reading and a few happy memories.

D.Q.
Addington, 1992

Good to the last drop. Goldie Hawn's Judy Benjamin does a belly-flop landing in the cause of laughter during *Private Benjamin*

Acknowledgements

I would like to express my gratitude to Peter Brummell, of Farncombe, Surrey, England, and to Ann V. McKee, of Minneapolis, Minnesota, America, for their generous assistance in discovering numerous additional credits for those stars whose careers began in silent films.

I am also indebted to the staff of the British Film Institute's information, library and stills departments for their help in the compilation of this book, and to Timothy Auger, Pauline Snelson and all at Batsford for their continuing forbearance over deadlines.

Almost all the photographs in this book were originally issued to publicize or promote films or TV material made or distributed by the following companies, to whom I gladly offer acknowledgement: Allied Artists, American-International, Anglo-Amalgamated, Artificial Eye, Associated British-Pathé, ATP, ATV, Avco-Embassy, BIP, Brent-Walker, British and Dominions, British United Artists, Cannon-Classic, Carolco, Cinerama, Columbia, Walt Disney/Buena Vista, Eagle-Lion, Ealing Studios, EMI, Enterprise, Entertainment, Filmakers Associates, First Artists, First Independent, First National, Gainsborough, Gala, Gaumont/Gaumont-British, Goldwyn, Granada TV, Grand National, Hammer, HandMade, Hemdale, Hollywood Pictures, Lippert, London Films, London Weekend TV, Lorimar, Medusa, Metro-Goldwyn-Mayer, Miracle, Monogram, New Line, New World, Orion, Palace Pictures, Paramount, PRC, The Rank Organization, Rediffusion, Republic, RKO/RKO Radio, Hal Roach, Selznick, Touchstone Pictures, 20th Century-Fox, UIP, United Artists, Universal/Universal-International, Vestron, Virgin Films, Warner Brothers and Yorkshire TV.

Snappy chappie. Max Miller strikes a pose of unaccustomed elegance for a studio publicity shot of the 1930s

Tramcar trouble. When he took off his 'Lonesome Luke' moustache and donned a pair of spectacles, Harold Lloyd became a star. Here he demonstrates how not to be a popular passenger

ABBOTT, Bud (top)
(William Abbott) 1895–1974
and
COSTELLO, Lou
(Louis Cristillo) 1906–1959

We begin our journey through screen comedy with a sad story that shows at their worst the difficulties than can beset a long-time comedy partnership. Bud Abbott and Lou Costello were Hollywood's number one box-office attractions in the early 1940s. But personal friction set in soon after film fame, fuelled, according to most biographers, by Costello's selfish, self-opinionated unpredictability. Costello was the short, plump member of the team, apprehensive of approaching trouble and forever the victim of his partner's guile. He was a Hollywood stuntman in the late 1920s before putting on weight, becoming a hit in burlesque, and prising Abbott away from another partner to set up the team in 1931. The long, lean, dapper Abbott was a brilliant, laconic straight man with immaculate timing and the two men, both from New Jersey, got on well together in the early days. Moving from vaudeville to radio in 1938, they confounded the doubters by rocking the nation's ribs with their crosstalk routines, such as 'Who's On First?', in which Abbott would baffle and bewilder his tubby partner through a series of verbal misunderstandings. Their comedy was never subtle, but the sheer speed and vitality of their on-stage work took them to Hollywood in 1940, where their supporting roles in *One Night in the Tropics* confirmed them as star material. A series of makeshift comedies followed, revolving round variations on their vaudeville routines – *eight* films in 1941 and 1942 alone. This period contains their two best films, *Who Done It?*, a murder-mystery with some tasty guest stars, and *Pardon My Sarong*. The latter is perhaps their most original vehicle, casting them as bus drivers who take a bus and a yacht to a tropical island where suave crook Lionel Atwill has his eye on the tribal jewels. By now audiences were used to Lou Costello's manic cries of 'I'm a ba-a-a-d boy!', his quick flight into panic at the first sign of danger and his chickening out of any arguments with Abbott after puffing his cheeks and blustering for a few seconds. He would also be the perplexed loser in the duo's long two-handed conversations. One of the most famous, 'Susquehanna Hat Company', among the most lunatic (or annoying, according to taste), appears as late as 1944 in *In Society*. The settings, like *Society* were, *Sarong* excepted, hardly original. There was an army comedy, a navy comedy, a flying comedy, a ghost comedy, a western comedy and a gangster comedy. It made little difference to their adoring captive audience in the wartime years. They were America's top box-office attractions in 1942, and not far away in 1941, 1943 and 1944 either. By this time, they had acquired a talented dialogue writer, John Grant, with a bottomless fund of routines, and a wily agent, Eddie Sherman, who manoeuvred them a deal with Universal that included them getting 10 per cent of the profits on their early films. But it was money that brought about the first surface cracks in the partnership. After their initial film success, Costello, irked by previous financial disputes with his partner, threatened to break the partnership if he didn't receive 60 per cent of the take. Abbott was forced to concede. Costello's temperament was further soured by the loss

Bud Abbott (left) and Lou Costello find their dreams of becoming successful detectives go up in smoke in *Abbott and Costello Meet the Invisible Man*

of his infant son, who drowned in the family pool. On screen, the comics' success continued unabated through the war years. From 1945, their films began to attract fewer people and, in the same year, a more serious rift occurred, initially over a minor matter, that led to a split in the partnership lasting several months. Films featuring them less as a team were not a success, and they had returned to more conventional film farces by 1947. At this stage, their career enjoyed its last resurgence with such hits as *The Wistful Widow of Wagon Gap* and *Abbott and Costello Meet Frankenstein*. From 1949, however, the quality of their scripts declined and their studio seemed to lose interest in a team apparently unable to keep up with the times. Their last few films were released as second-features and the team split for good in 1957, a year after their final movie together, *Dance With Me, Henry*. An attempt to revive the partnership a year later apparently foundered on Costello's unwillingness to offer his ex-partner a proper salary, but in any case the little man's heart was failing and, soon after his one solo venture, *The Thirty-Foot Bride of Candy Rock*, he died from a heart attack in March 1959. Like Costello, Abbott did briefly try a comeback, but neither was funny without the other to play against. Abbott, a lifetime epileptic, died, after years of ill-health, from the effects of two strokes and a cancerous ulcer, in April 1974. He was 78 and had lived 25 years longer than his partner. It seems doubtful if either of them realised how much each owed to the other in terms of their success. Certainly, Bud Abbott never got to grips with his temperamental partner as a person. He once told an interviewer: 'You know, I never really understood Lou at all.'

1940: * *Caribbean Holiday. One Night in the Tropics. Buck Privates (GB: Rookies). In the Navy.* 1941: *Hold That Ghost. Keep 'Em Flying.* * *Meet the Stars No. 4.* 1942: *Ride 'Em Cowboy. 'Rio Rita. Pardon My Sarong. Who Done It?* 1943: *It Ain't Hay (GB: Money for Jam). Hit the Ice.* 1944: *Lost in a Harem. In Society.* 1945: *Here Come the Co-Eds. The Naughty Nineties. Bud Abbott and Lou Costello in Hollywood.* 1946: *Little Giant (GB: On the Carpet). The Time of Their Lives.* 1947: *Buck Privates Come Home (GB: Rookies Come Home). The Wistful Widow of Wagon Gap (GB: The Wistful Widow).* 1948: *The Noose Hangs High. Abbott and Costello Meet Frankenstein (GB: Abbott and Costello Meet the Ghosts).* 1949: *Mexican Hayride. Africa Screams. Abbott and Costello Meet the Killer, Boris Karloff.* 1950: *Abbott and Costello in the Foreign Legion.* 1951: *Abbott and Costello Meet the Invisible Man. Comin' Round the Mountain.* 1952: *Jack and the Beanstalk. Lost in Alaska.* 1953: *Abbott and Costello Meet Captain Kidd. Abbott and Costello Go to Mars. Abbott and Costello Meet Dr Jekyll and Mr Hyde.* 1954: * *Screen Snapshots No. 225.* 1955: *Abbott and Costello Meet the Keystone*

Kops. *Abbott and Costello Meet the Mummy.* 1956: *Dance with Me, Henry.*
Costello alone. 1959: *The Thirty-Foot Bride of Candy Rock.*
Abbott alone. 1946: *The Ghost Steps Out.* 1950: *The Real McCoy.*

ADAMS, Edie
(Elizabeth Edith Enke) 1927–
A bright, round-faced, friendly-looking American singer-comedienne, who would surely have played a lot more wisecracking friends of the heroine if she had been born a decade earlier. A star graduate of music and drama schools, she had also won talent and beauty contests before breaking into television. Her vivacity, good looks and sense of humour soon boosted her to stardom, when she appeared (initially as a vocalist, billed Edith Adams) on several comedy/variety shows with moustachioed comedian Ernie Kovacs (qv), beginning in 1951 with *Kovacs on the Corner*. Between *Kovacs Unlimited* (1952–53) and *The Ernie Kovacs Show* (1955–56) Adams also made herself a name on Broadway as Rosalind Russell's glamorous sister Eileen in the musical *Wonderful Town*. Later she returned to the stage to create the role of Daisy Mae in *Li'l Abner*. She married Kovacs, whose first marriage had ended five years earlier, in 1954 but, after a meteoric and extravagant career, he was killed in a car crash in 1962. Allegedly, it took Edie five years to pay off the high-living comedian's gambling debts. In the mid 1960s she had her own TV show and by this time she had also made a belated film debut. But the movies never really made the most of her raucous, rasping, throwaway style of humour. She remained a TV and nightclub attraction, winning more fans for her on-target impressions of other stars. Later she married a bandleader, Pete Condoli (who was once wed to Betty Hutton). The cinema too often emphasised Edie Adams's sex appeal at the expense of her comic talents (largely because it saw her as a supporting actress rather than a star), and she has only sporadically appeared in the medium since 1960. But she continues to turn up in TV movies and series, in eye-catching guest roles.

1958: * *Showdown at Ulcer Gulch.* 1960: *The Apartment.* 1961: *Lover Come Back.* 1963: *Call Me Bwana. It's a Mad, Mad, Mad, Mad World. Under the Yum Yum Tree. Love with the Proper Stranger.* 1964: *The Best Man.* 1966: *Made in Paris. The Oscar.* 1967: *The Honey Pot.* 1972: *Evil Roy Slade (TV).* 1975: *The Return of Joe Forrester (TV).* 1978: *Up in Smoke. Racquet.* 1979: *Fast Friends (TV). Superdome (TV).* 1980: *The Happy Hooker Goes to Hollywood. Box Office. A Cry for Love (TV). Portrait of an Escort (TV). Make Me an Offer (TV).* 1983: *Shooting Stars (TV).* 1984: *Ernie Kovacs – Between the Laughter (TV).* 1986: *Neat and Tidy (TV).* 1989: *Jake Spanner – Private Eye (TV).*

ADRIAN, Iris
(I. A. Hostetter) 1912–
Plump-cheeked, fluffily pretty little American character actress who started her show business career in a chorus line at 14 years old. Movie cameras saw her mostly as a cheap blonde who had a ready remark for any come-on by the hero. After three years dancing in shows in her native California, Adrian graduated to the Ziegfeld Follies. There were a couple of small film roles around this time, but the major part of her movie career began after a cross-country dancing tour with a company headed by George Raft, then as well known for his dancing as his gangster films. Raft brought Adrian with him to Hollywood for a role in *Rhumba*, and she quickly settled in as a film regular. Playing hard-bitten shopgirls and dancers, she became the mistress of the sharp retort. Her characters, when they weren't just called Maisie or Daisy, sported such names as Gold Dust Gertie and Choo Choo Devine. She was still playing gangsters' girls as late as 1953 in *The City is Dark*, where her paramour turned out to be Charles Bronson. Iris Adrian worked with most of the great comedians in turn (her favourite was Jack Benny, qv) and rounded off her career with a few wisecracking, plumpish matrons for the Disney studio, where she finished her movie days. Iris Adrian matched words with the best – and was more than a match for most.

Bud Abbott hands out the spiel. Lou Costello looks prepared to be handed a licking. But he has unseen help in *Abbott and Costello Meet the Invisible Man*

Gracie swivels while George burns...his seat. Fred stays as debonair as ever George Burns, Gracie Allen and Fred Astaire in *A Damsel in Distress*

Reach for the girl... Woody Allen and Olga Georges-Picot seem to be playing to the camera: it's a matter of *Love and Death*

Turning the cinema into an aisle of joy. Diane Keaton and Woody Allen are falling in love again in Allen's black-and-white classic, *Manhattan*

1928: * Chasing Husbands. 1930: Paramount on Parade. Let's Go Native. * The Freshman's Goat. 1932: * If I'm Elected. * College Cuties. 1934: * Raring to Go/* Tearing to Go. 1935: Rhumba/Rumba. Stolen Harmony. The Gay Deception. Murder at Glen Athol (GB: The Criminal Within). Grand Exit. 1936: A Message to Garcia. One Rainy Afternoon. Lady Luck. Our Relations. Stage Struck. Mister Cinderella. Gold Diggers of 1937. 1937: * Man to Man. 1939: One Third of a Nation. Back Door to Heaven. 1940: Meet the Wildcat. Go West/Marx Brothers Go West. 1941: Horror Island. The Lady from Cheyenne. Meet the Champ. Too Many Blondes. Road to Zanzibar. Wild Geese Calling. New York Town. Sing Another Chorus. Hard Guy. Swing It Soldier (GB: Radio Revels of 1942). I Killed That Man. 1942: Roxie Hart. To the Shores of Tripoli. Rings on Her Fingers. Juke Box Jenny. Fingers at the Window. Broadway. Moonlight Masquerade. Orchestra Wives. Highways by Night. The McGuerins from Brooklyn. Calaboose. Thunder Birds. 1943: Ladies' Day. The Crystal Ball. He's My Guy. His Butler's Sister. Taxi, Mister. Lady of Burlesque (GB: Striptease Lady). Action in the North Atlantic. Hers to Hold. Submarine Base. Spotlight Scandals. Career Girl. 1944: Million Dollar Kid. Shake Hands with Murder Once Upon a Time. Swing Hostess. The Singing Sheriff. The Woman in the Window. Bluebeard. I'm from Arkansas. Alaska. 1945: It's a Pleasure. Road to Alcatraz. Steppin' in Society. Boston Blackie's Rendezvous (GB: Blackie's Rendezvous). The Stork Club. The Trouble with Women (released 1947). 1946: The Bamboo Blonde. Cross My Heart. Vacation in Reno. 1947: Fall Guy. Love and Learn. Philo Vance Returns. The Wistful Widow of Wagon Gap (GB: The Wistful Widow). 1948: * How to Clean House. Out of the Storm. Smart Woman. The Paleface. 1949: Miss Mink of 1949. Flamingo Road. My Dream is Yours. The Lovable Cheat. † Two Knights in Brooklyn/Two Mugs from Brooklyn. Mighty Joe Young. Sky Dragon. Trail of the Yukon. Tough Assignment. I Married a Communist (GB: The Woman on Pier 13). Always Leave Them Laughing. There's a Girl in My Heart. 1950: Blondie's Hero. Joe Palooka in Humphrey Takes a Chance (GB: Humphrey Takes a Chance). Once a Thief. Sideshow. Hi-Jacked. * Foy Meets Girl. 1951: Stop That Cab. GI Jane. Varieties on Parade. The Racket. My Favorite Spy. 1952: Carson City. The Big Trees. * Heebie Gee Gees. 1953: Take the High Ground. Crime Wave (GB: The City Is Dark). The Misadventures of Buster Keaton (TV. GB: cinemas). 1954: Highway Dragnet. The Fast and the Furious. * So You Want to Know Your Relatives. 1956: * So You Want to be Pretty. 1957: The Helen Morgan Story (GB: Both Ends of the Candle). Carnival Rock. 1958: The Buccaneer. 1961: Blue Hawaii. The Errand Boy. 1964: Fate is the Hunter. That Darn Cat! 1967: The Odd Couple. 1968: The Love Bug. 1970: The Barefoot Executive. 1972: Scandalous John. 1974: The Apple Dumpling Gang. 1976: Freaky Friday. The Shaggy DA. No Deposit, No Return. 1978: Getting Married (TV). 1980: Herbie Goes Bananas. Murder Can Hurt You! (TV). 1981: Paternity.

† Alternative GB titles for combined version of The McGuerins from Brooklyn/Taxi, Mister.

ALLEN, Chesney
See FLANAGAN, Bud and ALLEN, Chesney

ALLEN, Fred
(John Sullivan) 1894–1956
A tall, lugubrious, dark-haired, baggy-eyed American stand-up comedian who proved immensely popular on radio, then used his browbeaten features to launch a screen image that never quite took off. Allen created a character of a born pessimist beset by life's misfortunes – an image later elaborated on by Britain's Tony Hancock (qv) – but his vaudeville and radio appearances also allowed room for his special brand of dry humour. Most of his dialogue throughout his career was written by Allen himself. It took the Massachusetts-born comic quite a while to establish himself – and to arrive at his stage name. At various stages of his early career he called himself Paul Huckle, Freddie James and Fred St James before settling on Fred Allen in 1927. On stage his patter was sometimes interrupted by a mournful display of failed legerdemain – he was for a while billed as 'the world's worst juggler'. In 1927 he was part of a compering team called Allen and York; at other times his wife, Portland Hoffa, was his straight girl. She was still feeding him the lines when he began what was to be a magnificent radio career. Soon, he and Jack Benny (qv) were the two top comics on radio, locked in a legendary 'feud', which was entirely the making of their producers and, like most ventures of its kind, marvellously funny. He made his major film debut in Thanks a Million, as the fast-talking, fast-thinking manager of a group of travelling entertainers. In 1940 the Allen-Benny feud was carefully spilled over into a not-too-successful feature film, Love Thy Neighbor. Better was It's in the Bag!, a variation on the old chestnut The 12 Chairs, with Fred as a flea-circus promoter who inherits a hidden fortune. Again, his scenes with Benny (this time a guest star) were the funniest, but again it didn't lead to more cinema work. Just too much of a straight man in films, Allen often left many of the laughs to zany cameos from others. Not that he minded too much, continuing throughout his career to do his best work in radio, where he had uninterrupted success with his peculiarly cynical looks at life, freely loaded with puns and comic metaphors. He had just begun to make inroads into television as a master of ceremonies and droll member of panel games, when a heart attack killed him at 61.

1929: * Fred Allen's Prize Playettes. 1930: * The Still Alarm. 1931: * The Installment Collection. 1935: Thanks a Million. 1938: Sally, Irene and Mary. 1940: Love Thy Neighbor. 1944: It's in the Bag! (GB: The Fifth Chair). 1952: We're Not Married. O. Henry's Full House (GB: Full House). 1956: * Fabulous Hollywood.

ALLEN, Gracie 1902–1964
Although not unattractive, Gracie Allen was, like many great screen comediennes, certainly not conventionally pretty. Her prominent chin puts one in mind of Britain's Australian-born Cicely Courtneidge (qv) to whom she bears a faint resemblance. In the manner of raising laughter, however, the two women were very different. Born in San Francisco, Gracie was the daughter of vaudevillian parents, and it wasn't long before she and her sisters had worked up an act of their own. But they were still seeking the breakthrough to the big time when a friend introduced Gracie to budding comedian George Burns (qv), six years her senior. They formed a crosstalk act with Gracie as the straight girl, but when George saw she was getting as many laughs as he was they switched roles and the act took off with the public at once. Gracie's secret lay in her quickly timed and delivered 'scatter-brained' responses to George's increasingly thwarted efforts to conduct a sensible conversation. The team had already hit the big time when its partners married in 1925. Gracie and George began making short films in 1929 and made their radio debut the following year. Protagonists came and went in these films and shows, but Gracie defeated them all with her unique brand

of innocent illogic. The little-girl voice she used proved the final weapon in her armoury. In the cinema, Burns and Allen worked for Paramount, a studio that regarded them largely as 'added attractions' and rarely gave them top-class vehicles of their own. They quit making films as a team in 1939 (Gracie making one or two interesting solo appearances) and reshaped their radio show in the war years into a husband-and-wife format that was to serve them well when they entered television in 1950. *The George Burns and Gracie Allen Show* ran from 1950 to 1958 on TV and was always high in the ratings. Gracie was at the centre of things, secure in an off-kilter world of her own and never lost for an answer even if it was never the one the questioner expected. Tired of the TV treadmill by 1958 – 'I quit the movies to stop getting up at six a.m. and here I am getting up at five' – Gracie announced her retirement. She had enjoyed six years of it when a heart attack felled her a month after her 62nd birthday. Gracie was once dubbed 'the smartest dumbbell in show business history'. But others could have vied for that title and the truth was that there never was anyone quite like Gracie Allen. She seemed to have a sweet belief in the idiotic things she came out with that no-one could shake. Her unique personality is perhaps summed up in a line from *International House*, one of her early films: 'I've got a good mind', says Burns of Gracie, 'to get a different nurse.' 'No, no, doctor', replies co-star Franklin Pangborn (*qv*). 'This one is different enough.'

1929: * Lamb Chops. 1930: * Fit to be Tied. * Pulling a Bone. 1931: * The Antique Shop. * Once Over Light. * One Hundred Per Cent Service. 1932: The Big Broadcast. * Hollywood on Parade A−4. * Oh My Operation. * The Babbling Book. 1933: International House. College Humor. * Let's Dance. * Walking the Baby. 1934: We're Not Dressing. Six of a Kind. Many Happy Returns. 1935: Love in Bloom. Here Comes Cookie. The Big Broadcast of 1936. 1936: College Holiday. The Big Broadcast of 1937. 1937: A Damsel in Distress. 1938: College Swing (GB: Swing, Teacher, Swing). 1939: The Gracie Allen Murder Case. Honolulu. 1941: Mr and Mrs North. 1944: Two Girls and a Sailor. 1954: * Screen Snapshots No. 224.

Woody Allen presses on with his dreams of holding a mannequin in his arms in *Bananas*

ALLEN, Woody

(Allen Konigsberg) 1935−

It now seems unlikely that Woody Allen will ever make us laugh out loud again. He clearly has nothing but contempt for the fan whom he made (via his self-written script) say to him in *Stardust Memories*: 'I prefer you in your earlier, funnier films.' And yet Allen has been a unique clown for modern times. Ambitious to be achievers, his early characters are defeated by their own neuroses and insecurities. Circumstances crowd in on most of our comic heroes. But Woody's twitching heaps of the late 1960s and early 1970s bring about their own downfalls. One can well believe it when he chickens out of a confrontation, telling his companion that 'If you want me, I'll be at home on the floor having an anxiety attack.' Small, bespectacled and balding from his late twenties, Allen had the looks to substantiate the image he put over to his audiences as one of life's victims. Born in Brooklyn, New York, the young Woody was soon escaping from the real world of being bullied at school into an imaginary world of words. 'I was always the one who wrote essays and read them out loud in front of the class', he has said, and indeed his teachers thought some of his writing so funny that they encouraged him to send gags and sketches to newspapers, magazines and show business personalities. He poured out material at an amazing rate. The jokes and anecdotes he sold for five dollars a time would sometimes earn him as much as a thousand dollars a week, even as a teenager. In his early twenties Allen was already writing regular material for top TV comedy shows; Neil Simon and Mel Brooks (*qv*) were among his fellow-writers at the time. Appearing before an audience was something else again, especially in anticipation. Once out on stage, though, Woody would captivate his listeners with an off-centre, self-deprecating, sometimes Goonish kind of humour they hadn't heard before from an American stand-up comic. Films came perhaps later than they might have done. There was an uncertain start in a supporting role in *What's New Pussycat?* (1965), for which he also contributed the screenplay, although it is probably his worst writing for the cinema. Undoubtedly he learned from that, but it was four more years before the first Woody Allen comedy proper arrived in the shape of *Take the Money and Run*, a study of the world's worst bank-robber that also incorporated themes from Woody's childhood. Even though the humour, as always in his comedies, was of the hit and miss variety, it was already apparent that Allen could come up with visual as well as verbal gems: for instance when the attempted robbery fails because the bank staff cannot read Woody's threatening note, and where he tries to break out of prison using a gun made of soap and black polish which proceeds to turn to a foaming heap in his hand as it begins to rain. The most successful of his patchwork comedies came in the 1970s — *Play It Again, Sam* (adapted from his own play), the futuristic *Sleeper*, and the ultra-satirical *Love and Death*, set in Napoleonic times and mocking numerous other movies. This was, however, to be the last full-blooded Woody Allen comedy. It was followed by *Annie Hall*, in which the comedy was blended with a romantic nostalgic seriousness. Received with rather mysterious rapture, it won four Oscars including best actress (Diane Keaton, who had starred in Woody's previous three films and was his long-time companion after the breakup of his two marriages), best picture, best screenplay and best director. Woody Allen failed to show at the Oscar ceremonies, although he was said to be in town somewhere, playing with his jazz combo. Followed by the equally overrated *Manhattan*, *Annie Hall* set the pattern for the remainder of Allen's career to date. The most successful of his subsequent films have been *Zelig* (an unusual serio-comic masterpiece which showed the direction in which his career should perhaps have been heading) and *Radio Days*, warm reminiscences of his own wartime upbringing, to which he supplied a wittily sentimental narration. Of Allen's three completely serious ventures as director only, *Interiors* was a morose misfire and *September* a crashing bore. He now lives with the actress Mia Farrow. She has appeared in the last ten films that he has directed, most centrally and successfully in *The Purple Rose of Cairo* and *Alice*.

1965: What's New Pussycat? 1966: What's Up Tiger Lily? 1967: Casino Royale. 1969: † *Take the Money and Run. 1971:* † *Bananas. 1972:* † *Everything You Always Wanted to Know About Sex* * But Were Afraid to Ask. Play It Again, Sam. 1974:* † *Sleeper. 1975:* † *Love and Death. 1976: The Front. 1977:* † *Annie Hall. 1979:* † *Manhattan. 1980:* † *Stardust Memories. To Woody Allen, from Europe with Love. 1982:* † *A Midsummer Night's Sex Comedy. 1983:* † *Zelig. 1984:* † *Broadway Danny Rose. 1986:* † *Hannah and Her Sisters. 50 Years of Action. 1987:* † *Radio Days (narrator only). King Lear. 1989:* ‡ *New York Stories.* † *Crimes and Misdemeanors. 1991: Scenes from a Mall.*
Also as director. *1978: Interiors. 1985: The Purple Rose of Cairo. 1988: September. Another Woman. 1990: Alice. 1991: Shadows and Fog.*
† And directed.
‡ And co-directed.

ALLISTER, Claud
(William C. Palmer) 1891–1970
Tall, dark, dapper British comic character actor with beaming smile (but sad eyes) who donned a monocle, showed his teeth and 'I say old chap'-ed his way through dozens of debonair dandies in his peak cinema period, from 1929 to 1941. No more perfect Algy Longworth in the Bulldog Drummond stories could ever have existed than Allister, and he played the role several times, bringing to all his 'silly asses' a touch of warmth that other players type-cast in similar roles just didn't have. Allister, born in Blackheath, a salubrious London suburb, and raised in a manner underlined by his dry, upper-crust tones, began his working life as a clerk in the Stock Exchange. His folks expected him to make 'something in the City' of himself, but Allister was more attracted to amateur dramatics, and acting had soon taken over his life. He made his London stage debut in 1905 and became a typical leading actor of the time, with 'boot polish' hair, and always immaculately dressed. In America at the beginning of sound, he made his film debut (as Algy, naturally) in the 1929 *Bulldog Drummond*, and thereafter alternated between British and American films before eventually settling in Hollywood for good in 1949 and retiring there in 1955.

1929: Bulldog Drummond. The Trial of Mary Dugan. Charming Sinners. Three Live Ghosts.
1930: Monte Carlo. The Florodora Girl (GB: The Gay Nineties). The Czar of Broadway. Slightly Scarlet. In the Next Room. Such Men Are Dangerous. Murder Will Out. Ladies Love Brutes. Reaching for the Moon. 1931: I Like Your Nerve. Platinum Blonde. * *On the Loose. Captain Applejack. Meet the Wife. Papa Loves Mama.* * *Roughhouse Rhythm. 1932: The Midshipmaid (US: Midshipmaid Gob). Two White Arms (US: Wives Beware). Diamond Cut Diamond (US: Blame the Woman). The Return of Raffles. The Unexpected Father. Medicine Man. 1933: The Private Life of Henry VIII. Excess Baggage. That's My Wife. Sleeping Car. 1934: The Lady is Willing. Those Were the Days. The Return of Bulldog Drummond. The Private Life of Don Juan. 1935: The Dark Angel. Three Live Ghosts (and 1929 film). 1936: Dracula's Daughter. Yellowstone. 1937: Bulldog Drummond at Bay.* * *Oh What a Knight. The Awful Truth. Let's Make a Night of It. Danger — Love at Work. Radio Parade of 1937. 1938: Men Are Such Fools. Storm over Bengal. Kentucky Moonshine (GB: Three Men and a Girl). The Blonde Cheat. 1939: Arrest Bulldog Drummond! Captain Fury. 1940: Pride and Prejudice. Lillian Russell. 1941: Charley's Aunt. The Reluctant Dragon. Confirm or Deny. A Yank in the RAF. Never Give a Sucker an Even Break (GB: What a Man!). 1943: Forever and a Day. The Hundred Pound Window. 1944: Kiss the Bride Goodbye. 1945: Don Chicago. Dumb Dora Discovers Tobacco (US: Fag End). 1946: Gaiety George. 1948. Quartet. The First Gentleman (US: Affairs of a Rogue). 1949: The Adventures of Ichabod and Mr Toad (voice only). 1951: Hong Kong. 1952: Down Among the Sheltering Palms (filmed 1950). 1953: Kiss Me, Kate! 1954: The Black Shield of Falworth.*

ANDERSON, Eddie 'Rochester'
1905–1977
Stocky, hoarse-voiced Eddie Anderson was a middle-range vaudeville entertainer who had played a handful of small comic roles in films when he appeared on Jack Benny's radio show in 1937 and made an instant nationwide impression. Anderson was promptly signed up as Benny's perennially harassed manservant Rochester, a role which gave him the name by which he con-

tinued to be known in show business for the next 30 years. 'Rochester' obviously had his master sized up, and had scant respect for his frequent moanings and groanings. He appeared with Benny (*qv*) in four subsequent films. By now, his dry delivery, rolling eyes and panic-soothing squeaks had made him a personality in his own right, and M-G-M gave him the leading role in their all-black musical *Cabin in the Sky*. Anderson was Little Joe, torn between God and the devil. A popular figure in wartime films, Anderson went back to radio, television and Benny when it was over. The son of a minstrel and a high-wire artist, he had begun his career dancing in a chorus line before joining all-black revues and minstrel shows. He came to Hollywood in the early 1930s. Fame, and 'Massa Benny', was just around the corner.

1932: Hat Check Girl (GB: Embassy Girl). What Price Hollywood? 1934: Behold My Wife! 1935: Transient Lady (GB: False Witness). 1936: Two in a Crowd. Green Pastures. Rainbow on the River. Three Men on a Horse. Show Boat. 1937: Melody for Two. Bill Cracks Down (GB: Men of Steel). On Such a Night. White Bondage. Over the Goal. One Mile from Heaven. 1938: Kentucky. Restless Living. You Can't Take It with You. Gold Diggers in Paris (GB: The Great Impostors). Jezebel. Thanks for the Memory. Going Places. Exposed. Strange Faces. 1939: Honolulu. You Can't Cheat an Honest Man. Gone with the Wind. Man About Town. 1940: Buck Benny Rides Again. Love Thy Neighbor. 1941: Topper Returns. Birth of the Blues. Kiss the Boys Goodbye. 1942: Tales of Manhattan. Spar-Spangled Rhythm. 1943: The Meanest Man in the World. Cabin in the Sky. What's Buzzin' Cousin? 1944: Broadway Rhythm. 1945: Brewster's Millions. I Love a Bandleader (GB: Memory for Two). 1946: The Show-Off. The Sailor Takes a Wife. 1957: Green Pastures (TV remake). 1963: It's a Mad, Mad, Mad, Mad World.

The potent box-office combination of Fatty Arbuckle and Charlie Chaplin in one of their numerous films together at the Keystone Studio in 1914

character stars. But the genial Andrews had a useful second string to his bow that most similar players couldn't muster: he could endow palely-smiling villains with a genuine sense of deadly menace. Andrews came originally from the deep South of the United States; his father was an Episcopalian minister in his native state of Georgia. Edward never wanted to be anything but an actor and made his stage debut as a teenager, appearing on Broadway for the first time at 21. There were many more successful appearances in plays before Hollywood called him for top character roles 20 years later. He started as cold, florid, bad guys, only later proving himself a master of exasperation and panic. Andrews worked steadily until his death from a heart attack at 70.

1955: The Phenix City Story (GB: The Phoenix City Story). 1956: Tea and Sympathy. The Harder They Fall. These Wilder Years. The Unguarded Moment. Tension at Table Rock. 1957: Hot Summer Night. Three Brave Men. The Tattered Dress. Trooper Hook. 1958: The Fiend That Walked the West. 1959: Night of the Quarter Moon. 1960: Elmer Gantry. 1961: The Young Doctors. The Absent-Minded Professor. The Young Savages. Advise and Consent. Love in a Goldfish Bowl. 1962: Son of Flubber. 40 Pounds of Trouble. 1963: The Man from Galveston (TV. GB: cinemas). The Thrill of It All. A Tiger Walks. 1964: The Brass Bottle. Good Neighbor Sam. Kisses for My President. Send Me No Flowers. Youngblood Hawke. 1965: Fluffy. 1966: The Glass Bottom Boat. Birds Do It. 1969: The Over-the-Hill Gang (TV). The Trouble with Girls. 1970: The Intruders (TV). Tora! Tora! Tora! 1971: Million Dollar Duck. How to Frame a Figg. Travis Logan DA (TV). 1972: Now You See Him Now You Don't. Avanti! 1973: Charley and the Angel. 1975: The Photographer. Swiss

Family Robinson (TV). 1976: How to Break Up a Happy Divorce (TV). 1977: Don't Push, I'll Charge When I'm Ready (TV. Filmed in 1969). 1978: Freedom Riders (TV). My Undercover Years with the Ku Klux Klan (TV). Seniors. Lacy and the Mississippi Queen (TV). 1979: Supertrain (TV. Later: Express to Terror). 1980: The Final Countdown. 1984: Gremlins. Sixteen Candles.

ARBUCKLE, Roscoe 'Fatty'
1887–1933
A plump, light-haired, boyish-looking American comedian of wary expression, froglike smile and surprising agility, Arbuckle was among the most popular of Hollywood's silent clowns until his career was ruined by scandal in 1921. The fat man was also a director of some inventiveness, a talent he was glad to fall back on when on-screen exposure was denied to him in the 1920s. Born in Kansas, the young Roscoe always found pleasure in making people laugh. He was performing in travelling carnivals as a teenager, graduating to burlesque halls in his twenties. Taking

ANDREWS, Edward 1914–1985
Usually benevolent, bespectacled and beaming (and occasionally bewildered), avuncular Edward Andrews became in middle age one of the world's best comedy

'extra' work in Hollywood from 1908, the roly-poly comic had inevitably rolled into Mack Sennett's Keystone comedy studio by 1913, rubbing shoulders with such silent funsters as Ford Sterling, Mabel Normand and Charlie Chaplin (all *qv*). There was the occasional early appearance as a Keystone Kop, but Fatty's personal popularity with audiences was quickly apparent, and he began making his own series of shorts from 1913, often with Normand as co-star. The 'Fatty and Mabel' films are endearing short comedies with small unexpected sentimental and affectionate touches amid the slapstick. Arbuckle is said to have co-directed many of these early films with Normand and the credited director, Eddie Dillon. Both stars had the happy knack of seeming appealingly natural on camera. As well as being nimble on his feet, Arbuckle was clever with his hands for a large man. No sausage-fingers he. He could hit people with custard pies thrown in two directions at once, hit a target with knives flicked over his shoulder and roll a cigarette with just two fingers. His liking for appearing in drag often had him looking like Toad disguised as a washer-woman in *The Wind in the Willows*. He was certainly much-loved – for the time being. With his move into independent production in 1917 Fatty took as his partners his young nephew, Al St John (*qv*) and a promising young poker-faced acrobatic comedian called Buster Keaton (also *qv*). The new team made more than a dozen priceless comedies together before Keaton went his own way, a year before the Arbuckle scandal broke. It was late 1921, and Fatty was holding a typically lavish and orgiastic party at a San Francisco hotel. A few days later, a minor actress who had been at the party died from internal ruptures which the State, charging Arbuckle with manslaughter, alleged that the 23-stone actor's sexual attentions had caused. After two trials had both ended with the jury unable to reach a verdict, Arbuckle's ordeal was finally ended when a third trial jury acquitted him, together with an unprecedented apology. However, the hefty star found his career before the cameras on permanent hold and, after several years directing comedies under the pseudonym of William B. Goodrich, he returned to acting (making six shorts) only a year before his death from a heart attack. Ironically, in the very week of his sudden death he had signed a contract with Warner Brothers to make his first feature film in a starring role since *Leap Year* in 1921 (and that was released the following year only in Europe). Angel-faced, with eyebrows like boxers' cuts, Arbuckle believed in slapstick rather than subtlety – anything for the sudden laugh. But he never got a chance to develop that theory in a decade which produced his ex-partner Buster Keaton's best work.

1910: The Sanatorium/The Clinic. 1913: The Gangsters. Passions, He Had Three. The Waiters' Picnic. Help! Help! Hydrophobia. A Bandit. For the Love of Mabel. The Telltale Light. A Noise from the Deep. Love and Courage. The Riot. Mabel's New Hero. Fatty's Day Off. Mabel's Dramatic Debut. The Gypsy Queen. Mother's Boy. The Faithful Taxicab. A Quiet Little Wedding. Fatty at San Diego. Fatty Joins the Force. The Woman Haters. Fatty's Flirtations. He Would a-Hunting Go. 1914: A Misplaced Foot. The Under Sheriff. A Flirt's Mistake. In the Clutches of a Gang. Rebecca's Wedding Day. A Film Johnnie. Tango Tangles. A Rural Demon. His Favorite Pastime. Barnyard Flirtations. Chicken Chaser. A Suspended Ordeal. The Water Dog. The Alarm. The Knockout. Our Country Cousin. Fatty and Minnie-Haw-Haw. Fatty and the Heiress. Fatty's Finish. The Sky Pirate. Caught in a Flue. The Baggage Smasher. Those Happy Days. That Minstrel Man. Those Country Kids. Fatty's Gift. The Masquerade. A Brand New Hero. The Rounders. Fatty's Debut. Fatty Again. [†] *Tillie's Punctured Romance. Killing Horace. Their Ups and Downs. Zip the Dodger. An Incompetent Hero. Lovers' Post Office. The Sea Nymphs. Fatty's Jonah Day. Fatty's Wine Party. 1915: Leading Lizzy Astray. Among the Mourners. Shotguns That Kick. Fatty's Magic Party. Mabel and Fatty's Wash Day. Rum and Wallpaper. Mabel and Fatty's Simple Life. Fatty and Mabel at the San Diego Exposition. Mabel, Fatty and the Law. Fatty's New Role. Colored Villainy. Fatty and Mabel's Married Life. Fatty's Reckless Fling. Fatty's Chance Acquaintance. Love in Armor. Fatty's Faithful Fido. That Little Band of Gold. When Love Took Wings. Mabel and Fatty Viewing the World's Fair at San Francisco. Miss Fatty's Seaside Lovers. The Little Teacher. Fatty's Plucky Pup. Fatty's Tin Type Tangle. Fickle Fatty's Fall. 1916: The Village Scandal. Fatty and the Broadway Stars. Fatty and Mabel Adrift. He Did and He Didn't. Bright Lights/ The Lure of Broadway. The Other Man. His Wife's Mistakes. The Waiters' Ball. A Creampuff Romance/A Reckless Romeo. Rebecca's Wedding Day. 1917: The Butcher Boy. Rough House. His Wedding Night. Fatty at Coney Island. Out West. Oh! Doctor. A Country Hero. 1918: The Bell Boy. Goodnight Nurse. Moonshine. The Cook. The Sheriff. Camping Out. 1919: A Desert Hero. Backstage. The Garage. The Hayseed. The Pullman Porter. Love. The Bank Clerk. 1920:* [†] *Life of the Party.* [†] *The Round-Up.* [†] *The Traveling Salesman.* [†] *Brewster's Millions.* [†] *Crazy to Marry. 1921:* [†] *Gasoline Gus.* [†] *The Dollar a Year Man.* [†] *The Fast Freight/Freight Prepaid. 1922:* [†] *Leap Year/Skirt Shy. 1923:* [†] *Hollywood. 1925:* [†] *Go West. 1932: Hey Pop. 1933: How've You Bean? Buzzin' Around. Close Relations. Tomalio. In the Dough.*
As director. *1916: The Moonshiners. 1925: The Tourist. The Movies. The Fighting Dude. 1926: Cleaning Up. Home Cured. My Stars. His Private Life. Fool's Luck. One Sunday Morning. 1927: Peaceful Oscar.* [†] *The Red Mill.* [†] *Special Delivery. 1930: Won by a Neck. Three Hollywood Girls. Si Si Senor. Up a Tree. 1931: Crashing Hollywood. The Lure of Hollywood. Windy Riley Goes Hollywood. Honeymoon Trio. Queenie of Hollywood. Pete and Repeat. Ex-Plumber. Marriage Rows. The Back Page. That's My Line. Up Pops the Duke. Beach Pajamas. Take 'Em and Shake 'Em. That's My Meat. One Quiet Night. Once a Hero. The Tamale Vendor. Smart Work. Idle Roomers. 1932: Hollywood Luck. Anybody's Goat. Moonlight and Cactus. Keep Laughing. Bridge Wives. Mother's Holiday. Niagara Falls. Hollywood Lights. Gigolettes. It's a Cinch.*

All shorts except [†] features.

ARDEN, Eve
(Eunice Quedens) 1912–1990

Most audiences felt better about a film if they knew Eve Arden was in it. They could depend on sharp barbs smartly delivered by a waspish-looking blonde lady who normally played the heroine's best friend. The tall, elegant actress from California's Mill Valley was acting in stock companies at 16, but a career turnabout had made her a Ziegfeld girl five years later, and she stayed with Mr Ziegfeld's famous Follies for a further two years. She had played a couple of early film roles under her real name, but it was her role as a bitchy character appropriately called Eve in 1937's *Stage Door* (which gave a similar opportunity to Lucille Ball, *qv*) that set the pattern of her film career and had producers queuing for her services if, alas, almost always in supporting roles. Most of these were in comedies and musicals, but it was for a straighter role, as Joan Crawford's confidante in *Mildred Pierce*, that she received her only nomination for an Academy Award. Solo success, however, did come in television, in the 1950s with *Our Miss Brooks*, and in the 1960s with *Mothers-in-Law*, two very successful comedy series. Capable of zanier comedy than she often played, Eve Arden never quite found the one screen vehicle that might have made her a top comedienne of the cinema, even though she was voted best comedienne in films in a *Motion Pictures* poll for seven consecutive years from 1948 to 1954. She went on playing colourful, larger-than-life characters on stage, including stints as star of *Hello, Dolly!* and *Auntie Mame*. But, as later interviews showed, Arden didn't like the stereotyped image of the smart gal with the whipcrack wisecrack with which she found herself stuck: 'I never really cared for that kind of character', she told one interviewer. 'I certainly don't think it was me. I really think I'm kinder than that. My friends will tell you that I'm a very mild person!' After an unsuccessful first marriage, Eve remained married to her second husband, minor actor Brooks West, from 1951 to his death in 1984. She herself died from heart failure in November 1990, after more than a year of suffering from cancer and heart problems. Eve Arden was always evasive about her age which, officially 78 at her death, may in fact have been 82.

1929: † Song of Love. 1933: † Dancing Lady. 1937. Oh, Doctor. Stage Door. 1938: Coconut Grove. Letter of Introduction. Having Wonderful Time. Women in the Wind. 1939: Big Town Czar. The Forgotten Women. Eternally Yours. At the Circus. 1940: A Child is Born. Slightly Honorable. Comrade X. No, No, Nanette. 1941: Ziegfeld Girl. That Uncertain Feeling. She Couldn't Say No. She Knew All the Answers. San Antonio Rose. Sing for Your Supper. Manpower. Whistling in the Dark. 1942: Last of the Duanes. Obliging Young Lady. Bedtime Story. 1943: Hit Parade of 1943. Let's Face It. 1944: Cover Girl. The Doughgirls. My Reputation (released 1946). 1945: Pan Americana. Earl Carroll's Vanities. Mildred Pierce. Patrick the Great. 1946: The Kid from Brooklyn. Night and Day. 1947: Song of Scheherezade. The Arnelo Affair. The Unfaithful. 1948: The Voice of the Turtle. One Touch of Venus. Whiplash. 1949: My Dream is Yours. The Lady Takes a Sailor. 1950: Paid in Full. Curtain Call at Cactus Creek (GB: Take the Stage). Tea for Two. Three Husbands. 1951: Goodbye, My Fancy. 1952: We're Not Married. 1953: The Lady Wants Mink. 1954: * Hollywood Life. 1956: Our Miss Brooks. 1959: Anatomy of a Murder. 1960: The Dark at the Top of the Stairs. 1965: Sergeant Deadhead. 1969: In Name Only (TV). 1972: A Very Missing Person (TV). All My Darling Daughters (TV). 1973: Mother of the Bride (TV). 1975: The Strongest Man in the World. 1978: A Guide for the Married Woman (TV). Grease. 1980: The Dream Merchants (TV). 1981: Under the Rainbow. Pandemonium/Thursday the 12th. 1982: Grease 2.

ARTHUR, George K.
See DANE, Karl and ARTHUR, George K.

ASKEY, Arthur 1900–1982
A diminutive, well-scrubbed, bespectacled, dark-haired British comedian with a treasure-chest full of catch-phrases, a silly laugh and an endearing habit of ending his act with a daft novelty song. The ever-smiling, ever-buoyant Askey had a chin worthy of Jack Hulbert or Stan Laurel (both qv), little eyes that popped around behind big horn-rimmed glasses and funny walks that sent his early concert-party audiences into fits of laughter. Sam Askey's little boy started his working life as a clerk with the Liverpool Education Committee, and never quite lost the regional accent that permeated his light but timbrous speaking voice with a kind of twang. His facility for making people laugh soon led him to the world of concert-parties and pierrots and he had become a top seaside entertainer by 1926. He also enjoyed playing pantomime dames, an activity he kept up till the very end of his career. National fame came in January 1938 with the first broadcast of Band Waggon, the first British radio comedy show to present its stars (Askey and Richard Murdoch – qv) in situations, rather than as stand-up comics. They 'lived' on the top of Broadcasting House with their goat Lewis. Their 'char' Mrs Bagwash and her daughter Nausea were other integral characters and the programme quickly became so popular that it was moved from its regular Sunday evening slot when vicars complained that it was affecting their attendances. Films had to follow, inevitably beginning with Band Waggon (1939), although it had little to do with the original show, and continuing through the war years. Askey's characters in them were characterised by a playfulness and an inability to leave things alone, as when he scrambles the BBC pips in Back Room Boy (1942). The standard of Askey's films, however, dropped away quite quickly, and he was understandably so disappointed with the last, Bees in Paradise, in 1944, that he made no more films for a decade, returning to stage and radio. On radio he found a new partner in magician-comedian David Nixon, and the Askey catch-phrases – 'I thank you', 'Don't be filthy', 'Hello playmates' and 'Here and now, before your very eyes' became national watchwords. A film version of his stage success The Love Match brought Askey back to films in 1954 and a few more ramshackle movie vehicles followed. Though the little man kept joking to the end, his last few years were painful ones. Death finally came from gangrene after he had both legs amputated to try to stop its spread. An unworthy end for a comedian who, on film or stage, never seemed to stop moving.

1937: * Pathé Pictorial No. 115 (The Bee). Calling All Stars. 1939: Band Waggon. 1940: Charley's (Big-Hearted) Aunt. 1941: The Ghost Train. I Thank You. 1942: Back Room Boy. * The Nose Has It. King Arthur Was a Gentleman. 1943: Miss London Ltd. 1944: Bees in Paradise. 1954: The Love Match. 1955: Ramsbottom Rides Again. 1956: * Skilful Soccer. 1958: Make Mine a Million. 1959: Friends and Neighbours. 1972: The Alf Garnett Saga. 1977: * End of Term. 1978: Rosie Dixon – Night Nurse. 1982: The Pantomime Dame.

Anyone else would be paddling. But diminutive Arthur Askey is nearly up to his knees as he fishes for mermaids in Back Room Boy

ATES, Roscoe 1892–1962

Like one or two other minor American comedians of the screen, slight, scrawny, bug-eyed, wispy-haired, rubber-faced Roscoe Ates enjoyed two film careers: one as a comedy foil for the stars, and another as a comic sidekick for 'B' movie cowboy heroes. The little man from Grange, Mississippi had quite an eye for the ladies (he married four times, his last wife being 40 years his junior) and once said that that was where most of his money had gone. He certainly had little cash left to show for his life when he died from lung cancer at the age of 70. A violin and voice training student in his youth, Ates suffered from a speech impediment that made him stutter. According to Roscoe, he cured the affliction by the endless recitation of tongue-twisters in front of a mirror. In a rather bizarre twist, he later made a stammer part of his act in vaudeville and, then, the cinema. In the 1930s his putty features, pathetic gestures, jug ears and humble demeanour made him ideal material for henpecks and he was good at cringing before the tongue-lashing of some of Hollywood's most formidable harridans. His career was drifting in the 1940s, though, when he signed up to make westerns as the bumbling, guitar-playing Soapy, sidekick to singing cowboy Eddie Dean. Ates made fifteen of the Dean westerns between 1946 and 1948. From 1957 he was semi-retired.

*1929: South Sea Rose. 1930. Reducing. The Lone Star Ranger. Caught Short. The Big House. City Girl. Billy the Kid. Love in the Rough. 1931: The Great Lover. Cracked Nuts. The Big Shot (GB: The Optimist). The Champ. A Free Soul. Cimarron. Too Many Cooks. Politics. 1932: * Shampoo the Magician. * Never the Twins Shall Meet. Freaks. Ladies of the Jury. The Rainbow Trail. Young Bride/ Love Starved/Veneer. Roadhouse Murder. Hold 'Em, Jail! Come On, Danger. Deported. 1933: Renegades of the West. The Past of Mary Holmes. The Cheyenne Kid. Golden Harvest. Alice in Wonderland. What! No Beer? Scarlet River. Lucky Devils. * Hollywood on Parade B–3. 1934: Woman in the Dark. She Made Her Bed. The Merry Wives of Reno. 1935: The People's Enemy. 1936: God's Country and the Woman. Fair Exchange. 1938: Riders of the*

*Black Hills. The Great Adventures of Wild Bill Hickok (serial). 1939: Three Texas Steers (GB. Danger Rides the Range). Gone With the Wind. Rancho Grande. 1940: Fireman, Save My Choo-Choo. * You're Next. Cowboy from Sundown. Captain Caution. Untamed. I Want a Divorce. Chad Hanna. 1941: I'll Sell My Life. Ziegfeld Girl. * Glove Affair. Birth of the Blues. Mountain Moonlight (GB: Moving in Society). She Knew All the Answers. Sullivan's Travels. Robin Hood of the Pecos. Reg'lar Fellers. Bad Men of Missouri. One Foot in Heaven. 1942: The Palm Beach Story. The Affairs of Jimmy Valentine. 1944: Can't Help Singing. 1946: Colorado Serenade. Down Missouri Way. Driftin' River. Tumbleweed Trail. Wild West. Stars Over Texas. 1947: Wild Country. Range Beyond the Blue. West to Glory. Black Hills. Shadow Valley. 1948: Check Your Guns. Tornado Range. The Westward Trail. Inner Sanctum. The Hawk of Powder River. Prairie Outlaws. The Tioga Kid. Thunder in the Pines. 1950: The Hills of Oklahoma. Father's Wild Game. 1951: Honeychile. 1952: The Blazing Forest. 1953: Those Redheads from Seattle. The Stranger Wore a Gun. 1955: Lucy Gallant. Abbott and Costello Meet the Keystone Kops. Come Next Spring. 1956: The Birds and the Bees. The Kettles in the Ozarks. Meet Me in Las Vegas (GB: Viva Las Vegas!). 1957: Run of the Arrow. The Big Caper. Short Cut to Hell. 1958. The Sheepman. 1961: The Silent Call. The Errand Boy.*

AUER, Mischa
(M. Ounskowsky) 1905–1967

This lanky, pop-eyed, loose-limbed, Russian-born character player with dark hair, pencil moustache and anxious expression became an integral part of the Hollywood scene in the 1930s and early 1940s, even if his name was rarely seen above the title. The stars had to look to their laurels when sharing dialogue with such a deft scene-stealer. Born to a family of musicians, Auer had as grandfather a famous violinist, from whom he took his stage name. When Mischa was 15, his grandfather brought him to America to complete his education; he was to stay for almost 30

years. After Broadway success at 23, Mischa accepted a Paramount contract and embarked on a film career. At first he donned a sneer and played sneaky villains, but producers soon spotted his comedy potential. The breakthrough to bigger roles came with his gorilla impersonation as Carlo, the perpetual-motion parasite in *My Man Godfrey* (1936), a performance that brought him an Oscar nomination and a whole rash of arm-waving, English-fracturing, eccentric foreigners, culminating in his biggest and best role, as the way-out neighbour of Joan Bennett in *Twin Beds* (1942). Demands for his services slackened in post-war years, especially with the demise of the screwball comedy. From 1949 Auer became a wanderer, seeking work wherever there were interesting film roles – in England, France and Italy, where he died from a heart attack at only 61. Like so many of his characters, he had been something of a wayward and likeable genius.

1928: Something Always Happens. The Mighty. Marquis Preferred. 1929: Fame and the Devil. The Studio Murder Mystery. 1930: The Benson Murder Case. Inside the Lines. The Lady from Nowhere. Just Imagine. Women Love Once. Paramount on Parade. The Unholy Garden. 1931: Drums of Jeopardy. The Yellow Ticket (GB: The Yellow Passport). King of the Wild (serial). Delicious. No Limit. The Midnight Patrol. Command Performance. 1932: Last of the Mohicans (serial). The Intruder. Mata Hari. Sinister Hands. Murder at Dawn (GB: The Death Ray). No Greater Love (GB: Divine Love). Drifting Souls. Scarlet Dawn. Arsène Lupin. The Unwritten Law. The Monster Walks. Call Her Savage. Western Code. Beauty Parlor. 1933: Rasputin and the Empress (GB: Rasputin the Mad Monk). Dangerously Yours. Sucker Money (GB: Victims of the Beyond). Tarzan the Fearless (serial). Infernal Machine. Corruption. Gabriel Over the White House. The Flaming Signal. After Tonight (GB: Sealed Lips). Cradle Song. Girl Without a Room. Storm at Daybreak. 1934: Wharf Angel. The Crosby Case (GB: The Crosby Murder Case). Viva Villa! Bulldog Drummond Strikes Back. Change of Heart. Stamboul Quest. Student Year. Woman Condemned. 1935: Mystery Woman. Lives of a Bengal Lancer. Clive of India. The Adventures of Rex and Rinty (serial). Anna Karenina. Condemned to Live. Biography of a Bachelor Girl. The Crusades. I Dream Too Much. 1936: Murder in the Fleet. The House of 1000 Candles. One Rainy Afternoon. The Princess Comes Across. Winterset. The Gay Desperado. We're Only Human. Here Comes Trouble. Tough Guy. My Man Godfrey. Sons o' Guns. 1937: That Girl from Paris. Three Smart Girls. Top of the Town. We Have Our Moments. Pick a Star. Marry the Girl. Merry-Go-Round. Vogues of 1938. 1938: 100 Men and a Girl. Service de Luxe. It's All Yours. The Rage of Paris. You Can't Take It with You. Little Tough Guys in Society. Sweethearts. 1939: East Side of Heaven. Unexpected Father (GB: Sandy Takes a Bow). Destry Rides Again. * Three and a Day. 1940: Alias the Deacon. Sandy is a Lady. Public Deb Number One. Margie. Spring Parade. Trail of the Vigilantes. Seven Sinners. 1941: Flame of New Orleans. Cracked Nuts. Hold That Ghost! Moonlight in Hawaii. Hellzapoppin. Sing Another Chorus. 1942: Don't Get Personal. Twin Beds. 1943: Around the World. 1944: Lady in the Dark. Up in Mabel's Room. 1945: A Royal Scandal (GB: Czarina). Brewster's Millions. And Then There Were None (GB: Ten Little Niggers). 1946: Sentimental Journey. She Wrote the Book. 1947: For You I Die. 1948: Sofia. 1949: Al diavolo la celebrita. 1951: The Sky is Red. 1952: Song of Paris (US: Bachelor in Paris). 1954: Mr Arkadin (GB: Confidential Report). Escalier de service. 1955: Frou-Frou. Treize à table. L'impossible M. Pipelet. Futures vedettes (GB: Sweet Sixteen). Cette sacrée gamine (GB and US: Mam'zelle Pigalle). 1956: Mannequins de Paris. La polka des menottes. En effeuillant la marguerite (GB: Mam'selle Striptease. US: Please, Mr Balzac). 1957: Le tombeur. The Monte Carlo Story. 1958: Nathalie, agent secret (GB and US: The Foxiest Girl in Paris). Tabarin. Sacrée jeunesse. A pied, à cheval et en spoutnik (GB: Hold Tight for the Satellite. US: A Dog, a Mouse and a Sputnik). 1962: We Joined the Navy. Les femmes d'abord (US: Ladies First). * The King's Breakfast. 1964: What Ever Happened to Baby Toto? Queste pazza, pazze, pazze donne. 1966: The Christmas That Almost Wasn't. Par amore . . . par magia. Drop Dead, Darling (US: Arrivederci, Baby).

As anxious as ever, Mischa Auer (right), with the help of Francis Lederer, tries to foist an inheritance on reluctant heiress Madeleine Carroll in It's All Yours

AYKROYD, Dan 1951–

Tall, laconic, floppily dark-haired, straight-faced and latterly weighty American comedian who almost always works in harness with other light comedians of equal star value. Aykroyd can fell opponents with a withering glance, has good comic timing and a nice deadpan leer, and is often funniest when not leaning on the ruderies on which he sometimes relies. Born in Canada, Aykroyd had a somewhat troubled childhood that included being expelled from school, before finding his niche as a comic actor, and later joining the group of comics on television's late 1970s cult hit Saturday Night Live, several of whom would go on to dominate American film comedy in the following decade. Aykroyd formed a particularly felicitous partnership there with sawn-off, chubby, abrasive John Belushi (qv). Their creation of the iconoclastically awful Blues Brothers, with their dark suits and pork-pie hats and even darker glasses, was a great popular success. They transferred these creations to the big screen with some reward; the film The Blues Brothers made a lot of money but only a small profit because of its high initial cost of some $30 million. But it established Belushi and Aykroyd as a scatological Abbott and Costello (qv) for the 1980s. After one more film, Neighbors, the partnership was severed by Belushi's early death. One wondered whether Aykroyd could survive alone. For a while, he did seem to be struggling for a workable screen identity, and is still happiest doing collaborative work – in recent times with different partners in turn, among them Bill Murray, Chevy Chase (both qv), Walter Matthau, Tom Hanks (qv) and John Candy (qv). 'My strength is in collaboration', he has insisted. 'I enjoy the kinship of an ensemble.' Such films as Nothing But Trouble, though (which he also directed), have let Aykroyd's theory down. On the other hand, he surprised many with a low-key straight acting performance in Driving Miss Daisy which won him an Oscar nomination. Now heavier than in his Saturday Night Live days, but just as harumscarum in his poker-faced way, Aykroyd has commendably been going for more variations in comedy in recent years,

His fine fendered friend...no, this isn't Miss Daisy (that was Jessica Tandy), but this is the film for which Dan Aykroyd got an Oscar nomination, *Driving Miss Daisy*

Agatha's frisky. Butler Humphrey (Bob Hope) discovers that wild, wild westerner, Agatha Floud (Lucille Ball) has decided he's the man for her, in *Fancy Pants*

Chute the works. Even the ingenious Monty Banks finds this express delivery more than he can handle, in his silent comedy hit *Atta Boy*

even if the miss rate continues to outweigh the hits. He's married to the actress Donna Dixon.

1975: Love at First Sight. 1979: '1941'. Mr Mike's Mondo Video. 1980: The Blues Brothers. 1981: Neighbors. 1982: It Came from Hollywood (video). 1983: Doctor Detroit. Trading Places. The Twilight Zone (GB: Twilight Zone the Movie). 1984: Ghost Busters. Indiana Jones and the Temple of Doom. 1985: Into the Night. Spies Like Us. 1987: Dragnet. The Couch Trip. 1988: The Great Outdoors. Caddyshack II. My Stepmother Is an Alien. 1989: Loose Cannons. Ghostbusters II. Driving Miss Daisy. 1990: Nothing But Trouble (and directed). Masters of Menace. 1991: My Girl. This is My Life. 1992: Charlie. Sneakers.

A hair-raising time for Dan Aykroyd as he plans a prison break with a little help from Victoria Jackson in *The Couch Trip*

BACKUS, Jim 1913–1989

Raucous-voiced, heftily-built, wide-nosed American comedy actor with a background in radio. Backus's mere presence in any scene commanded amused attention, and several successful television series ensured his continual presence in the living-rooms of viewers on both sides of the Atlantic. But if the Backus features, creased equally convincingly into beam or scowl, created a score of memorable characters, the Backus voice surely created a hundred more. Besides appearing in more than 2,000 radio broadcasts, he became known world-wide as the voice of the short-sighted cartoon character Mr Magoo. Backus handled affability and irascibility with equal ease, but Magoo added another string to his vocal bow – bemusement. Backus was born in Cleveland, Ohio. As a boy his great passion was golf, although he found time to graduate from the American Academy of Dramatic Arts in 1933. He started his career on radio in Cleveland, first as an announcer, then as a character actor. In 1936 he moved into New York City radio, and remained there for ten years (apart from one minor film role) until a show he was doing with Alan Young (in which Backus played a character called Hubert Updyke) moved to California. Hollywood heard the Backus voice, and liked the face that went with it. As a result he was soon in dozens of films in mainly comic character roles – though he proved he could handle drama too, in such roles as James Dean's father in *Rebel Without a Cause*. Apart from his Magoo characterisation, though, Backus remains best remembered for numerous television series, all of which were enlivened by his abrasive presence. He was Joan Davis's long-suffering husband in *I Married Joan* (1952–55), a bungling news editor in *Hot Off the Wire/ The Jim Backus Show* (1960), a pompous, vague millionaire in *Gilligan's Island* (1964–67) and Dagwood's apoplectic boss in the brief TV revival of *Blondie* (1968–69). Backus reprised his *Gilligan's Island* characterisation of the blustery Thurston Howell III in several latter-day TV movies, but was semi-retired from the mid 1980s.

1942: The Pied Piper. 1949: One Last Fling. The Great Lover. Father Was a Fullback. Easy Living. A Dangerous Profession. Ma and Pa Kettle Go to Town (GB: Going to Town). 1950: Customs Agent. Emergency Wedding (GB: Jealousy). The Hollywood Story. Bright Victory (GB: Lights Out). The Killer That Stalked New York (GB: The Frightened City). 1951: I Want You. Iron Man. Half Angel. The Man with a Cloak. M. His Kind of Woman. I'll See You in My Dreams. 1952: Pat and Mike. Deadline USA (GB: Deadline). Here Come the Nelsons. The Rose Bowl Story. Don't Bother to Knock. Androcles and the Lion. Above and Beyond. Angel Face. I Love Melvin. 1953: Geraldine. 1954: Deep in My Heart. 1955: Francis in the Navy. Rebel Without a Cause. The Square Jungle. 1956: The Great Man. Meet Me in Las Vegas (GB: Viva Las Vegas!). The Naked Hills. You Can't Run Away from It. The Opposite Sex. The Girl He Left Behind. 1957: Top Secret Affair (GB: Their Secret Affair). Man of a Thousand Faces. Eighteen and Anxious. The Pied Piper of Hamelin (TV. GB: cinemas). 1958: The High Cost of Loving. Free Week-End (TV). Macabre. 1959: The Big Operator. The Wild and the Innocent. 1001 Arabian Nights (voice only). A Private's Affair. Ask Any Girl. 1960: Ice Palace. 1962: The Wonderful World of the Brothers Grimm. The Horizontal Lieutenant. Boys' Night Out. Zotz! Critic's Choice. 1963: Sunday in New York. Johnny Cool. The Wheeler Dealers (GB: Separate Beds). It's a Mad, Mad, Mad, Mad World. Operation Bikini. My Six Loves. Advance to the Rear (GB: Company of Cowards). 1964: John Goldfarb, Please Come Home. 1965: Fluffy. Billie. 1966: Hurry Sundown. 1967: Don't Make Waves. 1968: Hello Down There. Where Were You When the Lights Went Out? 1969: The Cockeyed Cowboys of Calico

*County (GB: TV, as A Woman for Charlie).
Wake Me When the War is Over (TV). 1970:
Myra Breckinridge. 1971: Getting Away from
It All (TV). The Magic Carpet (TV). 1972:
Now You See Him Now You Don't. 1973: The
Girl Most Likely To (TV). 1974: Miracle on
34th Street (TV). 1975: The Return of Joe
Forrester (TV). Friday Foster. Crazy Mama.
1976: The Feather and Father Gang (TV).
1977: Pete's Dragon. 1978: Good Guys Wear
Black. Return to Gilligan's Island (TV). 1979:
Seven from Heaven. The Rebels (TV).
The Castaways on Gilligan's Island (TV). The
Gossip Columnist (TV). Chomps. There Goes
the Bride. Angel's Brigade. 1981: Jayne Mans-
field — An American Tragedy (TV). The Harlem
Globetrotters on Gilligan's Island (TV). 1982:
Slapstick (US: Slapstick of Another Kind).
1984: Prince Jack.*

BALL, Lucille 1911–1989

An unpretty but attractive red-haired
American comedienne with expressive features and a large mouth that could hilariously portray various stages of sadness,
ecstasy, anguish, hysteria or despair. The
sadness for audiences was that it took her so
long to get to the very top. The stagestruck
teenager from Jamestown, New York began
in show business as early as 1926. She got
jobs in chorus lines but got fired from them,
then made a successful career as a model.
Two years in hospitals and a wheelchair
following a car crash would have blunted
most girls' ambition but not this one's. She
got back into modelling and had clawed her
way into tiny film roles by 1933. Drifting
from United Artists to Columbia and on to
RKO, it was three years before Lucy was
being given even small featured roles. Her
best part to date came in *Stage Door* (1937);
most of her roles at this stage were wisecracking dames, some way removed from
the broader type of clowning at which she
would prove herself so adept. There were a
few meaty dramatic parts, in *Five Came Back*
(1939), *The Big Street* (1942) and *The Dark
Corner* (1946). That was the year she stole
the show in a comedy role in *Easy to Wed* at
MGM, her fourth home studio. But it
wasn't until 1949, when she was at least
38 — one source gives her year of birth as
1908 — that things at last started to move in
the right direction. In two Columbia comedies (she'd left MGM in 1947), *Miss
Grant Takes Richmond* (in Britain *Innocence is
Bliss*) and *The Fuller Brush Girl* (in Britain
The Affairs of Sally), both made in 1949,
Lucy showed she could dominate a film and
make an audience laugh by comedy of action
and reaction. Her willingness to throw herself about in the cause of laughter was
further demonstrated by two comedies that
co-starred her with Bob Hope, *Sorrowful
Jones* (1949) and, especially, *Fancy Pants*
(1950), her biggest box-office success up to
that point. In 1951 Lucy and her husband.
Cuban bandleader Desi Arnaz, whom she
had married in 1940, decided on the strength
of a running skit they had performed on his
recent cross-country tour, to draw up the
format for a television show together. The
result was *I Love Lucy*, which debuted in

Heavily disguised from nose to toe, Lucille Ball impersonates a cleaning lady for an episode
of *I Love Lucy*

October 1951 and quickly became the most popular television comedy series of its time. At last Lucy was in her element. As Arnaz's accident-prone and predicament-prone wife, Lucy was endearingly goofy, game for anything and always able to upstage the odd guest star, such as Harpo Marx or John Wayne. Under her guidance the fun on *I Love Lucy* was fast and furious, and continued so for another six years. The couple divorced in 1960 and Arnaz sold out his interest in their very prosperous production company Desilu. Lucy made a couple more films with Bob Hope, but television was obviously her forte and she starred there in *Here's Lucy* from 1962 to 1974, giving her all in the cause of laughter. Performing less often in her last years, Lucille Ball had still come a long way from the time, 62 years ago, when she enrolled in her first drama school: 'I was a tongue-tied teenager spellbound by the school's star pupil – Bette Davis.' She died in 1989 following open heart surgery.

*1933: Broadway Thru a Keyhole. Blood Money. Roman Scandals. 1934: Moulin Rouge. Nana. Bottoms Up. Hold That Girl. Bulldog Drummond Strikes Back. The Affairs of Cellini. Kid Millions. Broadway Bill (GB: Strictly Confidential). Jealousy. Men of the Night. Fugitive Lady. The Whole Town's Talking (GB: Passport to Fame). * Perfectly Mismated. * Three Little Pigskins. 1935: Carnival. Roberta. Old Man Rhythm. * His Old Flame. Top Hat. The Three Musketeers. I Dream Too Much. * A Night at the Biltmore Bowl. 1936: * Dummy Ache. * One Live Ghost. * Swing It. Chatterbox. Follow the Fleet. The Farmer in the Dell. Bunker Bean (GB: His Majesty Bunker Bean). That Girl from Paris. * So and Sew. Winterset. 1937: Don't Tell the Wife. Stage Door. 1938: Joy of Living. Go Chase Yourself. Having Wonderful Time. The Affairs of Annabel. Room Service. The Next Time I Marry. 1939: Annabel Takes a Tour. Beauty for the Asking. Twelve Crowded Hours. Panama Lady. Five Came Back. That's Right, You're Wrong. 1940: The Marines Fly High. You Can't Fool Your Wife. Dance, Girl, Dance. Too Many Girls. 1941: A Girl, a Guy and a Gob (GB: The Navy Steps Out). Look Who's Laughing. 1942: Valley of the Sun. The Big Street. Seven Days' Leave. 1943: Dubarry Was a Lady. Best Foot Forward. Thousands Cheer. 1944: Meet the People. Ziegfeld Follies (released 1946). 1945: Without Love. Bud Abbott and Lou Costello in Hollywood. 1946: The Dark Corner. Easy to Wed. Two Smart People. Lover Come Back. 1947: Lured (GB: Personal Column). Her Husband's Affairs. 1949: Sorrowful Jones. Easy Living. Miss Grant Takes Richmond (GB: Innocence is Bliss). 1950: A Woman of Distinction. Fancy Pants. The Fuller Brush Girl (GB: The Affairs of Sally). 1951: The Magic Carpet. 1954: The Long, Long Trailer. 1956: Forever, Darling. 1960: The Facts of Life. 1963: Critic's Choice. 1967: A Guide for the Married Man. 1968: Yours, Mine and Ours. 1973: Mame. 1985: Stone Pillow (TV).*

BANKS, Monty
(Mario Bianchi) 1897–1950

Diminutive (5 ft 4½ in), moustachioed, dark, dapper Italian-born comic and director who first came to America at the age of 17 as a comic dancer. He began making small appearances in Mack Sennett films while still in his teens, but it was 1923 before he got a few starring comedies of his own. In these he was typically a quite elegant, but hapless hero, who won through against adversity in the end. In these ever-hopeful characters, blinking twitchily at their adversaries, but endowed with a special kind of innocence that was to see them through, one can see Banks's influence on other, more prominent comedians who followed close behind – notably Raymond Griffith and Harry Langdon (both *qv*). Despite this commendable building of character through a myriad of tiny mannerisms Banks never really did more than flirt with films as a star. He married actress Gladys Frazin in Hollywood (she was to commit suicide years after their divorce by throwing herself out of her apartment window) but went to Britain in the late 1920s with an eye to pursuing his ambitions as a director, having performed there as an eccentric dancer as early as 1912. Here he became publicly and then privately associated with Gracie Fields (*qv*). He continued a sporadic acting career, married Fields and directed her in several of her major musicals, in addition to making dozens of other minor comedies. With the advent of war the Bankses fled to America to avoid his possible internment as an alien. His last attempt at direction was made there: a latter-day, ramshackle Laurel and Hardy (*qv*) comedy, *Great Guns*. In 1950 Banks suffered a heart attack while on board the Orient Express travelling through his native Italy, and died, by now quite overshadowed by his more famous wife.

Silents (incomplete). *1916: * The Bright Lights. * The Moonshiners. * The Waiters' Ball. 1918: * The Geezer of Berlin. 1920: Poor Simp. * Don't Park Here. 1923: * Always Late. * Covered Schooner. * Southbound Ltd. * Taxi Please. 1925: * Keep Smiling. * Racing Luck. 1926: * Atta Boy! 1927: * Horse Shoes. * Play Safe! A Perfect Gentleman. * Flying*

Luck. 1928: Adam's Apple (US: Honeymoon Ahead). Weekend Wives. Atlantic.
Sound. *1930: The Compulsory Husband. 1932: Tonight's the Night. For the Love of Mike. 1933: You Made Me Love You. 1934: The Girl in Possession. The Church Mouse. 1935: So You Won't Talk. Man of the Moment. 1936: Queen of Hearts. Honeymoon Merry-Go-Round. 1941: † Blood and Sand. 1945: † A Bell for Adano.*
As director. *1928: Cocktails. 1930: * Amateur Night in London. Eve's Fall. The New Waiter. The Musical Beauty Shop. * The Jerry Builders. The Compulsory Husband. Not So Quiet on the Western Front. Kiss Me Sergeant. Why Sailors Leave Home. The Black Hand Gang. Almost a Honeymoon. 1931: Old Soldiers Never Die. What a Night! My Wife's Family. Poor Old Bill. 1932: Tonight's the Night. Money for Nothing. For the Love of Mike. 1933: Leave It to Me. Heads We Go (US: The Charming Deceiver). You Made Me Love You. 1934: Falling in Love. The Girl in Possession. The Church Mouse. Father and Son. 1935: Hello Sweetheart. Man of the Moment. Eighteen Minutes. No Limit. 1936: Queen of Hearts. Keep Your Seats, Please. 1938: We're Going to Be Rich. Keep Smiling (US: Smiling Along). 1939: Shipyard Sally. 1941: Great Guns.*
† As William Montague.

BANNER, John
(Johann Banner) 1910–1973

Chubby, pigeon-cheeked Austrian-born actor, in Hollywood from 1938. His broken English for a long time imperilled his American show business career but in the end it proved his salvation, when he took the nation by storm as the plumply inefficient Sergeant Hans Schultz in the long-running *Hogan's Heroes*. Schultz's menacing bluster was believed by no-one, least of all the inmates of Stalag 13, of which they were actually more in control than the Germans. Banner, Austrian by birth, was acting in Switzerland when the Nazi invasion of Austria decided him to head for America. A chance meeting with other European players in similar straits in New York gained him an early stage job on a revue, but it was four years before he managed an entry into films, playing mostly unpleasant Germans in a sporadic film career that never went any-where, even after his television success. However, his success as Schultz brought him financial security (*Hogan's Heroes* ran from 1965 to 1971), as well as scores of imitators. There was a second, mildly successful TV series for Banner in *The Chicago Teddy Bears* (1971), in which, in the footsteps of the similarly multi-jowled S. Z. Sakall (*qv*), he played Uncle Latzi, partner to star Dean Jones (*qv*) in a Chicago speak-easy of the 1920s. Having found success late in life, Banner did not live to enjoy its fruits in retirement, dying of an intestinal haemorrhage on his 63rd birthday.

1942: Once Upon a Honeymoon. Seven Miles from Alcatraz. The Moon Is Down. 1943: Tonight We Raid Calais. The Fallen Sparrow. 1946: Black Angel. Rendezvous. 1948: To the Victor. My Girl Tisa. 1950: Guilty of Treason (GB: Treason). 1953: The Juggler. 1955: The Rains of Ranchipur. 1958: The Beast of Budapest. 1959: The Blue Angel. 1960: The Story of Ruth. 1961: 20,000 Eyes. Operation Eichmann. Hitler. 1962: The Interns. 1963: The Yellow Canary. 1964: 36 Hours. 1968: The Wicked Dreams of Paula Schultz. 1970: Togetherness.

BARKER, Eric 1912–1990
A thinking man's comedian who was ad-mired by critics without ever quite becoming the darling of radio audiences, hesitantly handsome Eric Barker found a new string to his bow in his mid forties as a comic character actor in films. Neat, dark, some-times bespectacled Barker struggled in pre-war years as an impressionist on in between girlie acts at London's Windmill Theatre. Came the war, and Barker's career took off in *Merry-Go-Round*, an Army/RAF/Navy radio show that also gave birth to *Much-Binding-in-the-Marsh* and *Stand Easy*. Barker's Navy segment, *HMS Waterlogged*, which he wrote as well as starred in, brought to the fore his nimble wit, and a perfect sense of timing, whether chiming in sharply or hesitantly. The programme (which co-starred Barker's wife, dancer Pearl Hackney) continued after the war as *Waterlogged Spa*, the first (and certainly most riotous) of sev-

eral Barker radio shows, which also included *Barker's Folly* and the endearingly rambling *Just Fancy*. In 1956 Barker took up a career as a top character player in British comedy movies, working with the Boulting Brothers (he won a British Academy Award in their *Brothers in Law*), Launder and Gilliat in the St Trinian's films, and on the 'Carry On', 'Doctor' and 'Dentist' comedies. In these he was often seen as a busybody, down-trodden husband or petty official. Once jokingly self-billed as Eric 'Heartthrob' Barker, his catch-phrases included 'Steady Barker!' (also the title of his autobiography) and 'Carry on Smokin'.' A stroke in 1966 restricted Barker's later appearances, although he made a good recovery. He had an actress daughter, Petronella Barker.

*1936: Carry On London. 1937: West End Frolics. Concert Party. 1938: On Velvet. 1956: Brothers in Law. 1957: Happy is the Bride! 1958: Blue Murder at St Trinian's. Carry On Sergeant. * A Clean Sweep. Bachelor of Hearts. 1959: Left, Right and Centre. 1960: Carry On Constable. Dentist in the Chair. Watch Your Stern. The Pure Hell of St Trinian's. 1961: Dentist on the Job (US: Get On with It!). Nearly a Nasty Accident. Raising the Wind. On the Fiddle (US: Operation Snafu). 1962: Carry On Cruising. The Fast Lady. On the Beat. 1963: The Mouse on the Moon. Heavens Above! Father Came Too. 1964: The Bargee. Carry On Spying. Ferry 'Cross the Mersey. 1965: Three Hats for Lisa. Those Magnificent Men in Their Flying Machines. 1966: Doctor in Clover. The Great St Trinian's Train Robbery. Maroc 7. 1969: Twinky (US: Lola). 1970: There's a Girl in My Soup. Cool It Carol! (US: The Dirtiest Girl I Ever Met). 1972: That's Your Funeral. 1978: The Chiffy Kids (second series). Carry On Emmannuelle.*

BARKER, Ronnie 1929–
Big, beaming, bespectacled British com-edian, latterly with white hair — often seen as lechers, con-men and other types not quite on the level. An expert at one-liners, and an arch-portrayer of snappy or per-plexed lecturers hurrying through some baffling or tongue-twisting harangue. After early struggles in repertory, Barker became

popular on radio and particularly television, where he had several successful series: *Por-ridge*, *Open All Hours*, *The Magnificent Evans* and especially *The Two Ronnies*, a sketch-and-variety show which teamed him with the diminutive Ronnie Corbett (*qv*), and ran for more than 20 years, placing the emphasis on red-nosed comedy and smart plays-on-words. Revelling in the occasional mon-strous female disguise, Barker kept an admirably straight face in the unlikeliest of situations, proving himself no mean actor in the process. He came to the fore too late for success as a film character star, however (he was very much a supporting player in his early movie years), and, apart from the film version of *Porridge*, was never given a movie vehicle of his own. He retired in 1988.

*1953: * The Silent Witness. 1958: Wonderful Things! 1962: Kill Or Cure. 1963: The Cracksman. Doctor in Distress. Father Came Too. 1964: The Bargee. A Home of Your Own. 1965: Runaway Railway. 1967: The Man Outside. A Ghost of a Chance. 1968: * Two Off the Cuff (voice only). 1970: Futtock's End. 1971: The Magnificent Seven Deadly Sins. 1976: Robin and Marian. 1979: Porridge.*

BEERY, Wallace 1886–1949
As rough-and-ready as many of the charac-ters he played, Beery was a great lummox of a man who rode roughshod over life. His penchant for ad-libbing lines horrified di-rectors and co-stars alike but he paid them no attention. He was a major star of Holly-wood in its early sound years, often as a tough guy with feet of clay. Before and after his prime period Beery was often to be seen in 'series' comedies, usually team efforts that paired him with equally homely and vigorous partners. The younger brother of prime silent-screen villain Noah Beery, Wallace worked in a circus in his teenage years but by 1904 had followed Noah to New York and a stage career. In 1914 he joined Essanay Studios at the princely sum of 75 dollars a week, and played a Swedish housemaid called Sweedie in a popular series of one-reel comedies in which Beery would mug and grimace away like mad as perhaps the cinema's least likely girl on record. The

Swcedic comedies had fizzled out by 1916, and Beery worked with other comedians, married Gloria Swanson in the same year (it lasted two years), sought work as a director, and finally began to establish himself as a leering heavy and character star. Another series of comedies, opposite skinny Raymond Hatton, from 1925 to 1928, was followed by a call from M-G-M, for whom he worked (from 1929) for the remaining 20 years of his life. The head of the studio, Louis B. Mayer, was so appalled by Beery's lack of finesse that he had him actually at the studio as little as possible: 'Get him in, make the picture and get him out' was Mayer's comment on one of his biggest box-office stars. It was at this studio that Beery formed a massively popular team with veteran Marie Dressler (qv) in Min and Bill and Tugboat Annie, and steamrollered his way through more serious roles in The Big House, The Champ (winning an Oscar as a washed-up boxer), Grand Hotel, Dinner at Eight, The Secret Six and Viva Villa!. As his box-office power waned, Beery reverted to amiable comedy, making the first of several films with raucous Marjorie Main (qv) in 1940. He was still turning out rugged action-comedies up to the time he succumbed to a heart attack at 63. Hollywood's lovable slob, who played variations of his real self on screen throughout his career, had made few demands. 'Just spell the name right', he once told an M-G-M executive, 'and give me my snooze in the afternoon.' To a reporter he said: 'My mug has been my fortune. You can't get luckier than that.'

If an unexpected message were to come out from behind him, Wallace Beery looks in danger of falling overboard in this scene from his great popular success *Tugboat Annie*

1914: * *Sweedie and the Lord.* * *Sweedie and the Double Exposure.* * *Sweedie's Skate.* * *Sweedie Springs a Surprise.* * *The Fickleness of Sweedie.* * *Sweedie Learns to Swim.* * *She Landed a Big One.* * *Sweedie and the Trouble Maker.* * *Sweedie at the Fair.* * *Madame Double X.* * *The Plum Tree.* * *Sweedie the Swatter.* * *The Fable of the Bush League Lover Who Failed to Qualify.* * *The Broken Pledge.* * *Chick Evans Links with Sweedie.* 1915: * *Sweedie's Suicide.* * *Sweedie and Her Dog.* * *Two Hearts That Beat as Ten.* * *Sweedie's Hopeless Love.* * *Sweedie Goes to College.* * *Love and Trouble.* * *Sweedie Learns to Ride.* * *Sweedie's Hero.* * *The Slim Princess.* * *Sweedie in Vaudeville.* * *Sweedie's Finish.* 1916: * *Sweedie the Janitor.* * *Teddy at the Throttle.* * *A Dash of Courage.* 1917: * *Cactus Nell.* * *The Clever Dummy.* * *Maggie's First False Step. Patria* (serial). *The Little American.* 1918: *Johanna Enlists.* 1919: *The Love Burglar. The Unpardonable Sin. Life Line. Soldier of Fortune. Behind the Door. Victory. The Virgin of Stamboul.* 1920: *The Mollycoddle. The Roundup. The Last of the Mohicans. The Rookies Return.* 1921: *The Four Horsemen of the Apocalypse. 813. Patsy. A Tale of Two Worlds. The Golden Snare. The Last Trail.* 1922: *Wild Honey. The Man from Hell's River. The Rosary. The Sagebrush Trail. Ridin' Wild. I Am the Law. Robin Hood. Trouble Associated. Hurricane's Gal. Only a Shop Girl.* 1923:

Stormswept. The Flame of Life. Bavu. Ashes of Vengeance. Drifting. The Eternal Struggle. The Spanish Dancer. The Three Ages. Richard, the Lion-Hearted. Drums of Jeopardy. White Tiger. 1924: *The Sea Hawk. Unseen Hands. Madonna of the Streets. Dynamite Smith. Another Man's Woman. The Red Lily. The Signal Tower. So Big.* 1925: *Let Women Alone. The Great Divide. Coming Through. The Devil's Cargo. Adventure. The Lost World. The Night Club. Rugged Water. In the Name of Love. Pony Express.* 1926: *Behind the Front. Volcano. Old Ironsides* (GB: *Sons of the Sea*). *We're in the Navy Now. The Wanderer.* 1927: *Casey at the Bat. Fireman, Save My Child. Now We're in the Air.* 1928: *Wife Savers. Partners in Crime. The Big Killing. Beggars of Life.* 1929: *Chinatown Nights. Stairs of Sand. River of Romance.* 1930: *Way for a Sailor. Billy the Kid. A Lady's Morals* (GB: *Jenny Lind*). *The Big House. Min and Bill.* 1931:

The Secret Six. Hell Divers. The Champ. 1932: *Grand Hotel. Flesh.* * *The Stolen Jools* (GB: *The Slippery Pearls*). 1933: *Dinner at Eight. Tugboat Annie. The Bowery.* 1934: *The Mighty Barnum. Viva Villa! Treasure Island.* 1935: *West Point of the Air. China Seas. Ah, Wilderness! O'Shaughnessy's Boy.* 1936: *A Message to Garcia. Old Hutch.* 1937: *Good Old Soak. Slave Ship.* 1938: *Bad Man of Brimstone. Port of Seven Seas. Stablemates.* 1939: *Stand Up and Fight.* * *Screen Snapshots No. 77. Sergeant Madden. Thunder Afloat.* 1940: *The Man from Dakota* (GB: *Arouse and Beware*). *Twenty Mule Team. Wyoming* (GB: *Bad Man of Wyoming*). 1941: *The Bad Man* (GB: *Two Gun Cupid*). *Barnacle Bill. The Bugle Sounds.* 1942: *Jackass Mail.* 1943: *Salute to the Marines.* 1944: *Rationing. Barbary Coast Gent.* 1945: *This Man's Navy.* 1946: *Bad Bascomb. The Mighty McGurk.* 1948: *Alias a Gentleman. A Date with Judy.* 1949: *Big Jack.*

BELUSHI, John 1949–1982

Dark, chubby, uncouth-type American comedian who built up an enormous following on TV in the late 1970s. But there were to be few films: dangerous living and a consequent early death robbed John Belushi of an undoubted high-level participation in the lively movie comedy scene of the 1980s and beyond. A hot box-office draw in partnership with Dan Aykroyd (qv), Belushi, a hard-cursing Lou Costello (qv) for the 1980s, moved into films via success on the rule-breaking late-night TV comedy show *Saturday Night Live*. As with Costello, Belushi's films did better at the box-office than with critics. His comedy techniques were unsubtle, but still convulsed the majority of audiences, especially in his native America. However, after only a few years of stardom he was found dead from an overdose of cocaine and other drugs. A film about his volatile life, *Wired*, appeared in 1988. His brother Jim Belushi (1951–) became popular in blue-collar comedy and thriller roles in the late 1980s and early 1990s.

1975: *Le honte de la jungle* (GB: *Jungle Burger*. US: *Shame of the Jungle*. Voice only). 1978: *National Lampoon's Animal House*. *Goin' South*. *Old Boyfriends*. 1979: *1941*. 1980: *The Blues Brothers*. 1981: *Neighbors*. *Continental Divide*.

BENCHLEY, Robert 1889–1945

A humorist rather than a comedian, Robert Benchley's was one of the driest wits that ever invaded Hollywood. Blissfully befuddled in most of his appearances, Benchley's sense of comic timing was God given, and there can have been few actors who relished the idea of having him in the same scene. Through 30 years, if you were looking for an after-dinner speaker who would reduce the company to uncontrollable laughter, then Benchley was your man. A Harvard graduate of 1912, he began in advertising, but within a couple of years became associate editor of New York's *Tribune* Sunday magazine. But it was as a columnist for *New York World* and especially *The New Yorker* through the 1920s that he made his name. He began a spellbinding series of

film shorts in 1928, appearing first as a meandering lecturer, and later as the narrator and protagonist of the *How to* series which, of course, were really about 'how not to'. His bumbling appearances in features, rolling off inspired idiocies that he must surely have written himself, were occasions for the audience to savour but must have produced a sinking feeling in the heart of many a fellow-player. The same roly-poly features that could express sly triumph after another victorious verbal dogfight could easily be made to crumple in bewilderment as a thoroughly bemused Benchley lost another of his battles in the *How to* series, one of which, *How to Sleep* (1935), took an Oscar. He would probably have happily continued demonstrating how to make cinema audiences fall victim to a sudden chortle had not a cerebral haemorrhage killed him at 56. Benchley's long-time alcoholism was never a problem in his film appearances. On the contrary, it lent a raucous edge to his rasping wit.

1928: * *The Treasurer's Report*. * *The Sex Life of the Polyp*. * *The Spellbinder*. 1929: * *Furnace Trouble*. * *Lesson Number One*. * *Stewed, Fried and Boiled*. 1933: *Headline Shooter* (GB: *Evidence in Camera*). *Rafter Romance*. * *Your Technocracy and Mine*. *Dancing Lady*. 1934: *The Social Register*. 1935: *China Seas*. * *How to Sleep*. * *How to Break 90 At Croquet*. 1936: * *How to Behave*. * *How to Train a Dog*. * *How to Vote*. * *How to be a Detective*. *Piccadilly Jim*. 1937: *Live, Love and Learn*. * *The Romance of Digestion*. *Broadway Melody of 1938*. * *How to Start the Day*. * *A Night at the Movies*. 1938: * *Music Made Simple*. * *How to Figure Income Tax*. * *An Evening Alone*. * *The Courtship of the Newt*. * *Opening Day*. * *Mental Poise*. * *An Hour for Lunch*. * *How to Raise a Baby*. * *How to Read*. * *How to Watch Football*. * *How to Sub-let*. 1939: * *How to Eat*. * *Dark Magic*. * *Home Early*. * *The Day of Rest*. * *See Your Doctor*. 1940: * *Home Movies*. * *That Inferior Feeling*. * *The Trouble with Husbands*. *Foreign Correspondent*. *Hired Wife*. 1941: *Bedtime Story*. *Nice Girl? The Reluctant Dragon*. *Three Girls About Town*. *You'll Never Get Rich*. * *How to Take a Vacation*. * *Waiting for Baby*. * *Crime Control*.

* *The Forgotten Man*. 1942: * *Nothing But Nerves*. * *The Witness*. * *The Man's Angle*. * *Keeping in Shape*. *I Married a Witch*. *The Major and the Minor*. *Take a Letter, Darling* (GB: *The Green-Eyed Woman*). 1943: *Flesh and Fantasy*. *The Sky's the Limit*. *Song of Russia*. *Young and Willing*. * *My Tomato*. * *No News Is Good News*. 1944: * *Important Business*. * *The National Barn Dance*. * *Why, Daddy?* *Her Primitive Man*. *Janie*. *Practically Yours*. *See Here, Private Hargrove*. *It's in the Bag!* (GB: *The Fifth Chair*). 1945: *Duffy's Tavern*. *Kiss and Tell*. *Pan-Americana*. *Snafu* (GB: *Welcome Home*). *Week-End at the Waldorf*. * *Hollywood Victory Caravan*. * *I'm a Civilian Here Myself*. *Road to Utopia*. * *Boogie Woogie*. 1946: *Janie Gets Married*. *The Bride Wore Boots*.

BENDIX, William 1906–1964

The big lug that everybody loved in the 1940s and 1950s, barrel-chested, fairhaired, small-eyed William Bendix came to the screen playing dumb gorillas who could be comic or violently dramatic. But it was only on television a decade later that he proved his worth as an audience-pulling comedy star. It was then that Bendix's instinctive sense of comic timing, in both verbal and visual terms. really hit home. Far from the dim-witted, blue-collar bozos that he usually portrayed, to which his soft Manhattan accent gave the perfect vocal accompaniment, Bendix was a welleducated man whose father Max, a professional violinist, was at one time conductor of the Metropolitan Opera orchestra. Burly Bill Bendix, however, pursued no musical ambitions (although he was good at baseball and played semi-professional) and even took to running a grocery store for a while until turning to acting in his late twenties. He made his Broadway debut (as an Irish policeman) with the New York Theatre Guild in 1939. Bendix's first films were comedies for the Hal Roach Studio that cast him as a dozy cab-driver, but wartime producers looked at his bulk, big nose and set expression and saw him in more menacing roles. Variously vicious and friendly types in such Alan Ladd action films as *The Glass Key*, *China*, *Two Years Before the Mast* and

The Blue Dahlia (beating Ladd, lashing him, or going nuts in *Dahlia* with the 'monkey music' inside his head) made Bendix part of the Paramount scene. He did some comedy for them, too, and was a very funny and likeable Sir Sagramore in Bing Crosby's *A Connecticut Yankee in King Arthur's Court*. It was two small comedies at other studios that showed Bendix as a solo performer able to take charge of comedy of chaos and reduce an audience to tears of laughter. One was *The Life of Riley*, with Bendix as Chester A. Riley, a character he had created in a long-running radio series in 1944, the other *Kill the Umpire!*, a visual and verbal riot about a baseball umpire, with a script by Frank Tashlin. *The Life of Riley* also became a very popular TV series, with Jackie Gleason (*qv*) at first playing the harassed family man who was his own worst enemy. Bendix took over the role in January 1953 and played it until the series ended in 1958, giving the nation another catch-phrase: 'What a revoltin' development!' which would be passed on to the cartoon character Sylvester the cat. In the year the series ended Bendix made another film with Alan Ladd, *The Deep Six*, but both men were now past the peak of their popularity. In the few years remaining to him Bendix made films in England, launched a comedy and juggling nightclub act with two partners and starred in a Broadway musical, *Take Me Along*. In December 1964, Bendix was taken to hospital suffering from lobar pneumonia and died within a week. He was the kind of actor it was always a pleasure to find in films, whether the role was big or small.

1941: *Woman of the Year*. 1942: *The McGuerins from Brooklyn. Who Done It? Brooklyn Orchid. Wake Island. The Glass Key. Star Spangled Rhythm*. 1943: *China. The Crystal Ball. Hostages. Taxi, Mister. Guadalcanal Diary. Lifeboat*. 1944: *The Hairy Ape.* * *Skirmish on the Home Front. Abroad with Two Yanks. Greenwich Village. It's in the Bag!* (GB: *The Fifth Chair*). 1945: *Duffy's Tavern. Don Juan Quilligan. A Bell for Adano. Calcutta* (released 1947). *The Blue Dahlia*. 1946: *Two Years Before the Mast. The Dark Corner. Sentimental Journey. White Tie and Tails. I'll Be Yours*. 1947: *Blaze of Noon. Where There's Life. Variety Girl. The Web*. 1948: *The Time of Your Life. Race Street. The Babe Ruth Story*. 1949: *The Life of Riley. A Connecticut Yankee in King Arthur's Court* (GB: *A Yankee in King Arthur's Court*). *The Big Steal*. ‡ *Two Knights in Brooklyn/Two Mugs from Brooklyn. Streets of Laredo. Cover Up. Johnny Holiday*. 1950: *Kill the Umpire! Gambling House*. 1951: *Submarine Command. Detective Story*. 1952: *Blackbeard the Pirate. A Girl in Every Port. Macao*. 1954: *Dangerous Mission*. 1955: *Crashout*. * *Hollywood Shower of Stars*. 1956: *Battle Stations. Going His Way* (narrator only). 1958: *The Deep Six*. 1959: *A Quiet Game of Cards* (TV). *Idle on Parade* (US: *Idol on Parade*). *The Rough and the Smooth* (US: *Portrait of a Sinner*). 1961: *Johnny Nobody. The Phoney American* (GB: *It's a Great Life*). 1962: *Boys' Night Out*. * *Cash on the Barrel Head*. 1963: *The Young and the Brave. For Love or Money. Law of the Lawless*. 1964: *Young Fury*.

‡ Combined GB version of *The McGuerins from Brooklyn/Taxi, Mister*.

BENNY, Jack

(Benjamin Kubelsky) 1894–1974

Solemn-faced American stand-up comedian, most successful on radio but a frequent visitor to the cinema screen until 1945. Benny feigned meanness, crotchetiness, vainness, age-consciousness (he was always 39) and easily-hurt feelings as part of his comic armoury. There were also his bad violin-playing (which he didn't really have to feign) and his long silences, usually while he pretended to torment over comprehension or an answer. The standard of Benny's material wasn't always high but since he could work wonders without saying anything it didn't often matter. He began his career in entertainment with the intention of becoming a musician but, with the advent of World War One, he enlisted in the US Navy and discovered new talents as a comic. Back in civilian life Benny began a vaudeville career under the name Ben K. Benny, combining his violin-playing with comedy, as did the British-based radio comedians Vic Oliver and Ted Ray (*qv*). But Benny's style was uniquely droll and almost always self-deprecating. He was making film shorts by 1928 and was soon a star on radio, combining with his wife (from 1927) Mary Livingstone (real name: Sadye Marks). In the 1930s the radio show became America's (and probably the world's) most popular comedy programme and Benny began to make more positive film appearances that traded on his established image. The cinema never quite captured Benny's appeal and his films were rarely more than lightly enjoyable, with the exception of the occasional gem such as *To Be or Not to Be* in 1942. That gave Benny a chance to be a bit more than just a comedian as a Polish ham actor dodging the Nazis. But he really needed an audience to milk and television proved just the ticket. *The Jack Benny Show* began in 1950, using much the same formula as the radio show (and much the same cast, including Eddie 'Rochester' Anderson (*qv*) and Mary Livingstone). Benny just stood there, with that pained look (and equally pained voice), seeming to let the others do the work and suffering visibly from life's vicissitudes and unfairnesses. Benny's scriptwriters were at their best in the way

The very name of Jackson strikes terror into the hearts of William Bendix (right) and Lionel Jeffries (seated) in *Idle on Parade*

they were always thinking of new ways to take comic advantage of his parsimoniousness. Once they had Benny walking home at night when held up by what we would nowadays call a mugger. The robber tells Benny that it's his money or his life — then, angered by the lack of reply, repeats the threat. Benny, tetchily, blurts out that he's thinking it over. And we believe him. The TV show finished in 1965 and Benny made sporadic guest appearances on stage, in films and on TV before his death from stomach cancer on Boxing Day 1974. Ironically, one of his more famous poses was that he hated Christmas time because of the money he had to fork out on presents. In private life, not unexpectedly, this narcissistic Scrooge was actually a modest and generous man.

*1928: * Bright Moments. 1929: Hollywood Revue of 1929. * The Songwriters' Revue. 1930: Strictly Modern. * The Rounder. Chasing Rainbows. Medicine Man. 1931: * A Broadway Romeo. * Cab Waiting. * Taxi Tangle. 1933: Mr Broadway. 1934: Transatlantic Merry-Go-Round. 1935: Broadway Melody of 1936. It's in the Air. 1936: * Broadway Highlights No. 1. The Big Broadcast of 1937. College Holiday. 1937: Artists and Models. Manhattan Merry-Go-Round (GB: Manhattan Music Box). 1938: Artists and Models Abroad (GB: Stranded in Paris). 1939: Man About Town. 1940: Buck Benny Rides Again. Love Thy Neighbor. 1941: Charley's Aunt. 1942: To Be or Not To Be. George Washington Slept Here. 1943: * Show Business at War. * Screen Snapshots No. 109. The Meanest Man in the World. 1944: Hollywood Canteen. It's in the Bag! (GB: The Fifth Chair). 1945: The Horn Blows at Midnight. 1946: Without Reservations. 1948: * Screen Snapshots No. 166. * Radio Broadcasting Today. 1949: The Lucky Stiff. The Great Lover. * A Rainy Day in Hollywood. 1952: Somebody Loves Me. * Memorial to Al Jolson (narrator only). 1953: * Hollywood's Pair of Jacks. 1954: Susan Slept Here. 1955: The Seven Little Foys. 1957: Beau James. 1958: * Fabulous Hollywood. * The Mouse That Jack Built. 1959: Who Was That Lady? 1962: Gypsy. 1963: It's a Mad, Mad, Mad, Mad World. 1967: A Guide for the Married Man. 1972: The Man.*

BERGEN, Edgar 1903–1978

Another of the great American radio stars of the 1930s, Edgar Bergen was, like Britain's Peter Brough, a phenomenon — a ventriloquist who earned his greatest fame in a medium where no-one could see him. Dark, debonair, stocky and thin-mouthed, Bergen (father of the actress Candice Bergen) became interested in ventriloquism while still at high school, after spending 25 cents on a copy of Hermann's Wizard Manual. It was his only outlay towards getting up an act until he bought his first (and most famous) dummy, the wiseacre Charlie McCarthy. McCarthy helped Bergen pay his way through university before they launched a show business career together, hitting the

vaudeville circuit in 1925 and radio a few years later. There were a couple of experimental film shorts in 1930 and a whole cluster for Vitaphone a few years later. McCarthy was the funny man, naturally, Bergen providing him with an endless stream of witticisms that centred on the fact that he was, after all, a wooden doll, and inventing some ingenious byplay between McCarthy and guest stars on their radio show, which by this time included another Bergen doll, the slow-witted Mortimer Snerd. Bergen won a special Oscar for his creation of McCarthy in 1937, the same year the wooden wit toppled Jack Benny (qv) from his position as American radio's most popular entertainer. Bergen and McCarthy often tangled with W. C. Fields (qv) on these shows, and there was a classic Christmas 1937 confrontation with Mae West ('Ya certainly did kiss me, Charlie. I got marks to prove it. An' splinters too') that brought howls of outrage from religious associations and got West banned from radio. But Bergen himself was moving on to feature films, starring with Fields (who sets Bergen, McCarthy and Snerd adrift in a balloon) in *You Can't Cheat an Honest Man*, and shining in several other movies before providing himself with a dual career as a post-war nightclub entertainer and occasional character actor in films and TV. Bergen was half-way through his farewell engagement, at Las Vegas, before a planned retirement when he died from a heart attack in his sleep. Charlie McCarthy, silenced at last, was bequeathed by his master to the Smithsonian Institution.

*1930: * The Operation. * The Office Scandal. 1933: * Africa Speaks . . . English. * Free and Easy. 1934: * At the Races. * Pure Feud. 1935: * All American Drawback. * Two Boobs in a Balloon. 1936: * 2 Minutes to Play. 1938: The Goldwyn Follies. A Letter of Introduction. 1939: Charlie McCarthy, Detective. You Can't Cheat an Honest Man. 1941: Look Who's Laughing. 1942: Here We Go Again. 1943: Stage Door Canteen. 1944: Song of the Open Road. 1947: Fun and Fancy Free. 1948: I Remember Mama. 1949: Captain China. 1950: * Charlie McCarthy and Mortimer Snerd in Sweden. 1964: The Hanged Man*

(TV. GB: cinemas). 1965: One-Way Wahine. 1967: Don't Make Waves. Rogue's Gallery. 1969: The Phynx. 1971: The Homecoming (TV). 1975: Won Ton Ton, the Dog Who Saved Hollywood. 1979: The Muppet Movie.

BERLE, Milton
(M. Berlinger) 1908–

'Mr Television', 'Uncle Miltie', 'Mr Tuesday night', a blast from our television past. All that remains of Milton Berle in the memory now is that huge grin, standing on its own, like the only part of the Cheshire Cat that Alice could sometimes see. Yet in his day Uncle Miltie cleared the nation's streets as they flocked to the box each Tuesday for eight years from 1948 to 1956. He'd worked hard for his success — 35 years' hard, from a start at five as the bounciest pupil of the Professional Children's School in New York. With his sister he toured the vaudeville circuit as a boy, while his showbiz mother also got the appealing-looking kid roles in silent pictures. He played his first stage role at 12 and was performing on Broadway the following year. Vaudeville sketches with a comic called Jack Duffy sent him on his way as a comedian, and he had a successful solo act at New York's Palace Theatre by 1931. There were films in Hollywood from 1937 but they were mostly minor. Many of them came in the war years when practically every American comedian with some kind of reputation in radio or nightclubs was shunted into films to try to cheer up wartime audiences. The best of these cut-and-paste movies, none of which lasted much longer than an hour, was *Over My Dead Body*, with Berle as a private eye who accidentally frames himself for murder. Another, *Whispering Ghosts*, follows the same formula — radio sleuth forced to play detective in real life — that was popularised by Red Skelton (qv) in the 'Whistling' series. Berle's biggest film enterprise came after he had established himself as a major comic cheese on both radio and television. *Always Leave Them Laughing*, with its story of the rise and fall of a self-opinionated comic, not only contains some of Berle's classic routines but reflects in its title his personal philosophy. Berle would do anything for a laugh, whether it involved coming on stage as a woman, or in a barrel. He had no great individuality, save his own geniality, but his beaming smile filled American living-rooms from 1948 to 1956, his show, fashioned along lines similar to old-style vaudeville, frequently topping the charts. His latter years have been mainly spent as comedian on the nightclub circuit, a TV comeback in the late 1960s proving unsuccessful – but there have also been several typically extrovert cameo appearances in films. Seventy-nine years an entertainer: if there's a show business long-service award then 'Uncle Miltie' has surely earned it. Berle has said that he appeared in over 50 silent films as a boy. Records of these are scanty, and the list that follows is certainly incomplete. Two of the films Berle asserts he made are titles he lists as *The Maid's Night Out*, with Mabel Normand, and *Birthright*, with Flora Finch. While Berle undoubtedly appeared with both ladies, these particular titles do not seem to exist. The Normand film may be *Betty Becomes a Maid* (1911).

Silents (incomplete). *1914: Tess of the Storm Country. The Perils of Pauline (serial). Tillie's Punctured Romance. Bunny's Little Brother. 1915: Fanchon the Cricket. 1916: Easy Street. 1917: Rebecca of Sunnybrook Farm. The Little Brother. 1919: The Wishing Ring Man. Eyes on Youth. 1920: The Mark of Zorro. Humoresque. 1921: Love's Penalty. 1922: Divorce Coupons. The Beauty Shop. Quincy Adams Sawyer. 1923: Ruth of the Range (serial). 1925: Lena Rivers. 1926. Sparrows. Beverly of Graustark.*
Sound (complete). *1932: * Poppin' the Cork. 1937: New Faces of 1937. 1938: Radio City Revels. 1941: Tall, Dark and Handsome. Sun Valley Serenade. Rise and Shine. 1942: Whispering Ghosts. A Gentleman at Heart. 1943: Over My Dead Body. Margin for Error. 1945: The Dolly Sisters. 1949: Always Leave Them Laughing. 1960: Let's Make Love. The Bellboy. 1963: It's a Mad, Mad, Mad, Mad World. 1965: The Loved One. 1966: The Oscar. Don't Worry, We'll Think of a Title. 1967: The Happening. The Silent Treatment. Who's Minding the Mint? 1968: Where Angels Go, Trouble Follows. For Singles Only. 1969: Can Hieronymous Merkin Ever Forget Mercy Humppe and Find True Happiness? Seven in Darkness (TV). The April Fools. 1970: Love, American Style (TV). 1971: Journey Back to Oz (voice only). 1972: Evil Roy Slade (TV). 1974: Lepke. 1975: The Legend of Valentino (TV). Won Ton Ton, the Dog Who Saved Hollywood. 1978: The Muppet Movie. 1979: 'Hey Abbott' (TV). 1983: Smorgasbord. 1988: Side by Side (TV). 1991: Autobahn (US: Trabbi Goes to Hollywood).*

BEVAN, Billy

(William Bevan Harris) 1887–1957
Australian star of silent comedy shorts, with a big moon face (decorated by king-size toothbrush moustache) atop a stumpy body, raised eyebrows and dark hair and with an energetic clowning style. A graduate from the university of Sydney, Bevan gained some experience with a light opera company founded by his friend Snub Pollard (*qv*), whom he followed to Hollywood in 1917. Signing with the Mack Sennett studio, Bevan was soon a popular star of comedy shorts, although his tiny stature was dwarfed even by some of the Sennett bathing beauties. Forever on the run through chase sequences, the tiny Bevan cut a sympathetic character as a David attempting to get the better of the Goliaths after his skin. Surprisingly, clips from Bevan films turn up in latter-day compilations of silent comedy just as often as those from films by acknowledged comedy kings, indicating the durability of the always-on-the-move style of comedy he patented in his pictures. People still treasure the sequence in the 1925 hit *Super-Hooper-Dyne Lizzies* in which Bevan, pushing his car after it has broken down, picks up sundry other vehicles without apparently noticing the added weight, until he pushes the entire cortege over the edge of a cliff. By this time, however, Bevan was being forced to share the spotlight with another Sennett comic, Andy Clyde (*qv*). Although many of these films were fast-paced and funny, Clyde was their mainspring – and he had a moustache that was even bigger than Bevan's! Clyde was to leave Sennett in 1932 but by this time Billy Bevan had already settled into the second phase of his cinema career, as a largely comic character actor. He usually had only a scene or two, often as a perplexed policeman – something of a joke considering his height which would have got him rejected from almost any police force in the world. After 20 years in this new mould Bevan eventually retired in the early 1950s, but was able to enjoy only a few years of taking life easy before a heart ailment killed him at 69.

*1920: * Let 'Er Go. *‡ The Quack Doctor. * My Goodness. Love, Honor and Behave. * It's a Boy. * A Fireside Brewer. 1921: * Love and Doughnuts. * Be Reasonable. * By Heck. * A Stray from the Steerage. A Small Town Idol. 1922: * Home-Made Movies. * Gymnasium Jim. * The Duck Hunter. * Oh Daddy. * On Patrol. * Ma and Pa. * When Summer Comes. The Crossroads of New York. 1923: The Extra Girl. * Nip and Tuck. * Inbad the Sailor. 1924: The White Sin. * Wandering Waistlines. * Wall Street Blues. * Lizzies of the Field. * The Cannon Ball Express. * One Spooky Night. 1925: * Honeymoon Hardships. * The Lion's Whiskers. * Skinners in Silk. * The Iron Nag. * Butter Fingers. * From Rags to Britches. * Giddap. * Super-Hooper-Dyne Lizzies. * Sneezing Beezers. * Over There-Abouts. 1926: * Circus Today. * Whispering Whiskers. * Ice Cold Cocos. * Trimmed in Gold. * Wandering Willies. * Fight Night. * Hayfoot, Strawfoot. * Muscle Bound Music. * A Sea Dog's Tale. * Masked Mamas. * Hubby's Quiet Little Game. * Hoboken to Hollywood. * The Divorce Dodger. * Flirty Four-Flushers. 1927: * Peaches and Plumbers. * Should Sleepwalkers Marry? * Easy Pickings. * Gold Digger of Weepah. * The Bull Fighter. * Cured in the Excitement. * The Golf Nut. A Small Town Princess. 1928: Motorboat Mamas. * Motoring Mamas. * Blindfold. * The Best Man. * The Bicycle Flirt. * His Unlucky Night. * Caught in the Kitchen. * Hubby's Latest Alibi. * The Lion's Roar. * The Beach Club. Riley the Cop. * His New Steno. * Hubby's Week-End Trip. 1929: High Voltage. * Foolish Husbands. * Pink Pajamas. * Calling Hubby's Bluff. * Button My Back. * Don't Get Jealous. The Sky Hawks. * The Trespasser. 1930: * Scotch. Journey's End. For the Love o' Lil (GB: For the Love of Lil). Temptation (GB: So Like a Woman). Peacock Alley. For the Defense. 1931: Born to Love. Transatlantic. * Ashore from the Steerage. * Bungalow Troubles. 1932: Sky Devils. Me and My Gal (GB: Pier 13). The Silent Witness. Payment Deferred. Vanity Fair. * Honeymoon Beach. * Spot on the Rug. 1933: Looking Forward (GB: Service). * The Big Squeal. Alice in Wonderland. Cavalcade. Luxury Liner. * Uncle Jake. A Study in Scarlet. Midnight Club. Too Much Harmony. The Way to Love. Peg o' My Heart. 1934: Bulldog Drummond Strikes Back. The Lost Patrol. Shock. One More River (GB: Over The River). Caravan. Limehouse Blues. 1935: Black Sheep. A Tale of Two Cities. The Last Outpost. Mystery Woman. Widow from Monte Carlo. 1936: Mr Deeds Goes to Town. The Song and Dance Man. Lloyds of London. Dracula's Daughter. Piccadilly Jim. Private Number (GB: Secret Interlude). God's Country and the Woman. 1937: Slave Ship. Another Dawn. Personal Property (GB: The Man in Possession). The Sheik Steps Out. The Wrong Road. Riding on Air. The Soldier and the Lady (GB: Michael Strogoff) 1938: Arrest Bulldog Drummond. The Girl of the Golden West. The Young in Heart. Mysterious Mr Moto. Shadows over Shanghai. Blonde Cheat. Bringing Up Baby. 1939: Pack Up Your Troubles (GB: We're in the Army Now). Captain Fury. We Are Not Alone. Let Freedom Ring. Grand Jury Secrets. 1940: The Invisible Man Returns. The Earl of Chicago. The Long Voyage Home. Tin Pan Alley. 1941: One Night in Lisbon. Shining Victory. Dr Jekyll and Mr Hyde. Confirm or Deny. Suspicion. Scotland Yard. Penny Serenade. 1942: This*

Above All. I Married a Witch. Mrs Miniver. The Man Who Wouldn't Die. Counter Espionage. London Blackout Murders (GB: Secret Motive). 1943: Young and Willing. Holy Matrimony. Forever and a Day. The Return of the Vampire. Jane Eyre. Appointment in Berlin. 1944: Once Upon a Time. The Pearl of Death. The Lodger. National Velvet. The Invisible Man's Revenge. South of Dixie. Tonight and Every Night. 1945: The Picture of Dorian Gray. The Woman in Green. 1946: Devotion (completed 1943). Cluny Brown. Terror by Night. 1947: Moss Rose. The Swordsman. It Had to Be You. Love from a Stranger (GB: A Stranger Walked In). 1948: The Black Arrow. Let's Live a Little. 1949: The Secret Garden. The Secret of St Ives. Tell It to the Judge. That Forsyte Woman (GB: The Forsyte Saga). 1950: Rogues of Sherwood Forest. The Fortunes of Captain Blood.

‡ And co-directed

BLORE, Eric 1887–1959

Eric Blore's characters in films were often the height of servility. And how they suffered. Half the time, though, they almost seemed to like it. And when pushed too far the turning worm could be relied on for a few whiplash wisecracks of its own. The British-born actor with the cringing, crumpled mouth − which in real life could crease into an affable smile − would have made the perfect Uriah Heep in *David Copperfield*. Instead, he settled for becoming one of Hollywood's best-known screen butlers. Having first joined a stock company in Australia, and given up his career in insurance, Blore built up a formidable record of appearances in plays and revues on the London stage before going to America in 1923. He began appearing in films from the beginning of the sound era but it was his fussy assistant hotel manager in *Flying Down to Rio* in 1933 which launched him properly on to a film career. He played in four more Ginger Rogers−Fred Astaire musicals during the 1930s and although in retrospect it seems he was a butler in all of them in fact he was a manservant only in *Top Hat*, in which he introduces himself with the famous greeting 'We are Bates'. In 1939 he returned to Britain for the starring role in *A Gentleman's Gentleman*, inevitably as a scheming

butler. But the film was not too well received and Blore returned to Hollywood where he soon became involved in the long-running 'Lone Wolf' series as valet/assistant/Man Friday to the hero, played initially by Warren William and later by Gerald Mohr. And although Blore may never have played Uriah Heep he achieved the next best thing in 1949 by becoming the voice of Kenneth Grahame's Toad from *The Wind in the Willows*, in Disney's *The Adventures of Ichabod and Mr Toad*. Blore took life more easily after 1950, making only occasional appearances in films and on television. After 1955 he retired altogether but died a few years later from a heart attack at 71.

*1920: * A Night Out and a Day In. 1926: The Great Gatsby. 1930: Laughter. My Sin. 1931: Tarnished Lady. 1933: Flying Down to Rio. 1934: The Gay Divorcee (GB: The Gay Divorce). Limehouse Blues. 1935: Behold My Wife. Folies Bergère (GB: The Man from the Folies Bergère). The Casino Murder Case. Top Hat. Diamond Jim. Old Man Rhythm. I Dream Too Much. To Beat the Band. Seven Keys to Baldpate. The Good Fairy. 1936: Two in the Dark. The Ex-Mrs Bradford. Sons o' Guns. Piccadilly Jim. Swing Time. Smartest Girl in Town. Quality Street. 1937: The Soldier and the Lady (GB: Michael Strogoff). Shall We Dance? It's Love I'm After. Hitting a New High. Breakfast for Two. 1938: The Joy of Living. Swiss Miss. A Desperate Adventure (GB: It Happened in Paris). 1939: $1,000 a Touchdown. Island of Lost Men. A Gentleman's Gentleman. 1940: The Man Who Wouldn't Talk. The Lone Wolf Strikes. Music in My Heart. Till We Meet Again. The Boys from Syracuse. The Lone Wolf Meets a Lady. Earl of Puddlestone (GB: Jolly Old Higgins). South of Suez. 1941: The Lone Wolf Keeps a Date. The Lady Eve. The Lone Wolf Takes a Chance. Road to Zanzibar. Red Head. Lady Scarface. New York Town. Three Girls about Town. Confirm or Deny. The Shanghai Gesture. 1942: Sullivan's Travels. Secrets of the Lone Wolf (GB: Secrets). The Moon and Sixpence. Counter-Espionage. 1943: Forever and a Day. * Heavenly Music. Happy Go Lucky. Submarine Base. Holy Matrimony. One Dangerous Night. Passport to Suez. The Sky's the Limit. 1944: San Diego, I Love You. 1945: Penthouse Rhythm. Easy to Look At. 1946: Two Sisters from Boston. Kitty. Men in Her Diary. The Notorious Lone Wolf. Abie's Irish Rose. 1947: The Lone Wolf in Mexico. Winter Wonderland. The Lone Wolf in London. 1948: Romance on the High Seas (GB: It's Magic). 1949: Love Happy (later Kleptomaniacs). Adventures of Ichabod and Mr Toad (voice only). 1950: Fancy Pants. 1952: Babes in Baghdad. 1955: Bowery to Baghdad.*

BLUE, Ben

(B. Bernstein) 1901–1975

Lugubrious, long-faced, dark-haired, Canadian-born vaudeville comedian who never quite made a permanent niche for himself in films, but brightened many a dud

one by wandering on and threading one of his stage routines into the plot. He was, however, a comic of moments, unable to establish a character for himself in the cinema. Even efforts to establish himself as a star comic in the world of two-reel comedies proved miserable failures. It was probably because he was funny *doing* things, and a brilliant mime, but just couldn't come across in films as a sympathetic character. Elastic-limbed Blue originally hailed from Montreal but was performing in vaudeville and even on the New York musical-comedy stage while still in his mid teens. From the late 1920s he also appeared in Vitaphone and Hal Roach shorts, Roach pairing him with plumply wheezing Billy Gilbert (*qv*) in a series of two-reelers as 'The Taxi Boys'. But the boys seemed to be competing for laughs rather than operating as a team and the series never realised its potential. Blue's first feature film, *The Arcadians*, was made in England and it gave him a rare starring role. Back in Hollywood though, and after the failure of 'The Taxi Boys', he found himself having to settle for caemo appearances and comic sidekicks. He continued meandering in and out of movies until the late 1940s, thereafter turning to TV and nightclub work. He even had his own nightclub at one time but the venture was a financial failure which finally folded in 1967 after eight years of struggle. Blue made one final film appearance after that, a hilarious running gag as an apartment dweller trying painfully and in vain to complete a shave during the New York blackout, in *Where Were You When the Lights Went Out?*

*1927: The Arcadians/Land of Heart's Desire. 1930: * One Big Night. 1932: * Strange Inner-Tube. * What Price Taxi? 1933: * Rummy. * Thundering Taxis. * Taxi Barons. * Nothing But the Truth. * Wreckety Wreck. * Call Her Sausage. 1934: College Rhythm. 1936: Follow Your Heart. College Holiday. 1937: Turn off the Moon. Top of the Town. High, Wide and Handsome. Artists and Models. Thrill of a Lifetime. 1938: College Swing (GB: Swing, Teacher, Swing). The Big Broadcast of 1938. Cocoanut Grove. 1939: Paris Honeymoon. 1942: Panama Hattil. For Me and My Gal (GB: For Me and My Girl). 1943: Thousands*

*Cheer. 1944: Two Girls and a Sailor. Broadway Rhythm. 1945: * Badminton. 1946: Two Sisters from Boston. Easy to Wed. 1947: My Wild Irish Rose. 1948: One Sunday Afternoon. 1963: It's a Mad, Mad, Mad World. 1966: The Russians Are Coming, the Russians Are Coming. The Busy Body. 1967: A Guide for the Married Man. 1968: Where Were You When the Lights Went Out?*

BOLAND, Mary
(Marie Anne Boland) 1880–1965
A round-faced blonde with peaches-and-cream complexion and pleasantly middle-aged looks, Mary Boland was one of Hollywood's finest exponents of the hen-pecking, selfish, social-climbing and addle-brained (but, for all that, lovable) middle-class mama. In a series of 14 films opposite the huffly-snuffly Charlie Ruggles (*qv*), she became one of the cinema's best-loved character comediennes of the 1930s. Generous of girth and mellifluous of speech (rising easily to a cackle, a giggle or hysteria), she was born in Philadelphia to an actor who soon gave up the insecurity of the profession for interior decorating. His daughter, however, prospered. Known at first as a dramatic star on stage (and in a few insignificant silent films), she became established as a comedy player after her roaring success in 1923 in the play *Meet the Wife*, a title that just about summed up her career, and could have applied to a number of the successful sound films she subsequently made. Another long-running daughter hit, *Cradle Snatchers*, followed, but it was her role as the well-dressed, sophisticated, witty, romance-beset heroine of the Broadway comedy *The Vinegar Tree*, which ran for more than 200 performances in 1930, that brought her back to Hollywood. Almost immediately she found herself in the same casts as Charlie Ruggles. It was their pairing in the multi-story *If I Had a Million*, in 1932, that convinced Paramount they had a potent team on their hands. The result was the delightful *Mama Loves Papa*. Ruggles was a dapper, moustachioed little man who specialised in the meek and the mild. Although he was only 5 ft 5 in, Boland had no problems achieving an amusing physical dominance. In fact, most of her 'other

halves' in screen comedy would be small. Boland's aspirations to a place in high society, as she fluttered and flustered across the screen to the constant irritation of anything-for-a-quiet-life Ruggles, coupled with a funny script that somehow touched base with ordinary life, assured the new team of a good run. They made numerous co-features together for the rest of the decade, and one very popular major production – *Ruggles of Red Gap*, in which they supported Charles Laughton as the English butler won in a bet by their upstart western family. Boland made sure that pretentiousness and insincerity dripped from every pore of her flippertigibbet Effie Floud. In between film assignments, Boland returned to Broadway for a four-month run (she became ill and had to leave before her contract was up) of the Cole Porter musical *Jubilee*. Playing a mythical queen who takes a 'Roman holiday' from her duties, she moved one critic to say that 'Breezy and . . . gloriously ridiculous, she's possessed of a vitality and comic skill which annihilate dullness. She is the one real comedian of this troupe.' Despite these raves it was back to programmers at Paramount, where *People Will Talk* and *Early to Bed* (in which she dragoons Ruggles into marriage after a 20-year engagement) were popular, but the series gradually tailed away. Boland made a handful of films in the 1940s but spent most of her time in the theatre, where she remained until her retirement in 1955. One of her latter-day theatrical appearances was a last starring duet with Ruggles in a play called *One Fine Day*. Her last film, the underrated *Guilty Bystander*, gave Boland a chance to play heavily dramatic, in the change of pace she always relished. Looking appropriately fat and raddled, she was the proprietress of a shabby, shady hotel who turns out to be the chief villain, the mysterious boss of a contraband ring. Seedy private eye Zachary Scott eventually unmasks her and turns her over to the police. Boland was splendidly nasty, turning over the ambitious flutterbrain she always played to reveal a dark underside: a sharp-witted old harridan who amassed her wealth from the wrong side of the law. Indulging her passion for bridge more and more in the last years of her life, Boland, whom co-star Ruggles once called 'a dear and clever woman', died in her sleep at 85. Ironically, the movie queen of manic matriarchs had never married.

1915: The Edge of the Abyss. 1916: The Stepping Stone. The Price of Happiness. Big Jim Garrity. 1918: His Temporary Wife. The Prodigal Wife. A Woman's Experience. 1931: Personal Maid. Secrets of a Secretary. 1932: The Night of June 13th. Trouble in Paradise. Evenings for Sale. If I Had a Million. Night After Night. 1933: Three-Cornered Moon. The Solitaire Man. Mama Loves Papa. 1934: Six of a Kind. Melody in Spring. Four Frightened People. Stingaree. Down to Their Last Yacht (GB: Hawaiian Nights). The Pursuit of Hap-

piness. Here Comes the Groom. 1935: People Will Talk. Two for Tonight. Ruggles of Red Gap. The Big Broadcast of 1936: Wives Never Know. Early to Bed. College Holiday. A Son Comes Home. 1937: Marry the Girl. Mama Runs Wild. There Goes the Groom. Danger – Love at Work. 1938: Little Tough Guys in Society. Artists and Models Abroad (GB: Stranded in Paris). 1939: The Magnificent Fraud. Boy Trouble. The Women. Night Work. 1940: He Married His Wife. One Night in the Tropics. New Moon. Pride and Prejudice. Hit Parade of 1941. 1944: Nothing But Trouble. In Our Time. Forever Yours. They Shall Have Faith (GB: The Right to Live). 1948: Julia Misbehaves. 1950: Guilty Bystander.

THE BOWERY BOYS
GORCEY, Leo (top) 1915–1969
HALL, Huntz
(Henry Hall) 1920–
and various others
A group of fast-talking, wisecracking, bickering, would-be little tough guys from Brooklyn whose films were never more than programme fillers but who have built up cult following over the years. The leader was Leo Gorcey as Slip, who always had ideas above his station, and would murder (or moida) the Queen's English with such phrases as 'Can ya pitcha dat?'. He was little, chunky, round-faced, spoke out of the corner of his mouth and wore bow-ties and a trilby with the brim turned back. His chief lieutenant was tall, fair-haired, goofy, big-nosed Huntz Hall as Satch, whose ideas

were even more gormless, and whose remarks were usually rewarded by him being hit over the head with Slip's hat. Like his cohorts, who, Hall and David Gorcey (Leo's younger brother) apart, varied from film to film, Gorcey's character was 'allergic' to 'woik' and relied on harebrained schemes to make a fast buck. The Boys hung out at Louie's sweet shop and drove around in a battered 1910 car. Their style was anything but subtle, but all their films were short and swift. Gorcey's Malapropisms and Hall's gyrating lips were their principal sources of humour. Gorcey's actor father, Bernard (who played the long-suffering Louie in the films) emigrated to America from his native Switzerland and became an actor there. Despite being president of his high school drama class, the younger Gorcey showed little inclination to follow his father's profession. Gorcey Sr insisted that his son read for a part as one of the slum kids in the 1935 play *Dead End*. Leo still wasn't interested – until he lost his job as a plumber's mate. He got a part as one of the rival gang to the Dead End Kids, and eventually inherited the major role of Spit. Playing alongside him was Huntz Hall, a vacant-looking blond youth who had made his stage debut at one year old, and attended the Professional Children's School. Later, Huntz was a boy soprano with the Madison Square Quintette. After their run in the play had finished, six of the 'Dead End Kids' went to Hollywood to make the film version. They were never to go back to the stage. Warners cashed in on their image after *Dead End* by putting them into other crime-oriented films, such as *Angels with Dirty Faces*, *Hell's Kitchen* and *Angels Wash Their Faces*. Then they were shunted off into 'B' features. Gorcey became a member of the East Side Kids. Hall was with the Dead End Kids and the Little Tough Guys. Later, though, he joined the East Side Kids in a new series of comedies in which Gorcey, as Muggs, and Hall, as Glimpy, would be the leading figures. The first was *Bowery Blitzkrieg*, in 1941, and the series went on until *Come Out Fighting*, in 1945. During this period, the 'Kids' were mostly involved with gangsters and crooked promoters, but when they regrouped as the Bowery Boys, and began a new series of comedies with *Live Wires*, the comedy was much more general, in keeping with the themes tackled by other comedy teams, as can be seen by the titles: *Spook Busters, News Hounds, Smugglers' Cove, Master Minds, Hold That Baby, Crazy Over Horses, Private Eyes, Jungle Gents, Jail Busters, Spy Chasers* and so forth. In real life, the gang behaved very much as on screen, tearing around in fast cars (Gorcey had 18 citations for traffic offences before he was 21), chasing women (Gorcey was married five times – 'I married them all' he once said – and Hall three, often to showgirls) and undergoing minor brushes with the law. Hall was busted for marijuana possession in 1948 (but later exonerated), while charges were also

dropped against Gorcey after he had taken a couple of shots at the second Mrs G for hiring two detectives to search his home. By the time his third marriage ended in 1956, Gorcey had developed a severe drinking problem, exacerbated by the death of his father the previous year in a car crash. His speech is clearly impaired in his last Bowery Boys film, *Crashing Las Vegas* and after it he quit Hollywood for years, seeking solace on his ranch, where he raised chickens, cattle and pigs. After his fourth divorce in 1964, Gorcey tried to get back into show business in partnership with Huntz Hall. They made a few cameo appearances together but noone would take a chance on them in a solo film. The years of heavy drinking had taken their toll of Gorcey, and he died of liver failure just an hour before his 54th birthday. Hall, in later life a model citizen, stayed in the acting business, and became a wealthy man through his investments in offshore oil. He had a son who became an episcopal priest. Most of the other sometime members of the 'Kids' and 'Boys', like Bennie Bartlett, Gabriel Dell (with whom Hall had a nightclub stand-up comedy act in the early 1950s) and Billy Benedict, stayed in show business. But David Gorcey (sometimes known as David Condon), younger brother of Leo, became a clergyman, and Bernard Punsly became a doctor. As Slip might have said: 'Can ya pitcha dat?'

Gorcey and Hall together. *1937: Dead End. 1938: Crime School. Angels with Dirty Faces. 1939: Hell's Kitchen. Angels Wash Their Faces. The Battle of City Hall. They Made Me a Criminal. The Dead End Kids on Dress Parade. Invisible Stripes. 1940: That Gang of Mine. Gallant Sons. Boys of the City. East Side Kids. Angels with Broken Wings. Junior G-Men (serial). Pride of the Bowery (GB: Here We Go Again). 1941: Sea Raiders (serial). Bowery Blitzkrieg (GB: Stand and Deliver). Spooks Run Wild. 1942: Mr Wise Guy. Sunday Punch. Smart Alecks. 'Neath Brooklyn Bridge. Let's Get Tough. Junior G-Men of the Air (serial). 1943: Clancy Street Boys. Mr Muggs Steps Out. Follow the Leader. 1944: Block Busters. Bowery Chumps. The Million Dollar Kid. 1945: Mr Muggs Rides Again. Docks of New York. Come Out Fighting. Live Wires. 1946: Mr Hex (GB: Pride of the Bowery). In Fast Company. Spook Busters. Bowery Bombshell. 1947: Hard-Boiled Mahoney. News Hounds (GB: News Hound). Pride of Broadway. Bowery Buckaroos. 1948: Jinx Money. Angels' Alley. Trouble Makers. Smugglers' Cove. 1949: Angels in Disguise. Fighting Fools. Master Minds. Hold That Baby. 1950: Blues Busters. Blonde Dynamite. Triple Trouble. Lucky Losers. 1951: Ghost Chasers. Bowery Battalion. Crazy Over Horses. Let's Go Navy. 1952: Here Come the Marines. Hold That Line. No Holds Barred. Feudin' Fools. 1953: Jalopy. Loose in London. Clipped Wings. Private Eyes. 1954: Paris Playboys. The Bowery Boys Meet the Monsters. Jungle Gents. 1955: Bowery to Bagdad. High Society. Jail Busters. Spy Chasers. 1956: Dig*

That Uranium. Crashing Las Vegas. 1965: Second Fiddle to a Steel Guitar. 1969: The Phynx.
Gorcey alone. *1937: Portia on Trial (GB: The Trial of Portia Merriman). Headin' East. 1938: Mannequin. 1939: Private Detective. 1941: Road to Zanzibar. Down in San Diego. 1942: Born to Sing. Maisie Gets Her Man (GB: She Gets Her Man). 1943: Destroyer. 1945: One Exciting Night. Midnight Manhunt. 1963: It's a Mad, Mad, Mad, Mad World.*
Hall alone. *1938: Little Tough Guy. 1939: Call a Messenger. The Return of Doctor X. 1940: Give Us Wings. You're Not So Tough. 1941: Hit the Road. Zis Boom Bah. Mob Town. 1942: Junior Army. Private Buckaroo. Tough as They Come. 1943: Mug Town. Kid Dynamite. Keep 'em Slugging. Ghosts on the Loose. 1945: Wonder Man. A Walk in the Sun. Bring on the Girls. 1956: Hold That Hypnotist. 1957: Spook Chasers. Looking for Danger. Up in Smoke. 1958: In the Money. 1967: Gentle Giant. 1971: Escape (TV). 1974: Herbie Rides Again. The Manchu Eagle Murder Caper Mystery. 1975: Won Ton Ton, the Dog Who Saved Hollywood. 1977: Valentino. 1979: Gas Pump Girls. 1982: The Escape Artist. 1984: The Ratings Game (TV). 1986: Cyclone. 1991: Auntie Lee's Meat Pies.*

BRACKEN, Eddie 1920–
Forever identified with nervous Norval in *The Miracle of Morgan's Creek*, stocky, dynamic Eddie Bracken shot to fame in the mid 1940s playing dopey, sub-Mickey Rooney types who stumbled over their own nervous energy but still managed to end up with the girl. If there was a screen male equivalent of a dizzy dame, then Bracken was it. Unfortunately Bracken was unable to widen his range, and the image proved insufficiently attractive to sustain his screen career far past the decade. Since then life has been a struggle for the little man who once rode high in the public opinion polls as the sort-of-hero of two of director Preston Sturges's most popular films. Bracken was born into a show business life (in a suburb of New York), getting educated at the NY Professional Children's School, and appearing in one- and two-reel comedy films as a child. Some of these were alleged to be in

'Our Gang' films but, as complete records of this series exist without mention of Bracken in any of the casts, it seems more likely that he participated in one of the many other 'kiddie' series of late silent days, such as the New York Kiddie Troopers films. He made his Broadway debut at 11 and by 1938 was making a name for himself as bumbling boys-next-door in such shows as *Brother Rat* and *What a Life*. After a couple of minor film forays, Bracken was signed by Paramount in 1941 and almost immediately established his persona of the willing if incompetent eager beaver who was sometimes the hero's best friend, but always his own worst enemy. The two films for Sturges (*Hail the Conquering Hero* was the other) proved the highlights of these wartime years, but Bracken's standing immediately started to slip with the end of the conflict. The standard of his material in these post-war years was by and large poor, and his unvarying character began to appear irksome rather than endearing. He was out of films altogether by 1953. Since then Bracken has found only marginally better days in TV and on the stage, making more than his fair share of flops. Even these activities, though, were more successful than some of his disastrous business ventures, one of which, the crash of a chain of New England theatres, is said to have cost his company around $2 million. Throughout his trials and tribulations Bracken's bubbly personality has never lost its cheerfulness. In September 1989 he celebrated his golden wedding; he and his wife, ex-actress Connie Nickerson, have five children.

Sound films. *1938: Brother Rat. 1940: Too Many Girls. 1941: Life With Henry. Caught in the Draft. Reaching for the Sun. 1942: The Fleet's In. Sweater Girl. Star Spangled Rhythm. 1943: Young and Willing. Happy Go Lucky. 1944: The Miracle of Morgan's Creek. Hail the Conquering Hero. Rainbow Island. 1945: Bring on the Girls. Duffy's Tavern. Hold That Blonde. Out of This World. 1947: Ladies' Man. 1948: Fun on a Weekend. 1949: The Girl from Jones Beach. 1950: Summer Stock (GB: If You Feel Like Singing). 1951: Two Tickets to Broadway. * Hollywood on a Sunday Afternoon. 1952: We're Not Married. About Face. 1953: A Slight Case of Larceny. 1961: Wild, Wild World. 1962: A Summer Sunday. 1971: Shinbone Alley (voice only). 1983: National Lampoon's Vacation. 1991: Oscar. 1992: Home Alone: Lost in New York.*

BRAMBELL, Wilfrid 1912–1985

Scraggy in aspect and miserly in the manner of the parts he played, Irish-born Brambell remained a little-known character actor until he was 50. Then, with one of the two leading roles in *Steptoe and Son*, one of the most successful British TV comedy series of all time, Brambell suddenly became a national figure. Although only 13 years older than the actor chosen to play his son, Harry H. Corbett, Brambell fitted the part of the

sexagenarian skinflint rag-and-bone merchant like an old knitted glove. Running the gamut from cackling gleefully at the success of some scheme, through jeering at his son's amorous ambitions or grandiose plans, to pop-eyed horror and cringing servility when occasionally hoist with his own petard, Brambell *lived* through 12 years of TV, two (strangely unsuccessful) films and a subsequent series on radio as Albert Steptoe. Brambell's mother was an opera singer and his first stage appearance was as a child singer, entertaining World War One troops with his mother. Before and after World War Two, Brambell built up wide experience in repertory, first in his native Dublin, later in Swansea and Bristol before beginning a London stage career in 1950. It was on stage that, years later, he would eventually realise his ambition of playing the supreme miser, Ebenezer Scrooge in *A Christmas Carol*. He won his *Steptoe* role, appropriately, on the strength of his performance as a down-and-out in a TV play, *Doss House*. Seizing on the role of the scurrilous, scheming, toothless old codger referred to by his own son as a 'dirty old man', Brambell created his own niche in entertainment history. His infrequent film appearances were never as memorable.

1935: The 39 Steps. 1946: Odd Man Out. 1948: Another Shore. 1956: Dry Rot. 1957: The Story of Esther Costello (US: Golden Virgin). 1958: The Salvage Gang. 1959: Serious Charge (US: A Touch of Hell). 1960: Urge to Kill. 1961: The Sinister Man. Flame in the Streets. What a Whopper! * The Grand Junction Case. 1962: In Search of the Castaways. The Boys. The Fast Lady. 1963: The Small World of Sammy Lee. Crooks in Cloisters. The Three Lives of Thomasina. Go Kart Go! 1964: A Hard Day's Night. 1965: San Ferry Ann. 1966: Where the Bullets Fly. Mano di velluto. 1968: Witchfinder-General (US: The Conqueror Worm). Lionheart. Cry Wolf. 1969: * The Undertakers. Carry On Again, Doctor. 1970: Some Will, Some Won't. 1972: Steptoe and Son. 1973: Steptoe and Son Ride Again. Holiday on the Buses. 1978: The Adventures of Picasso. 1980: High Rise Donkey. 1981: Island of Adventure. 1983: * Death and Transfiguration. Sword of the Valiant.

BRENDEL, El
(Elmer Brendel) 1890–1964

A bogus Swede from Philadelphia, this dark, skinny, sad-looking American comedian's speciality was at least unusual. In films, he was more successful in brief supporting roles in major features than in the starring two-reel comedies he later made, films that cast him as the innocent immigrant placed in situations of personal peril that required him to widen his eyes and babble fearfully in splintered 'Scandinavian'. He was a vaude-villian in his early twenties, soon developing a facility with his fake Swedish accent that consumed his entire act. His routine had them in stitches, and he remained a popular performer on variety bills until he decided to step sideways into Broadway musicals in the early 1920s. Dialect comedians, however, rarely repeat stage, radio or TV success in films. Brendel actually did better than most and his nonsense songs in early sound films seldom failed to raise a smile. In his own starring short comedies, though, Brendel's stammering Swede soon wore thin. In the early 1940s, Columbia teamed him with burly Tom Kennedy in 'fright' comedies, one of which, *Sweet Spirits of the Nighter* actually got an 'H' (for horror) certificate from the British censor! Brendel's best solo effort of the period was *Love at First Fright*, in which his rookie radio announcer is mistakenly seized on by a family of homicidal hillbillies as a long-lost relative. In the mid 1940s, he was given a new partner in the once-great baby-faced comic Harry Langdon (*qv*). But both men were past their prime and, unlike some other older performers such as Edgar Kennedy and Leon Errol (both *qv*) who could be funny in themselves, very much at the mercy of their material. However, one of his later shorts, *The Blitz Kiss*, was (albeit rather mysteriously) nominated for an Academy Award. After being dropped from Columbia's comedy shorts roster Brendel went back to nightclub and stage work, doing only the odd role in films before his retirement in the late 1950s. He died from a heart attack.

1926: The Campus Flirt. You Never Know Women. Man of the Forest. 1927: Arizona

*Bound. Rolled Stockings. Too Many Crooks. Wings. Ten Modern Commandments. 1929: Sunny Side Up. The Cock-Eyed World. Hot for Paris. Frozen Justice. * Beau Night. 1930: The Golden Calf. Just Imagine. Happy Days. The Big Trail. New Movietone Follies of 1930. 1931: Mr Lemon of Orange. Women of All Nations. Delicious. The Spider. Six Cylinder Love. * The Stolen Jools (GB: The Slippery Pearls). 1932: West of Broadway. Handle with Care. Disorderly Conduct. 1933: Hot Pepper. My Lips Betray. The Last Trail. Olsen's Big Moment. 1934: The Meanest Gal in Town. 1935: * Broadway Brevities (series). * Hollywood on Parade B−4. * What! No Men? 1936: * Ay Tank Ay Go. * Lonesome Trailer. Career Woman. God's Country and the Woman. 1937: The Holy Terror. * The Super Snooper. Blonde Trouble. 1938: Little Miss Broadway. Happy Landing. Valley of the Giants. 1939: Code of the Streets. Risky Business. House of Fear. Spirit of Culver (GB: Man's Heritage). Call a Messenger. 1940: If I Had My Way. Captain Caution. Gallant Sons. 1941: * Ready, Willing but Unable. * Yumpin' Yiminy! * Love at First Fright. * The Blitz Kiss. * Sweet Spirits of the Nighter. 1942: * Olaf Laughs Last. * Phoney Cronies. * Ham and Yeggs. 1943: * His Wedding Scare. * I Spied for You. * Boobs in the Night. * A Rookie's Cookie. 1944: Machine Gun Mama. * Defective Detectives. * Pick a Peck of Plumbers. * Mopey Dope. I'm from Arkansas. 1945: * Pistol-Packin' Nitwits. * Snooper Service. 1949: The Beautiful Blonde from Bashful Bend. 1953: Paris Model. 1956: The She-Creature.*

BRESSLAW, Bernard 1933−

Long-faced, dark-eyed, hulkingly built British cockney character star whose speciality in thick-skulled, sweet-natured types brought him fame at an early age on TV's *The Army Game*. The son of a tailor's presser from Stepney, Bresslaw became hooked on acting after being taken weekly by his mother to the Hackney Empire. At 19 he himself was on the London stage in a play called *Wrestler's Honeymoon*. But it closed after three days! The 6 ft 6 in Bresslaw should have realised he was destined for comedy after a nasty mishap during a stage

version of *The Hasty Heart*: 'I forgot to duck while going on stage for a particularly emotional scene. The door frame wasn't fixed firmly and I made my entrance with it draped around me.' In 1957 he was picked to play the gormless, kiss-curled Private 'Popeye' Popplewell in *The Army Game*. The series ran for five years and Bresslaw's was the biggest of several personal successes in it. There was a spin-off film *I Only Arsked!* (Popeye's catchphrase) and an unsuccessful solo vehicle *The Ugly Duckling*. It cast him as the dim-witted descendant of Dr Jekyll who accidentally stumbles on his father's famous formula. With his hair rapidly disappearing, Bresslaw's comedy career suffered a lull in the early 1960s but he was soon back, bigger, balder and more blustering, as a regular and welcome member of the tight-knit company in the 'Carry On' films. In *Carry On Up the Jungle* he appeared as Upsidasi, the least likely native warrior on record. He stayed with the gang from 1965 to 1975 but was just as happy on stage and TV, where he has been seen in recent times in ever more belligerent roles.

*1954: Men of Sherwood Forest. 1955: The Glass Cage (US: The Glass Tomb). 1956: Up in the World. 1957: High Tide at Noon. 1958: Blood of the Vampire. I Only Arsked! 1959: The Ugly Duckling. Too Many Crooks. 1963: It's All Happening. 1965: Carry On Cowboy. Morgan − a Suitable Case for Treatment. 1966: * Round the Bend. Carry On Screaming. 1967: Follow That Camel. Carry On Doctor. 1968: Carry On Up the Khyber. 1969: Carry On Camping. Moon Zero Two. Carry On Up the Jungle. Spring and Port Wine. 1970: Carry On Loving. 1971: Up Pompeii. The Magnificent Seven Deadly Sins. Carry On At Your Convenience. Blinker's Spy Spotter. 1972: Carry On Matron. Carry On Abroad. 1973: Carry On Girls. 1974: Vampira (US: Old Dracula). Carry On Dick. 1975: One of Our Dinosaurs is Missing. Carry On Behind. 1976: Joseph Andrews. 1977: Jabberwocky. Behind the Iron Mask (GB: The Fifth Musketeer). 1980: Hawk the Slayer. 1983: Krull. 1992: Leon the Pig Farmer.*

BRICE, Fanny
(F. Borach) 1891−1951

Although she made only a handful of films, New York's ugly duckling Fanny Brice ironically became a household name to filmgoers years after her death when Barbra Streisand won an Oscar for portraying her in the 1968 film *Funny Girl*. An integral part of several Ziegfeld Follies shows down the years, Fanny never fitted in on the Hollywood scene. Born to a French father and Hungarian mother, the gawky, big-footed Fanny (she once played an alligator) was entertaining at 13, singing and clowning in a peculiarly Jewish way ('Irving Berlin taught me. I would never have had any idea of doing a song with a Jewish accent. I couldn't even speak the language'). She was playing in the *Ziegfeld Follies of 1910* at 18. As no-

one knew how to pronounce her surname, she borrowed Brice from an Irish neighbour. A brilliant visual comedienne with an elastic, duck-like face, Fanny was also capable of putting across a sentimental song with considerable emotional appeal. Her private life was fiery and it was a pity that she hit as many headlines over her long-running affair with gambler/criminal Nicky Arnstein as she did with her performances. She had met Arnstein (born in Norway as Julius Arndt Stein) when she was 19. They lived together until he was able to get a divorce, apart from a period when he was jailed on grand larceny counts from 1915 to 1917. They married in 1918, but a further jail sentence for Arnstein followed from 1923 to 1925 and the couple divorced in 1928. Fanny later married (and divorced) showman-composer Billy Rose. Meanwhile she continued being the most unusual female star Florenz Ziegfeld ever had. In between Follies stints that would last for a record period of 27 years, Fanny made a few tentative attempts to break into movies. Critics liked her singing of such classics as *My Man* and *Second Hand Rose* but found her exaggerated antics needed more subtlety for a transfer from stage to screen. Had she broken into films on a permanent basis the likelihood is that Fanny would have found herself straitjacketed into the same kind of cornball comedy as Joan Davis (whom Fanny once said she would like to play her in a film biopic) or Judy Canova (both *qv*). As it was, her remaining appearances were minor, like her crazy Russian maid in *Everybody Sing*, and a woman trying to retrieve a winning lottery ticket in the all-star *Ziegfeld Follies*. That title was appropriate: for more than two decades Fanny was an indispensable part of the Follies. On one occasion, when she went down with a severe cold, the management cancelled the entire show for two nights. It was during the Follies that she evolved her most popular character − Baby Snooks, a human monster, who gave her much opportunity for eye-rolling, face-pulling and mock baby-talk. She took the character with her into a long-running radio show. It was still playing when she suffered a brain haemorrhage at 59, dying five days later.

Edgar Bergen seems to have the inside track with the star of the show, Vera Zorina, in *The Goldwyn Follies*. Alas, she has eyes only for the wooden charms of Charlie McCarthy

Light fantastic. George Burns and Walter Matthau, as two feuding music hall comics, do the Dr Krankheit sketch in *The Sunshine Boys*

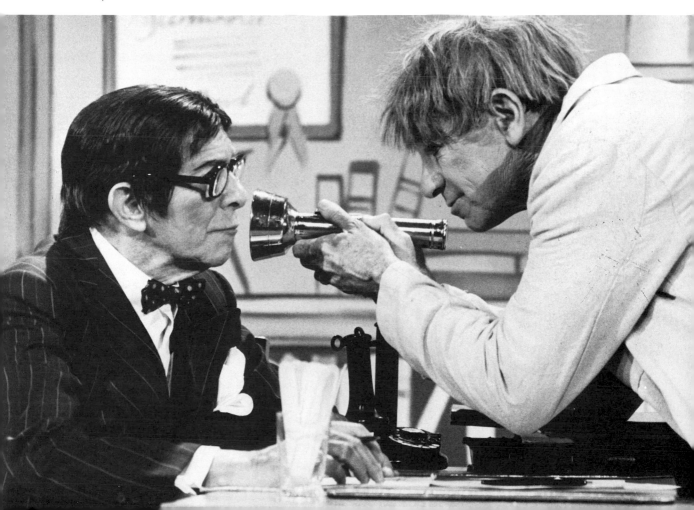

The balloon goes up. George Burns's God, familiar cigar in hand, prepares to ascend to the heavens in a publicity shot for one of his *Oh, God!* films

1928: My Man. 1929: * Night Club. 1930: Be Yourself. The Man from Blankley's. 1934: Crime Without Passion. 1935: * Broadway Highlights No. 1. 1936: The Great Ziegfeld. 1938: Everybody Sing. 1944: Ziegfeld Follies (released 1946).

BROOKS, Mel
(Melvin Kaminsky) 1926–

Volatile, incorrigibly enthusiastic Jewish-American – 'I am sensationally Jewish' he says – writer, director and entertainer with wide, beaming face that can crumple itself into any number of other expressions. Adept at writing cutting one-liners, Brooks started out as a stand-up comedian at 15 in Jewish holiday resorts after the same places had convulsed with laughter at his attempts at straight acting. But gradually his career as a writer for other comedians took over, and took off spectacularly from 1949 (to 1954) with his association with Sid Caesar's TV series *Your Show of Shows*. Caesar (qv) was a sharp and versatile comedian but few could have failed completely with such a chance assembly of writers including Brooks, Neil Simon, Carl Reiner, Woody Allen (qv) and Larry Gelbart. Brooks longed for success on the other side of the camera, and found it in 1960 with a sketch about a 2,000-year-old man which swiftly became an oft-repeated classic. Film success was longer in coming, but he made it (and took a sideswipe at Neo-Nazi organisations at the same time) in 1967 with *The Producers*, a word-of-mouth comedy hit that won him a 'best screenplay' Academy Award and included the classic spoof show 'Springtime for Hitler'. Now Brooks hit his stride, becoming a performer in his own movies, mixing pastiches of film classics with rudeness and irreverence, breaking down comedy taboos in a series of hit-and-miss sideswipes at anything within range, alienating the few but convulsing the many. Whether you like your foolery to be crude or subtle, Brooks has something to offer everyone, if not perhaps everything to offer someone. Latterly, his films have become American equivalents of the British 'Carry On' series, albeit faster, coarser, noisier and more frequently on target. Most modern American comics have this ratio of success and failure in their own scripts, but

Brooks is more of a realist about it than most. 'You can't get lucky all the time', he says. 'I am wild and ad lib and so I must house it. I try to create a very strong structure and then leave room inside it for insanity. It's like jazz you see: an arrangement with solos.' He has been married to the Oscar-winning actress Anne Bancroft – 'Sometimes I wake her up at three in the morning because I've thought of something funny' – since 1964.

1963: * The Critic (narrator only). 1967: Putney Swope. 1970: The Twelve Chairs. 1974: Blazing Saddles. 1976: Silent Movie. 1977: High Anxiety. 1978: The Muppet Movie. 1981: History of the World Part I. 1983: To Be or Not To Be. 1987: Spaceballs. 1990: Look Who's Talking Too (voice only). 1991: Life Stinks.
As director. 1967: The Producers. 1970: The Twelve Chairs. 1974: Blazing Saddles. Young Frankenstein. 1976: Silent Movie. 1977: High Anxiety. 1981: History of the World Part I. 1987: Spaceballs. 1991: Life Stinks.

BROWN, Joe E. 1892–1973

Dark-haired, ever-smiling, rubber-limbed American comic whose snub nose seemingly drifted half a mile away from his letter-box mouth, said to be the widest in show business. In the 1930s his deceptively simple style of humour made him a great favourite with small-town audiences, and it was only through ill-advised career moves during the decade that his career as a star film comedian was not longer. A circus acrobat at nine (with his family's blessing!), Brown eventually broke away from his troupe to create a solo act that had more comedy involved. He hit Broadway in 1920 and was an established star there by the time Hollywood beckoned with the coming of sound. After an indifferent start in the film capital, Joe E. (the E. stood for Evans) settled at Warner Brothers from 1929 and did much of his best screen work there. Often he played the timid innocent abroad who won the girl more by the divine hand of providence than anything else. There are echoes of Keaton and Lloyd in Joe's Warner films, although he had a warmth that those great comedians some-

times lacked. Like them, Brown was a great all-round athlete (and sports enthusiast) who worked in as much physical comedy as possible. He played baseball stars, polo players, javelin throwers, sprinters, cyclists, wrestlers and more besides. The Warner comedies put Joe E. Brown among America's top ten box-office draws for 1935 and 1936 (he had also been there in 1932). But after *Polo Joe*, one of his lesser vehicles for the studio, Joe declined a new contract to go into independent features. 'I listened to what turned out to be bad advice', he said in later years, 'and turned a deaf ear to what turned out to be good advice. It was disastrous.' His screen career lingered on for another eight years, breaking off after one of his better comedies of the war years, *Casanova in Burlesque*. But he enjoyed success on stage (notably in *Harvey*) and in nightclubs, and played a clown in a popular TV series of the early 1950s, *The Circus Hour*. And there were a few more film roles, most notably as the dotty millionaire romancing Jack Lemmon-in-drag in *Some Like It Hot*. An ardent suitor, Brown's wide grin is undimmed even by the final revelation that Lemmon is a woman. 'Ah well', he shrugs, 'nobody's perfect.' Towards the end of his life, Joe E. Brown was severely afflicted by arthritis, anathema to a man who had always prided himself on his agility. But he had a long (58 years) and happy marriage, and his wife was with him when he died some time after suffering a stroke. The title of his autobiography was *Laughter Is a Wonderful Thing* and Joe E. Brown had spent a lifetime proving it.

1928: * Don't Be Jealous. Crooks Can't Win. Hit of the Show. The Circus Kid. Take Me Home. Dressed to Kill. 1929: On with the Show. Painted Faces. My Lady's Past. * The Dancing Instructor. Molly and Me. Sunny Side Up. My Lady's Past. Sally. The Cock-Eyed World. Protection. The Ghost Talks. 1930: Song of the West. Hold Everything. Top Speed. Lottery Bride. Maybe It's Love. * Screen Snapshots No. 5. 1931: Going Wild. Sit Tight. Broad Minded. * Screen Snapshots No. 8. Local Boy Makes Good. 1932: Fireman, Save My Child. You Said a Mouthful. The Tenderfoot. * The Putter. * The Stolen Jools (GB: The Slippery Pearls). 1933: Elmer the Great. Son of a Sailor. * Hollywood on Parade A–8. 1934: A Very Honorable Guy. The Circus Clown. Six-Day Bike Rider. * Hollywood on Parade B–6. 1935: Alibi Ike. Bright Lights (GB: Funny Face). A Midsummer Night's Dream. 1936: Sons o' Guns. Earthworm Tractors (GB: A Natural Born Salesman). Polo Joe. 1937: When's Your Birthday? Riding on Air (GB: All is Confusion). 1938: Wide Open Faces. The Gladiator. Flirting with Fate. 1939: $1,000 a Touchdown. 1940: * Rodeo Dough. Beware, Spooks! So You Won't Talk. 1942: Shut My Big Mouth. Joan of Ozark (GB: Queen of Spies). The Daring Young Man. 1943: Chatterbox. 1944: Pin-Up Girl. Hollywood Canteen. Casanova in Burlesque. 1947: The Tender

Joe E. Brown usually faced the camera so as to get the maximum advantage of one of the widest mouths in the world — so he didn't often get to kiss the girl. Here Alice White finds out that Joe is *A Very Honorable Guy*

maybe at another studio, they might have continued usefully as a team for another 10 or 12 years in short subjects.

Together. *1943: The Adventures of a Rookie. Rookies in Burma. Gangway for Tomorrow. Mexican Spitfire's Blessed Event. 1944: Step Lively. The Girl Rush. Seven Days Ashore. 1945: Radio Stars on Parade. Zombies on Broadway (GB: Loonies on Broadway). 1946: Vacation in Reno. Genius at Work. 1961: The Absent-Minded Professor.*

Brown alone. *1943: * Radio Runaround. Petticoat Larceny. The Seventh Victim. Around the World. 1944: The Girl in the Case. 1946: Notorious. From This Day Forward. 1948: * Bachelor Blues. * Backstage Follies. Family Honeymoon. 1949: Come to the Stable. 1950: * Brooklyn Buckaroos. * Photo Phonies. * Put Some Money in the Pot. * Tinhorn Troubadors. 1951: As Young As You Feel. * From Rogues to Riches. 1954: The High and the Mighty. 1956: The Wild Dakotas. 1957: Untamed Youth. The Joker is Wild. 1958: Wink of an Eye. The Left-Handed Gun. 1959: Holiday for Lovers. Westbound. The Best of Everything.*

Carney alone. *1943: Mr Lucky. Gildersleeve's Bad Day. 1947: The Pretender. 1949: Hideout. 1959: Li'l Abner. 1960: North to Alaska. The Schnook (GB: Double Trouble). 1962: Swingin' Along (revised version of The Schnook). 1963: Son of Flubber. It's a Mad, Mad, Mad, Mad World. 1965: Sylvia. The Adventures of Bullwhip Griffin. 1967: Monkeys, Go Home! Blackbeard's Ghost. 1973: Herbie Rides Again.*

*Years. 1951: Show Boat. 1952: * Memories of Famous Hollywood Comedians (narrator only). 1954: * Hollywood Fathers. 1956: Around the World in 80 Days. 1959: Some Like It Hot. 1963: It's a Mad, Mad, Mad, Mad World. The Comedy of Terrors.*

BROWN, Wally (right) 1898–1961
and
CARNEY, Alan
(David Bougal) 1911–1973

A makeshift comedy team fabricated by RKO in the early 1940s as low-budget rivals to Bud Abbott and Lou Costello (*qv*). Two dark-haired, flush-faced vaudevillians who became comic character actors, the fast-talking Brown and the scrunch-faced Carney had barely signed contracts at the studio before they were thrown together as a team. They made 11 films together before the contracts ran out and they went their separate ways. Brown was the straight man and Carney the figure of fun. Just like Abbott and Costello they joined the army for their starring debut, in *The Adventures of a Rookie*, and stayed there for a sequel, *Rookies in Burma*. Their comedies thereafter provided bottom-of-the-bill fare for entertainment-starved audiences in the war years. And they even went out on a vaudeville tour with each other, knitting together some of their old stage routines. After two horror comedies, with such co-stars as Bela Lugosi and Lionel Atwill, the team fell victim to the new post-war policy of major studios — to make fewer bottom-budget films running only an hour or so. Brown made quite a few more two-reeler comedies, mostly in harness with Scottish-born comedian Jack Kirkwood (1895–1964), but the team had little more impact than Brown and Carney. Both Wally Brown and Alan Carney stayed on in films and TV (Carney starred in a TV comedy series called *Take It From Me*) to the ends of their not very considerable days — both men succumbed to heart attacks in their early sixties. Their vigorous playing together was too broad to sustain a major film although,

BUNNY, John 1863–1915

Generally accepted as America's first star film comic. A corpulent comedian with crooked teeth and greying fair hair, Bunny looked like a cherubic Alfred Hitchcock. The son of British immigrants to America, the young Bunny ran away from home to join a travelling minstrel show. Later he joined touring companies to become a legitimate actor and was a respected actor-manager when he offered his services to the Vitagraph Company to make a series of starring short comedies in 1910. Audiences were soon won over by the roguish charm and genial personality of this middle-aged man who tipped the scales at more than 300 pounds. Towards the end of the year (by which time he was earning $1,000 a week), he made his first film with his oft-time co-star Flora Finch, a scrawny British actress who portrayed his ferocious nagging wife. Their films together were sometimes called 'Bunnyfinches' or 'Bunnygraphs'. Typically Bunny's film character anticipated that of Leon Errol (*qv*) (who was as thin as Bunny was fat) in the 1930s and 1940s. An eager philanderer forever trying to escape being found out by his wife, Bunny would become hopelessly entangled in social embarrassments with the collision of his twin lives. Yet he always remained a sympathetic character. At the end of 1912 Bunny's international fame was demonstrated by his popularity on a trip to Britain to star as Samuel Pickwick in a version of Dickens' *The Pickwick Papers*. With his solid background in the theatre, Bunny would have probably continued on through the silent era and into sound films as a character player had not Bright's Disease killed him at 51. Just as a pantomine dame captures his audience with outlandish absurdity, so Bunny's larger-than-life warmth and sense of fun beamed out from the screen.

1910: Jack Fat and Jim Slim at Coney Island. He Who Laughs. Cupid and the Motor Boat. Doctor Cupid. The New Stenographer. The Subduing of Mrs Nag. In Neighboring Kingdoms. 1911: A Queen for a Day. Captain Barnacle's Courtship. The Widow Visits Springtown. An Unexpected Review. The Return of Widow Pogson's Husband. In the Arctic Night. Her Crowning Glory. Winsor Mackay's Drawings. The Woes of a Wealthy Widow. The Gossip. Selecting His Heiress. Two Overcoats. The Ventriloquist's Trunk. Intrepid Davy. The Politician's Dream. Treasure Trove. The Wrong Patient. Her Sister's Children. Ups and Downs. Kitty and the Cowboys. The Gossip. Madge of the Mountains. In the Clutches of a Vapor Bath. The Leading Lady. † *Vanity Fair. The Old Doll. The Latent Spark. Captain Barnacle's Baby. The Hundred Dollar Bill. The Tired, Absent-Minded Man. Her Hero. The Missing Will. A Slight Mistake. Hypnotizing the Hypnotist. 1912: A Cure for Pokeritis. Stenographer Wanted. Bunny and the Twins. The Awakening of Jones. Leap Year Proposals. Pandora's Box. The First Woman Jury in America. Irene's Infatuation. Diamond Cut Diamond. Her Old Sweetheart. The Suit of Armor. Umbrellas to Mend. How He Papered the Room. Suing Susan. Thou Shalt Not Covet. Martha's Rebellion. Red Ink Tragedy. Pseudo Sultan. Bunny's Suicide. A Persistent Lover. Freckles. Doctor Bridget. The First Violin. His Mother-in-Law. Chased by Bloodhounds. Burnt Cork. Ida's Christmas. The Troublesome Stepdaughters. The Unknown Violinist. Lovesick Maidens of Cuddleton. Cork and Vicinity. Who Stole Bunny's Umbrella? Chumps. Captain Barnacle's Messmate. I Deal, the Diver. The Honeymooners. Mr Bolter's Infatuation. Captain Jenks' Dilemma. Captain Jenks' Diplomacy. Working for Hubby. Who's to Win? At Scrog-*

ginses' Corner. Bunny and the Dogs. An Eventful Elopement. Michael McShane, Matchmaker. Mr Bolter's Niece. 1913: Three Black Bags. John Tobin's Sweetheart. There's Music in the Hair. And His Wife Came Back. † *The Pickwick Papers (also shown as three shorter films). Hubby Buys a Baby. His Honor, the Mayor. Bunny's Dilemma. The Wonderful Statue. He Answered the Ad. Bunny's Birthday Surprise. Cupid's Hired Man. Love's Quarantine. When the Press Speaks. The Pickpocket. Which Way Did He Go? A Gentleman of Fashion. The Feudists. The Girl at the Lunch Counter. Those Troublesome Tresses. Stenographer Troubles. The Locket. The Fortune. A Millinery Bomb. Suspicious Henry. Hubby's Toothache. The Schemers. The Autocrat of Flapjack Junction. Ma's Apron Strings. The Man Higher Up. Seeing Double. Bunny and the Bunny Hug. Bunny of the Derby. Bunny's Mistake. Bunny for the Cause. Bunny Blarneyed. Flaming Hearts. Bunny's Honeymoon. Bunny Versus Cutey. Bunny As a Reporter. His Tired Uncle. One Good Joke Deserves Another. Bunny and the Pirates. 1914: Bunny's Mistake. Mr Bunny in Disguise. Bunny's Scheme. The Golf Game and the Bonnet. A Change in Baggage Checks. Bunco Bill's Visit. Bunny Buys a Harem. Love's Old Dream. Polishing Up. The Vases of Hymen. Tangled Tangoists. The Old Maid's Baby. Bunny Buys a Hat for His Bride. The Old Fire House and the New Fire Chief. Hearts and Diamonds. Father's Flirtation. Such a Hunter. Bunny Attempts Suicide. Bunny's Swell Affair. Private Bunny. Personal Introductions. The Misadventures of a Mighty Monarch. Bunny's Birthday. A Train of Incidents. Bunny Backslides. Bunny's Little Brother. Pigs is Pigs. Bachelor Buttons. Love, Luck and Gasoline. Sheep's Clothing. Setting the Style. 1915: How Cissy Made Good. To John Bunny's. Bunny in Bunnyland.*

All shorts except † features.

BURKE, Billie
(Mary William Burke) 1885–1970
Not many great beauties of the stage carve out latter-day careers as character comediennes but Billie Burke was a notable Hollywood exception. But then, for all her beauty, fun did run strongly through her veins; her father, Billy Burke, was a cel-

ebrated singing clown with the Barnum and Bailey circus. After touring Europe at 17 Billie made her London stage debut in 1903 and took Broadway by storm five years later, making her name in light, frothy, wittily-written romantic plays. She married the stage 'Follies' impresario Florenz Ziegfeld in 1914 (he died in 1932), after which she took on a few leads in silent films. With Ziegfeld's death, Billie returned full-time to the screen, the scatterbrained society wife of John Barrymore in *A Bill of Divorcement* setting her up for a whole series of flighty, fluttery, feather-brained matrons, which she played with a brilliant light touch. Somewhere in the middle of this long run came the role by which many filmgoers still remember her − Glinda the Good Witch in *The Wizard of Oz*. In the 1940s she made a couple of starring two-reeler comedy shorts and played Don Taylor's twittering mother in the very successful M-G-M films *Father of the Bride* and *Father's Little Dividend*. She tried television but eventually retired in 1960 'because acting just wasn't any fun any more'. She published two volumes of reminiscences, *With a Feather on My Nose* and *With Powder on My Nose*.

*1915: Peggy. 1916: Gloria's Romance (serial). 1917: The Land of Promise. The Mysterious Miss Terry. Arms and the Girl. 1918: Eve's Daughter. In Pursuit of Polly. The Make Believe Wife. Let's Get a Divorce. 1919: Good Gracious, Annabelle. The Misleading Widow. Wanted − a Husband. 1920: Sadie Love. Away Goes Prudence. 1921: The Education of Elizabeth. The Frisky Mrs Johnson. 1929: Glorifying the American Girl. 1930: Ranch House Blues. 1932: A Bill of Divorcement. 1933: Christopher Strong. Dinner at Eight. Only Yesterday. 1934: Finishing School. Where Sinners Meet (GB: The Dover Road). We're Rich Again. Forsaking All Others. Only Eight Hours. 1935: Becky Sharp. Doubting Thomas. A Feather in Her Hat. Society Doctor. She Couldn't Take It (GB: Woman Tamer). Splendor. After Office Hours. 1936: Piccadilly Jim. My American Wife. Craig's Wife. 1937: Parnell. Navy Blue and Gold. Topper. The Bride Wore Red. 1938: Everybody Sing. The Young in Heart. Merrily We Live. 1939: Topper Takes a Trip. The Wizard of Oz. The Bridal Suite. Eternally Yours. Remember? Zenobia (GB: Elephants Never Forget). 1940: And One Was Beautiful. Irene. Hullabaloo. Dulcy. The Ghost Comes Home. The Captain is a Lady. 1941: Topper Returns. One Night in Lisbon. The Man Who Came to Dinner. 1942: The Wild Man of Borneo. What's Cookin'? (GB: Wake Up and Dream). They All Kissed the Bride. Girl Trouble. 1943: Hi Diddle Diddle. So's Your Uncle. You're a Lucky Fellow, Mr Smith. Gildersleeve on Broadway. 1944: Laramie Trail. 1945: Swing Out, Sister. The Cheaters. 1946: Breakfast in Hollywood (GB: The Mad Hatter). The Bachelor's Daughters. 1948: * Silly Billy. * Billie Gets Her Man. 1949: The Barkleys of Broadway. 1950: And Baby Makes Three. Father of the Bride. Three*

Husbands. The Boy from Indiana (GB: Blaze of Glory). 1951: Father's Little Dividend. Darling, How Could You? (GB: Rendezvous). 1953: Small Town Girl. 1957: The Star-Wagon (TV). 1958: Rumors of Evening (TV). 1959: The Young Philadelphians (GB: The City Jungle). 1960: Sergeant Rutledge. Pepe.

BURNABY, Davy 1881–1949

This portly and popular light-haired British comedian, of monocled eye and avuncular manner, was chiefly a star of stage revues, although he made his mark in radio and found steady work in the British cinema of the 1930s as a top supporting player. Affably addle-brained, Burnaby in his comic style was in some ways the ancestor of an even larger British comedian, Fred Emney (qv), who also had a sporadic cinema career. Burnaby's characters were less irascible than Emney's would be, and he usually played benign buffoons. A busy man in all spheres of show business, Burnaby, who made the perfect squire on screen, was also an author and songwriter. With the British film industry floundering at the end of the 1930s, Burnaby found roles for his roly-poly talents less easy to find and went back to the stage. Ill-health limited his appearances in later years and he died from a heart attack at 68. Show business obituaries for him were not as large as they might have been, as Burnaby's good friend and fellow character comedian Will Hay (qv) — much the bigger star in cinema terms — had died on the same day.

1929: The Devil's Maze. The Co-Optimists. 1933: Just My Luck. The Wishbone. That's My Wife. Cleaning Up. Three Men in a Boat. The Right to Live. Strike It Rich. A Shot in the Dark. 1934: * Screen Vaudeville No. 1. On the Air. Murder at the Inn. The Man I Want. Keep It Quiet. How's Chances? Are You a Mason? Radio Parade of 1935 (US: Radio Pirates). 1935: * Equity Musical Revue (series). Stormy Weather. Dandy Dick. We've Got to Have Love. * When the Cat's Away. Boys Will Be Boys. While Parents Sleep. 1936: The Marriage of Corbal (US: Prisoner of Corbal). 1937: Song of the Road. Feather Your Nest. Calling All Stars. Song of the Forge. Talking Feet. Leave It

To Me. 1938: Second Best Bed. Chips. Many Tanks Mr Atkins. Kicking the Moon Around (US: The Playboy). 1939: Come on George.

BURNETTE, Smiley
(Lester Burnette) 1911–1967

Eager-to-please, plump and jovial, Smiley Burnette was one of the most popular of the comic sidekicks in 'B' westerns of the 1930s, 1940s and 1950s. With his black stetson turned up at the front and down at the back he was also one of the most easily recognisable. A quick-fire joke teller with a frog-like voice second only to that of Andy Devine, the enterprising young Burnette was running his own Illinois radio station at 19, telling shaggy-dog stories and playing guitar. His talents came to the attention of country-and-western singer Gene Autry, who offered to double Burnette's salary if he would back him on his own radio programme. Burnette accepted, and a partnership was forged that was to last, on and off, for more than 20 years. Autry and Burnette came to films together in 1934 and were soon given western vehicles of their own. Burnette appropriately played a character called Frog. After more than 70 films together the team split and Burnette went on to play comedy foil to other screen westerners including Charles Starrett, Bob Livingston, Roy Rogers, Sunset Carson and Allan 'Rocky' Lane. In 1953 his career came full circle when he rejoined Autry for what were to be their last six westerns for the cinema. Burnette was appearing as a regular on the TV comedy Petticoat Junction in the 1960s when he learned he had leukaemia, the disease that was to kill him at 55. During his short lifetime the raw-throated funster wrote more than 350 songs, many with a western flavour, some of which were used by the 'singing cowboys' who rode the screen in the 1930s, 1940s and 1950s. He also boasted of being able to play 50 different instruments, was one of the few secondary westerners to almost always be billed above the title, had a comic-strip magazine devoted to his imaginary exploits and was placed respectably high in the list of top money-making 'B' western stars from 1940 to the end of his film career.

1934: In Old Santa Fe. Mystery Mountain (serial). 1935: The Phantom Empire (serial). Tumbling Tumbleweeds. Waterfront Lady. Melody Trail. The Sagebrush Troubadour. The Singing Vagabond. The Adventures of Rex and Rinty (serial). Streamline Express. Harmony Lane. 1936: Hitch Hike Lady (GB: Eventful Journey). Doughnuts and Society (GB: Stepping into Society). Red River Valley. Comin' Round the Mountain. Oh, Susannah! The Singing Cowboy. Guns and Guitars. Ride, Ranger, Ride. The Big Show. The Old Corral (GB: Texas Serenade). Hearts in Bondage. A Man Betrayed. The Border Patrolman. 1937: Round-Up Time in Texas. Rootin' Tootin' Rhythm (GB: Rhythm on the Ranch). Git Along Little Dogies (GB: Serenade of the West). Yodelin' Kid from Pine Ridge (GB: The Hero of Pine Ridge). Public Cowboy No. 1. Boots and Saddles. Manhattan Merry-Go-Round (GB: Manhattan Music Box). Springtime in the Rockies. Larceny on the Air. Dick Tracy (serial). Meet the Boy Friend. 1938: The Old Barn Dance. Gold Mine in the Sky. Man from Music Mountain. Prairie Moon. Rhythm of the Saddle. Western Jamboree. The Hollywood Stadium Mystery. Under Western Skies. Billy the Kid Returns. 1939: Home on the Prairie. Mexicali Rose. Blue Montana Skies. Mountain Rhythm. Colorado Sunset. In Old Monterey. Rovin' Tumbleweeds. South of the Border. 1940: Rancho Grande. Gaucho Serenade. Carolina Moon. Ride, Tenderfoot, Ride. Men with Steel Faces (GB: Couldn't Possibly Happen). 1941: Ridin' on a Rainbow. Back in the Saddle. The Singing Hills. Sunset in Wyoming. Under Fiesta Stars. Down Mexico Way. Sierra Sue. 1942: Cowboy Serenade (GB: Serenade of the West). Heart of the Rio Grande. Home in Wyoming. Stardust on the Sage. Call of the Canyon. Bells of Capistrano. Heart of the Golden West. 1943: Idaho. Beyond the Last Frontier. King of the Cowboys. Silver Spurs. 1944: Beneath Western Skies. Call of the Rockies. The Laramie Trail. Code of the Prairie. Pride of the Plains. Bordertown Trail. Firebrands of Arizona. 1946: Roaring Rangers (GB: False Hero). Galloping Thunder (GB: On Boot Hill). Frontier Gun Law (GB: Menacing Shadows). Two-Fisted Stranger. South of the Chisholm Trail. Heading West (GB: The Cheat's Last Throw). Terror Trail (GB: Hands of Menace). Gunning for Vengeance (GB: Jail Break). The Desert Horseman (GB: Checkmate). Landrush (GB: The Claw Strikes). The Fighting Frontiersman (GB: Golden Lady). 1947: The Lone Hand Texan (GB: The Cheat). Prairie Raiders (GB: The Forger). Riders of the Lone Star. The Buckaroo from Powder River. West of Dodge City (GB: The Sea Wall). Law of the Canyon (GB: The Price of Crime). The Stranger from Ponca City. The Last Days of Boot Hill. 1948: Whirlwind Raiders (GB: State Police). Phantom Valley. Blazing Across the Pecos (GB: Under Arrest). El Dorado Pass (GB: Desperate Men). West of Sonora. Six Gun Law. Trail to Laredo (GB: Sign of the Dagger). Quick on the Trigger (GB: Condemned in Error). 1949: Desert Vigilante. Challenge of the Range (GB: Moonlight Raid). Horsemen of the Sierras (GB: Remember Me). Bandits of El Dorado (GB:

Tricked). The Blazing Trail (GB: The Forged Will). South of Death Valley (GB: River of Poison). Laramie. Renegades of the Sage (GB: The Fort). 1950: Trail of the Rustlers (GB: Lost River). Streets of Ghost Town. Outcasts of Black Mesa (GB: The Clue). Across the Badlands (GB: The Challenge). Raiders of Tomahawk Creek (GB: Circle of Fear). Texas Dynamo (GB: Suspected). Lightning Guns (GB: Taking Sides). Frontier Outpost. 1951: Whirlwind. Fort Savage Raiders. Prairie Roundup. Bonanza Town (GB: Two-Fisted Agent). The Kid from Amarillo (GB: Silver Chains). Riding the Outlaw Trail. Snake River Desperadoes. Cyclone Fury. Pecos River (GB: Without Risk). 1952: Junction City. Smoky Canyon. The Hawk of Wild River. The Rough, Tough West. Laramie Mountains (GB: Mountain Desperadoes). The Kid from Broken Gun. 1953: Winning of the West. On Top of Old Smoky. Pack Train. Goldtown Ghost Riders. Saginaw Trail. Last of the Pony Riders.

BURNS, Bob 'Bazooka' 1890–1956

In the realm of homespun American humour, Bob Burns followed hard on the heels of Will Rogers (*qv*) – although he enjoyed only half of Rogers' success. Chubby-faced, with dark, tightly curly hair, large brown eyes and humorous lips that seemed to be permanently parted, chunkily-built Burns hailed originally from Van Buren in Arkansas. After a university education that belied the naive characters he often portrayed, Burns broke into show business telling dry, rambling, shaggy-dog stories about Arkansas country folk, earning himself the nickname 'The Arkansas Philosopher'. His personal charm was considerable. He also invented a musical instrument called a bazooka, which he claimed to have made out of gas pipes and a whiskey funnel. Burns made the jump from vaudeville to radio in the early 1930s and was soon one of the country's most popular comics, especially with mid-western audiences. He was tried out in films (he had done extra work in Hollywood in the very early days of Biograph Studio, around 1913) and given one or two vehicles of his own. These invariably cast the drawling Burns as a well-meaning citizen whose innate goodness and common sense enabled him to outwit the villains, and set everyone else's lives to rights. After the war Burns went back to radio and nightclub entertaining, singing, joking, philosophising and playing the bazooka and the mandolin (which he had first played professionally in Van Buren at the age of 14). He died from cancer, not back in Arkansas, but in his adopted California.

1931: Quick Millions. 1935: The Phantom Empire (GB: Radio Ranch). The Singing Vagabond. * Restless Knights. 1936: The Courageous Avenger. Rhythm on the Range. Guns and Guitars. The Big Broadcast of 1937. 1937: Waikiki Wedding. Wells Fargo. Git Along Little Dogies (GB: Serenade of the West). Public Cowboy No. 1. Yodelin' Kid from Pine Ridge (GB: The Hero of Pine Ridge). Hit the Saddle. 1938: Mountain Music. Tropic Holiday. Radio City Revels. The Arkansas Traveler. 1939: Our Leading Citizen. I'm From Missouri. Rovin' Tumbleweed. 1940: Alias the Deacon. Prairie Schooners (GB: Through the Storm). Comin' Round the Mountain. 1942: The Hillbilly Deacon. Call of the Canyon. * Soaring Stars. 1944: Belle of the Yukon. Mystery Man.

BURNS, George

(Nathan Birnbaum) 1896–

Was it George Burns or Groucho Marx who said 'I still chase girls at my age, but only if they're going downhill'? No matter. Both had the same straight stare and deadpan delivery behind the long cigar. If there were a hint of mockery about their stance, it came only from a flick of the ash from the end of the cigar as the punch-line came to rest. Still filming at 92 (in *18 Again!*), Burns has become a national institution in his native America. The ninth of 12 children from a family of Lower East Side New Yorkers, he entered show business at seven as a singer with the Pee Wee Quartet, four kids who backed an amateur hopeful in song contests and at restaurants. As a teenager in vaudeville, for Burns it was a case of a song and a smile. He was part of numerous double and triple acts, often changing his name from one engagement to the next, sometimes, he says, to pull the wool over the eyes of a theatre manager who hadn't liked him under the previous name. His last partner before he met and married Gracie Allen (*qv*) was a comic called Billy Lorraine. The partnership was already cracking up and George willingly joined forces with the 22-year-old Gracie, succeeding swiftly with the public once he switched to being her straight man. Somehow, though, it seemed that George always got in some cutting barbs of his own as Gracie wittered on along some new labyrinthine path. A brief account of their career together can be found under the section on Gracie Allen, although it should be added that George was usually the script-man – the brains behind her craziness. Her death in 1964, after six years in retirement, was only the beginning of George's second show business career, one that really took off at 79 when he made his first on-screen appearance for 30 years in *The Sunshine Boys*. This comedy of irascibility teamed Burns with Walter Matthau as veteran vaudevillians brought together for a reunion, even though they haven't spoken to each other in years, and included some raucous, rasping recreations of old vaudeville routines. When George Burns received an Academy Award for the film two months after his 80th birthday, he became the oldest Oscar-winner in Academy history. There have been ten more comedy films since then, including three as a cigar-puffing God, a role he hopes to play again in the planned *God Takes a Holiday*. George says his favourite ages are '94, 95 and 96 in that order' and that he has to live to 100, since he's booked to play the London Palladium in 1996. He's still busy with guest spots in nightclubs. In 1989 he said: 'I'm a very fortunate man. I love what I do for a living. And I do everything doctors tell me not to. I drink martinis and coffee. I smoke cigars too. Let's face it, at my age, if I don't hold on to something, I may fall down. Do I keep to a special diet? Sure – food.' Also: 'It's been fun working on my own, but tougher. With Gracie, I had the easiest job of any straight man in history. I only had to know two lines – "How's your brother?" and "Your brother did *what?*"'

1929: * Lamb Chops. 1930: * Fit to be Tied. * Pulling a Bone. 1931: * The Antique Shop. * Once Over, Light. * One Hundred Per Cent Service. 1932: The Big Broadcast. * Oh My Operation. * The Babbling Book. * Hollywood on Parade A–2. 1933: International House. College Humor. * Patents Pending. * Let's Dance. * Walking the Baby. 1934: We're Not Dressing. Six of a Kind. Many Happy Returns. 1935: Love in Bloom. Here Comes Cookie. The Big Broadcast of 1936. 1936: College Holiday. The Big Broadcast of 1937. A Damsel in Distress. 1938: College Swing (GB: Swing, Teacher, Swing). 1939: Honolulu. 1944: Two Girls and a Sailor. 1954: * Screen Snapshots No. 224. 1956: The Solid Gold Cadillac (narrator only). 1975: The Sunshine Boys. 1977: Oh, God! 1978: Sergeant Pepper's Lonely Hearts Club Band. The Comedy Company

Deadpan dancing from George Burns (right) as Fred Astaire and Gracie Allen smile for the camera in the musical comedy *A Damsel in Distress*

Forsaking All Others. Bulldog Drummond Strikes Back. 1935: Ruggles of Red Gap. The Night is Young. Baby Face Harrington. Orchids to You. Magnificent Obsession. 1936: Half Angel. We Went to College. Rainbow on the River. The Moon's Our Home. 1937: Swing High, Swing Low. Every Day's a Holiday. 1938: Thanks for the Memory. 1939: Let Freedom Ring. 1940: The Boys from Syracuse. Second Chorus. 1941: Road Show. Blonde Inspiration. * There's Nothing to It. Sis Hopkins. 1942: What's Cookin'? (GB: Wake Up and Dream). Night in New Orleans. Give Out, Sisters. 1943: Always a Bridesmaid. The Sultan's Daughter. This is the Army. 1944: Follow the Boys. Bermuda Mystery. Dixie Jamboree.

BUTTERWORTH, Peter 1919–1979

Built like a little barrel, Britain's bumbling Peter Butterworth spent much of his career cracking jokes for children but is now best recalled for the films which filled much of the latter part of his relatively short life — as a member of the famous 'Carry On' team. After brief theatrical experience, Manchester-born Butterworth became, with the outbreak of World War Two, a pilot in the Fleet Air Arm. Shot down off the Dutch coast in 1941, he spent the next four years as a prisoner-of-war, becoming noted for his escape attempts. He took part in vaulting over a gym horse in an escape that later formed the basis for *The Wooden Horse* (1950), and participated in a concert party — his first experience as a comedian — while fellow-prisoners were attempting to tunnel to freedom: an incident re-created in *The Colditz Story* (1954). It was always a source of some amusement to Butterworth that he was turned down for a part in *The Wooden Horse* because he was 'the wrong type'. By this time, though, he had become established as a patter comedian in concert parties, road shows and, from 1948, television. His work in children's television from 1950 — *Saturday Special*, *Peter's Troubles*, etc. — soon took precedence over his relatively infrequent appearances in character roles in films, though he made a few starring two-reeler comedies in the 1950s. He married attractive impressionist Janet

BUTTERWORTH, Charles 1896–1946

A supporting comedian who is now almost forgotten, Butterworth, an American who began his career as a journalist, made his name playing the elegant fool and singing silly songs in well-dressed Broadway musicals and comedies. With the coming of sound Hollywood quickly pounced on his talents and he was soon typed there as twittering, dithering, wealthy bachelors, all far too indecisive ever to get the girl. With his pencil-slim figure, dignified bearing, doleful expression and streak of fair hair that seemed forever hanging on by its follicles, he was perfect in his chosen role. And when given a leading role Butterworth was a real pleasure to watch. Especially memorable was his mild-mannered clerk in *Baby Face Harrington* (1935) who gets mixed up with gangsters and finds himself mistaken for Public Enemy Number 2! His George Van Bassingwell the same year in *Ruggles of Red Gap* was another memorable gem. With the end of the 1930s and the fading of the screwball comedy, Butterworth began to be seen in films less worthy of his talents. And he hadn't made a movie of any description for a couple of years when he died in a car crash in June 1946. He was 49.

1930: The Life of the Party. Illicit. 1931: Side Show. The Bargain. The Mad Genius. * The Stolen Jools (GB: The Slippery Pearls). 1932: Beauty and the Boss. Love Me Tonight. Manhattan Parade. 1933: The Nuisance (GB: Accidents Wanted). Penthouse (GB: Crooks in Clover). My Weakness. 1934: Student Tour. Hollywood Party. The Cat and the Fiddle.

(TV). Movie Movie. 1979: Just You and Me, Kid. Going in Style. 1980: Oh, God! Book II. 1983: Two of a Kind (TV). 1984: Oh, God! You Devil. 1988: 18 Again! 1989: George Burns: His Wit and Wisdom (video).

Charles Butterworth made a superb Algy in *Bulldog Drummond Strikes Back*. Here he prepares to help Ronald Colman's Bulldog dispose of Wilson Benge

Unaccustomed as he is to luxury... Eddie Cantor prepares to take his own picture in one of his smash musical-comedies, *Kid Millions*

John Candy plays a detective with a liking (but not a knack) for disguise in *Who's Harry Crumb?* When you're Candy's size, disguises tend to be irrelevant

Brown, another children's TV favourite, in 1949, and they remained married until his death. Butterworth was a latecomer to the 'Carry On' series — his first was *Carry On Cowboy* in 1965 — but he was soon an ever-present, appearing in 16 of the film farces, including the last, *Carry On Emmannuelle*, in 1978. Butterworth was appearing in panto-mime in Coventry when he had a heart attack while preparing for bed. His body was not found until the following afternoon. Butterworth's character in films was typically that of the dithering, bungling incompetent, a minor official who maintained a cheerful countenance as he blundered dim-wittedly through the plot. He became especially adept at duologues with fellow-members of the 'Carry On' gang, often unexpectedly sneaking laughs from under the noses of those billed above him.

1948: William Comes to Town. 1949: The Adventures of Jane. Murder at the Windmill (US: Murder at the Burlesque). Miss Pilgrim's Progress. 1950: Circle of Danger. Night and the City. Paul Temple's Triumph. Mr Drake's Duck. The Body Said No! 1951: The Case of the Missing Scene. Old Mother Riley's Jungle Treasure. Appointment with Venus (US: Island Rescue). Saturday Island (US: Island of Desire). 1952: Penny Princess. Is Your Honeymoon Really Necessary? 1953: * Watch Out! * A Good Pull-Up. Will Any Gentleman? 1954: * Five O'Clock Finish. The Gay Dog. 1955: * Playground Express. Fun at St Fanny's. * Black in the Face. * That's an Order. 1958: Blow Your Own Trumpet. tom thumb. 1960: The Spider's Web. Escort for Hire. 1961: The Day the Earth Caught Fire. Murder She Said. 1962: Fate Takes a Hand. The Prince and the Pauper. She'll Have to Go (US: Maid for Murder). Live Now — Pay Later. Kill or Cure. 1963: The Horse without a Head. The Rescue Squad. Doctor in Distress. 1964: Never Mention Murder. A Home of Your Own. 1965: Carry on Cowboy. The Amorous Adventures of Moll Flanders. 1966: A Funny Thing Happened on the Way to the Forum. Carry On Screaming. 1967: Don't Lose Your Head. Follow That Camel. * Ouch! Danny the Dragon. 1968: Carry On Doctor. Prudence and the Pill. Carry On Up the Khyber. 1970: Carry On Camping. Carry On Again, Doctor. 1970: Carry On Henry. Carry On Loving. 1971: The Magnificent Seven Deadly Sins. 1972: Carry On Abroad. Bless This House. 1973: Carry On Girls. 1974: Carry On Dick. 1975: Carry On Behind. 1976: Carry On England. The Ritz. Robin and Marian. 1977: What's Up Nurse? 1978: Carry On Emmannuelle. The First Great Train Robbery (US: The Great Train Robbery).

BUTTONS, Red

(Aaron Schwatt) 1918–

Cheerful, red-haired, long-faced little American comedian-who-turned-actor. His manner seemed to set him on the road to play timid, mousey types, but he managed a good variety of roles after winning an Academy Award for *Sayonara*. And it's as a star character actor that Buttons seems to have left his mark, rather than as a star comedian. The son of European immigrants to New York, the livewire Buttons was an extrovert entertainer from an early age. He won his first amateur contest at 12, and was entertaining professionally at 16, taking his stage name from his first billing in Bronx burlesque: Red Buttons the Singing Bellboy. It was 1942 before he made Broadway, and then he was immediately drafted into the US Army. This led to his film debut in the screen version of the famous forces stage show *Winged Victory*. In 1952 he became the star of his own TV show which was initially a great success, with Red doing silly songs and dances and equally inane monologues. But its popularity began to fade after two seasons, even with such performers as Phyllis Kirk and Paul Lynde supporting Red in a situation comedy format, and the show folded in 1955. Buttons was actually out of work when offered the role of the tragic Airman Kelly in *Sayonara*. The Oscar it brought as best supporting actor was a career lifesaver. After that he appeared in many other films and TV movies, as well as taking solo spotlight in nightclubs. A second TV series, though, *The Double Life of Henry Phyfe*, was again a flop.

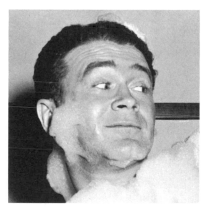

1944: Winged Victory. 1946: 13 Rue Madeleine. 1951: Footlight Varieties. 1957: Sayonara. 1958: Imitation General. 1959: The Big Circus. A Marriage of Strangers (TV). 1961: One, Two, Three. 1962: Hatari! Five Weeks in a Balloon. The Longest Day. Gay Purr-ee (voice only). 1963: A Ticklish Affair. 1964: Your Cheatin' Heart. 1965: Up From the Beach. Harlow. 1966: Stagecoach. 1969: They Shoot Horses, Don't They? 1970: Breakout (TV). 1971: Who Killed Mary What's 'er Name? 1972: The Poseidon Adventure. 1975: Gable and Lombard. The New Original Wonder Woman (TV). 1976: Louis Armstrong Chicago Style (TV). 1977: Viva Knievel! Pete's Dragon. 1978: Telethon (TV). Movie Movie. The Users (TV). VegaS (TV). 1979: Christmas in July (voice only). Chomps. 1980: When Time Ran Out ... 1981: Leave 'Em Laughing (TV). Side Show (TV). 1985: Reunion at Fairborough (TV), 1988: 18 Again! 1989: Into Thin Air. The Ambulance.

CAESAR, Sid 1922–

Sharp-chinned, dark-haired, fast-talking American comedian — a more wolfish-looking version of Britain's Bob Monkhouse and an enormous success on television. The cinema should have seized Caesar when he was hot, in the early 1950s, but it missed the opportunity and his later film appearances were insipid and lacked ambition. After early experience as a musician — playing saxophone and clarinet with dance bands, Caesar emerged from war service with the US Coast Guard as a wisecracking comedian with a formidable range of character impressions. He appeared in a Broadway show in 1947 and had broken into television by the following year. Early in 1949 TV's *Admiral Broadway Revue* united him for the first time with the versatile wide-mouthed comedienne Imogene Coca. The team stayed together for 90 minutes of variety that NBC started in 1950 and called *Your Show of Shows*. As much of a sudden hit as *Laugh-In* would be a couple of decades later, it featured Caesar excelling in parodies of current films and TV shows, as well as delivering monologues and mimes and being hilariously droll in the running role of 'the roving reporter'. The cast went their separate ways in 1954 but none of them re-captured the magic of those years. Ceasar himself, who had made his film debut in 1945 in the screen version of the forces show *Tars and Spars*, scoring with an amusing spoof of war movies, had several other TV shows centred on him but none brought him the same success. There was a mild attempt by director William Castle to give Caesar belated film stardom in 1966, but the two films they made together, *The Busy Body* and *The Spirit is Willing*, were too broad and engulfed Caesar's intimate style. The funniest Caesar moments on screen are nearly all contained in the compilation feature *Ten from Your Show of Shows* released in 1973. Since then, he has done extensive nightclub stints and made fairly frequent guest appearances in films and TV movies.

1945: Tars and Spars. 1947: The Guilt of Janet Ames. 1963: It's a Mad, Mad, Mad, Mad World. 1966: The Busy Body. The Spirit is Willing. 1967: A Guide for the Married Man. 1973: Ten from Your Show of Shows. 1974: Airport 1975. 1976: Flight to Holocaust (TV). Silent Movie. 1977: Fire Sale. Barnaby and Me. Curse of the Black Widow (TV). 1978: Grease. The Cheap Detective. 1980: The Fiendish Plot of Dr Fu Manchu. 1981: History of the World Part I. The Munsters' Revenge (TV). 1982: Grease 2. 1983: Over the Brooklyn Bridge. Cannonball Run II. 1985: Stoogemania. Love is Never Silent (TV). 1987: The Emperor's New Clothes. 1988: Freedom Fighter (TV). Side by Side (TV). 1991: The South Pacific Story.

CAMPBELL, Eric
see **CHAPLIN, Charlie**

CANDY, John 1950–
There hasn't been a really successful 'fat' comedian in films for a long time so the failure of John Candy's first real solo venture, *Who's Harry Crumb?*, was all the more disappointing. However, the failure was that of material rather than performer, and of a director who asked Candy to try too hard for laughs. Now past 40, Candy has experimented with some success in recent times with sentimental comedy, a genre which has defeated comedians down the ages. Light-haired, eager-looking and brash-talking — and very bulky — Candy was born and raised in Toronto, where he began his career with local stage performances and appear-ances in TV commercials. His comedy breakthrough came in 1972 when, by now having crossed the border between Canada and the United States, he joined the famous Chicago comedy troupe Second City. Second City began a very successful late-night television series, *SCTV*, in 1975. The series went into syndication with NBC and Candy, who stayed with it as a performer until 1983, won Emmys for comedy writing in 1982 and 1985. After a beginning in Canadian films, Candy's movies between 1980 and 1988 saw him mainly supporting such comedy stars as Bill Murray, Tom Hanks, Chevy Chase and Steve Martin (all *qv*), playing slobby, clumsy characters whose ham-fisted bonhomie embarrasses the star. In Mel Brooks' *Spaceballs*, Candy was typi-cally cast as a dog called Barf, but was allowed to run some interesting variations on his usual role in *Planes, Trains and Auto-mobiles*, in which his appalling and graceless cross-country traveller is skilfully turned over at the end by Candy to reveal a poignant and lonely side. It was an indicator of a subtle change in Candy's screen persona. By 1989 he was being given his own vehicles, these continuing by and large to show him in a more sympathetic light. *Uncle Buck* again revealed the carefully-concealed caring person beneath the slobbish exterior, and in *Only the Lonely* Candy was even allowed a screen romance with Ally Sheedy, drawing even more of a three-dimensional character than before, as a mother-dominated police-man. He was sympathetic again in *Delirious* (inventive, but a flop) and, despite stardom, continued to work at a furious rate, contribu-ting several cameos to films of the early 1990s. The best of this heaviest of light comedians may be yet to come.

1975: The Clown Murders. 1976: It Seemed Like a Good Idea at the Time. Find the Lady. 1977: Faceoff. 1978: The Silent Partner. 1979: Lost and Found. 1941. 1980: The Blues Brothers. 1981: Heavy Metal (voice only). Stripes. 1982: It Came from Hollywood (video). 1983: Strange Brew. National Lampoon's Vacation. Going Berserk. 1984: Splash. 1985: Sesame Street Presents: Follow That Bird. Brewster's Millions. Volunteers. Summer Rental. 1986: Armed and Dangerous. Little Shop of Horrors. Rocket Boy (TV). 1987: Spaceballs. Really Weird Tales (TV). Planes, Trains and Automobiles. 1988: The Great Outdoors. 1989: Who's Harry Crumb? Hot to Trot (voice only). Speed Zone. Uncle Buck. 1990: Home Alone. Nothing But Trouble. Masters of Menace. 1991: Delirious. Only the Lonely. The Rescuers Down Under (voice only). Career Opportunities (later One Wild Night). JFK. Once Upon a Crime. 1992: Bartholomew vs Neff.

CANOVA, Judy
(Juliet Canova) 1916–1983
There have been several zanies with operatic singing voices — Britain's Harry Secombe (*qv*) also springs to mind, and America's chestnut-haired, horse-faced Judy Canova.

a walking caricature of a girl, was another singer who just couldn't resist clowning around. Hillbillies and hayseeds were her stock in trade. She donned a gingham dress, a straw hat and oversized boots, wore her hair in pigtails or bangs, filled her act with cornball jokes and let rip. She once told an interviewer that 'some critics always thought my stuff was too corny, but the public bought it. I got started doing that country stuff as a teenager with my brother and sister, and I never could get out of it.' Whatever she thought of the 'cornball stuff', it brought her a healthy living for 30 years — and saw her through an unbelievable 16 years of starring roles in film comedies. It was all the more incredible because the second-feature comedy-musicals her studios mounted for her hardly ever gave Judy a chance to add impetus to her career — and her greatest following built up from a radio show. She was born the youngest of eight children to a cotton broker in Florida. Early operatic ambitions were stillborn after her father died and she was unable to go to music school. Instead she found herself teaching 'contor-tion dancing', which she herself had studied, before joining the family act (her sister Anne, brother Zeke and, later, brother Pete) who quickly switched from semi-classical har-mony to a hillbilly act when they found that their yodelling and 'hog-calling' was getting them bookings at New York clubs. Judy soon adopted her familiar guise of the brash little girl from Hicksville (although she wasn't that little, being 5 ft 6 in, fairly tall for the time, and quite solidly built). She hit Broadway with the rest of the family troupe in 1934, when one reviewer termed her 'quaint and enormously self-possessed'. With the voice that hit the back of the stalls and bounced back, she was hard not to pick out from the crowd. It was her habit of mangling songs, country style, though, that brought her to the attention of film studios and Warners handed her a small guest spot in their 1935 *In Caliente*, burlesquing one of the songs. It was her film debut at 18; the plain Jane from northern Florida had already come a long way. Four years later a solo screen career became a possibility for Judy after her Broadway success as the star of *Yokel Boy*, opposite Phil Silvers (*qv*) and

Buddy Ebsen. Judy didn't star in the film version even though it was made at the studio for whom she signed (Republic) and by a director she often worked with, Joseph Santley. In one of Hollywood's stranger quirks, Joan Davis (*qv*), who wasn't suited to the role, did it instead! Though Republic were a minor studio, they did offer Canova her own films, instead of guest roles in other people's. Production values and co-stars were good for the first three of Judy's four years there but the studio just didn't have the talents behind the camera to help her when she needed it most. Judy still dressed in gingham and calico and wore pigtails and straw hats; she even invented her own catch-phrase − 'You're telling I' − and sang a lot of hit songs in what, thought one critic, 'alternated between a whinny and an operatic soprano'. Her first two Republic films, *Scatterbrain* and *Sis Hopkins*, did exceptionally well at the box-office, especially in rural areas where Judy's crackerbarrel humour went down best. The latter was another remake of a Broadway classic, allowed Judy full scope for her imitation of a likeable backwoods bull in a china shop, and introduced one of her biggest hits *It Ain't Hay − It's the USA*. But her image was pretty unvarying and most of her films took a hammering from the critics. She turned down an M-G-M contract in 1942 (probably a wise decision) but the films she made for Columbia after leaving Republic were even worse and she turned to radio. By 1950 her show, cut to a familiar hillbilly format, was among the ten most popular on the air, with Judy getting $10,000 a programme. Republic lured her back with the promise of better things but, although they made her first two films under the new contract in colour and at A-feature length, Judy was on her own when it came to the scripts. In *Honeychile* she was a composer, and in *Oklahoma Annie* a gun-toting sheriff. Her unbridled energy just about carried the corny plots through but by the end of 1955 the Canova films were down to 70 minutes in black and white and she quit the studio for the second time. In the 1960s Judy finally managed to drop the hick-from-the-sticks image, changed the colour of her hair and did TV and nightclub work. One critic described her as 'looking and sounding like a country Dinah Shore'. She died after a heart attack at 67, leaving two daughters, Diana (a comedy actress) and Juliet. She once told a producer on radio that she wanted to sing 'the Miseries from *Il Trovatore*' on his show. 'You mean the *Miserere*' said the producer stuffily. Judy grinned. 'You ain't heard me sing it yet,' she said.

1935: In Caliente. Going Highbrow. Broadway Gondolier. 1937: Artists and Models. Thrill of a Lifetime. 1940: Scatterbrain. 1941: Sis Hopkins. Puddin' Head (GB: Judy Goes to Town). * Meet Roy Rogers. 1942: Joan of Ozark (GB: The Queen of Spies). True to the Army.

Sleepytime Gal. 1943: Chatterbox. Sleepy Lagoon. 1944: Louisiana Hayride. * Screen Snapshots No. 24. 1945: Hit the Hay. 1946: Singin' in the Corn. * Famous Hollywood Mothers. * Radio Characters of 1946. 1951: Honeychile. 1952: Oklahoma Annie. 1953: The WAC from Walla Walla (GB: Army Capers). 1954: Untamed Heiress. 1955: Carolina Cannonball. 1956: Lay That Rifle Down. 1960: The Adventures of Huckleberry Finn. 1976: Cannonball (GB: Carquake).

CANTOR, Eddie,
(Isidor Iskowitz) 1892–1964
With dark, floppy hair, dark, popping eyes that seemed to have a sea of white about them, slight build, surprised face and bushy eyebrows, New York's Eddie Cantor looked like a member of a gangster family who was just too meek and mild to follow in the Godfather's footsteps. He had a light, attractive singing voice, a uniquely skippety, almost effete way of careering through a dance routine and a breathless delivery of funny dialogue that was all his own. Through the 1920s and 1930s Cantor and Al Jolson, another Jewish entertainer, were great rivals. Both sang in blackface and both appeared in musical hits on Broadway and in the cinema. But Cantor was the comedian of the two, diligently seeking the funny angle in everything and making himself the centrepiece of some lavish and inventive entertainments. Cantor's Russian immigrant parents had died when he was young, and his early school-leaving days were spent working as a messenger boy in Wall Street. He was fired for messing about too much and entertaining other employees with impromptu impersonations of Broadway celebrities. Show business was clearly calling the young Iskowitz and he began entertaining for a living at 14, working for a while as a singing waiter before, at 16, he began his long stage career in a juvenile revue. It would be another eight years before he made it to the top on Broadway, in a show called *Midnight Frolics*. Another eight years passed before Cantor starred in *Kid Boots*, the comedy musical that was finally to bring him to Hollywood two years later. The film version was, of course, shorn of its songs as films were still a year short of bursting into sound. Cantor, as a caddy at a country club who falls for swimming instructress Clara Bow (at her most provocative), did his little-boy-lost act to some effect, but the show wasn't the same without dialogue or songs. With the coming of sound, however, Cantor joined forces with producer Samuel Goldwyn to make *Whoopee!* In two-colour Technicolor, it was the first of several annual beanfeasts from the Cantor-Goldwyn combination, each replete with songs, comedy

Close curtain call for Eddie Cantor and Virginia Field in this scene from *Ali Baba Goes to Town*

routines, dance direction by Busby Berkeley and bevies of beautiful girls. The teenage Betty Grable had spots in the first two, *Whoopee!* and *Palmy Days*. 'More girls, more fun . . . and more Cantor than you've ever seen before' promised the Goldwyn machine's publicity for *Palmy Days*. It was the film that gave Cantor a better variety of comedy routines than any other. There was his usual blackface routine, a hilarious scene involving his poker-faced playing of a one-man band, a Keystone Kops-style chase and a chance to play the fool in drag with the Goldwyn Girls. And George Raft was the villain! The formula was now established: a zany setting, lines of pretty girls, Busby Berkeley dances, the occasional splash of colour, a blackface number for Cantor in an unspectacular score which usually included just one big hit, and new comedy routines, the best of which, in the next film, *The Kid from Spain*, brought a Buster Keaton-style performance from Cantor as a man on the run forced to pose as a famous matador. The musical numbers were even more lavish in *Roman Scandals*, in which quite a few funny things happened to Eddie on the way to the forum. He also had a huge song hit with *Keep Young and Beautiful*. Much of *Palmy Days* had been set in a bakery, but the last great Goldwyn-Cantor frolic, *Kid Millions*, outdid this by bursting into colour at the end in the middle of an ice-cream factory. It was two years before Cantor's next film, and the pause was fatal. The vogue for whacky comedy-musicals was fading, and *Strike Me Pink* is probably Eddie's worst screen effort. Despite the presence of Ethel Merman as co-star, the only thing memorable about the film is the slapstick chase finale. Over at Fox the following year (1937), Cantor reworked his *Roman Scandals* format in *Ali Baba Goes to Town*, in which he plays a tourist who gets lost in the desert, gets a part in an 'eastern' film, falls asleep and dreams he is Ali Baba in old Baghdad. It was a genial romp, the last highpoint of Cantor's screen career, with one escalatingly funny scene, played deadpan by the star. When the villain's troops are attacking Baghdad, Cantor flies out to meet them on his magic carpet, carrying a rope dipped in oil, which he lights and dangles over their heads, causing their horses to panic. What he doesn't know is that he has set fire to his own carpet, which is slowly burning away behind him! Cantor's few further films are mostly nostalgic looks back at his glory days. A film biography in 1953 was nowhere near the success that *The Jolson Story* had been a few years before. By then Cantor himself had been largely side-lined with a heart attack in 1952 and, despite the award of a special Oscar for 'distinguished service to the film industry' in 1953, he seemed a distant figure when he died at 72 from another heart attack. Through it all, though, Cantor never lost the essential guilelessness and vitality that made so many of his appearances endearing

and invigorating. And no-one could (with the inevitable raised eyebrow) say 'Really?' in quite the same fashion.

*1926: Kid Boots. 1927: * The Speed Hound. Follies. Special Delivery. 1929: Glorifying the American Girl. * That Party in Person. * Getting a Ticket. 1930: Whoopee! * Insurance. 1931: Palmy Days. 1932: The Kid from Spain. 1933: Roman Scandals. 1934: Kid Millions. * Hollywood Cavalcade. * Screen Snapshots No. 11. 1936: Strike Me Pink. 1937: Ali Baba Goes to Town. 1940: Forty Little Mothers. 1943: Thank Your Lucky Stars. 1944: Hollywood Canteen. Show Business. 1945: Rhapsody in Blue. 1948: If You Knew Susie. 1952: The Story of Will Rogers. 1953: The Eddie Cantor Story. 1956: Seidman and Son (TV).*

CARMICHAEL, Ian 1920–
The innocent abroad, the lamb to the slaughter, the hapless hooray-Henry whose triumphs at the end confound those who had taken advantage of his innocence and laughed at him behind their hands. These were the images with which Ian Carmichael, a light comedian from stage revue, took the British cinema by storm in the 1950s, and established himself, albeit for a few short years, as a major star. The strangulated vowels with which Carmichael suggested a game of tennis, or made a remark so gauche as to send his elders and tormentors into fits of laughter, emanated not from Surrey or some smart London suburb, but from the effort of stifling his native Yorkshire accent, something he managed to resurrect in later life. Fair-haired, with wide blue eyes and a faintly vacuous grin, Carmichael was born in Hull to an optician. He always wanted to act, studied at RADA and was on stage at 19. He had already played his first revue before volunteering for army service in 1941. He returned to the theatre in 1947 and began getting some very small roles in films. He started appearing regularly in revue from 1951, utilising talents as a light singer and dancer to augment his facility for evoking laughter. 'Even as a schoolboy,' he once said, 'I could make people laugh. Noël Coward described it as a talent to amuse. It's a talent I've enjoyed, but it got sharpened

up during my association with a comic actor called Leo Franklyn, with whom I toured for 30 weeks in an operetta just after the war. He showed me how to time my laughs and how to play an audience.' Carmichael continued in revue for three years but, ironically, it was his first straight play after that which gave him his big break in films. He was the harassed TV producer in the farce *Simon and Laura*, about a married couple who portray an idyllic existence on TV but fight like cat and dog in real life. The cinema leaped at the chance to satirise its upstart rival, and Carmichael repeated his role in the film version. Both Rank, who made it, and the Boulting Brothers spotted his potential straight away. Rank gave him a comedy so awful – *The Big Money* – that they couldn't even show it. But the Boultings did better. They made him the guileless recruit Stanley Windrush in their *Private's Progress*, which was a funnier and more perceptive comedy about army life than the British cinema had previously seen. Its huge success prompted the producers to transfer practically half the cast to a legal comedy called *Brothers in Law*, which was actually much funnier, and featured Carmichael as a barrister wet behind the ears and completely lacking in confidence. Carmichael, who looked years younger than his real age, skilfully displayed dithering determination and induced laughter and audience sympathy at the same time. His reward was perhaps his best-remembered role: Kingsley Amis's *Lucky Jim*, a working-class university lecturer who gets up everybody's nose, not least that of Terry-Thomas (qv) who, in almost all of Carmichael's best films, plays the cheat and bounder who initially outwits him but is finally confounded. He, Carmichael and the Boultings had another hit with *Happy is the Bride!* A cameo-filled account of the disastrous run-up to a marriage, it was a remake of the 1940 success *Quiet Wedding*. At this point Rank, doubtless to Carmichael's embarrassment, decided to resurrect *The Big Money*, which cast him, in a red wig, as an inept thief in a family of successful ones. It did a little business on the strength of his name, and probably slightly damaged his career. For the moment, though, all was well. Launder and Gilliat, another solid British film team, took him on for a funny political satire, *Left, Right and Centre*, and then he was back in his Stanley Windrush role in *I'm All Right, Jack*, the Boulting Brothers' cutting thrust at trade unions, which won a British Oscar for its screenplay. Carmichael was again, to the life, the amiable, vulnerable blunderer caught between warring factions (the unions and the bosses) far more guileful than himself. Terry-Thomas was with him again as the chief bounder at the *School for Scoundrels*, in which Carmichael had everyone rooting for him as he delightfully turned the tables. At this point, Carmichael had taken over from Alec Guinness (qv) as Britain's hottest comedy bet. But there were bad times just

Informing the police — or trying to find out the cricket score? Ian Carmichael (left) and Arthur Lowe are Englishmen abroad in *The Lady Vanishes*

Under the sign of the double cross...Adenoid Hynkel (Charlie Chaplin), power-lord of Tomania, salutes his loyal subjects in *The Great Dictator*

In his only solo appearance after the death of his long-time partner Paul McCullough, Bobby Clark wore real spectacles for the first time for his role in *The Goldwyn Follies*. Here he gets a little closer to Helen Jepson

Ian Carmichael neglects to give himself wobble room in this scene from *Brothers in Law*. Nicholas Parsons stands by for the crash

around the corner. With the Boultings losing their touch, Carmichael went to British Lion for his next four films, none of which did much. The Boultings called him back, but only for a cameo in their *Heavens Above!* The star was Peter Sellers (*qv*), who had overtaken Carmichael in popularity just as Carmichael had overtaken Guinness. Films after that were few, but Carmichael was still well-liked and appeared in two television sagas, one playing P. G. Wodehouse's Bertie Wooster, a role for which he might have been born (although, ideally, a few years earlier), and the other as Dorothy Sayers' debonair detective Lord Peter Wimsey. In the 1970s he returned to his native Yorkshire but, since the early death at 61 of his wife of 40 years in 1983, he has made the occasional excursion to the London acting scene.

1948: Bond Street. 1949: Trottie True (US: Gay Lady). Dear Mr Prohack. 1952: Time Gentlemen Please! Ghost Ship. Miss Robin Hood. 1953: Meet Mr Lucifer. 1954: The Colditz Story. Betrayed. 1955: Storm Over the Nile. Private's Progress. 1956: Brothers in Law. The Big Money. 1957: Lucky Jim. Happy is the Bride! 1959: Left, Right and Centre. I'm All Right, Jack. School for Scoundrels. 1960: Light Up the Sky. 1961: Double Bunk. 1962: The Amorous Prawn. 1963: Heavens Above! Hide and Seek. 1964: The Case of the 44s. 1967: Smashing Time. 1971: The Magnificent Seven Deadly Sins. 1973: From Beyond the Grave. 1979: The Lady Vanishes. 1989: Diamond Skulls (US: Dark Obsession).

CARNEY, Alan
See BROWN, Wally and CARNEY, Alan

CARSON, Jack
(John Elmer Carson) 1910–1963
'I was the perennial goofball. The good-natured meathead. I was the guy in the movie who never got the girl.' Thus good-natured Jack Carson summed up his 25-year movie career. But there was more to Carson, once rather extravagantly billed by his studio as 'Our number one comedy star!', as his occasional more serious parts showed. He could be insidiously mean, or arouse pity, with equal conviction. In his Warner years, though, which spanned the whole of the 1940s, the public image Carson projected was that of a genial ham, typified by the amusing *It's a Great Feeling*, actually set

at Warner Brothers studios, in which Carson plays himself, a star who no-one at the studio wants to make a picture with. Many famous stars do walk-ons to look horrified at the prospect and one, Jane Wyman (who really had done a couple of comedies with Carson) actually passes out! Carson originally hailed from Canada but his family moved across the border to Milwaukee, Wisconsin when he was a child. Big and beefy, his first appearance on stage was as Hercules in a school play. By the mid 1930s, though, he was an experienced vaudevillian, appearing in a double act with Dave Willock, who would follow him to Hollywood and become a character player. He was signed in 1937 by RKO 'where I lost Ginger Rogers more times than Fred Astaire won her'. He moved on to Warners in 1941. Here he played best chums, obnoxious braggarts, hopeful blunderers, over-hearty associates and one really meaty role, as Albert Runkel, the brash but sensitive vaudevillian driven to suicide by the machinations of Ida Lupino in *The Hard Way*. Another of his co-stars in this film was genial singer Dennis Morgan, who also hailed from Wisconsin. The two men, good personal friends, would make ten films together, including one actually called *Two Guys from Milwaukee*. Ironically, it was just after leaving Warners in 1950 that Carson made his funniest film, appropriately called *The Good Humor Man* (although Good Humor was a brand of American ice-cream). It remains one of the funniest slapstick comedies ever made in the sound era, full of side-splitting sight gags behind which one detects the hand of screenwriter Frank Tashlin, a former cartoonist. It was also on this film that Carson met the third of his four wives, actress Lola Albright, to whom he was married from 1952 to 1958. After some good dramatic performances in the 1950s, including Gooper in *Cat on a Hot Tin Roof*, Carson returned to the stage, but in August 1962 he collapsed while rehearsing a play. Terminal stomach cancer was diagnosed. However, Carson managed to complete one more film, the Disney comedy *Sammy the Way-Out Seal*, before his death in January 1963.

*1935: * Knife No. 5. Circle of Death. 1937: * A Rented Riot. Stage Door. You Only Live Once. Stand-In. It Could Happen to You. Reported Missing. Too Many Wives. On Again, Off Again. † A Damsel in Distress. High Flyers. Music for Madame. The Toast of New York. 1938: The Saint in New York. Vivacious Lady. Carefree. This Marriage Business. The Girl Downstairs. Condemned Women. Go Chase Yourself. Crashing Hollywood. Law of the Underworld. Everybody's Doing It. Night Spot. Having Wonderful Time. Maid's Night Out. Quick Money. She's Got Everything. Bringing Up Baby. Mr Doodle Kicks Off. 1939: Destry Rides Again. Fifth Avenue Girl. The Kid from Texas. The Escape. The Honeymoon's Over. Mr Smith Goes to Washington. Legion of Lost Flyers. 1940: I Take This Woman. The Girl in*

313. *Shooting High. Sandy Gets Her Man. Alias the Deacon. Enemy Agent (GB: Secret Enemy). Queen of the Mob. Typhoon. Love Thy Neighbor. Parole Fixer. Lucky Partners. Young As You Feel.* 1941: *Mr and Mrs Smith. Love Crazy. The Strawberry Blonde. The Bride Came C.O.D. Blues in the Night. Navy Blues.* 1942: *Larceny Inc. Wings for the Eagle. Gentleman Jim. The Hard Way. The Male Animal.* 1943: *Thank Your Lucky Stars. Princess O'Rourke. Arsenic and Old Lace.* 1944: *Shine On, Harvest Moon. The Doughgirls. Hollywood Canteen.* * *The Shining Future. Make Your Own Bed.* * *Road to Glory.* 1945: *Roughly Speaking. Mildred Pierce.* 1946: *The Time, the Place and the Girl. One More Tomorrow. Two Guys from Milwaukee (GB: Royal Flush).* 1947: *Love and Learn.* * *So You Want to be in Pictures.* 1948: *Always Together. Two Guys from Texas (GB: Two Texas Knights). Romance on the High Seas (GB: It's Magic). April Showers.* 1949: *John Loves Mary. My Dream is Yours. It's a Great Feeling.* * *Rough but Hopeful.* 1950: *Bright Leaf. The Good Humor Man.* 1951: *The Groom Wore Spurs. Mr Universe.* 1953: *Dangerous When Wet.* 1954: *A Star is Born. Red Garters. Phffft!* * *Hollywood Cowboy Stars.* 1955: *Ain't Misbehavin'. Magnificent Roughnecks. Bottom of the Bottle (GB: Beyond the River).* 1957: *The Tattered Dress. Three Men on a Horse (TV). The Tarnished Angels.* 1958: *Rally Round the Flag, Boys. Cat on a Hot Tin Roof. The Long March (TV).* 1960: *The Bramble Bush.* 1961: *King of the Roaring Twenties (GB: The Big Bankroll).* 1962: *Sammy the Way-Out Seal (TV. GB: cinemas).*

† Scenes deleted from final release print.

CATLETT, Walter 1889–1960

Bulky, dry-humoured, light-haired, plum-nosed American comedian whose frame and face bore witness to more than 100 professional bouts as a boxer in between early acting stints. Hollywood used Catlett mostly in amusing supporting roles, but there were a few starring shorts for him in the 1930s and a cute little run of 'father' comedies in post-war years. The most jovial of men, destined to become one of Hollywood's great *bon viveurs*, Catlett, born in San Francisco, was the son of a man who, at one time or another had taken such diverse occupations

as mining engineer, banker and wine merchant. None of these posts had anything to do with show business, but his son Walter had a natural flair for mimicry and, at the early age of eight, was performing comic songs at a church fair. The manager of The Little Brownies, a theatrical group, saw the prodigal performer five years later and asked his parents if he could join them. After a few months with the Brownies, Catlett joined Power's Australian Lilliputians, touring Australia with Gilbert and Sullivan shows. Back in San Francisco he played boy roles on stage until his voice broke; then he exploited a roguish sense of humour (and a fund of material gathered on stage tours) to branch out on his own as a stand-up comedian. He was still battling for laughs at the Tivoli Opera House in San Francisco on the day of the great earthquake of 1906. Catlett, an inveterate teller of tall tales, would later joke about that putting a brake on his career, but he was certainly out of work at 18. He joined the Marines, but was discharged because of inadequate eyesight. At that stage he took up boxing and fought a bout a week for two years before his eyesight again took a hand, forcing him to quit. Broke but determined to get back to show business, Catlett had an amazing slice of luck — if you can call the grisly discovery of a body while fishing good luck. There was a small reward for the discovery of the missing man, and with it Catlett went to New York. Working steadily on Broadway from 1911 — there was a minor film debut in a 1912 New York-shot silent — Catlett had his first major success in the 1916 show *So Long Letty*. From then on he found himself in one hit after another, including a stint with the Ziegfeld Follies. He made his first trip abroad to feature in the 1919 London show *Baby Bunting*, and scored an enormous personal success. After 17 years as a Broadway resident, Catlett started to pay more and more attention to Hollywood. He was always a welcome sight with his big, beaming, bespectacled face as would-be rascals who tended to flush and fluster under pressure. Walter decided he liked it in California. A chain smoker, confirmed drinker and lover of good food and attractive women (he married three times), Catlett was also (over-) fond of gambling and found that the Hollywood lifestyle suited him, even if it left him permanently penniless. He obviously treated his pets like himself; for many years he had a famous cat, Fritz, who tipped the scales at 22 pounds. He was happy in featured roles in films, and found a welcome creative freedom when starring in a series of shorts for Mack Sennett (by then releasing through Paramount). Often appearing with fussy Franklin Pangborn (*qv*), Catlett played mostly errant fathers and wayward uncles in these amusing trifles, which allowed the maximum leeway for his own blustery style of humour. Catlett worked feverishly for the next decade, but slowed up a bit as the wartime film boom began to fade from 1945.

A few years later he became involved with a popular series of small-town comedies opposite plumply puffing Raymond Walburn. Walburn was an old codger called Henry, and Catlett his friend the Mayor, who ill-advisedly joined him in some of his hare-brained misadventures. The man who was once described by a reviewer as 'a package of firecracker laughs' died at 71 shortly after having a stroke. Of the many colourful stories he told about himself, the one about a burglary at his new Long Island house is certainly true. Catlett was away performing in a Broadway musical-comedy and returned to find practically the entire contents of his property had been stolen. That Christmas he played in a charity show at Sing Sing prison with Fred Astaire and other stars. One of the convicts was asking for signed photographs of everyone — except Walter. Astaire asked him why. Said the prisoner: 'I got one of him already. I took it when I cleared out his house.'

1912: *The Leopard Lady.* 1924: *Second Youth.* 1926: *Summer Bachelors.* 1927: *The Music Master.* 1929: *Why Leave Home?/Imagine My Embarrassment. Married in Hollywood.* 1930: *The Florodora Girl (GB: The Gay Nineties). The Big Party. The Golden Calf. Happy Days. Let's Go Places.* * *Aunts in the Pants.* * *Camping Out.* 1931: *The Front Page. Platinum Blonde. Palmy Days. The Maker of Men. Yellow. Goldfish Bowl.* 1932: * *So This is Harris.* * *Bring 'Em Back Sober.* * *Oh! My Operation. The Expert. Cock of the Air. Big City Blues. It's Tough to Be Famous. Back Street. Rockabye. Rain. Okay, America (GB: Penalty of Fame). Free, White and 21. Sport Parade.* 1933: * *The Big Fibber.* * *Meet the Champ.* * *Daddy Knows Best.* * *Dream Stuff.* * *Husbands' Reunion.* * *Roadhouse Queen.* * *One Awful Night.* * *Private Wives.* * *Caliente Love. Mama Loves Papa. Only Yesterday. Arizona to Broadway. Private Jones. Olsen's Big Moment.* 1934: * *Elmer Steps Out.* * *Get Along Little Hubby. Lightning Strikes Twice. Unknown Blonde. The Captain Hates the Sea.* 1935: *Every Night at Eight. The Affair of Susan. A Tale of Two Cities.* 1936: * *Fibbing Fibbers. We Went to College (GB: The Old School Tie). I Loved a Soldier. Follow Your Heart. Sing Me a Love Song. Cain and Mabel. Banjo on My Knee. Mr Deeds Goes to Town.* 1937: *Four Days' Wonder. On the Avenue. Wake Up and Live. Varsity Show. Love is News. Love Under Fire. Every Day's a Holiday. Danger — Love at Work. Come Up Smiling.* 1938: *Bringing Up Baby. Going Places.* 1939: *Kid Nightingale. Zaza. Exile Express.* * *Static in the Attic.* 1940: *Pop Always Pays. Li'l Abner (GB: Trouble Chaser). Remedy for Riches. Comin' Round the Mountain. Spring Parade. Half a Sinner. The Quarterback.* * *You're Next.* * *Blondes and Blunders. Pinocchio (voice only).* 1941: *You're the One. Honeymoon for Three. Horror Island. Sing Another Chorus. Wild Bill Hickok Rides. Wild Man of Borneo. Million Dollar Baby. It Started with Eve. Hello Sucker. Manpower. Bad Men of Missouri. Unfinished Business. Steel Against*

the Sky. 1942: Star Spangled Rhythm. My Gal
Sal. They Got Me Covered. Between Us Girls.
Maisie Gets Her Man (GB: She Gets Her
Man). Yankee Doodle Dandy. Give Out, Sisters.
Hearts of the Golden West. 1943: Hit Parade of
1943. West Side Kid. How's About It? Fired
Wife. His Butler's Sister. Cowboy in Manhat-
tan. Get Going. 1944: I Love a Soldier. Hat
Check Honey. Pardon My Rhythm. Up in Arms.
Ghost Catchers. Lady, Let's Dance! Hi, Beauti-
ful (GB: Pass to Romance). My Gal Loves
Music. Three is a Family. Her Primitive Man.
Lake Placid Serenade. 1945: I Love a Band-
leader (GB: Memory for Two). The Man Who
Walked Alone. 1946: Riverboat Rhythm.
Slightly Scandalous. 1947: I'll Be Yours. 1948:
Mr Reckless. Are You With It? The Boy with
Green Hair. 1949: Leave It to Henry. Look for
the Silver Lining. The Inspector General. Henry
the Rainmaker. Dancing in the Dark. 1950:
Father's Wild Game. Father Makes Good.
1951: Here Comes the Groom. Honeychile.
Father Takes the Air. 1956: Davy Crockett and
the River Pirates. Friendly Persuasion. 1957:
Beau James.

CHAPLIN, Charlie
(later Sir Charles) 1889–1977

A small, soulful-looking British-born
pantomimist with masses of black, curly hair,
Chaplin had already enjoyed considerable
acclaim in both British and American music-
halls before he donned a bowler hat, cane,
baggy pants and toothbrush moustache and
became the most famous screen comedian
Hollywood has ever known. His reputation,
at one time greatly over-inflated, has suffered somewhat in recent years but it is
almost impossible not to laugh outright at
some of the well-timed early slapstick
routines, especially those involving the
gigantic Eric Campbell. And some of his set
pieces are masterpieces of invention. However, once pathos got the better of his comic
inspiration Chaplin was never the same
force. He stayed too long at the party, leaving
us with the impression of a dyspeptic old
man. Post-war cinemagoers watching
Chaplin for the first time in one of his
contemporary features could be forgiven for
wondering what the fuss was all about. Not-
withstanding recent reappraisals of his
talents, Chaplin has generally maintained

his reputation as the greatest film comedian
of all time. Certainly in his heyday no-one
was more consistent at bringing the house
down. Chaplin was born in London to an
entertainer of the same name, a popular
singer of 'dramatic and descriptive ballads'.
Charlie and his half-brother Sydney were
deserted by their father when Charlie was
one and after their mother had a nervous
breakdown the boys found themselves first
in a poor-school for orphans and destitute
children and later entertaining on the streets
for pennies. At eight, Charlie Chaplin became a professional entertainer, as one of
the 'Eight Lancashire Lads', a clog-dancing
act in which only its newest recruit had
never been north of London. He remained
with the dancing troupe for several seasons
before he began undertaking solo work. At
11 he reached London's Hippodrome
Theatre in pantomime, playing the kitchen
cat in Cinderella. He was a big success.
From then on, Chaplin left dancing behind
and became a boy actor, often appearing in
straight plays over the next six years. His
first contact with slapstick came in 1906
when he joined the cast of The Casey Circus,
a sequel to the long-running farce Casey's
Court. Chaplin stole the show with his impression of the effect of 'electric cures' (then
a hot topic of public debate) on 'the working
man'. After touring for more than a year
with The Casey Circus, Chaplin found a slot
with entrepreneur Fred Karno, purveyor of
slapstick revues to the nation. Another of
Karno's up-and-coming comedians was
Stan Jefferson, later to become Stan Laurel
(qv). Chaplin's first revue with the company
was London Suburbia. Later he and Laurel
appeared together in one of Karno's most
famous productions, Mumming Birds, sailing

to America with the show in 1910. It was
retitled A Night in an English Music Hall and
did so well that a second tour took place in
1912. There was a follow-up show in 1913
and it was during this that Mack Sennett
(qv), boss of Hollywood's Keystone comedy
studio, spotted Chaplin and offered him a
contract at $150 a week – even though it
appears that he thought the comedian's
name was Charlie Chaffin. 'Chaffin' accepted. Chaplin's first view of his initial
Keystone film, Making a Living, was of a
comedian jumping from what seemed a great
height into a net that broke. 'Is this an
acrobatic role?' enquired the newcomer
nervously. However, personal agility was
very much part of Chaplin's armoury when,
after a couple of hiccups, he hit his stride in
films. His major character – the tramp –
soon evolved, complete with holey boots
that flapped to left and right in response to
their owner's flat-footed, foot-sore walk.
The year with Keystone established him as
internationally famous film comedian, and
he began to direct his own films, at first in
collaboration with frequent co-star Mabel
Normand (qv), then on his own. These
were cut very much to the Keystone format
but they helped to establish many of the
distinctive characteristics of Chaplin's
screen character: the shyness which he used
to attract women; the indomitability against
overwhelming odds; the downtrodden
wretchedness when up against it; and the
inventive mind that helped his character
overcome the vicissitudes of life as well as
turn the tables on clumsy bullies. He made
35 films in his Keystone year, including
the first feature-length comedy, Tillie's
Punctured Romance. He was a top name at
the end of it and when Sennett refused his

Having eaten his own boot, Charlie Chaplin keeps his feet warm in the oven in his 1925
classic The Gold Rush

demand of $1,000 a week Chaplin moved on to Essanay where they offered him even more without being asked. His first film for them bore an appropriate title: *His New Job*. Chaplin's Essanay period was to see the beginning of his associations with Ben Turpin (as comic sidekick), Eric Campbell (as villain) and Edna Purviance (as female lead). Although Turpin would pursue his own career, and Campbell be killed in a car crash in 1917, Purviance would stay with Chaplin until 1923 and become his best-remembered leading lady. Chaplin's two years at Essanay contain such gems as *The Champion*, *The Tramp*, *Work*, *The Bank* and *Police* but after a further dispute over money he moved on to Mutual, where nearly all the best-known titles from his pre-1920 period would be made. In the first of these, *The Floorwalker*, Chaplin had the action revolve round a moving staircase, an idea that would be echoed by other comedians in later years, notably Buster Keaton (*qv*) in *The Electric House*. After *The Fireman*, Chaplin made *The Vagabond*, which foreshadows the inter-twining of comedy and pathos which was to become an ever-present theme in his later films. Charlie's tramp falls for Edna, who is then found to be the long-lost daughter of a rich woman. She goes off leaving him heart-broken but returns to sweep him off to riches and happiness. That was the ending Chaplin decided on after rejecting an original in which he throws himself in the river, is rescued by a hag-faced woman, and throws himself back in again. For the moment, though, sentiment was to be kept sufficiently at bay to remain an enjoyable element of the whole spectrum of Chaplin's talent. In *One A.M.*, he reprised an old stage act in a one-man show as a drunken toff; *The Count* finds

him having fun with food – another recurring theme; while *The Pawnshop* contains one of his finest scenes, in which he dissects an alarm clock brought in by a prospective pawnee. *The Rink* was another extension of one of Chaplin's Karno routines, but a very funny one, with the comedian surprisingly graceful on skates. That was followed by one of Chaplin's best films, *Easy Street*. Campbell, a gigantic Scot who had also performed with Karno, proved the perfect adversary in this tale of a lawless ghetto street where Charlie volunteers as the local policeman. It contains the famous chase sequence that ends when Chaplin overcomes Campbell by putting his head in the top of a street lamp and turning the gas on. Wonderful comic timing between Chaplin and Campbell distinguishes both this and the next, *The Cure*, set at a health farm and containing more belly-laughs than perhaps any other Chaplin comedy, including an encounter between the two men in a revolving door. It was all crammed into 20 minutes' screen time – but already Chaplin was feeling restricted by the two-reel format, as evidenced by his having to cut his next film, *The Immigrant*, from an original 45 minutes. What was left, though, does contain the classic encounter between Chaplin as an impoverished immigrant and Campbell as the waiter whose foot is planted firmly on Charlie's only coin. After *The Adventurer*, which featured him as a convict on the run who breaks into high society, Chaplin signed with First National, who had promised him a studio of his own. No longer tied to a schedule, the gaps between Chaplin's comedies rapidly grew longer. Although he had promised to deliver eight films in 16 months, there was never a chance of such a deadline

being met. Nonetheless, his comedies remained reasonably frequent until *The Pilgrim* in 1923, after which the gap stretched to years rather than months. In one of his First National films, *Shoulder Arms* (the one in which Chaplin's soldier disguises himself as a tree), shooting took so long that Chaplin, who was planning the film as his first five-reeler, had to cut that ambition short to beat the end of World War One! In two other First Nationals, *A Dog's Life* and *The Kid* (his first feature), Chaplin defied the odds against acting with animals and children to share the honours with such scene-stealing performers as Scraps the Dog and little Jackie Coogan. Coogan, who had acted with Chaplin in the film that preceded *The Kid*, *A Day's Pleasure*, immediately became one of the world's favourite child stars. *The Pilgrim* was completed in September 1922, and with it Chaplin concluded the First National deal. The next Chaplin comedy did not appear until August 1925, but it is possibly his best, *The Gold Rush*. Chaplin is still the Tramp, but now in the Klondike, prospecting for gold in 1898. Sharing a cabin with Big Jim (Mack Swain), who has just struck gold, he prepares a celebratory dinner of boiled boot and, in perhaps the most famous of all Chaplin eating scenes, he treats the nails like bones, the laces like spaghetti and the sole like a steak. The only drawback is that he has to sleep with his foot in the oven. Among the film's other notable routines are the sequence in which Swain sees Chaplin as a giant turkey; Chaplin's 'dance' performed by two rolls on the ends of the forks he holds; and the final uproarious nonsense in and out of the cabin perched on the edge of a snow-clad cliff. Enormously costly, the film still made a profit of more than $2 million. It has been the most reissued of Chaplin's features and was his own favourite. He followed it with *The Circus*, a minor venture for which, ironically, he was handed an Academy Award, and, in 1931, *City Lights*. Considered by many to be his best film, it's memorable today for Chaplin's unusually delicate way of handling the sentiment involved in the Tramp's romance with a blind flower-seller, and for a comic boxing match, but not for much else. It was however a financial smash-hit, and Chaplin's last, all the more amazing considering it was made as a silent, as was the next, *Modern Times*, a funnier film about man versus machine with Chaplin's last real appearance as the Tramp. It made a modest profit, and so did *The Great Dictator*, a timely but now tiresome piece about a Hitler-like dictator and his double, with a hectoring final speech from Chaplin about the rights of man guaranteed to have you fleeing from the cinema. In post-war years Chaplin decided he had to come out from behind the Tramp. The only results of this approach were the almost unwatchable *Monsieur Verdoux*, with Chaplin as a mass-murderer, *Limelight*, a partial return to form but overrated, and *A King in New York*, poor by Chaplin's standards but

Charlie Chaplin's king is unimpressed by the attentions of Dawn Addams' flirtatious photographer in *A King in New York*

otherwise an average if overlong comedy which reflected the comedian's desire to hit back at an America that had banned him in 1952 from returning to its shores on moral grounds. Such morals charges as existed involved Chaplin's pro-Russia stance during World War Two, which got him into trouble with the Senate Un-American Activities Committee, and his predilection for young girls, whether as co-stars or marriage partners, or both. His first wife was 16, his second 16, his third (Paulette Goddard) 22 and his last (Oona O'Neill) 17. He had also made many enemies and had angered authorities by never adopting American citizenship. Chaplin settled in Switzerland where he spent most of the remainder of his life and where he died on Christmas Day 1977. Although he had vowed never to return to America, he did make a short visit in 1972 to accept a special Oscar. Of Chaplin's ten children, several had film acting careers at varying levels, most notably Sydney (1925–) and Geraldine (1944–).

1914: Making a Living. Kid Auto Races at Venice. Mabel's Strange Predicament. Between Showers. A Film Johnnie. Tango Tangles. His Favorite Pastime. Cruel, Cruel Love. The Star Boarder. Mabel at the Wheel. Twenty Minutes of Love. The Knockout. † *Tillie's Punctured Romance. Caught in a Cabaret. Caught in the Rain. A Busy Day. The Fatal Mallet. Her Friend the Bandit. Mabel's Busy Day. Mabel's Married Life. Laughing Gas. The Property Man. The Face on the Bar-Room Floor. Recreation. The Masquerader. His New Profession. The Rounders. The New Janitor. Those Love Pangs. Dough and Dynamite. Gentlemen of Nerve. His Musical Career. His Trysting Place. Getting Acquainted. His Prehistoric Past. 1915: His New Job. A Night Out. The Champion. In the Park. A Jitney Elopement. The Tramp. By the Sea. His Regeneration. Work. A Woman. The Bank. Shanghaied. A Night in the Show.* † *Carmen/Charlie Chaplin's Burlesque on Carmen. 1916: Police. The Floorwalker. The Fireman. The Vagabond. One A.M. The Count. The Pawn Shop. Behind the Screen. The Rink. 1917: Easy Street. The Cure. The Immigrant. The Adventurer. 1918: How to Make Movies. The Bond. A Dog's Life. Triple Trouble.* † *Shoulder Arms. Charles Chaplin in a Liberty Loan Appeal. 1919: Sunnyside. A Day's Pleasure. 1920:* † *The Kid.* † *The Mollycoddle. 1921:* † *The Nut. The Idle Class. 1922: Pay Day. Nice and Friendly. 1923:* † *The Pilgrim.* † *Souls for Sale.* † *A Woman of Paris. 1925:* † *The Gold Rush. 1926:* † *A Woman of the Sea. 1927:* † *The Circus. 1928:* † *Show People.* † *The Woman Disputed. 1931:* † *City Lights. 1936:* † *Modern Times. 1940:* † *The Great Dictator. 1947:* † *Monsieur Verdoux. 1951:* † *Limelight. 1957:* † *A King in New York. 1966:* † *A Countess from Hong Kong.*
As narrator of compilation film. *1959: The Chaplin Revue.*
Chaplin directed (or co-directed) all the

above except the first 13, plus *His Regeneration, The Nut, Souls for Sale* and *Show People.*

All shorts except † features.

CHASE, Charley
(Charles Parrott) 1893–1940
Skinny but dapper, bespectacled, slick-haired American Charley Chase ranked only just below the best of the comedians that came to fame in the 1920s and stayed around for the next two decades. The accident-prone man-about-town was his most consistently funny characterisation, but he could switch to playing a henpeck, a nuisance or a busybody with almost equal success. Frustrations over his failure to reach the very top undoubtedly contributed to the early death of one of Hollywood's most inventive and talented – his efforts as scriptwriter, songwriter and director were by no means negligible – comic minds. Born in Maryland, Chase had already taken to vaudeville at 16 with a versatile act involving singing, dancing, playing the banjo and giving out with mournful comic monologues. His cheery personality propelled the engaging entertainer to Broadway as early as 1912. He entered films in 1914, initially with the Mack Sennett studio as a supporting performer but later with Triangle and Fox, who saw his main talent as being the ingenious contributions he could make behind the camera. So in that same year, 1914, Chase began a 25-year parallel career directing other comedians, often being credited in this capacity under his real name. It was Hal Roach who suggested that Chase try again as an on-screen comedian. Charley returned from his Christmas holiday at the end of 1923 to find himself assigned to star in one-reel comedies. He would go on to make more than 150 comedy films of three reels or less in the next 17 years. Initially (and later) these were directed by Chase's brother James Parrott. In between many gems were made by Leo McCarey, later to win three Oscars. Both directors also worked extensively with Chase's contemporaries on the Roach lot, Laurel and Hardy (*qv*), whom Charley supported in their classic 1933 feature *Sons of the Desert*. Many Chase com-

edies have a resemblance in structure to some of the best Laurel and Hardys in that they are composed of escalating disasters. *All Wet*, in 1924, is the first of several 'Chases' in which cars sink in pools or simply fall to pieces. *Girl Grief* (1932) – Chase's screen persona adapted easily to sound – has a lot of girls and even more cats and ends with Charley covered in the latter after enemies have spread catnip over his bed. Chase's years at the Roach fun factory ended in 1936 after attempts to get him started in features (shorts were being phased out) were interpreted as misfires. The studio let him go and though Chase managed to find a home at Columbia, where he worked professionally enough for his last four years, he was never the same man. Drinking came with disillusionment and there were times in the late 1930s when, especially in his work as director, Chase seemed to be flying on automatic pilot. As one fellow-worker put it: 'When Charley directed a picture, he'd always use the first take and just get on with the next. We always knew we'd get home early, which was nice at the time, but it was a hell of a sloppy way to make a picture.' While Chase's innate comic sense ensured that his stuff was often very funny, especially in visual terms, his screen characters were never as endearing as those of Laurel and Hardy, and often considerably more irritating. His funny little songs were a nice touch but after he left Roach these almost dried up. Drying *out* was something Chase could not do. He ignored doctors' warnings to quit drinking (especially after the failure of the play he had gone into after leaving Columbia in 1940) and died from a heart attack at 46. Fellow-comedian Billy Gilbert (*qv*) once said that Chase was 'a genial but somehow sad man who simply couldn't understand why people didn't rate him up there with Chaplin, Keaton and Lloyd. He felt that his talent was never fully appreciated.'

1914: The Anglers. The Knockout. The Masquerader. Dough and Dynamite. His New Profession. The Rounders. His Musical Career. Gentlemen of Nerve. † *Tillie's Punctured Romance. Our Country Cousin. Mabel's New Job. Her Last Chance. Cursed By His Beauty. 1915: Only a Farmer's Daughter. Hash House Mashers. Love in Armor. Do-Re-Mi-Fa. Love, Loot and Crash. Settled at the Seaside. A Versatile Villain. The Rent Jumpers. The Hunt. His Father's Footsteps. Fatty and the Broadway Stars. The Little Teacher. Fatty's Reckless Fling. 1916: A Dash of Courage. 1917: Her Torpedoed Love. Chased into Love. 1918: Hello Trouble. 1919: Ship Ahoy. 1920: Kids Is Kids. 1923:* † *Long Live the King.* † *King of the Wild Horses. 1924: At First Sight. One of the Family. Just a Minute. A Perfect Lady. Hard Knocks. Powder and Smoke. Don't Forget. Love's Detour. April Fool. The Fraidy Cat. Publicity Pays. Why Husbands Go Mad. Position Wanted. Young Oldfield. Jeffries Jr. Stolen Goods. Ten Minute Egg. Sweet Daddy. Seeing Nellie Home. Why*

Men Work. The Poor Fish. Sittin' Pretty. Outdoor Pajamas. Too Many Mamas. All Wet. Bungalow Boobs. Accidental Accidents. The Royal Razz. 1925: The Rat's Knuckles. Hello Baby. Fighting Fluid. Plain and Fancy Girls. Is Marriage the Bunk? The Family Entrance. Looking for Sally. Big Red Riding Hood. Should Husbands Be Watched? Hard Boiled. Bad Boy. Innocent Husbands. Isn't Life Terrible? What Price Goofy? No Father to Guide Him. The Caretaker's Daughter. Thundering Fleas. His Wooden Wedding. The Uneasy Three. 1926: There Ain't No Santa Claus. Charley, My Boy. Dog Shy. Mama Behave. Mum's the Word. Long Fliv the King. Mighty Like a Moose. Bromo and Juliet. Crazy Like a Fox. Tell 'em Nothing. Be Your Age. 1927: Us. Many Scrappy Returns. A One-Mama Man. The Call of the Cuckoos. Are Brunettes Safe? Bigger and Better Blondes. Forgotten Sweeties. Fluttering Hearts. What Women Did for Me. Now I'll Tell One. The String of Strings. Assistant Wives. The Lighter That Failed. The Way of All Pants. Never the Dames Shall Meet. 1928: Aching Youths. All for Nothing. Limousine Love. Imagine My Embarrassment. The Fight Pest. Is Everybody Happy? The Booster. All Parts. Chasing Husbands. The Family Group. 1929: Ruby Love. Off to Buffalo. Movie Night. Thin Twins. The Big Squawk. [†] *Modern Love.* [†] *You Can't Buy Love. Crazy Feet. Leaping Love. Snappy Sneezer. Stepping Out. Great Gobs. 1930: The Real McCoy. Whispering Whoopee. Fifty Million Husbands. Fast Work. All Teed Up. Girl Shock. Dollar Dizzy. Looser Than Loose. High Cs. 1931: Rough Seas. The Pip from Pittsburgh. Thundering Tenors. One of the Smiths. The Panic Is On. Skip the Maloo! Hasty Marriage. What a Bozo! 1932: The Tabasco Kid. First in War. In Walked Charley. The Nickel Nurser. Young Ironsides. Girl Grief. Now We'll Tell One. Mr Bride. 1933: Fallen Arches. Nature in the Wrong. Arabian Tights. His Silent Racket. Sherman Said It. Midsummer Mush. Luncheon at Twelve.* [†] *Sons of the Desert (GB: Fraternally Yours). 1934: I'll Take Vanilla. Another Wild Idea. The Cracked Iceman. Four Parts. It Happened One Day. Something Simple. You Said a Hatful! Fate's Fathead. The Chases of Pimple Street. 1935: The Four Star Boarder. Okay Toots! Poker at Eight. Manhattan Monkey Business. Nurse to You. Public Ghost No. 1. Southern Exposure. 1936: Life Hesitates at 40. The Count Takes the Count. Vamp 'Til Ready. On the Wrong Trek. Neighborhood House (abridged from feature-length).* [†] *Kelly the Second. 1937: Hollywood Party. The Grand Hooter. From Bad to Worse. The Wrong Miss Wright. Calling All Doctors. The Big Squirt. Man Bites Lovebug. 1938: Time Out for Trouble. The Mind Needer. Many Sappy Returns. The Nightshirt Bandit. Pie à la Maid. 1939: The Sap Takes a Wrap. The Chump Takes a Bump. Rattling Romeo. Skinny the Moocher. Teacher's Pest. The Awful Goof. Mutiny on the Body. 1940: The Heckler. South of the Boudoir. His Bridal Fright.*

As director (incomplete). *1914: The Anglers. 1915: Do-Re-Mi-Fa. The Hunt. Dirty Work in a Laundry. Only a Messenger Boy. 1916: A*

Dash of Courage. There's Many a Fool. 1917: Chased Into Love. 1918: Hello Trouble. 1919: Hop the Bellhop. The Handy Man, Bright and Early. The Straight and Narrow, Playmates. Ship Ahoy! All at Sea. 1920: Why Go Home? Kids Is Kids. Live and Learn. 1921: His Best Girl. Blue Sunday. The Big Game. The Hustler. 1922: In the Movies. Days of Old. The Dumb Bell. The Stone Age. 1923: Sold at Auction. The Courtship of Miles Sandwich. Jes' Passin' Through. Jack Frost. 1933: The Bargain of the Century. Sherman Said It. Midsummer Mush. Luncheon at Twelve. 1934: I'll Take Vanilla. Another Wild Idea. The Cracked Iceman. Four Parts. It Happened One Day. Something Simple. You Said a Hatful! Fate's Fathead. The Chases of Pimple Street. 1935: The Four Star Boarder. Okay Toots! Poker at Eight. Manhattan Monkey Business. Nurse to You. Public Ghost No. 1. Southern Exposure. 1936: Life Hesitates at 40. The Count Takes the Count. Vamp 'Til Ready. On the Wrong Trek. Neighborhood House (abridged from feature-length). 1937: Oh, What a Knight! 1938: The Old Raid Mule. Tassels in the Air. Ankles Away. Flat Foot Stooges. Half-Way to Hollywood. Violent is the Word for Curly. Mutts to You. A Nag in the Bag. 1939: Mutiny on the Body. Boom Goes the Groom. Saved by the Belle. Static in the Attic.

All shorts except [†] features.

CHASE, Chevy
(Cornelius Chase) 1944–
Although consistently more successful in films on his own than in harness with other comedians, it now seems that Chevy Chase is destined not to reach the topmost level of international screen comedians. Yet his laid-back humour has been highly effective on the screen, especially in the 'National Lampoon' and 'Fletch' films. A struggling comedy writer until his late twenties, the unusually tall, widely-beaming, dark-haired Chase brought his toothy, moon-faced good looks, high forehead and aggressive style to the front of the camera while working for the innovative American TV series *Saturday Night Live*. The New Yorker soon became a national celebrity and a double Emmy winner with the show. His big-screen career seemed well under way with two starring

roles opposite Goldie Hawn in the comedies *Foul Play* and *Seems Like Old Times*, in which Chase was revealed as a slightly zany light romantic lead with a laconic line in humour. But promising-looking ventures misfired in the next few years and Chase didn't have a major hit with his own name at the head of the cast until the warm and wacky *National Lampoon's Vacation*. After a dazzling tour-de-force as the snoopy reporter in the comedy-thriller *Fletch*, proving equally adept at comedy and thrills and donning a number of sometimes baffling disguises, Chase seemed set for a good run of star roles. What in fact followed were a number of co-starring roles with such other popular comedians as Dan Aykroyd and Steve Martin (both qv). It was five years before Chase regained the lost ground, although it took sequels to successful originals to do it. *Fletch Lives* was largely disappointing, but performed well at the box-office. *National Lampoon's Christmas Vacation* was hilarious in patches but did less well financially, due in part to the fact that it was hardly exported abroad. Again, though, Chase faltered. Despite a previous failure with Aykroyd, the two got together for another flop, *Nothing But Trouble*, a film whose many title changes before release did it little good. However, given the right dialogue and situations, Chase has proved he can be very funny at both verbal and physical comedy. Like most comedians, he's willing to try anything. 'Hey, listen', he once said. 'I'll get a laugh picking my nose if I have to, because part of the art of humour is the sudden surprise. Pratfalls are one way of springing a surprise that I love to do; they work for me because I'm big and I don't look like the kind of guy who stumbles. That makes the resultant comeuppance all the funnier.'

1974: The Groove Tube. 1976: Tunnelvision. 1978: Foul Play. 1980: Caddyshack. Oh, Heavenly Dog. Seems Like Old Times. 1981: Modern Problems. Under the Rainbow. 1983: Deal of the Century. National Lampoon's Vacation. 1984: Fletch. 1985: National Lampoon's European Vacation. Sesame Street Presents: Follow That Bird. Spies Like Us. 1986: ¡Three Amigos! 1987: Rolling in the Aisles. 1988: Funny Farm. The Couch Trip. Caddyshack II. 1989: Fletch Lives. National Lampoon's Christmas Vacation (GB: National Lampoon's Winter Holiday). 1990: Nothing But Trouble. 1991: L.A. Story. Memoirs of an Invisible Man.

CHEECH and CHONG
Richard 'Cheech' Marin (left) 1946–
and
Thomas (Tommy) Chong 1941–
After 16 years together this latest Hollywood comedy double-act now seems to have gone its separate ways. Though hated by the critics, the initial film efforts of this Abbott and Costello for the drug generation went down well with the American public, even if they failed to travel. Hairy, incoherent and

forever smoking pot, the humour of Cheech and Chong was coarse but catching and a succession of their satirical LPs became million sellers. Canadian-born Chong was a rock guitarist with a fancy for becoming an entrepreneur. At one time he opened a bistro in Vancouver, then took over his brother's nightclub in the same city and turned it into a centre for improvised comedy. Marin, nicknamed 'Cheech' after a hot Mexican starter, joined him there in a group of musician-comedians who called themselves City Works. Marin had come to Canada from his native United States to avoid conscription for the war in Vietnam. The two men formed a rock band after City Works split up, interspersing – and sometimes interrupting – the music with 'spaced-out' comedy routines. Now using the name Cheech and Chong, they furthered their career in California, where they were signed for records and made a series of hit albums, most notably *Let's Make a New Dope Deal*. Although their scatological humour could be very funny in short bursts, their attempt at a film career soon showed up its limitations. Their first films were successful in America, but died in other parts of the world. Soon the American audience drifted away as well, and the team split up in 1985, ironically after its most successful appearance in films, supporting the stars as running-gag burglars in Martin Scorsese's *After Hours*. Since then the two men have sporadically pursued a career in films, Marin as a wild-eyed co-star in offbeat comedies and Chong, who directed most of their films, as an actor-director. It looks, though, as if their glory days may have gone. Chong's daughter, Rae Dawn Chong, is a star actress whose career in recent times has been rather more successful than her father's.

Together. *1978: Up in Smoke. 1980: Cheech and Chong's Next Movie (GB: Cheech and Chong's Close Encounters). 1981: Cheech and Chong's Nice Dreams. 1982: It Came from Hollywood (V). Things Are Tough All Over. 1983: Still Smokin'. Yellowbeard. 1984: Cheech and Chong's The Corsican Brothers. 1985: After Hours.*
Cheech alone. *1985: Echo Park. 1987: Fatal Beauty.* † *Born in East LA. 1988: Oliver &*

Company (voice only). 1989: Ghostbusters II. Rude Awakening. Troop Beverly Hills. 1990: The Shrimp on the Barbie. Mother Goose Rock 'n' Rhyme (TV). Chong alone. *1989:* † *Far Out Man (Cheech in 'bit' cameo). Tripwire. 1992: Life After Sex.*

(V) Video
† And directed.

CLARK, Bobby (top) 1888–1960
and
McCULLOUGH, Paul 1883–1936

Two of the wildest American comics outside The Marx Brothers (*qv*), Bobby Clark and Paul McCullough were unusual in that they first came together as a team when Clark was only 12. The lunatic duo stayed together on stage for 35 years, and did almost all their best work there, despite making three dozen films varying from one-reelers to feature length. They worked fast and with breathtaking energy, in routines of physical and verbal comedy (often conceived by Clark) that required hairsbreadth timing. Two small, nimble men – though McCullough was the stockier of the two – they started doing acrobatic tumbling at school in Springfield, Ohio, an establishment they soon left to pursue a show business career. They worked in minstrel troupes and circuses. Under the Big Top they did everything from juggling midgets to spinning an entire act round their endeavours to put a chair on a table. Moving into vaudeville, Clark and McCullough dropped most of their acrobatics in favour of straight comic work. They developed their trademark appearances, Clark having painted-on glasses over a wide, sharkish grin, a collection of hats and canes, an all-enveloping overcoat and a cigar he seemed able to make appear and disappear at will. McCullough, too, had an extraordinary range of hats – boaters, stetsons, even little woolly numbers, all worn with a fur coat, which was likely to conceal a snazzy matching waistcoat and tie. He also had a painted-on toothbrush moustache, and was given to paroxysms of explosive laughter. Together they looked the incarnations of mischievous devilment. They were a hit on stage in London during World War One, then returned to the States to take a Broadway bow in 1922. With the

coming of sound to the cinema, Clark and McCullough went to Hollywood where they made a number of comedy shorts for Fox that relied chiefly on their well-oiled stage routines. By this time Clark was established as the comic of the team, with McCullough as the straight man. Not happy with their first Hollywood experience, they returned to Broadway and appeared in several more successful revue-style shows before being lured back to RKO under a contract that allowed them to make two-reel comedies in the summer and perform on Broadway in the winter. Many of these films were made by Mark Sandrich, an experienced short-subject director who would later work with Wheeler and Woolsey (*qv*), before directing the cream of the Fred Astaire–Ginger Rogers musicals. Clark scripted most of these short comedies at RKO, which shifted their emphasis from slapstick to verbal humour as they progressed but were always fast and furious, with the unexpected (indeed ridiculous) always happening. In 1935, after the comedians had toured with a stage version of *George White's Scandals*, McCullough suffered a nervous breakdown. By March 1936 he appeared to have recovered when he suddenly committed suicide on the way home from the sanitarium by slashing his wrists and throat with a barber's razor. Clark withdrew from show business for a while then returned as a solo act, staying on Broadway for many years and making a name for himself as the master of the ad lib and pieces of comic business involving various inanimate props or sleight of hand. Later still, he made several appearances in revivals of restoration comedy before his death from a heart attack at 71. He was fondly remembered by stage comedy fans but films never quite captured Clark and McCullough's unique brand of manic mayhem.

1928: * *The Interview*. * *The Honor System*. 1929: * *The Bath Between*. *The Diplomats*. *Waltzing Around*. *Clark and McCullough in Holland*. * *Belle of Samoa*. * *Beneath the Law*. *The Medicine Men*. * *Music Fiends*. * *Knights Out*. * *All Steamed Up*. * *Hired and Fired*. * *Detectives Wanted*. 1931: * *Chesterfield Celebrities*. * *False Roomers*. * *A Melon-Drama*. * *Scratch As Catch Can*. * *The Iceman's Ball*. * *The Millionaire Cat*. * *Jitters, the Butler*. 1933: * *Hokus Focus*. * *The Druggist's Dilemma*. * *The Gay Nighties*. * *Kickin' the Crown Around*. * *Fits in a Fiddle*. * *Snug in the Jug*. 1934: * *Hey Nanny Nanny*. * *In the Devil's Doghouse*. * *Bedlam of Beards*. * *Love and Hisses*. * *Odor in the Court*. * *Everything's Ducky*. * *In a Pig's Eye*. 1935: * *Flying Down to Zero*. * *Alibi Bye Bye*. Clark alone. 1938: *The Goldwyn Follies*.

CLEESE, John 1939–

Spindly, straight-backed, grasshopper-like British comic actor with thinning dark hair, hollow eyes, annoyed expression and snapping, upper-class tones. Perhaps the funniest British star of his generation, his films and TV appearances have been too few for the liking of his fans. The son of a Somerset insurance salesman, Cleese (the family name was changed from Cheese in 1915) was 6 ft tall at 12 years old, 'a timid, weedy kid with no way of fading into the

What more appropriate place to find six Pythons than in the jungle? Terry Jones, Terry Gilliam, Michael Palin, John Cleese, Eric Idle and Graham Chapman (left to right) live up to the title of *And Now for Something Completely Different*

background'. Seven years and five inches later, he joined the Cambridge University Footlights revue and shattered forever his parents' dreams of him becoming a solicitor. Excelling at characters who express annoyance at being found funny, Cleese broke through on television with other university-reared comedians in the anarchic TV series *Monty Python's Flying Circus*. He could be beautifully straight-faced about idiotic subjects: a famous sketch about a man complaining about being sold a dead parrot was repeated in a subsequent Python film. Above all, his body language – all knees and elbows – was hilarious. Film roles, though, remained largely snooty cameos, even after his tremendous TV success as Basil Fawlty of *Fawlty Towers*, the monstrous seaside hotelier described by one writer as 'a unique exhibit in the comedy chamber of horrors'. The Fawlty half-hours are little miracles of invention, characterisation and comic timing, and in them Cleese proved himself a master of sarcasm and one of comedy's great escalating panickers, a man whose snide unflappable gradually crumbled as he attempted to put fingers in an ever-increasing number of holes in a dam in the face of a flood of impending disaster. The Fawlty creation was unusual in that he remained a fairly unsympathetic character. Cleese re-proved the theory that you didn't have to play lovable idiots to get laughs in the films *Privates on Parade* and *Clockwise*. In 1988 he had his first really big box-office hit with *A Fish Called Wanda*, a caper comedy which, like most of his material, Cleese wrote himself. He was at one time married to American-born actress Connie Booth, his co-writer and co-star in *Fawlty Towers*.

1968: *Interlude (shown 1967)*. *The Bliss of Mrs Blossom*. *The Best House in London*. 1969:

The Magic Christian. 1970: *The Rise and Rise of Michael Rimmer*. *The Statue*. 1971: *And Now for Something Completely Different*. 1972: *The Love Ban (originally It's a Two-Foot-Six-Inch-Above-the-Ground World)*. 1974: *Romance with a Double Bass*. 1975: *Monty Python and the Holy Grail*. 1976: *Pleasure at Her Majesty's (US: Monty Python Meets Beyond the Fringe)*. 1977: *The Strange Case of the End of Civilization As We Know It (TV)*. 1979: *Monty Python's Life of Brian*. † * *Away from It All (narrator only)*. *The Secret Policeman's Ball*. 1980: *The Taming of the Shrew (TV)*. 1981: *The Great Muppet Caper*. *Time Bandits*. *Monty Python Live at the Hollywood Bowl*. 1982: *The Secret Policeman's Other Ball*. *Privates on Parade*. 1983: *Monty Python's Meaning of Life*. *Yellowbeard*. 1985: *Silverado*. *Clockwise*. 1987: *The Secret Policeman's Third Ball*. 1988: *A Fish Called Wanda*. *The Big Picture*. 1989: *Erik the Viking*. 1990: *Bullseye!* 1991: *An American Tail 2: Fievel Goes West (voice only)*.

† And co-directed.

CLYDE, Andy 1892–1967

This sawn-off, scraggy Scotsman was a hairier version of the irascible Jimmy Finlayson (*qv*). In fact, the two had been friends in their native Scotland and it was Finlayson, established at the Mack Sennett studio by 1923 (and on the verge of a move to Hal Roach) who set up the opening for his pal Andy to come to Hollywood and start work with Sennett's slapstick empire. Although gainfully employed through the last of the silent years, Clyde came into his own with the coming of sound, when he rose from being a 'second banana' in other stars' two-reel comedies, and developed a character of his own that became a focus of vest-pocket comedies at the Sennett,

Fishing for compliments. Jewel thief Jamie Lee Curtis uses her obvious charms to persuade Archie (John Cleese) help her recover some lost loot, in *A Fish Called Wanda*

With Henry (George Cole) still in a state of hypnosis, his wife (Veronica Hurst) is amazed to find he's made a pass at the maid (Joan Sims, in her screen debut). From *Will Any Gentleman...?*

Two-ton treble. Robbie Coltrane gives voice as Annabelle, the transvestite hostess of a glitzy nightclub, in *The Fruit Machine*

Educational and Columbia studios for nearly three decades, years in which Clyde was often doubling up as a grizzled character actor in minor westerns. Adopting a walrus moustache, rimless spectacles and an unkempt, unshaven appearance, Andy created a naive old buffer, often with an eye for a pretty girl, whose own daughter always seemed to be threatening to elope. Starting to play this character — 'Pop', as he was usually called — when he was 38, Clyde remained comfortably at home with it until he made his last two-reeler comedy in 1956. Unhappy with his standing at Sennett, Clyde moved to other studios from 1932, continuing to turn out much the same kind of homespun comedy. The best of his short programme-fillers are the early films he made at Columbia during the 1934-36 period. *Alimony Aches*, *In the Dog House*, *Caught in the Act* and *It Always Happens* are still pleasantly amusing today, as is *Peppery Salt*, which has a side-splitting (and expensive-looking) sight gag when a wharfside diner is accidentally attached to a ship which rips it away from the pier and tows it out to sea. Later comedies, in which the Clyde character remains as dishevelled as ever and a trifle more bemused into the bargain, were all too often recyclings of the ones made in earlier years, complete with footage from them. In between them, he also made a name for himself in the 'B' western genre, as a tall-tale-telling comic sidekick. Andy left movies behind in 1956 but kept busy for the remainder of his life as a welcome regular in such television series as *The Real McCoys*, *No Time for Sergeants* and *Lassie*. He died at 75 in Los Angeles, just like his friend Jimmy Finlayson, both far away from the native land whose accent they never completely lost.

1924: * *One Spooky Night*. * *Wall Street Blues*. * *His New Mama*. * *Wandering Waistlines*. * *Lizzies of the Field*. * *The Cannon Ball Express*. 1925: * *Honeymoon Hardships*. * *Giddap*. * *The Lion's Whiskers*. * *From Rags to Britches*. * *Butter Fingers*. * *Skinners in Silk*. * *The Iron Nag*. * *Sneezing Beezers*. * *Super-Hooper-Dyne Lizzies*. * *Over There-Abouts*. 1926: * *Circus Today*. * *Whispering Whiskers*. * *Ice Cold Cocos*. * *Trimmed in Gold*.

* *Wandering Willies*. * *Fight Night*. * *Hayfoot, Strawfoot*. * *Muscle Bound Music*. * *A Sea Dog's Tale*. * *Masked Mamas*. * *Hubby's Quiet Little Game*. * *Hoboken to Hollywood*. * *The Divorce Dodger*. * *Flirty Four-Flushers*. 1927: * *Peaches and Plumbers*. * *Should Sleepwalkers Marry?* * *Easy Pickings*. * *Gold Digger of Weepah*. * *The Bull Fighter*. * *Cured in the Excitement*. * *The Golf Nut*. 1928: *Branded Man*. *The Goodbye Kiss*. * *Blindfold*. * *Motorboat Mamas*. 1929: *Midnight Daddies*. *Should a Girl Marry?* *Ships of the Night*. * *The Bride's Relations*. * *The Old Barn*. * *Whirls and Girls*. * *The Bee's Buzz*. * *The Big Palooka*. * *Girl Crazy*. * *The Barber's Daughter*. * *The Constabule*. * *The Lunkhead*. * *The Golfers*. * *A Hollywood Star*. * *Clancy at the Bat*. * *The New Halfback*. * *Uppercut O'Brien*. 1930: * *Scotch*. * *Sugar Plum Papa*. * *Bulls and Bears*. * *Match Play*. * *Radio Kisses*. * *Fat Wives to Thin*. * *Campus Crushes*. * *Goodbye Legs*. * *The Chumps*. * *Hello, Television*. * *Average Husband*. * *Vacation Loves*. * *The Bluffer*. * *Grandma's Girl*. * *Take Your Medicine*. * *Don't Bite Your Dentist*. * *Racket Cheers*. * *Bulls and Bears*. * *No, No, Lady*. 1931: * *The College Vamp*. * *The Dog Doctor*. * *In Conference*. * *Just a Bear*. * *The Cow-Catcher's Daughter*. * *Ghost Parade*. * *Monkey Business in Africa (GB: Gorilla Love)*. * *Fainting Lover*. * *Too Many Husbands*. * *The Cannonball* * *Speed*. * *The Great Pie Mystery*. * *Taxi Troubles*. * *All-American Kickback*. * *Half Holiday*. 1932: *Million Dollar Legs*. * *Shopping with Wifie*. * *Heavens! My Husband*. * *Speed in the Gay Nineties*. * *The Boudoir Butler*. * *Alaska Love*. * *For the Love of Ludwig*. * *His Royal Shyness*. * *The Giddy Age*. * *Sunkissed Sweeties*. * *A Fool About Women*. * *Boy, Oh Boy*. 1933: * *Artists' Muddles*. * *Feeling Rosy*. * *Loose Relations*. * *The Big Squeal*. * *Dora's Dunkin' Donuts*. * *His Weak Moment*. * *Frozen Assets*. * *An Old Gypsy Custom*. 1934: *The Little Minister*. * *Super Snooper*. * *Hello, Prosperity*. * *Half-Baked Relations*. * *It's the Cat's*. * *In the Dog House*. 1935: * *I'm a Father*. *Annie Oakley*. *McFadden's Flats*. *The Village Tale*. * *Old Sawbones*. * *Tramp, Tramp, Tramp*. * *Alimony Aches*. * *It Always Happens*. * *Hot Paprika*. 1936: *Two in a Crowd*. *Yellow Dust*. *Red Lights Ahead*. *Straight from the Shoulder*. * *Caught in the Act*. * *Share the Wealth*. * *Peppery Salt*. * *Mister Smarty*. * *Am I Having Fun!* * *Love Comes to Mooneyville*. * *Knee Action*. 1937: *The Barrier*. * *Stuck in the Sticks*. * *My Little Feller*. * *Lodge Night*. * *Gracie at the Bat*. * *He Done His Duty*. 1938: * *The Old Raid Mule*. * *Jump, Chump, Jump*. * *Ankles Away*. * *Soul of a Heel*. * *Not Guilty Enough*. * *Home on the Rage*. 1939: *It's a Wonderful World*. *Bad Lands*. * *Swing, You Swingers*. * *Boom Goes the Groom*. * *Now It Can Be Sold*. * *Trouble Finds Andy Clyde*. * *All-American Blondes*. * *Andy Clyde Gets Spring Chicken*. 1940: *Abe Lincoln in Illinois (GB: Spirit of the People)*. *Cherokee Strip (GB: Fighting Marshal)*. *Three Men from Texas*. * *Mr Clyde Goes to Broadway*. * *Money Squawks*. * *Boobs in the Woods*. * *Fireman,

Save My Choo Choo*. * *A Bundle of Bliss*. * *The Watchman Takes a Wife*. 1941: *In Old Colorado*. *Doomed Caravan*. *Pirates on Horseback*. *Border Vigilantes*. *Wide Open Town*. *Secrets of the Wasteland*. *Stick to Your Guns*. *Twilight on the Trail*. *Outlaws of the Desert*. *Riders of the Timberline*. * *Ring and the Belle*. * *Yankee Doodle Andy*. * *Host to a Ghost*. * *Lovable Trouble*. 1942: *Undercover Man*. *Lost Canyon*. *This Above All*. * *Sappy Birthday*. * *How Spry I Am*. * *All Work and No Pay*. * *Sappy Pappy*. 1943: *The Leather Burners*. *Hoppy Serves a Writ*. *Border Patrol*. *False Colors*. *Colt Comrades*. *Bar 20*. *Riders of the Deadline*. * *Wolf in Thief's Clothing*. * *A Maid Made Mad*. * *Farmer for a Day*. * *He Was Only Feudin'*. 1944: *Texas Masquerade*. *Lumberjack*. *Forty Thieves*. *Mystery Man*. * *His Tale is Told*. * *You Were Never Uglier*. * *Gold Is Where You Lose It*. * *Heather and Yon*. 1945: *Roughly Speaking*. *Son of the Prairie*. * *Two Local Yokels*. * *A Miner Affair*. * *The Blonde Stayed On*. * *Spook to Me*. 1946: *The Devil's Playground*. *Fools' Gold*. *The Green Years*. *Unexpected Guest*. *Dangerous Venture*. *The Plainsman and the Lady*. *That Texas Jamboree (GB: Medicine Man)*. *Throw a Saddle on a Star*. * *Andy Plays Hooky*. 1947: *Hoppy's Holiday*. *The Marauders*. * *Two Jills and a Jack*. * *Wife to Spare*. 1948: * *Eight-Ball Andy*. * *Go Chase Yourself*. *Silent Conflict*. *The Dead Don't Dream*. *Strange Gamble*. *Sinister Journey*. *False Paradise*. *Borrowed Trouble*. 1949: *Crashing Thru*. *Riders of the Dusk*. *Shadows of the West*. *Range Land*. *Haunted Trails*. * *Sunk in the Sink*. 1950: * *Marinated Mariner*. * *A Blunderful Time*. *Gunslingers*. *Arizona Territory*. *Canyon Raiders*. *Cherokee Uprising*. *Fence Riders*. *Outlaws of Texas*. *Silver Raiders*. 1951: *Abilene Trail*. * *Blonde Atom Bomb*. 1952: * *A Blissful Blunder*. * *Hooked and Rooked*. * *The Fresh Painter*. 1953: * *Pardon My Wrench*. * *Love's A-Poppin'*. * *Oh Say, Can You Sue*. 1954: * *Two April Fools*. 1955: * *Scratch, Scratch, Scratch*. * *One Spooky Night*. *The Road to Denver*. *Carolina Cannonball*. 1956: * *Andy Goes Wild*. * *Pardon My Nightshirt*.

COLE, George 1925–

Despite the fact that he has proved himself time and again to be a thoughtful and effective serious actor, almost all of this fretful-looking British actor's successes have been in comedy vein. Born in London, Cole was first seen as a teenage actor with dark, wavy, unruly hair and cockney accent, having answered an advert in a paper for a child player in a West End musical, and getting the job of understudy for the part. His first film, *Cottage to Let*, made when he was not quite 16, brought him to the attention of Alastair Sim (*qv*), who guided him in his early career. The two men made 11 films together and became lifelong friends. He was in the Royal Air Force from 1944 to 1947 but, now able to switch the London accent on and off at the drop of a lopsided smile, soon took up the threads of his career again after the war. His first big comedy success in films was in *Laughter in Paradise* in 1951, as a meek bank clerk who has to pretend to hold up his own bank to fulfil the conditions of an inheritance. This established one half of his split comic persona – as the well-intentioned young man who, despite being all fingers and thumbs, blunders through in the end. Reprising it the following year in *Top Secret*, as a bumbling sanitary engineer who picks up a case containing atomic secrets and takes it to Moscow, he estab.'shed himself as a name the public would pay to see. Transferring the character to radio, he sank it into nervous perennial bachelor David Bliss in *A Life of Bliss*, one of the longest-running radio comedy series in history. Beginning in 1953, it ran until 1969. Meanwhile, in 1954, Cole had created the other side of his comedy coin with Flash Harry, the ever-optimistic spiv in the 'St Trinian's' films. Later he extended the characterisation to create Arthur Daley, the salesman from whom you'd least like to buy a second-hand car, in another long-running series *Minder* – this time on television. Cole's comedy characters are brought to life by clever use of body language: facial tics, expressive hands and shifts of the shoulders all come into play to create rascals and ditherers alike. The most likeable and co-operative of stars, he has also tried his hand at heavy drama and stage musicals. He married actresses Eileen Moore (from 1954 to 1966) and Penny Morrell (from 1968 on).

1941: *Cottage to Let* (US: *Bombsite Stolen*). 1942: *Those Kids from Town*. 1943: * *Fiddling Fuel*. *The Demi-Paradise* (US: *Adventure for Two*). 1944: *Henry V*. 1945: *Journey Together*. 1948: *My Brother's Keeper*. *Quartet*. 1949: *The Spider and the Fly*. 1950: *Morning Departure* (US: *Operation Disaster*). *Gone to Earth* (US: *The Wild Heart*). 1951: *Flesh and Blood*. *Laughter in Paradise*. *Scrooge* (US: *A Christmas Carol*). *Lady Godiva Rides Again*. 1952: *The Happy Family* (US: *Mr Lord Says No)*. *Who Goes There!* (US: *The Passionate Sentry*). *Top Secret* (US: *Mr Potts Goes to Moscow*). *Folly to Be Wise*. 1953: *Will Any Gentleman . . .? The Intruder*. *Our Girl Friday* (US: *The Adventures of Sadie*). *The Clue of the Missing Ape*. 1954: *An Inspector Calls*. *Happy*

Ever After (US: *Tonight's the Night*). The *Belles of St Trinian's*. *A Prize of Gold*. 1955: *Where There's a Will*. *The Constant Husband*. *The Adventures of Quentin Durward*. 1956: *It's a Wonderful World*. *The Green Man*. *The Weapon*. 1957: *Blue Murder at St Trinian's*. 1959: *Too Many Crooks. Don't Panic Chaps! The Bridal Path*. 1960: *The Pure Hell of St Trinian's*. 1961: *The Anatomist*. 1963: *Dr Syn Alias the Scarecrow* (US: TV, as *The Scarecrow of Romney Marsh*). *Cleopatra*. 1964: *One Way Pendulum*. 1965: *The Legend of Young Dick Turpin*. 1966: *The Great St Trinian's Train Robbery*. 1968: * *The Green Shoes*. 1970: *The Vampire Lovers*. 1971: *Fright*. 1972: *Madigan: The London Beat* (TV). 1973: *Take Me High*. 1976: *The Blue Bird*. 1983: * *Perishing Solicitors*. 1985: *Minder on the Orient Express* (TV).

COLONNA, Jerry
(Gerardo Colonna) 1904–1986

Beaming, hugely-moustached American musician and comedian with big, bulging, bullfrog eyes and a voice like a high-pitched klaxon entering harbour. Colonna was playing drums in a jazz band at 13, and a year later led an orchestra that played at weddings and socials. Such enterprise was clearly headed for the top in show business. Colonna, now a specialist on the trombone, soon gained assignments with better-known bands, becoming known for the comedy and novelty songs he was also capable of injecting into a gig. From 1931, Colonna played as trombonist with the CBS staff orchestra in New York. By the middle of the decade, though, his side-splitting (and ear-splitting) comic interventions were making themselves felt on such radio comedy and music programmes as those hosted by Fred Allen (*qv*) and Bing Crosby. In 1938 Colonna joined Bob Hope's (*qv*) radio show as a regular, the two men forming a bond of friendship that lasted for life. Colonna also took his catch-phrase – 'Whassamatter, you crazy or something' – into the movies, playing prominent roles in several Paramount frolics of the time, and taking cameos in three Hope-Crosby 'Road' movies. His appearances were dynamic, to say the least. His fame spread with his caterwauling

singing on records, one of which, *Ebb Tide*, sold more than half a million copies. He could hold one of his deafening notes for almost a minute and a quarter. It was sad that for a man who always seemed to be happy Colonna should suffer so much with ill-health in his latter days. He suffered a disabling stroke in 1966 – for a long time he could use only his right hand – and was hospitalised for the last seven years of his life after a heart attack in 1979. His death came from kidney failure. Bob Hope was at his bedside when he died. A popular, demonstrative and big-hearted man who simply couldn't resist a gag appearance or the chance to show off in the nicest possible way, Colonna was given the highest USAF award, the Scroll of Appreciation, for his work with the armed forces in wartime.

1937: *52nd Street*. *Rosalie*. 1938: *College Swing* (GB: *Swing, Teacher, Swing*). *Little Miss Broadway*. *Garden of the Moon*. *Valley of the Giants*. * *The Star Reporter No. 2*. 1939: *Naughty But Nice*. *Sweepstakes Winner*. 1940: *Road to Singapore*. *Comin' Round the Mountain*. 1941: *Melody and Moonlight*. *You're the One*. *Sis Hopkins*. *Ice-Capades*. 1942: *True to the Army*. *Priorities on Parade*. *Ice-Capades Revue* (GB: *Rhythm Hits the Ice*). 1943: *Star-Spangled Rhythm*. 1944: *Atlantic City. It's in the Bag!* (GB: *The Fifth Chair*). 1946: *Make Mine Music*. 1947: *Road to Rio*. 1950: *Alice in Wonderland* (voice only). 1951: *Kentucky Jubilee*. 1955: *Meet Me in Las Vegas* (GB: *Viva Las Vegas!*). 1958: *Andy Hardy Comes Home*. 1961: *The Road to Hong Kong*. 1977: *Don't Push, I'll Charge When I'm Ready*.

COLTRANE, Robbie
(Robin Macmillan) 1950–

Giant-sized (6 ft 2 in, 20 stones), black-haired, Scottish-born comedian of abrasive character and equal talents in comedy and drama. The small, hostile eyes beneath low brows in a large, round face meant that, despite success in small-screen comedy series, Coltrane was often seen in his early films in outrageous, unsympathetic or downright nasty roles. Then, unexpectedly, he began to break through to comedy stardom at the end of the 1980s, much as another heavyweight, the rather more genial John Candy (*qv*), was doing on the other side of the Atlantic. As with Candy, top roles have enabled Coltrane to project a more sympathetic image, something he has managed with impressive ease. This most socialist of entertainers was born in Glasgow and educated at a public school in Perthshire. His rebellious attitudes on completing his education soon led him to express his views in aggressively comic style as a stand-up comedian. After a period in America in the late 1970s, there were numerous successes on British TV in such programmes as *The Comic Strip Presents*, *The Young Ones*, *A Kick Up the Eighties* and *Tutti Frutti*. In films, though, even if he were always unmistakeable (even as a transvestite nightclub queen in *The Fruit Machine*), he was becoming established as a leading character actor and all-purpose, nefarious ne'er-do-well. His Falstaff in Kenneth Branagh's award-winning *Henry V* brought Coltrane's work before a wider public, and he had his first outright comedy lead in harness with long, lean, startled-looking Eric Idle (*qv*) in the occasionally hilarious *Nuns on the Run*. In 1989 and 1990 Coltrane returned to America to make films, still describing himself as 'a character actor – the kind of face that everybody likes, but nobody fancies!' But Beverly d'Angelo's character fancied him all right in *The Pope Must Die* (although this failed in America) and the face itself became ever more familiar to the British public through TV commercials. Coltrane's present elevated status, which promises to make him a leading comedy force in the 1990s, is a far cry from his self-confessed 'worst moment' when, opening the bill for a pop group, he had bottles thrown at him and was booed off stage. 'They just wanted rock 'n' roll', he recalls with some sympathy. 'Not some fat Scot telling jokes. But I cried and cried.'

1979: * *Balham – Gateway to the South.* 1980: *Flash Gordon.* 1981: *Subway Riders.* 1982: *The Ghost Dance. Scrubbers.* 1983: *Krull.* 1984: *Chinese Boxes. Loose Connections.* 1985: *Revolution. National Lampoon's European Vacation. Defence of the Realm. Caravaggio. The Supergrass.* 1986: *Absolute Beginners. Mona Lisa.* 1987: *The Secret Policeman's Third Ball. Eat the Rich.* 1988: *The Fruit Machine. The Strike. Midnight Breaks. Bert Rigby, You're a Fool.* 1989: *Slipstream. Danny, the Champion of the World (US: TV). Lenny Live and Unleashed. Let It Ride. Henry V.* 1990: *Nuns on the Run. Perfectly Normal.* 1991: *The Pope Must Die (US: The Pope Must Diet). Triple Bogey on a Par 5 Hole. Alive and Kicking (TV).*

CONKLIN, Chester
(Jules Cowles) 1888–1971

A tiny, bag-eyed, sandy-haired, putty-nosed, balding American clown and comic actor, who sported a huge moustache in his days as a silent comedy king. Born in Iowa,

Conklin was originally intended for the priesthood, but was bitten by the entertainment bug and left home at 16 to go on the stage. Appearing in travelling road shows, Conklin soon realised his talent for comedy. His nimble limbs, tiny stature and mournful features eventually qualified him for a job as a clown with the Al G. Barnes Circus, where he was a great success. In 1913 he decided to try his luck in films and signed on at Mack Sennett's Keystone Studio. At this home of silent slapstick Conklin supported Charlie Chaplin (*qv*) and Mabel Normand (*qv*) in many of their early comedies. He also joined the Keystone Kops (he was, of course, far too small to have ever been a real one) and teamed with massive Mack Swain (*qv*) in the 'Ambrose and Walrus' two-reel comedies. These contrasted the boisterous Ambrose (Swain, weighing in at 280 pounds) with Conklin's mischievous Walrus (weighing in at 120 pounds) who usually contrived to get the better of their battles. Most of all, though, Conklin enjoyed his stints with the Keystone Kops. Many years later he told an interviewer: 'They couldn't make comedies these days like the ones the Kops appeared in. We'd set up our cameras in any street in Los Angeles, and, if a crowd gathered, we'd hire a few real cops on the spot to keep people away. We'd add on jokes and gags as we went along. Sennett was a great comedy producer because he'd laugh at what you were doing all the time. So you'd break your neck to make him smile.' In other films, Conklin had the lead in a series of two-reelers about Mr Droppington, a meek and mild little chap to whom the worst was always happening. The character wasn't catchy enough to make Conklin one of the major stars of the silent era like Chaplin and Harold Lloyd (*qv*), but the little man hung on as a leading figure in two-reel comedy until almost the end of the silent days. In the early 1920s, however, Chester was already making inroads into taking straight acting roles. He was in early versions of *Desire* and *Anna Christie*, and played ZaSu Pitts' (*qv*) father in Erich Von Stroheim's much-mauled classic *Greed*. With the 1930s, Conklin's appearances gradually grew less frequent – although he had his own brief series of two-reel comedies for Paramount in the early days of sound. These were hectic doses of slapstick in which Conklin invariably brought down half the scenery before the end. The most notable of his feature films from this decade saw him sharing, in Charlie Chaplin's *Modern Times*, the famous sequence where Charlie becomes trapped in factory machinery. Later still, whenever a group of comedy old-stagers needed to be got together, for example in *Hollywood Cavalcade* in 1939, Conklin was there, in this case reprising his old role as a Keystone Kop. In 1961, it seemed that Chester had finally disappeared from the scene, when he went into a nursing home. Four years later, in true Keystone

style, he eloped to Las Vegas with another resident of the home, a 65-year-old who became his fourth wife. They enjoyed half a dozen years of marriage before Conklin's death at 83. Essentially a silent clown, Conklin could still make you laugh in comedy cameos in later films – the ageing process held up by that huge brush moustache on so small a face.

1914: * *Back to Nature Girls.* * *Her Private Husband.* * *The Great Nickel Robbery.* * *Those Dangerous Eyes.* * *Making a Living.* * *Mabel's Strange Predicament.* * *Between Showers.* * *Tango Tangles.* * *Cruel, Cruel Love.* * *Mabel at the Wheel.* * *Twenty Minutes of Love.* * *False Alarm.* * *Business is Business.* * *Laughing Gas.* * *The Piper.* * *His Son's Wife.* * *Caught in a Cabaret.* * *The Face on the Barroom Floor.* * *Dough and Dynamite.* * *Mabel's Busy Day.* * *Step Lively Please.* * *The First Heir.* * *Mabel's New Job.* * *Those Love Pangs.* * *Gentlemen of Nerve.* * *Curses! They Remarked.* * *The Love Thief.* * *His Taking Ways.* * *How Heroes Are Made.* * *Home Rule.* * *Soft Boiled Yegg.* * *Rural Cinderella.* * *The Love Egg.* * *Country Chicken.* * *Perfect Villain.* * *A Colored Girl's Love.* * *Wild West Love. Tillie's Punctured Romance.* * *The Masquerader.* * *The Anglers.* 1915: * *Love, Speed and Thrills.* * *Hushing the Scandal.* * *Ambrose's Sour Grapes.* * *Hash House Mashers.* * *A One Night Stand.* * *The Best of Enemies.* * *A Woman.* * *Bulldog Yale.* * *Shot in the Excitement.* * *The Home Breakers.* * *The Cannon Ball.* * *Caught in a Park.* * *Droppington's Devilish Dream.* * *Wilful Ambrose.* * *When Ambrose Dared Walrus.* * *A Bird's a Bird.* * *Hearts and Planets.* * *Ambrose's Fury.* * *Droppington's Family Tree.* * *Ambrose's Lofty Perch.* * *A Hash House Fraud.* * *Do-Re-Mi-Fa.* * *The Battle of Ambrose and Walrus.* * *Saved by the Wireless.* 1916: * *Cinders of Love.* * *Dizzy Heights and Daring Hearts.* * *A Tugboat Romeo.* * *Bucking Society.* * *His First False Step.* 1917: * *The Pullman Bride.* * *A Clever Dummy.* * *Dodging His Doom.* * *An International Sneak.* * *Cactus Nell.* * *The Pawnbroker's Heart.* 1918: * *It Pays to Exercise.* * *Ladies First.* * *The Village Chestnut.* 1919: * *Uncle Tom's Cabin.* * *Yankee Doodle in Berlin.* * *Uncle Tom Without a Cabin.* 1920: * *Chicken a la Cabaret.* * *Lightweight Lover. Married

Life. * You Wouldn't Believe it. 1921: * Skirts. 1923: Desire. Anna Christie. Souls for Sale. Tea – With a Kick. 1924: Greed. Galloping Fish. The Fire Patrol. Another Man's Wife. North of Nevada. 1925: The Phantom of the Opera. A Woman of the World. The Great Love. The Pleasure Buyers. The Masked Bride. Battling Bunyon. Where Was I? The Winding Stair. The Great Jewel Robbery. One Year to Live. My Neighbor's Wife. Under the Rouge. The Gold Rush. 1926: Behind the Front. The Wilderness Woman. Say It Again. We're in the Navy Now. The Duchess of Buffalo. More Pay, Less Work. The Nervous Wreck. A Social Celebrity. Fascinating Youth. The Lady of the Harem. Midnight Lovers. Sybil. 1927: Rubber Heels. A Kiss in a Taxi. McFadden's Flats. Cabaret. Two Flaming Youths (GB: The Side Show). Tell It to Sweeney. Silk Stockings. Drums of the Desert. 1928: Tillie's Punctured Romance (Remake. GB: Marie's Millions). Fools for Luck. Gentlemen Prefer Blondes. The Big Noise. Variety. Taxi 13. The Haunted House. Trick of Hearts. Feel My Pulse. Horseman of the Plains. Beau Broadway. 1929: Fast Company. The House of Horror. The Studio Murder Mystery. The Virginian. Marquis Preferred. Stairs of Sand. Sunset Pass. Shanghai Rose (GB: The Secret Woman). Show of Shows. 1930: Swing High. * Chester Conklin in The Master Sweeper. * Cleaning Up. * The Love Trader. 1931: * Gents of Leisure. * Studio Sap. * Taxi. * The New Yorker. * Stout Hearts and Willing Hands. Her Majesty Love. * The Thirteenth Alarm. 1933: Hallelujah, I'm a Bum (GB: Hallelujah I'm a Tramp). 1935: * Keystone Hotel. * La Fiesta de Santa Barbara. 1936: Call of the Prairie. Modern Times. The Preview Murder Mystery. 1937: Sing Cowboy Sing. Hotel Haywire. Forlorn River. 1938: Every Day's a Holiday. * Flatfoot Stooges. * A Nag in the Bag. 1939: * Mutiny on the Body. Hollywood Cavalcade. Zenobia (GB: Elephants Never Forget). * The Teacher's Pet. 1940: The Great Dictator. Li'l Abner. * You're Next. Adventures of Red Ryder (serial). 1941: Honolulu Lu. Goodnight Sweetheart. Harmon of Michigan. * Dutiful But Dumb. Sullivan's Travels. 1942: In Old California. * Piano Mooner. Here Comes Mr Jordan. * College Belles. Valley of the Sun. The Palm Beach Story. Sons of the Pioneers. 1943: * Phony Express. * His Wedding Scare. Around the World. Sagebrush Law. 1944: Knickerbocker Holiday. The Yellow Rose of Texas. The Man from Frisco. Can't Help Singing. The Miracle of Morgan's Creek. Adventures of Mark Twain. Hail the Conquering Hero. Sunday Dinner for a Soldier. 1945: Bud Abbott and Lou Costello in Hollywood. * Micro Phonies. The Trouble with Women (released 1947). 1946: She Wrote the Book. The Hoodlum Saint. Singin' in the Corn. Little Giant (GB: On the Carpet). The Best Years of Our Lives. Fear. 1947: Song of Scheherazade. The Perils of Pauline. Springtime in the Sierras. The Song of the Wasteland. 1948: * A Pinch in Time. 1949: Jackpot Jitters (GB: Jiggs and Maggie in Jackpot Jitters). The Beautiful Blonde from Bashful Bend. The Golden Stallion. 1950: Fancy Pants. Joe Palooka in

Humphrey Takes a Chance (GB: Humphrey Takes a Chance). Never a Dull Moment. 1951: Here Comes the Groom. 1952: Son of Paleface. * Happy Go Wacky. 1953: * So You Want to Be a Musician. 1955: The Beast with a Million Eyes. Apache Woman. 1957: Paradise Alley (released 1962). 1958: Rock-a-Bye Baby. 1966: A Big Hand for the Little Lady (GB: Big Deal at Dodge City).

CONNOR, Kenneth 1918–

Distinctive little British comic actor with dark curly hair and crumpled features. Trained in Shakespeare at the Bristol and London Old Vics, his concert-party background reasserted itself in the 1950s when he ran up a whole range of radio characters who were usually thorns in the side of the star of the show, most often Ted Ray (qv). Connor's characters could be stuffy, downtrodden, lecherous or just plain pains-in-the-butt. To them all he brought a unique set of twanging tones, and his 'old codgers' were masterpieces of observation. As a film comedian he was never asked to carry a solo vehicle but he was close a couple of times and also proved a valuable member of the 'Carry On' casts in two long stints with the famous series. Born in London, Connor was the son of a naval officer who ran concert parties. By the time he was 11 he was doing a double act with his brother, both in his father's shows and charity revues. Later he decided to become a serious actor and won a gold medal at the Central School of Music and Drama. After six years as a wartime infantry gunner he resumed a career in stage drama but his talent for comic character voices was his greatest asset and, from 1953, he became the 'man of many voices' on the long-running radio series Ray's a Laugh, creating such characters as the shopkeeper Sidney Mincing and the oddjob man Herbert Toil. His catchphrases 'Do you mind?' and (on TV) 'Oh, mate!' became national watchwords. An original member of the 'Carry On' film casts, he left the series in 1964 to concentrate on theatre work, returning five years later to play the quivering old men that he no longer needed makeup to play visually as well as vocally. His favourite role, though, is a theatrical one: the Fool in King Lear.

1939: Poison Pen. 1949: The Chiltern Hundreds (US: The Amazing Mr Beecham). 1950: Don't Say Die/Never Say Die. 1952: The Beggar's Opera. Elstree Story (voice only). There Was a Young Lady. Miss Robin Hood. 1953: Marilyn (later Roadhouse Girl). 1954: The Black Rider. 1955: The Ladykillers. 1957: Davy. 1958: Carry on Sergeant. 1959: Make Mine a Million. Carry on Nurse. Carry on Teacher. 1960: Carry on Constable. Dentist in the Chair. Watch Your Stern. His and Hers. 1961: Carry on Regardless. A Weekend with Lulu. Nearly a Nasty Accident. Dentist on the Job (US: Get on with It!). What a Carve Up! (US: Home Sweet Homicide). 1962: Carry on Cruising. 1963: Carry on Cabby. 1964: Gonks Go Beat. Carry on Cleo. 1965: How to Undress in Public without Undue Embarrassment. 1967: Danny the Dragon (serial, voice only). 1968: Captain Nemo and the Underwater City. 1969: Carry on Up the Jungle. 1970: Rhubarb. Carry on Henry. 1972: Carry on Matron. Carry on Abroad. 1973: Carry on Girls. 1974: Carry on Dick. 1975: Carry on Behind. 1976: Carry on England. 1978: Carry on Emmanuelle.

CONRIED, Hans 1917–1982

In some ways the John Cleese (qv) of his day, but without the same degree of huge personal success, this lean, tall, knobble-jointed American character comedian whose startled eyes dominated an 'easily-offended' look, popped up in all sorts of cameos as waiters, photographers, teachers, clerks, publicity men and people who generally thought themselves above their station in life. His distinctive haughty tones and mastery of any number of accents (most of them put to comic use) made him a great favourite on American radio throughout the 1940s and early 1950s. A series of film roles in 1953 almost boosted him to star parts but it was TV that most gainfully employed him from 1958 until his death from a heart ailment at 65. Conried was born in Maryland and started acting on radio at 18. It proved a useful second string to his bow throughout a rather spotty film career in which he would rush in and out of films like a man on roller skates. With the onset of World War Two, and given his sharp features, Germanic name and facility for European voices, Nazis

Kenneth Connor feels tempted to prove that a bird in the hand could be one in the bush as well, in *Carry On Up the Jungle*

For he's a brolly good fellow. Sir Mortimer (Peter Cook) demonstrates his scheme to save fellow Britons from nuclear fall-out, in *Whoops Apocalypse*

Spotty server. With Cicely Courtneidge as the new maid at his mansion, nightclub king Sam Hardy looks prepared for the worst in *Aunt Sally*

reached out and claimed him for several years. 'I played so many of them', he once recalled, 'that I probably went to sleep in a turtle-neck sweater.' He was doubtless quite pleased to get away from films for some real wartime service that put him on the other side. The 1950s brought a renewal of film interest in Conried's eccentric talents, especially when he was given the leading role of the mad piano teacher in the fantasy-musical *The 5,000 Fingers of Dr T*. But, fearful of a box-office flop (which they had anyway), studio heads had the entire film cut and reshaped, trimming or eliminating 11 musical numbers. The result was a pretty odd kettle of fish, although Conried was splendidly megalomaniac and twitchy in the leading role. He was near the top of the cast in all his films that year, but the breakthrough to stardom didn't come, and he returned to what he termed 'bizarre characters'. 'I got a lot of those parts', he suggests, 'simply because there weren't many bizarre, eccentric character players of my age. Crazy younger people were in short supply!' He had already played several guest roles in TV's *The Danny Thomas Show* when he was offered a regular role in 1958. He appeared as Uncle Tonoose, the explosive, oddball patriarch of Thomas's TV family. The series ran until 1965, returning in a different format in the 1970/71 TV season. The modest Conried once described his career as 'hardly interesting'. There are many, though, who wouldn't agree.

1938: Dramatic School. 1939: It's a Wonderful World. On Borrowed Time. Never Say Die. 1940: Dulcy. Bitter Sweet. The Great Dictator. 1941: Maisie Was a Lady. Unexpected Uncle. Blondie in Society (GB: Henpecked). Underground. The Gay Falcon. Weekend for Three.

A Date with the Falcon. 1942: Joan of Paris. Saboteur. The Wife Takes a Flyer (GB: A Yank in Dutch). * The Greatest Gift. The Falcon Takes Over. Pacific Rendezvous. Blondie's Blessed Event (GB: A Bundle of Trouble). Journey into Fear. Underground Agent. The Big Street. Once Upon A Honeymoon. Nightmare. 1943: Hostages. Crazy House. Hitler's Children. A Lady Takes a Chance. His Butler's Sister. 1944: Passage to Marseille. Mrs Parkington. 1947: The Senator Was Indiscreet (GB: Mr Ashton Was Indiscreet). 1948: Design for Death (narrator only). 1949: The Barkleys of Broadway. My Friend Irma. Bride for Sale. On the Town. 1950: Jet Pilot (released 1957). Nancy Goes to Rio. Summer Stock (GB: If You Feel Like Singing). 1951: Rich, Young and Pretty. Texas Carnival. The Light Touch. Too Young to Kiss. Behave Yourself! New Mexico. I'll See You in My Dreams. 1952: Three for Bedroom C. The World in His Arms. Big Jim McLain. 1953: Peter Pan (voice only). Siren of Bagdad. The Affairs of Dobie Gillis. The Twonky. The 5,000 Fingers of Dr T. 1954: Davy Crockett, King of the Wild Frontier. 1955: You're Never Too Young. 1956: The Birds and the Bees. Bus Stop. Miracle on 34th Street (TV. GB: cinemas). 1957: The Monster That Challenged the World. 1958: The Big Beat. Rock-a-Bye Baby. 1959: Juke Box Rhythm. 1001 Arabian Nights (voice only). 1961: Judgment at Nuremberg. 1963: My Six Loves. 1964: Robin and the Seven Hoods. The Patsy. 1968: The Jay Ward Intergalactic Film Festival (voice only). 1969: Wake Me When the War is Over (TV). * Up is Down (narrator only). 1970: The Phantom Tollbooth (voice only). 1973: The Brothers O'Toole (GB: TV). 1976. The Shaggy DA. 1978: The Cat from Outer Space. 1980: Oh, God! Book II. 1981: * Once Upon a Mouse (narrator only). American Dream (TV). Through the Magic Pyramid (TV).

Hans Conried (as Dr Terwilliger) feels that Peter Lind Hayes is getting up his nose in *The 5,000 Fingers of Dr T*

COOK, Peter 1937–

Long, lugubrious, pale, dark-haired mournful-looking British satirist and revue artist who formed a university partnership with the tiny, multi-talented Dudley Moore (*qv*) that lasted for 20 years. One never thinks of Cook as a film comedian at all, although he has cropped up in quite a number of movies through the years. But his film career has been a thing of rags and patches. Cook elected to stay in Britain when Moore went to Hollywood and came close to super-stardom. His stork-like features were better suited to cameos and character roles, and the weight he put on in middle-age put David Warner-style leading roles out of the question. Born in the seaside town of Torquay, Cook was a bright lad whose father was in the British colonial service. The junior Cook read languages at Cambridge University with the intention of joining the Foreign Office on graduation. But at university he fell in with some of the brightest satirists of his generation, including Moore, Alan Bennett and Jonathan Miller, the four combining on the soon-famous *Beyond the Fringe* stage shows. On television, Cook soon became popular as the gloomy, plaintive, raincoated philosopher E. L. Wisty, then teamed with Moore in the milestone comedy show *Not Only . . . But Also*, of which only a few segments now survive. Cook and Moore's most popular items were the hilarious duologues between their cloth-capped chatters Pete and Dud, plangently making both sense and nonsense out of life. Cook found it easier to keep a straight face than his frequently corpsing partner. They moved into films in tandem but, apart from *Bedazzled*, a partial failure whose best moments stemmed directly from their television routines, they were limited to featured appearances. Cook also became involved with the satirical magazine *Private Eye*, as a director and contributor, sharing in its fluctuating fortunes down the years. In his fifties, Cook continues to be an astringent comedy writer and sardonic baiter of the establishment. It's a shame that much of his best work is probably forever lost thanks to British television's lack of decent storage space.

1958: *Bachelor of Hearts.* 1966: *The Wrong Box.* 1967: *Bedazzled.* * *Think 20th.* 1968: *A Dandy in Aspic.* 1969: *The Bed Sitting Room. Monte Carlo or Bust!* (US: *Those Daring Young Men in Their Jaunty Jalopies*). 1970: *The Rise and Rise of Michael Rimmer.* 1972: *The Adventures of Barry McKenzie.* 1976: *Find the Lady. Pleasure at Her Majesty's* (US: *Monty Python Meets Beyond the Fringe*). 1977: *The Hound of the Baskervilles.* 1979: *The Secret Policeman's Ball.* 1981: *Derek and Clive Get the Horn.* 1983: *Scandalous! Yellowbeard.* 1984: *Supergirl. The Secret Policeman's Private Parts.* 1987: *The Princess Bride.* 1988: *Without a Clue.* 1989: *Getting It Right.*

CORBETT, Ronnie 1930–
An appropriately short entry for sixty-one inches of bespectacled devilment. Like his oft-time partner, big Ronnie Barker (*qv*), Scotland's wee Ronnie Corbett has had leading roles in film comedies without quite becoming a film star. On television though, especially in harness with the other Ronnie, he was dynamite. Born and brought up in Edinburgh, the son of a baker, he first got bitten by the entertainment bug at his church youth club, where he did a couple of pantomimes, drew lots of laughs and realised where his talents lay. On leaving school, however, he worked as a civil servant at the Ministry of Agriculture until he was called up for National Service with the RAF. Here he ran shows for the forces and, after demobilisation, headed for London, where he worked in clubs, ran a bar, even did bookings for tennis courts in Regent's Park. The only film part he could find in these early years was as a schoolboy in the Ronald Shiner (*qv*) comedy *Top of the Form*. As the 1950s progressed, he became used to working in tandem with other comedians, notably Danny La Rue, Stanley Baxter and Bernard Bresslaw (*qv*). There was work for the children's TV programme *Crackerjack*, and another film, *Rockets Galore*, a Scottish comedy which gave him an engaging cameo role. On TV, he appeared in several programmes with presenter David Frost. It was Frost who first had the idea of teaming Corbett with Barker on his ITV show *The Frost Report*. Impressed, rival channel BBC

snapped them up for their own series, *The Two Ronnies*, which hit huge heights of popularity, and ran from 1971 to Barker's retirement in 1988. In the seventies Corbett had a couple of films more or less spun round his talents but neither was good enough to make him a top film attraction. *Some Will, Some Won't* was a less funny remake of the classic 1951 comedy *Laughter in Paradise. No Sex, Please — We're British* was a leery farce, adapted from a stage success that relied heavily on two statuesque girls running around in scanties. Corbett was at the centre of a plot that involved the erroneous delivery of pornography to a bank. 'I suppose', he says, 'that I've always capitalised on being small, but I never liked dressing in silly clothes or getting bashed about. That never appealed to me because it's undignified. I think what makes people laugh is that this little thing called Ronnie Corbett is pretending to be dignified and normally built. 'The only outsize thing I wear is my glasses.'

1952: *Top of the Form.* 1958: *Rockets Galore* (US: *Mad Little Island*). 1962: *Operation Snatch.* 1967: *Casino Royale.* 1968: *Monsieur LeCoq.* 1970: *Some Will, Some Won't. The Rise and Rise of Michael Rimmer.* 1973: *No Sex, Please — We're British.* 1975: *The Picnic.*

COSBY, Bill
See **PRYOR, Richard**

COURTNEIDGE, Dame Cicely
(Esmerelda C. Courtneidge) 1893–1980
Small and angular with a knowing look, irresistible confidence and energy, a resolute singing voice that could rebound from the back of the hall and a strutting dance/walk reminiscent of James Cagney, Cicely Courtneidge's strength was as an impersonator, a chameleon of endless variety and vitality. Her best asset was her own personality. Singularly unsuited with her wide mouth, large jaw and low forehead, to be a romantic ingenue, that was the hole into which Courtneidge found herself uncomfortably pigeoned for the first ten years of her adult career. Named after the comic opera in which her Scots-born actor-manager father and actress mother were touring through Australia at the time of her birth, Courtneidge first trod the boards at eight, as a

fairy in *A Midsummer Night's Dream*. She was already then billed as Cicely (her middle name, after a grandmother). Making her adult debut in the London theatre at 16, it soon became obvious that she was a spirited young actress who could sing and dance as well as speak lines. But it wasn't until 1917, on the instigation of her husband Jack Hulbert (*qv*), whom she had married the previous year, that she ventured to try her luck in variety halls as a solo artist. She sang military songs and danced a bit. The jokes came later and were mostly provided by Hulbert, then doing army service. 'I was too nervous to try them out at first and even then I couldn't believe it when the big laughs started coming.' She became a top billboard attraction, often assuming eccentric, hectoring characters within the act, or appearing in slyly-observed drag. Hulbert, too, forsook straight acting on his return from World War One to exploit talents as a dancer, laughter-maker and light singer, and husband and wife appeared in their first revue together, *Ring Up*, before Courtneidge continued her career in the halls. Audiences warmed to her friendliness and indomitable energy and she spent two more years touring on variety bills before the opportunity came in 1923 to rejoin Hulbert in a stage show that would put both entertainers at the top of the tree. It was called *The Little Revue Starts at Nine O'Clock*. There were three more outstanding shows, *By-the-Way, Clowns in Clover* and *The House That Jack Built*, before, with sound films, Courtneidge found herself dividing her services between the theatre, the music-hall and the cinema. Throughout the early and middle 1930s Courtneidge made films both in harness with Hulbert (though never as the romantic lead, preferring to flit through the plot in a series of outrageous disguises) or, on her own, in musical comedies that she would seize by the scruff of the neck and turn into virtually one-woman shows. Courtneidge may have lacked finesse in these films but, like most good comediennes, she would do anything for a laugh. There were funny faces to be pulled, comic voices to be assumed, and usually a hit song or two around the corner. You could often rely on her to turn up in military drag, which she did in *Soldiers of the King* and *Me and Marlborough*, among others. If some of the other cast members sometimes looked exhausted trying to keep up with her, who could blame them? Hulbert and Courtneidge were both patently unsuited to Hollywood films — they could only have been, at best, character players in the long run — but Courtneidge did give it a go in 1935 with a minor M-G-M vehicle, *The Perfect Gentleman* (in Britain, *The Imperfect Lady*), which predictably proved an unhappy experience. The production values of her films fell away in the later 1930s, together with the failing fortunes of the British film industry, and her only post-1937 film as a musical-comedy star was another movie version of a successful

The indefatigable Cicely Courtneidge ties to impress impresario Sam Hardy by posing as a French star in *Aunt Sally*

stage show with her husband, *Under Your Hat*. The Hulberts returned to the stage permanently at this juncture, appearing together in several wartime revues, most notably *Under the Counter*, which ran from 1945 to 1949 and was a hit all over the world – except America. The apogee of Courtneidge's career came in 1950, when Ivor Novello wrote a show specifically for her, *Gay's the Word* (Gay was the name of her character) and gave her her best-remembered song, *Vitality*, whose words acknowledged Courtneidge's own strengths as well as her shortcomings ('They had vigour, they were bigger, they had wonderful attack . . . They could thrill you, they could fill you with their energy and verve'). There were more films, most of them mistakes or tattered echoes of past glories (except for her excellent vignette in *The L-Shaped Room*) and some very respectable stage work into her eighties. She never considered retirement. 'I'll go on', she said in 1974, 'as long as the public wants me. There are always times when the public needs a laugh. And if you've made your name in comedy, well, why waste it?'

1928: * British Screen Tatler No. 10. 1930: Elstree Calling. 1931: The Ghost Train. 1932: Jack's the Boy (US: Night and Day). Happy Ever After. 1933: Soldiers of the King (US: The Woman in Command). Falling for You. Aunt Sally (US: Along Came Sally). 1934: Things Are Looking Up. 1935: Me and Marlborough. The Perfect Gentleman (GB: The Imperfect Lady). 1936: Everybody Dance. 1937: Take My Tip. 1940: Under Your Hat. 1955: Miss Tulip Stays the Night. 1960: The Spider's Web. 1962: The L-Shaped Room. 1965: Those Magnificent Men in Their Flying Machines. 1966: The Wrong Box. 1972: Not Now Darling.

CRIBBINS, Bernard 1928–
Donkey-faced, curly-haired British comic character star and revue artist with mournful smile, often seen as 'anxious' types in films. Also a singer of novelty songs, a popular narrator of children's stories and an eccentric comedian who has had his own TV series, Cribbins has been an actor since he

was 14; it was then that he became a student player with his local Lancashire repertory company. His light, distinctive voice could adapt itself to all shades and accents and this, combined with his bloodhound features and sense of fast comedy timing, had made him a London revue star by the 1950s. The 1960s, however, was his period of greatest public acclaim. He made progress towards leading film roles – especially in *The Wrong Arm of the Law* (as Nervous O'Toole), *Carry on Jack*, *The Mouse on the Moon*, *Carry on Spying* and *Crooks in Cloisters*, and invaded the pop charts with such inventive numbers as *Hole in the Ground*, *Right Said Fred* and *Gossip Calypso*. 'The songs were amazing accidents', he says. 'I want to be judged as a comedy actor – and that's about the most serious thing you can be.' Recently he has been back in comedy character roles. At the beginning of the 1980s he appeared with great success as an ineffective detective in a TV movie called *Dangerous Davies – The Last Detective*. A pity it didn't lead to a series.

1957: Yangtse Incident (US: Battle Hell). Davy. 1958: Dunkirk. 1959: Make Mine a Million. Tommy the Toreador. 1960: Two Way Stretch. Visa to Canton (US: Passport to China). The World of Suzie Wong. The Girl on the Boat. 1961: Nothing Barred. The Best of Enemies. 1962: The Fast Lady. The Wrong Arm of the Law. 1963: The Mouse on the Moon. Crooks in Cloisters. Carry on Jack (US: Carry on Venus). 1964: Carry on Spying. Allez France (US: The Counterfeit Constable). A Home of Your Own. 1965: She. You Must Be Joking! Cup Fever. 1966: The Sandwich Man. Daleks – Invasion Earth 2150 AD. 1967: Casino Royale. A Ghost of a Chance. Don't Raise the Bridge, Lower the River. 1969: * The Undertakers. 1970: The Railway Children. 1972: Frenzy. 1973: Yesterday and Today. 1976: Night Ferry. 1978: The Water Babies. The Adventures of Picasso. 1980: Dangerous Davies – The Last Detective (TV).

CRYSTAL, Billy 1947–
It's surprising (and disappointing) how long it took this fuzzy-haired, clown-faced American comedian to get around to starring

in film comedy hits. Now it looks as though he's here to stay — for a little while at least. A slightly mournful-looking little guy with a mobile mouth that can produce a huge smile, Crystal came from a vaguely show-bizzy background. His father was involved in the business as the producer of jazz concerts. The Crystal family also owned and ran a jazz record label, Commodore. Crystal Junior, however, was never interested in playing music. After education at New York University, he became involved with a local theatre group, then formed a comedy trio, The Three Cs, that toured clubs, coffee bars and colleges. By 1974 he was out on his own as a stand-up comedian, building up a formidable variety of characters which he would work into his act on a regular basis. A success in the medium, he decided he wanted to combine life on the road with stop-offs to make movies. The first film he ever saw, he says, was *The Court Jester*, almost non-stop hilarity with Danny Kaye (*qv*). The role was one that would be ideally suited to the grown-up Crystal, vaguely cowardly, vaguely heroic. For the moment, however, the breakthrough lay elsewhere. At the age of 30, he landed up in a TV comedy series, as Richard Mulligan's gay son-in-law Jodie in *Soap*. The show was wildly successful, and Crystal the biggest star to emerge from it. But not immediately, more's the pity. First, there was *Rabbit Test*, a dismal comedy about a pregnant man, then some TV stuff. Then the sharply funny *This Is Spinal Tap*, which wasn't a Crystal vehicle, but which was directed by Rob Reiner, who would remember Crystal when it mattered. For the time being, though, he went back to stand-up comedy. Much of Crystal's best on-stage routines come from the period that followed, and quite a lot of them are available in video, most notably *Billy Crystal: A Comic's Line*, from 1984, which contains his touchingly funny impression of a little boy left on his own at home. Crystal's return to films was somewhat fortuitous. The producers of a buddy-buddy cop movie, *Running Scared*, had rather ambitiously wanted Paul Newman and Gene Hackman for the leading roles. With neither available, a new director, Peter Hyams, took hold of the project, and did his own casting. What more natural for the roles of two tough cops than a comedian and a dancer? You may well ask, but Crystal and Gregory Hines got the parts and it wasn't bad. At any rate, Crystal was back in movies. He did a cameo under mounds of makeup in Rob Reiner's *The Princess Bride*, and then found a male co-star six inches shorter than himself in Danny DeVito (*qv*) for the partially successful *Throw Momma from the Train*, a comic variation on *Strangers on a Train*. He tried a comedy-weepie in *Memories of Me*. It was unsuccessful. Not so a romantic comedy, Reiner's *When Harry Met Sally . . .*, which was one of the biggies of its year, and contained some very funny scenes; Crystal was more relaxed and likeable on screen

than before. Two years later, *City Slickers* was another big hit. Although it had lots of funny lines, this was a poignant and sometimes exciting story about three urban workaholics who, dissatisfied with their lives at 39, take a two-week 'holiday' on an arranged cattle drive. The picture gave Crystal the opportunity to be sad, funny, heroic and silly, all the things that go towards the make-up in his best characters. The film's box-office success gave him the clout to direct the next one, *Mr Saturday Night*, as well as star.

1977: *Death Flight/SST Death Flight/Disaster in the Sky* (TV). 1978: *Rabbit Test. Human Feelings* (TV). 1979: *Breaking Up is Hard to Do* (TV). *Animalympics* (voice only). 1980: *Enola Gay: The Men, the Mission, the Atomic Bomb* (TV). 1983: *This is Spinal Tap.* 1986: *Running Scared.* 1987: *The Princess Bride. Throw Momma from the Train.* 1988: *Memories of Me.* 1989: *When Harry Met Sally . . . Midnight Train to Moscow* (TV). 1991: *City Slickers.* 1992: *Mr Saturday Night (and directed)*.

DALE, Charlie
See **SMITH, Joe and DALE Charlie**

DALE, Jim
(James Smith) 1935 –
A tall, gangling, youthful-looking, rubber-faced, dark-haired Briton who has followed in Michael Crawford's footsteps as a laughter-getter who turned all-round entertainer. Still in demand as a stage star in exhausting musical roles in his late fifties, there aren't many branches of show business that this energetic enthusiast hasn't had a go at. The son of a foundryman from the English Midlands, Dale was smitten by show business when his father brought him to London during the latter stages of World War Two to see Lupino Lane (*qv*) in *Me and My Gal*, a role that more than 40 years later Dale would inherit on Broadway. 'I saw this little man', Dale recalled, 'come out on the stage in a crown and robes, and I knew I wanted to be like him, to make people laugh.' From then on until he was 16

Dale devoted much of his out-of-school time to dancing lessons. Briefly an office boy on leaving school, he soon quit to become a full-time comedian on the northern club circuit. He was touring London music-halls (the few that were left) as a bottom-of-the-bill comedian by 1953. Two years national service in the RAF followed, after which he entered television, estimated in 1961 to be the only entertainer to have appeared in more than 1,000 shows. He was appearing as warm-up comedian in the tea-time TV pop music show *6-5 Special* in 1956 when he ended his spot by grabbing Tommy Steele's guitar and doing a parody of a song. The producers liked it so much that they booked him to appear in the next show — as a singer. Soon Dale had rocketed to fame with such chart-topping songs as *Be My Girl*. Dale knew the bubble was bound to go pop, and lost little time in moving into comedy acting, playing light Shakespearian roles on stage and, from 1963, giving the 'Carry On' films the one thing they had missed — a semi-straight juvenile lead. Perhaps his best for them was the central role in *Carry On Cowboy*, as the drainage engineer from East Finchley who somehow finds himself in the wild west having to take on the feared Rumpo Kid (Sidney James) in a gun duel. At this time he also worked as a disc jockey and made progress as a script-writer and songwriter: his song *Georgy Girl*, for the film of the same name, won an Oscar nomination. As a comedian, Dale's strengths had been his engaging personality, his facial contortions and acrobatic skills. He was able to put all these assets to good use when he played the lead in *Barnum* in America, co-incidentally the same show with which Michael Crawford made a hit in Britain. Having left the 'Carry On' team in 1970, Dale also played the lead in one or two more bitingly satirical film comedies such as *The National Health*. In America, there was a film or two for the Disney studio. In one of them, *Hot Lead and Cold Feet*, Dale repeated his tightrope walk from *Barnum* — except that this time it was across a canyon. His insistence on doing such hazardous scenes himself earned him honorary membership of the Association of Hollywood Stuntmen. Dale's first marriage ended in 1980 after 23

Stubble trouble. Kim Greist doubtless wishes Billy Crystal would get rid of that designer seven o'clock shadow in *Throw Momma from the Train*

Danny De Vito crosses swords with Penelope Ann Miller (below). She walks out (above) when he tries to seduce her with soft lights and (not so) sweet music, in *Other People's Money*

years. He's now married to an American and lives permanently in New York. He has said in interviews that his first film role was in a picture called *Break-In* in 1957. However, the film doesn't exist under that title. It may be a film called *Time Lock*, although Dale certainly isn't visible in the print shown recently on TV.

1958: 6-5 Special. 1961: Raising the Wind. 1962: Nurse on Wheels. The Iron Maiden (US: The Swingin' Maiden). 1963: Carry On Cabby. Carry On Jack (US: Carry On Venus). 1964: Carry On Spying. Carry On Cleo. 1965: The Big Job. Carry On Cowboy. 1966: Carry On Screaming. Don't Lose Your Head. The Winter's Tale. 1967: The Plank. Follow That Camel. Carry On Doctor. 1969: Lock Up Your Daughters! Carry On Again, Doctor. 1972: Adolf Hitler – My Part in His Downfall. 1973: Digby – The Biggest Dog in the World. The National Health. 1976: Joseph Andrews. 1977: Pete's Dragon. 1978: Hot Lead and Cold Feet. 1979: The Spaceman and King Arthur (US: Unidentified Flying Oddball). 1983: Scandalous!

DALEY, Cass
(Katherine Daley) 1915–1975
Cass Daley was the wild American singer-comedienne with the buck teeth who both entertained and convulsed wartime audiences at the same time. She was also just about the only lady funster who has used a shapely bottom to comic effect! But she came on too strong for supporting parts, and leading roles for her sort of 'gal' were so scarce that she found far greater fame in nightclubs and on radio. Very much in the same mould as Martha Raye and Judy Canova (both *qv*), though with a touch more charm when she chose, Cass Daley was born in Philadelphia. Nicknamed Bucky at school because of her protruding teeth, she soon developed twin talents for singing and impersonation. At 16 she got a job in a New Jersey nightclub as a hat-check girl and cigarette girl, and had soon wangled herself a small singing spot with the floor show as well. Her aptitude for comedy was nurtured in partnership with another budding comic, Red Skelton (*qv*), when she moved on to

another nightclub. She then went on to play in vaudeville and on Broadway for what she described as 'nine good years', including a star spot in the 1937 Ziegfeld Follies, replacing Judy Canova. At 26 Daley was signed by Paramount as part of their roster of stars for escapist wartime entertainment. She spent the next few years belting out songs, cavorting wildly around the scenery and often falling on her much-publicised bottom. Sometimes she was teamed with stringy Gil Lamb (*qv*), at others with chubby, nervous Eddie Bracken (also *qv*). This series of distinctly non-classics (though they all made a profit) included *The Fleet's In, Riding High* and *Out of This World*. She enjoyed a profitable loan-out to Universal for *Crazy House* with Olsen and Johnson (*qv*) (being marginally more crazy than they were) and was a popular guest artist in all-star entertainments of the day. But when her one shot at leading lady status (opposite Bracken in *Ladies' Man*) was a flop, capering Cass's Paramount days were over. After *Red Garters* in 1954 she retired to raise a family, although there were a few comebacks in film character roles and Broadway musical revivals after 1966. She died in a freak accident at her home, a fall on to a glass resulting in fatal injuries to her neck.

1942: The Fleet's In. Star Spangled Rhythm. 1943: Riding High (GB: Melody Inn). Crazy House. 1945: Duffy's Tavern. Out of This World. 1947: Variety Girl. Ladies' Man. 1951: Here Comes the Groom. 1954: Red Garters. 1966: The Spirit is Willing. 1969: The Phynx. 1970: Norwood.

DANE, Karl (top)
(Karl Daen) 1886–1934
and
ARTHUR, George K.
(G.K.A. Brest) 1899–
A long and short Hollywood comedy team that flourished briefly with Metro-Goldwyn-Mayer at the end of the silent era. Both participants were young enough to have continued into sound films for a lengthy period, but that was not to be. Karl Dane was indeed a Dane, a big, hefty, gangling lump of a man from Copenhagen who acted

in his father's theatre as a teenager and didn't arrive in America until 1917. His aim was to try his fortune in silent films, for his thick Scandinavian accent barred him from success in the theatre. But he had little luck until his role as John Gilbert's tobacco-chewing comrade in the World War One classic *The Big Parade* drew the public's attention to his distinctive features. Coming in at five stone lighter and nine and a half inches shorter than his future partner, boyish, pop-eyed George Arthur was a Scot from Aberdeen who ironed out his Scottish accent with education at Rugby School, and trained for the stage in Shakespearian drama. At 21 he was cast in the title role of the first screen version of H.G. Wells' *Kipps*. The film was a great success but it didn't make Arthur into a major figure of British cinema in the 1920s. He played successfully in the leading roles of other bright little comedies for Stoll but was seen in supporting roles in bigger films. In 1923 he decided to try his luck in Hollywood, but had mixed fortunes until he approached Josef Von Sternberg, then still with little experience of directing, to make a film. Ultra-cheap but innovative, *The Salvation Hunters*, a simple story of everyday life, grossed 40 times its cost of $5,000. Following this success, Arthur appeared in numerous light comedies through the late 1920s. In 1925 he appeared for the first time with Dane in *Lights of Old Broadway*, and they officially became a team two years later in *Rookies*. Awkward, hulking Dane, with his dreamy leer of a smile, and jack-in-the-box Arthur made a popular pair, cashing in on their extreme physical differences to create an innocently appealing kind of Flagg-and-Quirt comedy. There were six more films together before sound became inevitable. It soon became clear that Dane's heavy accent would no longer permit him to continue in leading roles. By the end of 1931 his career had virtually collapsed. He tried making a living by carpentry but by 1934 had become first a mechanic, then the operator of a hot-dog stand. Depressed by his lack of prospects, Dane shot himself at 47. Arthur, too, struggled. After a few character roles in the early 1930s he decided to go into the business side of films and became a financier and distributor of short subjects. Later, he ventured into production.

Together. *1925: Lights of Old Broadway. 1926: Bardelys the Magnificent. 1927: Rookies. 1928: Detectives. Baby Mine. Brotherly Love. Circus Rookies. 1929: All at Sea. China Bound. 1931: * The Lease Breakers. * Shove Off. * A Put Up Job. 1932: *Summer Daze.*

Dane alone. *1918: My Four Years in Germany. To Hell with the Kaiser. 1925: The Big Parade. His Secretary. The Everlasting Whisper. La Boheme. 1926: Son of the Sheik. The Scarlet Letter. War Paint. Monte Carlo. 1927: The Red Mill. Slide, Kelly, Slide. The Enemy. 1928: Show People. The Trail of 98. Alias Jimmy Valentine. Wyoming. 1929: Speedway.*

Hollywood Revue of 1929. The Duke Steps Out. The Voice of the Storm. The Gob. 1930: Montana Moon. The Big House. Navy Blues. Free and Easy. Numbered Men. Billy the Kid. On to Singapore. 1932: Speak Easily. 1933: The Whispering Shadow (serial). Arthur alone. *1920: Kipps. 1921: A Dear Fool. 1922: Lamp in the Desert. Wheels of Chance. Flames of Passion. Love's Influence. 1923: Paddy The Next Best Thing. *The Cause of All the Trouble. Madness of Youth. Hollywood. 1924: Flames of Desire. 1925: The Salvation Hunters. Lady of the Night. Sun Up. Her Sister from Paris. 1926: Irene. Kiki. The Boob. The Exquisite Sinner. The Boy Friend. The Waning Sex. 1927: Lovers. Tillie the Toiler. Spring Fever. The Gingham Girl. The Student Prince. 1929: The Last of Mrs Cheyney. 1930: Chasing Rainbows. 1932: Where is This Lady? 1933: Blind Adventure. Looking Forward (GB: Service). Oliver Twist. 1934: Riptide. 1935: Vanessa Her Love Story.*

DANGERFIELD, Rodney

(Jacob Cohen) 1921—

Not many film careers take off at 60, but this pop-eyed, bulbous, self-deprecating and often casually vulgar American stand-up comedian can say that he made one film at the age of 65 that took more than $90 million at the American box-office alone. It's an ordeal as well as an experience watching Dangerfield on screen, since the man has so much nervous energy that he simply can't keep still even when not delivering lines. A blue-collar equivalent of Britain's Tony Hancock (*qv*), Dangerfield is said to be at his best as a stand-up comic, spouting an endless stream of one-liners against himself. He tells his audience of when he was a child: 'I got lost on the beach once. A cop helped me look for my parents. "You think we'll find them?" I asked him. He said: "I don't know kid. There are so many places they could hide".' Dangerfield's real childhood was lived uneventfully above a store in the Queens district of New York; his mother looked after him, the parents having split when he was very young. At 18 he had decided to be a comedian and hit the route trodden by another young Jewish entertainer, Danny Kaye, a few years

before — the Catskill Mountains holiday resorts known as the Borscht Belt. 'I actually started writing jokes when I was 15', he remembers, 'as an escape from reality. Comedy is often a camouflage for depression and it certainly was for me.' At 28, still on the Borscht Belt, Dangerfield was no longer able to disguise the depression and quit the business. Twelve years, two children and a divorce later, he started all over again. He soon quit touring to raise his children and used his savings to open a New York nightclub which, with himself as its main attraction, became, to his surprise and relief, a success. Soon, with TV appearances and records, Dangerfield found himself in the big time. There was a film debut at 49, in *The Projectionist*, but, although Dangerfield was third-billed as the tyrannical cinema manager (and, in a dual role, as a serial villain, 'The Bat'), it was primarily a vehicle for chubby Chuck McCann's impressions. Dangerfield's first starring comedy was the dreadful *Easy Money*, but *Back to School*, the one that made all the money, was better, with Dangerfield as a bull-in-a-china-shop, self-made millionaire, who gets himself educated at 60 to encourage his son. Dangerfield's dialogue, as usual, consists almost entirely of an endless stream of one-liners, though they're not delivered with the ease and confidence he displays on stage; and it seems unlikely that he'll make many more movies. He describes the business of making a film as 'hard work and unrewarding. When you play to a camera instead of to an audience you don't get the emotional satisfaction. Without any response it's hard to tell what works.' In recent times Dangerfield has been back in nightclub work (the list below does not include several video compilations of such appearances), but now telling jokes about old age: 'I told my doctor that when I woke up in the morning I couldn't stand looking at myself in the mirror. He said: "At least we know your vision is perfect."'

1970: The Projectionist. 1977: Benny and Barney: Las Vegas Undercover (TV). 1980: Caddyshack. 1983: Easy Money. 1986: Back to School. 1987: Moving. 1991: Rover Dangerfield (voice only). Nuthin' Goes Right. 1992: Ladybugs.

DANIELS, Bebe

(Virginia Daniels) 1901—1971

A dark-haired, bubbling, vivacious and energetic American comedienne who played hundreds of comedy skits with just two leading men at either end of her career. In between, for many years, she was a light dramatic actress. But it's for the laughter — and the unique Daniels laugh — that she'll be remembered. Born in Texas of a Scottish father and Spanish mother, Bebe was on stage as a child with her mother's touring company and grew up to be both quick-witted and to use her face expressively in comedy. She made her screen debut at

seven, and played Dorothy in an early film of *The Wizard of Oz* two years later. There were a couple of other roles as a child while she was completing her education at a Los Angeles convent school. Bebe's teenage talents came to the attention of comedy producer Hal Roach and, just a few months past her 15th birthday, she was signed to become leading lady in Harold Lloyd's 'Lonesome Luke' two-reeler comedies. Lloyd (*qv*) had still to discover the 'spectacles' character that would bring him world fame, but the Luke comedies were doing very nicely. From May 1916 until October 1919 Bebe Daniels appeared opposite Lloyd in almost all his films, nearly 150 of them. Her freshness, youth and obvious enjoyment of the medium contributed much to their success. After she signed with Cecil B. De Mille, Daniels became a leading light in silent films, starring opposite most of the top men of the 1920s (including Rudolph Valentino) in a spirited assortment of romantic, dramatic and comic roles. She had an elfin appeal that made the public warm to her and gave her a more likeable image than that of Gloria Swanson, her more sophisticated rival in the field of comedy and romance. Sound revealed her abilities as a singer, too. But the 1930s neglected her comic talents, and her career rather resembled that of the star she played in her best-remembered film of the period, *42nd Street*: the musical queen on the skids who is eventually replaced by Ruby Keeler. She had married Ben Lyon, an actor of moderate talent but genial personality, in 1930, and in 1935 they came to Britain to get their careers going in a fresh direction — comedy. With Bebe doing the writing, they toured British music-halls from 1936 to 1939 with a husband-and-wife cross-talking act vaguely reminiscent of the kind of material with which George Burns and Gracie Allen (both *qv*) were working on the other side of the Atlantic. Their routines were fast-moving, polished and funny by the time they made the first of several appearances on radio's *Music Hall* in 1939. After successfully launching a long series of comedy programmes on Radio Luxembourg, they appeared in the stage comedy show *Haw-Haw!*, then started a radio show (written by themselves) called *Hi Gang!* Co-starring them with fiddle-playing comedian Vic Oliver, the show's three-handed patter and quickfire, quick-witted style made it a huge success; the Lyons became great popular favourites and honorary Britons as the show ran non-stop through air raids and blackouts for more than a year. A film, *Hi Gang!*, starring Bebe and Ben as rival entertainers chasing an inheritance in England, came out in 1941. During the war years there were more radio and stage shows and tours to entertain the troops. Bebe enjoyed several long stage runs in *Panama Hattie*, Cole Porter's Broadway musical that starred Ethel Merman on the American stage and Ann Sothern on film. With the singing, clowning and acting involved in one show, it remained Bebe's favourite role. After the war she returned to America, producing and appearing in a film (*The Fabulous Joe*) for her old boss Hal Roach. But she and Lyon soon found themselves anxious to return to Britain, where they set up permanent home from 1949. A nostalgic farewell series of *Hi Gang!* that year was soon to be followed by another radio show, *Life with the Lyons*, again co-written by Bebe, which featured her husband and her two children, the glamorous Barbara and the mischievous Richard. A study of constant domestic chaos, it abounded in rich supporting characters and ran uninterrupted from 1950

to 1961. Bebe introduced herself as 'Bebe Daniels Lyon' and built up a new range of catch-phrases for herself, including 'I'm fed up. Up, up, up, up, up!' The programme begat two films, a film serial, a television series and a stage show. For the last decade of her life, Bebe was constantly in poor health, eventually dying from a brain haemorrhage. In 1946 she had been awarded the American Medal of Freedom in recognition of her work in organising American overseas productions for the Allied forces in Europe.

1908: * *A Common Enemy.* *1910:* *The Wizard of Oz.* *1914:* *The Savage.* *Anne of the Golden West.* *1916:* * *Luke Laughs Last.* * *Luke Foils the Villain.* * *Luke and the Rural Roughnecks.* * *Luke's Double.* * *Luke Pipes the Pippins.* * *Luke and the Bomb Throwers.* * *Luke's Late Lunchers.* * *Luke's Fatal Flivver.* * *Luke's Washful Waiting.* * *Luke Rides Roughshod.* * *Luke Crystal Gazer.* * *Luke's Lost Lamb.* * *Luke Does the Midway.* * *Luke and the Mermaids.* * *Luke Joins the Navy.* * *Luke's Society Mix-Up.* * *Luke and the Bang-Tails.* * *Luke's Speedy Club Life.* * *Luke, the Chauffeur.* * *Luke's Newsie Knockout.* * *Luke, Gladiator.* * *Luke's Preparedness Preparations.* * *Luke, Patent Provider.* * *Luke Locates the Loot.* * *Luke's Fireworks Fizzle.* * *Luke's Movie Muddle.* * *Luke's Shattered Sleep.* *1917:* * *Luke's Busy Day.* * *Luke's Trolley Troubles.* * *Lonesome Luke, Lawyer.* * *Luke's Last

Liberty.* * *Luke Wins Ye Ladye Faire.* * *Lonesome Luke on Tin Can Alley.* * *Lonesome Luke's Lively Life.* * *Lonesome Luke's Honeymoon.* * *Lonesome Luke, Plumber.* * *Stop! Luke! Listen!* * *Lonesome Luke, Messenger.* * *Lonesome Luke, Mechanic.* * *Lonesome Luke's Wild Women.* * *Lonesome Luke Loses Patients.* * *Lonesome Luke From London to Laramie.* * *Over the Fence.* * *Pinched.* * *By the Sad Sea Waves.* * *Birds of a Feather.* * *Bliss.* * *Rainbow Island.* * *Love, Laughs and Lather.* * *The Flirt.* * *Clubs are Trumps.* * *All Aboard.* * *We Never Sleep.* * *Move On.* * *Bashful.* * *The Tip.* *1918:* * *The Big Idea.* * *The Lamb.* * *Hit Him Again.* * *Beat It.* * *A Gasoline Wedding.* * *Let's Go.* * *Look Pleasant, Please.* * *On the Jump.* * *Here Come the Girls.* * *Follow the Crowd.* * *Pipe the Whiskers.* * *It's a Wild Life.* * *Hey There!* * *Kicked Out.* * *The Non-Stop Kid.* * *Two-Gun Gussie.* * *Fireman, Save My Child.* * *That's Him.* * *The City Slicker.* * *Sic 'Em Towser.* * *Somewhere in Turkey.* * *Bride and Gloom.* * *Are Crooks Dishonest?* * *An Ozark Romance.* * *Kicking the Germ Out of Germany.* * *Two Scrambled.* * *Bees in His Bonnet.* * *Swing Your Partners.* * *Why Pick On Me?* * *Nothing But Trouble.* * *Hear 'Em Rave.* * *Take a Chance.* * *She Loves Me Not.* *1919:* * *Wanted: $5,000.* * *Going! Going! Gone!* * *Ask Father.* * *On the Fire.* * *I'm on My Way.* * *Look Out Below.* * *The Dutiful Dub.* * *Next Aisle Over.* * *A Sammy in Siberia.* * *Young Mr Jazz.* * *Just Dropped In.* * *Crack Your Heels.* * *Si, Senor.* * *Before Breakfast.* * *The Marathon.* * *Swat the Cook.* * *Off the Trolley.* * *Spring Fever.* * *Billy Blazes Esquire.* * *At the Old Stage Door.* * *A Jazzed Honeymoon.* * *Chop Suey and Co.* * *Count Your Change.* * *Heap Big Chief.* * *Don't Shove.* * *Be My Wife.* * *The Rajah.* * *He Leads, Others Follow.* * *Soft Money.* * *Count the Votes.* * *Pay Your Dues.* * *His Only Father.* * *Never Touched Me.* * *Just Neighbors.* * *Bumping into Broadway.* *Male and Female* (GB: *The Admirable Crichton*), *Everywoman.* *Captain Kidd's Kids.* *1920:* *Sick Abed.* *Feet of Clay.* *Why Change Your Wife?* *The Dancin' Fool.* *1921:* *The Affairs of Anatol* (GB: *A Prodigal Knight*). *Oh Lady, Lady.* *She Couldn't Help It.* *One Wild Week.* *The Speed Girl.* *Ducks and Drakes.* *You Never Can Tell.* *The March Hare.* *Two Weeks with Pay.* *1922:* *Nancy from Nowhere.* *The Game Chicken.* *Nice People.* *North of the Rio Grande.* *Singed Wings.* *Pink Gods.* * *A Trip to Paramounttown.* *1923:* *The Exciters.* *The World's Applause.* *Glimpses of the Moon.* *His Children's Children.* *1924:* *Sinners in Heaven.* *Daring Youth.* *Dangerous Money.* *Monsieur Beaucaire.* *Argentine Love.* *Heritage of the Desert.* *Unguarded Women.* *1925:* *The Manicure Girl.* *The Crowded Hour.* *Wild, Wild Susan.* *Lovers in Quarantine.* *Miss Bluebeard.* *1926:* *The Splendid Crime.* *Stranded in Paris.* *Mrs Brewster's Millions.* *The Palm Beach Girl.* *Volcano.* *The Campus Flirt.* *1927:* *She's a Sheik.* *A Kiss in a Taxi.* *Senorita.* *Swim, Girl, Swim.* *1928:* *Feel My Pulse.* *The Fifty-Fifty Girl.* *Take Me Home.* *What a Night!* *Hot News.* *1929:* *Rio Rita.* *1930:* *Alias French Gertie* (GB: *Love Finds a Way*). *Dixiana.* *Love Comes Along.*

Bebe Daniels appeared in a number of straighter roles in between her films with Harold Lloyd and her later fame as a radio comedienne. Here she is with Lloyd Hughes in *Love Comes Along*

Lawful Larceny. 1931: *Reaching for the Moon.* * *Screen Snapshots No. 7. My Past. The Maltese Falcon. Honor of the Family.* 1932: *Silver Dollar.* * *Radio Girl.* * *The Stolen Jools* (GB: *The Slippery Pearls*). 1933: * *Hollywood on Parade B-3. 42nd Street.* * *Hollywood on Parade B-7. Cocktail Hour. The Song You Gave Me. A Southern Maid.* 1934: *Counsellor at Law. Registered Nurse.* 1935: *Music is Magic.* 1936: *Not Wanted on Voyage* (US: *Trickery on the High Seas*). 1938: *The Return of Carol Deane.* 1941: *Hi Gang!* 1947: *The Fabulous Joe.* 1953: *Life with the Lyons* (US: *Family Affair*). 1954: *Adventures with the Lyons* (serial). *The Lyons in Paris.*

DAVIS, Joan
(Madonna Josephine 'Jo' Davis)
1907–1961
Angular, raw-boned, gawky, homely-looking, arrow-nosed, scrape-voiced American funny woman Joan Davis undoubtedly made the most of the 'gifts' that nature gave her. Even as a child she had started out as an acrobatic comic dancer, her deep-chestnut hair adding an unexpected touch of glamour to her rubber-limbed contortions. She was billed as 'the cyclonic Josephine Davis' and the whirlwind pace of her comedy never stopped from then on. While her limbs would flail around seemingly out of control Joan had in fact got her timing down to a fine art. One of her *pièces de résistance* involved her staggering around the stage balancing a huge pile of teetering plates which never quite fell. Charlie Chaplin (*qv*) was her comic hero but she didn't achieve her ambition of becoming a female Chaplin in films, not attaining the 'marquee value' to carry anything more than second-feature comedies on her own. It was television that made her a major star in the 1950s, when she was second only to Lucille Ball in the female clown ratings — before her hectic work- and lifestyles caught up with her. From 1934, she began to get featured spots in films, coming on as a goofy phone operator, secretary, messenger girl or dancer. Later she also took wisecracking roles as the heroine's best friend. Mostly, though, she was a man-hungry female that

men ran a mile from. The *New York Times* 'discovered' her in one of these early roles, describing her as 'a strange female curtain-climber with a trick of punching herself on the jaw and a curious resemblance to Olive Oyl in the Popeye cartoons'. 'The lady with the collapsible legs', as another critic called her, went on stealing scenes from the stars — even from Abbott and Costello (*qv*) in *Hold That Ghost* — before getting leading roles in minor Columbia comedies from 1941. She also had the lead in *Yokel Boy* for Republic the following year, in the role Republic star Judy Canova (*qv*) had made her own on Broadway. But Joan was unsuited to hillbilly humour and, at 69 minutes, the studio could hardly have been said to be doing justice to the original. The best of Joan's 1940s vehicles was not for Columbia but over at Universal, where she teamed with the equally rubber-faced Leon Errol (*qv*) in *She Gets Her Man* in 1945. This is a knock-about farce with almost as many laughs per frame as another slapstick feast of the period, Jack Carson's (*qv*). *The Good Humor Man.* Joan is the daughter of a famous detective and finds herself required almost single-handed to put an end to a city-wide crime wave triggered off by 'the blowpipe murderer'. The plot gives Joan the opportunity to fall foul of a record number of inanimate objects, as well as participate in several different sorts of chases and fights in which her acrobatic abilities and willingness to do any kind of physical comedy were given full rein. There were a couple of 'semi-A' features opposite Eddie Cantor (*qv*), *Show Business* and *If You Knew Susie*, but when the Columbia films hit an all-time low with *Harem Girl* (1952) Joan decided that, at 45, it was time to turn to situation comedy on television. The format of *I Married Joan* was not too dissimilar to that of *I Love Lucy*, which had debuted to enormous success the previous year. Joan was the well-meaning wife of a judge (Jim Backus, *qv*) whose every effort to help him turned to total disaster. She then had to retrieve or conceal the disaster in some way, involving her in some wildly comic escapades — like finding herself in a dryer at the local laundry. The show was a considerable success, although by 1954 Joan was complaining of the pressures of the demanding schedules of a weekly show of which she was not only the star but effectively executive producer. Her only daughter Beverly appeared in *I Married Joan* too, while Joan's ex-husband (her only marriage had ended in divorce after 17 years) wrote for the show. However, in 1955 Joan quit, pleading physical exhaustion. She went into semi-retirement at her Palm Springs and Bel Air homes, but was probably already showing signs of the heart weakness that was to kill her at 53, when she had a sudden heart attack and died within a day. Two years later Davis's mother, her daughter Beverly and her two grandchildren were all killed in a fire. 'I was never bothered by my lack of glamour', Joan said in her

early days. 'I know I'll last longer than the rest.'

1935: * *Way Up Thar. Millions in the Air.* 1936: *Bunker Bean* (GB: *His Majesty Bunker Bean*). 1937: *The Holy Terror. On the Avenue. Nancy Steele is Missing. The Great Hospital Mystery. Time Out for Romance. Thin Ice* (GB: *Lovely to Look At*). *Life Begins in College* (GB: *The Joy Parade*). *Love and Hisses. Angel's Holiday. You Can't Have Everything. Wake Up and Live. Sing and Be Happy.* 1938: *Hold That Co-Ed* (GB: *Hold That Girl*). *Tail Spin. Sally, Irene and Mary. Josette. My Lucky Star. Just Around the Corner.* 1939: *Day-Time Wife. Too Busy to Work.* 1940: *Free, Blonde and 21. Sailor's Lady. Manhattan Heartbeat.* 1941: *Sun Valley Serenade. Hold That Ghost. Two Latins from Manhattan. For Beauty's Sake.* 1942: *Yokel Boy* (GB: *Hitting the Headlines*). *Sweetheart of the Fleet.* 1943: *He's My Guy. Two Senoritas from Chicago. Around the World.* 1944: *Beautiful But Broke. Show Business. Kansas City Kitty.* 1945: *George White's Scandals. She Gets Her Man.* 1946: *She Wrote the Book.* 1948: *If You Knew Susie.* 1949: *Make Mine Laughs. The Traveling Saleswoman.* 1950: *Love That Brute.* 1951: *The Groom Wore Spurs.* 1952: *Harem Girl.*

DE FUNÈS, Louis
(Carlos L. de F. Galarza) 1908–1983
A twitchy, rat-like man of short stature, immense energy, fiery temper and flashing eyes, Louis de Funès vied with Fernandel (*qv*) for the position of France's top comedian in the 1950s and 1960s. Both made something of an international name for themselves and, while Fernandel was more beloved, de Funès could always point to the fact that 10 of the 50 best-grossing French films between 1955 and 1975 starred himself. Born in France of Portuguese parentage, de Funès did a number of casual jobs before beginning his career proper as a designer and decorator. After World War Two he changed his mind and took an acting course at the René Simon School. When his funds ran out before he had completed the course, de Funès left the school and, wanting to stay in show business, tried making a living as a bar-room pianist.

Louis de Funès finds that trying to deal with modern contraptions has led to disaster in *The Mad Adventures of 'Rabbi' Jacob*

He had already obtained a few small roles in films, and was to obtain more through the offices of actor Daniel Gelin, a friend from acting school. De Funès also made the acquaintance of Fernandel, who gave him roles in some of his comedies, most notably his international success *The Sheep Has Five Legs*. 'While I was still unknown', de Funès recalled later, 'I tried to colour by details, mimes and gestures, the little parts which I was given. That's how I developed my art of comedy, which I thought was always at its best without words.' It was ten years before de Funès was given comedy vehicles of his own, but his popularity quickly gained ground as a kind of gallic Groucho Marx (*qv*), with shifty look, loping walk and ferret-like air. He perfected a rapid blinking and twitching of the eyes and face, which could convey doubt, cunning, lechery, ignorance or annoyance. A French journalist of the 1950s found that 'to watch him work is a fascinating experience. On set, his concentration is absolute. He tries things out, starts again, goes off like a rocket, repeats himself, stops dead. He's a complete show in himself and the production team has a hard job trying to keep a straight face.' In British and American markets hungry for double-feature material during this decade, de Funès found his comedies, like those of Fernandel, being shown outside France with some success. He made English-speaking audiences laugh as: a black-market butcher in *Pig Across Paris/Three Bags Full*; and a village poacher outwitting authorities in *Vive Monsieur Blaireau*. Also popular around this

time were *Lock Up the Spoons* and *A Hair in the Soup/Crazy in the Noodle*. World-wide success evaded de Funès for the next few years but he regained his standing with the 'gendarme comedies', the first of which appeared in 1964 (he played a bullying but big-hearted and gullible gendarme), which were interspersed with such other international hits as *The Sucker* and *The Mad Adventures of 'Rabbi' Jacob*. Success had come late to de Funès, but he made up for it by maintaining a hectic schedule into the 1970s, until a heart attack forced him to slow down. He managed another popular 'gendarme' comedy, the sixth, before ill-health finally ended his film career at 72. He enjoyed a few years' retirement busying himself at his favourite pastime. As he once said, 'If I were not an actor, I would have loved to have been a gardener.'

1945: La tentation de Barloizon. 1946: Six heures à perdre. Dernier refuge. Antoine et Antoinette. 1947: Croiseau pour l'inconnu. 1948: Du Gueslin. Millionaires d'un jour. 1949: Pas de weekend pour notre amour. Un certain monsieur. Je n'aime que toi. Vient de paraître. Ademai au poste frontière. Au revoir, M. Grock. Rendez-vous avec la chance. Mission à Tanger. 1950: Le roi du bla-bla-bla. Boniface somnambule (GB: The Sleepwalker). Bibi Fricotin. L'amant de paille. La rue sans loi. Folie douce. La rose rouge. 1951: Pas de vacances pour M. le maire. Ma femme est formidable. Ils etaient cinq. Boîte à vendre. Le poison. Les joueurs. Champions junior. M. Leguignon lampist. Les sept péchés capitaux (GB and US: The Seven Deadly Sins). Le dindon. Agence matrimoniale. Un amour de parapluie. 1952: L'amour n'est pas un péché. Le huitième art et la manière. Monsieur Taxi. J'ai été trois fois. Moineaux de Paris. La fugue de M. Perle. Légère et court vêtue. Elle et moi. Au diable la vertu. La vie d'un honnête homme (US: The Virtuous Scoundrel). 1953: Dortoir les grandes. Le vire. L'étrange désire de M. Bard. Mon frangin du Sénégal. Capitaine Pantoufle. Le blé en herbe (GB: Ripening Seed. US: The Game of Love). Le chevalier de la nuit. Mam'zelle Nitouche (GB: Oh, No, Mam'zelle). Tourments. Innocents in Paris. Le secret d'Hélène Marimon. Faites-moi confiance. Les compagnes de la nuit. Les corsaires du Bois de Boulogne. Les hommes ne pensent qu'à ça. 1954: Les Impures. Huis clos. Les pépées font la loi. Les intrigantes. Napoléon. Frou-Frou. Poisson d'avril. La reine Margot. La mouton a cinq pattes (GB and US: The Sheep Has Five Legs). Ah! Les belles bacchantes (GB and US: Peek-a-Boo). Scènes du ménage. Escalier de service. Papa, Mama, the Maid and I. 1955: L'impossible M. Pipelet. Geschichtes eines Fotomodells. La bande à Papa. Papa, Mama, My Wife and I. Les hussards. Si Paris nous était conté. Bébés à gogos. La loi des rues. 1956: Courte tête. La traversée de Paris (GB: Pig Across Paris, US: Three Bags Full). Les truands (GB: Lock Up the Spoons). 1957: Ni vu, ni connu (GB: Vive Monsieur Blaireau). Comme un cheveu sur la soupe (GB: A Hair in the Soup. US: Crazy in the Noodle). 1958: Taxi, roulotte et corrida (GB: Taxi). La vie à deux. 1959: Fripouillards et cie. A pied, à cheval et en spoutnik (GB: Hold Tight for the Satellite. US: A Dog, a Mouse and a Sputnik). Mon pote le gitan. Certains l'aiment froide. Toto à Madrid. 1960: Les tortillards. Candide. La capitaine Fracasse. Dans l'eau qui fait des bulles. 1961: La belle americaine. Le crime ne paie pas. Le diable et les dix commandements (GB and US: The Devil and the 10 Commandments). La vendetta. Carambolages. Les veinards. Le gentleman d'Epsom/Les grands seigneurs. Nous irons à Deauville. Un clair de lune à mauberge. 1963: Pouic-Pouic. Faites sauter la banque. 1964: Le gendarme de Saint-Tropez. Fantômas. Une souris chez les hommes. 1965: Le corniaud (GB and US: The Sucker). Fantômas se déchaîne (GB: Fantomas Strikes Back). Les bons vivants. A Gendarme in New York. 1966: La grande vadrouille (GB and US: Don't Look Now, We're Being Shot At!). Fantômas contre Scotland Yard. 1967: Les grandes vacances. Le gendarme et les gendarmettes (GB, as The Gendarme Wore Skirts). US: How to Be an Honest Cop). Le grand restaurant. Oscar. Le petit baigneur. 1968: Le gendarme se marie. Le tatoué. 1969: Hibernatus. 1970: L'homme-orchestre. Le gendarme en balade. Sur un arbre perché. 1971: La folie des grandeurs (GB: Delusions of Grandeur). Jo (US: The Gazebo). 1972: Die Dummen streiche der Reichen. 1973: Les aventures de Rabbi Jacob (GB and US: The Mad Adventures of 'Rabbi' Jacob). 1975: L'aile ou la cuisse. 1976: Crocodile. 1977: La zizanie. 1978: Le gendarme et les extra-terrestres (GB: TV, as The Spaceman of St Tropez). 1980: L'avare.

DeLUISE, Dom 1933–

An American character star who specialises in outrageous grotesques. Balding, plump and chubby-cheeked, he has been popping up in films as a gleeful comic demon for nearly 30 years. Brooklyn-born, DeLuise began his career as a straight actor but soon began to make a comic mark on television. From the late 1950s he was seen on the long-running *Garry Moore Show* as Dominick the Great, a ham-fisted conjuror. His first major film chance came in Frank Tashlin's *The Glass Bottom Boat*, as a spy called Julius, sharing with the star, Doris Day, a scene of escalating silliness in which he steps into a huge cake, and they both end up with one foot in the same metal bucket. The Hollywood of 30 years before would, from there on in, have used DeLuise in cameos at the rate of about one film a month. Instead, he continued to be seen mainly on television, including a short run as the star of his own show in 1968, co-starring with his comedy actress wife Carol Arthur. The 1970s began a long association with producer/star Mel Brooks and with Brooks's one-time protegé Gene Wilder (both *qv*). For one or the other, DeLuise played juicy roles in *The Twelve Chairs*, *Blazing Saddles*, *Silent Movie*, *The World's Greatest Lover* and *History of the World Part I*, culminating in a rather over-enthusiastic drag act in Wilder's *Haunted Honeymoon*. There were also several comedies opposite Burt Reynolds, which allowed both stars to ham it up, and DeLuise's debut as star and director with *Hot Stuff*. A not unamusing little number about Miami cops fencing stolen goods, it was promising enough to suggest that some of Brooks' and Wilder's later comedies might have been funnier (and more human) if DeLuise had directed them rather than their stars. In recent times DeLuise's giggling, gurgling tones have been used in several major cartoon features, in which his tendency to go over the top in characterisation has a happier impact than in live-action comedy.

1963: Diary of a Bachelor. 1964: Fail Safe. The Ordeal of Thomas Moon (unreleased). 1966: The Glass Bottom Boat. The Busy Body. 1968: What's So Bad About Feeling Good? The Twelve Chairs. 1970: Norwood. 1971: Who Is Harry Kellerman and Why is He Saying These Terrible Things About Me? 1972: Every Little Crook and Nanny. Evil Roy Slade (TV). 1974: Only with Married Men (TV). Blazing Saddles. 1975: The Adventure of Sherlock Holmes' Smarter Brother. 1976: Silent Movie. 1977: The World's Greatest Lover. Sextette. 1978: The Cheap Detective. The End. 1979: The Muppet Movie. Hot Stuff (and directed). The Last Married Couple in America. Diary of a Young Comic (TV). 1980: Wholly Moses! Smokey and the Bandit II (GB: Smokey and the Bandit Ride Again). The Cannonball Run. Fatso. 1981: History of the World Part I. 1982: The Secret of NIMH (voice only). The Best Little Whorehouse in Texas. 1983: Cannonball Run II. Happy (TV). 1984: Johnny Dangerously. 1986: Haunted Honeymoon. An American Tail (voice only). 1987: Ben, Bonzo, Mo and Big Bad Joe. My African Adventure. Spaceballs (voice only). Un tassinaro in New York/Italian Taxi Driver. Going Bananas. 1988: Oliver & Company (voice only). All Dogs Go to Heaven (voice only). 1989: Loose Cannons. 1990: The Princess and the Dwarf. Happy Ever After (voice only). 1991: Autobahn (US: Trabbi Goes to Hollywood). An American Tail: Fievel Goest West (voice only). Almost Pregnant.

DeVITO, Danny 1944–

Hollywood's most unlikely superstar funny-man of the late 1980s, as well as its smallest, DeVito's ever-present sense of humour leads him to see the funny side of things and disregard the long struggle to reach the top. 'Let's face it', he told one writer, 'the competition is pretty flimsy for roles around five feet.' Such effervescent qualities kept DeVito going through the lean years when it looked as though a career of bit parts and supporting roles would be the best he could manage. But, now almost bald, with homely looks and a figure that would surely float over Victoria Falls, DeVito has always been a non-stop bundle of mesmeric energy. As a kid in 1950s New Jersey the young DeVito hung out in cinemas when he wasn't in his father's pool parlour with his pals, performing what they called 'street theatre'. 'My own father threw me out', DeVito recalled, 'on account of we were driving the customers away instead of pulling 'em in.' After acting in school plays, including a 'real sincere' portrait of St Francis of Assisi, DeVito studied at the American Academy of Dramatic Arts. Unable to get work following graduation, DeVito brought a ticket to Hollywood, where 'I was sure chic people gathered round the pool were just waiting for a five-foot Italian to walk into their lives. Guess what? I was wrong.' No film or TV offers were forthcoming and two more years of unemployment drove him back to New York. Here he did get some stage work and struck up a friendship with another young actor, Michael Douglas, that was to have an important effect on his career. He moved in with actress Rhea Perlman (1949–   ) – they married in 1981 – and got a small part in a film, a turkey called *Lady Liberty*, in 1971, which he actually went to Italy to make. 'It was a "tiny" role', he tells you. 'No really, it was.' Just as well. Through the Douglas family collection he also got a part in Michael's father Kirk Douglas's *Scalawag* in 1973, but it was another bomb. His supporting role in the stage version of *One Flew Over the Cuckoo's Nest* was the one that really shaped his future. Michael Douglas came to see his performance and insisted that DeVito re-create the role of Martini in the forthcoming film version that Douglas was producing. Regular movie employment began to come DeVito's way, mostly in abrasive, blue-collar roles that called for lots of bad language. As a comic actor, though, he made his biggest strides in a long-running TV series *Taxi*, which began in 1978 and cast him as Louis, a little Hitler of a dispatcher. The series ran for five years and after it was over DeVito completed his climb to the top as a movie funny-man when he burst into the spotlight as the ham-fisted but lovable crook Ralph in Michael Douglas's *Romancing the Stone* and *The Jewel of the Nile*. Then Disney's successful Touchstone Pictures arm put the seal on DeVito's success by giving him leads in *Ruthless People* and *Tin Men*, both as relentless, whirling, egocentric rough diamonds firing on all cylinders. DeVito had directed a couple of shorts and a TV movie in his earlier days, but his new-found clout gave him a chance to direct two major black comedies in the late 1980s. *Throw Momma from the Train* and *The War of the Roses*, in both of which he also played principal roles. 'I guess', says DeVito, 'that my idea of doing a movie in Hollywood is not exactly the same as everybody else's. I'm interested in moving the camera, and I love figuring out scenes with other actors to find some lower, darker, hidden, but still funny side of the characters. That's what makes it fun.' In front of the camera, the DeVito style of visual comedy – increasing frenzy as events gang up unfairly against him – wasn't seen again for a couple of years, until he made *Other People's Money* in 1991. Then he was cast as the Penguin in Warners' second *Batman* film.

1969: *The Sterile Cuckoo* (GB: *Pookie*). 1970: *Dreams of Glass*. 1971: *La mortadella/Lady Liberty*. 1973: *Scalawag. Hurry Up, Or I'll Be 30*. 1975: *One Flew Over the Cuckoo's Nest.* *† *Minestrone*. 1976: *The Van. Car Wash*. 1977: * † *The Sound Sleeper. The World's Greatest Lover*. 1978: *Goin' South*. 1979: *Valentine* (TV). 1981: *Going Ape*. 1983: *Terms of Endearment*. 1984: *Romancing the Stone.* † *The Ratings Game* (TV). *Johnny Dangerously*. 1985: *The Jewel of the Nile. Head Office*. 1986: *Ruthless People. Wise Guys*. 1987: *Tin Men.* † *Throw Momma from the Train*. 1988: *Twins*. 1989: † *The War of the Roses*. 1991: *Other People's Money. Jack the Bear*. 1992: † *Hoffa. Batman Returns*.

† Also directed

DE WOLFE, Billy
(William Jones) 1907–1974

Tall, dark, faintly apologetic American comedian, who specialised on stage in female impersonation and miming escalating disasters, but was usually seen in films as prissy and pious suitors who lost the girl to the hero. He had gappy teeth, a long-lipped leer, and a moustache once described by columnist Walter Winchell as resembling a seagull in flight. Far too few films made room for his amusing antics. Born in Massachusetts, he was taken back to Wales by his Welsh parents for the next nine years, before they returned to Massachusetts to become American citizens. At 18 Billy was hired as a dancer, taking his stage name from that of the manager at his first theatre. Later, he took a partner and played in a dancing act around vaudeville. It was during a five-year stay in England in the 1930s, though, that he perfected the eccentric dancing and comedy act that was to make him a star. During these routines De Wolfe would have his audiences in stitches doing an impression of trying to get in and out of a girdle, or presenting the entire staff of a cheap nightclub, from head waiter to chorus girl. He was soon much in demand at top clubs across the country. Films latched on to De Wolfe late. He was well into his thirties and doing wartime service with the US Navy before he made a couple of films for Paramount, who signed him up for more. *Blue*

Skies, one of the first, contains his classic 'Mrs Murgatroyd' skit, in which he takes off a middle-aged housewife with a heavy load of shopping, who stops at a cocktail bar to take the weight off her feet, and has a few snorts of Scotch to help her on her way. De Wolfe often used the character on stage, always calling her Mrs Murgatroyd. In between club work, De Wolfe popped back and forth to Paramount, playing the same role, Joan Caulfield's easily-flustered would-be beau Albert Kummer in *Dear Ruth* and *Dear Wife*, and appearing in a second sequel (without Caulfield), *Dear Brat*. Films soon petered out but De Wolfe remained a force to be reckoned with in clubs and variety halls. In the mid 1950s he appeared at the Palladium in London, doing his Mrs Murgatroyd sketch. In 1957 he was a member of the cast of the very last Ziegfeld Follies. He died from lung cancer at 67, leaving nearly a quarter of a million dollars – but no survivors to inherit it.

1943: *Dixie*. 1944: *Miss Susie Slagle's* (released 1946). 1945: *Duffy's Tavern*. 1946: *Blue Skies. Our Hearts Were Growing Up*. 1947: *The Perils of Pauline. Dear Ruth. Variety Girl*. 1948: *Isn't It Romantic?* 1949: *Dear Wife*. 1950: *Tea for Two*. 1951: *Dear Brat. Lullaby of Broadway*. 1953: *Call Me Madam*. 1965: *Billie*. 1973: *The World's Greatest Athlete*.

DILLER, Phyllis
(née Driver) 1917–

It was never likely that the witch-like American zany Phyllis Diller could succeed in the movies for very long. The essence of her appeal on stage lay in her self-deprecating remarks and her approach to telling a story, which she would cap with several short punch-lines, piled one on top of the other. Like other madcap, all-stops-out comediennes, such as Martha Raye (*qv*), Phyllis was always welcome in cameo roles but had an outsize personality that could hardly be squeezed into a series of different characters. Her personal success story, though, is extraordinary. Born in Ohio to parents who hoped she would do something in music, Phyllis quit her final course two months before she was to take a music

degree, in order to marry Sherwood Diller. The Dillers had five children before Phyllis launched her show business career, beginning by entertaining in women's clubs, PTA and Red Cross shows and military bases while still working as a continuity writer for a radio station. From 1955, she quit other jobs, and began performing at nightclubs, joking, singing and playing piano or zither. She started piling up huge notebooks full of jokes, and variations on jokes. She invented characters like her husband Fang (he only had one tooth), her mother-in-law Moby Dick, her sister-in-law Captain Bligh and her neighbour Mrs Clean. Dressed in outrageous costumes and a blonde fright wig, and flourishing a bejewelled cigarette holder (a great irony; Diller is a vigorous anti-smoking campaigner in real life), she regaled her audiences with such jokes as 'I went bathing nude on the beach the other day. It took me 20 minutes to get arrested.' She formed a friendship with her idol Bob Hope (*qv*) and he helped her make a number of attempts to get a screen career started. But the great man was past his prime and the films were critical flops and only marginal money-makers. Nor did she have much luck with her own vehicle, *Did You Hear the One About the Traveling Saleslady?* and actually did her best film work in a straight role as a nagging wife in *The Adding Machine*. Television ventures were only marginally more successful and Diller remained at her best knocking them in the aisles at night spots; once you start laughing at the lady, it's difficult to stop. She divorced her first husband in 1965 and married singer Warde Donovan.

1961: *Splendor in the Grass*. 1965: *The Fat Spy*. 1966: * *Hollywood Star Spangled Revue. Boy, Did I Get a Wrong Number*. 1967: *Eight on the Lam* (GB: *Eight on the Run*). *Mad Monster Party* (voice only). 1968: *The Private Navy of Sergeant O'Farrell. Did You Hear the One About the Traveling Saleslady?* 1969: *The Adding Machine*. 1970: *Love American Style* (TV). 1982: *Pink Motel* (GB: *Motel*). 1988: *Dr Hackenstein*. 1990: *The Boneyard. The Nutcracker* (voice only). *Happily Ever After* (voice only). 1991: *Pucker Up and Bark Like a Dog. Wisecracks*. 1992: *The Perfect Man*.

DRAKE, Charlie
(Charles Springall) 1925–

Diminutive (5 ft 1 in), whirlwind British comedian with a frizz of wild fair hair and light, plaintive voice. From humble beginnings and an early career as a children's entertainer, Drake sprang to prominence in the late 1950s as some kind of demon imp who could wreck the safest of occasions. He used to preface his introductions with a yelp of 'Hello, my darlings'. Born in the centre of London, where for many years he had a flat overlooking Leicester Square, Drake was singing for the family supper at the age of eight, and gained experience with his trapeze artist father soon afterwards. At 14 he left

school and became an electrician's mate. 'On my first day', he recalled, 'I went into this room, and stuck a screwdriver right through the wallpaper. Paper, plaster and about 50 gallons of water fell on me. It was a burst pipe, and I must admit I've been getting laughs out of water gags ever since. That's how I started being a comic, I suppose. I'd be asked to knock a nail in the wall and I'd end up wrecking the room. I'd be asked to fix a fuse and half of the Elephant and Castle would be blacked out.' These early experiences were not to go to waste, even though Drake was plagued by accidents and disasters for the rest of his professional life. After wartime service with the RAF, he set about a show business career. Bookings on radio and in variety halls were sparse for the next three years – at one time he resorted to driving a tractor for a living. Then he ran into solid, 6 ft 6 in Jack Edwardes, a Margate-born comic who had been struggling for a similar period. The new team got their first job on TV in 1950, and became favourites on BBC children's variety shows. By 1955 they had invented the characters of Mick and Montmorency, vaguely based on Laurel and Hardy. They had bowler hats and overalls and were the world's worst at whatever they were hired to do. In turn, they were part of programmes called *Jobstoppers*, *Jolly Good Time* and *Mick and Montmorency*. The physical contrast of the two men, coupled with their little-devil mischief and simple slapstick had made them the top children's attraction on TV by 1958, when Drake decided to resume a solo career. To his surprise, he quickly found himself a national figure. Ratings for his TV show were very high, and he broke into films as the star of a series of comedies from Associated-British that included the painful *Sands of the Desert* and *Petticoat Pirates* and the rather better *The Cracksman*. In the last of these three, Charlie had a real character to play in the shape of a gullible master locksmith who gets into all sorts of trouble, including prison, because he can't resist picking a challenging lock. The best scene in the film was pure silent comedy, with Charlie, out to get some bird seed for his cell mate's budgerigars, picking practically every lock in the prison, ending with a long line of convicts trailing behind him in the hope that he'll lead them to freedom. Better things should have followed. Instead, Drake returned to television with his series *The Worker*, a slightly more sophisticated variant on his Montmorency character. The series, beginning in 1965, was a success but Drake began having accidents doing stunts and several times ended up in hospital. A further film, *Mister Ten Per Cent*, was a dispiriting flop. He decided to quit comedy in 1968 but returned after a period of 'retirement' to do another series of *The Charlie Drake Show* on TV. A few years later, however, the little man with the falsetto voice took the plunge into straight acting. Later still, he admitted he had lost all the money he earned as a comic through gambling. 'Now', he said in the late 1980s, 'I live a very different life but I'm happy. I don't gamble any more. When you've gambled at the rate I did, there's not much of a thrill in having a fiver each way.' He has given richly-embroidered portrayals in some classic serials on TV and in 1991 cropped up in the leading role of a TV film, *Filipina Love Girls*, in a rascally role far removed from the innocent image of his slapstick days.

1954: The Golden Link. 1960: Sands of the Desert. 1961: Petticoat Pirates. 1963: The Cracksman. 1967: Mister Ten Per Cent. 1974: Professor Popper's Problem (serial). 1991: Filipina Love Girls (TV).

DRESSLER, Marie
(Leila Koerber) 1869–1934
Hulking Canadian-born Hollywood comedienne who despite a visage that could easily be made fearsome could also be quite a charmer when she chose. After an extremely chequered career she made a sensational comeback in her sixties to become the world's number one box-office star for the last four years of her life. Despite her father's objections, the young Marie – she took her stage name from a distant dead relative – had joined a small-time stock company at 14. She also sang in grand opera before her Broadway debut in 1892 and later sang raucous songs in vaudeville. She was a star playing heavyweight harridans by her mid forties and was invited to Hollywood in 1914 to do a feature-length farce based on one of her stage successes. The film, *Tillie's Punctured Romance*, was a great success, especially as it teamed Marie with the popular Charlie Chaplin and Mabel Normand (both *qv*). But subsequent two-reelers did less well, and she was black-balled out of films – and almost out of show business – after she became involved in the 1917 strike that led to the formation of Actors' Equity. She worked in France and did another Broadway show in 1923, but was out of work in 1926 and thinking of taking a job outside acting when an old friend, script-writer Frances Marion, came to her rescue with a screenplay written especially for Marie, *The Callahans and the Murphys*. The film teamed her with pawky, crow-voiced, buck-toothed Polly Moran (*qv*), a successful vaudeville comedienne. They played two frowzy, gin-swilling dames, the film's alcoholic content running it into trouble with anti-drink societies and causing its eventual withdrawal. But Marie stayed in Hollywood, played some good supporting roles and later made five more popular comedies with Moran, *Bringing Up Father*, *Politics*, *Reducing*, *Caught Short* and *Prosperity*. The film that took her back to the top was *Anna Christie* in which, as the waterfront slattern Marthy, she even stole scenes from Greta Garbo making her talkie debut. M-G-M now prepared star vehicles for her, not only opposite Moran but, more importantly, in a film called *Min and Bill*, opposite the equally raucous and lovable Wallace Beery (*qv*). Beery played a dockside down-and-out, Marie the tough-shelled proprietress of a waterfront hotel. Their salty exchanges radiated real warmth and humour and there was tragedy in the story, too, when Marie is forced to kill the vicious mother of the young girl she has brought up as her own. Dressler took an Oscar as best actress for the film and suddenly the studio was billing the barrel-shaped old vaudevillian as 'the world's greatest actress'. She and Beery sparred against each other again in *Tugboat Annie*, with Marie as the salty skipper and Beery as her indolent husband. She also made *Dinner at Eight*, in which she had the famous final exchange with brassy Jean Harlow who complains about machinery taking over every profession. Marie does a studied double-take and says: 'My dear, that is something you need never worry about'. She became enormously popular with the studio and everyone was devastated in 1934 when she learned she was dying from cancer. She just managed to complete her autobiography (which was published posthumously): *The Life Story of an Ugly Duckling*.

*1914: Tillie's Punctured Romance. 1915: * Tillie's Tomato Surprise. 1916: * Tillie's Day Off. * Tillie's Divorce Case. * Tillie's Love Affair. * Elopement. * Night Out. 1917: * Tillie Wakes Up. * The Scrublady. 1918: * The*

Rough waters of true love are soon smoothed over when rambunctious Annie (Marie Dressler) takes the helm of the tugboat *Narcissus* in *Tugboat Annie*

Even such seasoned stagers as Jimmy Durante (right) and fellow-comedian El Brendel (*qv*) have to work hard not to be upstaged by Shirley Temple in *Little Miss Broadway*

Itching to wander. Tom Ewell is handed a little friendly advice from unkempt Robert Strauss on how to deal with wandering women in *The Seven-Year Itch*

Fancy meeting you here... Gracie Fields and John Loder don some very fancy dress for one of their stage numbers in *Queen of Hearts*

*Agonies of Agnes. * Fired! * The Cross Red Nurse. 1926: The Joy Girl. 1927: The Callahans and the Murphys. Breakfast at Sunrise. 1928: The Patsy (GB: The Politic Flapper). Bringing Up Father. 1929: The Vagabond Lover. * Dangerous Females. The Divine Lady. Hollywood Revue of 1929. 1930: Chasing Rainbows. The Girl Said No. One Romantic Night. Let Us Be Gay. Caught Short. Anna Christie. Min and Bill. * The Voice of Hollywood. The Swan. The March of Time. Call of the Flesh. Derelict. 1931: Reducing. Politics. 1932: Prosperity. Emma. * Jackie Cooper's Christmas (GB: The Christmas Party). 1933: Tugboat Annie. Dinner at Eight. The Late Christopher Bean. 1934: * Hollywood on Parade No. 13.*

DUMONT, Margaret
(Daisy Baker) 1889–1965
Few character comediennes have played people with such stuffy, faintly silly names as the tall, stately Margaret Dumont, whose characters were certainly among the most easily flattered in films (mainly by a succession of very eccentric comedians headed by Groucho Marx, *qv*). Sybilla Crum, Jasmine Bell-Rivington, Emily Upjohn, Mrs Hemoglobin, Cecilia Croxton-Lynch, Florence Faulkener, Mrs Rittenhouse and many more were all played by the lady whose high-society demeanour belied her Brooklyn background. Originally trained as a light opera singer, she made her Broadway debut in 1908. There was a tour of Europe, an isolated silent film and more plays and musical revues before she was accepted for a part in the second big Marx Brothers stage comedy hit *The Cocoanuts* in 1925. 'I was told', she said later, 'that they wanted an actress with dignity and poise.' She didn't realise then that the dignity would be constantly deflated and the poise quickly undermined. 'After three weeks as Groucho's leading lady', she remembered, 'I nearly had a nervous breakdown.' But she soon developed a great affection for the brothers, never minded being the fall guy and sailed, stately as a galleon, through seven of their films. With arched eyebrows and lowered lids, she could be bemused and charmed at the same time, and expressed feigned out-

rage to perfection. Although she proved a perfect partner for the Marx Brothers, her natural comic aplomb was such that she also worked easily with such disparate comedians as Jack Benny, Abbott and Costello, Laurel and Hardy, W. C. Fields, Wheeler and Woolsey, Red Skelton and Danny Kaye (all *qv*). As late as 1962 she was still presenting one of her distinctively named characters: Persephone Updike in *Zotz!* Groucho once said that Margaret Dumont was 'the same off stage as on – the austere, dignified, charming dowager duchess. She must like me – our friendship even survived me putting frogs in her bath during a stage show.' The lady who could always take it with a smile died from a heart attack in Hollywood at 75 – just a few days after making her final showbiz appearance, in a TV sketch with Groucho.

1917: A Tale of Two Cities. 1929: The Cocoanuts. 1930: Animal Crackers. 1931: The Girl Habit. 1933: Duck Soup. 1934: Gridiron Flash (GB: Luck of the Game). Kentucky Kernels (GB: Triple Trouble). Fifteen Wives (GB: The Man with the Electric Voice). 1935: After Office Hours. A Night at the Opera. Orchids to You. Rendezvous. 1936: Anything Goes. The Song and Dance Man. 1937: A Day at the Races. Wise Girl. Youth on Parole. High Flyers. The Life of the Party. 1938: Dramatic School. 1939: The Women. At the Circus/The Marx Brothers at the Circus. 1941: For Beauty's Sake. The Big Store. Never Give a Sucker an Even Break. 1942: Born to Sing. About Face. Rhythm Parade. Sing Your Worries Away. 1943:

The Dancing Masters. 1944: † Tales of Manhattan. Seven Days Ashore. Up in Arms. Bathing Beauty. 1945: Sunset in El Dorado. Billy Rose's Diamond Horseshoe (GB: Diamond Horseshoe). The Horn Blows at Midnight. 1946: Little Giant (GB: On the Carpet). Susie Steps Out. 1952: Three for Bedroom C. Stop, You're Killing Me. 1956: Shake, Rattle and Rock. 1958: Auntie Mame. 1962: Zotz! 1964: What a Way to Go!

† Scene deleted from final release print.

DURANTE, Jimmy 1893–1980
Energetic, piano-playing, frizz-haired, wild-eyed little New Yorker whose gravel voice and nose like a plum tomato contributed greatly to a highly individual personality. Though he struggled to carry film comedies by himself, he brightened up many more of them as a co-star or guest performer. He was nicknamed 'Schnozzle' on account of his nose, which he himself referred to as 'de big beak' and which never ceased to bother him, even when it was helping him to earn a handsome living. Not that he didn't milk it for every laugh that was going. When someone told him that something was 'right under his nose' Durante's reply was invariably: 'Don't be indefinite!' The nose was insured with Lloyds of London for $1 million. The son of a travelling carnival man, Durante demonstrated an early talent for the piano, and was playing ragtime in Bowery nightclubs at 16. Later he added foot-tapping comic songs, performed at the piano, to his repertoire. Teaming up with two other vaudevillians, Lou Clayton and Eddie

Jimmy Durante finds the lost chord. George M. Cohan stands for president. Claudette Colbert just takes it easy in *The Phantom President*

Jackson, he soon became a name and opened his own Manhattan club when he was 30. By 1929 Durante had made Broadway, following at least one joke in every performance with one of his favourite catch-phrases: 'I've got a million of 'em.' At other times, beaming and raising eyes to the skies, he would complain that 'Everybody wants to get into the act.' His closing line was normally: 'Good night Mrs Calabash – wherever you are.' Poor material robbed Durante of major stardom in the 1930s, revealing his inability to carry moderate pictures by himself. Given the opportunity, though, he frequently stole the limelight from those billed above him. He kept on cropping up, enlivening often dull M-G-M musicals with one of his novelty songs, the most popular being *Inka Dink a Dink* and *I'm the Guy Who Found the Lost Chord*. In nightclubs he remained as energetic and popular as ever, cocking a snook at everything and everybody in top hat, white tie and tails, and working well into his seventies. There were a million good-looking guys in the world, he told his audiences, but only one Durante. He was right.

*1930: Roadhouse Nights. 1931: The Cuban Love Song. The New Adventures of Get-Rich-Quick Wallingford. 1932: The Wet Parade. The Passionate Plumber. Speak Easily. * Hollywood on Parade B-3. The Phantom President. Blondie of the Follies. 1933: Hell Below. What! No Beer? Meet the Baron. Broadway to Hollywood (GB: Ring Up the Curtain). 1934: George White's Scandals. She Learned About Sailors. Hollywood Party. Strictly Dynamite. Palooka (GB: The Great Schnozzle). Student Tour. Carnival. 1936: Land without Music (US: Forbidden Music). 1938: Start Cheering. Little Miss Broadway. Sally, Irene and Mary. 1940: Melody Ranch. You're in the Army Now. The Man Who Came to Dinner. 1944: Two Girls and a Sailor. Music for Millions. 1946: Two Sisters from Boston. 1947: It Happened in Brooklyn. This Time for Keeps. 1948: On an Island with You. 1950: The Milkman. The Great Rupert. 1957: Beau James. 1960: Pepe. 1961: Il giudizio universale (US: The Last Judgment). 1962: Billy Rose's Jumbo (GB: Jumbo). 1963: It's a Mad, Mad, Mad, Mad World.*

EDWARDS, 'Professor' Jimmy
1920–1988

A big, bluff, blustering British comedian, with white smile beneath a huge handlebar moustache, a hectoring manner, thinning brown hair and a large, round face. A huge star on radio, he was never *quite* the same attraction in films and TV. After wartime service with the Royal Air Force, during which he was awarded the Distinguished Flying Cross, Edwards became a stand-up comedian at London's Windmill Theatre. He also played the trombone in his act, which saw the beginnings of his long series of catch-phrases, all delivered in fruitily well-educated tones which typified the public's view of the wartime airman. 'Greetings, gentlefolk', which introduced his act, and 'Wake up at the back there', delivered in his character of an aggressive schoolmaster, were two of the earliest. Around this time he also made his film debut as the leading character, a radio commentator, in *Trouble in the Air*, a crude low-budget comedy. But radio would occupy his attention over the next few years. He was one of the three stars (the others were both Australians – Dick Bentley and Joy Nichols) of a wittily-written, fast-moving half-hour radio show called *Take It from Here*, which became the successor to ITMA as Britain's most popular programme. His most famous character came as the series progressed through its 12-year (1948–60) run. It was the working-class Pa Glum, forever bursting in on his unfortunate son Ron (Bentley) and girlfriend Eth (June Whitfield, who had by this time taken over as the show's comedienne) just as they were having a bit of slap and tickle. Before the show had ended, Edwards had diversified into television, taking his schoolmaster character into a series called *Whack-O!* He played Professor Edwards, head of a school supposedly for 'the sons of gentlefolk'. He browbeat his staff to disguise his own ignorance, and his accountant was more likely to be turf than chartered. The cast made a film of the series, *Bottoms Up!*, and it later became a radio programme. Meanwhile, on the film front, Edwards was less consistent. *Murder at the Windmill* took him back to his old stamping ground, but he had to wait until

1952 for his next starring role, in the poorly received *Treasure Hunt*. Films tried to straitjacket him into character roles instead of letting him be more or less himself at the centre of things: thus his mission as one of Jerome K. Jerome's *Three Men in a Boat* was doomed from the outset. Apart from *Bottoms Up!*, Edwards' most successful film was perhaps 1961's *Nearly a Nasty Accident*. He was for once astutely cast as an RAF group-captain driven to exasperation and beyond by the antics of an accident-prone airman, played by Kenneth Connor (*qv*). The rest of Edwards' film career was made up of unsatisfactory scraps and snaps. But by this time he had already become entrenched in the long-running radio panel game *Does the Team Think?* which he also devised and in which he headed a team of four comedians making mincemeat of questions from the audience which were rarely serious. It ran from 1957 to 1976. Revelations of Edwards' bisexuality created some unsavoury headlines in the later years of his life, but the disclosure made little impact on his popularity. He had a West End theatre hit in harness with Eric Sykes (*qv*) in *Big Bad Mouse*, touring the provinces with various versions of the farce (replete with Edwards ad libs which often reduced the plot to confusion) for several seasons thereafter. He died from bronchial pneumonia.

*1948: Trouble in the Air. 1949: Murder at the Windmill (US: Murder at the Burlesque). Helter Skelter. 1952: Treasure Hunt. * Sport and Speed. 1953: Innocents in Paris. 1955: An Alligator Named Daisy. 1956: Three Men in a Boat. 1959: Bottoms Up! 1961: Nearly a Nasty Accident. 1967: The Plank. A Ghost of a Chance. 1968: Lionheart. 1969: The Bed Sitting Room. 1970: Rhubarb. 1971: The Magnificent Six and a Half (3rd series). 1972: Anoop and the Elephant.*

EMERY, Dick 1917–1983

Stardom came late and ill-health early for this wolfish-looking British comedian with barking tones gained from an upper-class background and wartime service with the RAF. Dark-haired (later almost white) and stocky, Emery was the son of entertainers

Callen and Emery and joined in their act as a child. As a juvenile, he appeared in pantomimes and summer shows. Blessed with a strong singing voice, he had early ambitions for an opera career, but had settled for singing and clowning on variety bills by the time World War Two came along. During hostilities he appeared in Gang Shows and other forces' entertainments. When the war was over, Emery, like so many post-war British comedians, picked up the threads of his career as a stand-up comic at the Windmill Theatre, before transferring his talents to radio. Here he became a man of many voices, usually listed at the end of the supporting cast but with as much to do in various capacities as anyone else. As a solo he was not successful at this time but did join fellow comedians from *The Goon Show* in a couple of film shorts. Success in the radio series *Educating Archie* from 1956 to 1959 gave him a wider following and he began to build up the repertoire of outrageous characters which would get a bigger showcase when he landed his own show. But that wouldn't happen until 1963; in the meantime he played camera-hogging cameos in several British comedy films and starred in a minor number called *A Taste of Money*. *The Dick Emery Show* began on BBC-TV in 1963 and would continue until shortly before the comedian's death. In 1964 he also began a starring radio series, *Emery at Large*, but it was the ability to add visual interpretations of his broad comic characters to the funny voices that was to make him a viewers' favourite. Best-liked were con men, old codgers and appearances in drag, notably including the man-eating peroxide blonde Mandy with her catchphrase: 'Ooh, you *are* awful. But I like you!' There was a starring feature film, *Ooh ... You Are Awful*, in 1972, a Bob Hope-style chase comedy which allowed Emery to play the main role as well as seven appearances in disguise. The same year he was voted TV Entertainer of the Year, but missed the awards ceremony when he was rushed to hospital. It was the beginning of years of health scares, Emery suffering from heart trouble, stomach disorders and eye problems which needed a series of operations. He was no luckier in love, being married five times,

all to showgirls. He was living with his sixth partner, a showgirl 30 years his junior, at the time of his death. He became ill with a lung infection in December 1982 and died the following month, from respiratory problems associated with gout and blood poisoning. Ironically, Emery had always been a keep-fit fanatic, building a gymnasium and sauna in his garden.

1953: * The Super Secret Service. 1955: * The Case of the Mukkinese Battlehorn. 1959: Follow a Star. 1960: Light Up the Sky. A Taste of Money. 1962: Mrs Gibbons' Boys. Crooks Anonymous. The Wrong Arm of the Law. * The Plain Man's Guide to Advertising (voice only). The Fast Lady. 1963: Just for Fun. 1965: The Knack ... and how to get it. The Big Job. 1966: The Wrong Box. 1967: River Rivals (serial). Yellow Submarine (voice only). 1968: Baby Love. 1970: Loot. 1972: Ooh ... You Are Awful (US: Get Charlie Tully). 1976: Find the Lady.

EMNEY, Fred 1900–1980
Had a meeting with Charlie Chaplin in Hollywood in the early 1920s gone according to plan, it's likely that 20-stone British comedian Fred Emney would have added dozens of films to the list that follows this brief glance at his career. But Emney was thrown out of the studio by a disbelieving doorman and the two men did not meet again for 50 years. Emney reminded the great man of the disastrous appointment. 'Good heavens' Chaplin is reputed to have said, 'You're late.' But it was appropriate that the best of Emney should have been seen on English stages and in (too few) British films. For the big man with a grumbling wheeze of a voice was essentially English. The monocle and cigar were ever present, although the dress alternated between top hat and tails and cloth cap and plus-fours. And even when smartly attired he, and his hair, were always vaguely dishevelled. The son of a famous character comedian, also called Fred, Emney junior was born in Liverpool and took to the stage at 15. He quickly outgrew the page-boy's uniform he wore in his first show and a year later was playing the squire in *Puss in Boots* at a London theatre. His

American trip lasted from 1920 to 1931 and included a long sojourn in Canada, where Emney perfected his most successful stage act, playing the piano and bumbling disconnected inanities at the same time. Such carefully-rehearsed incoherence had Canadian and American audiences in stitches and Emney returned to Britain without a movie to his name but with his personal reputation enhanced. An association with the superstar entertainer Jack Buchanan provided Emney with a new breakthrough in popularity in 1934. Buchanan cast Emney as Lord Leatherhead in his stage smash *Mr Whittington*, and the heavyweight huffer was an enormous hit. He went into Buchanan's next two film vehicles, *Brewster's Millions* and *Come Out of the Pantry*, and became a welcome part of the British film scene for the remainder of the pre-war years. He had a good leading role in the lively *Let's Make a Night of It*, as a man who inherits a nightclub (it was also one of his few major films), but he played character parts in *Jane Steps Out*, *Hold My Hand* and *Yes, Madam?*, and supported Buchanan again in *The Middle Watch*. The Buchanan connection continued through the war years as the entertainers toured together in such shows as *Top Hat and Tails* and *It's Time to Dance*. At Christmas times, Emney returned to pantomime. Entrenched in the theatre as he was, Emney's screen career seemed to be a thing of the past. It was revived to an extent by the success of his 1954–55 TV series *Emney Enterprises*. There was a leading role as a headmaster in a film farce, *Fun at St Fanny's*, but the script, part-written by Emney himself, was poor and, after a surprisingly successful stint as ringmaster with Chipperfield's Circus, Emney was confined to eccentric character parts in increasingly unworthy film comedies. He was perhaps at his best in stage shows of the 1950s, such as *Blue for a Boy* and *Happy as a King* in which he would dazzle his audiences with a series of outrageous outfits (in one show he appeared as a dowager, complete with moustache, monocle and cigar), register disbelief with the twitch of an eyelid, a blank stare or the flick of a cigar, and pump his sausage fingers up and down the keys of the piano. Emney was too big a man ever to entirely lose his inherent dignity, no matter what amazing antics he got up to on stage. In later years his mere appearance was enough to set his audiences smiling. Emney once said that 'I suppose I'm a comic because I haven't got enough brain to be anything duller. I've never known why they laugh. I've been lucky enough to just stroll on stage and say "Good evening" and they start laughing. It's wonderful for your confidence.'

1934: Brewster's Millions. 1935: Come Out of the Pantry. 1937: Let's Make a Night of It. The Lilac Domino. 1938: Just Like a Woman. Jane Steps Out. Hold My Hand. Yes, Madam? 1939: Just William. She Couldn't Say No. The Middle Watch. 1940: * Goofer Trouble. 1942: Let the

People Sing. 1955: Fun at St Fanny's. 1962: The Fast Lady. 1963: Father Came Too. 1964: A Home of Your Own. I've Gotta Horse. 1965: San Ferry Ann. Bunny Lake is Missing. Those Magnificent Men in Their Flying Machines. 1966: The Sandwich Man. 1968: Oliver! 1969: The Italian Job. Lock Up Your Daughters! The Magic Christian. Under the Table You Must Go. 1970: Doctor in Trouble. 1971: Up the Chastity Belt. 1973: Mistress Pamela. 1974: The Amorous Milkman. 1977: Adventures of a Private Eye.

ERROL, Leon 1881–1951

This balding Australian comedian with his shifty weasel's face and indiarubber features, body and (especially when playing drunk, which was often) legs, came very late to film fame but remained a popular two-reel star and top supporting comedian over a period of almost 20 years, a period that would have undoubtedly have been extended in television but for his sudden death. In America from an early age, Errol was a Ziegfeld Follies comic at 30, and was soon showing audiences that he could be funny with even the most minimal material. A versatile performer, his quickfire delivery disguised a nimble comic brain, and he was as much a perfectionist as the major figures of silent screen comedy at the time. Errol's own appearances in silents were limited to supporting parts, and it seemed he wouldn't be given a chance to prove his worth in a comedy series of his own when, at 52 and with sound well established, that began to happen. His character of the nervous henpecked drunk, forever trying to escape the wrath of his wife over his latest peccadillo, was quickly established on screen but Errol always fought to widen the formula, playing some pretty unusual variations within it, including one film in which he is driven to mass murder by a wife who's forever playing bridge. His facility with disguises, impersonations and dual roles also helped to keep his short comedies fresh over a period of 19 years. During this time, Errol also became involved in top roles in two long-running 'B' movie feature series, the 'Mexican Spitfire' films with Lupe Velez, and the 'Joe Palooka' boxing farces with Joe Kirkwood. At 70 the

man who always looked on screen as if he were about to keel over in an alcoholic haze, but never quite did, collapsed suddenly while returning from a hunting trip. It was a heart attack and Errol, who had just set up a deal to try the new medium of TV in a half-hour show, was dead before he could take on this final challenge.

1924: Yolanda. 1925: Clothes Make the Pirate. Sally. 1927: The Lunatic at Large. 1929: One Heavenly Night. 1930: * Let's Merge. Paramount on Parade. Queen of Scandal. Only Saps Work. 1931: Her Majesty, Love. Finn and Hattie. * Practice Shots. 1933: Alice in Wonderland. * Poor Fish. * Three Little Swigs. * Hold Your Temper. 1934: We're Not Dressing. The Notorious Sophie Lang. The Captain Hates the Sea. * No More Bridge. * Autobuyography. * Service with a Smile. * Good Morning, Eve. * Perfectly Mismated. * Fixing a Stew. * One Too Many. 1935: Princess O'Hara. Coronado. * Hit and Rum. * Salesmanship Ahoy. * Home Work. * Honeymoon Bridge. * Counselitis. 1936: * Down the Ribber. * Pirate Party on Catalina Isle. * Wholesailing Along. * One Live Ghost. 1937: * Wife Insurance. Make a Wish. * Wrong Romance. * Should Wives Work? * A Rented Riot. * Dummy Owner. 1938: * His Pest Friend. * The Jitters. * Stage Fright. * Major Difficulties. * Crime Rave. * Berth Quakes. 1939: The Girl from Mexico. Career. Dancing Co-Ed (GB: Every Other Inch a Lady). Mexican Spitfire. * Home Boner. * Moving Vanities. * Ring Madness. * Wrong Room. * Truth Aches. * Scrappily Married. 1940: * Bested by a Beard. * He Asked for It. * Tattle Television. * The Fired Man. Pop Always Pays. Mexican Spitfire Out West. The Golden Fleecing. 1941: Six Lessons from Madame La Zonga. Where Did You Get That Girl? Hurry, Charlie, Hurry. Mexican Spitfire's Baby. Melody Lane. Moonlight in Hawaii. Never Give a Sucker an Even Break (GB: What a Man!). * When Wifie's Away. * A Polo Phony. * A Panic in the Parlor. * Man I Cured. * Home Work (and 1935 film). * Who's a Dummy? 1942: Mexican Spitfire at Sea. * Wedded Blitz. * Hold 'Em Jail. Mexican Spitfire Sees a Ghost. * Framing Father. * Mail Trouble. * Dear! Dear! * Pretty Dolly. Mexican Spitfire's Elephant. 1943: * Double Up. * A Family Feud. * Gem Jams. * Radio Runaround. Cowboy in Manhattan. Strictly in the Groove. * Seeing Nellie Home. * Cutie on Duty. * Wedtime Stories. Mexican Spitfire's Blessed Event. Higher and Higher. Follow the Band. Gals Inc. 1944: Hat Check Honey. The Invisible Man's Revenge. Slightly Terrific. Twilight on the Prairie. Babes on Swing Street. * Say Uncle. * Poppa Knows Worst. * Prices Unlimited. * Girls, Girls, Girls. * Triple Trouble. * He Forgot to Remember. 1945: She Gets Her Man. What a Blonde! Under Western Skies. Mama Loves Papa. * Birthday Blues. * Let's Go Stepping. * It Shouldn't Happen to a Dog. * Double Honeymoon. * Beware of Redheads. 1946: Riverboat Rhythm. * Oh, Professor, Behave. * Maid Trouble. * Twin Husbands. * I'll Take Milk.

* Follow That Blonde. Joe Palooka, Champ. Gentleman Joe Palooka. 1947: * Borrowed Blonde. * Wife Tames Wolf. * In Room 303. * Hired Husband. * Blondes Away. Joe Palooka in the Knockout. 1948: The Noose Hangs High. Variety Time. * Bet Your Life. * Don't Fool Your Wife. Joe Palooka in Fighting Mad. * Secretary Trouble. * Bachelor Blues. * Uninvited Blonde. * Backstage Follies. 1949: Joe Palooka in the Big Fight. * Dad Always Pays. * Cactus Cut-Up. * I Can't Remember. * Oil's Well That Ends Well. Joe Palooka in the Counterpunch. * Sweet Cheat. * Shocking Affair. Joe Palooka Meets Humphrey. 1950: * High and Dizzy. Joe Palooka in Humphrey Takes a Chance/Humphrey Takes a Chance. * Texas Tough Guy. * Spooky Wooky. Joe Palooka in the Squared Circle (GB: The Squared Circle). 1951: Chinatown Chump. * Punchy Pancho. * One Wild Night. * Deal Me In. * Lord Epping Returns. * Too Many Wives. Footlight Varieties.

ETAIX, Pierre 1928–

Probably, few filmgoers today have heard of this dark, sad-eyed, poker-faced, stick-like French mime comedian. But for a few years in the early 1960s it did seem that there might be room for a new Buster Keaton (qv) in the modern cinema. Alas, that only applied to short subjects and Etaix has not directed a film now for more than 20 years, although he continues to crop up in wordless cameos in other people's movies. An artist by training, Etaix became a set designer, a cartoonist and an illustrator of books before meeting his mentor Jacques Tati (qv) in the early 1950s. Etaix worked with Tati in his long-in-production Mon Oncle, designing some sets and costumes and drawing a storyboard of the film, which finally appeared in 1958. Etaix also appeared as a crowd player in several scenes. The experience fired Etaix with the enthusiasm to tackle some film work of his own. Basing his character loosely on that of his idol Keaton, he constructed a series of side-splitting comedies on the 'one dàrn thing after another' theme, in which the common man fights against a series of disasters only to be overwhelmed by them in the final frame. These little gems, among them Rupture and Happy Anniversary, were widely distributed throughout the world and gained Etaix something of a reputation both among critics and among those filmgoers who chanced on one of his films in their supporting programme. His first feature, *The Suitor*, was still much in the silent comedy tradition and contains, as well as Etaix's own mournful persona at its best, a good collection of splendidly-timed wheezes and inventive comic ideas. From this promising beginning, however, little developed. Etaix's other features all have their moments but there are fewer of them and the overall tone is one of sadness and melancholy. The pace, too, is sometimes fatally slow, allowing our attention to slip away so that the funny moments lose some of their impact. After 1970 Etaix seemed to lose interest in the cinema, he and his wife, actress Annie Fratellini, devoting their time to Etaix's 'Ecole du Cirque', where he taught clowning and mimicry. From the mid 1980s there were a few more of Etaix's film vignettes, but no sign of a permanent return to the cinema in a more productive role. At his best Etaix was a peerless purveyor of escalating comic chaos with some highly original ideas built into stories of men for whom nothing would go right. As a direct descendant of Max Linder (*qv*), one wonders if Etaix could have spent his whole career happily making uproarious movie shorts. Ambition, alas, is often a dangerous thing.

*1956: Mon oncle/My Uncle. 1959: Pickpocket. 1960: Le pèlerinage. 1961: Tire-au-flanc 62. *† Rupture. *† Happy Anniversary. 1962: † Le soupirant/The Suitor. 1963: Une grosse tête. *† Insomnia. *† Nous n'irons plus au bois. 1964: † Yoyo. 1965: † As Long As You're Healthy. 1966: Le voleur. 1969: * La mayonnaise. 1970: † Pays de cocagne. 1971: The Day the Clown Cried (unfinished). *† La Polonaise. 1973: ‡ Bel ordure. 1974: Sérieux comme le plaisir. 1986: Max mon amour. 1987: L'âge de monsieur est avancé. 1990: Henry and June.*

† And directed.

‡ Scenes deleted from final release print.

EVANS, Fred 1889–1951

The most successful British film comedian of early silent times, Fred Evans' career ran roughly parallel to that of Hollywood's John Bunny (*qv*). In fact Evans had such a splendidly Dickensian face that it's almost surprising that Bunny didn't find room for his fellow-comic in his British-made version of *The Pickwick Papers*, released in 1913. The nephew of music-hall comedian Will Evans, who also made a few films, Fred was a film man through and through. At 18 he was an acrobatic bit player in British slapstick comedies. His athletic high jinks and broad comic style soon brought him to leading roles. But it was really Fred Evans' face, rather than his talent, that sustained his popularity with the British public over an eight-year period. A forerunner of Joe E. Brown (*qv*) facially, Evans had a cavernous

clown's mouth, smooth, dark, centre-parted hair, little narrow eyes and an engaging sense of the absurd. As befitted his looks, he began his starring comedies as a character called Charley Smiler but he soon stumbled on his most famous incarnation – Pimple, an all-fingers-and-thumbs everyman, who was just as likely to be involved in contemporary problems, historical skits, or with famous fictitious characters. The public swallowed Evans' simple antics whole. He co-directed and co-wrote almost all of his films with his younger brother Joe, and if their style was unsubtle and their action rough-and-tumble they seemed to hit the public funnybone. Scores of these comedies played to full houses until their appeal finally began to fade in 1917. Evans made sporadic attempts to make 'Pimple' comedies on a larger scale, but the image was passé. There was an opportunity to return to the circus where he had started as a boy clown when he was just four years old but as far as films were concerned Evans did his last work in the 1930s just as he had started – as a bit player and extra.

(All shorts.) *1910: A Costly Gift. The Last of the Dandy. The Marriage of Muggins VC. As Prescribed by the Doctor. Prison Reform. 1911: How Puny Peter Became Strong. Charley Smiler Joins the Boy Scouts. Charley Smiler Takes Brain Food. Charley Smiler Competes in a Cycle Race. Charley Smiler Takes Up Ju Jitsu. Charley Smiler is Robbed (US: Smiler Loses His Wallet). Stop the Fight! Charley Smiler is Stage Struck (US: Smiler Has Stage Fever). 1912: Wanted – A Wife and Child. Charley Smiler's Love Affair. Charley Smiler Asks Papa. Cowboy Mad. The Little General. Charley Smiler at the Picnic. Charley Smiler Catches a Tartar. Fifty Years After. A Novel Burglary. Fred's Police Force. The Taming of Big Ben. The Whistling Bet. Grand Harlequinade. Pimple's Extraordinary Story. Pimple Does the Turkey Trot. Pimple and the Snake. Pimple Wins a Bet. Pimple Gets a Quid (US: Pimple's Taxi Twister). Pimple's Fire Brigade. Pimple Becomes an Acrobat. Pimple As a Cinema Actor. Pimple As a Rent Collector. Pimple As a Ballet Dancer. Pimple's Motor Bike. 1913: Pimple P. C. Pimple Goes a-Busking. Pimple Detective. Pimple and Galatea. Pimple Writes a Cinema*

Plot. Pimple Meets Captain Scuttle. Miss Pimple Suffragette. Pimple: The Indian Massacre. Pimple's Complaint. Two to One on Pimple. Pimple's Sporting Chance. Pimple's Motor Trap. Pimple Takes a Picture. Pimple's Waterloo. Pimple Gets the Sack. Pimple's Wonderful Gramophone. Pimple's Rest Cure. Pimple and the Gorilla. Pimple Joins the Army. Tragedy in Pimple's Life. Dicke Turpin's Ride to Yorke. Pimple Does the Hat Trick. A Bathroom Problem. Pimple's Wife. Pimple Goes Fishing. When Pimple Was Young. Pimple the Sport. Pimple Gets the Jumps. Pimple's Inferno. Once Upon a Time. Slippery Pimple. Lt Pimple on Secret Service. How Pimple Saved Kissing Cup. Pimple's Ivanhoe. Pimple's Great Bull Fight. Pimple's Midnight Ramble. Pimple the Suicide. Pimple's New Job. 1914: Pimple the Gentleman Burglar. Lt Pimple at the Stolen Submarine. Pimple's Humanity. Pimple: His First Sweetheart. Pimple Elopes. Lt Pimple's Dash for the Pole. Young Pimple's Schooldays. Pimple in the Grip of the Law. Pimple in the Hands of the London Crook. The House of Distemperley. Pimple Goes to Paris. Young Pimple and His Little Sister. The Battle of Gettysownback. How Pimple Won the Derby. Lt Pimple's Sealed Orders. The Whitewashers. Pimple Midst Raging Beasts. Lt Pimple Goes to Mexico. Pimple's Burglar Scare. Stolen Honours. Pimple in Society. Pimple's Trousers. Pimple's Advice. Big Chief Little Pimple. Pimple Turns Honest. Pimple Anarchist. Bronco Pimple. Pimple Counter Jumper. Pimple's Vengeance. Pimple Pinched. Pimple's Last Resource. Pimple Beats Jack Johnson. Pimple's Escape from Portland. Lt Pimple Gunrunner. Pimple MP. Pimple's Proposal. Pimple's Charge of the Light Brigade. Pimple Enlists. Lt Pimple and the Stolen Invention. Pimple's Great Fire. Pimple's Prison. Pimple, Special Constable. Lt Pimple King of the Cannibal Islands. The Clowns of Europe. Pimple's Leap to Fortune. Inspector Pimple. How Lt Pimple Captured the Kaiser. Pimple and the Stolen Plans. Pimple on Football. Young Pimple's Frolics. Pimple the Spiritualist. Trilby, by Pimple and Co. 1915: Pimple in the Kilties. Mrs Raffles, née Pimple. Judge Pimple. Sexton Pimple. Pimple's Storyette. Pimple's Dream of Victory. Pimple Child Stealer. Pimple the Bad Girl of the Family. Flash Pimple the Master Crook. Pimple Copped. Pimple's Million Dollar Mystery. Pimple's The Man Who Stayed at Home. Pimple's Past. Pimple's The Case of Johnny Walker. Pimple's Three Weeks. Pimple's Royal Divorce. Pimple's Rival. Pimple's Peril. Pimple's Dilemma. Pimple's Holiday. Tally Ho, Pimple. Pimple's Scrap of Paper. The Smugglers. The Kaiser Captures Pimple. Driven by Hunger. For Her Brother's Sake. Pimple's Boy Scout. Mademoiselle Pimple. Pimple's Burlesque of the Still Alarm. Pimple Has One. Pimple's Good Turn. Ragtime Cowboy Pimple. Pimple's Willit Wasit Isit. Pimple's Some Burglar. Pimple's Motor Tour. Pimple's Three O'Clock Race. Pimple Up the Pole. Pimple's Road to Ruin. Pimple Explains. Pimple's Three. Was Pimple Wright? Pimple Sees Ghosts. Pimple's Uncle. Pimple Acts. Pimple Will Treat. Pimple Gets the Hump. Pimple's Artful Dodge.

Aladdin. 1916: Pimple's Crime. Pimple's Part. Pimple's Great Adventure. Pimple Ends It. Pimple's Double. Pimple's Zeppelin Scare. Pimple Splits the Difference. Pimple's Arm of the Law. Pimple's Pink Forms. Pimple, Himself and Others. Pimple Poor But Dishonest. Pimple as Hamlet. Pimple's A Woman in the Case. Pimple's Midsummer Night's Dream. Pimple's Tenth Commandment. Diamond Cut Diamond. Pimple's Silver Lagoon. Pimple's Monkey Business. Pimple's Clutching Hand. Pimple's Nautical Story. The Merry Wives of Pimple. 1917: Pimple's Senseless Censoring. Pimple's The Whip. Pimple's Motor Tour. Pimple's Mystery of the Closed Door. Some Dancer. Saving Raffles. Pimple's Tableaux Vivants. Pimple − His Voluntary Corps. Pimple's Romance. Pimple's Lady Godiva. Pimple's Pitter Patter. Pimple's The Woman Who Did. Oliver Twisted. 1918: Pimple's Better 'Ole. Rations. Inns and Outs. 1920: Pimple's Topical Gazette. 1922: Pimple's Three Musketeers.

EWELL, Tom
(Samuel Yewell Tompkins) 1909−

In retrospect, one thinks of Tom Ewell as the Man in the Light Suit, with the face of a demented monkey, forever chasing desirable women but never quite getting there. This image has been fostered by 20th Century-Fox casting him opposite its three big blondes of the 1950s: Marilyn Monroe (in *The Seven Year Itch*), Sheree North (in *The Lieutenant Wore Skirts*) and Jayne Mansfield (in *The Girl Can't Help It*). In fact Ewell mixed his ordinary Joes with a number of cynical observers, the latter role being one he was perhaps well qualified to play after such a lengthy climb to the top. He began acting on stage at 19, completing a number of years in stock before dropping out of the business for a while to try his luck as a salesman at Macy's. Returning to acting, he made Broadway by 1934 and stayed there for 14 years (war service intervening) without ever having a hit. Towards the end of the 1930s Ewell began to demonstrate that his forte was comedy, and it was in this vein that he had his first major success in 1947 with the stage version of *John Loves Mary*. Ewell missed out on the film version of *John Loves Mary*: he was busy making an auspicious

major film debut, alongside two other newish talents who had struggled to make it, David Wayne and Judy Holliday, all supporting Spencer Tracy and Katharine Hepburn in *Adam's Rib*. After a few further supporting roles, Ewell was reunited with Wayne in the army comedy *Up Front*, based on Bill Mauldin's cartoon characters Willie and Joe, and followed by a sequel (without Wayne) called *Back at the Front*. Ewell then left films to return to the stage in his greatest Broadway success, as Richard Sherman in *The Seven Year Itch*. He repeated his role in the 1955 screen version, as the sheep in wolf's clothing whose imagination is far worse than his bite. This and the other mid 1950s films admirably demonstrate Ewell's quiet, crumpled style of getting the laughs, feeding by reaction off others in the scene. By now, however, he was well into his forties and when the quality of his roles quickly fell away again he was only too glad to return to his first love, the stage. An attempt to do a TV situation comedy series in 1960, as an estate agent living in a woman-dominated household, was not successful.

1940: They Knew What They Wanted. 1941: Desert Bandit/The Kansas Kid. 1949: * Caribbean Capers. * Southward Ho! Ho! Adam's Rib. 1950: An American Guerilla in the Philippines (GB: I Shall Return). Mr Music. A Life of Her Own. 1951: Up Front. Finders Keepers. 1952: Lost in Alaska. Back at the Front (GB: Willie and Joe in Tokyo). 1955: The Seven Year Itch. The Lieutenant Wore Skirts. 1956: The Great American Pastime. The Girl Can't Help It. 1958: A Nice Little Bank That Should Be Robbed (GB: How to Rob a Bank). 1961: Tender is the Night. 1962: State Fair. 1965: * Wonders of Kentucky (narrator only). 1969: Suppose They Gave a War

and Nobody Came. 1971: To Find a Man. 1972: They Only Kill Their Masters. 1974: † The Great Gatsby. The Spy Who Returned from the Dead. 1975: Promise Him Anything (TV). 1979: Return of the Mod Squad (TV). 1983: Easy Money.

† Scenes deleted from final release print.

FAZENDA, Louise 1889−1962
A zany, likeable, low-browed (and low-brow!), sharp-eyed, light-haired American hillbilly-style slapstick comedienne in silent comedies, with extravagant gestures and a remarkable range of facial expressions. Tall for the early twentieth century (she was 5 ft 6 in) and willowy, the convent-educated Fazenda had already had some stage experience when she decided to try for a career in films. Her appealingly equine features (her voluptuous figure was rarely revealed) were soon put into leading roles by Universal; stills from one of her earliest, the now-lost *Mike and Jake at the Beach*, show her towering over diminutive co-star Bobby Vernon.

An unusually well-dressed Louise Fazenda in one of the last roles of her career, opposite pugnacious Nat Pendleton in Swing *Your Lady*

She moved to Sennett in 1915, where she played comedy eccentrics in support of such stars as Mack Swain and Fatty Arbuckle (both *qv*). Soon, though, she was second only to Mabel Normand (*qv*) in the studio's small roster of female comedy stars. Playing mostly gangling, rustic, knockabout roles, Louise thrust her angular limbs out in all directions and did all her own stunts. Insurance companies today would never allow her to attempt such comedy action as jumping from heights, being dragged by runaway horses and vehicles, and throwing herself with abandon into comic fight sequences. More often than not, in the course of the action, Fazenda could be relied upon to lose her voluminous bloomers! Although the height of her popularity was around 1917 and 1918 — often co-starring with fellow-grotesque Charlie Murray (*qv*), Fazenda stayed with Mack Sennett until 1922. One of her most successful roles for Sennett was as the extravagant, gingham-clad heroine of *Down on the Farm* in 1920, sporting an extraordinary hairdo with several pigtails that went off in all directions. In the 1920s Fazenda was seen in top character roles, often as eccentric domestics, sometimes as maneaters. One of her best chances came in 1928 in the old Marie Dressler (*qv*) role in the remake of *Tillie's Punctured Romance*, with the equally idiosyncratic W. C. Fields (*qv*) in the part formerly played by Charlie Chaplin (*qv*). But the plot was totally revamped and the misconceived venture was a deserved flop. Louise did, however, get her own series of simple slapstick comedies for Paramount/Christie and for RKO in the early 1930s. In 1926 Louise had married for the second and last time at the age of 36. Her husband was the ten-years-younger producer Hal Wallis, whose career would later overshadow hers. Although shamefully marginalised in most of her sound feature films, Fazenda continued to play zany character parts in movies until the end of the 1930s. She and Wallis remained married until shortly before her death from a cerebral haemorrhage at the age of 72. Four years later Wallis married actress Martha Hyer.

*1913: * The Cheese Special. * Mike and Jake at the Beach. * Almost an Actress. 1914:*

*Hubby's Cure. * Traffic in Soles. * Love and Graft. 1915: * Ambrose's Fury. * Ambrose's Little Hatchet. * The Great Vacuum Robbery. * A Versatile Villain. * Wilful Ambrose. * That Little Band of Gold. * Ambrose's Lofty Perch. * A Bear Affair. * Crossed Love and Swords. * A Hash House Fraud. * Stark Mad. * Fatty's Tin Type Tangle. * A Game Old Knight. 1916: * Summer Girl. * Bombs and Brides. * The Judge. * His Hereafter. * A Love Riot. * Her Marble Heart. * Pills of Peril. * A la Cabaret. * The Feathered Nest. * Maid Mad. 1917: * Her Fame and Shame. * Her Torpedoed Love. * The Summer Girls. * Maggie's First False Step. * His Precious Life. * The Betrayal of Maggie. 1918: * Her Screen Idol. * The Kitchen Lady. * The Village Smithy. * Her First Mistake. * The Village Chestnut. 1919: * Hearts and Flowers. A House Divided. * Treating 'em Rough. * Back to the Kitchen. * It's a Boy. * Fireside Brewer. * Wedding Bells Out of Tune. * Astray from Steerage. 1920: Down on the Farm. Married Life. 1921: * A Small Town Idol. The Foolish Age. 1922: * The Beauty Shop. Quincy Adams Sawyer. The Beautiful and Damned. 1923: The Gold Diggers. The Spoilers. Main Street. The Fog. Mary of the Movies. The Old Fool. The Spider and the Rose. Tea — with a Kick. The Wanters. 1924: Being Respectable. Abraham Lincoln/ The Dramatic Life of Abraham Lincoln. This Woman. True As Steel. Galloping Fish. Listen, Lester. The Lighthouse by the Sea. 1925: Bobbed Hair. Déclassée/The Social Exile. The Night Club. Grounds for Divorce. Hogan's Alley. A Broadway Butterfly. Cheaper to Marry. The Love Hours. Compromise. 1926: The Lady of the Harem. The Bat. Loose Ankles (GB: Ladies at Play). Footloose Widows. Millionaires. The Passionate Quest. Miss Nobody. The Old Soak. 1927: The Cradle Snatchers. Babs Comes Home. A Sailor's Sweetheart. Finger Prints. Gay Old Bird. The Red Mill. Simple Sis. A Texas Steer. 1928: The Terror. Tillie's Punctured Romance (GB: Marie's Millions). Outcast. It's All Greek to Me. Five and Ten Cent Annie. Pay As You Enter. Heart to Heart. Riley the Cop. Domestic Troubles. Vamping Venus. Noah's Ark. Stark Mad (and 1915 short of same title). 1929: The Desert Song. The House of Horror. Hot Stuff. Hard to Get. Show of Shows. On with the Show. * Faro Nell; or, In Old California. * Hot Lemonade. The Broadway Hoofer (GB: Dancing Feet). 1930: Leathernecking (GB: Present Arms). * The Bearded Lady. * A Fall to Arms. * Pure and Simple. * So This is Paris Green. * Too Hot to Handle. Rain or Shine. No, No, Nanette. Bride of the Regiment (GB: Lady of the Rose). Gold Diggers of Broadway. Loose Ankles (and 1926 film of same title). Viennese Nights. High Society Blues. Spring is Here. Wide Open. 1931: * Blondes Prefer Bonds. * The Itching Hour. * Second Hand Kisses. Misbehaving Ladies. Gun Smoke. Cuban Love Song. * The Stolen Jools (GB: The Slippery Pearls). The Mad Parade (GB: Forgotten Women). Newly Rich (GB: Forbidden Adventure). 1932: * Hesitating Love. * Union Wages. Once in a Lifetime. Racing Youth. The Unwritten Law. 1933: Alice in Wonderland.*

*Hunting Trouble. * Out of Gas. * Stung Again. * A Divorce Courtship. * Quiet Please. * Walking Back Home. 1934: Wonder Bar. Caravan. Mountain Music. 1935: Broadway Gondolier. The Casino Murder Case. Bad Boy. The Winning Ticket. The Widow from Monte Carlo. 1936: Colleen. Doughnuts and Society (GB: Stepping into Society). I Married a Doctor. 1937: Ready, Willing and Able. * Once Over Lightly. The Road Back/Return of the Hero. First Lady. Merry-Go-Round of 1938. Ever Since Eve. 1938: Swing Your Lady. Down on the Farm (and 1920 film of same title). 1939: The Old Maid. * A Small Town Idol (1921 film revised for sound). 1951: * Memories of Famous Hollywood Comedians (previously unshown footage).*

FELD, Fritz
(F. Feilchenfeld) 1900–

This Berlin-born actor with round features, unruly moustache and a streak of dark hair, turned up as butlers, waiters, orchestra conductors, noblemen, maîtres d', hotel managers, composers and music teachers. The only thing they had in common was that you couldn't take any of them seriously. Feld made his debut in the 1920 German classic *Der Golem* as a court jester, and has been making people laugh ever since. Told on his first application to a drama school that he would never make an actor because he lisped, Feld lost little time in proving people wrong. The son of a printer, he was already assistant to the great Max Reinhardt when the famous director brought his company to America in 1922. Feld stayed on in the States, making occasional acting appearances on stage and in films, but working mainly in a series of behind-the-scenes jobs, directing stage shows or acting as dialogue director in films. It was when Feld was assisting Ernst Lubitsch, then production chief at Paramount, that he returned, almost by accident, to acting — and audiences (and producers) quickly picked up on what they had been missing. Feld leaned forward, rubbed his hands, jabbered in his Berlin-tinged accent, clicked his heels, smacked his head in despair, or slapped his mouth to imitate a champagne cork popping. His fuss-budget, sarcastic waiters and hotel managers became legendary. 'Every studio', he once remembered, 'wanted at one time to cast me as a waiter or maître d'.' Sensibly, he sought a wider range and provided scores of comic cameos before his work rate slowed in the late 1950s. His feet seemed never to leave the ground as he slid into a scene, stole the laughs and slid out again. A co-founder of the Hollywood Playhouse, Feld, who threatens at time of writing to go on making appearances in films and TV into his nineties, has been married to the character actress Virginia Christine since 1940.

*1920: Der Golem: Wie er in die Welt kam. Dämen der Welt. 1921: Christian Wahnschaffe. 1925: The Swan. 1928:. The Dove. * The Sorcerer's Apprentice. The Leopard Lady. The Last Command. A Ship Comes In (GB: His Country). Blindfold. 1929: One Hysterical Night (GB: No, No, Napoleon). The Charlatan. Broadway. Black Magic. 1937: I Met Him in Paris. Expensive Husbands. Hollywood Hotel. Tovarich. True Confession. Lancer Spy. 1938: Go Chase Yourself. Campus Confessions (GB: Fast Play). Romance in the Dark. Bringing Up Baby. The Affairs of Annabel. Artists and Models Abroad (GB: Stranded in Paris). Gold Diggers in Paris (GB: The Gay Impostors). I'll Give a Million. * Out Where the Stars Begin. 1939: Idiot's Delight. At the Circus/Marx Brothers at the Circus. When Tomorrow Comes. Little Accident. * Springtime in the Movies. * Quiet, Please. Everything Happens at Night. 1940: It's a Date. Millionaire Playboy. Victory. Little Old New York. Ma, He's Making Eyes at Me. I Was an Adventuress. Sandy is a Lady. 1941: Four Jacks and a Jill. Come Live with Me. World Premiere. Mexican Spitfire's Baby. Three Sons o' Guns. You Belong to Me (GB: Good Morning, Doctor!). Skylark. 1942: Shut My Big Mouth. Sleepytime Gal. Maisie Gets Her Man (GB: She Gets Her Man). Iceland (GB: Katina). 1943: Henry Aldrich Swings It (GB: Henry Swings It). Phantom of the Opera. Holy Matrimony. 1944: Knickerbocker Holiday. Passport to Adventure. Take It Big. Ever Since Venus. 1945: The Great John L (GB: A Man Called Sullivan). George White's Scandals. Captain Tugboat Annie. 1946: Catman of Paris (filmed 1940). I've Always Loved You. Wife of Monte Cristo. Her Sister's Secret. Gentleman Joe Palooka. 1947: Carnival in Costa Rica. * Cupid Goes Nuts. The Secret Life of Walter Mitty. Fun on a Weekend. 1948: If You Knew Susie. The Noose Hangs High. Julia Misbehaves. Trouble Makers. My Girl Tisa. You Gotta Stay Happy. Mexican Hayride. 1949: The Lovable Cheat. The Great Lover. Appointment with Danger (released 1951). 1950: The Jackpot. Belle of Old Mexico. Riding High. 1951: Missing Women. Rhythm Inn. Kentucky Jubilee. Sky High. Little Egypt (GB: Chicago Masquerade). My Favorite Spy. * So You Want to Enjoy Life. * So You Want to be a Doctor. Journey into Light. 1952: Aaron Slick from Punkin Crick (GB: Marshmallow Moon). The Star. O. Henry's Full House (GB: Full House). Has Anybody Seen My Gal. 1953: * So You Want to be a Musician. Casanova's Big Night.*

*Call Me Madam. Crime Wave (GB: The City is Dark). The French Line. 1954: Riding Shotgun. Living It Up. Paris Playboys. 1955: Jail Busters. 1956: * So You Want to be Pretty. 1957: Up in Smoke. 1959: Juke Box Rhythm. Don't Give Up the Ship. 1961: Ladies' Man. Pocketful of Miracles. The Errand Boy. 1963: Promises! Promises! Wives and Lovers. Who's Minding the Store? Four for Texas. The Miracle of Santa's White Reindeer. 1964: The Patsy. 1965: Harlow. 1966: Three on a Couch. Penelope. Way . . . Way Out. Made in Paris. Fame is the Name of the Game (TV). 1967: Caprice. Barefoot in the Park. 1968: The Wicked Dreams of Paula Schultz. 1969: The Comic. Hello, Dolly! The Computer Wore Tennis Shoes. The Phynx. 1970: Which Way to the Front? (Ja! Ja! Mein General, But Which Way to the Front?). 1972: Call Her Mom (TV). 1973: Herbie Rides Again. 1974: Only with Married Men (TV). 1975: The Strongest Man in the World. The Sunshine Boys. Won Ton Ton, the Dog Who Saved Hollywood. 1976: Silent Movie. Freaky Friday. 1977: The World's Greatest Lover. 1980: Herbie Goes Bananas. 1981: History of the World Part I. † . . . All the Marbles (GB: The California Dolls). 1982: Heidi's Song (voice only). 1983: Last of the Great Survivors (TV). 1986: † A Fine Mess. 1987: Barfly. 1989: Get Smart, Again (TV). B-Men (TV).*

† Scenes deleted from final release print.

FELDMAN, Marty 1933–1982

A tiny, bug-eyed, hook-nosed British writer and comedian with wild frizzy light hair, Feldman's intimately demonic personality was ideally suited to the television screen, and it was in this medium that he achieved his greatest popularity. Feldman began his show business career as a musician but a meeting with Spike Milligan (qv), then a founder-member of radio's celebrated The Goon Show, persuaded him to make a career in comedy. He soon broke into radio writing, his greatest success coming with the radio series Round the Horne in the mid 1960s. Later in the decade he switched to performing and quickly made a name for himself in his own TV series Marty. Bowler-hatted and loose-limbed, his pale, watery eyes

gleamed manically as he launched some new scheme as a kind of devil's innocent. The programmes leaned heavily on visual humour: Feldman's idol was Buster Keaton (qv) and he aimed to emulate his lasting stardom, although Feldman's fiendish open grin contrasted markedly with Keaton's impassive looks. Feldman could probably have remained entrenched in television for the decade, but he was anxious to seek wider horizons. His first starring venture in films, Every Home Should Have One, tiresomely smutty, was an unpromising start. But Feldman did better when he accepted featured roles in Mel Brooks and/or Gene Wilder hits: Young Frankenstein, The Adventure of Sherlock Holmes' Smarter Brother and Silent Movie. His finest film moments probably come as the hunchback in the Frankenstein film. Asked if his hump will impede him carrying luggage, he is affronted. 'Hump?' he enquires. 'What hump?' But he then directed two flops in which he also played leading roles: The Last Remake of Beau Geste and In God We Trust. Both films were stronger on ideas than in script and execution. In Hollywood he became involved in the drugs scene, and there was a failed suicide attempt in 1980 when his star career seemed to have evaporated. But he had returned to featured comedy roles by the time of his death in Mexico from a heart attack, for which some blamed a very heavy smoking habit rather than his work schedule. He was buried in Forest Lawns, California, not far from his hero Buster Keaton. His sister is the revue star Fenella Fielding (1932–), a sometime participant in 'Carry On' films.

1969: The Bed Sitting Room. 1970: Every Home Should Have One. 1971: The Magnificent 7 Deadly Sins. 1974: Young Frankenstein. 1975: The Adventure of Sherlock Holmes' Smarter Brother. 40 gradi all'ombra (GB and US: Sex with a Smile). 1976: Silent Movie. 1977: † The Last Remake of Beau Geste. 1979: † In God We Trust. 1982: Slapstick/Slapstick of Another Kind. 1983: Yellowbeard.

† Also directed

FERNANDEL
(Fernand Contandin) 1903–1971

A tall, lugubrious, stoop-shouldered, horse-featured Frenchman with engaging manner and tombstone smile. Despite the generally higher standing of Jacques Tati (qv) and other pioneering French film-makers, Fernandel was the only continental comic actor to become a box-office attraction with general audiences in Britain and America during the post-war years. Although many of his comedies were of saucy or dubious content, Fernandel's knowing innocence disarmed prudes and doubters. He was never less than lovable, and on his award of the Légion d'honneur he was cited as 'Le Marchand de Bonheur' — as one writer translated it, pedlar of joy. Born in

Marseilles, Fernandel was interested from childhood in entertaining people and organised children's stage performances in the city while still a schoolboy. His father was a local café singer who wanted his son to work in a bank and for a while the younger Contandin did just that. After military service, however, Fernandel made up his mind to be an entertainer and turned professional at 19, working as a singer and comedian in music-halls, cafés and stage revues throughout the south of France before reaching Paris in 1928 and taking the city by storm. He made a name for himself as a skilful comic character actor in numerous French films throughout the 1930s but it was not until the post-war years that his career began to make strides on the international market. From 1949, especially with *Casimir* and *Monsieur Boniface*, Fernandel's facial contortions and warm personality reached an increasingly wider audience in both Britain and the United States. And with the introduction of longer, brighter double-bills, used in the fight against television, Fernandel's elastic face was seen on marquees at major city houses on both sides of the Atlantic. This was the period of his greatest popular appeal. Besides the broader comedies, he branched out a little to play the wily parish priest in the Don Camillo comedies, made in Italy, in which Fernandel's character constantly engaged in a battle of wits and wills with the town's Communist mayor. Other successes of the period included *The Red Inn*, *An Artist with Ladies*, *Forbidden Fruit*, *Public Enemy No. 1*, *The Sheep Has Five Legs* (in which he played six roles, a father and his five sons), *Ali-Baba*, *Fernandel the Dressmaker*, *The Two of Us*, and *The Cow and I*. Many of these were the forerunners of the continental brand of rural sex comedies popular a decade later, and could not have succeeded without Fernandel's impish charisma at the helm. There was also a venture with the Hollywood star Bob Hope (*qv*), *Paris Holiday*, in 1958, but the two comedians were so different it was a struggle to make the mixture work. Fernandel's career was quieter in the 1960s and there were fewer international hits, although he remained as much-loved as ever in France. Knowing that he had in-

curable lung cancer, he attempted to make one more Don Camillo film (the sixth, it was also intended to be the last) but became too ill to complete it. The project unfortunately could not be salvaged without him. He died in February 1971 at his luxury Paris apartment, with his wife Henriette at his side. He once said: 'I love loud ties, pretty girls and making fun of myself. Having the brain of a small bureaucrat and the head of a large horse makes that pretty easy. I also have pretensions to being a serious actor!' Occasionally Fernandel was allowed to show that these might have been more than mere pretensions had he not been happier being a master of fun.

1930: Le blanc et le noir. La fine combine. Coeur de lilas. On purge bébé. La meilleure bobonne. 1931: Attaque nocturne. Paris-Béguin. Restez dîner. J'ai quelque chose à vous dire. Pas un mot à ma femme. Beau jour de noces. Le veine d'Anatole. Une brume piquante. Bric-a-brac et cie. 1932: Le jugement de minuit Lidoire. Les gaietés de l'escadron. Le parteuse de pain. Le rosier de Madame Husson. 1933: L'ordonnance. L'homme sans nom. Le coq du régiment. Ad-hémar aviateur. 1934: Le garrison amoureuse. Angèle. Ma ruche. Nuit de folies. D'amour et d'eau fraîche. Le chéri de sa concierge. Les bleus de la marine. L'hôtel du libre exchange. 1935: Le train de huit heures. Le cavalier Lafleur. Ferdinand le noceur. Les gaietés de la finance. Jim la Houlette. 1936: Les rois du sport. Les dégourdis de la onzième. François premier. Josette. Un de la légion. 1937: Ignace. Regain. Hercule. Un carnet de bal (US: Life Dances On). Ernest le rebelle. 1938: Barnabé. Schpountz. Tricoche et Cacdet. Raphaël le Tatoué. Les cinq sous de Lavarède. 1939: Christine. Berlingot et cie. C'était moi. Fric-Frac. 1940: Monsieur Hector. L'héritier de Montdésir. La fille du puisatier. L'acrobate. Un chapeau de paille d'Italie. L'âge d'or. 1941: La nuit merveilleuse. Le club des soupirants. Les petits viens. Une vie de chien. 1942: La bonne étoile. Simplet. Ne le criez pas sur les toits. 1943: Adrien. La cavalcade des heures. Guignol, marionette de France. 1944: Les gueux du paradis. Naïs. Irma la voyante. 1945: L'aventure de Cabasson. La carrière du grand café. Le mystère Saint-Val. 1946: Pétrus. Coeur du coq. Comédians ambulants. 1947: Édition spéciale. Emile l'Africain. 1948: Si ça peut vous faire plaisir. L'armoire volante. 1949: Je suis de la revue. On demande un assassin. Casimir. L'heroïque Monsieur Boniface. 1950: Topaze. Meurtres. Tu m'as sauvé la vie. Uniformes et grandes manoeuvres. Boniface somnambule (GB: The Sleepwalker). 1951: Le Red Inn/L'auberge rouge. † Adhémar. La table aux crevés (GB: Village Feud). The Little World of Don Camillo. 1952: Coiffeur pour dames (GB: An Artist with Ladies). Forbidden Fruit. Le boulanger de Valargue. The Return of Don Camillo. 1953: Carnaval. Santarellina. Mam'zelle Nitouche. Public Enemy No. 1. 1954: The Sheep Has Five Legs. Ali-Baba. Le printemps, l'automne et l'amour. 1955: La grande bagarre de Don Camillo (GB: Don Camillo's Last Round).

1956: Le couturier de ces dames (GB: Fernandel the Dressmaker). Honoré de Marseille. Quatres pas dans les nuages. L'art d'être papa (TV). Around the World in 80 Days. L'homme à l'imperméable. 1957: Ex: fugue pour clarinette. Le chômeur de Clochemerle. Sénéchal the Magnificent. 1958: Paris Holiday. Le vie à deux (GB: The Two of Us). La loi c'est la loi. The Cow and I. Le grand chef. Le confident de ces dames. Sous le ciel de Provence. 1959: Crésus. Les vignes du Seigneur. 1960: Le caïd. Cocagne. Dynamite Jack. 1961: Don Camillo Monseigneur. Cet imbécile de Rimoldi. L'assassin est dans l'annaire. Il giudizio universale. 1962: En avant la musique. The Devil and the 10 Commandments. Voyage to Biarritz. 1963: La cuisine du beurre (US: My Wife's Husband). Blague dans le coin. 1964: L'âge ingrat. Relaxe-toi, chérie. Le bon roi Dagobert. 1965: La bourse et la vie. Don Camillo in Moscow. 1966: Le voyage du père. 1967: L'homme à la Buick. 1970: Heureux qui comme Ulysse. 1971: The Last of Don Camillo/Don Camillo, Peppone e i Giovanni d'oggi (unfinished).

† And directed

FIELD, Sid 1904–1950
An enormously successful British comedian of music-hall and stage shows of the 1940s, with dark hair, curved eyebrows, green animal eyes and a mobile, Punchinello face. The three films he made before his early death do little to preserve his unique appeal. Born in Edgbaston on April Fool's Day, Field was an on-stage boy comedian at 12 but he toiled away for many years without being anything more than an amusing provincial comic. It was with the addition to his act of tall, imperious Jerry Desmonde as straight man that Field turned the corner. Desmonde, who would later perform a similar service for Norman Wisdom (*qv*), joined Field in 1942. The following year they performed at London's Prince of Wales Theatre in the revue *Strike a New Note*. Although there were nominally no stars in the production when it started, within three weeks Field's name was up in lights. The show ran for 18 months and he followed it with two more long-running hits: *Strike It Again* and *Piccadilly Hayride*. Suddenly Field was *the* funny-man to see in London's West

End, and they were clinging to the rafters to get a glimpse of him. Field would shamble on in some enormous overcoat with padded shoulders and launch into one of his ludicrously funny routines. Looking back on the sketches in his first big movie, an enormous (and enormously expensive) turkey called *London Town*, it's hard to see what all the fuss was about. But one important element is missing: laughter. Field fed on cumulative audience laughter; the more they laughed, the more daring and extrovert the antics became. His enthusiasm was infectious. A second film, *Cardboard Cavalier*, was rather more enjoyable, although it muffled Field's impact by trying to make him a character comedian. He was allowed, however, a few enjoyable one-liners which demonstrated his droll sense of the absurd. Like Wisdom a decade later, Field was a sucker for a sentimental song and had a melodious if not outstanding voice. His best-known number was *You Can't Keep a Good Dreamer Down*, Sid Field was also a drinker and a compulsive worrier: the failure of his films disappointed and disillusioned him. Both weaknesses may have contributed to his death from a heart attack at 45. His favourite catch-phrase was 'What a performance!' With Field on stage, it always was.

1940: *That's the Ticket*. 1946: *London Town* (US: *My Heart Goes Crazy*). 1948: *Cardboard Cavalier*.

FIELDING, Fenella
see FELDMAN, Marty

FIELDS, Dame Gracie
(Grace Stansfield) 1898−1979

One of the earliest examples in show business of the irrepressible born clown who just happens to have a marvellous singing voice as well. Another Briton, Sir Harry Secombe (*qv*), springs to mind in the same category. Secombe, however, was never as big a star as 'Our Gracie' in her prime, a prime that might have lasted a good deal longer but for the unlucky circumstances of her second marriage. Dark and chirpy, with a strong chin and unruly curls that spilled over her forehead, Gracie Fields became

Smashing time. Kit (Gracie Fields) shows husband Dobbie (Victor McLaglen) what she thinks of his latest hare-brained gold-rush scheme, in *We're Going to be Rich*

Britain's highest-paid film star of the 1930s − an unlikely pinnacle for a girl born above a fish and chip shop in the backstreets of Rochdale in Lancashire. The shop belonged the Gracie's grandmother, a local character known as Chip Sarah. Her mother, Jenny Stansfield, was anxious for her children to escape their workaday environment. Stagestruck herself when younger, she was now a cotton-mill worker. Capitalising on her daughter's singing voice, she entered Gracie for her first talent content at seven − and saw her tie for first place. When Gracie became a 'half-timer' at school at 12 her mother made sure the girl entertained at local clubs in the evenings as well as doing her four hours at the mill. Gracie first became part of a juvenile concert-party troupe, then branched out as a solo act at 15, still working in her spare time at the mill or selling ribbons at a local drapery store. It was at that stage that her bubbling, un-putdownable sense of fun led her to start clowning around with her musical numbers. The mixture of seriousness, sentiment and wild burlesque, wrapped up in such a likeable, bubbly personality, soon began to exert a grip on the public throughout the north of England. She began regularly interspersing ballads with comic songs and at 20 became the star of a touring revue, *The Tower of London*. The show ran to packed houses for five years across Britain before hitting London and putting its star at the top of her profession. Her Lancashire accent − which she never lost − proved no bar to national popularity. With the coming of sound, it was inevitable that Gracie's sense of fun and her voice − half-way between a chirrup and an operatic soprano of remarkable clarity − had to be seen and heard in films. She made just over one a year throughout the 1930s,

and the titles reflected their homespun, Depression-killing appeal: *Sally in our Alley* (based on the title of her most popular song), *Looking on the Bright Side*, *Sing As We Go*, *Queen of Hearts*, *Keep Smiling*, *Shipyard Sally* and others. Typically, she played a working girl turning the tables on tyrannical bosses. Towards the end of the decade there was an association with Hollywood's 20th Century-Fox, intended to broaden her international appeal. After a visit to Hollywood, Gracie decreed that these films should be made in Britain. 1940 proved a decisive year in the career of the nation's sweetheart. She divorced her first husband and married director/comedian Monty Banks (*qv*), fleeing with him to America when it became obvious he would be interned as an alien with the entry of Italy into the war on the Axis side. 'Every British paper screamed that I was a traitor', she remembered in later years. 'I was stunned.' Eventually, there were a couple of comedy films in Hollywood, in which she performed with distinction opposite irascible Monty Woolley. She travelled the Commonwealth and entertained the troops. Now based on the isle of Capri − she never returned to Britain to live − she regained something of a foothold in British show business and the affections of the people from the late 1940s on. Banks died in 1950 and two years later Gracie married Boris Alperovici, a Rumanian-born radio mechanic who had been a neighbour of the Bankses on Capri. She remained in demand for concerts until the end of her life, returning to Rochdale in 1978 to open a theatre named after her, and singing one of her greatest comedy hits, *The Biggest Aspidistra in the World*. Finally created Dame in 1979 − an honour which under happier circumstances would have come much earlier; she was a CBE as early as 1938 – she died from a heart attack later the same year on her beloved Capri.

1931: Sally in our Alley. 1932: Looking on the Bright Side. 1933: This Week of Grace. 1934: Love, Life and Laughter. Sing As We Go. 1935: Look Up and Laugh. 1936: Queen of Hearts. 1937: The Show Goes On. 1938: We're Going to be Rich. Keep Smiling (US: Smiling Along). 1939: Shipyard Sally. 1943: Stage Door Canteen. Holy Matrimony. 1944: Molly and Me. 1945: Paris Underground (GB: Madame Pimpernel).

FIELDS, W. C.

(William Claude Dukenfield) 1879–1946
A solidly-built, sandy-haired, plum-nosed American comedian with a voice like a rusty saw and a deep distrust of his fellow man, Fields was an endearing character in spite of the image he presented on screen, which was decidedly less sympathetic than that of most screen comedians. Chiefly, Fields was seen either as a covertly whisky-swilling henpeck, or as a conniving charlatan, lying and cheating to keep himself above the breadline. Somewhere along the plots of his films (often sketched out by himself on the backs of envelopes), his dislike of small children, animals and bankers would probably make itself apparent. His usual expression was a scowl. Dialogue would come from the side of his mouth, and smiles were rare: they usually indicated some underhand triumph over a particularly hated opponent. This might be a wife, mother-in-law or simply *the* law. Only drinking companions were true friends. The breadline was something Fields himself never even reached during his early years of fending for himself, after he ran away from home at the age of 11. He lived by his wits, often sustaining beatings that led to the beginning of the famous bulbous nose. But he had one show business skill – he was adept at juggling (which he had been practising since he was nine) and sleight of hand. It was these dexterities that landed him jobs in fairs and circuses, in between helping to put up tents and shows and generally mess out. While still in his teens, he successfully auditioned

for vaudeville and began a long career on stage; he adopted the name W. C. Fields and was billed initially as a 'comic juggler'. By 20 he had worked his way to the top of the bill at local variety houses. At the turn of the century he went on a European tour with great success, entertaining at the Palace Theatre in London (and, for a special command performance, at Buckingham Palace) and at the Folies Bergère in Paris, where he shared billing with Maurice Chevalier. Back in the United States, he could tour the country as a top-liner, now being billed as 'the silent humorist' as well as 'the comic juggler'. He was making about $100 a week, and it was around this time, travelling from city to city, that he began depositing money in banks all over America, eventually amassing some 700 accounts under various names, ever distrustful of financial sharks around him. Fields had made his Broadway debut in 1905 but it was his appearance in Irving Berlin's *Watch Your Step* in 1914 that made him a major star of the Great White Way, and led to an invitation to make his first films. These proved to be two shorts, *Pool Sharks* (based on his famous vaudeville routine) and *His Lordship's Dilemma*. Any thoughts that might have been hatching among producers and Fields himself about a prolonged film career at this stage were nipped in the bud by the showman Florenz Ziegfeld who signed the comedian up that year (1915) for his famous Follies show. Fields remained a popular regular with the Follies for seven seasons. It was during the early days of this run that he first introduced dialogue into his act. To begin with, as Eddie Cantor (*qv*) a fellow Ziegfeld star recalled, this was in the form of passing ad libs, commenting on assistants or other performers coming on and off the stage. These had the audiences in such stitches that Fields was persuaded that funny lines added to the attractions of his act. 'Once he'd started', Cantor remembered, 'there was no stopping him.' An individual triumph for Fields in the Broadway show that followed, *Poppy* (1923/24), led to a renewal of Hollywood interest and he appeared in a number of silent comedies that exploited the best of his stage material, including *Sally of the Sawdust*, a film version of *Poppy*. For a while it seemed that Hollywood might see Fields as an entertainer in the Will Rogers (*qv*) tradition, but Fields was too rascally, roguish and rough-edged to be another Rogers. In 1928 he began his last major stage run, with the *Earl Carroll Vanities*. It was during this run that he was taken to court for allegedly ill-treating a canary in one of his sketches: something straight out of a W. C. Fields storyline for the movies (Fields was acquitted). What the Fields personality had really been waiting for in films was sound. In the spring of 1930 he went to Hollywood (all but one of his previous films had been made at studios on the other side of the country) to make a short film, *The Golf Specialist*, based on another of his funniest routines. Although

crudely filmed – it would be done much more cinematically a few years later in another Fields comedy – the sketch introduced audiences to the Fields style of delivery, and such famous lines as 'Keep your eye on the ball', 'Keep your wrists close together' and 'I've never struck a woman – not even my own mother'. There's also the 'pie' incident, which provokes Fields to observe, 'Imagine bringing a pie to the golf course. A pint, yes, but a pie, never!' Fields decided that Hollywood, with its warm climate and relaxed atmosphere, was the place for him. But it was several years before he was really to make a mark in his own starring feature films. He discarded the clip-on moustache he had worn for years and, armed with a revised image, launched himself on a movie career. At first, his aggressive style of comedy was seen at its best in two-reelers: *The Fatal Glass of Beer*, *The Barber Shop*, *The Pharmacist* and, especially, *The Dentist*, in which he has to locate a small mouth lost somewhere in a vast black beard. His appearances in features were mainly extended cameos in such all-star ventures as *International House* and *Alice in Wonderland* (as Humpty-Dumpty), which left his fans frustrated at too little Fields footage in the film. In 1934, however, Paramount gave the old curmudgeon his head. *You're Telling Me!* and *It's a Gift* both presented Fields as the browbeaten local businessman who miraculously triumphs over a sea of nagging women in the end. The former contains another version of the golfing sketch and the latter (considered by many to be Fields' most consistently funny film) has the classic encounter with the blind man who wrecks his store. *The Old Fashioned Way* gives us Fields in his other guise, the wily old fox, in this instance the proprietor and star of a travelling troupe of actors who haven't been paid in months, and who only keep in work by staying one jump ahead of the law. Here we see another Fields trait, that of fake courtesy to the opposite sex when they may be of use to him, although, out of her earshot, he describes prospective backer Jan Duggan as 'all dressed up like a well-kept grave'. Fields fans by this time were also becoming fond of his euphemistic oaths, among them 'Godfrey Daniel!', 'Mother of Pearl!' and 'Drat!'. And there were usually barbs-in-passing against babies, black people, policemen, motorists, wives and mothers-in-law. 'It must be hard', says a character to him in *The Man on the Flying Trapeze*, 'to lose your mother-in-law.' Fields considers. 'Yes it is', he rumbles. 'Very hard. Almost impossible.' There were also top character roles for Fields in *Mississippi* and *David Copperfield* (an incomparable Micawber) and a remake of *Sally of the Sawdust*, reverting to the original title *Poppy*. But by 1936 Fields' health was in decline, finally undermined by years of alcoholic abuse. Doctors were another breed of men Fields disliked, and he only consulted them when absolutely necessary. Severely weakened by a long bout of pneumonia, Fields told a friend in 1937 that he expected 'the fellow in the bright nightgown' (a Fieldsian euphemism for death) to collect him before the end of the year. But, to the relief of his supporters, Fields was to cheat the grim reaper for another decade. His renewed popularity in a well-arranged radio 'feud' with ventriloquist Edgar Bergen's famous doll Charlie McCarthy (qv) brought him to Universal Studios, where he made four increasingly harebrained comedies, three as a chiseller-in-chief on the run from his creditors, the other in his familiar guise of the liquor-befuddled henpeck. The latter, The Bank Dick, is generally seen as Fields' last classic. He has an awful wife, a domineering mother-in-law, a brat of a daughter, and magical alcoholic interludes in the Black Pussy Cat Café. In It's a Gift it was an orange grove which came to his rescue. In The Bank Dick it's a 'beefsteak mine', Fields' investments having become increasingly idiotic with the years. The film with Bergen and McCarthy, You Can't Cheat an Honest Man, in which Fields played a circus-owner called Larson E. Whipsnade and also appeared in drag as a trick rider called Buffalo Bella, was more successful than Fields' venture with Mae West, My Little Chickadee, though this too had its moments. Asked by an Indian if poker is a game of chance, Fields takes his measure in a flash and replies: 'Not the way I play it, no-o.' The last film at Universal, Never Give a Sucker an Even Break, was a comedy too surreal for the studio, who hacked large chunks out of it, chopping it down to under an hour to send it out as a second-feature. Fields' star career was played out. His health was again failing, and his last few films consisted of guest spots and a sequence (in Tales of Manhattan) that was cut entirely from the finished film. The day he hated above all others, because it stood for the (unnecessary) spending of money on one's fellow men, was Christmas Day. So it was perhaps appropriate that when the fellow in the bright nightgown finally arrived to collect the old buzzard, who had dropsy and a severe kidney ailment, it was on 25 December. Today his films are more frequently revived than those of most of his contemporaries.

1915: * Pool Sharks. * His Lordship's Dilemma. 1924: Janice Meredith (GB: The Beautiful Rebel). 1925: Sally of the Sawdust. That Royle Girl. 1926: So's Your Old Man. It's the Old Army Game. 1927: The Potters. Running Wild. Two Flaming Youths (GB: The Side Show). 1928: Tillie's Punctured Romance (GB: Marie's Millions). Fools for Luck. 1930: * The Golf Specialist. 1931: Her Majesty Love. 1932: * The Dentist. If I Had a Million. Million Dollar Legs. 1933: The Fatal Glass of Beer. * The Pharmacist. * Hip Action. * Hollywood on Parade (B7). * The Barber Shop. International House. Tillie and Gus. Alice in Wonderland. 1934: Six of a Kind. You're Telling Me! The Old Fashioned Way. It's a Gift. Mrs Wiggs of the Cabbage Patch. 1935: David Copperfield. Mississippi. The Man on the Flying Trapeze (GB: The Memory Expert). 1936: Poppy. 1938: The Big Broadcast of 1938. 1939: You Can't Cheat an Honest Man. 1940: My Little Chickadee. The Bank Dick (GB: The Bank Detective). 1941: Never Give a Sucker an Even Break. 1942: Tales of Manhattan (sequence deleted). 1944: Follow the Boys. Song of the Open Road. Sensations of 1945.

FINLAYSON, James 1887–1953

A scraggy Scotsman with a walrus moustache and the most baleful squint in the business, James (or Jimmy) Finlayson is one of the few comedians in screen history who owes his comic immortality to other comedians. As the antagonist of Laurel and Hardy (qv) in many of their best comedies, Finlayson, who hadn't quite made it to the top under his own steam, became famous for his exaggerated reactions to disaster, topped by what he called his 'double take and fade away'. This facial contortion consisted of 'Fin' screwing one eye up and widening the other at the same time, as he expressed incredulity at what Sylvester the cartoon cat would have called 'another revoltin' development'. Born in Falkirk, Finlayson was the son of a well-to-do iron foundry owner who looked to his son to follow him into the family business. But though the bright youth was sent by his parents to study engineering at Edinburgh University he was drawn to the stage soon after graduation and quickly developed into a popular light comedy player. He went to Broadway in 1916 with a show called Bunty Pulls the Strings and liked the American show-business environment so much that he decided to stay when the play completed its 18-month run. Gravitating to California by 1919, he joined the Mack Sennett studio, playing in all kinds of comedies there. In 1923 he made a significant move across to the Hal Roach lot. Something of a dapper Dan in his early Hollywood films, Finlayson soon developed the wizened features, bushy moustache and balding head that would help make him a star character comedian with Roach. He was a leading light of the All-Stars comedies there, from which Laurel and Hardy graduated to stardom as a team. Finlayson, whose acting style was basically less relaxed, at least in verbal terms, soon became their most formidable foil. Their film feuds with Fin probably reached their height with Big Business, in 1929, in which they pursue the unlikely career of selling Christmas trees in summer. Calling at Finlayson's house, they receive the cold shoulder and, after he cuts up one of their trees, an orgy of destruction ensues that involves the eventual demolition of both

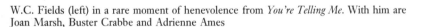

W.C. Fields (left) in a rare moment of benevolence from You're Telling Me. With him are Joan Marsh, Buster Crabbe and Adrienne Ames

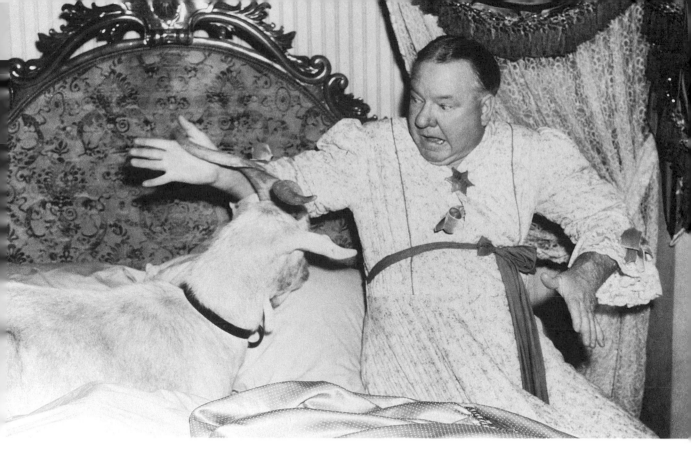

'Godfrey Daniel!' Twillie (W.C. Fields) finds that intended bedmate, Mae West, appears to have metamorphosed into a goat in *My Little Chickadee*

Bud Flanagan, complete with as moth-eaten a fur coat as even he ever wore, and Chesney Allen find themselves 'underneath the arches' for the last time in *Life is a Circus*

George Formby soon discovers that the referee is the least popular person at an ice-hockey match in *I See Ice*. Big Cyril Ritchard clearly has the upper hand

Feeling ropy. George Formby finds that all-in wrestling has him on the ropes in *Trouble Brewing*. Gun McNaughton reckons it's time for plan B

Laurel and Hardy's car and the front of Finlayson's house. It's Finlayson who gets the last close-up, as his adversaries' 'peace-offering' cigar explodes in his face. There were to be 33 films altogether for Finlayson with Stan and Ollie, the sequence being interrupted for a while in 1934–35 when the Scot worked in England, appearing in several minor low-budget comedy films there. Then he returned to Hollywood to take up his role again as the butt of Laurel and Hardy's bunglings. Few comedians were as amusingly apoplectic in defeat. Laurel and Hardy's departure from the Roach studio was the end of an era for many of the comedy players who were their contemporaries there. Finlayson stayed on in Hollywood, making around a dozen more minor appearances before his death from a heart attack at 66.

*1919: * Love's False Faces. * Why Beaches Are Popular. 1920: Married Life. Down on the Farm. 1921: *A Small Town Idol. Home Talent. 1922: The Crossroads of New York. Home Made Movies. * The Counter Jumper. 1923: Hollywood. * White Wings. * Roughest Africa. A Man About Town. * The Soilers. * The Barnyard. * No Wedding Bells. 1924: * Near Dublin. * Wide Open Spaces/Wild Bill Hiccup. * Brothers Under the Chin. * Smithy. * Rupert of Hee-Haw/Rupert of Cole-Slaw. 1925: Welcome Home. * Official Officers. * Mary, Queen of Tots. * Yes, Yes, Nanette. * Unfriendly Enemies. * Moonlight and Noses. * Hard Boiled. Innocent. * Thundering Fleas. * Husbands. * The Caretaker's Daughter. 1926: * Madame Mystery. * Never Too Old. * The Merry Widower. * Wise Guys Prefer Brunettes. * Raggedy Rose. * The Nickel Hopper. 1927: * Seeing the World. * With Love and Hisses. * Love 'Em and Weep. * Do Detectives Think? * Hats Off. * Flying Elephants. * Sugar Daddies. * The Call of the Cuckoos. * The Second Hundred Years. No Man's Law. 1928: Lady Be Good. Ladies' Night in a Turkish Bath (GB: Ladies' Night). Show Girl. Bachelor's Paradise. * Should Tall Men Marry? * Galloping Ghosts. 1929: * Liberty. * Big Business. * Men o' War. * The Hoose Gow. Two Weeks Off. Hard to Get. Wall Street. * Fast Freight. 1930: * Dollar Dizzy. * Night Owls. *Another Fine Mess. For the Defense. Young Eagles. Flight Commander. The Dawn Patrol. 1931: Big Business Girl. * One of the Smiths. * False Roomers. * A Melon-Drama. * Catch As Catch Can. * Oh! Oh! Cleopatra. * Scratch As Catch Can. * One Good Turn. * Our Wife. * Chicken Come Home. * The Hasty Marriage. Pardon Us (GB: Jailbirds). * Stout Hearts and Willing Hands. 1932: * The Chimp. * Boy, Oh Boy. * Trouble from Abroad. † * Any Old Port. * The Iceman's Ball. Pack Up Your Troubles. * So This Is Harris. * Thru Thin and Thicket, or Who's Zoo in Africa. Thunder Below. * The Millionaire Cat. * Union Wages. * Jitters, the Butler. 1933: The Devil's Brother (GB: Fra Diavolo). * Mush and Milk. * Me and My Pal. * His Silent Racket. * The*

*Druggist's Dilemma. * The Gay Nighties. The Girl in Possession. Dick Turpin. Strictly in Confidence. 1934: What Happened to Harkness. Oh! No, Doctor. Big Business (and 1929 short). Father and Son. Nine Forty Five. Trouble in Store. 1935: Handle with Care. Who's Your Father? * Thicker Than Water. Bonnie Scotland. *Manhattan Monkey Business. 1936: The Bohemian Girl. Our Relations. * Life Hesitates at 40. 1937: All Over Town. Pick a Star. Way Out West. Toast of New York. Angel. 1938: Carefree. * False Roomers. Block-Heads. Wise Girl. 1939: The Great Victor Herbert. The Flying Deuces. A Small Town Idol (revised sound version of 1921 film). Hollywood Cavalcade. A Chump at Oxford. 1939–40: Raffles. 1940: Foreign Correspondent. Saps at Sea. 1941: Nice Girl? One Night in Lisbon. 1942: To Be or Not To Be. 1943: Yanks Ahoy! 1946: Till the Clouds Roll By. 1947: The Perils of Pauline. Thunder in the Valley (GB: Bob, Son of Battle). 1948: Grand Canyon Trail. Julia Misbehaves. 1950: Royal Wedding (GB: Wedding Bells). 1951: Here Comes the Groom.*

† Scenes deleted from final release print.

FLANAGAN, Bud (above)
(Reuben Weintrop, later Robert Winthrop) 1896–1968
and
ALLEN, Chesney 1893–1982
At once vulgar and endearing, these two giants of the English music-halls first met by accident in 1917 (the same year Laurel had a first chance encounter with Hardy on film) although, on the evidence of later years, both men only barely remembered it. They had been born under very different circumstances and it was something of a miracle that they ended up together. Flanagan was born in London to poor Polish Jews and at the age of 13 was trying to break into show

business as Fargo the Boy Wizard. He failed. A year later he ran away from home and worked his passage to America. He was a messenger boy, a boxer (Canvasback Cohen) and a newsboy. He got a single line in a play as a bellhop, and consolidated his foothold in show business with a revue that went round the world. After service in World War One he returned to London with a new name, stolen from a much-hated Irish sergeant, but no notable success. He worked as a cab driver before running into Allen again and forming a team. Chesney Allen's vaguely transatlantic twang probably owed something to his Somerset-born father but he himself was born in Brighton and began his working life as a solicitor's clerk. He started acting in local repertory, then moved on to become the straight man in a series of double acts. These led him, after wartime service as a cavalryman, to London's Criterion Theatre with Florrie Forde's troupe, and it was near here that he ran into Flanagan for the second time. The two men teamed up in 1920 and soon began to make progress as a polished act with the accent on madcap humour. Everything about Flanagan (except his height) was big: his girth, his mouth, his nose, his face, his eyebrows. He soon assumed his familiar garb: shabby racoon fur coat that reached nearly to the ground, topped by pork-pie hat or boater with snapped-up brim. Chesney Allen, on the other hand, who bore a passing resemblance to the American straight man Bud Abbott (qv), was snappily dressed and usually egged Flanagan on to some new mayhem (or punch-line) in reassuring, confidential tones. Their big breakthrough as a team came in 1929. Then in the early 1930s they merged with other comedy teams to form the Crazy Gang, which maintained a reign of constant pandemonium in several London shows of that decade. With and without the Gang, Flanagan and Allen made a number of ramshackle comedy romps from the beginning of the 1930s to the end of the war years. The films with the Gang on board reflect more the undiluted anarchy of the stage shows – British relatives of Olsen and Johnson's (qv) Hellzapoppin. The films with Bud and Ches on their own tend to be on the sentimental side, and contain some of their million-selling songs, always lilting, often nostalgic, patriotic or redolent of hard times: Underneath the Arches, Strolling, Run Rabbit Run, The Umbrella Man, Dreaming and Hang Out Your Washing on the Siegfried Line. Flanagan's light East End cockney voice could carry a song as easily as descend to a demonic chuckle and Allen harmonised by emphasising various syllables. They were a formidable team of duettists as well as comedians. Favourites of the British royal family, who were known to ask them not to tone down their ruderies when they attended one of their performances, Bud and Ches split in 1946 because the straight man was plagued with arthritis and could no longer perform on stage. Ironically he would out-

Bud Flanagan (at rear) and The Crazy Gang are up their frozen wastes in trouble when staring down the barrels of Moore Marriott's pistols in *The Frozen Limits*

live every member of the Gang. But Flanagan carried on. After all, he had the Crazy Gang. And their stage shows continued, seven more of them between 1947 and 1962, when the Gang bade farewell to their devoted audiences. There was even another film, in 1958, *Life is a Circus*, with Allen in a guest role. It was a remake of one of the Gang's funniest – *Alf's Button Afloat*. The chaos the comedians wrought was always impeccably timed and well-rehearsed. The stage shows and the funniest of the films were warm, spontaneous-seeming, non-stop fun in the broad working-class manner of the times. The shows ceased in 1962 and the Gang more or less retired, Flanagan spending time on his boxing promotions. He died from a heart attack at 72, 14 years before his laconic partner, who proved sprightly enough to make personal appearances into his mid eighties. Flanagan was Jewish, an inveterate practical joker, a gambler, a spendthrift and a human dynamo. Allen was a Christian, a sobersides, careful with money, not funny in himself and the businessman of the entire Gang, whose accounts he assiduously logged. 'And yet', Allen once said, 'our personalities complemented each other perfectly. It was a wonderful combination.'

*1932: * The Bailiffs. 1933: * They're Off. * The Dreamers. 1934: Wild Boy. 1935: A Fire Has Been Arranged. 1937: Underneath The Arches. O-Kay for Sound. 1938: Alf's Button Afloat. 1939: The Frozen Limits. 1940: Gasbags. 1941: * Listen to Britain. * The Crazy Gang Argue About Lending Money (Gaumont-British newsreel). 1942: We'll Smile Again. 1943: Theatre Royal. 1944: Dreaming. 1945: Here Comes the Sun. 1958: Dunkirk. Life is a Circus.*

Flanagan alone. *1951: Judgment Deferred. 1963: The Wild Affair.*

FORDE, Walter
(Thomas Seymour) 1896–1984
Britain's only major screen comedian of the 1920s, stocky, nimble, impish, light-haired Walter Forde, perhaps disappointed by his efforts in sound films, elected instead to become a director – with amazing success. A lively little man with a passing resemblance to Spencer Tracy, Forde was born in Yorkshire and, after having some lyrics for songs published, became a music-hall entertainer in the north of England. Initially he was a pianist (including a cinema stint accompanying silent movies), but improvised more and more comedy into his act. Contributing scenarios to films, he was persuaded to step in front of the camera in 1920, in three two-reeler films he devised himself. Forde was an admirer of Harold Lloyd (*qv*) and that soon began to show in his own work, in which he is the little man

forced into unwanted feats of derring-do only for his bravery to go unappreciated. He went to Hollywood in 1923 and worked for Universal, without becoming anything of a name. Returning to Britain in 1925, he recommended work on his two-reel comedies, usually as the willing young trier who somehow gets the hand of his employer's daughter in the end. He was still doing it in his first feature, *Wait and See*. Sound was approaching and the title of Forde's next feature was both appropriate and prophetic: *What Next?* had him fleeing the attentions of a maniac collector after accidentally buying an old candlestick the madman desperately needs. As a mixture of chills and chuckles, it was his best and most sophisticated work to date. The next, *Would You Believe It?*, was also silent, but Forde bowed to the inevitable and had sound added six months later. However, words robbed Forde's comedy of much of its subtlety, and his interest in performing was rapidly waning. He had already begun directing films in which he did not appear and Gainsborough were soon assigning him to their more prestigious projects. The enthusiastic reviews he gathered for *The Ringer* and *The Ghost Train* convinced both himself and his studio that the right decision had been made. Forde's best film as director was probably *Rome Express*, in 1932, an archetypal train thriller in which the direction was acclaimed by one critic as 'masterly'. But it was in comedy that he was predictably most consistent. There were four films with Jack Hulbert and several with Gordon Harker (both *qv*), most notably two of the three popular Inspector Hornleigh capers. In wartime years, however, Forde's two films that attempted to launch Tommy Handley (*qv*) as a major film comedian proved disappointing, and he was not the same force thereafter, taking an early retirement that lasted 35 years.

*1920: † * The Handy Man. † * Fishing for Trouble. † * Never Say Die. 1921: * Walter's Winning Ways. * Walter Finds a Father. 1922: ‡ * Walter Wins a Wager. *‡ Walter's Trying Frolic. ‡ * Walter Makes a Movie. † * Walter Wants Work. 1923–5: * Unidentified Universal shorts. 1925: *Walter's Paying Policy. 1926: * Walter's Worries. * Walter the Sleuth. * Walter's Day Out. * Walter Tells the Tale. * Walter the Prodigal. 1928: † Wait and See. † What Next? 1929: † Would You Believe It? 1930: You'd Be Surprised.*

† Also directed
‡ Also co-directed

Also as director. *1929: The Silent House. 1930: Red Pearls. The Last Hour. Lord Richard in the Pantry. Bed and Breakfast. 1931: The Ringer. Splinters in the Navy. Third Time Lucky. The Ghost Train. Condemned to Death. 1932: Lord Babs. Jack's the Boy (US: Night and Day). Rome Express. 1933: Orders is Orders. 1934: Chu Chin Chow. Jack Ahoy! 1935: Bulldog Jack (US: Alias Bulldog Drummond). Brown on Resolution (later: For*

Ever England. US: Born for Glory). King of the Damned. 1936: Land without Music (US: Forbidden Music). 1938: Kicking the Moon Around (US: The Playboy). The Gaunt Stranger (US: The Phantom Strikes). 1939: Inspector Hornleigh on Holiday. Let's Be Famous. The Four Just Men (US: The Secret Four). Cheer Boys Cheer. 1940: Saloon Bar. Sailors Three (US: Three Cockeyed Sailors). Charley's (Big-Hearted) Aunt. Neutral Port. Gasbags. 1941: The Ghost Train (remake). Inspector Hornleigh Goes to It (US: Mail Train). Atlantic Ferry (US: Sons of the Sea). 1942: Flying Fortress. * Go to Blazes. The Peterville Diamond. 1943: It's That Man Again. Time Flies. 1947: Master of Bankdam. 1949: Cardboard Cavalier.

FORMBY, George
(G. Booth) 1904–1961

It was hard not to like this unlikely superstar comedian from the heart of the north of England. The huge, friendly grin and shy manner were two reasons – in films he always had two left feet with girls as well as everything else – but it was his musical talents that set the warbler from Wigan apart from the rest. No-one else strummed a ukulele quite so heartily, nor had such a repertoire of comic songs with wittily-written, ingenious and seemingly endless verses. Formby wasn't a great joke teller, but it was these songs, and the warmth of a personality that seemed introverted and amazed at his success that first made him a star. The son of another singer-comedian, James Booth, who changed his name to George Formby in the early 1900s, the younger Formby was seen by his father as a budding jockey. He became an apprentice at a stable at the age of seven, but after his father's death in 1921 he quickly threw up horse-racing for a life on the stage. He married Beryl Hoy, one half of a singing sister act, and she became both a bane and a blessing to him. Beryl's overbearing nature and constant jealousy meant that the marriage itself was a happy one for only a few years. But she made a brilliant business manager, always seeming to know what was best for her husband's career, and helping him to accumulate far more money than he

might have done with someone else. After he had become a music-hall star in his native Lancashire, he and Beryl appeared in a film together, *Boots! Boots!*, a ramshackle affair set in a hotel (where George was the boot boy), but mostly shot in a room over a garage in Manchester. Hardly subtle, but with effective knockabout comedy, the film made a considerable profit on its tiny initial investment. Following a second Manchester-made comedy, *Off the Dole*, in which Beryl also co-starred, George was taken up nationally by a major studio – ATP, later to become more famous as Ealing Studios. His first two appearances had been as a character called John Willie, but for the rest of his film career his characters would all be called George. George's helplessness in the face of adversity, the slight figure that made women want to mother him, the face that could be gormless when he looked dismayed and stuck his lower lip out, or beguiling when he flashed that toothy smile, plus those million-selling naughty-but-nice strumalong songs, had audiences queueing down the street after George's first ATP film *No Limit*. It cast him as a chimney sweep who becomes a motor-cycling

champion and featured the hit song *Riding at the TT Races*. It was two years later that he hit it big again with *Keep Fit*, which helped take him to the number one box-office position among British stars; it was one he would hold from 1937 to 1943. Meanwhile the film hits flowed: *I See Ice, It's in the Air, Come on George, Trouble Brewing, Let George Do It, Spare a Copper* and *Turned Out Nice Again* were all monster money-spinners. George's flapping limbs, co-ordinated only when strumming a song, flailed their way into the most unlikely situations, including a wrestling match in which he had trouble disentangling himself from the knots into which his opponent had tied him. Sport was something his body could never fathom, and helplessly attempting to referee a ferocious ice hockey match in *I See Ice* was probably George's finest hour. With the films came the songs: *Hitting the Highspots Now, Keep Fit, Fanlight Fanny, Leaning on a Lamp, When I'm Cleaning Windows* and many more. The films were directed at a rattling pace by Marcel Varnel, a key figure in the development of British comedy who also made the best films of Will Hay and Flanagan and Allen/the Crazy Gang (all *qv*). Formby took

Maid to measure — for handcuffs? Police sergeant George Carney has George Formby (left) in a tight corner in *Come On George*

Varnel with him when he moved across the way from ATP to Columbia-British, an ill-advised move since the new company could lavish neither the tender loving care nor the technical discipline on George's vehicles that he had come to take for granted at Ealing. His last film, *George in Civvy Street*, released in 1946, was stale and uninspired. His health was failing and his personal life a misery: he had begun an unofficial separation from Beryl that would last to her death in 1960. Varnel died in a car crash in 1947 at the early age of 53 and George decided his film days were over. Apart from the decline in his own popularity, George was right. Ealing were embarking on a different kind of comedy, and George's brand of slapstick wouldn't become popular again until it was taken up by another all-fingers-and-thumbs singing fool, Norman Wisdom (*qv*) seven years later. By this time, George had revived his stage career with a highly successful revue *Zip Goes a Million*. Again his health let him down: he collapsed with a coronary thrombosis in 1952, but he made a comeback in the autumn of the following year and proved a popular top-of-the-bill in summer seaside seasons for the rest of his days. In 1960 he even had another song hit, *Happy-Go-Lucky Me*. Beryl died in December of that year and George soon announced plans to marry his love of many years, a schoolteacher. But three months later he himself was dead from a heart attack. Strangely enough, Formby's mother, a robust old soul, outlived him by 20 years, reaching the age of 102. She it was who gave George his most famous catch-line. Trapped by the bad guys and in a hopeless situation, George always had flailing panic and a stammering cry of 'M-m-m-mother!' to fall back on.

*1915: By the Shortest of Heads. 1934: Boots! Boots! 1935: Off the Dole. No Limit. 1936: Keep Your Seats Please. 1937: Keep Fit. Feather Your Nest. 1938: I See Ice. * Cavalcade of the Stars. It's in the Air (US: George Takes the Air). 1939: Come on George. Trouble Brewing. 1940: Let George Do It (US: The Hell with Hitler). Spare a Copper. 1941: Turned Out Nice Again. South American George. 1942: Much Too Shy. 1943: Bell Bottom George. Get Cracking. 1944: He Snoops to Conquer. 1945: I Didn't Do It. 1946: George in Civvy Street.*

FREEMAN, Kathleen 1920–

This cheery, chubby-faced American character actress was to Jerry Lewis what Margaret Dumont was to Groucho Marx (all *qv*). A female foil, a lucky charm, a game getter of laughs, and the long-suffering recipient of the consequences of her co-star's misfortunes. Light-haired, with a milkmaid's face and buxom build, Kathleen broke into films after drama school and repertory training, followed by experience in stock. There was an early glimpse of her as strap-hanging commuter in *The Naked City*; with her youthful looks, she could play

bobby-soxers and college girls even in her late twenties, and enjoyed steady work in minor roles. In 1950's *Lonely Hearts Bandits* she took advantage of a rare leading role as a girl duped by a fake matrimonial agency. She began playing more comedy from the early 1950s, her first encounter with Jerry Lewis coming in 1954's *Three-Ring Circus*, when he was still in partnership with Dean Martin. There were to be appearances in ten more Lewis comedies over the next 15 years. As she entered young middle age, Freeman came into her own as a comedy player. In *The Ladies' Man* (1961), she was Katie, the plain girl among a host of pretty ones. From then on, jowls sagging, eyebrows arched, her mouth was either wide open in outrage, or snapped shut in an expression that boded ill for some poor miscreant – usually Lewis. He fell foul of her dragons in *The Nutty Professor*, *The Disorderly Orderly*, *Three on a Couch* and more: the films were the funnier for it. She became a latter-day mistress of the double-take. From 1966 she began to mix television with films, making regular appearances in *Hogan's Heroes*, *The Beverly Hillbillies* and *Lotsa Luck*, the latter a mid-seventies version of the British comedy hit *On the Buses*, casting her as the bossy, autocratic mother of Dom DeLuise (*qv*). In her early seventies, Freeman remains a busy working actress, still very much her old, ebullient self in cameo roles.

*1948: * Annie Was a Wonder. The Naked City. The Saxon Charm. Casbah. Behind Locked Doors. 1949: Mr Belvedere Goes to College. The House by the River. 1950: A Life of Her Own. Lonely Hearts Bandits (GB: Lonely Heart Bandits). The Reformer and the Redhead. Once a Thief. No Man of Her Own. Cry Danger. 1951: Appointment with Danger (filmed 1949). A Place in the Sun. Cause for Alarm. Behave Yourself! The Wild Blue Yonder (GB: Thunder Across the Pacific). Kid Monk Baroni (GB: Young Paul Baroni). The Company She Keeps. Love is Better Than Ever (GB: The Light Fantastic). Let's Make It Legal. 1952: Talk About a Stranger. Singin' in the Rain. The Bad and the Beautiful. O. Henry's Full House (GB: Full House). The Greatest Show on Earth. Wait 'Til the Sun Shines, Nellie. The Prisoner of Zenda. Monkey Business. Bonzo*

Goes to College. 1953: She's Back on Broadway. The Magnetic Monster. Half a Hero. The Glass Web. The Affairs of Dobie Gillis. Dream Wife. The Glass Wall. A Perilous Journey. 1954: Athena. Three-Ring Circus. The Far Country. 1955: Artists and Models. 1956: Hollywood or Bust. 1957: The Midnight Story (GB: Appointment with a Shadow). Kiss Them for Me. Pawnee (GB: Pale Arrow). 1958: The Fly. Houseboat. Too Much, Too Soon. The Buccaneer. The Missouri Traveler. 1959: Don't Give Up the Ship. 1960: North to Alaska. 1961: The Ladies' Man. The Errand Boy. Wild Harvest. 1962: Madison Avenue. 1963: The Nutty Professor. Mail Order Bride (GB: West of Montana). 1964: The Rounders. The Disorderly Orderly. 1965: Marriage on the Rocks. 1966: Three on a Couch. 1967: Point Blank. The Helicopter Spies (TV. GB: cinemas). 1968: Hook, Line and Sinker. Support Your Local Sheriff! 1969: The Good Guys and the Bad Guys. Death of a Gunfighter. Le sorelle/So Evil My Sister. 1970: But I Don't Want to Get Married (TV). Myra Breckinridge. Hitched (TV. GB: Westward the Wagon). The Ballad of Cable Hogue. Which Way to the Front? (GB: Ja! Ja! Mein General! But Which Way to the Front?). 1971: Head On. Support Your Local Gunfighter. Where Does It Hurt? 1972: Stand Up and Be Counted. Call Her Mom (TV). 1973: Unholy Rollers. Your Three Minutes Are Up. 1974: The Daughters of Joshua Cabe Return (TV). 1975: The Strongest Man in the World. 1978: The Norseman. 1980: The Blues Brothers. 1986: The Malibu Bikini Shop (completed 1984). The Best of Times. 1987: Innerspace. In the Mood (later and GB: The Woo Woo Kid). 1988: Glitz (TV). 1989: Chances Are. 1990: Hollywood Chaos. The Princess and the Dwarf. Gremlins 2: The New Batch. Joey Takes a Cab. 1991: Tales from the Crypt (TV). The Willies.

FULLER, Leslie 1889–1948

A burly, bluff, beetle-browed British concert-party comedian with a horsey face, working-class image, and a fondness for too-tight tweeds. Concert-party comics, several of whom became quite popular in low-budget British comedies of the 1930s and 1940s, were mostly open-air types, who were just as likely to be found on the end of

Leslie Fuller gets that sinking feeling about young Peter Lawson's hat trick, in the early Fuller comedy *Bill's Legacy*

directed by Norman Lee, a comedy expert who also worked extensively with Fuller's contemporary Ernie Lotinga (*qv*). Lee once wrote that the main thing about a Fuller character was that it must be intensely human. 'As for the Fuller dialogue', he added, 'it need be neither scintillating nor witty — it is enough if it be funny. Broadly funny. A Fuller joke is often a familiar one, because Leslie believes that people laugh most heartily at the jokes they know best. So a creative mind is not quite so essential as a good memory!' Lee's Fuller vehicles are amiable, artless pictures and, made on a shoestring, they all showed a profit. Their success encouraged Fuller to make his own comedy films. *Strictly Illegal*, the first Leslie Fuller production, is passable fun in which bookmaker Fuller masquerades as a clergyman, but the series ran rapidly downhill and Fuller's popularity had diminished considerably by 1937. After a gap of two years, he found himself able to get only supporting roles or co-leads in poor bottom-of-the-barrel comedies. He had one decent role in *Front Line Kids* in 1942, but his last film, *What Do We Do Now?*, had him well down the cast as a cabby, in support of a nondescript comedian called George Moon. Fuller returned to the concert-party circuit. He was still living in Margate, his screen fame practically forgotten, when he died from a heart attack at 59. His first wife had died in 1931 and two years later Fuller had married actress Nan Bates, who had played a minor role in one of his films.

1930: Not So Quiet on the Western Front. Kiss Me Sergeant! Why Sailors Leave Home. 1931: Old Soldiers Never Die. Poor Old Bill. Bill's Legacy. What a Night! Tonight's the Night — Pass It On. 1932: Old Spanish Customers. The Last Coupon. 1933: Hawleys of High Street. The Pride of the Force. A Political Party. 1934: The Outcast. Lost in the Legion. Doctor's Orders. 1935: Strictly Illegal/Here Comes a Policeman. The Stoker. Captain Bill. 1936: One Good Turn. 1937: Boys Will Be Girls. 1939: The Middle Watch. 1940: Two Smart Men. 1941: My Wife's Family. 1942: Front Line Kids. 1945: What Do We Do Now?

a seaside pier as on a makeshift stage in your local park. Fuller was actually born at the seaside, in Margate (though some sources say Hackney) and lived all his life there. He began his career in seaside shows before World War One and was already a local name when he met another comedian (and later film character actor) called Syd Courtenay. Courtenay was also a writer of jokes and sketches. He began writing material for Fuller in 1919 and stayed with him through the greater part of his career. In these little anecdotes, Fuller was always a cheerful but unlucky blue-collar character called Bill, and he took the creation with him when BIP films beckoned in 1930. Raucous, boisterous and larger-than-life, Fuller made films that were never for sophisticates. The first half-dozen or so were very basic knockabout farces, casting him as Bill, with various surnames that always ended with 's', like Higgins, Biggles or Smithers. Fuller would usually play a soldier, a sailor or, in one instance, a travelling salesman loose in a haunted house. From 1932 the films assumed a slightly longer (70-minute) 'character' format. In *The Last Coupon*, one

of Fuller's few really good comedies, he was given an amusing script by Courtenay and Frank Launder and played a miner who thinks he's won a jackpot on the pools (he's mistaken). Around this time, Fuller started to develop the use of catch-phrases in his films: he could usually be relied upon to utter 'Dear, dear, dear!' somewhere in the course of the plot. Basic physical slapstick was the order of the day in Fuller's films, but occasionally he could show an inventive touch. In *Hawleys of High Street*, otherwise a lesser Courtenay-Launder effort, there's an uproarious battle between Fuller and Moore Marriott (*qv*), a draper and a butcher who are rivals at the local council elections. What makes this duel different is that it's carried out entirely with joints of meat. Fuller's liveliest films were made in 1933 and the early part of 1934. In *Pride of the Force*, he played twins, a policeman and a slow-witted farmhand. In *A Political Party*, one of two films Fuller made with the young John Mills, he was a chimney sweep standing for Parliament. In the other Mills film, *Doctor's Orders*, Fuller did well as Professor Pippin, a carnival quack. All three of these films were

FYFFE, Will 1884–1947

One of the most beloved of twentieth-century British comedians, Will Fyffe was a tubby, sandy-haired Scotsman of no great height whose homespun fun captivated music-hall audiences through four decades. In some ways Fyffe was a Scottish equivalent to the great American tale-teller Will Rogers (*qv*) and, strangely, both men were to come to tragic ends. In the cinema, both made their names in wryly humorous character roles. Will was born in Dundee, on Scotland's east coast, where his father Jack at first ran a penny arcade. The boy played his first acting roles at five in Jack's wooden 'geggies', a kind of mobile theatre. When Jack set out to reach a wider audience with his touring company Will, then seven, went with him. The lad travelled Scotland playing both boy and girl roles, such as Little Willie in *East Lynne* and Little Eva in *Uncle Tom's Cabin*. In the Boer War, the teenage Will recited Kipling to British troops in South Africa, while at 17 he became one of the youngest actors to tackle *Hamlet*, a role for which he was paid the princely sum of £2 a week! A year later, though, Will had decided to make comedy his stock in trade. He would often tell the story in later years that it was one line that had decided him when, as a judge in a farce, he had uttered the words: 'Let the murdered man give evidence' and brought the house down. Will's subtle, pawky humour had keen insight into humanity. He was soon a top-of-the-bill artist with his ripe, warm-hearted tales of a ship's engineer, a railway guard, a dock labourer, a Gretna Green blacksmith and a gamekeeper-turned-poacher. He also began to write the songs with which he completed his act. There was one called *I Belong to Glasgow*, which Will held back, hoping to sell it to another great Scottish entertainer Sir Harry Lauder. That never happened, and instead the song became Will Fyffe's signature tune as he staggered around the stage in a genial imitation of the archetypal drunken working-class Scot on a Saturday night in the city. Much later, there was another big song hit, *I'm 94 Today*. When Will entertained the troops in World War One, it wasn't with Kipling but with jokes, a task he undertook again in World War Two, being awarded a CBE for this work in 1942. In 1921 Will brought his act to London music-halls and was acclaimed by the then-critical London Palladium audience. A national star 'overnight', he was featured in the next Royal Command Performance and topped bills throughout the decade before making a brief film debut in 1930, then going to America to star on Broadway. A subtle humorist who 'never cracked a blue joke in m'life', Will didn't fit in to the American revue scene of the early 1930s. In 1932 he tore up a $1,000 a week contract and flew home to Scotland. He said of the show that made him do it: 'It had too much sex in it. I couldna stand it.' Back in Britain, he was gobbled up by the bustling cinema industry for both comic and dramatic character roles. There was a supporting role in a Stanley Lupino film, *Happy*, before he was given his own vehicle, albeit a silly 'B' called *Rolling Home*, as a whisky-swilling engineer. Generally speaking, most of Fyffe's comedies of the period were too broad to suit his style, and he only found the right blend of comedy and sentiment within films where he could build a sympathetic character, who might often be wily and stubborn as well. *Annie Laurie* and *Owd Bob* were the ones in which he showed up best, the latter leading to a Hollywood film, *Rulers of the Sea*, with Douglas Fairbanks Jr. Fyffe stole all his scenes as an endearing, wry-humoured steam-engine inventor, and returned to Britain with his reputation

enhanced. Journalists began to push Fyffe's claims to being a major British character star. There was a made-to-measure part as a nervous jeweller who rounds up a gang of crooks in *They Came By Night*, and two unorthodox portraits of Edgar Wallace's detective Mr J. G. Reeder. After flag-waving thrillers like *For Freedom* and *Neutral Port*, though, Fyffe was off entertaining British forces overseas again. He came back to find himself supporting American songstress Leni Lynn, playing her father and uncle in two unsuccessful attempts to launch her as a film star. Thereafter it was back to variety halls until 1947, when he was contracted for featured roles in *The Brothers* and *Bonnie Prince Charlie*. Will completed the first of these, but started to sustain dizzy spells and became too ill to continue the second (Finlay Currie replaced him). He was rushed into hospital where he had an emergency ear operation. He seemed to be recovering and went to recuperate at his favourite hotel overlooking the famous golf course at St Andrew's. He referred to it as 'the wee pub I keep doon at the golf links'. But while looking out of his second-floor window he seems to have been overcome by another fit of dizziness and fell to the ground below, sustaining injuries from which he later died. The Scotsman whom thousands felt they knew as a friend was much mourned. One critic said that his best films 'were homely, simple, quiet and richly entertaining in their character and humanity.' He could have added that Will Fyffe was a wise and witty man whose knowledge of human nature had enabled him to mine a rich vein of humour for the better part of his career.

1930: Elstree Calling. 1933: Happy. 1935: Rolling Home. 1936: Debt of Honour. King of Hearts. Love in Exile. Man of Yesterday. Annie Laurie. Well Done, Henry. 1937: Spring Handicap. Cotton Queen. Said O'Reilly to McNab (US: Sez O'Reilly to McNab). Owd Bob (US: To the Victor). 1939: Rulers of the Sea. The Mind of Mr Reeder (US: The Mysterious Mr Reeder). The Missing People. 1940: They Came by Night. For Freedom. Neutral Port. 1941: The Prime Minister. * Camp Concert. 1943: * Scottish Savings No. 2. 1944: Heaven is Round the Corner. Give Me the Stars. 1947: The Brothers.

GERRARD, Gene
(Eugene O'Sullivan) 1890–1971

Like many other British stage musical-comedy talents, breezy, debonair Gene Gerrard mixed stage and screen careers in the boom years of the early 1930s in the British cinema. When the standard of his vehicles began to fall away, he returned to the stage, but not for too long, retiring early to a home in the country. Many of his early successes stemmed from successful stage shows or works by P.G. Wodehouse. Here he was handsome, but often shy with the ladies, a sort of cross between Jack Buchanan and Harold Lloyd (*qv*) with a dry sense of humour and competent singing and dancing talents. But, as with many of Britain's 1930s stars, he was already in his forties when sound films came in, digesting most of the country's top stage talents. The son of a tailor, he began his career as a cutter in his father's shop in High Holborn, London. Dissatisfied with life there, he resolved to try for a stage career, and made his first appearance on the boards at the London Palladium in 1910 as boy stooge to the famous comedian George Mozart (1864–1947), himself later a popular character player in films. Gerrard remained with Mozart for five years, the partnership being broken when the younger man went into the army, serving in Italy for much of World

War One. Gradually coming to the fore in musical comedy on his return to civilian life (following a tour of Australia), Gerrard's career received a major boost when he wrote and produced *The Midnight Frolics*, in which he co-starred with the legendary Gertrude Lawrence. In 1925 he scored a great personal success in another revue, *Katya the Dancer*, which ran for more than 500 performances. He had made his film debut years before, working for producer Cecil Hepworth on several long-forgotten short subjects around 1912. His sound film debut came in May 1931 in a film whose title summed up his movie output: *Let's Love and Laugh*. He played a workshy toff who marries a chorus girl in a drunken revel. His studio, Elstree, impressed by this debut, decided to promote Gerrard as a musical-comedy star. Equally at home with comedy that was elegant or zany, Gerrard prospered for a while, co-directing several of his own films, including *Out of the Blue*, which introduced cinema audiences to Jessie Matthews. Most of these comedies were enlivened by Gerrard's friendly, energetic brand of fooling, but he never found the one outstanding vehicle that could have established him as a first-rank movie star. Early in 1936 a fire destroyed part of Elstree Studios and production there was curtailed. Elstree gave up its regular vehicles for Gerrard as part of the cutback, which would have taken place anyway with the impending movie slump. Like others, Gerrard found his brand of dry-martini tomfoolery going out of style; people were paying instead to see the broad roughhouse antics of George Formby (*qv*). He was back on stage in 1937, although there was a little film work for Warner Brothers' British studios in 1938. He seemed lost without comedy material in the sentimental *Glamour Girl* and then directed fellow comic Claude Hulbert (*qv*) in *It's in the Blood*; the rest of Hulbert's Warner comedies were made by Americans — not that they were that much more successful. Gerrard seemed more at home on stage in *Pelissier's Follies*, then became a regular in pantomime, playing the king in *Humpty Dumpty* in three successive years in cities around Britain. He retired to live in Devon in 1948.

*1912: * Unknown Hepworth productions. 1931: Let's Love and Laugh (US: Bridegroom for Two). My Wife's Family. Out of the Blue. 1932: Brother Alfred. Lucky Girl. Let Me Explain, Dear. 1933: Leave It to Me. The Love Nest. 1934: There Goes Susie (US: Scandals of Paris). 1935: It's a Bet. Joy Ride. Royal Cavalcade (US: Regal Cavalcade). The Guv'nor (US: Mr Hobo). No Monkey Business. 1936: Faithful. Where's Sally? Such Is Life. Wake Up Famous. 1938: Glamour Girl. 1945: Dumb Dora Discovers Tobacco.*

As director. *1936: Wake Up Famous. 1938: It's in the Blood.*

As co-director. *1931: Out of the Blue. 1932: Lucky Girl. Let Me Explain, Dear.*

GILBERT, Billy 1893–1971
Although he brightened many a scene, both in features and short comedies, big, blustering Billy Gilbert never became the star in movies that he had been in vaudeville. It was impossible, though, not to notice his appearances. At 280 lbs, the dark, moustachioed, puff-cheeked Gilbert seemed to fill a large proportion of the screen. His comic characters could be bad-tempered, explosive, pompous or plain daft. They turned up all over the place, but nowhere more effectively than in support of Laurel and Hardy with whom he made nine films, including *The Music Box* where his irascible Professor Theodore von Schwarzenhoffen ends the film by hacking his own piano to pieces. Gilbert originally hailed from Kentucky. The son of two Metropolitan Opera singers, he himself had talents as a writer (he later collaborated on many film scripts and wrote a play), singer and director. But it was as a comic that he made his name in vaudeville, developing a hilarious, will-he-won't-he sneezing routine that occupied several minutes of stage time, and so convulsed a young Walt Disney that years later he asked Gilbert to be the 'voice' of Sneezy the dwarf in *Snow White and the Seven Dwarfs*. During World War One Gilbert's straight man was for a while a dapper young performer called Bud Abbott (*qv*). But they had long since gone their separate ways by the time Gilbert (after a few isolated appearances in silents) came to Hollywood to start a career in sound films in 1929. He was to become a studio regular for the next 20 years. Gilbert would have seemed, with his huge girth, to be one half of a comedy team looking for the other, just as Hardy found Laurel. But although he worked with several other comics Gilbert once confessed that he never particularly relished the experience. In 1932 and 1933 Hal Roach tried pairing Gilbert with skinny, long-faced Ben Blue (*qv*) in a series called 'The Taxi Boys'. But each man seemed to be working for his own laughs and they never gelled as a team. Billy Gilbert found that what he enjoyed most was creating eccentric comic characters. He did it for Laurel and Hardy, Thelma Todd and ZaSu Pitts, the Ritz Brothers, the Marx Brothers, Olsen and Johnson (all *qv*) and many more.

His ambition was to work with Buster Keaton (*qv*) and as his film career was dwindling to a close he finally made it, the two appearing together in a TV sketch that *Variety* thought one of the funniest ever done on the small screen. In the same year (1952) Gilbert's first performed play, *Buttrio Square*, made its debut on Broadway, his second home since the late 1940s (he also directed two shows there). In real life the friendliest and heartiest of men, Gilbert retired in the early 1960s, dying following a stroke a few days after his 78th birthday.

*1916: Bubbles of Trouble. 1921: Dynamite Allen. 1927: * Smith's Pony. 1929: Noisy Neighbors. Woman from Hell. * The Woman Tamer. 1930: * The Doctor's Wife. * The Beauties. 1931: * Dogs is Dogs. * War Mamas. * Shiver My Timbers. * The Panic is On. * The Hasty Marriage. * One Good Turn. * A Melon-Drama. * Catch As Catch Can. * The Pajama Party. Chinatown After Dark. 1932: * Free Eats. * Spanky. * The Tabasco Kid. * What Price Taxi? * Young Ironsides. * Just a Pain in the Parlor. * Strange Inner-Tube. * Never the Twins Shall Meet. Pack Up Your Troubles. * The Nickel Nurser. * In Walked Charley. Blondie of the Follies. Million Dollar Legs. * First in War. * You're Telling Me. * County Hospital. * Their First Mistake. * The Chimp. * Strictly Unreliable. * The Music Box. * Seal Skins. * Sneak Easily. * On the Loose. * Red Noses. * Towed in a Hole. 1933: This Day and Age. * Fallen Arches. * The Big Fibber. * Rummy. * Wreckety Wreck. * Thundering Taxis. * Taxi Barons. * Nothing But the Truth. * Luncheon at Twelve. * Maids a la Mode. * The Bargain of the Century. *Asleep in the Fleet. * One Track Minds. Sons of the Desert (GB: Fraternally Yours. Voice only). 1934: Happy Landing (GB: Air Patrol). Peck's Bad Boy. Eight Girls in a Boat. Cockeyed Cavaliers. The Merry Widow. Evelyn Prentice. * Another Wild Idea (voice only). * The Cracked Iceman. * Them Thar Hills. * Men in Black. * Soup and Fish. * Roaming Vandals. * Tripping Through the Tropics. * Get Along Little Hubby. 1935: A Night at the Opera. Millions in the Air. Mad Love (GB: The Hands of Orlac). Escapade. * Just Another Murder. * Nurse to You. * His Bridal Sweet. * Pardon My Scotch. * His Old Flame. Hail Brother. Here Comes the Band. I Dream Too Much. 1936: Sutter's Gold. Parole! Love on the Run. Three of a Kind. Dangerous Waters. The Bride Walks Out. Grand Jury. The Big Game. Early to Bed. Night Waitress. Kelly the Second. * The Brain Busters. * So and Sew. Hi, Gaucho! Give Us This Night. The First Baby. Poor Little Rich Girl. F-Man. Devil Doll. My American Wife. One Rainy Afternoon. 1937: * Swing Fever. The Man Who Found Himself. The Outcasts of Poker Flat. Live, Love and Learn. Rosalie. We're on the Jury. Sea Devils. Music for Madame. China Passage. The Toast of New York. The Life of the Party. The Firefly. On the Avenue. Espionage. Broadway Melody of 1938. One Hundred Men and a Girl. Captains Courageous. Maytime. Fight for Your Lady.*

When You're in Love. Snow White and the Seven Dwarfs (voice only). 1938: Mr Doodle Kicks Off. She's Got Everything. My Lucky Star. The Girl Downstairs. Maid's Night Out. Joy of Living. Block-Heads. Angels with Dirty Faces. Happy Landing (and 1934 film of same title). Breaking the Ice. Peck's Bad Boy with the Circus. Army Girl (GB: The Last of the Cavalry). The Great Waltz. 1939: Forged Passport. Destry Rides Again. Rio. The Under-Pup. The Star Maker. Million Dollar Legs. 1940: Sing, Dance, Plenty Hot (GB: Melody Girl). The Great Dictator. His Girl Friday. Women in War. Scatterbrain. Safari. A Night at Earl Carroll's. Sandy is a Lady. Seven Sinners. A Little Bit of Heaven. Queen of the Mob. Cross Country Romance. The Villain Still Pursued Her. Tin Pan Alley. No, No, Nanette. 1941 * Crazy Like a Fox. Reaching for the Sun. New Wine (GB: The Great Awakening). One Night in Lisbon. Angels with Broken Wings. Model Wife. Week-End in Havana. * Meet Roy Rogers. Our City. 1942: Mr Wise Guy. Sleepytime Gal. Valley of the Sun. Song of the Islands. Arabian Nights. 1943: Shantytown. Crazy House. * Shot in the Escape. Spotlight Scandals. Always a Bridesmaid. Stage Door Canteen. 1944: * Ghost Crazy. * Wedded Bliss. Three of a Kind. Ever Since Venus. Three's a Family. Ghost Catchers. Crazy Knights. 1945: Anchors Aweigh. Trouble Chasers. 1947: Fun and Fancy Free (voice only). 1948: The Kissing Bandit. The Counterfeiters. 1949: Bride of Vengeance. 1952: Down Among the Sheltering Palms. 1961: Paradise Alley. 1962: Five Weeks in a Balloon.

GINGOLD, Hermione 1897–1987

With piercing wit, outrageous humour and rumbling tones, Britain's Hermione Gingold was always worth going to the theatre to see; her outfits were as colourful as her tongue and you never knew quite what she might say. It hadn't always been that way. For close to 30 years she had struggled along as an actress (following a debut at 11 in a children's play) with no outstanding success. It wasn't until the belated discovery of what Noël Coward would have called her 'talent to amuse' in the mid 1930s that she became the darling of London's revue audiences. Then and in the 1940s she

created a series of gargoyles and grotesques as flamboyant and cartoon-like as anything out of The Muppet Show. The blue eyes flashed, the lips curled and another stream of wicked repartee would find its mark. Her delivery was a scriptwriter's dream, and she was often to be seen in tandem with Hermione Baddeley ('The Two Hermiones'): their ad-lib shredding of Noël Coward's Fallen Angels was a nightly delight to London's theatregoers in 1949. Such a larger-than-life personality was obviously not entirely suited to radio, although she did build up a cult following with her sepulchral portrait of Drusilla Doom, pouring tea in her cobwebbed mansion in Mrs Doom's Diary, an early 1950s satire on the popular radio soap Mrs Dale's Diary. Richard Attenborough played Hermione's son! Although the stage was the only medium in which Hermione Gingold could operate at full throttle, her red-gold locks and malign smile were seen in a few films, especially after she began to spend more time in America in the 1950s. Her peak year for the cinema was 1958, when she played a witch in Bell, Book and Candle, and enjoyed her famous duet with Maurice Chevalier in Gigi, archly eyeing her partner as they sang I Remember It Well. She also gave enjoyably camp performances in The Music Man and A Little Night Music. One of those rare people who was as richly, wittily cutting in real life as on stage, Gingold was once asked by some hapless playwright what she thought of his work after a somewhat strained first night. 'My dear boy', replied Hermione in her most vibrant gurgle, 'in future I would advise you never to write anything more ambitious than a grocery list.' She died from heart disease at 89.

1936: Someone at the Door. 1937: Merry Comes to Town. 1938: Meet Mr Penny. 1943: The Butler's Dilemma. 1952: The Pickwick Papers. Cosh Boy (US: The Slasher). 1953: Our Girl Friday (US: The Adventures of Sadie). 1956: Around the World in 80 Days. 1958: Gigi. Bell, Book and Candle. 1961: The Naked Edge. The Music Man. 1962: Gay Purr-ee (voice only). 1964: I'd Rather Be Rich. 1965: Harvey Middleman, Fireman. Promise Her Anything. 1966: Munster Go Home! 1967: Jules Verne's Rocket to the Moon (US: Those Fantastic Flying Fools). 1971: Banyon (TV). 1976: A Little Night Music. 1984: Garbo Talks!

GLEASON, Jackie

(Herbert John Gleason) 1916–1987

If ever a man lived life to the full it was surely Jackie Gleason, the portly, pouch-faced, self-styled 'Great One' of American comedy. Apart from his wide-ranging activities as a comedian who created bombastic characters who were almost always deflated in the long run, he was: a prodigious composer and conductor of mostly forget-table light music whose albums sold millions; a world-class pool player who did all his

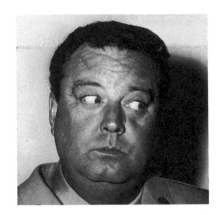

own trick shots in his most famous film, The Hustler, a food-and-wine glutton who once ate five stuffed lobsters at one dinner; an accomplished hypnotist; an inventor of innumerable published children's games; a writer of enormous energies; a designer of both jewellery and clothes; a lover of women who was three times married and could never resist a pretty face; a heavy smoker; and a prominent researcher into psychic phenomena. He also composed a ballet. Gleason never did anything by halves. After he persuaded the production company to let him take his long-running television show on location to Miami, he hired an entire train to travel down from New York and stuffed it with friends, chorus girls, champagne and gourmet food. Once asked what was the cause of his staggering variations in weight over the years, Gleason treated his interviewer to a withering glance and replied: 'eating'! Jackie Gleason came from a broken home in Brooklyn and was educated about equally in various local schools and pool halls in the district. At 15 he left school and pool behind by winning an amateur talent contest as a stand-up comic. This led to an engagement at a Newark nightclub where he became the master of barbed insults to customers, es-pecially those who talked when he was on. Spotted at a Manhattan club in 1940, he was signed up for films by Warner Brothers. But they, and other studios, gave him only nebulous supporting roles and within two years he was devoting his career to club and radio work. TV threw his career a lifeline. His first show as star, The Life of Riley, was cancelled after only one season. Ironically, another big man, William Bendix (qv), would make a success of it three years later. But in the meantime Gleason had found nation-wide fame on Cavalcade of Stars. This was basically a variety show but Gleason soon made it his own. He invented a variety of characters for its sketches — loudmouths, drunks, pessimists and henpecks. These were all rolled into one for his most famous characterisation: bus driver Ralph Kramden in The Honeymooners. Before that, Gleason had also invented 'The Bachelor', a series of mime routines in which the great American single slob tried, without success, to cope with the everyday things in life, like doing the laundry or preparing a meal. These sketches revealed Gleason's dexterity and subtlety, belying the bravura performances of his later career. *The Honeymooners* made its debut as a segment of *Cavalcade of Stars* in 1951. It used only sparse sets, relying on the personality of Gleason as Ralph, the boastful, bigoted, blustering schemer and dreamer, full of his own importance and impossible ambitions but doomed to failure or defeat before each episode was over. He was a combination of Britain's Hancock (*qv*) and Alf Garnett figures, and a forerunner in some ways of another immensely successful American television character, Archie Bunker. Gleason took the characterisation with him when he began his own show in 1952, and it remained an on-off segment of *The Jackie Gleason Show* until the programme expired in 1970. There was even a short spin-off series of *The Honeymooners* in the mid 1950s, with regulars Art Carney (as Gleason's sewerman friend) and Audrey Meadows (the wife who almost always got the better of him) to support him. Naturally Ralph, as with others of his ilk, would never escape his homespun surroundings. Gleason's film career flourished as a result

of his new popularity, although oddly his most successful roles were dramatic: his Minnesota Fats in *The Hustler* earned him an Oscar nomination; he was also excellent as the boxing manager in *Requiem for a Heavyweight*. Solo comedy ventures often leant too heavily on the sentimental side. Later he scored a hit with his overripe portrayal — Gleason was once called The Golden Ham — of Sheriff Buford T. Ford in three *Smokey and the Bandit* films. His last film, *Nothing in Common*, which paired the old comedy master with much younger star comedian Tom Hanks (they played father and son), was released just before Gleason's death from cancer of the liver.

1941: *Navy Blues*. 1942: [†] *Larceny Inc. All Through the Night. Lady Gangster. Escape from Crime. Orchestra Wives. Springtime in the Rockies*. 1950: *The Desert Hawk*. 1961: *The Million Dollar Incident (TV). The Hustler*. 1962: *Requiem for a Heavyweight (GB: Blood Money). Gigot*. 1963: *Papa's Delicate Condition. Soldier in the Rain*. 1968: *Skidoo*. 1969: *Don't Drink the Water. How to Commit Marriage*. 1970: *How Do I Love Thee?* 1977: *Mr Billion. Smokey and the Bandit*. 1980: *Smokey and the Bandit II (GB: Smokey and the*

Bandit Ride Again). 1982: *The Toy*. 1983: *Smokey and the Bandit — Part 3. The Sting II*. 1984: *Fools Die*. 1985: *Izzy and Moe (TV)*. 1986: *Nothing in Common*.

[†] As Jack C. Gleason.

GLEASON, James 1886–1959

A man who had almost as many strings to his bow as his namesake Jackie (*qv*), James Gleason was a skinny, wiry, narrow-headed New Yorker with shaggy eyebrows. He usually wore a small moustache and his characters — throughout the 1930s he played leads in second-features and character roles in major films — had a ready wisecrack for most occasions. Gleason was also a talented writer and director whose extensive army service in several campaigns had given him experience of people from all walks of life. His rasping accent helped paint convincing portraits of reporters, policemen, taxi drivers, fight managers, army sergeants and best friends with an acid sense of humour who could always cheer the hero up. The son of actors, Gleason spent time with his parents' stock company in between periods of army service. He saw action in both the Spanish-American War and World War One. After marriage, he and his wife Lucile acted together in stock in Oregon before Gleason's activities brought them to Broadway, where he wrote a number of plays and musicals, some of them later turned into films. With the coming of sound in the cinema, Gleason went to Hollywood where he starred in a number of two-reel comedies, most of them accounts of lowbrow Brooklynese antics. Gleason's whisky-and-water voice soon got him cast in top character roles as well. His sardonic smile, lantern jaw and nose like an Italian tomato, appeared, typically, beneath the brim of a trilby hat or plastic eyeshade. The homely features could also look puzzled, as they normally did as Inspector Oscar Piper, frequently beaten to the killer by school-ma'am sleuth Hildegarde Withers (played variously by Edna May Oliver and ZaSu Pitts, both *qv*) in a series of comedy-thrillers — with the accent on comedy — based on whodunnits written by Stuart Palmer. *The Penguin Pool Murder* was the first of these in

Sailors leave? Not while they're in company like this.
James Gleason (left) and Robert Armstrong feel like abandoning ship in *Suicide Fleet*

1932, and they continued until *The Plot Thickens* in 1936. In 1933 Gleason came to Britain to star in *Orders is Orders* with Charlotte Greenwood (*qv*) and was surprised at the star treatment and publicity his visit engendered. Two years after his last appearance as Oscar Piper, Gleason began another comedy series, *The Higgins Family*, this time with his wife Lucile and their son Russell. It proved successful enough for four more Higgins films to be made. Tragedy struck in 1945 when Russell fell to his death from a hotel window; he was 37. Two years later Lucile was dead from a heart attack at 61. Gleason himself continued to work. Half the time it seemed he was playing characters called Pop. He actually got shot, a rare indignity, in Cagney's *Come Fill the Cup*, but he was soon back to being understanding, lending James Stewart a shoulder to cry on in *The Jackpot*, and helping two children escape a murderous Robert Mitchum in *Night of the Hunter*. A television series of *The Higgins Family* was suggested, but Gleason declined. No doubt it would have brought back painful memories and he was in any case hampered on prolonged work schedules by the asthma that eventually brought about his death a little before his 73rd birthday. His demise came at around the same time as that of the old Hollywood, where his unforced timing and rapier delivery of a sardonically funny line had made him a welcome part of any film.

1922: *Polly of the Follies*. 1928: *The Count of Ten*. 1929: * *The Garden of Eatin'*. *High Voltage*. *Oh, Yeah!* (GB: *No Brakes*). *The Shannons of Broadway*. *His First Command*. *The Broadway Melody*. * *Fairways and Foul*. 1930: *The Swellhead* (GB: *Counted Out*). * *Don't Believe It*. *Big Money*. *What a Widow!* *Dumbbells in Ermine*. *The Matrimonial Bed* (GB: *A Matrimonial Problem*). * *No Brakes* (and 1929 feature). *Her Man*. *Puttin' on the Ritz*. 1931: *A Free Soul*. * *Where Canaries Sing Bass*. *Sweepstakes*. *The Big Gamble*. *Suicide Fleet*. * *Slow Poison*. * *Doomed to Win*. *It's a Wise Child*. *Beyond Victory*. 1932: * *Lights Out*. * *Battle Royal*. * *High Hats and Low Brows*. * *Stealin' Home*. * *Yoo Hoo*. *The Penguin Pool Murder* (GB: *The Penguin Pool Mystery*). *Fast Companions/Information Kid*. *The Crooked Circle*. * *Rule 'em and Weep*. *The All-American* (GB: *Sport of a Nation*). *Lady and Gent*. *Blondie of the Follies*. *The Devil is Driving*. 1933: *Orders is Orders*. *Hoopla*. *Clear All Wires*. *Billion Dollar Scandal*. * *Rockabye Cowboy*. * *Alias the Professor*. * *Mister Mugg*. * *Gleason's New Deal*. 1934: *Search for Beauty*. *Murder on the Blackboard*. *Change of Heart*. *The Meanest Gal in Town*. * *Pie for Two*. 1935: *Helldorado*. *Murder on a Honeymoon*. *Hot Tip*. *West Point of the Air*. 1936: *Murder on a Bridal Path*. *The Ex-Mrs Bradford*. *Don't Turn 'em Loose*. *The Plot Thickens* (GB: *The Swinging Pearl Mystery*). *The Big Game*. *Yours for the Asking*. *We're Only Human*. 1937: *Manhattan Merry-Go-Round* (GB: *Manhattan Music Box*). *Forty Naughty Girls*. 1938: *Army Girl* (GB: *The Last of the Cavalry*). *The Higgins Family*. 1939: *Should Husbands Work? The Covered Trailer*. *My Wife's Relatives*. *On Your Toes*. 1940: *Earl of Puddlestone* (GB: *Jolly Old Higgins*). *Grandpa Goes to Town*. *Money to Burn*. 1941: *Affectionately Yours*. *Meet John Doe*. *Nine Lives Are Not Enough*. *Here Comes Mr Jordan*. *Tanks a Million*. *Babes on Broadway*. *A Date with the Falcon*. 1942: *My Gal Sal*. *Hayfoot*. *Tales of Manhattan*. *Footlight Serenade*. *Manila Calling*. *The Falcon Takes Over*. *Tramp, Tramp, Tramp*. 1943: *Crash Dive*. *A Guy Named Joe*. *Arsenic and Old Lace*. 1944: *The Keys of the Kingdom*. *Once Upon a Time*. 1945: *The Clock* (GB: *Under the Clock*). *Captain Eddie*. *A Tree Grows in Brooklyn*. *This Man's Navy*. 1946: *The Hoodlum Saint*. *Lady Luck*. *The Well-Groomed Bride*. *Home Sweet Homicide*. 1947: *Down to Earth*. *The Homestretch*. *Tycoon*. *The Bishop's Wife*. 1948: *When My Baby Smiles at Me*. *The Return of October* (GB: *Date with Destiny*). *Smart Woman*. *The Dude Goes West*. 1949: *The Life of Riley*. *Bad Boy*. *Take One False Step*. *Miss Grant Takes Richmond* (GB: *Innocence is Bliss*). 1950: *Riding High*. * *Screen Snapshots No. 182*. *The Yellow Cab Man*. *Key to the City*. *The Jackpot*. *Joe Palooka in The Squared Circle* (GB: *The Squared Circle*). 1951: *Come Fill the Cup*. *Joe Palooka in The Triple Cross* (GB: *The Triple Cross*). *Two Gals and a Guy*. *I'll See You in My Dreams*. 1952: *What Price Glory? We're Not Married*. *The Story of Will Rogers*. 1953: *Movie Stuntmen* (GB: *Hollywood Thrill Makers*). *Forever Female*. 1954: *Suddenly!* 1955: *The Night of the Hunter*. *The Girl Rush*. 1956: *Star in the Dust*. 1957: *Spring Reunion*. *Loving You*. *Man in the Shadow* (GB: *Pay the Devil*). 1958: *The Female Animal*. *Once Upon a Horse*. *Man or Gun*. *Rock-a-Bye Baby*. *Money, Women and Guns*. *The Last Hurrah*. *The Time of Your Life* (TV).
As co-director. 1929: *Oh, Yeah!* (GB: *No Brakes*). 1935: *Hot Tip*.

GOLDBERG, Whoopi
(Caryn Johnson) 1949–
You get the feeling that, while nightclub audiences still see her as a very funny comedienne, Hollywood persists in treating Whoopi Goldberg as Mother Earth. The nearest the cinema has come to combining the two Whoopis was in *Ghost* – and for it she won an Academy Award. Born in New York, the girl with hair like a tarantula and the widest mouth in films since Joe E. Brown (*qv*) was acting when she was eight, at the Helena Rubinstein Children's Theatre. She says that even then she dreamed of winning an Oscar, and drove her mother and brother crazy by writing and reciting speeches of acceptance. In the late 1960s she got married, and 'into flower power, civil rights marches and radical politics'. Divorced, she flew west in search of an acting career, and joined the San Diego Repertory Company for six years, leaving in 1979 to act with the Spontaneous Combustion Group, an improvisational company. Two years later she went solo to create *The Spook Show*, working in Europe and America and ending up on Broadway in a show directed by Mike Nichols. She continued with her one-woman productions, in which she invented various provocative, funny or tragic characters, and made hit records too, winning a Grammy for best comedy album with a recording of one of her shows. Films seemed to have passed her by until Steven Spielberg chose her to play the naïve, tortured Celie, the heroine of *The Color Purple*. The comic side of her talent was revealed later that year in *Jumpin' Jack Flash*, directed by Penny Marshall, before she hit the jackpot with *Big*. The film wasn't too good (although it showcased Whoopi to good advantage), but it was a lot better than what followed. *Burglar*, *The Telephone* and *Fatal Beauty*, basically thrillers with moments of humour, all bombed. *Clara's Heart* and *The Long Walk Home* were better, except that they were virtually liberated versions of the kind of role Hattie McDaniel had been playing 50 years earlier. In *Homer & Eddie*, she was more at home as an escaped mental patient who makes life difficult for slightly retarded James Belushi. But the bitter-sweet comedy was scarcely seen outside its native America. Whoopi tried a TV sit-com – but then *Ghost* revived her flagging film fortunes. As the fake medium who finds to her terror that she really has a gift for it, Whoopi was the liveliest and funniest, not to mention most likeable thing in this somewhat overrated show. Deservedly the winner of the Oscar for Best Supporting Actress, Whoopi was able to deliver the much-practised acceptance speech at last. Subsequently, she was rather lost (and wasted) in the middling *Soapdish*, but gave the film world a taste of her standup comedy in *Wisecracks*.

1982: *Citizen*. 1986: *The Color Purple* (shown 1985). *Jumpin' Jack Flash*. 1987: *Burglar*. *The Telephone*. *Fatal Beauty*. 1988: *Scared Straight! 10 Years Later* (TV). *Clara's Heart*. *Homer & Eddie*. 1989: *Beverly Hills Brats*. *Kiss Shot* (TV). *The Long Walk Home*. 1990: *Ghost*. 1991: *Soapdish*. *Wisecracks*. 1992: *The Player*. *Sister Act*. *Sarafina! Freddy Goes to Washington* (voice only).

Guns and noses. James Gleason (right) and Robert Armstrong are at loggerheads in *Suicide Fleet*. Bill Boyd (centre, later to play Hopalong Cassidy) has the situation in hand

Duly drabbed up, Whoopi Goldberg made a sensational major film debut as Celie in Steven Spielberg's epic weepie *The Color Purple*. The laughs came later

Charlotte Greenwood gets friendly with an indignant Cyril Maude in *Orders Is Orders*. She could probably kick his hat off from where she's standing

Taxi on tap. Alec Guinness brings a blacked-up Bill Fraser back from his daydream in *The Captain's Paradise*

GORCEY, Leo
See **THE BOWERY BOYS**

GREENWOOD, Charlotte
(Frances C. Greenwood) 1890–1978

Tall, sandy-haired, horse-faced and long-legged (she once had a horse named after her) America's Charlotte Greenwood found life a kick — a high kick. Her party piece was a bounding, gangling dance routine during which she would swing her foot far above her head in the most casual of ways. She performed this in almost all of her stage and film successes. Her audiences loved it, and her. But Greenwood was much more than an eccentric dancer. She had a happy manner, a rich contralto voice and hearty, honeyed tones that made mincemeat of more than one hapless hero via a cutting piece of dialogue. Fans of Fox musicals of the 1940s relished her cameo appearances but she is probably best remembered as Aunt Eller in the film version of *Oklahoma!*, a part she missed on Broadway because of conflicting film schedules. She was born in Philadelphia into a family whose father deserted them when she was one year old. Via Connecticut and Virginia, she reached New York and a show business debut at 15, by which time she was already rangy and 5ft 9½in tall. She got a job in the back row of a chorus ('I'd have blotted them all out in the front') and gradually gained prominence on the vaudeville circuits, at first with a partner then as a solo turn, hitting Broadway at 22 in *The Passing Show of 1912*. Already she had developed the 'whirlwind gymnastic eccentricities', as one critic put it, that would be an endearing and enduring part of her appeal. She starred in a film, *Jane*, in 1915, as a maid forced to pose as the mistress of the house, and might have started a long screen career there and then had not a play been written for her which would give her a character she would portray, in different plays, over the next 25 years. The role of Letty in *So Long, Letty* (she herself was known to her friends as Lottie) was tailor-made for Greenwood's antics and way with a warmly witty line; it was followed by *Linger Longer, Letty, Let 'Er Go, Letty, Letty Pepper* and (most successful of all) *Leaning on Letty*.

Before the last of these made its appearance in 1935, committing Charlotte to the stage for another five years, she had resumed her film career. Co-starring with Bert Lahr, Buster Keaton and Eddie Cantor (all *qv*), Greenwood endowed playful predators with her own brand of charm. One critic, impressed with the Greenwood gyrations but obviously not totally won over, commented that her 'gymnastic activities and queer grimaces ... probably suit the peculiar humour of ... this film'. He was referring to *Baby Mine* (1928), but the words might have applied to any of Charlotte's appearances; she always looked as though she knew something the audience didn't and was enjoying herself without letting them in on the secret. Two successful musical shows at London's Drury Lane (with a British comedy, *Orders is Orders*, in between) and the five-year run of *Leaning on Letty* pre-dated Charlotte's most prolific spell in films, after she signed for 20th Century-Fox in 1940. These were mostly musicals, in which Charlotte would get a chance to do a speciality high-kick number and make with the wisecracks in support of one of Fox's three musical blondes — Alice Faye, Betty Grable or June Haver. After doing a Cole Porter musical, *Out of This World*, on stage in the early 1950s, Greenwood tried a couple more screen roles, the second of which, in *Oklahoma!*, gave her her last screen triumph. Aunt Eller, a warmer, wiser extension of her role in *Home in Indiana* a decade earlier, even allowed her room for a couple of the old high kicks; and few cinemagoers believed her when, at the end of one musical routine, she had to boom: 'That's about as far as I can go!' After two more films and some TV work, Greenwood retired in the early 1960s, devoting her latter days to her work for the Christian Science church. She was able to enjoy a happy retirement, too, living to be 87.

1915: Jane. 1928: Baby Mine. 1929: So Long, Letty. 1930: * Love Your Neighbor. * Girls Will Be Boys. 1931: Parlor, Bedroom and Bath (GB: Romeo in Pyjamas). Palmy Days. Stepping Out. Flying High (GB: Happy Landing). The Man in Possession. 1932: Cheaters at Play. 1933: Orders is Orders. 1940: Young People. Star Dust. Down Argentine Way. 1941: Moon Over Miami. Tall, Dark and Handsome. 1942: The Perfect Snob. Springtime in the Rockies. 1943: Dixie Dugan. The Gang's All Here (GB: The Girls He Left Behind). 1944: Up In Mabel's Room. Home in Indiana. 1946: Wake Up and Dream. 1947: Driftwood. 1949: The Great Dan Patch. Oh, You Beautiful Doll. 1950: Peggy. 1953: Dangerous When Wet. 1955: Oklahoma! 1956: The Opposite Sex. Glory.

GRENFELL Joyce
(née Phipps) 1910–1979

Joyce Grenfell was funny to look at and funny to listen to. She was also inimitably

Charlotte Greenwood discovers an unusual rest for a tricky shot in *Orders is Orders*. Cyril Maude can't wait to witness the results

British. Several of her comic monologues became classics of their kind, to be repeated over and over again on radio. Slim, dark, effusive, toothy and wittily literate, she once described herself as 'about eight feet tall with a face like a reflection in a spoon'. A talented writer who scripted all her own material, she began her career as a journalist – most successfully, too, progressing to radio critic of *The Observer* at only 26. But the other side of her talent – using her rich, gurgling tones, gift for mimicry and straight-faced laconic sense of humour to entertain friends and colleagues at parties and gatherings – soon led her to perform in revue. Her first solo act, in 1939, made her a nationally-known stage star almost overnight. Her work on stage and in radio – including the classic burlesque series on documentaries, *How*, co-starring Stephen Potter, a kind of English Robert Benchley (*qv*) – left her disappointingly little time for films. But from 1943 she did appear in a few, usually in cameo roles. In 1950 she created one of her most memorable characters, the gushing games mistress Gossage – 'Call me Sausage' – in *The Happiest Days of Your Life*. Touring with her one-woman shows continued to take up much of her year, although she found time to make three 'St Trinian's' comedies for the *Happiest Days* people, Frank Launder and Sidney Gilliat, all as the intrepid, if idiotic, policewoman Ruby Gates. She gave up films after 1964, and took her gallery of gentle grotesques around the world – to Australia, New Zealand, Singapore, Hong Kong, Switzerland, Canada and America, before returning to the London stage with a unique collection of songs and recitations. One national theatre critic wrote at the time that 'From Joyce Grenfell nobody is safe. Deviate by a hairsbreadth from the normal and you become a specimen in her collection. She has the ear to record every nuance of your talk and the tongue to reproduce it.' Joyce Grenfell's last years were unhappily painful ones. She lost an eye in 1972, her body painfully rejecting the replacement in the years that followed. She died from cancer in 1979, just before a New Year in which she was to have been made a Dame. Her best-loved comic song, *Stately As Two Galleons*, is still a regular record request, while her funniest monologue, *George: Don't Do That*, became the title of a collection of her humorous writings published in 1977. She also published two volumes of autobiography as well as collections of poetry.

*1943: The Lamp Still Burns. The Demi-Paradise (US: Adventure for Two). 1946: While the Sun Shines. 1948: * Designing Women. Alice in Wonderland (voice only). 1949: Poet's Pub. Scrapbook for 1933 (voice only). 1950: The Happiest Days of Your Life. Stage Fright. 1951: The Galloping Major. Laughter in Paradise. The Magic Box. 1952: The Pickwick Papers. 1953: Genevieve. The Million Pound Note (US: Man with a Million).*

1954: Forbidden Cargo. The Belles of St Trinian's. 1957: The Good Companions. Blue Murder at St Trinian's. 1958: Happy is the Bride! 1960: The Pure Hell of St Trinian's. 1962: The Old Dark House. 1964: The Yellow Rolls-Royce. The Americanization of Emily.

GRIFFITH, Raymond 1890–1957
Many of the silent screen masters approached the sound era with apprehension. Chaplin (*qv*) chose to ignore it; Buster Keaton (*qv*) had switched studios at the wrong time to cope with it; and it was no stage for Harry Langdon (*qv*) to attempt a comeback upon. Only Laurel and Hardy (*qv*), it seems, emerged the better for it. One silent clown, the elegant Raymond Griffith, had a special reason for viewing the coming of sound with total gloom. Permanently-damaged vocal chords meant that he could speak only in a hoarse whisper. As the last silents slipped away, Griffith prepared for a sad but inevitable move to the other side of the camera. Born to theatrical parents, Griffith had always been an all-rounder. He went to Vitagraph as a young writer and producer in 1914, then moved across to Mack Sennett. Here there were a few on-camera appearances, mainly in 1916, that revealed Griffith at 26 as far less dapper and neat than he would soon become. He remained a power behind the throne of Sennett comedy for another six years; few were his equal at developing original gags. Came the 1920s, and Griffith had developed, visually, into a sort of cross between Adolphe Menjou (with whom he once co-starred) and Max Linder (*qv*). He asked Sennett for a chance to act again and, with the screen personality he had been secretly developing, quickly became a star. As a leading comic Griffith presented a series of triumphs of suaveness and unflappability over calamitous events. He would provide the audience with a cliffhanger, get-yourself-out-of-this situation, then extract himself from peril with aplomb, usually in a way the audience were unlikely to guess. In *Hands Up!*, one of his best vehicles, he tossed plates in the air to avoid being executed by a firing squad, and taught Indians the Charleston while they were doing a war

dance round victims tied to the stake. Master of the sudden surprise, Griffith was always, agilely, despite his short, almost rotund stature, the man in command. His build and appearance – usually the elegant, top-hatted man-about-town – belied his ability to invent and perform some wonderful acrobatic comedy routines. And he was a master at subtle satire of some of Hollywood's sacred cows. Some mystery persists about Griffith's abrupt exit from the movies. His Paramount contract was cancelled in 1927, partly through a falling-out with the head of the studio, B. P. Schulberg. Griffith seems to have been keen to continue in comedy but, faced with the probability of being confined to supporting cameos, quit acting altogether. After a wordless gem as a dying soldier in *All Quiet on the Western Front*, Griffith spent the next ten years on the production side with Warners and, mainly, 20th Century-Fox, often going back to his old trade of inventing bits of comic business. Leaving Fox in 1941 to contribute to the war effort, the Boston-born Griffith did not return to the movie business in post-war years, opting it seems for an early retirement, leaving behind a busy, varied (he was a boy clown with Barnum and Bailey's Circus at 12) but in many ways unfulfilled career.

*1915: * Under New Management. * A Saphead's Revenge. * A Scandal at Sea. * Tears and Sunshine. 1916: * A Scoundrel's Toll/The Scoundrel's Tale. * The Surf Girl. * Cupid at the Polo Game. * Mr McIdiot's Assassination. * September Mourning. * Blue Blood But Black Skin. * Elevating Father. * The Bankruptcy of Boggs and Schultz. * A Busted Honeymoon. * How Stars Are Made. The Millionaire's Son. The Great Smash. 1917: * A Royal Rogue. * An Aerial Joy Ride. * His Foothill Folly. * False to the Finish. 1918: * Ruined by a Dumb Waiter. * His Double Life. * Mud. A Red-Haired Cupid. The Follies Girl. † * The Village Chestnut. 1922: Fools First. The Crossroads of New York (GB: For Love Or Money). Minnie. 1923: Souls for Sale. Red Lights. The Eternal Three. The Day of Faith. White Tiger. 1924: Poisoned Paradise: The Forbidden Story of Monte Carlo. Nellie, the Beautiful Cloak Model. The Dawn of a Tomorrow. Changing Husbands. Lily of the Dust. Open All Night (GB: One Parisian 'Knight'). 1925: Miss Bluebeard. When Winter Went. Forty Winks. The Night Club. Paths to Paradise. Fine Clothes. A Regular Fellow (later He's a Prince). 1926: Hands Up! Wet Paint (GB: Fresh Paint). You'd Be Surprised. The Waiter from the Ritz. 1927: Wedding Bills. Time to Love. 1929: Trent's Last Case. * Post Mortems. * The Sleeping Porch. 1930: All Quiet on the Western Front.*

† Also directed

GUINNESS, Sir Alec
(A. Guinness de Cuffe) 1914–
Guinness is perhaps no longer thought of today as a comedy star. But, had you been alive in Britain in the 1950s, you would have

had no doubt: here was the British cinema's brightest and most talented laughter-maker. Through his work in comedy, Guinness became a major star; and it is his comedies that are most often revived today on TV. In them he demonstrates both an amazing versatility and the lightest of comedy touches. Always firmly in character, he is a magnetic performer in these films. When the laughter had died down a little, and an opportunity came to escape from comedy, Guinness took it; he has by and large not been the same force in the cinema since 1960, although there have still been moments of inspiration. If Ealing Studios had stayed afloat, however, who knows what glories in character comedy Guinness might have achieved. He was born in London, where he threw up a job as an advertising copywriter in 1932 to go to acting school. Beginnings were small: his first stage appearance was a walk-on in 1934; the same year he made his first visit to a film studio to be an extra in the musical Evensong. It took Guinness five years to reach leading roles on stage, then there were another five years' war service with the Royal Navy, so it was 1946 before he made his film debut proper, playing the cocky Herbert Pocket (a role he had previously played on stage) in David Lean's masterly Great Expectations. From then on Guinness hardly ever looked the same from one film to the next. When he came on as himself, he was sometimes (though not always) less effective. No-one, before or since, has matched his horrifying Fagin in Lean's classic 1948 version of Oliver Twist; and then he began to make the Ealing comedies. Eight roles (all of them murdered by Dennis Price) in Kind Hearts and Coronets made him a household name. He was also box-office gold as the timid gardening writer involved with rampaging Welsh rugby fans in A Run for Your Money, gently funny (and finally tragic) in Last Holiday and disarmingly dotty as the boffin who invents an all-white material that never wears out in The Man in the White Suit, a comedy boosted by the wonderfully weird noises in Guinness's laboratory. Bespectacled, he co-starred with Stanley Holloway (qv) as mild-mannered masterminds who pull off an unlikely bullion robbery in the fast-moving (and immensely

popular) The Lavender Hill Mob. Guinness's reading of the role was exactly right and ensured audience sympathy all the way. For the next decade Guinness could do virtually no wrong. He was cheeky, dynamic and winning as The Card, a Potteries wheeler-dealer of the late nineteenth century, witty and suave as a bigamist in The Captain's Paradise; uncomfortable with wartime heroics in Malta Story; and back on form as a whimsical clerical detective in Father Brown. At this point Guinness capped his career in comedy by playing the Professor, leader of a gang of comically sinister bank robbers, in Ealing's The Ladykillers. With chalky make-up, black bags under his eyes, straggly hair, an extraordinary set of fake teeth and an ingratiating air, Guinness created a memorably comic grotesque. Among his 'boys' were Peter Sellers (qv) and Herbert Lom, who years later would appear together again in the Pink Panther comedies. Guinness, though then past his best, would have graced one of those. His Oscar for The Bridge on the River Kwai changed the public's conception of his talents. Strangely, after it he was no longer such a certainty at the box-office. Barnacle Bill, The Horse's Mouth and Our Man in Havana all had moments of high comedy, but none were winners at the tills. Knighted in 1959, Guinness received his last film critical applause for some time the following year for his hard-drinking Scots officer in Tunes of Glory, although in truth the portrayal seemed just a touch too far from reality. Very far from reality was his Japanese widower in A Majority of One, not a comedy (though it might have played better as one) and Guinness's first big flop since the underrated romantic comedy To Paris with Love years earlier. He went dramatic again in the solid HMS Defiant, and became a supporting player in epics. He tried comedy again with Situation Hopeless ...

But Not Serious and Hotel Paradiso, but touch and material deserted him; they were barely seen. Since then Guinness has been a top supporting star with an erratic level of performance. He became rich through his participation in the Star Wars series, the first film of which earned him an Oscar nomination. And he was excellent as the crusty old nobleman in the remake of Little Lord Fauntleroy. But his blind butler, Bensonmum, in Murder by Death, showed that he had long since forgotten how not to go over the top in comedy.

1934: Evensong (as extra). 1946: Great Expectations. 1948: Oliver Twist. 1949: Kind Hearts and Coronets. A Run for Your Money. 1950: Last Holiday. 1951: The Mudlark. The Lavender Hill Mob. The Man in the White Suit. 1952: The Card (US: The Promoter). 1953: The Captain's Paradise. * The Square Mile (narrator only). Malta Story. 1954: Father Brown (US: The Detective). The Stratford Adventure. To Paris with Love. 1955: The Prisoner. * Rowlandson's England (narrator only). The Ladykillers. 1956: The Swan. 1957: The Bridge on the River Kwai. Barnacle Bill (US: All at Sea). 1958: The Horse's Mouth. The Scapegoat. 1959: Our Man in Havana. 1960: Tunes of Glory. 1961: A Majority of One. 1962: HMS Defiant (US: Damn the Defiant!). Lawrence of Arabia. 1963: The Fall of the Roman Empire. 1965: Situation Hopeless ... But Not Serious. Doctor Zhivago. 1966: Hotel Paradiso. The Quiller Memorandum. 1967: The Comedians. 1970: Cromwell. Scrooge. 1972: Brother Sun, Sister Moon. 1973: Hitler: The Last Ten Days. 1976: Murder by Death. 1977: Star Wars. 1980: The Empire Strikes Back. Raise the Titanic! 1981: Little Lord Fauntleroy. 1983: Lovesick. Return of the Jedi. 1984: A Passage to India. 1987: Little Dorrit I. Little Dorrit II. 1988: A Handful of Dust. 1991: Kafka.

Glynis Johns (centre) and Petula Clark are just two of the Victorian ladies courted by the charismatic Alec Guinness in The Card

GUTTENBERG, Steve 1958–

Steve Guttenberg is a nice, likeable young man. But right now it's difficult to see which way his career is going. He says that 'the career I want is being the love interest', but the fact remains that all of his popular hits have been in comedy. He has made five sequels to previous comedy hits, but all of them as part of an ensemble. There's some evidence that the paying public is less ready to accept him as a solo attraction. One of Guttenberg's producers, Steve Woolley, from *High Spirits*, shares such reservations. 'People think of Steve as a funny guy, not as a serious actor', he says. 'Whatever Steve does, you keep expecting him to crack a joke. Once you have a smash like *Police Academy*, you can't change that image.' Blessed with boyish, smiling looks, Guttenberg prepared early for an acting career by attending the School of Performing Arts in New York, and studying under John Houseman at Julliard, as well as with Lee Strasberg and Uta Hagen – a formidable trio of acting teachers. After off-Broadway experience, Guttenberg moved to California, where he soon attracted minor film roles, most notably the spy who is killed at the beginning of *The Boys from Brazil*. He also had the lead in his first film, *The Chicken Chronicles*, a below-the-belt high-school comedy that enjoyed some minor success. Discouraged at not following up these successes with major roles, Guttenberg returned to New York with the idea of training to become a dentist. 'No sooner did I leave', he recalls, 'than I was suddenly in demand.' He didn't leave again. The breakthrough came with a starring role in Barry Levinson's *Diner*, as the chubby sports fanatic who makes his fiancée pass a sports trivia test before he'll marry her. An invisibility comedy, *The Man Who Wasn't There*, lived up to its name by hardly being seen, but Guttenberg followed it with *Police Academy* (as the parking lot attendant who becomes a police cadet), then *Cocoon* and *Short Circuit*. All three led to sequels, and Guttenberg's percentage of the *Police Academy* films made him wealthy. But not happy. He slimmed down by three stone in his quest for more romantic roles, and was rewarded with *The Bedroom Window*, a chillingly effective

Hitchcock-style thriller which unfortunately not many went to see. Indeed, its producers were so nervous of its prospects in Britain that they previewed it, then failed to give it a release. It was back to the Police Academy for Guttenberg, although the fourth in this six-film series proved to be his last. Instead of number five (which, after all, he had met in *Short Circuit!*), he made *3 Men and a Baby*, an enormous box-office hit which led to its trio of leading men, Guttenberg, Tom Selleck and Ted Danson, doing a follow-up, *3 Men and a Little Lady*. Guttenberg then made an attempt to launch his bright, eager personality in a vehicle of its own in the extremely lame *Don't Tell Her It's Me*, in which he must have thought that the role of a man who has lost his hair and his confidence, and regains both by impersonating a long-haired New Zealand biker, would be funny. It wasn't. Right now, what Guttenberg needs to be accepted as a comedy actor who can play other things is to get himself into the kind of roles that Tom Hanks (*qv*) has been playing. It remains to be seen whether or not he has the weight to do it.

1977: The Chicken Chronicles. Rollercoaster. The Last Chance. Something for Joey (TV). 1978: The Boys from Brazil. 1979: Players. 1980: Can't Stop the Music. To Race the Wind (TV). 1981: Miracle on Ice (TV). 1982: Diner. 1983: The Day After (TV). The Man Who Wasn't There. 1984: Police Academy. 1985: Police Academy 2: Their First Assignment. Cocoon. Bad Medicine. 1986: Short Circuit. Police Academy 3: Back in Training. Amazon Women on the Moon. 1987: Surrender. The Bedroom Window. Police Academy 4: Citizens on Patrol. 3 Men and a Baby. 1988: High Spirits. Cocoon: The Return. 1990: 3 Men and a Little Lady. Don't Tell Her It's Me. 1992: Freddie Goes to Washington (voice only). Change of Heart.

HACKETT, Buddy
(Leonard Hacker) 1924–

A tubby little black-haired American comedian in the Lou Costello (*qv*) mould, Brooklyn-born Buddy Hackett several times threatened to have a movie career, but never quite got there. Nimble of wit and extra-

ordinarily mobile of face, he nonetheless remained, in his few films at least, a second banana. One of the reasons was that, unlike Costello, Hackett never found a Bud Abbott (*qv*) with whom he could have teamed for top stardom. All in all though, Hackett remains a more endearing figure than Costello in films, even if he never had the same following. Hackett's father was an upholsterer and the son followed him into the family business – for a while. He became an apprentice comedian on the so-called Catskill Mountain 'Borscht Circuit' which nurtured many other Jewish comedians – doubling as a waiter at some of the resorts to supplement his meagre income. Soon, however, the roly-poly joker began to build a reputation. He broke into television in 1949 in a programme called *School House* and quickly became a top nightclub attraction. Universal signed him up for a couple of films, the first of which was a medium-budget musical, *Walking My Baby Back Home*. Hackett got good billing on the posters and stole the notices from the stars, Donald O'Connor (*qv*) and Janet Leigh. When a contract dispute with the studio's top stars, Abbott and Costello, resulted in them withdrawing from *Fireman, Save My Child*, Hackett and Hugh O'Brian were pitched into the breach. But the film was partially revamped to make room for Spike Jones and his City Slickers, and the Hackett-O'Brian team struck no sparks with the public – hardly surprising as O'Brian was just a manly action hero for the greater part of his career and had little experience in comedy. It was hard on Hackett, who returned to TV. He had his own series, *Stanley*, but then surprisingly played second fiddle to Jackie Gleason (*qv*) on *The Jackie Gleason Show*. At the end of the 1950s he had another little go at films, the first being *God's Little Acre* in which he had a dramatic role. The remainder were a mixture of featured roles and guest spots in comedies and musicals, the best of them being *The Music Man*. And he was one of many comics featured in Stanley Kramer's overblown *It's a Mad, Mad, Mad, Mad World*. Hackett's brand of amiable buffoonery was seen to its best advantage as Dean Jones' sidekick and mechanic in the phenomenally successful Walt Disney film

Black spot. Mahoney (Steve Guttenberg) gives Moses (Bubba Smith) a harrowing driving lesson in the smash-hit comedy *Police Academy*

Finny girl. Gus (Steve Guttenberg) seeks advice from his matchmaking sister Lizzie (Shelley Long) in *Don't Tell Her It's Me*

Sonnie Hale and Jessie Matthews (real-life husband and wife at the time) take stock of the latest disaster in the sexual deceptions of *First a Girl*

On his marks. . . Tony Hancock awaits the call to action while shooting his last major comedy vehicle, *The Punch and Judy Man*

The Love Bug. Surprisingly, it didn't lead to more assignments with the studio, and Hackett has since concentrated on nightclub and TV work. In 1978 director Robert C. Thompson decided to film Bob Thomas's fine, acerbic Abbott and Costello book *Bud and Lou* as a TV movie. There was really only one candidate to play Lou Costello. Buddy was fine in the role, even though he couldn't make the old A & C comedy routines seem funny. The only sadness was that he was clearly too old for it, but it was still the part of a lifetime. In the early 1980s Buddy starred in a TV revival of the old Groucho Marx (*qv*) quiz show *You Bet Your Life*. Films now seem a thing of the past for this effervescent comic jack-in-the-box, though his voice is still heard in cartoon features.

1953: Walking My Baby Back Home. 1954: Fireman, Save My Child. 1958: God's Little Acre. 1961: All Hands on Deck. Everything's Ducky. The Music Man. 1962: The Wonderful World of the Brothers Grimm. 1963: It's a Mad, Mad, Mad, Mad World. 1964: Muscle Beach Party. 1965: The Golden Head. 1968: The Love Bug. 1969: The Good Guys and the Bad Guys. 1977: Loose Shoes/Coming Attractions (released 1981). 1978: Bud and Lou (TV). 1988: Scrooged. 1989: The Little Mermaid (voice only).

With a smile and a song. Sonnie Hale's wheeler-dealing helps Jan Kiepura (right) win a bride in *My Song for You*

HALE, Sonnie

(John Robert Hale-Monro) 1902–1959
Britain's Sonnie Hale had great charm. With it and with his talents for singing, clowning, dancing, romancing and writing, he wooed and won not only a whole generation of theatregoers but also two of that generation's most graceful and beautiful stage stars. The son of musical-comedy star Robert Hale, and younger brother of comedienne Binnie (née Beatrice) Hale, he had worked his way up from the chorus to one of the West End of London's leading lights by the late 1920s, marrying blonde megastar Evelyn Laye in 1926. His most memorable performances were in spectacularly-staged shows at the London Pavilion, when he could be clowning in the ripest pantomime tradition one moment, then whip off his glasses to sing an

ineffably romantic duet with his leading lady. It was on one of these shows that he fell in love with his co-star, Jessie Matthews. Both were married to other stage stars, and the resultant divorce suit brought by Laye provoked many headlines, and temporarily damaged the Matthews and Hale careers. They married in 1931. The demand for top stage talent to make movies, however, brought them both to the cinema in the early years of sound. Hale's first film for five years was appropriately called *Happy Ever After*, and presented Hale and Jack Hulbert (*qv*) as two window-cleaners called Willie in love with the same girl: a formidable star quartet was completed by Lilian Harvey and Cicely Courtneidge (*qv*). Hale was teamed several times with his wife: *Friday the Thirteenth*, *Evergreen* (a film of their smash stage success), *First a Girl* and *It's Love Again*. Perhaps to his chagrin, he was never the romantic interest but always the comedy relief. His flawless timing and immaculate diction, though, scored less heavily on screen when it came to raising laughs. When Matthews' director Victor Saville left the studio, Hale took over the direction of her musicals. As a director, he was workmanlike and efficient, but he lacked inspiration and his wife's following began to fall away. There were a few more film comedy roles for Hale but at the beginning of World War Two he returned to the stage. Initially, he found difficulty re-establishing himself there in a changing atmosphere. He left Matthews in 1942 and they were divorced two years later.

By this time Hale had found a new calling – as a pantomime dame, a role he continued to fill enthusiastically for the next eight years. He also teamed with his sister in a very successful revue, *One, Two, Three!*, and a series of radio programmes, *All Hale* (1946–52), in which they played all the roles – 131 in the first series! There were a couple more films, though only in support of the stars (Tommy Trinder and Sid Field, both *qv*) and a reunion with Matthews in the 1955 production of the play *Nest of Robins*. Hale's gifts of wit, mimicry, charm and lightly-boiled lunacy were all seen to their best advantage in a 1956–7 tour with George Gershwin's *Lady Be Good*, which left theatregoers, said one writer 'with a delightful last glimpse of an almost forgotten comic attack'. Two years later he was dead, the victim of myelofibrosis, a rare blood disease.

*1927: * On with the Dance (series of shorts). * The Parting of the Ways. 1932: Happy Ever After. Tell Me Tonight (US: Be Mine Tonight). 1933: Friday the Thirteenth. Early to Bed. 1934: Evergreen. Wild Boy. Are You a Mason? My Song for You. My Heart is Calling. 1935: Marry the Girl. First a Girl. 1936: It's Love Again. 1938: The Gaunt Stranger (US: The Phantom Strikes). 1939: Let's Be Famous. 1944: Fiddlers Three. 1946: London Town (US: My Heart Goes Crazy).*
As director. *1937: Head Over Heels (US: Head Over Heels in Love). Gangway. 1938: Sailing Along.*

HALEY, Jack 1899–1979

Mild affability was the hallmark of genial Jack Haley's trade as a light comedian. Although a big name in revue, he never quite climbed to the top of the Hollywood tree, not even after he played the Tin Man in the classic 1939 version of *The Wizard of Oz*. This easy-going American entertainer was born John Joseph Haley in Boston. An angelic-looking child who sang as a boy soprano in choirs, he ran away from home after finishing high school, and became a song-plugger in Philadelphia before trying his luck on the vaudeville circuit with a song-and-comedy routine. He was on Broadway in musical comedies by the 1920s, scoring a notable personal success in *Follow Thru*, the film version of which in 1930 provided him with one of his earliest movie appearances. He made a few two-reel comedies as star in the early part of the decade, then was taken up by the major studios for co-star roles in cheerful comedies. He was ideally paired with chubby Jack Oakie (*qv*) as songwriters on the make in *Sitting Pretty* (1933), the success setting him up for a string of romantic comedy roles in co-features for the rest of the decade. Two of his most successful were opposite Shirley Temple in *Poor Little Rich Girl* (they sang *Military Man* together) and *Rebecca of Sunnybrook Farm*. Ironically circumstances caused Shirley to miss out on *The Wizard of Oz*, which jetted Haley to screen immortality. The film did little overall for his popularity, however, and he continued as the star of minor spoof comedy-chillers such as *One Body Too Many* and *Scared Stiff*, while supporting the stars in more expensive films. Haley used his money wisely and, having made a fortune from real estate, eased up on his workload after 1946, appearing only in the odd film or TV show, including material produced or directed by his son, Jack Haley Jr, an avid compiler of nostalgia specials. Happily married for many years to former Ziegfeld Follies dancer Florence McFadden, Haley died from a heart attack at 79.

*1927: Broadway Madness. 1930: * The 20th Amendment. * Harlequins. Follow Thru. 1932: * Sherlock's Home. * The Imperfect Lover.*

*Redheads on Parade. 1933: * Then Came the Yawn. * Wrongorilla. * Nothing But the Tooth. Sitting Pretty. Mr Broadway. 1934: Here Comes the Groom. 1935: The Girl Friend. Coronado. Spring Tonic. 1936: Pigskin Parade (GB: The Harmony Parade). Poor Little Rich Girl. F-Man. Mister Cinderella. 1937: Wake Up and Live. Pick a Star. She Had to Eat. Danger — Love at Work. 1938: Rebecca of Sunnybrook Farm. Alexander's Ragtime Band. Hold that Co-Ed (GB: Hold That Girl). Thanks for Everything. 1939: The Wizard of Oz. 1941: Moon Over Miami. Navy Blues. 1942: Beyond the Blue Horizon. 1943: Higher and Higher. 1944: One Body Too Many. 1945: George White's Scandals. People Are Funny. Scared Stiff. Sing Your Way Home. 1946: Vacation in Reno. 1949: Make Mine Laughs. 1958: No Time at All (TV). 1970: Norwood. 1972: Rolling Man (TV).*

HALL, Huntz
See **THE BOWERY BOYS**

HANCOCK, Tony 1924–1968

A tubby, hangdog British comedian in morose, Eeyore-like characterisations, who became enormously popular on radio and TV before discarding writers and co-stars alike and failing in films. Grouchy and bag-eyed, and always heading for a fall with his head in the clouds, Hancock is regarded by many as the greatest radio and television comedian of his day from any country. Born in Birmingham to a hotelier and part-time entertainer who died when he was still a boy, Hancock had already tried stand-up comedy at 16 and made his first radio broadcast in 1941. During wartime service with the RAF, he worked in ENSA concert parties and gang shows. On one of these, Hancock met Graham Stark (*qv*) with whom he would later co-star in situation comedy routines that foreshadowed the advent of the classic *Hancock's Half Hour*. After early post-war struggles he got a job as a comedian at the Windmill Theatre. Radio bookings began to come in from 1949. His characterisation of a long-suffering Scoutmaster in *Happy-Go-Lucky* (Stark and Bill Kerr, both

to be associated with him, were among the Scouts) was popular, as was his term as tutor to the ventriloquist's dummy Archie Andrews in *Educating Archie*, when his exasperated 'Flippin' kids' became a nationally repeated catchphrase. Two years later, in 1953, Hancock became the resident comedian on radio's *All-Star Bill*, working again with Stark and, for the first time, writers Ray Galton and Alan Simpson, who would create his 'character' and furnish him with all his best material. Egocentric and depressive, Hancock worried to an obsessive degree about relying too much on fellow performers. So Stark was missing when the first series of *Hancock's Half Hour* began in 1954, featuring a talented cast that included Sidney James, Hattie Jacques, Kenneth Williams (all *qv*) and Bill Kerr. It soon took off, more than can be said for Hancock's first film appearance, as a bandmaster in a deadly army comedy, *Orders Are Orders*. Later Hancock would tell of going to a cinema to see the film and asking if they had a seat in the circle. He was told he could have the first 15 rows. By great radio comedy acting, Hancock created a character of grandiose ambitions and huge cynicism, rooked by everyone and loved by no-one. This creation, frequently pictured in Homburg hat and astrakhan coat, wearing a predictably gloomy expression, was described by Galton and Simpson as 'a cunning, high-powered mug'. The character of Anthony Aloysius St John Hancock III was rude, arrogant, stubborn, childish and pompous — and much-loved by millions of listeners. The show went on until 1959 and ran on television from 1956, though Kerr, Williams and Jacques were phased out. The TV programmes, many of them two-handers for James and Hancock, were equally popular and became much-repeated classics. In 1960, at Hancock's insistence, James was dropped and, still scripted by Galton and Simpson, he went solo. Despite increasing dependence on alcohol, and often having to read his lines from cue cards, he turned out some wonderful half-hours, including *The Blood Donor*, *The Bowmans* and *The Radio Ham*. There was another film, *The Rebel*, also written by Galton and Simpson, casting Hancock as a London clerk who becomes an artist in Paris, but it was only partly successful. Galton and Simpson had partially written several other film ideas when Hancock decided not to work with them again, in films or TV. Instead, he did *The Punch and Judy Man*, a melancholy film comedy which cast him as a seaside entertainer with a nagging wife. It was too downbeat for his public, who stayed away in droves. That was really the end, although there was an abysmal TV series, *Hancock's*, and three episodes of a comedy series made in Australia, where he committed suicide with a combination of alcohol and pills. Like many other comedians, he had not known when the pinnacle of achievement had been reached.

1954: Orders Are Orders. 1961: The Rebel (US: Call Me Genius). 1962: The Punch and Judy Man. 1965: Those Magnificent Men in Their Flying Machines. 1966: The Wrong Box.

HANDL, Irene 1901–1987

Dumpy, delightful British character actress with brown, curly hair and plump, puffin-like features. A specialist in London land-ladies with mewling voices, she could make quite insignificant phrases seem funny. Her plaintive tones and unique way of brow-beating her fellow-players quickly stamped her out as a comedy player of distinction, although it wasn't until late in her career that people began to put a name to the face they knew so well. The daughter of an Austrian banker, she described her younger self as a plain-faced rebel who moved from school to school. 'No teacher wanted me.' Her French mother died when Irene was young, and she cared for her father until suddenly deciding to try for the stage in her early thirties, and enrolling at an acting school run by the sister of Dame Sybil Thorndike. She made her London stage debut in February 1937. The play closed in a fortnight but her next stage role ensured her continuous employment on stage, screen, radio and television for the next 40 years. This was Beer, the maid in *George and Margaret*, the only sane figure in the midst of a panicking family who are awaiting important guests (who are never seen). She repeated the role in the successful 1940 film version, by which time she was already on her way to being established as a regular contributor of funny cameos to British comedies and dramas in the war years. In post-war years she continued to play film roles, becoming more shapeless with each decade, as well as becoming an easily-identified radio voice on such shows as *Hello Playmates* and *Hancock's Half Hour*. With Tony Hancock (*qv*), she moved into tele-vision, but it was 1970 before she got a series of her own, *For the Love of Ada*, in harness with one-time quizmaster Wilfred Pickles, as two septuagenarians getting married. By this time she had published her first novel, *The Sioux*, which became a best-seller. It was followed by another. Also in the 1960s, she had her biggest theatrical hit in many years in the title role of *Goodnight, Mrs Puffin*, which she took on a world-wide tour after a two-year London run. It was much to her disappointment that it was never filmed. Cooks, gossips, busybodies and aggressive domestics of all shapes and ranks were her stock in trade. She played Madam Arcati the medium in a stage version of *Blithe Spirit*, and revelled in the role of David Warner's Marxist mum in *Morgan — a Suitable Case for Treatment*. She was just as good at being kind and nice as she was at being absolutely awful. Dying a few weeks before her 86th birthday, Irene Handl had never managed to get married, as much a source of surprise to her, apparently, as anyone else. 'It's one thing I just don't understand', she said. 'I can't understand why I didn't. It's extraordinary.' Perhaps Irene Handl, author, broadcaster, actress and personality, was just too busy.

*1937: Missing — Believed Married. The Vulture. 1938: Strange Boarders. The Terror. The Viper. 1939: Mrs Pym of Scotland Yard. On the Night of the Fire (US: The Fugitive). Inspector Hornleigh on Holiday (US: Inspector Hornleigh on Leave). Dr O'Dowd. 1940: The Girl in the News. Night Train to Munich (US: Night Train). George and Margaret. Gasbags. Spellbound (US: The Spell of Amy Nugent). 1941: Pimpernel Smith (US: Mister V). * Mr Proudfoot Shows a Light. 1942: Partners in Crime. Uncensored. 1943: I'll Walk Beside You. Rhythm Serenade. Get Cracking. The Flemish Farm. Millions Like Us. It's in the Bag. Dear Octopus (US: The Randolph Family). 1944: Welcome Mr Washington. Mr Emmanuel. English Without Tears (US: Her Man Gilbey). Kiss the Bride Goodbye. Give Us the Moon. Medal for the General. 1945: For You Alone. Great Day. Brief Encounter. The Shop at Sly Corner (US: The Code of Scotland Yard). 1946: I'll Turn to You. 1947: Temp-tation Harbour. The Hills of Donegal. 1948: Woman Hater. Silent Dust. No Orchids for Miss Blandish. The History of Mr Polly. Card-board Cavalier. 1949: The Fool and the Princess. Adam and Evelyne (US: Adam and Evalyn). For Them That Trespass. The Perfect Woman. Dark Secret. 1950: Stage Fright. 1951: One Wild Oat. Young Wives' Tale. 1952: Top Secret (US: Mr Potts Goes to Moscow). Treasure Hunt. 1953: The Wedding of Lilli Marlene. Meet Mr Lucifer. The Weak and the Wicked. Stryker of the Yard. The Accused. 1954: Duel in the Jungle. Burnt Evidence. The Case of the Second Shot. The Belles of St Trinian's. Mad About Men. A Kid for Two Farthings. 1955: Now and Forever. 1956: Who Done It? It's Never Too Late. The Silken Affair. Brothers in Law. Happy is the Bride! 1958: The Key. Law and Disorder. Carlton-Browne of the F.O. (US: Man in a Cocked Hat). Next to No Time! 1959: The Crowning Touch. Carry On Nurse. Inn for Trouble. I'm All Right, Jack. Desert Mice. Upstairs and Downstairs. Left, Right and Centre. School for Scoundrels. 1960: Two-Way Stretch. Carry On Constable. Make Mine Mink. Doctor in Love. A French Mistress. The Night We Got the Bird. No Kidding (US: Beware of Children). The Pure Hell of St Trinian's. 1961: Double Bunk. The Rebel (US: Call Me Genius). A Weekend with Lulu. Watch It Sailor! Nothing Barred. 1963: Heavens Above! Just for Fun. 1965: You Must Be Joking! 1966: Morgan —*

Tony Hancock in one of his typical moods of reflective melancholy in this off-set shot from *The Punch and Judy Man*. He seems to have ignored the 'No Parking' sign. But then Hancock ignored most advice in life

Irene Handl (right) in the film version of the great TV success of her later years, *For the Love of Ada*. With her are Wilfred Pickles, Barbara Mitchell and (rear) Jack Smethurst

A Suitable Case for Treatment (US: Morgan). The Wrong Box. 1967: Smashing Time. 1968: Lionheart. Wonderwall. 1969: The Italian Job. 1970: Doctor in Trouble. The Private Life of Sherlock Holmes. On a Clear Day You Can See Forever. 1972: For the Love of Ada. 1976: Confessions of a Driving Instructor. The Chiffy Kids (series). 1977: Come Play with Me. The Last Remake of Beau Geste. Adventures of a Private Eye. The Hound of the Baskervilles. Stand Up, Virgin Soldiers. 1979: The Great Rock 'n' Roll Swindle. 1980: Riding High. 1985: Hotel du Lac (TV). 1986: Absolute Beginners.

HANDLEY, Tommy 1894–1949

Button-bright Liverpudlian purveyor of puns and gobbledegook who became Britain's most famous comedian of the 1940s. Films were rare and never captured his special appeal, for Handley was essentially a vocal comedian who sometimes looked uncomfortable with visual gags. His rate of patter, though, was something else. Always word-perfect, he picked his way at a speed of knots through a complicated array of often non-sequitur plays on words usually written for him by Ted Kavanagh, a gag writer of like mind with whom he teamed up in the 1920s. Handley was already a rising comedian on the variety halls then; especially popular was his famous sketch *The Disorderly Room*, which he performed at the Royal Variety Show of 1924 (when it was broadcast, it was the first time his voice had been heard on radio). Listeners liked what they heard and Handley got his own series, *Radio Radiance*, the following year, opposite comedienne Jean Allistone, whom he later married and with whom he recorded the hysterical clucking song *Have You Seen My Chickens?* Further radio series included *Handley's Manoeuvres* and *Tommy's Tours*, and there was a feature film debut in the revue-style *Elstree Calling*, whose roster of acts had to suffer the intervention of Handley as a sort of master of ceremonies. In the early 1930s Handley formed a profitable partnership with fellow punster Ronald Frankau. They proved a popular pair of cross-talkers under the names Murgatroyd and Winterbottom, specialising in 'silly' commentaries on sporting events. There was even a film together, *Two Men in a Box*, which saw them performing much the same sort of function as had Handley in *Elstree Calling*. Films patently didn't know how to handle Handley, but radio was about to immortalize him. Kavanagh devised a comedy programme called *It's That Man Again* (soon to be shortened to *ITMA*) in which Handley rarely stopped talking as the axle around which revolved a stream of idiotic happenings. He himself reckoned the show delivered a joke every 11 seconds. How about 'Our Friday night concerts were a terrific success. For four pence you could get a catalogue, a cantata, a cream cornet, and a cold if you sat near the trombone. We played all the classics – The Charge of the Laundry by Liszt, Beethoven's Too Ripe Tomato, Elgar's Circumpump and Stance, Offenbach's Horses and Knees Up, Mother Brahms. Nobody stayed after the first bar – they made for the nearest one.'? With its delightful array of outlandish characters, *ITMA*'s audience was soon up to 30 million, and Handley himself was receiving 40,000 letters a year. New characters and settings came and went with the years and Tommy found time to make two more films, *It's That Man Again*, as the mayor of Foaming-in-the-Mouth, and *Time Flies*, a time-travel comedy which misfired despite script contributions from Kavanagh, and a plot that predated *Bill and Ted's Excellent Adventure* by 35 years. The new post-war *ITMA* setting, an island called *Tomtopia*, brought Handley's voice, at least, back to films in a short, *Tom Tom Topia*. But time was running out. Three days after the 310th show was broadcast, and three days before his 55th birthday, Handley died suddenly following a stroke. The 311th show, already scripted, was never broadcast. Handley never had time to regret his failed flirtation with films, though ironic references to it can still be found in his scripts. 'I played a divot in *The Good Earth*, but was replaced later! They finished me off with a good fat part – a frying-pan in *Goodbye Mr Chips!*'

*1928: * Pathé Pictorial No. 548. * Gaumont Mirror No. 94. 1930: Elstree Calling. 1933: * Making a Christmas Pudding. * A Tail of Tails (voice only). This is Paris! That Was!! (narrator only). 1934: * Hot Airman. 1936: * Leslie Jeffries and His Orchestra. 1937: * BBC Musicals No. 2. 1938: Two Men in a Box. 1942: It's That Man Again. 1943: Time Flies. Pictorial Revue of 1943. 1945: * Worker and Waterfront Magazine. * Tommy Handley's Victory Song. 1946: * Tom Tom Topia (voice only). 1949: Scrapbook for 1933.*

HANKS, Tom 1956–

Unlike most of his contemporaries on the film comedy scene, who are stand-up comedians turned comic actors, California's Tom Hanks is an actor who happens to be particularly adept at comedy. Funnily enough, Hanks once tried stand-up comedy in pursuance of the part he was about to play in *Punchline*. 'When I first got up to do it', he says, 'I knew I was going to be terrible and I was. I was really bad ... especially after being introduced as 'the guy from all those funny movies'. I couldn't wait to get off the stage. After about the ninth time, I felt a bit more comfortable. But I don't think I could make a living doing it. Believe

Knock-out patch. Miss Patch (Irene Handl) distracts the attention of a German guard while Gay (Dora Bryan) stands by with a spanner, in *Desert Mice*

They're talking about the fish/woman he loves. Allen (Tom Hanks) reads all about the capture of Madison the mermaid in *Splash*

Desert island risks. Robertson Hare (second from right), Kenneth More and George Cole understandably come to blows over Joan Collins in *Our Girl Friday*

me, the three hardest jobs in America are coal-mining, police work and stand-up comedy.' Not that Hanks has had to worry about that. The only hiccups in the career of this seemingly relaxed, happy man, who says he wakes up in the morning and feels good about life, have come when he has veered away from comedy into other fields. Tall and rangy, with dark, curly hair, large blue eyes and a mischievous mouth, Hanks got into acting while at university and, after a period of struggle in the late 1970s, won a regular spot on a TV sitcom called *Bosom Buddies*, in which he spent most episodes dressed as a woman. It was good training for comedy films, but it was four years before Hanks got one. And then it was only *Bachelor Party*, although he was easily the best thing in this teen-sex-drugs-stag party caper aimed at the drive-in market. There were quite a few good things about the next one, *Splash*, in which he fell in love with Daryl Hannah as a mermaid. Like all the best comedians — and comedy — Hanks combined an intelligently thought-out character with moments of believable wild madness. Add warmth and a certain wry charm, and he could now consider himself a star. But not yet one the public would necessarily pay to see, as evidenced by *The Man with One Red Shoe* (underrated, say the few people who have seen it), *Volunteers* and *Every Time We Say Goodbye*, the latter a mistaken attempt at slushy romance. All went straight to video outside America. In between times, there was *The Money Pit*, which certainly *was* underrated, teamed him with Shelley Long (*qv*) and demonstrated his engaging, and skilful sense of physical comedy, and *Nothing in Common*, a partial success opposite Jackie Gleason (*qv*), in a film which didn't quite get the balance of comedy and drama right. These did make some money, but peanuts compared to *Dragnet*, a cop caper which teamed him with Dan Aykroyd (*qv*) and, after a clever first 15 minutes, proved to be unsubtly old-fashioned; and certainly compared to *Big*, one of the major hits of 1988 and a big star role for Hanks as a 12-year-old boy's reincarnation in the body of a man. 'Making that character come alive', said Hanks, 'and appear real — that was a fun challenge.' Few actors could have expressed

childish delight so well, and Hanks was nominated for an Oscar, as he was the following year for *Punchline*. He was allowed to show both unsympathetic and goofy sides to his nature in that, but *The 'burbs* handed him just *too* dislikeable a character for it to be funny as well. *Joe vs the Volcano*, however, a cross between *1984* and *Road to Singapore*, was just dotty enough to make you laugh out loud every now and again. He was droll in *Turner & Hooch* as a cop with a slavering dog for a partner. At this point, Hanks' career took something of a wrong turn. William Hurt had to bow out of the film version of *The Bonfire of the Vanities* due to another film overrunning its schedule, and Hanks was substituted in a role to which, frankly, Hurt was far better suited. That, however, was only part of the reason why this film version of a best-seller was a flop. After that, eyebrows were rightly raised when Hanks was announced for the remake of a 1950s *film noir*, *Night and the City*. The role of a doomed man on the run appeared alien to his talents. Fortunately, the role eventually went to Robert De Niro, who seemed ideal, and Hanks, to the relief of everyone who enjoys laughing with him, zoomed off into an all-star comedy, *A League of Their Own*.

1980: He Knows You're Alone. 1982: Mazes and Monsters/Rona Jaffe's Mazes and Monsters (TV). 1984: Bachelor Party. Splash. 1985: Volunteers. The Man with One Red Shoe/ Mischief. The Money Pit. 1986: Nothing in Common. Every Time We Say Goodbye. 1987: Dragnet. 1988: Big. Punchline. 1989: The 'burbs. Turner & Hooch. 1990: Joe vs the Volcano. The Bonfire of the Vanities. 1992: A League of Their Own. Radio Flyer.

HARE, Robertson
(John R. Hare) 1891–1979

When a man whose name is Hare actually looks like a persecuted rabbit, then surely his future as a comic character star is assured. And so it was with Robertson Hare, inevitably known to his many friends as 'Bunny'. But it wasn't until he lost his hair and teamed with Ralph Lynn and Tom Walls (both *qv*) in the famous Aldwych farces that he became a major West End stage

attraction. As British as roast beef, Hare studied for the stage as a teenager and made his first professional appearance at 19. Two years later he had deserted London to gain experience in provincial touring companies. It was with one of these that he first played the leading role that was to become his favourite: 'Grumpy' Bullivant in *Grumpy*. Grumpy was a lovable, dyspeptic lawyer with a penchant for detection. Hare played the role several times on tours between 1914 and 1916. Years later, in 1930, a film version would be made in Hollywood by George Cukor but by that time Hare was securely entrenched in the Aldwych farces. These bastions of English stage farce began in the early 1920s. Written by Ben Travers and co-starring Walls and Lynn, they cast Hare as small, fussy, bespectacled serious little men of unquestionable morals against whom fate and his fellows would conspire. One of his catchphrases on stage was 'Indubitably!' But his most famous, ever-present at moments of greatest crisis, such as losing his trousers, was 'Oh, calamity!' Hare began playing in Travers's romps in 1922 and continued in them for 20 years, most of them beginning their runs at London's Aldwych Theatre before being transferred to film in abbreviated versions at the Gaumont-British studios. Hare played such characters as the Rev. Cathcart Sloley-Jones, Harold Twine, Oswald Veal, Ernest Ramsbotham, Edwin Stoatt, Clement Peck, Herbert Holly and Gilbert Augustus Pogson. All were among life's losers. Genuinely pitiable in distress, Hare found a new partner for his stage frolics in the 1940s, in the big, burly, bluff form of Alfred Drayton. But Drayton died in 1949, and a teaming of Hare with Stanley Holloway (*qv*) — for example in the 1951 film *One Wild Oat* — did not work out. But there were still occasional film ventures — a lineup of Hare, George Cole (*qv*), Kenneth More and Joan Collins in *Our Girl Friday* (1953) was popular even though the film itself was poor — and he enjoyed renewed popularity for a while in the late 1960s with his running role as the Archdeacon in a TV series called *All Gas and Gaiters*, which poked fun at the clergy. After he died at an actors' home in Middlesex, from bronchial pneumonia, he was described by his friend Ben Travers as 'the man who lived next door to everybody'. 'He was indulged by nature with a pedantic, reedy, almost clerical tone of voice which served him so well', Travers added. 'He was also, without exception, the worst golfer in the world, and a delight to play with — or, preferably, against.' Hare published an autobiography in 1957. It was called *Yours Indubitably*.

1930: Rookery Nook (US: One Embarrassing Night). On Approval. Tons of Money. Plunder. 1932: Thark. A Night Like This. Just My Luck. 1933: It's a Boy! A Cuckoo in the Nest. Turkey Time. Friday the Thirteenth. 1934: A Cup of Kindness. Are You a Mason? Dirty

Work. 1935: Oh Daddy! Fighting Stock. Stormy Weather. Car of Dreams. Foreign Affaires. 1936: Jack of All Trades. Pot Luck. You Must Get Married. Aren't Men Beasts! 1938: A Spot of Bother. 1939: So This is London. 1940: * Yesterday is Over Your Shoulder. 1941: Banana Ridge. 1942: Women Aren't Angels. 1944: He Snoops to Conquer. 1948: Things Happen at Night. 1951: One Wild Oat. The Magic Box. 1953: Our Girl Friday (US: The Adventures of Sadie). 1956: Three Men in a Boat. My Wife's Family. 1960: The Night We Got the Bird. 1961: Out of the Shadow. The Young Ones. 1962: Seven Keys. Crooks Anonymous. 1966: Hotel Paradiso. 1968: Salt and Pepper. 1971: Raising the Roof.

HARKER, Gordon 1885–1967

Although Britain's Gordon Harker was never a comedian, there were few films in which his characters could not be guaranteed to make you laugh. With jutting lower lip and built-in scowl, sandy-haired Harker's cockney features oozed truculence. Whether as policeman, crook or general rapscallion, though, it was hard not to like him. And prolific dramatist Edgar Wallace tailored a whole series of plays to Harker's particular talents. Few ugly, middle-aged men have proved hot bets at the box-office. But Harker, in common with Hollywood's Lee Marvin, in tougher vein, was certainly one of the select band. Born to a London family of scenic painters – his father and four of his five brothers were in the business of painting theatrical scenery – Gordon, too, worked for a while at the family studio, but started picking up what small parts he could at theatres where his family had provided scenery. In 1904 he went to Australia and worked for a touring company there until 1913. Harker returned to England where he soon found himself in the army with the outbreak of World War One. Serving in Gallipoli and Palestine, he was eventually invalided out soon after the cessation of hostilities. Picking up his career was hard and for a while the best he could do was understudy work. But he gradually began to make strides and the doorway to the big-time opened in 1926 when he was cast as an old lag, Sam Hackitt, in a stage version of

Wallace's thriller The Ringer, about a disguised crook out for revenge on his former partner. The following year, he entered films; he was to average four films a year for the next 15 years. His first three were for Alfred Hitchcock. These were silents, however, and only sound gave full value to Harker's fruity tones. His first Edgar Wallace film was The Squeaker, followed by The Ringer, The Calendar and The Frightened Lady (all repeats of roles he had created on stage). Britannia of Billingsgate and My Old Dutch were sagas of cockney life, and Hyde Park Corner, The Phantom Light, Saloon Bar and Once a Crook film versions of stage successes. From 1936 to 1941 Harker seemed to have the magic touch. He got some marvellous characters, and the scripts were sparkling. Or, at least, he helped to make them so, with a unique under-use of that marvellously expressive face, which sometimes made a virtue of immobility. This was the period in which he played the redoubtable Sergeant Elk (also created on stage) in two Wallace comedy-thrillers about a master-criminal called The Frog. Comedy-thriller was also the vein hit by the Inspector Hornleigh films, based on a radio series. Gordon was Hornleigh and Alastair Sim (qv) his cohort Sergeant Bingham, although, in truth, the roles might have been better cast the other way round. Very British and good fun, the films were hugely popular and could probably have gone on but for Harker's theatrical commitments. He played in Acacia Avenue (also filmed, as another tale of cockney life), then toured the country in productions of some of his greatest successes. A film comeback, in the farce Things Happen at Night, revealed that Harker's best movie days were done but, returning to the

stage, he was a splendid Doolittle in Pygmalion, and enjoyed one last great theatrical success as Albert, the wily waiter of Small Hotel. That, too, was filmed, if only in a pocket version. Harker, still game for work, was to have branched out into television in 1959 as Old Bill the night watchman in a series of W. W. Jacobs' Night Watchman stories. But he was injured in a fall in December 1958 and unable to take part. It was effectively the end of a long career, during which Harker's froglike features and mutters of 'Yus-s' were always guaranteed to raise a chuckle.

1927: The Ring. The Farmer's Wife. 1928: Champagne. The Wrecker. 1929: The Return of the Rat. The Crooked Billet. Taxi for Two. 1930: * All Riot on the Western Front. The 'W' Plan. Elstree Calling. Escape. The Squeaker. 1931: Third Time Lucky. The Sport of Kings. The Stronger Sex. Shadows. The Man They Could Not Arrest. The Ringer. The Calendar (US: Bachelor's Folly). The Professional Guilt. Condemned to Death. 1932: The Frightened Lady (US: Criminal at Large). Love on Wheels. White Face. Rome Express. 1933: Britannia of Billingsgate. Lucky Number. This is the Life. Friday the Thirteenth. 1934: My Old Dutch. Road House. Dirty Work. The Phantom Light. 1935: The Lad. Admirals All. Squibs. Hyde Park Corner. Boys Will Be Boys. The Amateur Gentleman. 1936: Wolf's Clothing. Two's Company. * The Story of Papworth. Millions. 1937: Beauty and the Barge. The Frog. 1938: Blondes for Danger. No Parking. Lightning Conductor. The Return of the Frog. Inspector Hornleigh. 1939: * Tommy Atkins. Inspector Hornleigh on Holiday. 1940: Saloon Bar. * Channel Incident. 1941: Inspector Hornleigh Goes to It (US: Mail Train). Once a Crook.

Will he get away with it? Store thief Gordon Harker hopes to escape detection in female disguise in Love on Wheels

Hornleigh (Gordon Harker) tries to crack the case, while Sgt Bingham (Alastair Sim) concentrates on his two-finger typing in *Inspector Hornleigh*

In *Foul Play*, Goldie Hawn is chivvied and chased by many, and helped by Chevy Chase! It was the first of their two successful films together

Inept lawyer Ben Stubbins (Will Hay) studies a tangled family tree in his office, which interests crooks as it's over a bank. With him is Hal Walters.

1943: *Warn That Man.* 1945: *29 Acacia Avenue* (US: *The Facts of Love*). 1948: *Things Happen at Night.* 1950: *Her Favourite Husband* (US: *The Taming of Dorothy*). *The Second Mate.* 1952: *Derby Day* (US: *Four Against Fate*). 1954: *Bang! You're Dead* (US: *Game of Danger*). 1955: *Out of the Clouds.* 1956: *A Touch of the Sun.* 1957: *Small Hotel.* 1959: *Left, Right and Centre.*

HAWN, Goldie 1945–

It's a pity America's Goldie Hawn has turned away from comedy to make thrillers in recent years. She's decent enough in these roles, but few comic actresses these days are as good with the physical business of evoking laughter. Her large blue eyes and vulnerable, doll-like features only serve to make you laugh the more at her misfortunes. 'Twas ever thus. In *Rowan and Martin's Laugh-In*, the freewheeling TV comedy show that made her a star from its inception in January 1968, she squeaked and giggled, and forgot her lines, and we all loved her for it. Poor, adorable Goldie. Still, there was evidence in real life that poor little Goldie knew what was good for her and had a solid business brain behind those wide, flapping blue eyes, and under the head of fluffy blonde hair. She had started out as a dancer, but was obviously so funny and endearing that making people laugh soon seemed the more lucrative option. She was suddenly a big movie star, too, when she won an Academy Award (best supporting actress) in *Cactus Flower*, only her second film. In a mixture of comedies and dramas, she certainly proved she could act, although the films themselves weren't all that popular, apart from *Shampoo* in 1975, which was more of a vehicle for Warren Beatty's sexual charisma. She followed that with *The Duchess and the Dirtwater Fox*, one of those promising ideas that sometimes fall on the screen with a damp thud. This western 'comedy' certainly did, despite the fact that Goldie was as effervescent as ever. She found the right blend of action and comedy with *Foul Play*, which also boosted the careers of Chevy Chase and Dudley Moore (both *qv*). She was vulnerable and funny, and it helped to have leading men who were basically comedians too. A much later, similar venture with a straight

leading man, Mel Gibson, hardly worked at all. At this point, the delicate flower took control of her own destiny by forming a production company. It made such Hawn vehicles as *Private Benjamin* and *Protocol*, tailor-made stuff that proved to be (often hilariously) funny for two-thirds of the way through, but went soft and sentimental at the end. *Wildcats*, with Goldie as a tough football coach whipping a school team of no-hopers into shape, was mostly delightful, but barely shown outside America because of the theme. She tried a change of pace with *Overboard*, opposite Kurt Russell, with whom she had lived since 1983 (her two marriages ended in divorce) and her personal charm and comedy sense made it work. She's a rich bitch who falls overboard from her yacht, suffers amnesia and changes personality for the better in the household of rough-hewn Russell and his sons. Her fans stayed away, and she didn't film again for three years, an annoying waste of time in her early forties. When she did come back, she played safe by pairing herself with Gibson in *Bird on a Wire*, and could congratulate herself when the (poor) film did well in monetary terms. Goldie now seems to see herself more in the kind of roles that Sally Field plays, which is a pity, since she is partially stifling talents that are peculiarly her own. Since 1987 she has become a filmographer's nightmare: Hawn projects have been announced, slated, even 'gone into production', then disappeared from view. She did make a Field-type thriller, *Criss-Cross*, which followed on another thriller, *Deceived*. Her fans were relieved when serendipity seemed to take a hand. Her friend Steve Martin (*qv*) lost his co-star when Meg Ryan bowed out of *The Housesitter*, and Goldie stepped into the breach. There's still time for Goldie to make us laugh some more with her own version of a wide-eyed disaster area.

1968: *The One and Only Genuine Original Family Band.* 1969: *Cactus Flower.* 1970: *There's a Girl in My Soup.* 1971: *$* (GB: *The Heist*). 1972: *Butterflies Are Free.* 1973: *The Sugarland Express.* 1974: *The Girl from Petrovka.* 1975: *Shampoo.* 1976: *The Duchess and the Dirtwater Fox.* 1978: *Travels with Anita* (US: *A Trip with Anita*). *Foul Play.* 1980: *Private Benjamin. Seems Like Old Times.* 1982: *Best Friends.* 1983: *Swing Shift.* 1984: *Protocol.* 1985: *Wildcats.* 1987: *Overboard.* 1990: *Bird on a Wire.* 1991: *Deceived.* 1992: *Criss-Cross. The Housesitter. Death Becomes Her.*

HAWTREY, Charles

(George C. Hartree) 1914–1988

Thin, dark-haired, British comic character star with dry, plaintive tones. He moved from what seemed a lifetime of skinny, snooty, trouble-making schoolboys in the late 1950s to become a regular member of the 'Carry On' films for 15 years. Pop-eyed

and bespectacled, thin lips, it seemed, permanently pursed in an expression of disapproval or in anticipation of trouble, Hawtrey came originally from a theatrical family based in Middlesex. At the age of six he was writing plays that he and friends would put on for anyone who would pay a penny. The stage was in his own back garden. But greater fame beckoned when he developed a fine soprano voice, joined an amateur operatic society and even made a record or two. There were roles in silent films, a first stage appearance at 11 and some training at drama school before he made his debut London stage appearance at 18. For a while Hawtrey tried producing but found it less satisfying and returned to acting. He gradually began to get a footing in the 'false boom' of the British cinema industry of the mid 1930s when versatile actors found themselves in great demand. But it was a series of films that Hawtrey made with Will Hay (*qv*) that made his name, defined his image and familiarised audiences with his face. Hay was Hawtrey's idol — he once said 'I learned everything I know from him' — and he even turned down a role in *Top of the Form* (1952), a remake of Hay's 1937 film *Good Morning, Boys!*, because he thought (rightly) that it cheapened the original. In between his five films with Hay, Hawtrey became a regular broadcaster, most notably on children's programmes as the voice of Norman Bones, boy detective. His light, earnest-sounding speaking voice enabled him to keep going in the role for several years after his debut in 1943. And there were numerous film performances, almost always in comic cameos, before his performance as an inept private soldier in *Carry On Sergeant* made him a regular member of the highly successful series of film farces until 1972. Knobbly-kneed and goggle-eyed, Hawtrey's characters in these films were vaguely camp and campily vague. He was always worth a smile and the running gag about him being tortured in *Carry On Henry* is the best thing in the film. Hawtrey's last years were far from happy. He became a heavy drinker and lost his place on the 'Carry On' team. Bitterly, he would tell friends that he had been dumped for being too old, an ironic fate for the perennial schoolboy. In his seventies, Hawtrey developed serious arterial problems. Revived after his heart stopped beating in September 1988, he was told that he would die unless both legs were removed. He refused the operation and died a month later. He lived alone in a terraced house in a Kent seaside town, seldom visited by old companions from the film world. A sad ending for the multi-talented youngster once billed as 'Master Charles Hawtrey − the Angel Voiced Choirboy'.

1922: † *Tell Your Children.* 1923: † *This Freedom.* 1932: † *Marry Me.* 1933: † *The Melody Maker.* 1935: * *Kiddies on Parade.* 1936: *Sabotage* (US: *The Woman Alone*). *Cheer Up! Well Done Henry.* 1937: *Good Morning, Boys!* (US: *Where There's a Will*). *The Gap. East of Ludgate Hill.* 1939: *Where's That Fire? Jailbirds.* 1941: *The Ghost of St Michael's. The Black Sheep of Whitehall.* 1942: *Let the People Sing. The Goose Steps Out. Much Too Shy.* 1943: *Bell Bottom George.* 1944: *A Canterbury Tale.* 1946: *Meet Me at Dawn.* 1947: *The End of the River.* 1948: *The Story of Shirley Yorke.* 1949: *Passport to Pimlico. Dark Secret.* 1950: *Room to Let.* 1951: *Smart Alec. The Galloping Major. Brandy for the Parson.* 1952: *Hammer the Toff. You're Only Young Twice!* 1954: *Five Days* (US: *Paid to Kill*). *To Dorothy a Son* (US: *Cash on Delivery*). 1955: *As Long As They're Happy. Man of the Moment. Timeslip* (US: *The Atomic Man*). *Simon and Laura. Jumping for Joy. Who Done It?* 1956: *The March Hare.* 1958: *Carry On Sergeant.* 1959: *I Only Arsked! Carry On Nurse. Carry On Teacher. Please Turn Over. Inn for Trouble.*

1960: *Carry On Constable.* 1961: *Carry On Regardless. Dentist on the Job* (US: *Get On with It!*). *What A Whopper!* 1963: *Carry On Cabby. Carry On Jack* (US: *Carry On Venus*). 1964: *Carry On Cleo. Carry On Spying.* 1965: *Carry On Cowboy.* 1966: *Carry On Screaming. Don't Lose Your Head.* 1967: *The Terrornauts. Follow That Camel. Carry On Doctor.* 1968: *Carry On Up the Khyber.* 1969: *Carry On Camping. Carry On Again, Doctor. Zeta One.* 1970: *Carry On Loving. Carry On Up the Jungle. Carry On Henry. Grasshopper Island* (TV). 1971: *Carry On at Your Convenience.* 1972: *Carry On Matron. Carry On Abroad.* As director. 1945: *What Do We Do Now? Dumb Dora Discovers Tobacco.*

† As Charles Hawtrey Jr

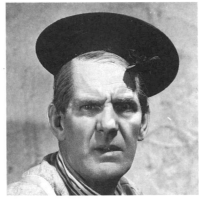

HAY, Will 1888−1949
Although a scholarly man in real life, with a passion for astronomy, Will Hay's comic

reputation rests on his portraits of seedy incompetence in figures who commanded authority but not respect. These included fire chiefs, police chiefs, prison wardens and stationmasters − but above all schoolteachers. Hay first introduced the schoolmaster character into his stage act in 1909 but it didn't become a regular part of his act until several years as a stand-up comic in the British halls and a long spell as a member of Fred Karno's troupe of crazy comedians. This early Hay was a long way from the man who would perfect the comedy of reaction, causing one writer to describe him as 'the best straight man there ever was'. He was born in the north of England, to a quite well-to-do and very un-show business family. His father was an engine fitter, his vivacious mother active in local politics. Young Will, married at 19, worked for a printing company while building a reputation as an after-dinner speaker and a joke-teller at local functions and 'smoking concerts'. He became a professional entertainer in 1909. Early versions of his school sketch were called 'Bend Down', but it was not until the early 1920s, when he called it 'The Fourth Form at St Michael's' and introduced other characters, that it really began to add momentum to his career. By 1925, he was the major star (and the biggest hit) of the year's Royal Variety Performance. Hay's school sketches were unusual for their day in that, by and large, they lacked punchlines, relying instead on a long series of absurd connections with previous lines, and the fact that the pupils were continually discomfiting their teacher. The secret lay in the timing. In 1927 Hay took the act to America, with considerable success. But, although sound comedy shorts were already popular before he returned to Britain, he remained aloof from film comedy until well into the 1930s. He felt that playing the schoolmaster on screen would quickly use up all his stage material. He accepted the magistrate in *Those Were the Days* in 1934 because, as much as anything else, it gave him a chance to break away from his most famous character. Now popular in radio, determined to pursue a cinema career, and completing his book on astronomy, *Through My Telescope*, Hay no longer had the time for regular stage tours. Further cheerful film romps followed. He played a country vicar in *Dandy Dick* and a broadcasting boss (his station was called NBG) in *Radio Parade of 1935*. He succumbed to a school comedy, *Boys Will Be Boys*, because the scripts were not based on his St Michael's characters but on the Narkover College created by the famous humorist Beachcomber (J. B. Morton). So it was that audiences saw Hay for the first time in full sail, complete with pince-nez, mortar-board, frustrated scowl, squinty eyes and pasted-over hair (at first Hay thinned his own hair, but later wore a 'balding' wig). As Dr Alec Smart, he typically obtains the position of headmaster with the help of false credentials − a device used,

Charles Hawtrey (centre) in rare relaxed mood in the company of Sidney James and Amanda Barrie in *Carry On Cabby*

with variations, in several other films. *Where There's a Will* found him as an incompetent lawyer, and *Windbag the Sailor* had him as bogus sea captain. The former teamed him for the first time with plump teenager Graham Moffatt (*qv*) and the latter with both Moffatt and Hay's other famous film protagonist, wheezy, toothless Moore Marriott (*qv*). But Hay's schoolmaster was still his most popular characterisation, and he appeared again in *Good Morning, Boys*, which featured Moffatt and Charles Hawtrey (*qv*) and found Hay for the first time under the direction of French-born Marcel Varnel, a brilliant comedy director who would go on to make eight of Hay's best. The school was Hay's old favourite, St Michael's. Hay, Varnel, Moffatt and Marriott all came together in Hay's next, *Oh, Mr Porter!*, which proved to be his most enduring comedy classic and contains the much-quoted line 'The next train's gone'. In this film, Hay leapt across the bridge between stage and screen comedy. Playing an inept station-master, he is banished to the obscure Irish station of Buggleskelly, where he soon sinks to the same level of corruption as co-workers Moffatt and Marriott and becomes involved with a gang of gun-runners and a ghost that isn't. Hay had been Dr Benjamin Twist in *Good Morning, Boys* (confusingly called *Where There's a Will* in America) and kept the character name for *Convict 99* and *Hey! Hey! USA*. The next three, *Old Bones of the River*, *Ask a Policeman* and *Where's That Fire*, all with Moffatt and Marriott, debunked the colonial service, the police force and the fire service respectively. Running second only to George Formby (*qv*) at the British box-office in 1940, Hay paused. Like other comedians before and after him, he worried about his 'stooges' becoming part of an unbreakable team, and taking the limelight away. He decided that Moffatt and Marriott were 'swamping him' and he'd make no more films with them. (During the war years they worked with other comedians, notably Arthur Askey (*qv*).) Meanwhile, Hay moved across from Gainsborough to Ealing. But his finest films were already behind him, and it was noticeable that the two best Ealing efforts, *The Ghost of St Michael's* and *My Learned Friend*, both teamed him with another excellent comedian, Claude Hulbert (*qv*). The first of these was also directed by his old friend Marcel Varnel, and featured the famous schoolmaster character, here called William Lamb, for the last time. In it, Hay abandoned, for the first time, his 'scratch' wig and showed his own full head of hair. After the completion of *My Learned Friend* in 1943, Hay underwent an operation for cancer and was not well enough to resume filming. Instead he returned to an old favourite, radio. There was also some theatre, but, because of his health, Hay was forced to opt out of top-billing in revue in favour of guest spots. By 1947 his health had improved sufficiently for him to talk to Marcel Varnel about making another film

together but early in the year Varnel was killed in a car crash and Hay's interest waned again. A few months later he had a stroke that left him physically crippled, and a further stroke killed him in the spring of 1949. Hay once said that he 'gloried in the idea of an inefficient man doggedly trying to do a job of which he is utterly incapable'. The portrait of that character was the cornerstone of his career.

*1933: * Know Your Apples. 1934: Those Were the Days. Radio Parade of 1935 (US: Radio Follies). 1935: Dandy Dick. Boys Will Be Boys. 1936: Where There's a Will. Windbag the Sailor. 1937: Good Morning, Boys! (US: Where There's a Will). Oh, Mr Porter! 1938: Convict 99. Hey! Hey! USA. Old Bones of the River. 1939: Ask a Policeman. Where's That Fire? 1941: The Ghost of St Michael's. † The Black Sheep of Whitehall. The Big Blockade. 1942: * Go to Blazes. † The Goose Steps Out. 1943: My Learned Friend.*

† And co-directed.

HEARNE, Richard 1908–1979

One of Britain's earliest and most-loved television comedians, Hearne became a star at 37 when he donned a droopy, fluffy white moustache and spectacles, sprinkled flour in his hair, and became an accident-prone character called Mr Pastry. His father was a

Will Hay finds himself holding the baby (pig) while on his way to his new job as stationmaster at Buggleskelly in *Oh, Mr Porter!*

clown, his mother an actress who carried her son on stage when he was a six-week-old baby. They joined a circus when Hearne was seven years old. 'That was my university', he once said. He studied ballet and acting and learned several dozen different ways of falling down. From the circus he graduated to variety and concert halls. Christmas usually brought appearances in pantomime and it was in one of these, *Dick Whittington*, that he made his London stage bow in 1932. He remained a popular part of London theatrical revue throughout the 1930s and the war years, often in befuddled roles or as downtrodden characters who merged with the wallpaper. There were a few minor film appearances and a starring film debut in 1943 in *The Butler's Dilemma*. Hearne appeared as a foolish gambler who has to agree to pose as a butler at a friend's gambling party to try and get himself out of trouble. But, despite an excellent cast — Judy Kelly, Henry Kendall, Ronald Shiner (*qv*), Francis L. Sullivan, Hermione Gingold (*qv*), Wally Patch, Ralph Truman, Wilfrid Hyde White and Marjorie Rhodes were also in it — the film had a poor script and was a dispiriting failure. Two years later Hearne's friend and mentor Fred Emney (*qv*) invented the character of Mr Pastry for the show *Big Boy*. It was a big hit and gave Hearne the positive image for which he had been searching. He played the role, with occasional variations, for the rest of his career. Postwar years saw him become a children's comedy favourite on TV in a series of simple slapstick situations in which he was the clumsy old codger who never got things done, creating havoc around him. This success led to a resumption of his film career, both in features, and in such shorts as *Mr Pastry Does the Laundry*. Again, response was not favourable. The 'slapstick grandfather', as one writer termed him, returned to the welcoming arms of TV. He

had his own series, and created such classic mime routines as 'The Lancers' and 'The Passing Out Ceremony'. In the mid 1950s, he also came as close to cracking the cinema nut as he would ever do. The secret was to use the ingredient which has proved the downfall of so many great comedians — pathos. But, as Pastry was a failed old man, the pathetic element was built in. *The Time of His Life*, which cast him as a long-term prisoner returning bewildered to society, and *Tons of Trouble*, where he was the eccentric oddjob man at a block of flats, were respectable blends of knockabout comedy and pathos based on character study. Hearne's hectic work schedule, however, permitted no more feature films. After spells in variety, pantomime and TV (and a long trip to Australia), his career ran full circle when he joined Chipperfields Circus in 1958, remaining, on and off, for 18 months. In 1960 Hearne started his own charity to raise funds to build swimming pools for handicapped children. With the help of his efforts, 116 pools were built. A heart attack in 1969 slowed down the rate of his appearances and shortly afterwards he retired to his home in the Kent countryside, bemoaning the rise of 'smut and permissiveness' in screen and stage comedy. The heart condition reappeared towards the end of the 1970s and another attack proved to be the end for the children's clown.

1934: Give Her a Ring. 1935: Dance Band. No Monkey Business. 1936: Millions. 1937: Splinters in the Air. 1943: Miss London Ltd. The Butler's Dilemma. 1948: One Night with You. Woman Hater. 1949: Helter Skelter. 1950: Something in the City. * Mr Pastry Does the Laundry. 1951: Captain Horatio Hornblower RN. Madame Louise. 1952: * What a Husband. Miss Robin Hood. 1955: The Time of His Life. 1956: Tons of Trouble. 1962: * The King's Breakfast.

HENSON, Leslie 1891–1957

Bullfrog-faced British concert-party and revue comedian with dark, receding hair and an appropriately croaky voice. Popular through many years on the London stage, he made a few frantically-paced farces for the cinema in the 1930s, romps which usually cast him as older than his real age and often saw him playing staid men having a fling. A broad comic with a florid complexion, basilisk eyes and an ingratiating personality, Henson made his stage bow in 1910 and was a great success a couple of years later in *Tonight's the Night*. His repertoire of funny faces was even wider than his wardrobe of funny hats, and he was frequently capable of rising above poor material with bursts of (sometimes ad-lib) individuality. By World War One Henson was well enough known to star in a few silent comedy shorts, but he remained primarily a man of the theatre in such shows as *Yes Uncle*, *Kissing Time*, *A Night Out* and *Nice Goings On*. His most successful sound films were made at the Gainsborough studios, then bossed by Michael Balcon. Several of these demonstrated his talents as a character comedian, the most successful being *It's a Boy!*, which fortuitously teamed him with Hollywood's Edward Everett Horton (*qv*) in the story of a crisis that nearly wrecks a wedding. As with other stage favourites, such as Jack Hulbert (*qv*), Lupino Lane (*qv*) and Jack Buchanan, Henson did not survive as a cinema star into the war years, and his larger-than-life personality was always more suited to the stage. He retained his popularity despite a largely poor choice of theatrical vehicles, and his fans cheered when he triumphed anew in 1951 in *And So to Bed*, a notable West End musical success in which he played the diarist Samuel Pepys. Henson followed up with another hit, the minor Victorian classic *The Diary of a Nobody*. Two heart attacks while on holiday in 1955 almost killed him, but he was determined to go on. He was rehearsing his role as Widow Twankey in a 1957 Christmas pantomime when another heart attack proved fatal. He was always amused to recount the fact that Henson's Throat had in the early 1940s become an accepted medical term for a certain kind of permanent

Convincing his wife that he's a city gent, Richard Hearne (left) leaves each day for his real job: pavement artist. Here he encounters fellow street trader Horace Kenney

Leslie Henson giving a typically rumbustious performance as a surgeon involved with a notorious nightclub singer (Frances Day) in *The Girl from Maxim's*

sore throat. 'My throat is all my own work', he once said. 'Just bad voice production, I'm afraid.'

1916: * Wanted a Widow. * The Real Thing at Last. The Lifeguardsman. 1920: * Broken Bottles. Alf's Button. 1924: Tons of Money. 1927: * On with the Dance (series). 1930: A Warm Corner. 1931: The Sport of Kings. 1933: It's a Boy! The Girl from Maxim's. 1935: Oh Daddy! 1943: The Demi-Paradise (US: Adventure for Two). 1956: Home and Away.

HERBERT, Hugh 1887–1952
Although subtlety was not the strongpoint of this stocky, ruddy-cheeked, dark-haired, flappable American comedian, he was a man of many talents who crammed an amazing amount of work into his 64 years. Comedian, comic actor, writer and director, he began as a stand-up comic in vaudeville, also making a reputation as a prolific supplier of jokes, sketches, playlets and plays. Almost 40 when he came to Hollywood, Herbert quickly created his best-known character, the excitable, fumbling, good-natured incompetent who was a pain in the side to all around him. His trademark was a noise that represented flustered embarrassment. It became known as 'Woo Woo!' and was normally accompanied by a raising of fluttering Herbert hands and a 'Bashful' style double-take. Mainly in prominent cameo roles in Hollywood, Herbert also starred in dozens of two-reel comedies and played occasional leading roles in minor comedies, notably a series for Universal from 1939 to 1942, the best of which is *La Conga Nights*. Not young enough to become a comic leading man in the Bob Hope (qv) style, Herbert never quite made the big time, although he was still making short comedies at the time of his death from a heart attack. He was Snout in the 1935 version of *A Midsummer Night's Dream*.

1927: * Realisation. * Solomon's Children. Husbands for Rent. 1928: * The Lemon. * On the Air. Lights of New York. * Mind Your Business. * The Prediction. * Miss Information. Caught in the Fog. 1929: * She Went for a Tramp. 1930: Danger Lights. Hook, Line and Sinker. Second Wife. The Sin Ship. 1931:
Traveling Husbands. Laugh and Get Rich. Cracked Nuts. Friends and Lovers. 1932: The Lost Squadron. * Shampoo the Magician. Faithless. Million Dollar Legs. 1933: Goldie Gets Along. * It's Spring. Diplomaniacs. Convention City. College Coach (GB: Football Coach). From Headquarters. Footlight Parade. Bureau of Missing Persons. Goodbye Again. Strictly Personal. She Had to Say Yes. 1934: Easy to Love. Dames. Fashions of 1934 (GB: Fashion Follies of 1934). Wonder Bar. Harold Teen (GB: The Dancing Fool). Kansas City Princess. The Merry Frinks (GB: The Happy Family). Sweet Adeline. The Merry Wives of Reno. Fog Over Frisco. 1935: Gold Diggers of 1935. * A Trip Thru a Hollywood Studio. The Traveling Saleslady. A Midsummer Night's Dream. We're in the Money. To Beat the Band. Miss Pacific Fleet. 1936: Colleen. Sing Me a Love Song. Love Begins at 20 (GB: All One Night). One Rainy Afternoon. We Went to College (GB: The Old School Tie). Mind Your Own Business. 1937: Sh! The Octopus. That Man's Here Again. Marry the Girl. The Perfect Specimen. Hollywood Hotel. Top of the Town. The Singing Marine. 1938: The Great Waltz. Men Are Such Fools. Four's a Crowd. Gold Diggers in Paris. 1939: The Little Accident. The Family Next Door. * Dad for a Day. Eternally Yours. The Lady's from Kentucky. 1940: La Conga Nights. Slightly Tempted. A Little Bit of Heaven. Hit Parade of 1941. The Villain Still Pursued Her. Private Affairs. 1941: The Black Cat. Hello Sucker. Hellzapoppin. Meet the Chump. Nobody's Fool. Badlands of Dakota. Mrs Wiggs of the Cabbage Patch. 1942: There's One Born Every Minute. You're Telling Me. Don't Get Personal. 1943: It's a Great Life. * Who's Hugh? * Pitchin' in the Kitchen. Stage Door Canteen. Beauty for Sale. 1944: Ever Since Venus. Music for Millions. * His Hotel Sweet. * Oh Baby! * Woo Woo. Kismet. 1945: One Way to Love. * Wife Decoy. * The Mayor's Husband. * When the Wife's Away. * Honeymoon Blues. 1946: * Get Along Little Zombie. 1947: * Tall, Dark and Gruesome. * Hot Heir. * Nervous Shakedown. * Should Husbands Marry? Carnegie Hall. Blondie in the Dough. 1948: A Miracle Can Happen (later On Our Merry Way). So This Is New York. One Touch of Venus. A Song Is Born. * A Punch in Time. The Girl from Manhattan. 1949: * Trapped by a Blonde. * Super Wolf. The Beautiful Blonde from Bashful Bend. 1950: * A Slip and a Miss. * A Knight and a Blonde. * One Shivery Night. 1951: * Woo Woo Blues. Havana Rose. * Trouble-in-Laws. * The Gink at the Sink.

HERMAN, Pee-wee
see REUBENS, Paul

HILL, Benny
(Alfred Hill) 1925–1992
A light-haired, blue-eyed, round-faced, tubby British comedian with mischievous grin who brings seaside-postcard humour to life. Benny Hill's film career, though, has

been surprisingly spotty considering his consistent popularity on television through four decades. But the nature of his material is sketchy, in all senses of the word, and so it was perhaps not surprising that one of his most popular film outings was a compilation of his TV material: a very rare occurrence even in British film comedy. The son and grandson of men who had both spent time as circus clowns, Hill was, at 13, an amateur entertainer in his native Southampton with a group called Bobby's Concert Party. But with the outbreak of World War Two the troupe disbanded, and Benny had to forage for audiences on his own. As a teenager he entertained in pubs, halls and − during the early years of the war − even in air-raid shelters, while pursuing post-school occupations of shop assistant in Woolworths, then milkman, complete with horse and cart. The latter occupation would, many years later, give him material for one of the most successful of his famous saucy songs. At this time, he was playing guitar and drums and singing, rather than cracking jokes. He even became a singer with a dance band. Trying for a career as a comic actor, he got a job at a theatre in the East End of London as an assistant stage manager, playing small roles in productions as well. During his war service he built up on-stage experience with the show *Stars in Battledress*, and switched to the music-hall stage in post-war years. His face became familiar as straight man to another comedian, Reg Varney (*qv*), but he was soon making strides as a stand-up comedian under his own steam, billed as 'Britain's brightest boy'. His breathless delivery and impish demeanour, together with a self-written fund of material, made him a headliner inside a couple of years. He was a popular radio guest from the early 1950s, and had his own TV show from 1953. It was destined to run, in one form or another, for 36 years. The cinema sat up and took notice, and Ealing Studios brought the prodigy to the screen in 1955 in *Who Done It?* Benny played an ice-rink sweeper who sets himself up as a detective after winning £100 and a bloodhound. Although rough-edged, the caper that resulted was wildly funny in parts and performed well at the British box-office.

However, Ealing was a fading force in the British cinema and Rank, who distributed their films, had its own star comedian in Norman Wisdom (*qv*). So it was that Hill returned to television, never again to make a film as solo star. The format of his TV show settled into something similar to that which would bring success to another British comedian, Dick Emery (*qv*), more than a decade later. The star appeared in a number of farcical disguises, proved slightly bland as a master of ceremonies, was surrounded with pretty girls (who chased whichever character he happened to be playing off the screen at the end) and amused with leery madrigals, often sung while dressed as a straw-sucking hayseed. One of these songs, *Ernie (the fastest milkman in the west)*, soared to number one in the British pop charts. There was the odd film appearance, in increasingly eccentric cameo roles as the years wore on, but for the most part it was simply *The Benny Hill Show*, its latter-day appearances becoming sporadic as good material became scarce. The show achieved an amazing worldwide popularity, which continued even after its mentors, Thames Television, dropped it from British schedules after 1989. Greta Garbo was supposedly one of its greatest fans and Hill has often defended its simple vulgarity in print. Asked how he saw himself on TV, he told one interviewer: 'I see several chins and a large tummy. That's why I rummage through supermarket shelves. It's not to see how much things cost, but to see how many calories they contain!' He was forced to ease up further on the calories after a heart attack in 1992, but died from a further attack on the same day as his friend and fellow comic Frankie Howerd (*qv*).

*1955: Who Done It? 1960: Light Up the Sky. 1965: Those Magnificent Men in Their Flying Machines. 1968: Chitty Chitty Bang Bang. 1969: The Italian Job. * The Waiters. 1974: The Best of Benny Hill (TV material reshown in cinemas). 1984: Benny and Friends (video). 1986: Le miracule.*

HOGAN, Paul 1940−
'I'm not a movie star − I just made a movie', said Australia's Paul Hogan, after the world-

wide success of *Crocodile Dundee*. And how right he was. Five years later, and at time of writing not another movie in sight to follow the first three, Hogan the movie star can clearly be said to have had his day. But what a day it was. Hogan the TV comedy sketch star is not particularly funny, compared with similar comedians around the world. But douse him in the magic dust of reality and Hogan is a bit of everything − funny, likeable, admirable and convincing in action, with a tongue and a timing that could, in its riposte, cut down a eucalyptus tree at 50 paces. This is the Hogan of *Crocodile Dundee*. The Hogan who, in one fell screenplay, got it all right at the same time. He was born the son of a professional soldier, and had no connection with show business until his early thirties, working in a succession of outdoor jobs that built up the permanent tan and weatherbeaten look, doubtless later sustainable by wealth. In 1972 he won a talent contest and quickly made headway in the business, getting a regular spot on TV and, soon, his own show. Fair-haired and blue-eyed, with an attractive smile, Hogan is, like America's Steve Martin (*qv*), handsome as comedians go, and films looked a natural further step. But the scripts offered were disappointing and in the end he decided to write his own. By the time it was ready, international audiences had seen him on TV's *The Paul Hogan Show*, on numerous lager adverts and in a TV mini-series called *Anzacs*, which was made in 1985. *Crocodile Dundee* was released the following year and became an enormous worldwide success. Hogan plays Mick Dundee, hero of Australian folklore and teller of tall tales. Some heroes are streetwise, but Dundee is outbackwise, and it's this talent that enables him to turn the tables both verbally and physically on his adversaries during the film. He's down to earth, kind and funny, a character you can regard with affection and sympathy. The feelgood fun that resulted from Dundee's adventures in Australia and, subsequently, New York, where he has little difficulty confounding muggers with a knife that's three times bigger than theirs, cost the equivalent of $6 million to make and took 20 times that at the box-offices of the world. Hogan was the third most popular star in the world at the end of 1986. But then Rodney Dangerfield (*qv*) was fourth. Such are the fleeting qualities of stardom. A sequel was inevitable, but *'Crocodile' Dundee II* (the American distributor had added the quotes the first time round) was less well received by critics and, to an extent, by audiences, although it made a healthy profit. This time Dundee and his American girl-friend (Linda Koslowski, whom Hogan made his second wife in real life) are involved with drug-runners. It's all entertaining enough, although a lot of the warmth has gone from the characters, and the script is already undermining Dundee's appeal in small ways. Hogan decided to put the Croc out to grass, and opted instead for *Almost an*

Just hanging around... *'Crocodile' Dundee* (Paul Hogan) tries to get his bearings in the midst of the busy traffic of an American city

This is a very young Stanley Holloway (though you couldn't really tell; he always looked the same age) with Else MacFarlane in the film version of *The Co-Optimists*

Angel, a bold comedy-fantasy that almost no-one went to see. At 52, with more money than he knows what to do with, and an eloquent ambassador for Australia in TV commercials, Hogan probably has no need to subject himself again to the backbreaking work of international comedy films. But, who knows? There may be life left in the old Croc yet.

1980: Fatty Finn. 1986: Crocodile Dundee (GB and US: 'Crocodile' Dundee). 1988: 'Crocodile' Dundee II. 1990: Almost an Angel.

HOLLIDAY, Judy
(Judith Tuvim) 1922–1965

The extraordinary thing about Judy Holliday is that while she made her name playing the dumbest of dumb blondes she was in real life the most intelligent and intellectual of women, well-educated and highbrow in tastes. That you would never have guessed it is a tribute to her comic acting abilities. Not even a blonde to begin with, New York-born Judy was too tall (and rather too plump) for the ballet career her mother had envisaged. Rejected by Yale Drama School despite a remarkably high IQ and undoubted talent, she left high school at 16 and took a menial job backstage with Orson Welles' famous Mercury Theatre. Soon, however, she and four friends (who included Betty Comden and Adolph Green, later to write many stage and film musicals) had formed a satirical musical-comedy group called the Revuers, which became the rage of Manhattan and stayed together for six years. It was in 1943 that a run at Hollywood's Trocadero Club brought the Revuers to the attention of film studio scouts. 'Everybody wanted Judy', Adolph Green once recalled. 'But she insisted they took us as a job lot.' The studio that took the 'job lot' was 20th Century-Fox, purveyor at that time of gaudy musicals to the wartime masses. The Revuers made their debut in one such offering, a Don Ameche–Carmen Miranda musical, *Greenwich Village*. When the film was released in 1944 the Revuers found that most of their footage had been left behind on the cutting-room floor. Judy was kept on as a solo for a couple of small assignments

but then went back to Broadway where she had a minor success in *Kiss Them for Me* and a major one in *Born Yesterday* (taking over at short notice from an ailing Jean Arthur), which provided her with the best-remembered role of her too-brief career. The play ran for nearly four years but Holliday was at first turned down for the film version, supposedly because of her weight problems. It was ironically her next film role, as a birdbrain court defendant in *Adam's Rib* (in which a character called her 'Fatso') that she convinced Columbia she was right for the part she had created in *Born Yesterday*. Shedding more than a stone to play her character, Billie Dawn, on screen, Judy was funny, touching, vulnerable, marvellously strident and wonderfully likeable as the ex-chorus girl mistress of Broderick Crawford's bullying, crass tycoon. She beat out some very hot competition (including Bette Davis and Anne Baxter in *All About Eve* and Gloria Swanson in *Sunset Boulevard*) to take the year's best actress Oscar. After a brush with the Senate Un-American Activities Committee – she got away with past Communist affiliations partly by charming the Committee with a reprise of her personality from *Born Yesterday* – Judy returned to films in *The Marrying Kind*, a comedy about a young couple about to divorce. That got only a limited release but her piece of political tightrope walking was forgotten when her next three screen comedies were all solid hits. *It Should Happen to You* was about a nobody who hires an enormous advertisement hoarding and puts her name on it. *Phffft!* ('the sound of a marriage breaking apart') was another romp about divorce. *The Solid Gold Cadillac* had her as a small-time stockholder who exposes the crooked dealings of the corporation in which she has shares. In the first two of these she co-starred with a just-starting Jack Lemmon (*qv*); the third paired her with her Broadway *Born Yesterday* co-star, Paul Douglas. In all three she gave bright, intelligent comedy performances that had the audience solidly on her side. Holliday should really have gone on to super-stardom after this, but the next comedy, *Full of Life*, about the misadventures of a very pregnant housewife, was deservedly unpopular, and probably helped her decide to return to Broadway where she starred in the musical *Bells Are Ringing* as the over-bright telephone girl who becomes involved in the problems of the clients of her answering service. She did make the film version of this but it was much less effective (and less musical) than the stage show. Holliday stayed on stage but success deserted her. So did her health. Breast cancer was diagnosed in 1960 and, despite a mastectomy, the cancer reoccurred. She worked little in her last two years and died a few days before her 43rd birthday. At her best, Judy Holliday played a comedy role as perfectly as it could be played. The legacy of her films is small but, as Billie Dawn might have put it, cherce.

*1938: † Too Much Johnson. 1944: Winged Victory. Greenwich Village. Something for the Boys. 1949: Adam's Rib. 1950: Born Yesterday. 1952: The Marrying Kind. 1953: It Should Happen to You. 1954: Phffft! * Extra Dollars. 1956: The Solid Gold Cadillac. Full of Life. 1960: Bells Are Ringing.*

† *Unreleased.*

HOLLOWAY, Stanley 1890–1982

A first-rate comedian, booming *basso* singer and poker-faced comic monologuist who turned out to be no mean actor, East London-born Stanley Holloway was a popular member of any entertainment for more than 50 years. From a cherubic-looking boy soprano who also entertained at parties with comic recitations, Holloway grew into a large man with a big, round, friendly face, cheerful grin and dark, slicked-back hair. He communicated easily with audiences and, as early as 1907, he could be found as a member of a pier-end concert-party troupe in one of England's east coast resorts. He remained with them for several years until snapped up by fellow-comedian Leslie Henson (*qv*) to feature in his rather more prestigious concert-party. Still holding thoughts of an operatic career, Holloway took time off to study classical singing in Italy. But the war intervened and he enlisted in the Connaught Rangers. Immediately after World War One, he made his debut in West End musical comedy. Stardom came as a prominent member of the long-running show *The Co-Optimists*, in which all the cast dressed as pierrots. The show began in 1921, ran until 1927, and was filmed (after a fashion) two years later. A second series of *The Co-Optimists* began in 1929, and with it Holloway's series of monologues and comic songs that became hits worldwide, selling thousands of records. Down the years, these included 'My Word You Do Look Queer', 'Albert and the Lion' (and several follow-ups), 'Brahn Boots', 'Pick Oop Tha' Musket Sam' (and several more about Sam Small), 'The Battle of Hastings', 'Runcorn Ferry', 'With 'er 'ead Tucked underneath 'er Arm (She Walks the Bloody Tower)' and 'The Dark Girl Dressed in Blue'. Holloway's collaborator on many of these was Marriott

Stanley Holloway looks to have the weight advantage in this altercation with Robertson Hare from *One Wild Oat*

Edgar (brother of novelist Edgar Wallace), who worked on many of Britain's biggest comedy film hits of the 1930s. Holloway himself made sporadic film appearances during the 1930s, in between playing in stage revues and pantomimes, but the most popular phase of his movie career (appropriately for a man who would make such a hit in *My Fair Lady*) came when he was cast in the 1941 film of George Bernard Shaw's *Major Barbara*. He was a comforting presence (and the narrator) in a tribute to the British spirit in the war, *Salute John Citizen*. But it was two years later, in 1944, that he became established as a favourite character star with the British masses, tackling the Germans in *The Way Ahead*, as the friendly neighbour in *This Happy Breed* and as the conceited Great Vance in the Victorian musical *Champagne Charlie*. His next two films were also blockbuster hits: *The Way to the Stars* and *Brief Encounter*. He was co-starred with another famous monologuist, Cyril Fletcher, in *Nicholas Nickleby*, and played the gravedigger in Laurence Olivier's *Hamlet*, before beginning a profitable association with Ealing Studios that saw him as an integral part of such comedy classics as *Passport to Pimlico*, *The Lavender Hill Mob* and *The Titfield Thunderbolt*. Ealing gave him his own vehicle in 1953, the star-studded *Meet Mr Lucifer*, with Holloway doubling as the devil and a pantomime demon king. But it was less successful and he returned to top character roles. His career as a comedian-singer-personality was crowned in 1956 when he was chased by authors Lerner and Loewe to play dustman Alfred P. Doolittle in *My Fair Lady*, the musical version of Shaw's *Pygmalion*. His authentic East

London tones and fine baritone were heard in the role for more than four years in London and on Broadway, becoming indelibly identified with such songs as *Wiv a Little Bit o' Luck* (later the title of his autobiography) and *Get Me to the Church on Time*. The re-creation of the role in the 1964 film brought Holloway his first (and only) Oscar nomination at the age of 74. Like Rex Harrison, his friend and co-star in *Major Barbara* and *My Fair Lady*, Holloway suffered from eye trouble in his last years, glaucoma meaning that he had to give up reading, and could only do his beloved crosswords with his wife reading the clues. But he remained as cheery as ever, staying an active entertainer well into his eighties. He had three daughters and a son by his first marriage, and a son, Julian, by his second. Julian co-starred with him in a successful US TV comedy show of the 1950s, *Our Man Higgins*, featuring the senior Holloway as a gentleman English butler serving an upstart American family. Even so, to the end his first love remained the theatre. 'It's the immediate impact on the audience that's so rewarding. You deliver a line, pause, wham! back comes the hoped-for laugh, or chuckle, or applause. Magic!'

1921: The Rotters. 1929: The Co-Optimists. 1933: Sleeping Car. Lily of Killarney (US: Bride of the Lake). The Girl from Maxim's. 1934: Road House. Love at Second Sight (US: The Girl Thief). Sing As We Go. D'Ye Ken John Peel (US: Captain Moonlight). In Town Tonight. 1935: * Sam and His Musket (voice only). Squibs. Play Up the Band. 1936: * Alf! Who Goes There? (voice only). * Sam's Medal (voice only). 1937: Song of the Forge. Our Island Nation. The Vicar of Bray. Sam Small Leaves Town. Cotton Queen. 1939: * Co-Operette. 1940: * Highlights of Variety No. 21. 1941: Major Barbara. 1942: Salute John Citizen. Sabotage at Sea. 1944: This Happy Breed. The Way Ahead. Champagne Charlie. 1945: The Way to the Stars (US: Johnny in the Clouds). Brief Encounter. Caesar and Cleopatra. 1946: Wanted for Murder. Carnival. 1947: Meet Me at Dawn. Nicholas Nickleby. 1948: One Night with You. Hamlet. Snowbound. Noose (US: The Silk Noose). Another Shore. The Winslow Boy. 1949: Passport to Pimlico. The Perfect Woman. 1950: Midnight Episode. 1951: Painter and Poet. One Wild Oat. The Lavender Hill Mob. * Sailor's Consolation (voice only). The Magic Box. Lady Godiva Rides Again. 1952: The Happy Family (US: Mr Lord Says No). Meet Me Tonight. 1953: The Beggar's Opera. The Titfield Thunderbolt. A Day to Remember. Meet Mr Lucifer. 1954: Fast and Loose. 1955: An Alligator Named Daisy. 1956: Jumping for Joy. 1958: Hello London. Alive and Kicking. 1959: No Trees in the Street (US: No Tree in the Street). 1960: No Love for Johnnie. 1961: On the Fiddle (US: Operation Snafu). 1964: My Fair Lady. 1965: In Harm's Way. Ten Little Indians. 1966: The Sandwich Man. 1968: Mrs Brown, You've Got a Lovely Daughter. 1969: Run a Crooked Mile (TV). How to Make It (GB: Target Harry). 1970: The Private Life of Sherlock Holmes. 1971: Flight of the Doves. 1972: Up the Front. 1976: Journey into Fear.

HOPE, Bob

(Leslie Hope) 1903 –

Dark-haired, British-born star comedian with slightly apprehensive good looks and an embryonic Cyrano de Bergerac nose. One of the great wisecrack artists of the screen, Hope was among the top ten money-making stars in America (and surely the world) from 1941 to 1953, the last 13 of his best 15 years at the top — an unparalleled box-office run. In recent days it has become fashionable to deride Hope as a man at the mercy of his material. Yet, over the years, he has been admired by comedians as diverse as Charlie Chaplin, W. C. Fields and Woody Allen (all qv). As long as this particular

Bob Hope has the feeling that he's been framed, after this minor falling-out with Madeleine Carroll in *My Favorite Blonde*

comic cobbler stuck to his last – the image of the cowardly braggart forever nervously joking in the face of danger, and winning the girl in the end even if he was sometimes willing to let her do the fighting for him – Hope had no match within his own range. His timing was his own – and immaculate, his jokes often carried topical references within the plot, or even, as confidence grew, stepped outside the plot to make comic comments about Paramount, or Bing Crosby, or Dorothy Lamour, or American politics, or show business – all of which he knew world audiences would appreciate. Only when he allowed his brilliant team of gag writers to begin recycling their old material, in the early 1950s, did the standard of Hope's comedies begin to drop towards the mediocre. Even so, he allowed himself to diversify too soon into a more sophisticated kind of comedy. Occasional throwbacks to the old style of Hope comedy revealed that it was still the best. But the golden era of the 1940s could never be consistently recaptured and Hope's final films are a sadly unnecessary coda to a triumphant career. Hope was born in Eltham, a London suburb, but was destined to live there only four years. The family soon moved to Bristol and two years later emigrated to America, settling in Cleveland, Ohio. At ten, Hope won a Chaplin imitation contest at a local park, and broke into show business at 17 as half of a comedy dance act with Lloyd Durbin (later to die from food poisoning). Fatty Arbuckle (*qv*) saw the teenagers and helped them get their first big break with *Hurley's Jolly Follies*, a vaudeville touring company. After reaching Broadway with another partner, George Byrne, Hope

went solo in 1928, billed as Lester T. Hope. The following year he changed his name to Bob and in 1930 failed his first movie test ('My nose came into the frame ten seconds before I did. I tried to climb over the studio wall so's I wouldn't have to go out the front gate'). On Broadway, however, he was more successful, appearing in vaudeville-style revues (in one of which, in 1932, he first teamed with Bing Crosby). He had his first major hit in 1933/4, with the lead in Jerome Kern's *Roberta*. Hope didn't get to appear in the 1935 film version but he was paged by Warner Brothers to do a number of slapped-together two-reel comedies, which he later said were so bad they should have been shown to public enemies to make them give themselves up. Paramount rescued his film career by signing him up in 1938. But, not having complete confidence in his ability, they put him into co-features, mainly with explosive Martha Raye (*qv*) and soulful Shirley Ross, who sang a duet with Hope that became his theme song: *Thanks for the Memory*. Although Hope is clearly struggling to find an established character in these films, they do have funny moments, notably *Never Say Die*, which casts him as John Kidley 'the big bean man', and for which Norman Panama and Melvin Frank wrote a variation on their famous duel scene ('There's a cross on the muzzle of the pistol with the bullet') that they would later rework to even better effect in *The Paleface* and (with Danny Kaye, *qv*) *The Court Jester*. The film that put Hope into the big league was still little more than a 'B' (it only ran 72 minutes), a remake of an old spooky-house mystery called *The Cat and the Canary*. For the first time, Hope was allowed to be

frightened of danger. As the lily-livered hero, he was thus able to set his style for the next 15 years: exaggerated, throwaway acting, with lines delivered as much to the audience as to his fellow-players, and never quite *within* the film, so that, whatever character he played, he was always Bob Hope – and you knew how he would react to any given situation. Paramount lost no time in putting him and leading lady Paulette Goddard into something similar: *The Ghost Breakers*. Hope shivered while audiences shook with laughter. Subsequent films from the studio contained more in-jokes and topical references, and ensured they put the new star into situations that quickly exposed the yellow streak running down the middle of his back. Some of these were the phenomenally successful 'Road' comedies that he made with Crosby and Dorothy Lamour (a radio singer who had become the queen of South Seas adventure-romances), another old acquaintance. These began by accident but soon developed into riotous ragbags of comedy in *Hellzapoppin* style after audiences started to flock to see them. Hope was always the wiseacre who came unstuck, was always surprised to lose Lamour to Crosby and, by thinking himself clever enough to rumble Crosby's schemes, always fell for them. The series abounded with impossible jokes (a snowy hill in *Road to Utopia* turns into the Paramount mountain) and, in keeping with Hope's style, 'outside the plot' references. In *Road to Morocco*, he complains to Crosby about his two-timing throughout the story. Crosby doesn't wish to know, but Hope points out that people who came into the cinema recently might have missed that part of the plot. For the next few years Hope hardly put a foot wrong, whether in thriller comedies (*They Got Me Covered*, *My Favorite Blonde*, *My Favorite Brunette*), comic westerns (*The Paleface*, *Son of Paleface*) or costume charades (*The Princess and the Pirate*, *Monsieur Beaucaire*). In *Pirate* he lost the girl to Crosby in the end even though Crosby wasn't in the story. 'How d'you like that?' Hope protests. 'I knock myself out for nine reels and some bit player from Paramount comes over and gets the girl. That's the last film I do for Goldwyn.' (It was.) It was when Hope seemed in personal control of the dialogue in this way that he held his greatest appeal. It was less evident in *Where There's Life*, his first critical flop (not that it lost money, merely made less than others) and in two uncomfortable ventures into Damon Runyon land, *Sorrowful Jones* and *The Lemon Drop Kid*. Basically, audiences didn't want to see Hope as an established character of fiction, they wanted to see him as Hope. Even so, he got away with *Fancy Pants* (a remake of *Ruggles of Red Gap*), which was much to his credit, though the edges of his comedy techniques were sometimes fuzzed by having to play it. In any case, in post-war years, there were also films in the more familiar Hope style: *Road to Rio*, *The Great Lover*, *My Favorite Spy*, *Road to Bali*. Many

Posing as 'Fearless Frazier The Human Rat', Bob Hope has his doubts about the stunt proposed by Bing Crosby at the beginning of *Road to Zanzibar*

Son of Paleface. Road to Bali. Off Limits (GB: Military Policemen). * A Sporting Oasis. 1953: Scared Stiff. Here Come the Girls. * Faith, Hope and Hogan. Casanova's Big Night. 1954: * Screen Snapshots No. 224. 1955: The Seven Little Foys. 1956: That Certain Feeling. The Iron Petticoat. 1957: Beau James. * The Heart of Show Business. 1958: Paris Holiday. * Showdown at Ulcer Gulch. 1959: The Five Pennies. Alias Jesse James. 1960: The Facts of Life. 1961: Bachelor in Paradise. * Kitty Caddy (voice only). The Road to Hong Kong. 1963: Critic's Choice. A Global Affair. Call Me Bwana. 1965: I'll Take Sweden. 1966: The Oscar. Boy, Did I Get a Wrong Number. * Hollywood Star-Spangled Revue. Not with My Wife, You Don't. 1967: Eight on the Lam (GB: Eight on the Run). The Movie Maker (TV). 1968: * Where There's Hope. The Private Navy of Sergeant O'Farrell. 1969: How to Commit Marriage. 1972: Cancel My Reservation. 1978: The Muppet Movie. 1979: Ken Murray's Shooting Stars. 1985: Spies Like Us. 1986: A Masterpiece of Murder (TV).

Hope films of the period boast guest appearances by other stars from the studio: Crosby in almost anything (including an executioner who takes much relish at the prospect of 'frying' Hope in the chair), Jane Russell (in *Road to Bali*) and Alan Ladd (a superb deadpan detective in *My Favorite Brunette*) among them. Hope has often cited the films of 1952/3 as the ones which resolved him to make the switch from outright comedy, though in fact they revive well — especially *Casanova's Big Night*, in which Hope rebels against going to the executioner's block and demands that the studio gives audiences a choice of a new, ultra-heroic ending (he snarls when they choose the old one). At any rate, he diversified. *The Seven Little Foys*, *That Certain Feeling* and *Beau James*, three of the early 'character' films, are pleasant enough, but Hope's heartiness rang less true without an army of gag-writers at his back. Paired with other star personalities, (Mickey Rooney (qv) in *Off Limits*, Katharine Hepburn in *The Iron Petticoat*, Fernandel (qv) in *Paris Holiday*), he seems unrelaxed and ill-at-ease. *Alias Jesse James*, a comic western with a marvellous climax (in which most of Hollywood's current cowboy stars come to Hope's rescue), was a welcome return to form, and *The Facts of Life* gave him a rare success outside farce. He gave *it* the best of his 'straight' performances and was in any case well partnered by his old colleague Lucille Ball (qv). Both Hope and Crosby would have done well to give up on films after the mediocre (if good-natured) *The Road to Hong Kong*, the last in that series. But Hope went on, forever in search of suitable material — though in truth only his youth and old character would have saved his films from becoming what one critic rather unkindly called 'the annual ordeal'. At his peak, though, few comedians

could handle a funny line with more aplomb. Hope was also a tireless entertainer of US troops all over the world and an indefatigable worker for charities, receiving special Oscars in 1940, 1944, 1952 and 1965. He joked that the ones they gave him said 'Made in Japan'. As for the post-1953 films, Hope should perhaps have heeded the dialogue handed to him two years earlier in *My Favorite Spy*, when his character is asked to take undue risks. 'That ain't my line of work', snaps Hope. 'I tell jokes. That's dangerous enough.'

1934: * Going Spanish. * Paree, Paree. * Soup for Nuts. 1935: * Watch the Birdie. * The Old Grey Mayor. 1936: * Double Exposure. * Calling All Tars. * Shop Talk. 1938: The Big Broadcast of 1938. College Swing (GB: Swing, Teacher, Swing). Give Me a Sailor. Thanks for the Memory. * Don't Hook Now. 1939: Never Say Die. Some Like It Hot. The Cat and the Canary. 1940: Road to Singapore. The Ghost Breakers. 1941: Caught in the Draft. * Cavalcade of the Academy Awards. Road to Zanzibar. Louisiana Purchase. Nothing But the Truth. 1942: My Favorite Blonde. Road to Morocco. Star Spangled Rhythm. They Got Me Covered. 1943: Let's Face It. Welcome to Britain. 1944: The Princess and the Pirate. * Memo for Joe. 1945: * All-Star Bond Rally. Road to Utopia. Duffy's Tavern. * Hollywood Victory Caravan. 1946: Monsieur Beaucaire. 1947: My Favorite Brunette. Variety Girl. Where There's Life. Road to Rio. 1948: * Radio Broadcasting Today. The Paleface. * Screen Snapshots No. 166. * Rough But Hopeful. 1949: * Honor Caddie. You Can Change the World. Sorrowful Jones. The Great Lover. 1950: Fancy Pants. * On Stage Everybody! 1951: My Favorite Spy. The Lemon Drop Kid. 1952: The Greatest Show on Earth.

HORTON, Edward Everett 1886–1970
This tall, stooping, dark-haired, thin-mouthed American comedy character star was a dapper flapper. Crisis would loom, and, with an 'Oh, dear!' or 'Oh, my!', Horton's characters, losing control of their arm movements in the process, would unfailingly fail to surmount it. Horton's confidential, rather furtive leer could be supplanted by a worried look like the dropping of a mask, invariably followed by dithering panic. Although his characters could rarely be relied upon to carry you through a storm, there was usually a happy ending in store for them. One of the screen masters of the 'double-take', Horton was born in New York, the son of a printer. He began playing the acting fool while still at Columbia University, ostensibly studying history and German. By 1906 he was singing and dancing in the chorus of Broadway musicals. For the next 15 years he built up experience in stock companies in several states. It was joining the Los Angeles Stock Company in 1919 that led to his making appearances in

Tepee or not tepee...Painless Peter Potter (Bob Hope) adopts an Indian disguise to try and evade capture by the dreaded Redskins in *The Paleface*

Edward Everett Horton (centre) goes into his worried penguin act. Mischa Auer and Mary Boland stand by for a crisis. From *Little Tough Guys in Society*

Tony (Bobby Howes) finds himself falling for his partner's secretary Jill (Jean Gillie), even after she has wrecked an important party, in *Sweet Devil*

silent films. His first role of note was in the initial screen version of *Ruggles of Red Gap*, as the English butler whisked out to the wild west by an American family of social climbers. That was in 1923 and was one of the every-now-and-again leading roles that he mixed in with top supporting cameos and starring parts in two-reel comedies. Two years later he again took centre spotlight as the daydreaming composer in *Beggar on Horseback*, a sort of second cousin to *The Secret Life of Walter Mitty*. Several things were to combine to make Horton one of America's busiest and most popular comedy figures in the 1930s. From 1931 he began appearing in the stage comedy *Springtime for Henry*, about the misfortunes of an ageing philanderer. Horton would ply the role from coast to coast, although it didn't come to Broadway until 20 years later — a record 'try-out'! From 1933 he travelled frequently to Britain, where he could find star roles in comedy films. Most notable of these was *The Man in the Mirror*, an ingenious fantasy about a dithering businessman whose image steps out of a mirror and does all the things for which he has never had the stomach. Horton's wholly credible performance as two contrasting individuals reflected his earlier work in the American *Lonely Wives*, about which one reviewer remarked that it seemed 'marvellous that the two persons on the screen could possibly be one and the same man'. Horton's highest profile at the time, however, was provided by his roles in the Fred Astaire–Ginger Rogers musicals. Horton was always Astaire's friend, or lawyer, or manager — a position, at any rate, that allowed him to share in the action throughout, and to do his familiar impersonation of a panicking penguin. It was also in the 1930s that he played the Mad Hatter in the 1933 *Alice in Wonderland* and took the same role in both versions of the sophisticated comedy *Holiday*. The 1940s continued his assignments as comedy relief in musicals, mainly in gaudy 20th Century-Fox offerings, opposite such stars as Betty Grable, John Payne, Alice Faye and Carmen Miranda. He rarely got a chance to demonstrate his stage training in the song-and-dance department, although there was a delightful duet with Grable in the Astaire–Rogers film *The Gay Divorcee* called *Let's K-Nock Knees*. When Grable became a bona-fide star, Horton also got the chance to prance a few steps in the finale of her 1942 musical *Springtime in the Rockies*, which gave film-goers the treat of Horton and Charlotte Greenwood (*qv*) on the same stage. The war years also brought one of his best-remembered characters: the fussbudget messenger 7013 who rushes Robert Montgomery off to Heaven too soon in *Here Comes Mr Jordan*. After 1948 Horton concentrated on the stage and TV. One of his most memorable appearances in the latter medium was as the wizened Indian chief Roaring Chicken in the comedy western series *F Troop*, which ran from 1965 to

1967. Horton worked on to the end (he died from cancer at 84). 'Retirement?' he once asked with mock astonishment. 'What's that? When nobody asks me any more, *then* I'll retire.'

*1920: Leave It to Me. 1922: The Ladder Jinx. Too Much Business. A Front Page Story. 1923: Ruggles of Red Gap. To the Ladies. Try and Get It. 1924: Flapper Wives. The Man Who Fights Alone. Helen's Babies. 1925: Marry Me. The Business of Love. Beggar on Horseback. The Nut-Cracker (GB: You Can't Fool Your Wife). 1926: The Whole Town's Talking. Poker Faces. La Bohème. 1927: Taxi! Taxi! * No Publicity. * Find the King. * Dad's Choice. 1928: * Miss Information. * Behind the Counter. Horse Shy. * Vacation Wives. * Call Again. * Scrambled Weddings. The Terror. 1929: Sonny Boy. The Hottentot. The Sap. The Aviator. * Trusting Wives. * Ask Dad. * Prince Gabby. * The Eligible Mr Bangs. * Good Medicine. 1930: * The Right Bed. Take the Heir. Wide Open. Holiday. Once a Gentleman. 1931: * The Great Junction Hotel. Reaching for the Moon. Lonely Wives. The Age for Love. Kiss Me Again (GB: Toast of the Legion). Six Cylinder Love. Smart Woman. The Front Page. 1932: Trouble in Paradise. But the Flesh is Weak. Roar of the Dragon. 1933: Soldiers of the King (US: The Woman in Command). It's a Boy! A Bedtime Story. The Way to Love. Design for Living. Alice in Wonderland. 1934: The Gay Divorcee (GB: The Gay Divorce). The Poor Rich. Ladies Should Listen. The Merry Widow. Kiss and Make Up. Easy to Love. Success at Any Price. Uncertain Lady. Sing and Like It. Smarty (GB: Hit Me Again). 1935: The Night is Young. In Caliente. Biography of a Bachelor*

Girl. Top Hat. $10 Raise (GB: Mr Faintheart). The Devil is a Woman. Going Highbrow. Little Big Shot. The Private Secretary. His Night Out. All the King's Horses. Your Uncle Dudley. 1936: The Man in the Mirror. The Singing Kid. Her Master's Voice. Hearts Divided. Nobody's Fool. 1937: Let's Make a Million. The King and the Chorus Girl (GB: Romance is Sacred). Lost Horizon. Shall We Dance? The Great Garrick. Hitting a New High. Wild Money. Oh, Doctor! Angel. The Perfect Specimen. Danger — Love at Work. 1938: Holiday/Unconventional Linda (GB: Free to Live). College Swing (GB: Swing, Teacher, Swing). Bluebeard's Eighth Wife. Little Tough Guys in Society. 1939: The Gang's All Here (US: The Amazing Mr Forrest). That's Right — You're Wrong. Paris Honeymoon. 1941: Ziegfeld Girl. You're the One. Bachelor Daddy/ Sandy Steps Out. Here Comes Mr Jordan. Sunny. Week-End for Three. The Body Disappears. 1942: I Married an Angel. The Magnificent Dope. Springtime in the Rockies. 1943: Forever and a Day. Thank Your Lucky Stars. The Gang's All Here (GB: The Girls He Left Behind). Arsenic and Old Lace. 1944: Her Primitive Man. Summer Storm. San Diego, I Love You. The Town Went Wild. Brazil. 1945: Steppin' in Society. Lady on a Train. 1946: Cinderella Jones. Faithful in My Fashion. Earl Carroll Sketchbook (GB: Hats Off to Rhythm). 1947: The Ghost Goes Wild. Down to Earth. Her Husband's Affairs. 1948: All My Sons. 1957: The Story of Mankind. Three Men on a Horse (TV). 1961: Pocketful of Miracles. 1963: It's a Mad, Mad, Mad, Mad World. 1964: Sex and the Single Girl. 1967: The Perils of Pauline. 1969: 2000 Years Later. 1970: Cold Turkey.

Wedding day blues for Edward Everett Horton (centre) when Albert Burdon turns up claiming to be his son in *It's a Boy!* Best man Leslie Henson (*qv*) looks sceptical

HOUSMAN, Arthur 1888–1942

One of the screen's great inebriates, Arthur Housman was the drunk's drunk. Seldom seen sober in well over a hundred films, this brown-haired, neatly moustachioed, bleary-eyed, arch-eyebrowed American actor with the common touch literally staggered to immortality. Invariably in light trilby with dark band, Housman was always the friendliest of drunks. There didn't seem to be a disagreeable bone in his body. And through it all he displayed perfect comic timing — especially in his encounters with Laurel and Hardy (qv). Born in New York, Housman was a stage actor in his early career. A little man with a florid complexion, he soon turned to comedy, and found work in films as early as 1912, achieving a degree of fame in the 'Waddy and Arty' one-reel comedies in 1914. After active service during World War One — it left him with a weak chest from which he never really recovered (in real life, he became a teetotaller) — Housman returned to the stage. From 1921, though, he began to take film work again, always in supporting roles, but always easily picked out from the crowd. In retrospect, it seems that he was in every other Laurel and Hardy comedy, although in fact he only made a few with 'the Boys': Scram!, Any Old Port, The Live Ghost, The Fixer-Uppers and the feature Our Relations, enjoying a memorably tipsy game of 'fist on fist' with them. He also tottered in and out of comedies starring other teams at the Hal Roach studio. If Housman's range was undeniably limited, he was a master of his craft in his own little world. His slurred diction and involuntary stumble were superb. He would probably have gone on making welcome cameo appearances into the 1950s but for contracting in the winter of 1941/2 the pneumonia from which he died.

*1912: What Happened to Mary (serial). * How a Horseshoe Upset a Happy Family. 1913: * When the Right Man Comes Along. * The Two Merchants. 1914: * On the Lazy Line (and other one-reelers in the 'Waddy and Arty' series). * Seth's Sweetheart. 1915: * The Champion Process Server. * A Spiritual Elopement. 1917: Red, White and Blue Blood. 1921: Clay Dollars. The Way of a Maid. Room*

*and Board. Worlds Apart. The Fighter. Is Life Worth Living? 1922: * The Snitching Hour. Man Wanted. Love's Masquerade. Destiny's Isle. Shadows of the Sea. The Prophet's Paradise. Why Announce Your Marriage? 1923: Under the Red Robe. Wife in Name Only. Male Wanted. 1924: Nellie (the Beautiful Cloak Model). Manhandled. 1925: Thunder Mountain. A Man Must Live. The Necessary Evil. The Coast of Folly. The Desert's Price. Night Life of New York. 1926: Braveheart. Whispering Wires. The Bat. The Midnight Kiss. Early to Wed. 1927: Publicity Madness. Bertha the Sewing Machine Girl. Rough House Rosie. Sunrise — A Song of Two Humans (GB: Sunrise). The Spotlight. Love Makes 'Em Wild. 1928: The Singing Fool. Happiness Ahead. Partners in Crime. Fools for Luck. Sins of the Fathers. 1929: Side Street (GB: Three Brothers). Queen of the Night Clubs. Broadway. Times Square (GB: The Street of Jazz). Fast Company. The Song of Love. 1930: Officer O'Brien. The Squealer. Feet First. Girl of the Golden West. 1931: Five and Ten (GB: Daughter of Luxury). Anybody's Blonde (GB: When Blonde Meets Blonde). Bachelor Girl. Night Life in Reno. Caught Plastered. Bachelor Apartment. 1932: Hat Check Girl (GB: Embassy Girl). No More Orchids. Movie Crazy. * Parlor, Bedroom and Wrath. Afraid to Talk. * Scram! * Any Old Port. 1933: She Done Him Wrong. The Intruder. Her Bodyguard. * Sing, Sinner, Sing. The Way to Love. * Good Housewrecking. 1934: Mrs Wiggs of the Cabbage Patch. Here is My Heart. * Elmer Steps Out. Success at Any Price. Kansas City Princess. The Merry Widow. * The Chases of Pimple Street. * Something Simple. * The Love Ghost. * Babes in the Goods. * Done in Oil. * Punch Drunks. 1935: Woman Wanted. Call of the Wild. * It Always Happens. * The Captain Hits the Ceiling. Hold 'Em Yale (GB: Uniform Lovers). Two for Tonight. Riffraff. Paris in Spring (GB: Paris Love Song). Here Comes Cookie (GB: The Plot Thickens). * The Fixer-Uppers. Diamond Jim. The Fire Trap. * Treasure Blues. * Sing, Sister, Sing. 1936: Our Relations. After the Thin Man. Wives Never Know. Show Boat. With Love and Kisses. Racing Blood. * Am I Having Fun! 1937: Double or Nothing. A Family Affair. Step Lively, Jeeves! 1938: Where the West Begins. Hard to Get. 1939: Navy Secrets. Broadway Serenade. They Made Me a Criminal. Blondie Takes A Vacation. 1940: Go West (GB: The Marx Brothers Go West). No Time for Comedy. 1941: Public Enemies. Billy the Kid.*

HOWARD, Sydney 1884–1946

A loose-chinned, brown-haired, pale-eyed, dumpy and very distinctive British comedian whose doleful, sometimes twisted expressions abounded in British comedy films of the 1930s, where he was likely to be found as henpecks or hapless menials who made good. As a scene-stealer in films where he was not the star, Howard proved to be almost in the same league as Alastair Sim

and Dame Margaret Rutherford (both qv). A Yorkshireman, Howard started his career far from show business as a paper merchant. But entertaining at clubs with his own brand of humour had led him to becoming a pierrot with a seaside concert party by his mid twenties. During World War One he was a member of the famous 'Splinters' concert-party troupe formed by serving soldiers to entertain troops on the battlefront. With the war over, Howard headed for the revue stage. There have always been mournful comedians on the British stage, and in radio and theatre, from Robb Wilton through Tony Hancock (qv) to today's Les Dawson. Howard was one of the best, his mouth forever downturned in an expression of misery or despair. He had a way of acting out the characters in his stories, which he augmented by a funny walk, arms delicately raised like those of a seal, plus inimitable speech and gestures. He was soon in demand nationally and became one of the nation's leading comedians after his biggest stage success, Hit the Deck, in 1927. Howard's first film in 1929 was a throwback to the past: Splinters, re-creating his army antics. There were two more 'Splinters' films in the 1930s, in both of which Howard took centre stage. Meanwhile he was taken up by producer Herbert Wilcox, for whose British and Dominions outfit Howard was to make nearly 20 films in the next eight years. Howard was mainly cast in these as mild, sad-faced characters who bore the indignities heaped upon them with patience but sometimes barely-disguised frustration. He had a droll way of delivering the most absurd line that had built him a sizeable fan following by the mid 1930s. His apologetic manner was underlined by the way he always said 'Pardon' following one of his frequent hiccups, but this worm could turn, and often did, to the delight of his followers, in the final reel of the film. Howard could quickly sketch in characters from all walks of life and Graham Greene once wrote about him as 'a real actor and a character of devastating pathos'. Howard rarely found the scripts to match his talents, and his last years in films were spent in juicy cameo roles, stealing scenes from the stars. In Once a Crook he played a Bible-thumping pickpocket called

Hallelujah Harry, and in *When We Are Married* he was in magnificent form as a drunken photographer. On the strength of these early 1940s' performances, a campaign was launched in certain sections of the British press to have Howard restored to stardom in his own vehicles, on the grounds that such individual comedians were too thin on the ground to allow them to languish in character roles. The campaign was nipped in the bud by Howard's early death from a heart attack but those behind it certainly had a point. His forays into sympathetic supporting roles – notably in Gracie Fields' (*qv*) *Shipyard Sally*, and his one Hollywood film, *Transatlantic Merry-Go-Round* (very much second fiddle to Jack Benny, *qv*) were among the least successful of his career. His fans preferred to remember him as the hapless ship's steward in *Trouble*, the blundering shopwalker in *Fame*, the north-country loom inventor loose in London in *Up for the Cup* or the insurance agent mistaken for a Ruritanian king in *It's a King*, a consistently funny take-off of *The Prisoner of Zenda*. A second look at Howard's work in comedy is long overdue.

1929: *Splinters*. 1930: *French Leave*. 1931: *Tilly of Bloomsbury*. *Almost a Divorce*. *Splinters in the Navy*. *Up for the Cup*. 1932: *The Mayor's Nest*. *It's a King!* 1933: *Up for the Derby*. *Night of the Garter*. *Trouble*. 1934: *It's a Cop!* *Transatlantic Merry-Go-Round*. 1935: *Where's George?/The Hope of His Side*. 1936: *Fame*. *Chick*. 1937: *Splinters in the Air*. *What a Man!* 1939: *Shipyard Sally*. 1940: *Tilly of Bloomsbury (remake)*. 1941: *Once a Crook*. * *Mr Proudfoot Shows a Light*. 1943: *When We Are Married*. 1945: *Flight from Folly*.

HOWARD, Tom (left) 1886–1955
Deadpan Hollywood humorist Tom Howard probably arrived too late in films to make himself a major name and few people remember him today. Hopefully, television showings of Frank Capra's 1930 comedy *Rain or Shine* both in Britain and America in the early 1990s will have won Howard a few more fans. Dark-haired, low-lidded, purse-lipped, tall, thin, and in his film roles, often

bowler-hatted and bespectacled, Howard originally hailed from County Tyrone in Ireland. After coming to America as a young man, he became known on the vaudeville circuit as a dry-voiced, dry-humoured monologuist. Howard would often have his audiences in fits by taking some absurd situation, and treating it in earnest, philosophical style after the manner of Will Rogers (*qv*). Through the 1920s, he starred in several editions of the *Greenwich Village Follies*, and graduated to Broadway late in the decade with James Gleason's wild hit circus comedy-musical *Rain or Shine*. Columbia decided to bring the show to the screen without its songs, but with original stars Joe Cook (Joseph Lopez, 1890–1959), seen serving Howard spaghetti in the picture, Tom Howard and Dave Chasen (1899–1973). Howard was Amos K. Shrewsberry, who comes to the circus to tally up its debts, but ends up, thanks to Cook's silver tongue, by investing in it instead. He also takes a shine to 'oriental dancer' Louise Fazenda (*qv*), who throws him out of her caravan. 'Well,' he philosophizes from a prone position, 'you gotta find these things out!' Cook went back to vaudeville (only making two more films), but Paramount found Howard a niche in their short comedies department, and he hung around for seven years, delighting audiences with his crackling, dry wit in the midst of a series of absurdly farcical situations. One of his best shorts came in 1931, with *My Wife's Jewelry*. Elaborating on an original story by Eddie Cantor (*qv*), Howard plays a gentleman burglar who, when caught, proceeds to indulge in polite but quite idiotic conversation with the owner of the house until the police arrive to take him away. In *Breaking Even*, a year later, we find Howard running a shop that's quite empty and sells nothing – eliminating all money worries at the time of the Depression. Britain's Monty Python gang, 40 years later, would have been proud of that idea. It was inevitable that Howard's distinctive voice should take him into radio and, as his interest in movies waned, he became the chairman of a panel game called *It Pays to be Ignorant*, which ran from the late 1930s to the end of the 1940s, when it transferred to television. The format was that Howard would pose some extremely simple and obvious questions to a panel of hand-picked idiot comedians, who would proceed to make a hash of them by going off at ridiculous tangents. One of the panellists was George Shelton (1884–1971), Howard's partner in many of his shorts. An equally successful British version of the show, *Ignorance is Bliss*, enjoyed an eight-year run after its 1946 debut. In the meantime, Howard and Shelton took the American show to TV, where it ran until the winter of 1951. By this time, its star was known as 'Professor' Tom Howard, and his wit was nimbler than ever. Many of Howard's shorts have been preserved, and are now available for television, showing audiences a comedian ahead of his time.

1930: *Rain or Shine*. * *The Pest*. * *Go Ahead and Sing*. * *The African Dodger*. 1931: * *My Wife's Jewelry*. * *The Mouse Trapper*. 1932: * *Breaking Even*. * *The Rookie*. * *The Acid Test*. * *The Vest with a Tale*. 1933: * *A Drug on the Market*. * *The Great Hokum Mystery*. * *Detective Tom Howard of the Suicide Squad*. 1934: * *Static*. * *The Big Meow*. * *A Good Scout*. 1935: * *Easy Money*. * *An Ear for Music*. * *Grooms in Gloom*. * *Time Out*. * *The Magic Word*. * *Stylish Stouts*. * *He's a Prince*. 1936: * *Where is Wall Street?*

HOWERD, Frankie
(Francis Howard) 1917–1992
In the days when all radio comedians were required to sign off with a song, it seemed strange that one who couldn't sing a note should have become radio's hottest property in the immediate post-war years. Born in York but raised in a London suburb, the screw-lipped, crab-faced, caterpillar-eyebrowed, curly-haired, mournful-looking Howerd first acted in a church dramatic society but, after failing an interview for a scholarship with the Royal Academy – 'I was so nervous I made a total mess of it' – he turned to comedy while serving in wartime with the Royal Artillery. After a dispiriting series of rejections – four of them by the famous *Carroll Levis Discoveries* radio show – he 'starved for six months', then began to get work as a bottom-of-the-bill comic on touring music-hall shows. His big break came in December 1946. Booked to appear on *Variety Bandbox*, a Sunday night peak-viewing radio slot that proved a breeding ground for those top comedians who progressed to being last on the bill, Howerd used his initial nervousness to his own advantage, grasping the microphone and stammering 'Ladies and gentle*men*.' It became one of his great catch-phrases, along with 'Titter ye *not*', 'Just make myself comfy' and 'I was am*azed*!'. Quickly progressing to the top of the bill, he became a resident comic on the show, furthering his popularity by an amusing 'arranged' feud with the other resident comedian, Derek Roy. Despite his comic appearance, dry delivery, loose-limbed body and occasional hilarious appearances in drag, films never quite found

a really funny script for Howerd, despite several such tries in the 1950s, and he was in guest spots by the following decade. It was a television show, *Up Pompeii!*, that revived his standing as a star comedian. Loosely based on *A Funny Thing Happened to Me on the Way to the Forum*, it cast Howerd as Lurcio, a slave in Roman times and a commentator on the idiocies, pomposity and lechery around him. Proving a master at leering confidences to the camera, Howerd was asked to repeat the role in a feature film. It was followed by two crassly inferior spin-offs, which not even Howerd could save but, as a coda to his career, he did also make in this period *The House in Nightmare Park*. In a role that perhaps suited him more than any other, this spoof horror thriller cast him as Foster Twelvetrees, an Edwardian ham actor and monologuist who becomes involved with a dottily homicidal family at their remote country mansion. Howerd was allowed the full range of his famous 'Ooohs' and 'Aaahs' as well as creating a cowardly boor that might well have boosted his film career had it been discovered two decades earlier. After that, he tackled a bit of all sorts including some Shakespeare, rolling those delicious gurgling tones round lines over which he might once have stumbled. 'As a boy', he once recalled, 'I suffered from a sort of speech dyslexia and when I was nervous everything came out in a jumble. I was very inarticulate. I still do have terrible nerves. Many people must think I'm stupid, though I'm not. I once took an intelligence test and found I had the IQ of a college professor. But everybody has weaknesses.' He was to appear in *Carry on Columbus* in 1992, but died from a heart attack before it could be made.

1954: The Runaway Bus. 1955: An Alligator Named Daisy. The Ladykillers. 1956: Jumping for Joy. A Touch of the Sun. 1958: Further Up the Creek. 1959: * Three Seasons. 1961: Watch It Sailor! 1962: The Fast Lady. The Cool Mikado. 1963: The Mouse on the Moon. 1966: The Great St Trinian's Train Robbery. 1967: Carry on Doctor. 1969: Carry on Up the Jungle. 1971: Up Pompeii. Up the Chastity Belt. 1972: Up the Front. 1973: The House in Nightmare Park (US: Crazy House). 1978: Sergeant Pepper's Lonely Hearts Club Band.

HOWES, Bobby 1895–1972

A small, agile, baby-faced, dark-haired British comedian, dancer and light singer who played young and foolish men-about-town and always seemed to be cast as characters called Jimmy, Bobby or Tommy. Essentially a man of the 1920s and 1930s, he prolonged his career in pantomime, and drew reflected fame as the father of singer-actress Sally Ann Howes. Born in London, Howes was on stage as early as 14, playing a Boy Scout in a revue sketch. For a while he made his way as an acrobatic dancer but by 1912 was part of a music-hall act called the Gotham Quartette, which went on country-

wide tours. After army service in World War One he returned to the Quartette, occasionally taking solo engagements, until one such made him a West End name. This was the Jack Hulbert–Cicely Courtneidge (both *qv*) show *The Little Revue Starts at 9*. Howes had worked with them the previous year (1922) on the tour of their revue *Pot Luck*, as supporting comedian. The supporting singer was Patricia Malone (Patricia Malone Clark), who shared his sharp sense of humour, and whom he married the following year. They both appeared with the Hulberts in *The Little Revue*, and Howes soon became an attraction in his own right, rising to West End stardom in the Hulbert-produced show *The Blue Train*, in 1927. Temperamental by nature − Hulbert, with whom he remained great friends, once kindly described him as 'erratic and impulsive' − Howes nonetheless projected a lovable personality on stage, as the shy innocent getting into all sorts of scrapes. The highly theatrical style he developed was to show up less well on screen, his personal charm working best on a live audience. Howes' first major film was one of his best. *Third Time Lucky*, made by ace comedy

director Walter Forde (*qv*), cast Howes as a timid clergyman compelled into acts of bravery in order to retrieve some blackmail letters. This successful version of a stage comedy led Howes to film a stage success of his own, *For the Love of Mike*, a musical farce with Howes as a bungling socialite forced to turn burglar to help the heiress he loves. The stage was again the source for Howes' next film, *Lord Babs*, a musical farce on a somewhat smaller scale than the previous films, with Bobby as a ship's steward feigning regression to babyhood in a bid to avoid marriage. But Howes' Stan Laurel-type mannerisms were obviously less effective on the screen and, unlike many of his musical-comedy contemporaries, he spent the majority of the 1930s on stage. Here his continuing successes encouraged Howes to transfer two more musical romps from stage to screen towards the end of the decade: *Please, Teacher!* and *Yes, Madam?* were both quite good fun, but failed to revive audience interest in Howes as a film attraction. Director Norman Lee, who made the *Josser* comedies with Ernie Lotinga, once laid out the formula for a Bobby Howes film for all aspiring Howes directors. 'It is always safe', Lee told his studio, 'to make Bobby the fool of the family, with aristocratic up-bringing and democratic leanings. If he is a rich young man chased by ... tough blondes and, in attempting to escape, meets ... the daughter of a policeman, success should be in sight. He will of course, despite his natural timidity, help her father round up a ... gang of Mayfair crooks, so everything will turn out hunky-dory. If you can make him an earl, it will help; then he can disguise himself as a bootblack, dance-band musician or something. And there will be a song or two as he rolls along.' Bobby made the first of several appearances as Buttons in *Cinderella* pantomimes in 1944 and scored

Bobby Howes feigns regression to babyhood in order to evade an unwanted marriage in *Lord Babs*. Everyone should have a nurse who looks like Jean Colin

another stage success alongside his old comrade Jack Hulbert two years later in *Here Come the Boys*. After a lull in his career in the early 1950s, he came back in a showy supporting role in the first British presentation of *Paint Your Wagon* in 1953, the show that made his daughter Sally Ann a musical star. In latter days Howes showed up well in a remake of the classic British musical *The Good Companions*, and returned to the West End in triumph in 1960 as Finian in *Finian's Rainbow*, a role he was to play several times during the decade, including a tour of Australia. His marriage to Patricia Malone ended in divorce.

1927: * On with the Dance (series of shorts). 1928: The Guns of Loos. 1931: Third Time Lucky. 1932: For the Love of Mike. Lord Babs. 1934: Over the Garden Wall. 1937: Please, Teacher! 1938: Yes, Madam? Sweet Devil. 1945: The Trojan Brothers. 1951: Happy-Go-Lovely. 1956: The Good Companions. 1961: Watch It, Sailor!

Claude Hulbert (left) and Will Hay discuss their chances of staying alive at a school where two previous headmasters have met sudden deaths in *The Ghost of St Michael's*

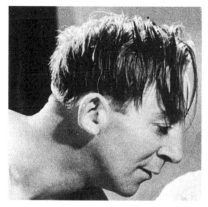

HULBERT, Claude 1900–1964

Less of a leading light than his brother Jack (*qv*), but more effective vocally and so a more popular broadcaster, moon-faced British funny-man Claude Hulbert starred in several minor comedies for the British cinema of the 1930s, as well as supporting his brother and other stars in bigger-budget romps. Born with a callow chin as opposed to his brother's jutting jaw, Claude's features, which he could easily change from affable to asinine, and mellifluous voice soon made him a favourite 'silly ass' of stage, radio and screen. A lesser-known side of his talent was as an acrobatic dancer who specialised in stage falls. But it was as a radio broadcaster, often in partnership with his wife, actress Enid Trevor (they married in 1924), that he was at his most relaxed. Their well-rehearsed domestic crosstalk was first heard on the radio in 1928 and thereafter they became frequent broadcasters, sometimes on variety bills. Educated at Cambridge, Claude became a leading member of the Footlights Revue and, on graduation, featured in a long list of musical-comedy stage successes, including *Fantasia*, *Primrose*, *Tell Me More*, *Sunny*, *Oh, Kay!*, *Kid Boots* and *Song of the Sea*. His unique quick-fire humour, coupled with a droll, amusing personality, adept at portraying nervousness, made his entrances eagerly awaited in some otherwise vacuous entertainments. Like other British musical-comedy talents, Claude found himself grabbed by the cinema for most of the 1930s. He began by supporting the Aldwych farceurs in *Thark* and *A Night Like This* before being handed his first lead in a weak B-film with Renee Houston and Binnie Barnes, *Their Night Out*. *Love at Second Sight* was little better and Hulbert returned to stealing scenes from the stars. He was the hero's well-meaning but bungling friend in most of these, his most successful solo film vehicle of the mid 1930s being *Hello Sweetheart*, a version of George M. Cohan's play *The Butter and Egg Man*, directed by former slapstick star Monty Banks (*qv*). Like most of Hulbert's starring comedies, however, its ambition was strictly small-scale; it seemed that British studios simply didn't see him as a major star. Things picked up a bit in 1936 with *Wolf's Clothing*, which starred him as a dithering diplomat, and *Honeymoon-Merry-Go-Round*, where he played a bumbling bridegroom who unintentionally becomes an ice-hockey star. Late the same year he made his first appearance as criminologist C. Gull in comedy-thrillers at the Warner British studio, where his leading lady was frequently the capable Lesley Brook. In 1937 Hulbert and Enid Trevor renewed their radio popularity in *At Home with the Hulberts*, the first domestic situation comedy series and a forerunner of *Life with the Lyons* more than a decade later. In films, he became a very capable partner for Will Hay (*qv*), after that comedian decided he wanted to do without his famous 'stooges', Moore Marriott and Graham Moffatt (both *qv*). Hay's two films with Hulbert, *The Ghost of St Michael's* and *My Learned Friend*, were the most successful of his later vehicles. Claude's film appearances, though, became scarcer as the 1940s wore on. He renewed a radio partnership with brother Jack, first heard in the 1920s in *The Hulbert Brothers*. The new series, *Hulbert House*, began in 1948. Its selling line ran: 'Jack, gay and debonair, gets himself in various spots of bother and Claude, trying hard to follow Jack's example, lands them both in greater difficulties'. The Hulberts knew how to play to each other's strengths and the series went well. Claude Hulbert's films, however, were, at best, modest and moderate, sadly lacking in budget, ambition and scriptual spark. It says something for his appeal that he survived so many, and still retained his popularity.

1928: Champagne. 1929: Naughty Husbands. 1932: A Night Like This. Thark. The Mayor's Nest. Let Me Explain Dear. The Face at the Window. 1933: Heads We Go (US: The Charming Deceiver). Radio Parade. Their Night Out. The Song You Gave Me. 1934: Love at Second Sight (US: The Girl Thief). The Girl in Possession. A Cup of Kindness. Big Business. Lilies of the Field. 1935: Hello Sweetheart. Man of the Moment. Bulldog Jack (US: Alias Bulldog Drummond). 1936: Where's Sally. Wolf's Clothing. The Interrupted Honeymoon. Hail and Farewell. Honeymoon Merry-Go-Round (formerly Olympic Honeymoon). Take a Chance. The Vulture. 1937: Ship's Concert. It's Not Cricket. You Live and Learn. 1938: Simply Terrific. It's in the Blood. The Viper. His Lordship Regrets. Many Tanks Mr Atkins. 1940: Sailors Three (US: Three Cockeyed Sailors). 1941: The Ghost of St Michael's. 1943: The Dummy Talks. My Learned Friend. 1946: London Town (US: My Heart Goes Crazy). 1947: The Ghosts of Berkeley Square. 1948: Under the Frozen Falls. 1949: Cardboard Cavalier. 1955: Fun at St Fanny's. 1960: Not a Hope in Hell.

HULBERT, Jack 1892–1978

Jack was jolly and jaunty – and very British. Irrepressibly cheerful, his talents enhanced the London stage for more than 60 years. From 1920 to 1950 he was at his best – he danced nimbly, could carry a tune and had an impeccable sense of comic timing – as one of the magic figures of a golden period for British revue theatre. And he also enjoyed a formidable and immensely popular film career, even though the major part of it was restricted to the 1930s. Above all, though, his face was his fortune: a huge crescent-moon of a thing that looked like a re-creation of Mr Punch without the ruddy cheeks, and swung from the high forehead down to a chin with which you could have almost dug the garden. Despite Hulbert's undoubted musical talents, this was a face made for comedy, and could express charm, determination or hurt bewilderment with equal persuasion. Organising amateur performances from an early age, featuring himself and his younger brother Claude (qv), Jack never thought of any other career but the stage – although his attention was briefly diverted by his exploits as a Cambridge oarsman while at university. At 19 he appeared at the famous New Theatre, Cambridge, in the title role of a comedy called *Jack Straw*. His own christian name seemed to express many of his likeable qualities, and it pursued him in the titles of several of his films. He made his professional debut at 21 in the musical *The Pearl Girl*, and his early experience both in this field and in Restoration comedy quickly established him as a musical star and comic actor rather than comedian. War service interrupted the flow of his career but, after the success of *The Little Revue Starts at Nine*, in 1923, both Hulbert and his co-star (and wife), Cicely Courtneidge (qv), found themselves established among Britain's brightest and most popular stage personalities. Another revue, *By-the-Way*, followed, which the Hulberts took to America, and, in 1927, perhaps their most spectacular success, *Clowns in Clover*. With the coming of sound, Hulbert's affable tones, lizard-lidded eyes, goofy grin and unique jawline began to make their presence felt in films as well. The move to films was partly dictated by financial

necessity. His partnership with producer Paul Murray had gone into liquidation, and Hulbert made himself responsible for paying back its five-figure debts. Films were a quick solution. Apart from a guest appearance in the all-star *Elstree Calling*, the first film up was the second of three versions of the old stage comedy-thriller classic *The Ghost Train*. Hulbert, playing the 'silly ass' who turns out to be a detective, re-wrote some of his dialogue to suit his style, and the film was a big popular hit. After a musical comedy, *Sunshine Susie*, Hulbert got his first genuine solo vehicle (and the first of the 'Jack' films), *Jack's the Boy*. Playing the hapless son of a police commissioner, Hulbert was at the top of his form, cavorting like a dancing giraffe through a story about jewel thieves, highlighted by the famous 'ladder' sequence, the traffic-stopping consequences of which anticipated the similar 'pole' sequence in Will Hay's (qv) *Where's That Fire?* Probably still Hulbert's best, the film landed him and his wife three-year contracts with Gaumont-British. In quick succession, it was on to *Happy Ever After*, *Love on Wheels*, *Falling for You* and then another big hit, *Jack Ahoy*. Able Seaman Hulbert got mixed up with revolutionaries, sang *My Hat's on the Side of My Head* and danced a hornpipe. The 'energy and high spirits', to which one contemporary critic referred were tested more than somewhat on the latter film when Hulbert was required to jump off Weymouth Quay into the English Channel – a sequence which required a number of fully-clothed soakings to get right. Up to this point Hulbert's best films had all been directed by stocky Walter Forde (qv), himself a former comedian. *The Camels Are Coming*, partly filmed in Egypt, wasn't, and it flopped,

proving Hulbert not indestructible at the box-office. It was back to Forde with a film that restored the balance in style: *Bulldog Jack*, in which passer-by Jack has to take over from the famous detective Bulldog Drummond on a case when the latter is hurt. A stylish mix of comedy and thrills, it had some riotously funny moments enhanced by Hulbert's graceful awkwardness, and an exciting climax in London's Underground. The results were less happy when Hulbert (co-)directed himself the following year (1936) in *Jack of All Trades*. In Hollywood with his wife, he turned down an RKO contract and returned to Britain to make his last really funny film, *Take My Tip*. As well as providing Hulbert with some of his most inventive dance routines, *Take My Tip* reunited him with Courtneidge, giving them both the opportunity to indulge in some extravagant disguises as they played swindled nobility trying to get their money back. From 1937 Hulbert became more and more involved in staging shows, often featuring his wife. But they were on stage together in 1938 in *Under Your Hat*, enjoying more silly disguises as an actor and actress involved with enemy agents. The show was filmed two years later. It was to be Hulbert's last movie musical-comedy. From 1940 on Hulbert devoted most of his time to theatrical production and direction. It was not until 1955 that he began appearing regularly again as an actor. There were a few more films which he would probably have been wiser not to make but which hardly tarnished the image of the breezy, cheerful chappie who had so brightened the 1930s. They did nothing to diminish the affection in which the Hulberts were held by their public and peers alike for the remainder of their days.

Jack Hulbert's ruse to pose as the manager of the shop where he works, to impress Leonora Corbett, seems to be working – so far, in *Love on Wheels*

The odds are lengthening on Take a Chance in the big race, much to the pleasure of tipster Alastair (Claude Hulbert, with chalk) who stands to win more than money, in *Take a Chance*

Jennifer (Lauren Hutton) finds that Wendell (Eric Idle) is very happy to have hidden from crooks in a vat of wine, in *Missing Pieces*

Titfer tat. Backstage battle between Daisy Delaware (Hattie Jacques) and fellow Gaiety Girl Trottie True (Jean Kent), in *Trottie True*. Bill Owen waits for the fur to fly

Sidney James in one of the many cockney crook roles he played before becoming a comedy star. Here he's Sharkey in *The Flanagan Boy*, a lurid mix of boxing, sex and murder

1928: * British Screen Tatler No. 10. 1930: Elstree Calling. 1931: The Ghost Train. Sunshine Susie (US: The Office Girl). 1932: Jack's the Boy (US: Night and Day). Love on Wheels. Happy Ever After. 1933: Falling for You. 1934: Jack Ahoy! The Camels Are Coming. 1935: Bulldog Jack (US: Alias Bulldog Drummond). 1936: Jack of All Trades (US: The Two of Us). 1937: Take My Tip. Paradise for Two (US: The Gaiety Girls). 1938: Kate Plus Ten. 1940: Under Your Hat. 1948: * Highwaymen. 1950: Into the Blue (US: The Man in the Dinghy) 1951: The Magic Box. 1955: Miss Tulip Stays the Night. 1960: The Spider's Web. 1972: Not Now Darling. The Cherry Picker.

'Sister' Eric Idle learns a few home truths from the confession of girlfriend Camille Coduri in this scene from Nuns on the Run

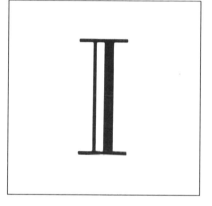

IDLE, Eric 1943–

With his amusingly anguished face, startled eyes, mobile body and deadly serious approach to lunacy, it's surprising that Britain's brown-haired Eric Idle has, of all the Monty Python gang, stayed out of the limelight for so long. He is of course a writer of comedy as much as a performer, so perhaps we can put that down to the many unfilmed screenplays that Idle lists in his biographical notes. Recently, though, he has been starring in films on both sides of the Atlantic, although it seems a little late for international stardom to claim him. Born in the north of England, Idle studied English Literature at Cambridge University, where he became involved with the Footlights group. His sole venture into straight acting – the world premiere of Henry Miller's I'm Just Wild about Harry, a legendary fiasco in which falling sets nearly maimed London critics in the front row of the stalls – must have convinced him that his future lay in comedy. From 1966 Idle began to write for TV and radio shows, most notably the innovative BBC-Radio series I'm Sorry I'll Read That Again. The following year he began an association with many of the comic players destined to be Monty Pythons in Do Not Adjust Your Set, an ITV comedy series that ran to a second season. Monty Python's Flying Circus came to BBC-TV in 1969 and stayed for three seasons, leading to numerous spin-offs, films and concerts, in most of which Idle took part. His limb-flapping style – close to over-acting without getting there – proved ideal for the far-out, innovative farces that the Pythons created. In the meantime, he himself starred in Rutland Weekend Television, which led to The Rutles, satirising the success of the pop group the Beatles. Film activities were largely restricted to Python films – he was very funny as the guard who struggles to remember a simple command in Monty Python and the Holy Grail – until ex-Python Terry Gilliam's spottily successful The Adventures of Baron Munchausen introduced Idle to a wider audience as the fast-running servant Berthold, a clown-like role for which Idle wore appropriate makeup – and had to run a lot. 'I read the script', he said at the time, 'and thought it was wonderful. I made the mistake of telling Terry it was wonderful and that he should make it at once. It's all my fault. I'm to blame, and I've suffered ever since by being in it.' At much the same time, Idle branched out into operetta by playing Ko-Ko in a production of Gilbert and Sullivan's The Mikado at the English National Opera. In 1990 Idle's long, lugubrious features made a very acceptable comedy team with plump-cheeked Robbie Coltrane (qv) in Nuns on the Run, in which Idle's brand of panic was seen to good advantage. An American venture, Too Much Sun, went less well – straight to video, in fact, in Britain. But there are more films to come. Divorced from actress Lynn Ashley, Idle is now married to American ex-model Tanya Kossvitch. 'Writing humour', he said in 1989, 'is not funny! For the past 25 years I've managed to make a living in humour. It's a skill you work at, and it evolves and develops with experience – like any skill. But it's an odd business.'

1967: * Albert Carter QOSO. 1971: And Now for Something Completely Different. 1975: Monty Python and the Holy Grail. 1976: Pleasure at Her Majesty's (US: Monty Python Meets Beyond the Fringe). 1977: To See Such Fun (TV). 1978: * Ging Gang Goolie (and directed). 1979: Monty Python's Life of Brian. The Secret Policeman's Ball. 1981: Time Bandits. 1982: Monty Python Live at the Hollywood Bowl. The Secret Policeman's Other Ball. 1983: Yellowbeard. Monty Python's The Meaning of Life. 1985: National Lampoon's European Vacation. 1986: The Transformers (voice only). 1987: The Adventures of Baron Munchausen. 1990: Nuns on the Run. Too Much Sun. 1991: Missing Pieces. 1992: Mom and Dad Save the World.

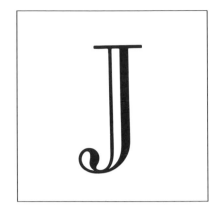

now!' ITMA was only one of three hugely popular radio comedy programmes with which Hattie was associated. She also played the interfering Agatha Dinglebody on the long-running *Educating Archie*, which introduced much fresh comedy talent, before moving on to become Grizelda Pugh, secretary to Tony Hancock (he had also been in *Educating Archie*) in the innovative *Hancock's Half Hour*. Meanwhile, a film career had started, at first with ripely-rounded and richly-sketched Dickensians in *Nicholas Nickleby*, *Oliver Twist*, *Scrooge* and *The Pickwick Papers*. In 1958 she was in the first 'Carry On' film, *Carry On Sergeant*. Now, she became extremely busy, keeping up her stage work, appearing in more than 30 film comedies over the next 15 years, and beginning a long-lasting TV series with Eric Sykes (they played sister and brother). The shows had a pasted-together quality but were regarded with affection by the British public, who kept them on air until Hattie's death from a heart attack at 56. Hattie married fellow comedy actor John le Mesurier (*qv*) in 1949, the marriage ending in an amicable divorce 16 years later. Le Mesurier was generous in his tributes at the time of her death, observing that 'Hat', as everyone called her, 'had a wealth of talent that was often underestimated'.

1946: Green for Danger. 1947: Nicholas Nickleby. 1948: Oliver Twist. 1949: Trottie True (US: Gay Lady). The Spider and the Fly. 1950: Waterfront (US: Waterfront Women). Chance of a Lifetime. 1951: Scrooge (US: A Christmas Carol). 1952: No Haunt for a Gentleman. Mother Riley Meets the Vampire (US: Vampire Over London). The Pickwick Papers. 1953: Our Girl Friday (US: The Adventures of Sadie). All Hallowe'en. 1954: The Love Lottery. Up to His Neck. 1955: As Long As They're Happy. Now and Forever. 1958: Carry On Sergeant. The Square Peg. 1959: Carry On Nurse. Carry On Teacher. Left, Right and Centre. The Night We Dropped a Clanger. The Navy Lark. Follow a Star. School for Scoundrels. 1960: Carry On Constable. Make Mine Mink. Watch Your Stern. 1961: Carry On Regardless. In the Doghouse. 1962: She'll Have to Go (US: Maid for Murder). The Punch and Judy Man. 1963: Carry On Cabby. 1967: The Bobo. The Plank. Carry On Doctor. 1968: Crooks and Coronets (US: Sophy's Place). 1969: Carry On Again, Doctor. The Magic Christian. Carry On Camping. Monte Carlo or Bust (US: Those Daring Young Men in Their Jaunty Jalopies). 1970: Carry On Loving. Rhubarb. 1971: Danger Point. Carry On at Your Convenience. 1972: Carry On Matron. Carry On Abroad. 1974: Three for All. Carry On Dick.

Matron Hattie Jacques is horrified at the uses Sidney James proposes for his penknife in *Carry On Again, Doctor*

JACQUES, Hattie
(Josephine Jacques) 1924–1980

A plump, tall, lovable, dark-haired British comedienne whose arched eyebrow and regal emphases convulsed many a stage, radio and film audience from her theatrical debut at the age of 20 to the last of her 14 appearances in 'Carry On' films 30 years later. Theatre fans knew her best as a succession of fairy queens at the famous Players Theatre. For radio listeners, she created richly memorable characters on comedy programmes with Tommy Handley, Tony Hancock and Eric Sykes (all *qv*). Filmgoers probably remember her as a formidable hospital matron in the four medical 'Carry Ons'. Born in Kent, she had a distinctly upper-class education, but at 18 was doing her bit for the war effort by working as a Red Cross nurse for two years. In August 1944 she made the first of many appearances at the Players Theatre, singing Victorian songs. In the next 18 years, she acted with what one critic called 'expansive relish' in many of the theatre's best revues, variety bills, plays and pantomimes. She was first heard regularly on radio in the 1940s' greatest comedy series, *ITMA*, which she joined in 1947. Her most popular character was the greedy schoolgirl Sophie Tuckshop, who would regale listeners with an account of her latest monstrous eating orgy, culminating in the reassurance: 'But I'm all right

JAMES, Sidney 1913–1976

Show business's most famous motto is, of course: 'The show must go on'. That rule was broken, however, when Sidney James died on the opening night of a new stage production of the comedy *The Mating Season*. Said the play's producer: 'This is one show that will not go on. Sid was irreplaceable.' This most loved of British film comedy actors, with his crumpled face, slitted eyes, disappearing tightly wavy hair and inimitable raucous laugh, was actually born in South Africa. His early life was spent in manual labour there: he was a coal heaver, a stevedore, a diamond polisher and a professional boxer. Batterings in the ring made his homely features even more so. During World War Two, as well as being an officer with an anti-tank regiment in the Middle East, Sid served with an entertainment unit, and decided to have a go at acting as a career, travelling to Britain in 1946 on his service gratuity. Breaking into repertory work almost straight away, he was soon grasped by the busy British post-war film industry, and became one of those faces that cropped up all over the place without you knowing the name to go with it. He could play shady East End characters, friendly cockneys or brash Americans with equal conviction, and his confident acting style soon put him into good featured roles. His first major comedy was *The Lavender Hill Mob*: he and Alfie Bass were the other two members of the bullion robbery gang headed by Alec Guinness and Stanley Holloway (both *qv*). In the same year (1951), he made two more film comedies, *Lady Godiva Rides Again* and *The Galloping Major*, and played a comic singing gangster in the London stage production of *Kiss Me Kate*. Sid was playing almost a role a month for British films in 1954 when he began the famous comedy partnership with Tony Hancock (*qv*), at first on radio, in *Hancock's Half Hour* (1954–9) as part of the gaggle of funny supporting players, then in tandem with Hancock on TV (1956–60) as the seedy duo living at 23, Railway Cuttings, East Cheam. This quickly became the most popular TV comedy series in Britain. James, with his deflating cry of 'Allo, 'Ancock', was soon getting as many laughs as his partner, much to the discomfort of the star, who eventually had Sid dropped from the show. Via a guest spot in another hit radio programme, *Educating Archie*, Sid bounced back into films to become a leading member of the 'Carry On' gang. He made 19 films with them altogether, but really came into his own in costume, superb as Henry VIII in *Carry On Henry*, but also incongruously and delightfully cast as the Rumpo Kid, the villain of *Carry On Cowboy*; Sir Rodney Ffing (alias the Black Fingernail), the scourge of the French in *Don't Lose Your Head*; Sir Sidney Ruff-Diamond in *Carry On Up the Khyber*; and Turpin the highwayman in *Carry On Dick*. Through all these, the grin, chortle and demeanour remained the same; and comic ripostes were fired at perfect speed. The characters were leering and lecherous ... and likeable. He was enjoyably Sid James in all of them and his entrances were something to be savoured. Latterly he enjoyed success at the head of casts of TV situation comedies, notably *George and the Dragon*, *Taxi* and *Bless This House*. He survived a heart attack in 1967 to offer audiences another nine years of a man who, in comedy at least, always seemed to have the answer. There was national grief when a second heart attack killed him at 62. Said 'Carry On' co-star Hattie Jacques (*qv*): 'He belied his TV and film image as a brash man. That image was everything Sid was not in real life.'

1947: Black Memory. The October Man. It Always Rains on Sunday. 1948: No Orchids for Miss Blandish. Night Beat. Once a Jolly Swagman (US: Maniacs on Wheels). The Small Back Room. 1949: Paper Orchid. The Man in Black. Give Us This Day (US: Salt to the Devil). 1950: Last Holiday. The Lady Craved Excitement. 1951: Talk of a Million (US: You Can't Beat the Irish). Lady Godiva Rides Again. The Lavender Hill Mob. The Magic Box. The Galloping Major. 1952: I Believe in You. Emergency Call (US: Hundred Hour Hunt). Gift Horse (US: Glory at Sea). Cosh Boy (US: The Slasher). Miss Robin Hood. Time Gentlemen Please! Father's Doing Fine. Venetian Bird (US: The Assassin). Tall Headlines. The Yellow Balloon. 1953: The Wedding of Lilli Marlene. Escape by Night. The Titfield Thunderbolt. The Square Ring. Will Any Gentleman ...? The Weak and the Wicked (US: Young and Willing). Park Plaza 605 (US: Norman Conquest). The Flanagan Boy (US: Bad Blonde). Is Your Honeymoon Really Necessary? 1954: The Rainbow Jacket. The House Across the Lake (US: Heatwave). Seagulls Over Sorrento (US: Crest of the Wave). The Crowded Day. Orders Are Orders. Aunt Clara. For Better, For Worse (US: Cocktails in the Kitchen). The Belles of St Trinian's. 1955: Out of the Clouds. Joe Macbeth. The Deep Blue Sea. A Kid for Two Farthings. The Glass Cage (US: The Glass Tomb). A Yank in Ermine. It's a Great Day. John and Julie. 1956: Ramsbottom Rides Again. The Extra Day. Wicked As They Come. The Iron Petticoat. Dry Rot. Trapeze. 1957: Quatermass II (US: Enemy from Space). Interpol (US: Pickup Alley). The Smallest Show on Earth. The Shiralee. Hell Drivers. Campbell's Kingdom. A King in New York. The Story of Esther Costello (US: The Golden Virgin). 1958: The Silent Enemy. Another Time, Another Place. Next to No Time! The Man Inside. I Was Monty's Double (US: Monty's Double). The Sheriff of Fractured Jaw.

Corn in Egypt. Just as well Sidney James and Amanda Barrie don't have to keep straight faces as they jostle for position in *Carry On Cleo*

1959: *Too Many Crooks. Make Mine a Million. The 39 Steps. Upstairs and Downstairs. Tommy the Toreador. Desert Mice. Idle on Parade (US: Idol on Parade). 1960: Carry On Constable. Watch Your Stern. And the Same to You. The Pure Hell of St Trinian's. 1961: Double Bunk. A Weekend with Lulu. The Green Helmet. What a Carve Up! (US: No Place Like Homicide). Raising the Wind (US: Roommates). What a Whopper! Carry On Regardless. 1962: Carry On Cruising. We Joined the Navy. 1963: Carry On Cabby. 1964: The Beauty Jungle (US: Contest Girl). Carry On Cleo. Three Hats for Lisa. 1965: The Big Job. Carry On Cowboy. 1966: Where the Bullets Fly. Don't Lose Your Head. 1967: Carry On Doctor. 1968: Carry On Up the Khyber. 1969: Carry On Again, Doctor. Carry On Camping. Carry On Up the Jungle. 1970: Carry On Loving. Carry On Henry. 1971: Carry On at Your Convenience. Tokoloshe, the Evil Spirit. 1972: Carry On Matron. Bless This House. Carry On Abroad. 1973: Carry On Girls. 1974: Carry On Dick.*

Lionel Jeffries (second right) seems to have the upper hand on his rival (Anthony Newley, second left) for the daughter (Anne Aubrey) of the CO (William Kendall) in *Idle on Parade*

JEFFRIES, Lionel 1926–

Bald-headed, often bewhiskered British comic character actor who, in his most rambunctious period (1956–65), was a merciless scene-stealer, liable to filch laughs from under the noses of the stars at the twitch of a muscle. Facial movement combined with an inimitable delivery of a line was Jeffries' comedy secret. As a straight character actor he was workmanlike and likeable but not as effective. As a laughter-getter he had a fearsome scowl, a ferocious double-take and a wondrous 'upside-down' tight-lipped grin that was liable to open up into massively-toothed smiles or leers. In the early 1960s he was often star-billed but good film roles were becoming scarce. Fortunately he turned his arm to directing and showed a delicate, fond and sure touch in making films with young players. A man of strong opinions, Jeffries has never suffered fools, nor weak scripts, gladly and often rewrote his own comedy material to the advantage of the film. His parents, very far removed from show business, were Salvation Army social workers, for a long time stationed in India. Jeffries himself spent a long period of his early manhood in the

Far East, as a regular soldier serving in Burma – the military bearing he acquired adding usefully to some of his more memorable comic creations. After working for the Rangoon radio station he decided to take up acting. 'I was the only bald student at RADA' he told an interviewer once. Still, he won the Kendall Medal there. He has in fact been bald since he was 19. 'Of course I was upset', he remembered. 'Tried a toupee once, too. But it looked like a dead moth on a boiled egg.' Married to an actress he met at RADA, Jeffries embarked on a stage and film career. After a fleeting role in Hitchcock's *Stage Fright*, he began to get regular film work in the early 1950s. There was a good role as a camp inmate in *The Colditz Story* and an amazing one in the B-feature *Windfall* in which, at 29, he played an old codger whose find of £2,000 only leads to trouble for his son and daughter. This remarkable performance did as much as anything to establish Jeffries on the film acting scene. He was on good form as George, one of the seamen involved in the ramshackle romp *The Baby and the Battleship* in 1956, and from this juncture began to be seen more often in comedy. He was a crook trying to get away with a fortune in gems hidden in a water-polo ball in *Blue Murder at St Trinian's*, appearing at one stage in quite convincing drag. He began a profitable three-film association with Peter Sellers in *Up the Creek*. In this first he was an affable cove called Steady Barker, but he really came into his own in *Two Way Stretch* and *The Wrong Arm of the Law*, as officious, obnoxious upholders of the law whose downfall was delightful. *Two Way Stretch* was a prison comedy that cast Jeffries as warden Sidney Crout; *The Wrong Arm of the Law* had him as Inspector Nosey Parker, both self-righteous, nostril-twitching, sadistically

comic bad guys who took pleasure in keeping their victims under the thumbscrew – but who had the tables spectacularly and hilariously turned on them. Jeffries was now at his peak of comic invention. His finest achievement was perhaps his Professor Cavor in *First Men in the Moon*, all huffles, snuffles and sudden switches of thought, an enchanting creation. Jeffries never quite stepped up to top spot in the cast after that, although there was more Jules Verne tomfoolery, and a good leading straight role in the underrated thriller *Eyewitness*, before he stepped behind the camera to make the wholly charming *The Railway Children*, reluctantly relinquishing the role of Perks the Porter (Bernard Cribbins (*qv*) played it) to concentrate on directing. Jeffries also contributed the script. For his next film as writer/director, Jeffries stepped back in time again to make another beguiling entertainment, *The Amazing Mr Blunden*, a cosy ghost story that underlined Jeffries' talent for extracting convincing performances from children. His few films since then were moderately well received but did not repeat the overwhelming popular success of the first two. Since the beginning of the 1980s he has been seen more frequently again as an actor, including the tackling of his first TV situation comedy series, *Father Charlie*, bringing him almost full circle to his beginnings: he played a convent's chaplain who's an ex-regimental sergeant major. 'I was constantly rewriting the words of the comedy characters I was given in the past', he once said, 'to bring them a comic humanity. Most of the people I played were men caught in desperation. In their hearts they knew that they were failures – but they would never admit it, even to themselves.' In real life Jeffries and failure have seldom been even on nodding terms.

Good king Sid. Unmistakeable in regal robes and beard, Sidney James enjoyed the role of a laugh-time as a cackling Henry VIII in *Carry On Henry*

One of Lionel Jeffries' early comedy roles was in *The Baby and the Battleship*. Here he is, extreme right, with fellow matelots including John Mills, Richard Attenborough and Bryan Forbes

Dean Jones beats a hasty retreat as he starts turning into an Old English sheepdog. Suzanne Pleshette leads him away, in Disney's *The Shaggy D.A.*

1949: Stage Fright. 1953: Will Any Gentleman . . .? 1954: The Colditz Story. The Black Rider. 1955: Windfall. No Smoking. The Quatermass Experiment (US: The Creeping Unknown). All for Mary. 1956: Jumping for Joy. Eyewitness. Bhowani Junction. Lust for Life. The Baby and the Battleship. Up in the World. The High Terrace. The Man in the Sky (US: Decision Against Time). 1957: The Vicious Circle (US: The Circle). Hour of Decision. Doctor at Large. Barnacle Bill (US: All at Sea). Blue Murder at St Trinian's. 1958: Law and Disorder. Dunkirk. Orders to Kill. Up the Creek. The Revenge of Frankenstein. Girls at Sea. The Nun's Story. Behind the Mask. Nowhere to Go. Life is a Circus. Further Up the Creek. 1959: Idle on Parade (US: Idol on Parade). Please Turn Over. Bobbikins. 1960: Two Way Stretch. The Trials of Oscar Wilde (US: The Man in the Green Carnation). Jazzboat. Let's Get Married. Tarzan the Magnificent. 1961: The Hellions. Fanny. 1962: Operation Snatch. Mrs Gibbons' Boys. Kill or Cure. The Notorious Landlady. The Wrong Arm of the Law. 1963: Call Me Bwana. The Scarlet Blade (US: The Crimson Blade). The Long Ships. 1964: First Men in the Moon. The Truth about Spring. Murder Ahoy. 1965: You Must Be Joking! The Secret of My Success. 1966: Drop Dead, Darling (US: Arrivederci Baby!). Oh Dad, Poor Dad, Mama's Hung You in the Closet and I'm Feeling So Sad. The Spy with a Cold Nose. 1967: Jules Verne's Rocket to the Moon (US: Those Fantastic Flying Fools). Camelot. 1968: Chitty Chitty Bang Bang. 1969: Twinky (US: Lola). Twelve Plus One/ The Twelve Chairs. 1970: Eyewitness (and 1956 film. US: Sudden Terror). 1971: Whoever Slew Auntie Roo? (US: Who Slew Auntie Roo?). 1974: Royal Flash. What Changed Charley Farthing. 1977: Wombling Free (voice only). 1978: The Water Babies (voice only). The Prisoner of Zenda. 1982: Ménage à Trois/Better Late Than Never. 1988: A Chorus of Disapproval. 1989: Danny, the Champion of the World (TV. GB: cinemas). Jekyll and Hyde (TV).

As director. 1970: The Railway Children 1972: The Amazing Mr Blunden. Baxter! 1977: Wombling Free. 1978: The Water Babies.

JENKINS, Allen
(Alfred McGonegal) 1890–1974

Allen Jenkins played gangsters — but almost none of them were to be taken seriously. Shifty-eyed, hook-nosed and horse-faced, with receding black hair slicked back and a voice that was pure Brooklyn, Jenkins could have stepped straight from the pages of any Damon Runyon story about those guys and dolls. With twisted lip and dim expression, this native New Yorker leered his way through dozens of crime films and comedies — always perfectly in character, whether as two-bit crook or equally slow-witted sidekick of the hero. Although his parents were musical-comedy performers Jenkins had no thoughts of an acting career until after working in shipyards up to the

end of World War One. He got into acting by the back door when he became a stage mechanic, then decided to enrol at the American Academy of Dramatic Art and was acting on Broadway by the mid 1920s. With the coming of sound, Hollywood soon added him to its roster of character players. He signed up with Warner Brothers, and stayed with the studio for ten years, playing in light-hearted gangster spoofs alongside all the studio's top stars, including Cagney, Bogart, Robinson and Bette Davis. It was Jenkins, as Louis, who said to her in *Marked Woman*: 'I positively guarantee you this was stolen from the best shop in town.' He was Perry Mason's assistant Spudsy in crime cases of the mid 1930s, then switched to RKO to become Goldie Locke, the sidekick of 'Falcon' George Sanders in detective thrillers of the early 1940s. He and owlish Hugh Herbert (*qv*) had the leading roles as dim detectives in the 1937 comedy *Sh! The Octopus*, but it didn't lead to a series. Jenkins continued making a good living as men on the make and soft-hearted thugs until the early 1950s, when he transferred his talents to television. From 1956 to 1957, he shared the lead with Jeannie Carson in the show *Hey Jeannie!*, playing a friendly cab driver showing a Scottish immigrant around New York. He slowed up after 1959, but was called back for a few courtesy appearances, most notably in company with several other gangster players from his era in the 'Man from UNCLE' telefilm, *The Spy with the Green Hat*. He completed his final role, as the telegrapher in the 1974 remake of *The Front Page*, shortly before his death in hospital, from complications following surgery.

*1931: * Straight and Narrow. The Girl Habit. 1932: Rackety Rax. Blessed Event. I Am a Fugitive from a Chain Gang. Three on a Match. * The Stolen Jools (GB: The Slippery Pearls). Lawyer Man. 1933: 42nd Street. Ladies They Talk About. The Mayor of Hell. Employees' Entrance. The Keyhole. Tomorrow at Seven. Professional Sweetheart (GB: Imaginary Sweetheart). The Mind Reader. Havana Widows. Hard to Handle. The Silk Express. Bureau of Missing Persons. Blondie Johnson. 1934: I've Got Your Number. Twenty Million Sweethearts. Happiness Ahead. The Merry*

*Frinks (GB: The Happy Family). The St Louis Kid (GB: A Perfect Weekend). The Case of the Howling Dog. Bedside. The Big Shakedown. Whirlpool. Jimmy the Gent. 1935: A Night at the Ritz. Miss Pacific Fleet. The Case of the Curious Bride. Page Miss Glory. The Irish in Us. Sweet Music. While the Patient Slept. The Case of the Lucky Legs. Broadway Hostess. I Live for Love (GB: I Live for You). 1936: The Singing Kid. Sing Me a Love Song. Three Men on a Horse. Sins of Man. Cain and Mabel. 1937: There Goes My Girl. Dance, Charlie, Dance. The Singing Marine. Marry the Girl. Dead End. Talent Scout. Ready, Willing and Able. Marked Woman. Ever Since Eve. The Perfect Specimen. Sh! The Octopus. 1938: A Slight Case of Murder. Swing Your Lady. Racket Busters. Heart of the North. Going Places. Gold Diggers in Paris (GB: The Gay Imposters). The Amazing Dr Clitterhouse. Hard to Get. Fools for Scandal. * For Auld Lang Syne. 1939: Sweepstakes Winner. Five Came Back. Torchy Plays with Dynamite. Naughty But Nice. Destry Rides Again. 1940: Oh, Johnny, How You Can Love. Meet the Wildcat. Brother Orchid. Margie. Tin Pan Alley. 1941: The Gay Falcon. Time Out for Rhythm. Footsteps in the Dark. Dive Bomber. Ball of Fire. Go West, Young Lady. A Date with the Falcon. 1942: Maisie Gets Her Man (GB: She Got Her Man). The Falcon Takes Over. Tortilla Flat. Eyes in the Night. They All Kissed the Bride. 1943: Stage Door Canteen. 1945: Wonder Man. Lady on a Train. 1946: Singin' in the Corn (GB: Give and Take). The Dark House. Meet Me on Broadway. 1947: The Case of the Babysitter. Fun on a Week-End. Easy Come, Easy Go. Wild Harvest. The Senator Was Indiscreet (GB: Mr Ashton Was Indiscreet). The Hat Box Mystery. 1948: The Inside Story. 1949: The Big Wheel. 1950: Bodyhold. 1951: Let's Go Navy. Crazy over Horses. Behave Yourself! 1952: The WAC from Walla Walla (GB: Army Capers). Oklahoma Annie. 1957: Three Men on a Horse (remake. TV). 1959: Pillow Talk. Chained for Life. 1963: It's a Mad, Mad, Mad, Mad World. 1964: I'd Rather Be Rich. Robin and the Seven Hoods. For Those Who Think Young. 1966: The Spy in the Green Hat (TV. GB: cinemas). 1967: Doctor, You've Got to Be Kidding! 1971: Getting Away from It All (TV). 1974: The Front Page.*

JEWEL, Jimmy (left, overleaf)
(James Marsh Jr) 1909–
and
WARRISS, Ben 1909–

Enormously popular cross-talking British comedians, vaguely in the Abbott and Costello (*qv*) mould, who might have made it big in British film comedy if only they had had the backing of a major studio. Jewel and Warriss were real-life cousins born in the same house in Sheffield. Many observers thought them the funniest act of their kind in Britain until Morecambe and Wise (*qv*) came to their peak. Beaky Ben had pop eyes, dark hair slicked back with cream and a hectoring manner. He wore smart blazers.

Dishevelled, sandy-haired Jimmy was the fall guy, enduring comic humiliation and taking it on the chin. He always got the blame, eyes blinking pitifully from crumpled features. They teamed in 1934 (in the stage revue *Revels of '34*) and by the war years had made their way to the London Palladium, where they starred in *Gangway* and *High Time*. Radio work followed, at first in *Navy Mixture* but, from 1947, in their greatest success, the long-running *Up the Pole*. This was initially set at a trading post in the Arctic, but underwent various changes of location during its six-year run. Buoyed by the success of *Up the Pole*, which made them national figures, Jewel and Warriss decided to try for a film career. Unfortunately, they made the decision to hitch up with the pinchpenny Mancunian Film Unit. That had made comedies with Frank Randle (*qv*) that had enjoyed success in the north of England, but had the reputation of producing films that contained more footage than fun. Such proved the case with the two Jewel and Warriss efforts, which ran 95 minutes but could have benefited from hefty trimming (not to mention better direction and script rewrites). Production values were notably absent from *What a Carry On!* (the pair's best-known catchphrase). This was an army comedy patterned very much after the old Randle vehicles, and gave the comedians little chance to deliver their own brand of fun. Rather, they found themselves straitjacketed into a formula alien to their innate craziness. The second film, *Let's Have a Murder*, was better, but not much. Poorly scripted, it had Jimmy and Ben as clumsy detectives investigating the murder of a singer. Disillusioned, they returned to radio and *Up the Pole*, later transferring the series to television. In 1958 and 1959 they returned to radio for *The Jewel and Warriss Show*, but the title betrayed its lack of invention and by the 1960s their appeal was clearly on the wane. The team split in 1966, leaving Jewel to pursue an increasingly profitable career as a character actor. There was also a TV series, *Nearest and Dearest*, with fellow north-country funster Hylda Baker, from which a film was made. Warriss dropped out of show

business for a while, running a successful restaurant near Bath. Later he too tried straight acting, as well as being master of ceremonies at old-time music-hall entertainments. Jewel, too, kept on acting, though he knew his limitations. 'One company offered me *King Lear* and *The Merchant of Venice*', he remembers, with a deadpan worthy of Jewel and Warriss at their best. 'I went out and bought both plays and couldn't understand a bloody word. It's no good doing things you won't enjoy – it's a sure bet the audience won't enjoy them either.'

Together. *1943: Rhythm Serenade. 1949: What a Carry On! 1950: Let's Have a Murder.* Jewel alone. *1970: The Man Who Had Power Over Women. 1972: Nearest and Dearest. 1984: Arthur's Hallowed Ground (TV). 1986: Rocinante. 1987: Hideaway (TV).*

JONES, Dean 1933–

Hollywood's best light comedian since Cary Grant, this brown-haired, friendly-looking, boyish singer-turned-actor threw it all up in 1980 to work for the charismatic worship movement. In his late fifties, though, Jones returned to films in telling character roles. Born in Alabama (other sources give 1930, 1935 and 1936!), Jones left home at 15 to make a career as a singer. There were few jobs around for a white blues singer in the American South of the late 1940s and Jones

found himself more often employed loading coal, cutting timber, picking cotton and washing dishes. But he did get his first engagement as a vocalist in a New Orleans nightclub, shortly before enlisting in the US Navy. (In a scenario more suited to one of his films, Jones spent four years in the navy without ever setting foot on a ship: he was assigned to an outfit operating targets for gunnery practice!) Resuming his career as a vocalist on resumption of civilian life, Jones was spotted and signed by M-G-M. But the heyday of studio musicals was over. 'I was signed as a singer', he once said. 'But my first job there was to kiss Leslie Caron (in *Gaby*). My second film (*These Wilder Years*) gave me one scene – with James Cagney. Cagney nursed me through it, and from then on the straight acting roles just grew.' Jones made more than a dozen films at the studio as a light dramatic actor before his contract lapsed. From 1960 he tried television, a medium which provided him with a key career switch when he won the leading role in the comedy series *Ensign O'Toole* (1962–3), as a junior officer who fancied himself an expert on every subject when it came to advice but who was seldom to be found when there was any actual work to be done. The series was a big hit and Jones returned to Hollywood an accredited comedy star. A profitable association with the Disney studio began in 1965, when Jones played the leading role as the allergy-beset FBI man opposite Hayley Mills in *That Darn Cat!* He would appear in nine more films for the studio, the most successful of which was undoubtedly *The Love Bug*, in which Jones was the owner of the Volkswagen car with a mind of its own. His fine, archetypally American voice (strange that he was never used for narrations) and range of facial expressions (crumpled bewilderment was the best) led to Jones making a major contribution to the studio's comedies in this period. *Snowball Express* was actually funnier (though less successful) than *The Love Bug* (and a better showcase for Jones's talents), and he appeared in one of the *Love Bug* sequels, *Herbie Goes to Monte Carlo*. Jones's conversion to religious work in the late 1970s meant that he made few films from then on. There was a sentimental TV film, *When Every Day Was the Fourth of July* (and a sequel), plus a starring role as Watergate conspirator Charles Colson in *Born Again*, the film that was supposed to open up major profits from the largely-untapped religious market, but didn't. It was 1991 before he reappeared, one of the few good things in a Danny DeVito (*qv*) misfire, *Other People's Money*. He followed that with a Charles Grodin comedy about a dog, *Beethoven*. One hopes there's time for a few more James Stewart-style harassed fathers before Jones's film comedy days are over.

1956: Gaby. These Wilder Years. The Opposite Sex. The Great American Pastime. The Rack. Somebody Up There Likes Me. Tea and

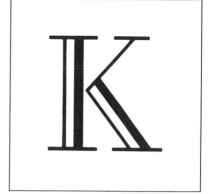

Dean Jones misses out on a welcoming kiss from screen wife Sandy Duncan in the Walt Disney comedy *Million Dollar Duck*

Sympathy. 1957: Ten Thousand Bedrooms. Designing Woman. Until They Sail. Jailhouse Rock. 1958: Handle with Care. Imitation General. Torpedo Run. 1959: Night of the Quarter Moon. Never So Few. 1963: The New Interns. Under the Yum Yum Tree. 1964: Two on a Guillotine. 1965: That Darn Cat! 1966: Any Wednesday (GB, abridged, as Bachelor Girl Apartment). The Ugly Dachshund. 1967: Monkeys, Go Home. Blackbeard's Ghost. 1968: The Horse in the Gray Flannel Suit. The Mickey Mouse Anniversary Show (narrator only). The Love Bug. 1970: Mr Superinvisible.

1971: Million Dollar Duck. The Great Man's Whiskers (TV). 1972: Snowball Express. 1973: Guess Who's Sleeping in My Bed. 1976: The Shaggy DA. 1977: Herbie Goes to Monte Carlo. Once Upon a Brothers Grimm (TV). 1978: When Every Day Was the Fourth of July (TV). Born Again. 1980: The Long Days of Summer (TV). 1991: Other People's Money. Beethoven.

JUSTICE, James Robertson
See **PHILLIPS, Leslie**

KAYE, Danny
(David Daniel Kaminsky) 1913–1987
A long-legged, anxious-looking, red-haired zany, Danny Kaye had, above all, a winning way with comic doggerel, a lot of which was woven into novelty songs. It was this talent, coupled with an engaging personality, that provided his passport to films after one failed attempt a few years earlier. Born to impoverished Russian immigrants who throughout their lives could speak no more than broken English, the gangling youth dropped out of school at 13 to become a 'clowning busboy' at summer resorts in the mountains around New York, combining waiting duties with taking part in shows. 'Those were lean years', Kaye once remembered. 'But eventually I did convince the owner of one resort that I could sing and tell jokes well enough to get a solo spot. After that, I was always trying to see Broadway producers, but I never got past the secretaries.' The lean years began to come to a close when Kaye met his future wife, Sylvia Fine, a talented lyricist with a wicked sense of humour, in 1937, after he'd been touring in revue for four years. She began to supply him with the kind of material that was to make his name. They married in 1940 and the following year Danny finally made it to Broadway as one of the stars of the musical *Lady in the Dark*. He stopped the show nightly with one of the earliest of Sylvia's tongue-twisting songs, *Tchaikowsky*,

Danny Kaye's Walter Mitty imagines himself a famous western hero in *The Secret Life of Walter Mitty*. The prairie rose is Virginia Mayo

of inspired lunacy. The next decade, however, brought *Hans Christian Andersen*, a bit dreamy and drippy in parts but with a brilliant score by Frank Loesser, and then a sparkling association with the Norman Panama—Melvin Frank team that produced the funny *Knock on Wood*, with Kaye as a ventriloquist fleeing spies, and his best film — *The Court Jester*. Kaye was able to use his mobile body in this medieval romp to demonstrate his ease and finesse with action comedy. There were catchy songs, the best supporting cast of any Kaye vehicle, and a marvellous duel with villainous Basil Rathbone in which snaps of a finger keep changing Kaye from hero to coward. But the film is justifiably best remembered for its jousting sequence, cleverly worked out and peppered with sight gags, with a side-splitting central motif in which knights Kaye and Robert Middleton are kept busy trying to keep a mental grip on the location of the pellet with the poison which one of them must drink after combat: 'The pellet with the poison's in the vessel with the pestle. The chalice from the palace has the brew that is true.' This holds good until the chalice from the palace is broken, and 'the flagon with the dragon' enters the lists. Panama and Frank had originally pinched the idea for the routine from Eddie Cantor's *Roman Scandals* in the early 1930s, and worked variations on it with two Bob Hope (*qv*) pistol duels in *Never Say Die* and *The Paleface*. Sentiment and slow pacing both played a part in the decline of Kaye's appeal to once-adoring audiences. Thankfully, neither appears in *The Court Jester*. Despite it, however, Kaye never regained the world-wide acclaim of the 1940s and only *The Man from the Diners' Club* (with a director, Frank Tashlin, who emphasised the star's zanier qualities) represented a partial return to his roots. Made in black and white on a much less lavish scale than the Goldwyn films, it's a failure that nevertheless bears re-viewing. At this point, Kaye allowed his other interests in life to take over — his work with children world-wide, and his fascination with conducting symphony orchestras. He died at 74 from a heart attack.

1937: * Dime a Dance. * Cupid Takes a Holiday. 1938: * Money on Your Life. * Getting an Eyeful. 1942: * Night Shift. 1944: Up in Arms. 1945: Wonder Man. 1946: The Kid from Brooklyn. 1947: The Secret Life of Walter Mitty. 1948: A Song is Born. 1949: The Inspector General. It's a Great Feeling. 1951: On the Riviera. 1952: Hans Christian Andersen . . . and the Dancer. 1953: Knock on Wood. 1954: * Assignment Children. White Christmas. * Hula from Hollywood. 1955: The Court Jester. 1958: Merry Andrew. Me and the Colonel. 1959: The Five Pennies. 1961: On the Double. 1963: The Man from the Diners' Club. 1969: The Madwoman of Chaillot. 1975: Peter Pan (TV). 1977: Pinocchio. 1981: Skokie (TV. GB: Once They Marched Through a Thousand Towns).

which contained the names of 50 Russian composers rattled off at bewildering speed, leaving laughing audiences little chance to distinguish fake Russian names from real. A few short films in 1937 and 1938 had led nowhere for Kaye, but now Hollywood began to think of giving him a second chance. He turned down an M-G-M contract and it was Bob Hope (*qv*) who landed the screen version of Kaye's 1942 Broadway hit *Let's Face It*. But movie mogul Sam Goldwyn had more original material in mind for Kaye and they began an often stormy nine-year partnership in 1944. Beginning with a nutty war comedy, *Up in Arms*, Kaye made some fun, funny, firecracker, free-wheeling entertainments for Goldwyn, Warners and Paramount over the next 12 years. The 1940s' films have worn less well, mixing embarrassments with moments

Jester moment. Danny Kaye's hero tries to remember that the pellet with the poison's in the vessel with the pestle. Angela Lansbury, Glynis Johns try to help him find the brew that is true in *The Court Jester*

Danny Kaye becomes involved with a circus, and refuses to take danger lion down in *Merry Andrew*. You wonder if the star may be as frightened as he looks

Way out, west. Buster Keaton displays pedal power while surveying his future in *Our Hospitality*. The pony seems destined to take little part

KAYE, Stubby 1918–

Blue-eyed and roly-poly, with seamless, un-lined features and an unquenchable good humour, Kaye is a star of the American musical-comedy stage who has occasionally lent his daft sense of humour and fine sing-ing voice to the cinema as well. A winner of the famous Major Bowes amateur contest on radio at only 20, Kaye turned pro-fessional, touring with the USO during World War Two, and entertaining in night-clubs in the late 1940s. He was also a success on the vaudeville circuit and, a natural for character comedy, made his Broadway bow in 1950 as Nicely-Nicely Johnson in *Guys and Dolls*. Besides clowning around, Kaye had the show-stopping song *Sit Down, You're Rocking the Boat*. He re-peated both performance and song in the 1955 film version. Other media rarely tempted him away from the theatre after that, although 1959 saw him play Marryin' Sam in the zany musical *Li'l Abner* (with another hit song, *Jubilation T. Cornpone*) and a running role as a songplugger in the TV comedy series *Love and Marriage*. A frequent visitor to Britain, he played Judge Mikado there in 1963 in Michael Winner's modern-dress version of Gilbert and Sullivan, *The Cool Mikado*. But a second British venture, *Cool It Carol!* was one from which he would have done better to stay away. He has con-tinued to fit occasional films into a busy schedule, one of the most recent having been the 1988 hit *Who Framed Roger Rabbit*. He played Marvin Acme, owner of the Acme Joke Company and enamoured of the cartoon vamp Jessica Rabbit. It's a pity Kaye didn't have a duet with Jessica in the film. It would surely have been a hit.

1953: Taxi. 1955: Guys and Dolls. 1956: You Can't Run Away from It. 1959: Li'l Abner. 1962: 40 Pounds of Trouble. 1963: The Cool Mikado. 1964: Sex and the Single Girl. 1965: Cat Ballou. 1967: The Way West. 1968: Sweet Charity. Can Hieronymous Merkin Ever Forget Mercy Humppe and Find True Happiness? 1969: The Cockeyed Cowboys of Calico County (GB: TV, as A Woman for Charlie). 1970: Cool It Carol! (US: The Dirtiest Girl I Ever Met). 1975: Six Pack Annie. 1981: Goldie and the Boxer Go to Hollywood (TV). 1984: Ellis Island (TV mini-series shortened for cinemas). 1988: Who Framed Roger Rabbit. The Big Knife (TV).

KEATON, Buster
(Joseph Keaton Jr) 1895–1966

Small, slight, dark, dapper American comedian (and accomplished acrobat) of slightly frowning countenance. Known as 'The Great Stone Face', Keaton was at his best during the silent days, when his inven-tiveness, filling the frame of the film with action stunts in various clever ways, was at its height. Later, circumstances combined to lead to a fall from grace. By the time that came Keaton had already spent half a life-time entertaining people. He was on stage at three with his vaudevillian parents, often stretching or contorting his body to make comic 'props' for their act. Buster soon became an expert tumbler, and the star of the trio. During the greater part of their time together (which ended in 1917) the act was known as 'Buster, assisted by Joe and Myra Keaton'. With the break-up of the act, Buster was made two offers: one for a season in a Shubert revue in New York, the other by fellow-comedian Fatty Arbuckle (qv) to come to Hollywood. Keaton became at first Arbuckle's stooge, then his junior partner and co-gagman, in a series of films running for three years (with an interruption for Keaton to do World War One military service). Physically at least, the Keaton–Arbuckle team resembled an earlier Laurel and Hardy (qv). On screen, Keaton was in charge of (and largely invented) the more surrealistic jokes, while Arbuckle dealt more in straightforward slapstick. When Arbuckle decided to move into features, Keaton was offered his own series of starring shorts by their producer, Joseph Schenk. It began a period of autonomy similar to that enjoyed later by Laurel and Hardy with Hal Roach, in that Schenk didn't interfere but let Buster get on with making films in his own way. Right from the start, these films (all shorts for four years with the exception of one feature) displayed a high degree of originality and hairsbreadth timing in the visual gags. The formula was simple: Buster would be beset, like Hamlet, by the slings and arrows of outrageous fortune, but would win through in the end, even if he never once broke into a smile. His early two-reelers include: *One Week*, in which a rival-in-love switches all the numbers on Buster's DIY housebuilding kit; *The High Sign*, in which he has to cope with a mistaken reputation as a sure shot; *The Electric House*, in which he tries unsuccessfully to cope with a house full of gadgets; *The Blacksmith*, in which he invents an assembly-line operation for out-fitting horses; *Cops*, with a wondrously-staged chase in which he's pursued by hundreds of baton-waving policemen; and *The Boat*, in which he undergoes the first of several unhappy encounters with water. In this last, Buster attempts to sail his home-made boat, having already demolished his house to get it out of the basement where he built it. Real-life disasters on the film in-cluded a boat that was designed to sink but wouldn't, and a floating boat that tended to go under at every other opportunity, taking the star with it. At one time it seemed that in most of the films he made the intrepid, perfection-seeking Keaton risked death from drowning. In his first feature after switching from shorts, *Our Hospitality*, Keaton has evaded the villains with the help of a rope still tied around him. He leaps on to the engine of a riverside train. He's caught between engine and tender as they become uncoupled, and the tender plunges into the river, becoming a makeshift boat. Buster hangs on until it shoots the rapids. Swept overboard with the rope still round him, he becomes bound up to a log. Heading down-stream at a rate of knots, Keaton and log become lodged in rocks at the top of a massive waterfall. He scrambles on to a ledge, only to see his girlfriend, who has followed him in a boat that's capsized, about to go over the falls. Swinging out on his rope at the moment she goes over, he grabs her in mid-air and hauls her to safety. Keaton remembered being less concerned at the time with the acrobatics than with the water-fall, which was man-made in the studio but had its perils. 'The big problem was that I swung out twice on the rope and turned upside-down as I caught her. When the full force of water comes down and hits you in that position, you really feel it. They had to pump me out each time I tried it, but we got there in the end.' As a film colleague of Keaton's once said, 'There wasn't anything Buster wouldn't do to set up a gag, once he was satisfied it was possible.' In *The Three Ages*, he careers down the side of a building, ultimately being projected through a window two storeys further down. Sliding across the room (it's a fire station), Keaton grabs the pole, slides down it and leaps on to the rear of a fire engine as it moves out. And while making his 1924 classic, *The Navigator*, Keaton worked in water 20 feet deep. 'You could only stay in for half-an-hour', he recalled. 'After that, you started to go numb and couldn't work properly.' One on-land sequence that gave him problems came the

The child Buster Keaton in vaudeville with his parents. The face is as expressionless as it was to be at the height of his fame

'Then I took up my place in front of the house and six powerful wind machines blew the front off. The crash was terrific. I couldn't see for dust but the shot was perfect. It was a one-take scene. You don't do these things twice.' Through all these masterpieces of ingenuity, Keaton never cracked his face, even in the quieter moments. But he could convey much by the twitch of a lip or an eyebrow, or the flicker of an eye, or by, in a rare moment of ecstasy, tossing his flat-topped boater into the air. But by 1928 the wind of change was in the air for Keaton, carrying with it the whiff of disaster. Joseph Schenk withdrew from independent production, and Keaton signed up with MGM where he soon found he had to operate the studio way, without his former freedom. The results were somewhat similar to those of Laurel and Hardy's departure from Roach a decade later, although Keaton started well enough; *The Cameraman* and *Spite Marriage* both showed many delightful touches, even if they were less individual and more cut to the studio formula. From then on, his reputation and stardom declined rapidly. *Free and Easy* is an untypical but mostly entertaining spoof on Hollywood, where Buster becomes a star. The plot was totally un-prophetic. The next, *Doughboys*, was awful, and so was everything else Keaton turned out over the next few years. Soon despairing of ever regaining his old control over his films, Keaton retreated into alcohol. His 11-year marriage to Natalie Talmadge (sister of Norma) fell apart, and they were divorced in 1932. His MGM contract was terminated the following year, primarily on account of his drinking. By 1935, Keaton was making a series of two-reel comedies for a minor company, far inferior to anything he had ever made before. The inspiration and the sparkle had completely gone. There was a brief period in a psychiatric clinic in 1937 and a further, dreadful, series of shorts for Columbia which somehow lasted until 1941. One or two of them, though, notably *Pest from the West* and *Nothing But Pleasure* (in which Buster tries to manoeuvre his car out of a tight space, unaware that the vehicle behind him has driven away) do show flashes of the Keaton of old. In 1940 he married his third wife, dancer Eleanor Norris, and the war years showed a slow climb back, if not to stardom, then to respectability, in a series of sometimes scene-stealing cameo roles in feature films. A series of live appearances at Paris's Medrano Circus from 1947 signalled the beginning of Keaton-worship that spread rapidly through France. Keaton's life, if not his career, was now back in focus. He started a television show in 1949 that ran for six months, and was much in demand for commercials, the occasional minor starring movie, guest spots in films, TV talk shows, industrial films and around-the-world travelling to host retrospectives of his films. MGM re-hired him, but tragically only as a gag-man to supply comic ideas in other people's — often Red Skelton's (*qv*) —

same year in *Sherlock Junior*. Keaton had to jump on to the handlebars of a speeding motorcycle. 'In one take', he remembered, 'I ran into a car, somersaulted through the air, and finished up with my bottom against the windscreen and legs through the roof.' Trains were often the setting for Buster's split-second feats of daredevil timing. One of his most famous silent comedies, *The General*, is an action-comedy entirely centred on one. But it's *Sherlock Junior* that contains his most brilliant and daring railroad work. Locked in the train's freeze-wagon, Keaton escapes from a skylight and runs along the train, jumping from carriage to carriage. Coming to the end of the train, he throws himself on to the chain of an overhead water-feed. His weight brings

down the feed and water cascades over him, washing him on to the track. As usual, nothing was faked and the last fall fractured Keaton's neck. But he got up and ran into the distance as per the script. Although there is great precision in all of Keaton's stuntwork — the scene of him dodging the avalanche of rocks in *Seven Chances* is an amazing piece of comic timing — his most famous dice with disaster is probably the house that falls around him in *Steamboat Bill Junior*, after he has been swept along a street in his bed by a cyclone. 'We built the front framework', Keaton told one writer, 'then laid it on the ground, and built a window space around me. We put it back on the house, and made a jagged edge where the cyclone would tear the framework away.

An all-too-apt pose for Buster Keaton for the MGM photographer in 1932. The doors were rapidly closing on his star career, and the studio let him go the following year

Inmates out. Michael Keaton (left), Peter Boyle, Stephen Furst and Christopher Lloyd are men(tal) with a mission, in *The Dream Team*

Mr Limpet (Don Knotts) talks to his favourite fellow-creatures: fish. Soon he'll become one, courtesy of some cartoon work, in *The Incredible Mr Limpet*

*Misadventures of Buster Keaton (TV, GB: cinemas). Limelight. 1952: Paradise for Buster. 1953: L'incantevole nemica. 1956: Around the World in 80 Days. 1960: The Adventures of Huckleberry Finn. 1962: Ten Girls Ago. 1963: It's a Mad, Mad, Mad, Mad World. * The Triumph of Lester Snapwell. 1964: Pajama Party. 1965: The Railrodder. Sergeant Deadhead. Buster Keaton Rides Again. Beach Blanket Bingo (GB: Malibu Beach). * Film. How to Stuff a Wild Bikini. Due Marines e uno generale (US: War Italian Style). 1966: A Funny Thing Happened on the Way to the Forum. * The Scribe.*

Also as director. *1938: * Hollywood Handicap. * Life in Sometown USA. * Streamlined Swing.*

[†]Also co-directed.
[‡] Also directed.

Keaton not making one of his own movies, but playing the title role in *The Cameraman*

comedies from 1943 to 1951, the year he appeared in support of Chaplin (*qv*) in *Limelight*. In 1960 he brought out an autobiography, *My Wonderful World of Slapstick*, and in the same year started an innovative series of TV beer commercials that worked variations on some of his best silent comedy routines. For all the activity, it was still a far cry from the glories of the 1920s. Still, at least after all the troubles Keaton managed to come up smiling or, in his case, unsmiling. He received a special Academy Award in 1959, and died from lung cancer in 1966.

*1917: * A Reckless Romeo. * The Butcher Boy * The Rough House. * His Wedding Night. * A Country Hero (released 1920). * Coney Island. * Oh Doctor! 1918: * Out West. * The Bell Boy. * Moonshine. * Good Night Nurse. * The Cook. 1919: * Love. * A Desert Hero. * Back Stage. * The Hayseed. * The Garage. 1920: * The Round Up.* [†] * One Week.* [†] * The High Sign. The Saphead. *[†] The Scarecrow.* [†] *Neighbors.* [†] *Convict 13. 1921:* [†] *Hard Luck.* [†] *The Goat.* [†] *The Boat.* [†] *The Paleface.* [†] *The Playhouse. 1922:* [†] *The Electric House.* [†] *The Frozen North.* [†] *My Wife's Relations.* [†] *The Blacksmith.* [†] *Daydreams.* [†] *Cops. 1923:* [†] *The Balloonatic.* [‡] *The Love Nest.* [†] *The Three Ages.* [†] *Our Hospitality. 1924:* [‡] *Sherlock Junior.* [†] *The Navigator. 1925:* [‡] *Seven Chances.* [‡] *Go West. 1926:* [†] *The General.* [‡] *Battling Butler. 1927: College. 1928: Steamboat Bill Junior. The Cameraman. 1929: Hollywood Revue of 1929 (and German version). Spite Marriage (and*

*French version). 1930: Free and Easy (and Spanish version). Doughboys (GB: Forward March). 1931: Parlor, Bedroom and Bath (GB: Romeo in Pyjamas. And German and French versions). Sidewalks of New York. 1932: Speak Easily. The Passionate Plumber (and French version). 1933: What! No Beer? * Hollywood on Parade A-6. 1934: Le roi des Champs-Elysées. 1935: L'horloger amoureux. The Invaders (US: An Old Spanish Custom). * La Fiesta de Santa Barbara. * Allez-Oop. * The Serenade. * The Gold Ghost. * Palooka from Paducah. * Hayseed Romance. * Stars and Stripes. * The E Flat Man. * One Run Elmer. 1936: * The Timid Young Man. * Three on a Limb. * Grand Slam Opera. * Blue Blazes. * The Chemist. Three Men on a Horse. * Mixed Magic. 1937: * Jail Bait. * Ditto. * Love Nest on Wheels. 1939: * Pest from the West. * Mooching through Georgia. The Jones Family in Hollywood. Hollywood Cavalcade. * Nothing But Pleasure. The Jones Family in Quick Millions. 1940: Li'l Abner (GB: Trouble Chaser). The Villain Still Pursued Her. * Pardon My Berth Marks. * The Spook Speaks. * The Taming of the Snood. New Moon (most scenes deleted). 1941: * His Ex Marks the Spot. * General Nuisance. * She's Oil Mine. * So You Won't Squawk. 1943: Forever and a Day. 1944: San Diego, I Love You. Two Girls and a Sailor (most scenes deleted). 1945: That Night with You. That's the Spirit. 1946: God's Country. El moderno Barba Azul. 1948: Un duel à mort. 1949: In the Good Old Summertime. The Lovable Cheat. You're My Everything. 1950: Sunset Boulevard. 1951: The*

KEATON, Michael
(M. Douglas) 1951–

At the inception of this book Michael Keaton's place looked secure. A few years on, and it seems marginal at best. A former stand-up comedian, he made his name as a comic actor of wild energy, then sought to widen his range with demanding straight roles, in some of which he has been highly effective. Keaton will need no reminding, though, that his major successes have all been in comedy. Of medium height and build, with receding fluffy dark hair, and the youngest of seven children from a Pittsburgh suburb, he studied speech at university, then went 'underground' as a local entertainer at Pittsburgh coffee-houses (one of his partners was Louis, the Dancing Chicken). Moving to Los Angeles in his mid twenties, he gained experience in comedy routines with the Comedy Store and the Second City Improvisational Workshop. He broke into TV in 1977 in the series *All's Fair*, as a super-hip presidential joke writer called Lanny Wolf. Two years later, he teamed with John Belushi's brother Jim in another series, *Working Stiffs*, about two Chicago janitors. It didn't run to more than a season, but Keaton had more luck with 'stiffs' in his first film, *Night Shift*, which was set in a mortuary. As an extraordinary wheeler-dealer called Billy Blaze, Keaton helped glum mortuary keeper Henry Winkler set

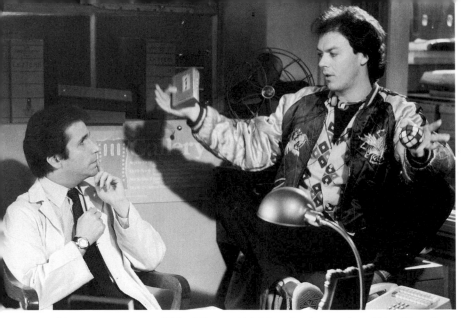

Mortuary entrepreneur Michael Keaton (right) launches into another of his wild profit-making schemes. Morgue-keeper Henry Winkler has yet to be convinced. From *Night Shift*.

up a call-girl racket from his land of slabs. It did unexpectedly well in America, but was pulled from a British release after preview – not the last time this would happen to a Keaton movie. The next one, *Mr Mom*, just about surfaced outside the United States where it was phenomenally successful, leading Keaton to be offered two other starring roles – in *Splash* and *Johnny Dangerously*. He chose the wrong one. The former made stars out of Tom Hanks (*qv*) and Daryl Hannah. The latter, a gangster comedy, began brightly and continued to have its moments, mainly thanks to Keaton's performance in the lead. He fell out with Mia Farrow and Woody Allen (*qv*), and left *The Purple Rose of Cairo* after only three days, but found a better comedy role in *Gung Ho*, the story of the culture clashes that result from Japanese taking over an American car factory. A dramatic role in *Touch and Go* was unsuccessful, and *The Squeeze* gave him a rare strike-out in comedy, so he needed the hit he got as *Beetlejuice*, playing a demented phantom (in *Drop Dead Fred*-style get-up) who helps two young fellow-ghosts rid their manse of unwelcome occupants. Keaton's manic antics as the 'bio-exorciser' were practically the whole show. Since then the only Keaton films seen widely outside America have been *The Dream Team* (his last comedy), *Pacific Heights* and the *Batman* sagas – playing the title role, although in the first film he would have seemed to have been better cast as the Joker, eventually played by Jack Nicholson. Distributors seemingly remain nervous of Keaton as a solo attraction, and even his eye-catching villain in *Pacific Heights* (a nastier outlet for his nervous energy) saw him, as in *Beetlejuice*, billed below the stars. Once a 'hot number' with actress Michelle

Pfeiffer, Keaton married actress Caroline McWilliams. The couple were recently divorced and Keaton picked up his relationship with Pfeiffer again after they co-starred in *Batman Returns*. Perhaps they could even try a comedy together.

1982: Night Shift. 1983: Mr Mom (GB: Mr Mum). 1984: Johnny Dangerously. 1985: Touch and Go. 1986: Gung Ho. 1987: The Squeeze. 1988: Beetlejuice. Clean and Sober. 1989: The Dream Team. Batman. 1990: Pacific Heights. 1991: One Good Cop. 1992: Batman Returns.

KELLY, Patsy
(Sarah Kelly) 1910–1981

Dumpy, diminutive, dark-haired, raucous-voiced American dancer and comedienne who was the daughter of a genuine, Irish-born, Manhattan policeman called Kelly. The likeable Kelly had her troubles off screen but, often with the help of her many friends, always bounced back. The dynamic

Patsy was at dancing school at ten, having been forced to give up an early ambition to be a fireman. Three years later she was the school's youngest instructor. She was on stage at 16 when auditioner Frank Fay (later to marry Barbara Stanwyck) preferred her to the Kelly brother she had come to help. She stayed with Fay for two years. Then a stint with a Will Rogers (*qv*) show on Broadway, *Three Cheers*, established her as a singing and dancing funny girl. Patsy had only flirted with films when an offer came in from Hal Roach to star in two-reel comedy shorts. His popular team of Thelma Todd and ZaSu Pitts (both *qv*) had been broken up when ZaSu left to do more feature film work. With the help of a pay rise, Todd was persuaded to remain and take on a new partner. The big-eyed, flap-eared, wise-cracking Patsy proved an ideal partner for the glamorous Thelma, and they made 21 films together between 1933 and Todd's 'mystery' death in December 1935. They usually played working girls whose attempts to climb the social ladder ended in what Laurel and Hardy (*qv*) would have called another nice mess. Patsy was obviously a natural for comic character roles in Hollywood films – although she showed in one film, *Kelly the Second* (the Kelly of the title was a boxer), that she could handle a sympathetic lead as well. Soon, though, she was an expert at playing cynical domestics in support of the stars. The biggest problem for the peppy Patsy's career was that she never found herself in a really good film. After 1943 she left Hollywood to sort out 'personal problems'. Although not a front-runner on the social scene, she had developed into a hard-drinking Kelly. Her sex life was somewhat secretive, although her lengthy relationship with Tallulah Bankhead caused a few raised eyebrows in its time. Patsy Kelly's disappearance (following five years of doing not very much) into road-show tours of musical comedies was a great loss to the cinema, a medium to which she didn't return until 1960. Her biggest triumph, however, was yet to come, when she co-starred in 1971 with childhood friend Ruby Keeler (they attended the same dancing school) in the smash-hit Broadway revival of *No, No, Nanette*, which ran for well over two years. The 'two old bags' (Kelly's description) were a roaring success. Patsy, of course, played a maid. One line from the show summed up most of her 'domestic' roles in films. 'You name it', she squawked, 'and I've cleaned it!' She died from cancer at 71.

*1929: A Single Man. 1931: * The Grand Dame. 1933: Going Hollywood. * Beauty and the Bus. * Air Fright. * Backs to Nature. 1934: * Maid in Hollywood. * Soup and Fish. The Countess of Monte Cristo. The Party's Over. * Babes in the Goods. * I'll Be Suing You. * Roaming Vandals. The Girl from Missouri (GB: 100 Per Cent Pure). * Three Chumps Ahead. Transatlantic Merry-Go-Round.*

Opened by Mistake. * *One Horse Farmers.* * *Done in Oil.* * *Bum Voyage* (GB: *Bon Voyage*). 1935: * *Treasure Blues.* * *The Tin Man.* * *Sing, Sister, Sing. Go into Your Dance* (GB: *Casino de Paree*). *Every Night at Eight. Page Miss Glory. Thanks a Million.* * *The Misses Stooge.* * *Slightly Static.* * *Top Flat.* * *Hot Money.* * *Twin Triplets.* * *All American Toothache.* 1936: *Private Number. Kelly the Second. Sing, Baby, Sing. Pigskin Parade* (GB: *Harmony Parade*). * *Pan Handlers.* * *Hill-Tillies.* * *At Sea Ashore.* 1937: *Nobody's Baby. Wake Up and Live. Pick a Star. Ever Since Eve.* 1938: *Merrily We Live. There Goes My Heart. The Cowboy and the Lady.* 1939: *The Gorilla.* 1940: *Hit Parade of 1941.* * *The Happiest Man on Earth. Road Show.* 1941: *Topper Returns. Broadway Limited.* 1942: *Playmates. Sing Your Worries Away. In Old California.* * *Screen Snapshots No. 99.* 1943: *My Son, the Hero. Ladies' Day. Danger! Women at Work.* 1947: * *Babies, They're Wonderful.* 1960: *Please Don't Eat the Daisies. The Crowded Sky.* 1964: *The Naked Kiss.* 1966: *Ghost in the Invisible Bikini.* 1967: *C'mon, Let's Live a Little.* 1968: *Rosemary's Baby.* 1969: *The Pigeon* (TV). *The Phynx.* 1976: *Freaky Friday.* 1978: *North Avenue Irregulars* (GB: *Hill's Angels*).

KENNEDY, Edgar 1890–1948
There was nothing subtle about pinkly bald Edgar Kennedy. He was always the same — exaggeratedly affable as a friend and quick to explode in times of trouble. Often an embarrassment in feature films, he was at his best in two-reelers, whether the butt of Laurel and Hardy's (*qv*) antics, or the star of the show as the average man whose do-it-yourself ideas end in disaster. In Laurel and Hardy's world he was usually a perplexed policeman, scratching his head in his efforts to unravel their latest chapter of cataclysmic chaos, though many remember him only as the gouty uncle whose bandaged foot is frequently to get their car going for a picnic in *Perfect Day.* It was during their association that Kennedy perfected his horrified reaction to their antics, which he called a 'slow burn', involving a delayed and emphasised reaction as the full ridiculous impact of the

situation sunk into his character's addled brain. He also directed a couple of their best shorts, as 'E. Livingston Kennedy'. Born in California, Kennedy began as a 'singing clown' in minstrel shows and vaudeville. His fluffy hair was already a thing of the past when he joined the Keystone studio towards the end of 1913. He played character roles in short comedies starring Mabel Normand, Charlie Chaplin and Fatty Arbuckle (all *qv*) and even served time as a Keystone Cop. But it wasn't until he joined the Hal Roach studio's 'All Star Comedies' in 1927 that Kennedy settled into Hollywood as a comedy star. From 1931 he starred in his own long-running series of comedy two-reelers at RKO, as 'The Average Man', an all-American chump, beset by foolish chatterbox wife, nagging mother-in-law and ne'er-do-well brother-in-law. These were fast-moving little pieces, buoyed up by the bumbling personality of Kennedy and the diverting dizziness of his wife, Florence Lake. Early in the series Kennedy's famous slow burn received a decorative variation in the form of a follow-up, involving a gesture of despair, glaring unbelievingly between his outstretched fingers as he passed his hand across his face — before exploding in a paroxysm of rage at the film's fadeout. Lake's departure from the series in 1937 proved quite a blow, and she returned in 1944 at the same time as a new director, Hal Yates. Yates had worked with Laurel and Hardy, and brought a new pace to the series, which now gave out with some of its best entries, including *Sleepless Tuesday,* an inspired, inventively sustained piece of foolishness in which Edgar is beset by his mother-in-law's radio. He attempts to sabotage it and fails, seizes it, has to get it back when he thinks there is money in it and finally smashes it to pieces (the tubes play *Stars and Stripes Forever* as they're smashed one by one) only to have his moment of triumph choked off as we see mother-in-law ordering a new radio even after 'The End' has appeared on screen. After he'd made more than a hundred of these shorts, the industry was shocked to hear that the popular Kennedy was suffering from terminal throat cancer. A testimonial dinner was arranged, ostensibly to celebrate his 35 years in films on 10 November 1948 — but he died 36 hours before it was due to be held.

1912: *Hoffmeyer's Legacy.* 1913: * *Mabel's Dramatic Career.* 1914: * *The Star Boarder.* * *Twenty Minutes of Love.* * *Caught in a Cabaret.* * *Those Love Pangs.* * *Dough and Dynamite.* * *Gentlemen of Nerve.* * *The Knockout. Tillie's Punctured Romance.* * *Our Country Cousin.* * *The Noise of Bombs.* * *Getting Acquainted.* 1915: * *A Game Old Knight.* * *The Great Vacuum Robbery.* * *Fatty's Tin Type Tangle.* * *Fickle Fatty's Fall.* 1916: * *His Hereafter.* * *His Bitter Pill.* * *Madcap Ambrose.* * *A Scoundrel's Tale.* * *Bombs.* * *Ambrose's Cup of Woe.* * *Bucking Society.* 1917: * *Her Fame and Shame.* * *Her Torpedoed Love.*

* *Oriental Love.* 1918: * *She Loved Him Plenty.* 1921: *Skirts.* 1922: *The Leather Pushers.* 1924: *The Night Message. The Battling Fool.* 1925: *Proud Heart/His People. The Golden Princess.* * *The Marriage Circus.* 1926: *My Old Dutch. The Better 'Ole. Across the Pacific. Going Crooked. Oh! What a Nurse.* 1927: * *Wedding Bills.* * *The Wrong Mr Right. Finger Prints. The Chinese Parrot.* 1928: * *A Pair of Tights.* * *Two Tars.* * *The Finishing Touch.* * *Leave 'Em Laughing.* * *The Family Group.* * *Limousine Love.* * *The Fight Pest.* * *Imagine My Embarrassment.* * *Is Everybody Happy?* (GB: *Everybody Happy?*). * *All Parts.* * *The Booster.* * *Chasing Husbands.* * *Should Married Men Go Home?* 1929: * *Moan and Groan Inc.* * *Great Gobs.* * *Hotter Than Hot.* * *Bacon Grabbers.* * *Dad's Day.* * *Hurdy Gurdy.* * *Unaccustomed As We Are.* * *Perfect Day. Angora Love. Trent's Last Case. They Had to See Paris. The Gay Old Bird. Going Crooked* (and 1926 film). * *Why Is a Plumber?* * *Thundering Toupees.* * *Off to Buffalo.* * *Dumb Daddies.* 1930: * *Night Owls.* * *The First Seven Years.* * *Shivering Shakespeare.* * *When the Wind Blows.* * *The Real McCoy.* * *All Teed Up.* * *Fifty Million Husbands.* * *Dollar Dizzy.* * *Girl Shock.* * *Looser Than Loose.* * *The Head Guy.* * *The Big Kick.* * *Bigger and Better.* * *Doctor's Orders.* * *Ladies Last.* 1931: * *All Gummed Up. Bad Company.* * *The Midnight Patrol.* * *High Gear.* * *Love Fever.* * *Lemon Meringue.* * *Rough House Rhythm.* * *Thanks Again.* * *Camping Out.* 1932: * *Parlor, Bedroom and Wrath.* * *Mother-in-Law's Day.* * *Bon Voyage.* * *Giggle Water.* * *The Golf Chump.* * *Fish Feathers.* * *Never the Twins Shall Meet. Carnival Boat. Hold 'Em Jail! Westward Passage. Rockabye. The Penguin Pool Murder* (GB: *The Penguin Pool Mystery*). *Little Orphan Annie.* 1933: * *Kickin' the Crown Around.* * *Art in the Raw.* * *The Merchant of Menace.* * *Good Housewrecking.* * *Quiet, Please.* * *What Fur.* * *Grin and Bear It. Professional Sweetheart. Duck Soup. Tillie and Gus. Scarlet River. Crossfire. Son of the Border.* 1934: * *Wrong Direction.* * *In-Laws Are Out.* * *Love on a Ladder.* * *A Blasted Event.* * *Poisoned Ivory. Kid Millions. All of Me. Twentieth Century. Flirting with Danger. Heat Lightning. Murder on the Blackboard. The Silver Streak. We're Rich Again. Money Means Nothing. Gridiron Flash* (GB: *Luck of the Game*). *King Kelly of the USA. The Marines Are Coming.* * *Brick-a-Brac.* 1935: * *A Night at the Biltmore Bowl.* * *South Seasickness.* * *Edgar Hamlet.* * *Sock Me to Sleep.* * *Happy Tho' Married.* * *In Love at 40.* * *Gobs of Trouble* (GB: *Navy Blues*). *The Cowboy Millionaire. Living on Velvet. Little Big Shot. Woman Wanted. In Person. $1,000 a Minute. The Bride Comes Home. Rendezvous at Midnight.* 1936: * *Gasaloons.* * *Will Power.* * *High Beer Pressure.* * *Vocalising.* * *Dummy Ache.* * *The Return of Jimmy Valentine. Three Men on a Horse. Small Town Girl. Mad Holiday. Fatal Lady. San Francisco. Yours for the Asking. Robin Hood of El Dorado.* 1937: * *Locks and Bonds.* * *Bad Housekeeping.* * *Dumb's the Word.* * *Hillbilly Goat.* * *Tramp*

Trouble. * Morning, Judge. * Edgar and Goliath. A Star is Born. When's Your Birthday? Super Sleuth. Double Wedding. True Confession. Hollywood Hotel. 1938: Hey! Hey! USA. Peck's Bad Boy with the Circus. The Black Doll. Scandal Street. * Beaux and Errors. * Ears of Experience. * False Roomers. * Kennedy's Castle. * Fool Coverage. * A Clean Sweep. 1939: * Maid to Order. * Kennedy the Great. * Clock Wise. * Baby Daze. * Feathered Pests. * Act Your Age. Little Accident. Everything's on Ice. Charlie McCarthy, Detective. Laugh It Off (GB: Lady Be Gay). It's a Wonderful World. 1940: * Mutiny in the County. * Slightly at Sea. * 'Taint Legal. * Sunk by the Census. * Trailer Tragedy. Dr Christian Meets the Women. Sandy is a Lady. The Quarterback. Margie. Remedy for Riches. Li'l Abner. Who Killed Aunt Maggie? Sandy Gets Her Man. 1941: * Drafted in the Depot. * It Happened All Night. * Mad About Moonshine. * An Apple in His Eye. * Westward Ho-Hum. * I'll Fix That. * A Quiet Fourth. Public Enemies. Blondie in Society (GB: Henpecked). The Bride Wore Crutches. 1942: Snuffy Smith, Yard Bird (GB: Snuffy Smith). Pardon My Stripes. There's One Born Every Minute. In Old California. Hillbilly Blitzkrieg. * Cooks and Crooks. * Inferior Decorator. * Heart Burn. * Two for the Money. * Duck Soup (and 1933 feature). * Rough on Rents. 1943: Cosmo Jones – Crime Smasher (GB: Crime Smasher). The Falcon Strikes Back. Air Raid Wardens. Hitler's Madman. The Girl from Monterey. Crazy House. * Hold Your Temper. * Indian Signs. * Hot Foot. * Not on My Account. * Unlucky Dog. * Prunes and Politics. 1944: * Love Your Landlord. * Radio Rampage. * The Kitchen Cynic. * Feather Your Nest. It Happened Tomorrow. The Great Alaskan Mystery (serial). 1945: * Alibi Baby. Anchors Aweigh. Captain Tugboat Annie. * You Drive Me Crazy. * Sleepless Tuesday. * What? No Cigarettes? * It's Your Move. * The Big Beef. * Mother-in-Law's Day (remake). 1946: Noisy Neighbors. * Wall Street Blues. * I'll Build It Myself. * Trouble or Nothing. * Social Terrors. The Sin of Harold Diddlebock (later and GB: Mad Wednesday!). * Do or Diet. 1947: * Heading for Trouble. * Television Turmoil. * Mind over Mouse. * Host to a Ghost. Heaven Only Knows. 1948: Variety Times. Unfaithfully Yours. * No More Relatives. * Brother Knows Best. * How to Clean House. * Dig That Gold. * Home Canning. * Contest Crazy. 1949: My Dream Is Yours.
As director (as E. Livingston Kennedy). 1925: † * The Marriage Circus. * Cupid's Boots. 1928: * From Soup to Nuts. * You're Darn Tootin' (GB: The Music Blasters). 1930: * All Teed Up. † Fifty Million Husbands. * Bigger and Better.

† Co-directed.

KNOTTS, Don 1924–

An undernourished-looking, dark-haired American comedian, with prominent lips, fish eyes, a squawk of a voice and (in his film and TV roles) an anxious, agitatedly nervous

manner. Very popular on TV, Knotts tried time and again to find a successful film vehicle, but never did. He was born in West Virginia and entered show business during his service with the US Army, when he became part of a show called Stars and Grapes. Offered a teaching fellowship on his release from the forces, Knotts opted instead to head for New York, where he began his professional career as a comedy ventriloquist. More nightclub and radio work followed, before he made his Broadway debut in the farce No Time for Sergeants, starring Andy Griffith; both re-created their roles in the film version in 1958, and struck up a friendship that led to Knotts being hired in 1960 as co-star on TV's The Andy Griffith Show. Knotts won three successive Emmy awards for his portrayal of Barney Fife, the

hyper-tense, inept deputy to Griffith's small-town sheriff. Don stayed with the show for six years, the meanwhile building up one or two more film credits. He scored a hit as the shoe salesman in Doris Day's Move Over, Darling, and tried his first starring comedy in The Incredible Mr Limpet, a mixture of comedy and cartoon that remains probably his most successful venture as solo star. With his departure from The Andy Griffith Show, Knotts signed up with Universal for a series of starring comedies. But there were two big problems: the material was weak and the films, at 100 minutes-plus, were all too long. Modestly successful in America, the films were released as second-features in other countries. Probably the best of them was The Shakiest Gun in the West, although that had been far funnier 20 years earlier as The Paleface. The series ended damply with How to Frame a Figg in 1971. After a run of his own show on television, Knotts joined forces with the Disney studio in a series of comedies that teamed him with other light comedians, most notably busy, buzzy little Tim Conway, who co-starred with him in four of them. Again the most successful was the first, The Apple Dumpling Gang, with Knotts and Conway as bungling western outlaws. These sidekick roles typically had Knotts, as before, soon disintegrating into dithering panic. There were two more comic westerns, Hot Lead and Cold Feet and The Apple Dumpling Gang Rides Again, and the series ended on quite a high note with The Private Eyes, casting Knotts

Wheely (Don Knotts) thinks twice about taking the short route down the mountain in Disney's Herbie Goes to Monte Carlo. The driver is Dean Jones.

and Conway as defective detectives caught up in an old-dark-house mystery, allowing Knotts plenty of room for his imitation of a petrified parrot. Knotts' most recent on-screen performance was a delightful one — back in his old role of Barney Fife in *Return to Mayberry*, a nostalgic update of *The Andy Griffith Show*. It had Knotts and Griffith running against each other for sheriff and reunited 16 actors from the original series.

1958: No Time for Sergeants. 1960: Wake Me When It's Over. 1961: The Last Time I Saw Archie. 1963: Move Over, Darling. The Incredible Mr Limpet. It's a Mad, Mad, Mad, Mad World. 1966: The Ghost and Mr Chicken. 1967: The Reluctant Astronaut. I Love a Mystery (TV). 1968: The Shakiest Gun in the West. 1969: The Love God? 1971: How to Frame a Figg. 1974: The Apple Dumpling Gang. 1976: No Deposit, No Return. Gus. 1977: Herbie Goes to Monte Carlo. 1978: Hot Lead and Cold Feet. 1979: The Apple Dumpling Gang Rides Again. The Prize Fighter. 1980: The Private Eyes. 1983: Cannonball Run II. 1986: Return to Mayberry (TV). 1987: Pinocchio and the Emperor of the Night (voice only).

KOVACS, Ernie 1919–1962

Inscribed on Kovacs' tombstone, following his death in a car crash at the age of 42, are the words 'Nothing in Moderation'. The comedian's epitaph summed up one of the most extravagant lifestyles of Hollywood; Kovacs' high life left his widow with tax and gambling debts of around $600,000. But he was funny; of that there's no doubt. In a custard-pie and yet intellectual way, and always explosive, whether starring in a TV comedy series or playing top comedy character roles — often as blustering, comic villains — in his too-few films. You even expected the huge cigar which the dark-haired, moustachioed, wolfishly-smiling Kovacs smoked most of the time to explode at any minute. He was born in New Jersey to Hungarian immigrants, and studied to be a straight actor at the American Academy of Dramatic Art in Manhattan. Kovacs almost died in 1940 from a combination of pleurisy and penumonia but recovered to become

the barnstorming young head of a group of travelling players, producing such blood-curdlers as *Dr Jekyll and Mr Hyde*. From 1942 to 1950, Kovacs worked for radio, beginning as an announcer but building a reputation for zany outside broadcasts that included such lunatic and hair-raising scrapes as lying on a railway line waiting for the train to come. His TV debut in 1950 was quickly followed by his first nationwide show, *Kovacs on the Corner*. The vocalist and leading lady on the show was Edie (then still Edith) Adams (*qv*), who became Kovacs' second wife (his first marriage had ended in 1949) in 1954. Kovacs and Adams went on to share more TV comedy shows, including *It's Time for Ernie, Ernie in Kovacsland, Kovacs Unlimited* and finally, inevitably, *The Ernie Kovacs Show*. In 1957 Kovacs won an Emmy for a TV show done entirely without dialogue, and was consequently offered a film contract by Columbia. His first movie was *Operation Mad Ball* (the first of several collaborations with Jack Lemmon, *qv*) as the loudmouthed, blowhard army captain who must be deceived as to the location of the ball of the title. He was an alcoholic author writing an exposé of witchcraft in Manhattan in *Bell, Book and Candle*, and then beautifully cast as 'the meanest man in the world' in the underrated frolic *It Happened to Jane*, trying to prevent Doris Day from getting her lobsters to market. Both of these films were with Lemmon, who might have co-starred again in later years with Kovacs, had he lived, in roles that would eventually be played by Walter Matthau. Undoubtedly, Kovacs and Lemmon would have made a great team in *The Odd Couple*. Lemmon thought Kovacs 'a man of immense talent'. When he made *Our Man in Havana* in 1959 one critic described him as 'Clark Gable with fangs . . . the perfect comedy menace'. Kovacs proved himself a useful straight actor in *Strangers When We Meet*, and deserved rather better for his first starring vehicle than the British *Five Golden Hours*, even though its director Mario Zampi had had a string of comedy hits in Britain. While continuing to be happier with the freedom he was allowed on television, Kovacs was nonetheless nego-tiating a deal to make another film with his *Havana* co-star Alec Guinness (*qv*) at the time of his sudden death. He was on his way home from a party on a wet January night when his station wagon skidded and crashed into a pole, fracturing his skull. One Hollywood paper noted that 'his zany tricks have never been matched . . . for Kovacs, living up to expectations was always a breeze'.

*1957: Operation Mad Ball. Topaze (TV). 1958: Bell, Book and Candle. * Showdown at Ulcer Gulch. 1959: It Happened to Jane (That Jane from Maine/Twinkle and Shine). Our Man in Havana. 1960: Wake Me When It's Over. Strangers When We Meet. Pepe. North to Alaska. 1961: Five Golden Hours. Sail a Crooked Ship.*

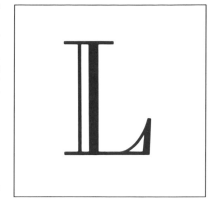

LAHR, Bert
(Irving Lahrheim) 1895–1967

The Cowardly Lion, of course. But, that role apart, Hollywood could hardly have been said to have made the most of this popular vaudevillian with his wonderfully expressive New Yorker's face and wry, engaging smile; he would have been per-fectly cast as a singing cabbie. But then Lahr loved performing on a live stage so maybe he wasn't too sorry that films so seldom beckoned. Dark-haired and pale-eyed with small, round features and a lopsided crescent grin, he left school at 15 to become one of the Seven Frolics. Lahr became a popular fool on the vaudeville and burlesque circuits in the 1920s, with a facility for accents and vocal gyrations, tempered by an inimitable gurgling laugh. He'd moved into Broadway revue by 1927, and proved a big hit in such shows as *George White's Music Hall Varieties*. Not very tall (around 5 ft 5 in), but jack-in-the-box bouncy, Lahr seemed a natural for starring roles in Holly-wood shorts and cameo roles in musical comedy. In fact, he had made only three two-reelers and seven feature films (and hadn't done a stage show for three years) when M-G-M plucked the little man from the threat of obscurity in 1939 and put him inside the lion's costume for *The Wizard of Oz*. Later the same year Lahr enjoyed one of his greatest stage successes in a dual role in the comedy-musical *Du Barry Was a Lady*, missing out on the subsequent film version, which was still enjoyable even after unfortunately ditching the original Cole Porter score. There were few further opportunities in films for this hobgoblin of humour. He had some good (but too few) comedy scenes with Marjorie Main (*qv*) in *Rose Marie*, which cast him as an unlikely Mountie, teamed with fellow top vaudeville comic Ed Wynn (*qv*) (who had a better rub of the film genie's lamp with his Disney character roles) in TV's *The Greatest Man Alive* and bade a nostalgic farewell in *The Night They Raided Minsky's*, a tribute to old-time burlesque (and indirectly to Lahr himself), dying (from an internal haemorrhage) before it was completed. Three years earlier he had triumphed in another of his favourite shows, *Foxy*, at his home-from-home, the Ziegfeld Theatre on Broadway. He was a man who always brought a smile to your face − with or without the lion's whiskers.

*1929: * Faint Heart. 1931: Flying High (GB: Happy Landing). 1933: Mr Broadway. 1934: * Hizzoner. 1936: * Gold Bricks. 1937: Merry-Go-Round of 1938. Love and Hisses. 1938: Just Around the Corner. Josette. 1939: Zaza. The Wizard of Oz. 1942: Sing Your Worries Away. Ship Ahoy. 1944: Meet the People. 1949: Always Leave Them Laughing. 1951: Mr Universe. 1954: Rose Marie. 1955: The Great Waltz (TV). The Second Greatest Sex. 1962: Ten Girls Ago. 1965: The Fantasticks (voice only). 1966: Thompson's Ghost (TV). 1968: The Night They Raided Minsky's.*

LAKE, Arthur
(A. Silverlake) 1905−
American comic actor with dark, rumpled hair, round face, squeaky voice and a baffled, sometimes desperate expression. His speciality was the All-American idiot. For millions this reached its finest representation in his long-running creation of Dagwood Bumstead in the *Blondie* films. Lake was in show business from childhood, and once said that it took him 30 years to become an overnight success. His father was a circus acrobat and his mother a legitimate actress. He appeared with one or the other throughout his childhood, and his mother was re-

sponsible for his screen debut when she got him a role in a 1917 film of *Jack and the Beanstalk*. Becoming a light actor, often in comedy, after leaving school, Lake soon began playing the odd role in films. His early ambitions to be a star comedian came and went with a moderately popular short series of two-reel comedies at the beginning of sound. Thereafter he was often to be found playing juveniles, even into his late twenties. The big break came in 1938, when the tall, gangling-limbed Lake was cast as the screen incarnation of the disaster-prone strip-cartoon character Dagwood, created by Chic Young, and married to Blondie (Penny Singleton), the greatest scatterbrain of all time. Their adventures were sufficiently rooted in reality, and the characters so familiar and well-loved through the pages of newspapers, that the Bumstead family's first adventure was an immense popular success. Costing less than $100,000, it grossed almost $10 million. Dagwood, Blondie, Daisy the Dog and Baby Dumpling (a role that saw Larry Simms grow up with the series) were clearly on the film scene to stay, as was Lake's croaky cry of 'Blond-eee!' at each fresh disaster. In fact the Blondie comedies became one of the longest-running series of all time, lasting 13 years and 28 more films. Lake was superbly in character throughout, one of the best transfers of a character from strip cartoon to live cinema on record. The series ended in 1950, and so did Lake's film career, producers being unwilling to see him in any other role. He even revived the character for a nine-month television series (with Pamela Britton as Blondie) in 1957. Lake proved himself right when he once said: 'When I don't play a dope, I don't work.' After that Lake, a careful investor, retired from the show business scene to enjoy life with his wife Patricia, niece of film star Marion Davies. He returned just once − for a short stage run of the musical *No, No, Nanette*, opposite his old Blondie sparring-partner Penny Singleton (*qv*).

*1917: Jack and the Beanstalk. Aladdin and the Wonderful Lamp. 1925: Where Was I? Sporting Life. 1926: Skinner's Dress Suit. 1927: The Cradle Snatchers. The Irresistible Lover. 1928: Stop That Man. The Count of Ten. Harold Teen. The Air Circus. Lilac Time. 1929: On with the Show! Dance Hall. Tanned Legs. * Doing His Stuff. * Night Owls. * His Girl's Wedding. 1930: * Some Show. * Her Bashful Beau. * Follow Me. Cheer Up and Smile. She's My Weakness. 1931: Indiscreet. 1933: Midshipman Jack. 1934: The Silver Streak. Girl o' My Dreams. * Glad to Beat You. 1935: Women Must Dress. Orchids to You. 1936: I Cover Chinatown. 1937: Annapolis Salute (GB: Salute to Romance). 23¹/₂ Hours Leave. Topper. Exiled to Shanghai. True Confession. 1938: Double Danger. Everybody's Doing It. There Goes My Heart. Blondie. 1939: Blondie Meets the Boss. Blondie Brings Up Baby. Blondie Takes a Vacation. 1940: Blondie on a Budget.*

Blondie Has Servant Trouble. Blondie Plays Cupid. 1941: Blondie Goes Latin (GB: Conga Swing). Blondie in Society (GB: Henpecked). 1942: Blondie for Victory (GB: Troubles Through Billets). Blondie Goes to College (GB: The Boss Said 'No'). Blondie's Blessed Event. (GB: A Bundle of Trouble). The Daring Young Man. 1943: Footlight Glamour. It's a Great Life. 1944: Sailor's Holiday. The Ghost That Walks Alone. Three is a Family. 1945: The Big Show-Off. Life with Blondie. Leave It to Blondie. 1946: Blondie's Lucky Day. Blondie Knows Best. Blondie's Big Moment. 1947: Blondie's Holiday. Blondie in the Dough. Blondie's Anniversary. 1948: Blondie's Secret. Blondie's Reward. 16 Fathoms Deep. 1949: Blondie Hits the Jackpot (GB: Hitting the Jackpot. Blondie's Big Deal (GB: The Big Deal). 1950: Beware of Blondie. Blondie's Hero.

LAMB, Gil 1904−
A spike-nosed, giraffe-legged, rubber-faced American comic and eccentric dancer with dark, curly hair, darting brown eyes and a prominent Adam's apple. Film studios seemed unwilling to take a chance on the energetic Lamb as a solo attraction, and he was confined to comic support in features and starring roles in two-reelers. But he stayed on the fringes of Hollywood, and the Disney studio later used him in a few comic cameo roles. Born in Minneapolis of French and English parentage, the tall, rangy Lamb was a music-mad youth who studied clarinet, saxophone and oboe in his spare time at night. After leaving college, he soon found himself a place in a dance band based in Chicago, and stayed with them until 1925. After leaving the band, he joined a vaudeville act as a saxophone player, and wound up in New York. Later he took to clowning with a harmonica, and developed a solo pantomime act in which he tangled himself up with a stage-full of musical instruments. As a novelty comedy act, he finally made it to Broadway in the late 1930s as part of Al Jolson's show *Hold on to Your Hats*. Before war broke out in Europe, Lamb went on a tour there, taking in Paris and Berlin − and London, where he looked up relatives. But he was back in America when Paramount signed him up for films in 1941. He still had

plenty of time for stage work, for the studio only used him in five films in four years — mostly as hayseeds or idiots, in harness with such contemporaries as Cass Daley and Eddie Bracken (both *qv*). In 1949 Lamb found a new home with RKO, who signed him to star in short comedies. These were strictly programme-fillers but they did make more of Lamb's physical dexterity than his feature films, gave him a chance to show he could be a fine, flapping panicker, and handed him decent co-stars in Carol Hughes, Claire Carleton and Andy Clyde (*qv*). The series lasted four years. A TV enterprise in the early 1950s, *The Gil Lamb Show*, was unsuccessful, and Gil returned to entertaining on a live stage, knocking them in the aisles with his musical instrument routine. Every now and again, when Hollywood needed a distinctively eccentric player for a minor appearance, films beckoned again, and the comedian remained active well into his seventies.

*1942: The Fleet's In. Star Spangled Rhythm. 1943: Riding High (GB: Melody Inn). 1944: Rainbow Island. 1945: Practically Yours. 1947: Hit Parade of 1947. 1949: Make Mine Laughs. Her Wonderful Lie. * Bashful Romeo. * Groan and Grunt. 1950: Joe Palooka in Humphrey Takes a Chance (GB: Humphrey Takes a Chance). * Night Club Daze. 1951: * Fast and Foolish. * Hollywood Honeymoon. 1952: * Baby Makes Two. * The Fresh Painter. * Ghost Buster. * Lost in a Turkish Bath. * Pardon My Wrench. 1956: The Boss. 1958: Terror in a Texas Town. 1961: Breakfast at Tiffany's. 1963: Bye Bye Birdie. 1964: Good Neighbor Sam. 1967: The Gnome-Mobile. Blackbeard's Ghost. 1968: The Love Bug. 1970: Norwood. The Boatniks. 1973: Terror Circus. 1975: Queen of the Stardust Ballroom (TV). 1976: Day of the Animals.*

LANE, Lupino
(Henry Lupino Lane) 1892−1959
The first stage show this author ever saw starred Lupino Lane in the umpteen hundredth performance of the musical *Me and My Girl*, with its hit song *The Lambeth Walk*. Tiny (he was 5 ft 3½ in tall), jaunty, dapper and confident, with amazing agility even in middle age, he was every inch the star of British theatre revue. The performance, just like all the others, was a huge popular success. The Lupinos and Lanes were an old stage family who traced their theatrical ancestry back to 1703 (brother Wallace Lupino was an actor-comedian, and cousin Stanley Lupino (*qv*) a stage revue star who made films in the 1930s). Lupino Lane, soon nicknamed 'Nipper' for obvious reasons, first trod the boards at four and quickly established himself as an acrobatic boy comic with a wonderful sense of physical timing. From 1915 he made a few one-reel comedies in Britain, frequently disguised as a woman or child, impersonations which, with the help of his mobile 'innocent' features and small build, he managed with more facility than most. Lane went to appear on the American stage in the early 1920s. Mid-way through the decade, he suddenly became a very successful Hollywood film comedian in two-reelers. His pale moon-face and guileless gaze, together with his bodily dexterity, led to some very inventive comedies, especially *Only Me*, in which, as the only performer, Lane played 23 disparate roles. Like Peter Sellers (*qv*) many years later, however, Lane never really established a comic personality of his own. With the coming of sound, it was quickly apparent that his raucous London tones did not match the silent images he had been projecting, and he soon decided to return to Britain, where he mixed stage and film work. Despite his reputation, the 1930s, film-wise, were a bit of a struggle, and he hit rock-bottom with *The Deputy Drummer*, a clodhopping comedy-musical in which Lane played a struggling composer whose greatest hit is called *Rhapsody in Pink*. The following year, though, he found *Me and My Girl* and, with it, a regular income for the rest of his life. His only remaining film was the screen version of it, called *The Lambeth Walk*, all prints of which seem to have been lost. The chipper, moustached, loud cockney charmer who starred in it seemed far removed from the beatific blunderer of those Hollywood shorts of the late 1920s.

*1915: * His Cooling Courtship. * Nipper's Busy Holiday. * The Man in Possession. * Nipper and the Curate. 1916: * A Wife in a Hurry. * Nipper's Busy Bee Time. * The Dummy. 1917: * Hello, Who's Your Lady Friend. * The Missing Link. * Splash Me Nicely. 1918: * Unexpected Treasure. * Trips and Tribunals. * His Busy Day. * His Salad Days. * Love and Lobster. 1919: * A Dreamland Frolic. * Clarence, Crooks and Chivalry. 1920: * A Night Out and a Day In. * A Lot About a Lottery. 1922: * The Broker. * The Reporter. 1923: * A Friendly Husband. 1924: Isn't Life Wonderful? 1925: * The Fighting Dude. * Maid in Morocco. 1926: * Fool's Luck. * His Private Life. * Time Flies. 1927: * Ship Mates. * Movieland. Monty of the Mounted. * Half-Pint Hero. * Naughty Boy. * Drama de Luxe. * Hello, Sailor. * Howdy Duke. 1928:*

*Hectic Days. * Fandango. * Fisticuffs. * Listen Sister. * Privates Beware. * Sword Points. * Roaming Romeo. 1929: * Joy Land. * Battling Sisters. * Fire Proof. * Only Me. * Summer Saps. * Purely Circumstantial. The Love Parade. The Show of Shows. * Buying a Gun. * Evolution of the Dance. 1930: Bride of the Regiment. Golden Dawn. The Yellow Mask. 1931:* † *Never Trouble Trouble.* † *No Lady. 1933: A Southern Maid. 1935: Who's Your Father? Trust the Navy. The Deputy Drummer. 1936: Hot News. 1939: The Lambeth Walk.*
† *And directed.*

Also as director. *1931: Love Lies. The Love Race. 1932: Innocents of Chicago (US: Why Saps Leave Home). Old Spanish Customers. The Maid of the Mountains. 1933: Letting in the Sunshine. Oh! What a Duchess.*

LANGDON, Harry 1884−1944
Few leading American comedians' stars shone as briefly as that of Harry Langdon. But, like the English comedian Tony Hancock (*qv*) many years later, Langdon brought his downfall on himself, by 'closing the door' on his collaborators, advisers and colleagues, going his own way, looking for something that was never there, at least in terms an audience could relate to. Like Hancock, he refused to stick with the character and formula that had brought him success. Unlike Hancock, Langdon had to suffer struggling on for another 16 years after the glory days were over. In his final films the little man America once adored looks tired and bewildered. As his best director, Frank Capra, commented: 'He never did understand what had happened to him and why.' Perhaps if the character of the guileless innocent had been lighted on by Langdon earlier in his career, things might have worked out differently. But Langdon was 40 before he came to the movies. When he reached the crisis, age, the coming of sound and his ambitions provided a lethal cocktail that poisoned his career. Born in Iowa to ardent Salvationists, Langdon ran away from home at 13 and joined up with various medicine and minstrel shows as juggler, blackface comedian, singer and dancer. He was even

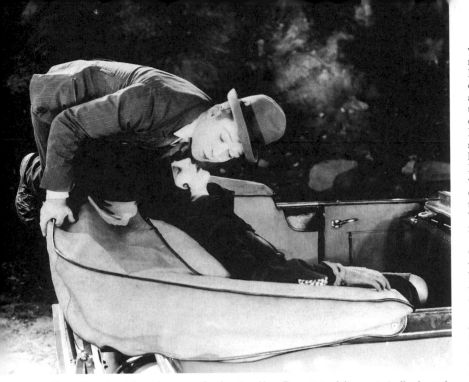

Harry Langdon takes advantage of a sleeping Alma Bennett to deliver a typically shy and unconventional Langdon kiss in *Long Pants*

employed for a while as a trapeze artist, then clown, with a circus. He also earned money as a cartoonist, a field in which his talent was undisputed, as his many pen portraits of Hollywood stars would later testify. Graduating to vaudeville, Langdon married (at 19) a fellow vaudevillian, Rose Mensolf, and devised a lengthy sketch, *Johnny's New Car* (involving a car that gradually comes to pieces), with which they toured the country for next 20 years, until a lucky (or unlucky) encounter with a film producer, Sol Lesser, brought Langdon to Hollywood. Lesser sold Langdon's contract to Mack Sennett and, with his baby face cloaking his age, Langdon was put into a succession of two-reel comedies as the innocent abroad, his eyes, eyebrows and mouth the only black smudges in a chalk-white face — a babylike character trying to cope with an unkind world. To the audience's delight, Langdon's characters bear a charm'ed life. Someone up there is indeed looking after this over-age child in tight jackets, baggy trousers and booted feet that turn the opposite way to Chaplin's (*qv*). By late 1925 Langdon had assembled a team around him, including writers Arthur Ripley, Frank Capra and Harry Edwards, with Edwards doing the directing. But after the three-reeler *Soldier Man* the quartet left Sennett and formed the Harry Langdon Corporation, moving to First National release. In the next two years Langdon produced his best work — and fell from grace. *Tramp, Tramp, Tramp* took him on a cross-country walking race for the love of Joan Crawford. Harry wins despite such minor

inconveniences as imprisonment and a cyclone. That film was directed by Edwards, but Capra took over for the next, *The Strong Man* — and the storms began. Frequently, it was Ripley and Langdon who thought the film should be made one way with Capra on the other side. Capra was right, as the results showed, but, even so, an increasingly acrimonious relationship developed in which Langdon, the introvert who once said 'I don't like people. I just like to be alone and think' would scream at Capra over what he considered the necessity for the films to contain more pathos and a more measured development. *The Strong Man* is an enchanting comedy about a Belgian soldier (Langdon) who is taken prisoner in World War One by a German circus strong man whose assistant he becomes in post-war times. Delights en route include Langdon trying to carry a golddigger up a long flight of stairs, trying to make a reputation as a weightlifter when his boss gets drunk, secretly enjoying the vamp's attempted seduction and wrecking an entire saloon at the film's climax. He becomes infatuated with another vamp in the last of the Capra films *Long Pants*, falling head over handle-bars for her while riding his bicycle up to — then round and round — her car. He even tries to help her escape from prison when she is quite rightly jailed for drug-smuggling. The title refers to the hero's first pair of long trousers — a tribute to Langdon that he could still get away with such a situation at 43. By now the situation between Langdon and Capra had become untenable. Both

were highly-strung, sensitive, egocentric men who believed that they knew best. Langdon decided that he could direct his own stuff just as well, and in a more peaceful atmosphere. He terminated Capra's contract. The director's reply was a vitriolic open letter to journalists denouncing Langdon's 'connected tantrums'. Hurt, stung and turning to other, less talented heads for advice when unsure of himself, Langdon made three more comedies which, while not entirely without merit, were unevenly paced and increasingly shunned by the public. He went back to making shorts. Then, broke and bemused, Langdon filed for bankruptcy in 1931. He was back by 1933, making cheap comedy two-reelers for Columbia and Educational, but the speed with which they were made must have baffled the little man. And age had caught up with him. While his old (tor)mentor Capra was reaching the heights with the first of three Oscars (for *It Happened One Night*), Langdon had lost the one quality that had put him at the top — his babylike innocence. There were trips to England and Australia, then he was back in Hollywood churning out the garbage. Occasionally he was directed by his old collaborators Harry Edwards and Arthur Ripley, but it made little difference. He wrote for Laurel and Hardy (*qv*) and earned money with cartoon work (including the caricatures on the opening credits of *Block-Heads* in 1938) and made a couple of clumsy feature comedies for poverty-row studio Monogram before the end came from a cerebral haemorrhage in December 1944. Langdon was 60 and looked every year of it in his last few films. One of his leading ladies once described Harry Langdon as 'a funny little wordless man'. She was referring to the real-life Harry, but it also summed up the best times of his blighted film career.

1918: The Master Mystery (serial). 1923: † **Johnny's New Car. *Picking Peaches. 1924: *Smile Please. *Feet of Mud. *Shanghaied Lovers. *Flickering Youth. *The Luck o' the Foolish. *All Night Long. *The Cat's Meow. *His New Mamma. *The First Hundred Years. *The Hansom Cabman. *The Sea Squawk. *Boobs in the Wood. 1925: *Plain Clothes. *Lucky Stars. *There He Goes. *His Marriage Wow. *Remember When? *Horace Greeley Jr. *The White Wing's Bride. 1926: *Saturday Afternoon. *Soldier Man. *Fiddlesticks. His First Flame. Ella Cinders. Tramp, Tramp, Tramp. The Strong Man. 1927: Long Pants. *Three's a Crowd. 1928:* † *The Chaser.* † *Heart Trouble. 1929: *Hotter Than Hot. *Shy Boy. *Skirt Shy. *The Head Guy. 1930: See America Thirst. A Soldier's Plaything (GB: A Soldier's Pay). *The Fighting Parson. *The Big Kick. *The King. *The Shrimp. *Voice of Hollywood No. 9. 1932: *The Big Flash. 1933: Hallelujah I'm a Bum (GB: Hallelujah I'm a Tramp). My Weakness. *Amateur Night. *The Hitch Hiker. *Knight Duty. *Tied for Life.*

* Hooks and Jabs. * Tired Feet. * Marriage Humor. † * The Stage Hand. * Leave It to Dad. 1934: * No Sleep on the Deep. * On Ice. * A Roaming Romeo. * A Circus Hoodoo. * Petting Preferred. * Council on De Fence. * Trimmed in Furs. * Shivers. * Hollywood on Parade B-6. 1935: Atlantic Adventure. * The Leathernecker. * His Marriage Mix-Up. * His Bridal Sweet. * I Don't Remember. 1937: Mad About Money (US: He Loved an Actress). 1938: * A Doggone Mixup. * Sue My Lawyer. There Goes My Heart. 1939: Zenobia (GB: Elephants Never Forget). 1940: Misbehaving Husbands. * Goodness! A Ghost. * Cold Turkey. * Sitting Pretty. 1941: Road Show. All-American Co-Ed. Double Trouble. * Beautiful Clothes. 1942: House of Errors. * What Makes Lizzie Dizzy. * Carry Harry. * Piano Mooners. * A Blitz on the Fritz. * Tireman, Spare My Tires. 1943: Spotlight Scandals. * Here Comes Mr Zerk. * Blonde and Groom. 1944: * Defective Detectives. * Mopey Dope. Block Busters. Hot Rhythm. * To Heir is Human. 1945: Pistol Packin' Nitwits. * Snooper Service. Swingin' on a Rainbow.

Also as director. 1937: Wise Guys.

† And directed.
‡ Unreleased.

Stan is happy that Ollie has found the mud puddle before their pet goat, in *Angora Love*

LAUREL, Stan (right)
(Arthur S. Jefferson) 1890–1965
and
HARDY, Oliver
(Norvell Hardy, later legally changed) 1892–1957

Probably the best-loved and most enduring comedians of the twentieth century, with a unique range of trademark mannerisms and catchphrases. Vagabonds strolling through life's vicissitudes, the pair (well, Ollie mainly) had aspirations to better things in life, but about the most their characters usually achieved in films was a suburban bungalow and a nagging wife: 'Look out! It's the wives!' became just one of the many phrases they had only to utter to set audiences giggling. Stan was a skinny Lancashire lad who became a skilled pantomimist in his teens and, after years with Fred Karno's riotous stage troupe, came to America with them (Charlie Chaplin (*qv*) was their leading comic) in 1910. The

company broke up when Chaplin left it to try his luck in films after a second US tour in 1912. Stan Laurel stayed in America. With various partners, he played successfully in vaudeville for the next five years, changing his name from Stan Jefferson to Stan Laurel around 1915. He was spotted for film comedies in 1917, and gained some success as a character called Hickory Hiram. Irregularities in Laurel's private life (the woman he lived with was unable to obtain a divorce) led to a couple of estrangements from the morals-conscious Hal Roach, who had hired him in 1917 and again in 1922. But the lady, actress Mae Dahlberg, returned to her native Australia in 1926, and Stan married another actress, Lois Nielsen, whereupon Roach took him back. The high-mindedness of Roach, however, was to be a running sore in his relationship with the free-living Stan, and years later was to lead to the premature decline of the Laurel and Hardy partnership. Oliver Hardy was a plump, outgoing kid from Georgia, fascinated both by his fellow man – 'I would sit in the lobby of my mother's hotel and just watch people go by' – and by the smell of show business, who ran away from home at the age of eight for a life as a boy singer in a travelling minstrel show. He returned home in time for at least part of a proper musical education at the Atlantic Conservatory. 'They were impressed I could hit high C.' His mother moved to the small Georgia town of Milledgeville when Hardy was 18, and he opened a cinema there for a living, managing it for three years. In 1913 he decided to try and break into films, and went to nearby Jacksonville where he hung out at the Lubin studios until they took him

on to do odds and ends in comedy shorts at 5 dollars a week. As the years passed, Hardy played the villain or 'second banana' or simply straight man to dozens of screen comedians, including Bobby Ray, Harry Myers, Billy West, Jimmy Aubrey and, most notably, Larry Semon (*qv*), to whose Scarecrow he played the Tin Man in the 1925 version of *The Wizard of Oz*. Hardy briefly tried making a living as a cabaret singer in 1917 but soon returned to films. By 1918 he was being billed as Oliver 'Babe' Hardy, having acquired his lifetime nickname and his new legal first name (after his father) around the same time. He was under long-term contract to Hal Roach when Laurel arrived back at the studio in 1926 and the long-standing partnership between them gradually evolved. Between 1927 and 1940, the team made around 90 films, mostly shorts, at the Roach studio. They became at once kings of escalating mayhem – especially in their early shorts – and a kind of comedy of personal relationships, which might be termed 'intimate idiocy'. At the same time 'the boys' (as most of their directors apparently called them) began developing individual 'gesture' trademarks that rarely failed to make their fans laugh. Laurel had the head scratch, which often indicated bewilderment. Then there was the prolonged eye-blink, which indicated a concentrated and unhappy attempt at thought. There was also the ear-wiggle and the skip when running, and he would sometimes resort to crying when bullied by Ollie over some misdemeanour. Most of Hardy's mannerisms stemmed from what he himself called 'the courtly behaviour of a southern gentleman'. There was the tie twiddle, usually when he was embarrassed, the flourish of the derby hat when preparing to do something (it was subsequently consigned to the crook of his arm), the imperious wave of his arm when indicating to Stan that he, Ollie, was to go first (normally heading into disaster) and of course the famous set of 'camera looks', which involved the camera focusing on Ollie's look of horror, exasperation or faint puzzlement at something Stan has done. One thing that always proved beyond the Ollie character was the expertise Stan possessed in physical 'magic', not only with the ear-wiggle, but blowing on to his finger to raise his hat, the handlock with middle fingers sticking out in opposite directions, the kneesie-earsie-nosie routine (involving pulling his nose with his left hand and his left ear with his right hand simultaneously) and, with the help of special effects, the striking flame with a thumb and finger. But Stan himself was always defeated by a simple thing like folding his arms, the interlocking of the arms somehow escaping him until they dropped to his sides. With sound films, which Laurel and Hardy took more in their stride than any other silent comedians, came the catchphrases. Ollie would admonish Stan 'Why don't you do something to help me?' or (after he did) 'Here's another nice mess you've gotten us into.' Stan would invariably reply 'Well, I couldn't help it', dissolving into tears. Whatever the boys touched was sure to turn to ashes in their films and, even when they got away with something, nemesis was destined to catch up with them at the fadeout, whether in the form of the mad chef from *Pack Up Your Troubles* or the gorilla in *Swiss Miss*. Their best feature film from the Roach period was probably *Way Out West*, in which they were unhindered either by an episodic plot or by musical interludes. That is, apart from two classical musical interpolations of their own, a soft-shoe shuffle to the backing of Chill Wills and the Avalon Boys and a rendition of *The Trail of the Lonesome Pine* that, years after their deaths, became an international pop chart hit. Laurel and Hardy probably made more end-to-end belly-laugh short films than any other comic or comics in film history. The most consistently inventive are (of the silents) *Leave 'Em Laughing, The Finishing Touch, From Soup to Nuts, You're Darn Tootin', Two Tars, Liberty, Bacon Grabbers* and *Big Business* and (of the sound shorts) *Men o' War, Perfect Day, Hog Wild, Helpmates, Early to Bed, The Music Box* (their only Oscar-winner), *Their First Mistake* and *Them Thar Hills*. Although Hal Roach left the boys to go their own way in the making of the films (though the men were equals as laughtermakers, Stan was the brains behind most of their ideas), he engaged Stan in a continuous running battle about his private life, and the two men severed their association in 1939, with Roach invoking a morals clause in the contract. Laurel and Hardy did sign to make two further Roach films on a two-off basis,

but then formed their own production company. It was never to make a picture. Rather than go back to Roach where, despite advancing years, they might have found a few more major films within their capabilities, the boys signed up with major studios, MGM and Fox, whom they soon found to be far more intractable than Roach ever was. The result is rather like watching good TV comedians, say Britain's Morecambe and Wise (*qv*) trying to perform on the screen. Without the intimacy and time for trying out gags, their impact is completely muffled. And so it was with Laurel and Hardy. Of their 1940s films, only *Nothing But Trouble* has a few funny moments, and these are formula action-slapstick stuff. Within the cocoon of the Roach organisation, however, Laurel and Hardy had always seemed real characters. They could be antagonistic towards each other but always presented a united front against a common foe. And their reactions towards each other always seemed genuine, never feigned. Hardy's opinion of the team bears this impression out. 'We had a lot of fun and did many, many crazy things in our pictures with Roach. But we were always real. Even in our shortest pictures, we tried to be real'.

Together. *1917: A Lucky Dog. 1921: The Rent Collector. 1926: Get 'Em Young. 45 Minutes from Hollywood. 1927: Duck Soup. Slipping Wives. Love 'Em and Weep. Why Girls Love Sailors. With Love and Hisses. Sailors, Beware!/Ship's Hero. Do Detectives Think?/The Bodyguard. Sugar Daddies. Flying Elephants. The Second Hundred Years. Call of the Cuckoos. Hats Off. Putting Pants on Philip.*

Let George Do It. The Battle of the Century. 1928: Leave 'Em Laughing. The Finishing Touch. From Soup to Nuts. You're Darn Tootin' (GB: The Music Blasters). Their Purple Moment. Should Married Men Go Home? Early to Bed. Two Tars. Habeas Corpus. We Faw Down (GB: We Slip Up). 1929: Liberty. Wrong Again. That's My Wife. Big Business. Unaccustomed As We Are. Double Whoopee. Berth Marks. Men o' War/Man o' War. Perfect Day. They Go Boom. Bacon Grabbers. Angora Love. [†] *The Hollywood Revue of 1929 (and German-language version). The Hoose-Gow. 1930: The Night Owls. Blotto. Brats. Below Zero.* [†] *The Rogue Song. Hog Wild (GB: Aerial Antics). The Laurel and Hardy Murder Case. Another Fine Mess. 1931: Be Big. Chicken Come Home/ Chickens Come Home. Laughing Gravy. The Stolen Jools (GB: The Slippery Pearls). Our Wife.* [†] *Pardon Us (GB: Jail Birds). Come Clean. One Good Turn.* [†] *Beau Hunks (GB: Beau Chumps). On the Loose. Helpmates. 1932: Any Old Port. The Music Box. The Chimp. County Hospital. Scram!* [†] *Pack Up Your Troubles. Their First Mistake. Towed in a Hole. 1933: Twice Two. Me and My Pal.* [†] *The Devil's Brother (GB: Fra Diavolo). The Midnight Patrol. Busy Bodies. Wild Poses. Dirty Work.* [†] *Sons of the Desert (GB: Fraternally Yours). 1934: Oliver the Eighth (GB: The Private Life of Oliver the Eighth).* [†] *Hollywood Party. Going Bye Bye! Them Thar Hills.* [†] *Babes in Toyland/March of the Wooden Soldiers. The Live Ghost. 1935: Tit for Tat. The Fixer Uppers. Thicker Than Water.* [†] *Bonnie Scotland. 1936:* [†] *The Bohemian Girl. On the Wrong Trek.* [†] *Our Relations. 1937:* [†] *Way Out West.* [†] *Pick a Star. 1938:* [†] *Swiss Miss.* [†] *Block-Heads. 1939:* [†] *The*

Stan puzzles over the problem of what to tell the wives when they get back home. Ollie is complacent about it, in *Our Relations*

Offending fenders. Stan Laurel and Oliver Hardy start taking the automobiles of their adversaries apart, in *Two Tars*

Stan Laurel shows Oliver Hardy the easy way to make a living stealing purses in *The Bohemian Girl*. When Ollie tries, it doesn't work so well...

Even when they spend a night out bowling, Felix (Jack Lemmon, right) and Oscar (Walter Matthau) can't get along, in *The Odd Couple*

Flying Deuces. †*A Chump at Oxford. 1940:* †*Saps at Sea. 1941:* †*Great Guns. 1942:* †*A-Haunting We Will Go. The Tree in a Test Tube. 1943:* †*Air Raid Wardens.* †*Jitterbugs.* †*The Dancing Masters. 1944:* †*The Big Noise.* †*Nothing But Trouble. 1945:* †*The Bull Fighters. 1951:* †*Atoll K (GB: Robinson Crusoeland. US: Utopia).*

Hardy alone. *1913: Outwitting Dad. 1914: Back to the Farm. Pins Are Lucky. The Soubrette and the Simp. The Smuggler's Daughter. The Female Cop. What He Forgot. Cupid's Target. Spaghetti and Lottery. Gus and the Anarchists. Shoddy the Tailor. The Rise of the Johnsons. Kidnapping the Kid. Mother's Baby Boy. Dobs at the Shore. 1915: The Paper Hanger's Helper. Spaghetti à la Mode. Charley's Aunt. Artists and Models. The Tramps. Prize Baby. An Expensive Visit. Cleaning Time. Mixed Flats. Safety Worst. The Twin Sister. Baby. Who Stole the Doggies? A Lucky Strike. The New Butler. Matilda's Legacy. Her Choice. The Cannibal King. What a Cinch! The Dead Letter. Avenging Bill. The Haunted Hat. The Simp and the Sophomores. Babe's Schooldays. Ethel's Romeos. A Bungalow Bungle. Three Rings and a Goat. A Rheumatic Joint. Something in Her Eye. A Janitor's Joyful Job. Fatty's Fatal Fun. Ups and Downs. This Way Out. Chickens. A Frenzied Finance. Busted Hearts. Clothes Make the Man. The New Adventures of J Rufus Wallingford (serial). 1916: A Sticky Affair. Bungles' Rainy Day. The Try-Out. One Two Many. Bungles Enforces the Law. The Serenade. Bungles' Elopement. Nerve and Gasoline. Bungles Lands a Job. Their Vacation. Mama's Boys. He Went and Won. A Special Delivery. A Battle Royal. All for a Girl. Hired and Fired. What's Sauce for the Goose. The Brave Ones. The Water Cure. Thirty Days. Baby Doll. The Schemers. Sea Dogs. Hungry Hearts. Edison Bugg's Invention. Never Again. Better Halves. A Day at School. A Terrible Tragedy. Spaghetti. Aunt Bill. The Heroes. It Happened in Pikersville. Human Hounds. Dreamy Knights. Life Savers. Their Honeymoon. An Aerial Joyride. Side Tracked. Stranded. Love and Duty. Artistic Atmosphere. The Reformer. Royal Blood. The Candy Trail. A Precious Parcel. A Maid to Order. Twin Flats. A Warm Reception. Pipe Dreams. Mother's Child. Prize Winners. Ambitious Ethel. The Guilty One. He Winked and Won. Fat and Fickle. 1917: Boycotted Baby. Wanted – A Bad Man. The Other Girl. The Love Bugs. Back Stage. The Hero. Doughnuts. Cupid's Rival. The Villain. The Millionaire. A Mix-Up in Hearts. The Goat. The Genius. The Stranger. The Fly Cop. The Modiste. The Star Boarder. The Chief Cook. The Candy Kid. The Station Master. The Hobo. The Pest. The Prospector. The Bandmaster. 1918: The Slave. The Artist. The Barber. The Chef. Hello Trouble. Painless Love. King Solomon. The Orderly. His Day Out. The Rogue. The Scholar. The Messenger. The Handy Man. Bright and Early. The Straight and Narrow. Playmates. Freckled Fish. 1919: Hop the Bellhop. Lions and Ladies. Mules and Mortgages. Tootsies and Tamales. Healthy and Happy. Flips and Flops. Yaps and Yokels. Mates*

and Models. Squabs and Squabbles. Bungs and Bunglers. Switches and Sweeties. Dames and Dentists. 1920: Maids and Muslin. Squeaks and Squawks. Fists and Fodder. Pals and Pugs. He Laughs Last. Springtime. The Decorator. His Jonah Day. The Back Yard. 1921: The Nuisance. The Tourist. The Blizzard. The Bakery. The Fall Guy. The Bell Hop. The Sawmill. 1922: Golf. †*Fortune's Mask. The Counter Jumper.* †*The Little Wildcat. 1923:* †*One Stolen Night. No Wedding Bells. The Barnyard.* †*Three Ages.* †*The King of the Wild Horses. 1924:* †*The Girl in the Limousine. Her Boy Friend. Kid Speed. 1925: Is Marriage the Bunk? Stick Around. Hop to It!* †*The Wizard of Oz. Isn't Life Terrible? Yes, Yes, Nanette. Should Sailors Marry? Enough to Do.* †*The Perfect Clown. Thundering Fleas. 1926:* †*Stop, Look and Listen. A Bankrupt Honeymoon. Madame Mystery. Say It with Babies. Long Fliv the King.* †*The Gentle Cyclone. A Sea Dog's Tale. Along Came Auntie. Crazy Like a Fox. Bromo and Juliet. Be Your Age. The Nickel Hopper. 1927: Should Men Walk Home? Why Girls Say No. The Honorable Mr Buggs.* †*No Man's Law. Baby Brother. Crazy to Act. Fluttering Hearts. The Lighter That Failed. Love 'Em and Feed 'Em. Assistant Wives. 1928: Galloping Ghosts. Barnum and Ringling Inc. 1932: Choo-Choo! (voice only). 1939:* †*Zenobia (GB: Elephants Never Forget). 1949:* †*The Fighting Kentuckian. 1950:* †*Riding High. 1952: Meet Bela Lugosi and Oliver Hardy.*

Laurel alone. *1917: Nuts in May. The Evolution of Fashion. 1918: Whose Zoo? Just Rambling Along. Phoney Photos. It's Great to be Crazy. Hickory Hiram. Huns and Hyphens. No Place Like Jail. Bears and Bad Men. Frauds and Frenzies. Do You Love Your Wife? 1919: Hustling for Health. Hoot Mon. Mixed Nuts. Scars and Stripes. 1922: The Pest. The Week-End Party. The Egg. Mud and Sand. 1923: When Knights Were Cold. The Noon Whistle. Pick and Shovel. Gas and Air. The Handy Man. A Man about Town. Scorching Sands. Roughest Africa. Mother's Joy. Collars and Cuffs. White Wings. Kill or Cure. Short Orders. The Whole Truth. Save the Ship. Frozen Hearts. Under Two Jags. The Soilers. Oranges and Lemons. 1924: Wild Bill Hiccup/Wide Open Spaces. Detained. Zeb vs. Paprika. Smithy. Near Dublin. Short Kilts. Rupert of Hee-Haw/Rupert of Cole-Slaw. West of Hot Dog. Postage Due. Brothers Under the Chin. Monsieur Don't Care. 1925: Madam Mix-Up/ Mandarin Mix-Up. Pie-Eyed. Navy Blue Days. The Sleuth. Half a Man. Somewhere in Wrong. The Snow Hawk. Twins. Dr Pyckle and Mr Pride. 1926: Atta Boy. On the Front Page (GB: The Editor). 1927: Seeing the World. Eve's Love Letters. Now I'll Tell One. Should Tall Men Marry?*

As director. *1925:* ‡*Yes, Yes, Nanette. Unfriendly Enemies. Moonlight and Noses. Wandering Papas. Enough to Do. 1926:* ‡*Madame Mystery.* ‡*Never Too Old. Wise Guys Prefer Brunettes.* ‡*The Merry Widower.* ‡*Raggedy Rose.*

All shorts except †features. ‡Co-directed.

le MESURIER, John 1912–1983
Popular, grey-haired (originally dark), worried-looking, gentle-voiced British comic character actor with distinctive flapping gestures, sometimes accompanied by an anxious purse of the lips and a mop of the brow. Once established in comedy, after years in straight acting, le Mesurier came much into demand on television as a straight-faced foil, especially to Tony Hancock (*qv*). Although he ended up making dozens of films, le Mesurier's longest association was with TV. He entered the industry in its infancy in 1938. More than 40 years later, he was highly praised for his leading role (one of his last) in *An Honourable Retirement*, as a retired civil servant who unintentionally becomes involved with spies. In films from 1948, le Mesurier often played shifty characters at first, in minor crime dramas. In one, *Blind Man's Bluff*, this most sophisticated of men was cast as 'Lefty Jones'! An involvement with the Boulting Brothers brought his talents to comedy. He made *Private's Progress*, *Brothers in Law* and *Happy is the Bride!* for the brothers. Then it was back to television for episodes of *Hancock's Half Hour* and *Hancock*. He was also in two films with the stormy, alcoholic Hancock: *The Rebel* and *The Punch and Judy Man*. Sometimes in these roles le Mesurier would pretend to be a calm, quietening influence. But the alarmed eyes would give him away. He was seldom seen to smile. From 1967 to 1977, le Mesurier reached the pinnacle of his popularity as the ever-fretting, always-expecting-the-worst Sergeant Wilson, a bank manager turned Home Guard soldier, in the long-running TV comedy series *Dad's Army*. The spin-off film in 1971 was one of the more successful of its kind. It was also in 1971 that John won a Best Actor on TV award for his performance in *The Traitor*. This most lugubrious of actors also made records that cashed in on his view of the world, as it came across through his comedy characters, most notably one called *What Is Going to Become of Us All?* Le Mesurier was married to Hattie Jacques (*qv*) from 1949 until 1965, and the couple remained on good terms after their divorce and his remarriage. He became more frail in his late sixties and died at 71 from an

abdominal illness. He had left an obituary notice for his second wife Joan to insert into the daily papers, informing his friends that he had 'conked out'. His best-selling autobiography, *A Jobbing Actor*, appeared posthumously in 1984.

*1948: Death in the Hand. Escape from Broadmoor. 1949: A Matter of Murder. Old Mother Riley's New Venture. 1950: Dark Interval. 1951: Never Take No for an Answer. Blind Man's Bluff. 1952: Mother Riley Meets the Vampire (US: Vampire Over London). 1953: House of Blackmail (voice only). * The Drayton Case. The Blue Parrot. Black 13. The Pleasure Garden. 1954: Dangerous Cargo. Stranger from Venus (US: Immediate Delivery). Beautiful Stranger (US: Twist of Fate). 1955: Police Dog. Josephine and Men. A Time to Kill. Private's Progress. 1956: The Battle of the River Plate (US: Pursuit of the Graf Spee). The Baby and the Battleship. Brothers in Law. The Good Companions. 1957: Happy is the Bride! These Dangerous Years (US: Dangerous Youth). High Flight. The Admirable Crichton (US: Paradise Lagoon). The Moonraker. The Man Who Wouldn't Talk. 1958: Law and Disorder. Another Time, Another Place. I Was Monty's Double (GB: Monty's Double). Gideon's Day (US: Gideon of Scotland Yard). Blind Spot. Man with a Gun. The Captain's Table. Blood of the Vampire. Too Many Crooks. Carlton-Browne of the FO (US: Man in a Cocked Hat). 1959: Operation Amsterdam. The Lady is a Square. Ben-Hur. A Touch of Larceny. I'm All Right, Jack. The Wreck of the Mary Deare. The Hound of the Baskervilles. Our Man in Havana. Shake Hands with the Devil. Follow a Star. Desert Mice. School for Scoundrels. 1960: Jack the Ripper. The Day They Robbed the Bank of England. Let's Get Married. Never Let Go. Dead Lucky. Doctor in Love. The Night We Got the Bird. The Pure Hell of St Trinians. The Bulldog Breed. 1961: Five Golden Hours. The Rebel (US: Call Me Genius). Very Important Person (US: A Coming Out Party). Don't Bother to Knock! (US: Why Bother to Knock?). Invasion Quartet. On the Fiddle (US: Operation Snafu). Village of Daughters. Mr Topaze (US: I Like Money). 1962: Hair of the Dog. Go to Blazes. Jigsaw. Flat Two. The Waltz of the Toreadors. Mrs Gibbons' Boys. Only Two Can Play. The Wrong Arm of the Law. We Joined the Navy. The Punch and Judy Man. 1963: The Pink Panther. In the Cool of the Day. Never Put It in Writing. Hot Enough for June (US: Agent 8¾). The Mouse on the Moon. The Main Attraction. 1964: The Moon-Spinners. 1965: The Early Bird. City Under the Sea (US: War Gods of the Deep). Cuckoo Patrol. Masquerade. Where the Spies Are. Those Magnificent Men in Their Flying Machines. The Liquidator. 1966: The Sandman. Eye of the Devil. Finders Keepers. Mr Ten Per Cent. The Wrong Box. Our Man in Marrakesh (US: Bang! Bang! You're Dead). 1967: * The Inn Way Out. The 25th Hour. Casino Royale. 1968: Salt and Pepper. 1969: * The Undertakers. The Italian Job. Midas Run (US: A Run on Gold). The Magic Christian. 1970:*

*Doctor in Trouble. On a Clear Day You Can See Forever. 1971: Dad's Army. 1972: The Garnett Saga. Au Pair Girls. 1974: Confessions of a Window Cleaner. Barry McKenzie Holds His Own. Three for All. Brief Encounter (TV). 1975: The Adventure of Sherlock Holmes' Smarter Brother. 1977: Stand Up, Virgin Soldiers. Jabberwocky. What's Up Nurse? 1978: Who is Killing the Great Chefs of Europe? (GB: Too Many Chefs). Rosie Dixon Night Nurse. 1979: The Spaceman and King Arthur (US: Unidentified Flying Oddball). 1980: The Fiendish Plot of Dr Fu Manchu. * Late Flowering Love. The Shillingbury Blowers (TV).*

LEMMON, Jack
(John Lemmon III) 1925–

As America's foremost comic *actor* of the post-1950 period, fast-talking, sharp-chinned, dark-haired, nervously-smiling Lemmon built up a formidable range of neurotics. What many of Lemmon's characters lacked was confidence in themselves. And they probably all rolled together into one in his classic portrayal of the houseproud Felix in one of his biggest hits *The Odd Couple*. The man whom director Billy Wilder once described as 'the divine clown' made a low-key start to his theatrical career after wartime service as a communications officer on an aircraft carrier. Strangely, Lemmon played comparatively little comedy up to the first thing that gained him a wider audience than before – a TV series, *That Wonderful Guy*, which began towards the end of 1949. He played an aspiring actor working as a (bungling) valet to a suave, sniffy drama critic. Following other TV comedy series opposite his first wife (1950–56), Cynthia Stone, such as *Heaven for Betsy* and *The Couple Next Door*, Lemmon signed up for films with Columbia, a company he'd remain with until 1964. In his first film, *It Should Happen to You*, opposite Judy Holliday (*qv*), the studio billed Lemmon on the posters as 'a guy you're gonna like'. The public soon confirmed the slogan. Lemmon undoubtedly was fun to be with in a movie, whether wheeler-dealing, panicking, or just going off in all directions like a human firecracker. His bundles of nervous energy usually packed charm and charisma as well. During

his formative years at Columbia Lemmon made a number of comedies with such stars as Holliday, Kim Novak and Ernie Kovacs (*qv*), few of which were liked by the critics (though they liked Lemmon), but all of them popular with the public: *Phffft!*, *Operation Mad Ball*, *Bell, Book and Candle* and *The Notorious Landlady*. Several of these films from Lemmon's first ten Hollywood years were made by Richard Quine, who had also directed his early screen tests. Lemmon also found his way rather mysteriously into a few lightweight musicals (most of Columbia's musicals were just that), but it was at other studios that he began to build a reputation as more than a master of light comedy. *Mister Roberts* won him the first of his two Oscars as the lecherous, unreliable, faintly unbalanced Ensign Pulver, destined eventually to hurl the hated captain's equally hated potted palm off the ship. Lemmon's frenetic, eye-catching, precisely-timed portrayal, full of minute detail and telling gestures, summed up the performances of his early years. Three more Oscar nominations in the four years from 1959 pushed Lemmon into the league of top money-making stars; he was scarcely out of the top ten for the next decade. The first of these was for *Some Like It Hot*, a comedy 'so brilliant … that I once fell off the couch laughing' said Lemmon, who savoured the script's witty lines and the chance to appear with devastating success in drag (as did co-star Tony Curtis), as well as act with Marilyn Monroe, in the story of two musicians on the run from the Mob. Lemmon was back to being the average Joe, in a sick world but not so honest, in *The Apartment*, in which he lends his key to superiors for amorous assignations in the cause of personal advancement. Lemmon indulged in several inventive comedy scenes – including straining spaghetti through a tennis racket – as well as showing his talent at appealing to our emotions. His yearning to prove himself as an all-round actor reached complete fruition with his alcoholic in *Days of Wine and Roses*, a creation that was funny, touching and pitiable all at the same time. The big-scale comedies that followed, including a strangely songless version of the Broadway musical *Irma La Douce*, were not the laugh riots their studios intended and it was left to Billy Wilder (director of *Some Like It Hot*) to boost Lemmon's career with *The Fortune Cookie* (in Britain, *Meet Whiplash Willie*) which cast him as an injured man at the mercy of his shyster lawyer. Walter Matthau won an Oscar in this role and the pair co-starred again in the very popular *The Odd Couple*. Lemmon, superbly fussy, employed his full range of blinks, grimaces and sudden bursts of comic malice. There followed a succession of disappointments, relieved for Lemmon himself, though not for filmgoers, by the aggressively downbeat *Save the Tiger*, a depressing film illuminated by his own biting, driving performance which won him a second Oscar. The lowpoint of this period was probably the hapless *Alex and the Gypsy*. This provided the (probably true) story of Lemmon asking Walter Matthau at a preview what he thought of the film. Matthau is said to have turned and growled 'Get out of it!' Lemmon's career had turned full circle from his early work in drama. The misses of his later years have been the comedies, and the hits have come in such tense, grabbed-from-the-headlines dramas as *The China Syndrome* and *Missing*. Now drifting into star cameos, Lemmon could become a wicked scene-stealer in his old age. As an actor who uses body language as well as the full gamut of facial expressions, he could have more talent in his little finger than some of the stars he supports. He's been married since 1960 to his second wife, actress Felicia Farr.

*1950: * Once Too Often. 1953: It Should Happen to You. 1954: Phffft! Three for the Show. 1955: Mister Roberts. My Sister Eileen. 1956: * Hollywood Bronc Busters. You Can't Run Away from It. 1957: Fire Down Below. Operation Mad Ball. The Mystery of 13 (TV).*

*1958: Bell, Book and Candle. Cowboy. Face of a Hero (TV). 1959: It Happened to Jane (That Jane from Maine/Twinkle and Shine). Some Like It Hot. 1960: The Wackiest Ship in the Army. The Apartment. Pepe. Stowaway in the Sky (narrator only, English-language version). 1962: The Notorious Landlady. Days of Wine and Roses. 1963: Irma La Douce. Under the Yum Yum Tree. 1964: Good Neighbor Sam. How to Murder Your Wife. 1965: The Great Race. 1966: The Fortune Cookie (GB: Meet Whiplash Willie). 1967: Luv. The Odd Couple. 1968: * There Comes a Day (narrator only). 1969: The April Fools. 1970: The Out-of-Towners. 1972: The War Between Men and Women. Avanti! 1973: * Wednesday. Save the Tiger. 1974: The Front Page. 1975: The Prisoner of Second Avenue. The Entertainer (TV). 1976: Alex and the Gypsy. 1977: Airport 77. 1978: The China Syndrome. 1979: Ken Murray's Shooting Stars. 1980: Portrait of a 60% Perfect Man. Tribute. 1981: Buddy Buddy. 1982: Missing. 1984: Mass Appeal. 1985: Macaroni. 1986: 'That's Life!' 1989: Dad. 1991: JFK. 1992: The Player. Glengarry Glen Ross. Father, Son and the Mistress. For Richer, For Poorer (TV).*

LEWIS, Jerry
(Joseph Levitch) 1926–

It was unfortunate for madcap American comedian Jerry Lewis that one of his most appealing points was his youth. It was the one thing that couldn't last. As he approached 40 and, long split from his partner Dean Martin, began directing his own films in the 1960s, his popularity gradually but noticeably began to wane. Although his pictures were still often touched by sparks of genius, they no longer contained the same kind of comedy that had first drawn audiences to nightclubs and cinemas. They weren't the entities that a strong production team and inventive director could produce — and they relied on Jerry alone to carry them. Born to show business parents, he was a sometime part of their act at five. Twelve years later he had already left school and embarked on a career as a (struggling) entertainer. With a high-pitched, squeaky voice, doleful features, an angular bone structure that never quite looked as though it connected up and a range of manic expressions, Lewis was a bull in search of a china shop. The shop came along in the shape of crooner Dean Martin. Almost ten years older than Lewis but equally struggling, Martin was receptive to the 20-year-old Lewis's idea of a partnership when they played on the same bills together in a windswept Atlantic City in 1946. The formula was simple: Martin warbled his songs and attempted to flex his charm as well as his tonsils but was consistently messed about by Lewis, whose antics (which frequently involved the orchestra as well) would drive the singer to despair. Universal briefly signed the hit comedy team up as a threat to the warring Abbott and Costello (*qv*). But it was over at Paramount that they made their film debuts — billed down the cast, just like Abbott and Costello in their first picture, but the attractions that everyone was going to *My Friend Irma* for. Most critics concurred that they were the only funny things in the film. They were in an ensemble sequel, *My Friend Irma Goes West*, and then struck out on their own. Just like Abbott and Costello, they started off with an army film and did a navy film and a ghost comedy in short order. Jerry had a memorable encounter with a

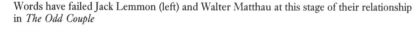

Words have failed Jack Lemmon (left) and Walter Matthau at this stage of their relationship in *The Odd Couple*

Jerry Lewis has terrible trouble with a trolley that develops a mind of its own, in *The Disorderly Orderly*

downhill for Lewis fairly rapidly in terms of his relationship with a popular audience. Pretentiousness crept in to an increasing degree, and the most mainline of these later movies, *Boeing Boeing*, an adaptation of a stage farce, proved a miserable mistake — although it might have had more bite and spark with Dean Martin as co-star instead of Tony Curtis. Public patience with the Lewis comedies (and private backing) seemed to run out with the beginning of the 1970s and the years that followed were full of unrealised or unreleased projects. The only time Lewis reached the general audiences that had once been his biggest fans was when he had a king-sized guest role in Robert De Niro's *The King of Comedy*. For years Lewis and Martin hardly spoke to one another, after a break-up almost as bitter as the final split between Abbott and Costello, their predecessors in world popularity. Each referred to the other as difficult and arrogant and each was probably right. In June 1989, however, they finally buried the hatchet at a massive bash in Las Vegas to celebrate Martin's birthday and the 40th anniversary of his entry into films. There was a giant cake, and it was presented to Martin by Jerry Lewis. If he came to terms with his ex-partner, though, it was clear that Jerry never really understood, or even accepted, his slide in popularity and the reasons for it. In a mid-1980s interview he asserted that 'a lot of people were hostile because I was a multifaceted, talented, wealthy, internationally famous genius. It was too much for them. I like me. I like what I became. I'm proud of what I've achieved, and I don't believe I've scratched the surface even yet. I may have an ego that's bigger than other people's but thank God for it, if that is what brought me to where I am today.'

1949: My Friend Irma. 1950: My Friend Irma Goes West. At War with the Army. 1951: That's My Boy. * Screen Snapshots No. 197. Sailor Beware. 1952: * Screen Snapshots No. 207. The Stooge. Jumping Jacks. Road to Bali. * Hollywood Fun Festival. 1953: Scared Stiff. The Caddy. 1954: Money from Home. Living It Up. Three Ring Circus. * Paramount Presents VistaVision. 1955: You're Never Too Young. Artists and Models. 1956: Pardners. Hollywood or Bust. * Hollywood Premiere. 1957: The Delicate Delinquent. The Sad Sack. 1958: Rock-a-Bye Baby. The Geisha Boy. 1959: Don't Give Up the Ship. Visit to a Small Planet. Li'l Abner. 1960: † The Bellboy. Cinderfella. 1961: † The Ladies' Man. † The Errand Boy. 1962: It'S Only Money. 1963: It's a Mad, Mad, Mad, Mad World. † The Nutty Professor. Who's Minding the Store? 1964: The Disorderly Orderly. † The Patsy. 1965: † The Family Jewels. Boeing-Boeing. 1966: † Three on a Couch. Way . . . Way Out. 1967: † The Big Mouth. Don't Raise the Bridge, Lower the River. 1968: ‡ The Silent Treatment. 1969: Hook, Line and Sinker. 1970: † Which Way to the Front? (GB: Ja, Ja, Mein General, But

soft-drink machine in *At War with the Army*, a cleverly-staged boxing match in *Sailor Beware* and did imitations of Humphrey Bogart and Carmen Miranda in *Scared Stiff*. In this early period the boys also made the underrated *The Stooge*, which foreshadowed their own break-up a few years later. This time, though, there's a happy ending, with Jerry returning at the last minute to help out his partner, whose gags are dying without the stooge he thought he didn't need. Some people didn't like the pathos but it certainly works better than the same element in most of Lewis's solo starring films. After 16 films together Martin and Lewis split up early in 1957. Jerry's first few films on his own — *The Delicate Delinquent*, *The Sad Sack* and *The Geisha Boy* in particular — were excellent, the last of the three providing the comedian with a continuing collaboration with Frank Tashlin, a director who had previously worked with Bob Hope (*qv*), and

specialised in hectic pacing and cartoon-like sight gags. Almost all of Lewis's best 1960s' work was to be with Tashlin. *It'S Only Money* contains the ridiculous attack of the lawn-mowers. *Who's Minding the Store?* has Jerry demonstrating a vacuum cleaner that sucks up everything including dogs. *The Disorderly Orderly* involves Jerry trying to locate a lost patient inside the plaster cast that was on his leg. From 1960 Lewis began increasingly to direct his films himself. Of these, the most successful in terms of laughs achieved are the first, *The Bellboy*, an unconnected series of gags, and the most commercial, *The Nutty Professor*, a gaudily-coloured Jekyll and Hyde story in which Jerry (in his Hyde persona) does a wicked impersonation of Dean Martin! The supporting cast of these later comedies often included the gorgonic, perpetually-outraged Kathleen Freeman (*qv*), a first-rate comic foil. After *The Disorderly Orderly* things went

Which Way to the Front?). 1971: † ‡ *The Day the Clown Cried. 1978:* ‡ *Levy Flies Away. 1979:* † ‡ *That's Life. Rascal Dazzle (narrator only). 1980:* † *Hardly Working. 1982: Slapstick (US: Slapstick of Another Kind). The King of Comedy. 1983:* † *Smorgasbord (Completed 1981. Later: Cracking Up). To Catch a . . . Cop! (The Defective Detective). 1984: Par où t'es rentré, on t'a pas vue sortir? 1987: Fight for Life (TV). 1989: Cookie. 1992: American Dreamers. Freddie Goes to Washington (voice only).*

† Also directed.
‡ Unreleased.

LILLIE, Beatrice 1894–1989

A long-faced, high-browed, brown-haired, athletic-looking, Canadian-born mistress of waspishly zany comedy and devastating asides, Beatrice Lillie could break an audience up by a pause in delivery, a twitch of the cheek, a raise of an eyebrow or a flash of those lively eyes. It's not surprising she made so few films, as she could hardly be relied upon to stick to a script, and even her most devoted audiences rarely had an idea of what she was likely to do at any given time. She was one of a kind, a law unto herself. Born in Toronto, she came to London at 19 to join her mother and sister and soon broke into show business as a chorus girl in London revues. Impresario André Charlot saw that what she was doing with a song had more to do with comedy than vocalising, and set out to make her a top comedienne. By the early 1920s, especially in the Little Theatre's *Nine O'Clock Revue*, 'Bea' Lillie was one of the darlings of London's West End theatre scene. She conquered America in 1924, and it was here that she got the majority of her few film chances. In *Exit Smiling*, her first Hollywood film in 1926, Lillie is stunningly funny without words as the jill-of-all-trades in a touring stock company. She dreams of playing the hip-swinging femme fatale in the company's famous production of *Flaming Women*, but instead is called on to do some real-life vamping to foil a devious villain. The scene where Lillie confounds the dastardly Harry Myers is among the most pricelessly (and bizarrely) funny pieces from Hollywood's silent era. Lillie made her first appearance in cabaret that same year, and her wickedly laid-back sense of humour was shared between Britain and America for the next few years. Her stand-up comedy style was Joyce Grenfell (*qv*) with claws. Professionally and privately, nobody crossed verbal swords with Lillie without being cut down. Rapier-sharp, her wit cut deep into all its targets. She combined with Noël Coward in 1928 in his hit show *This Year of Grace*, although she was the Master's despair at rehearsals, creating chaos out of his well-ordered preparations, and carrying it forward into the actual performance. Lillie's chaos, however, was much funnier than most other comedians' order. Back in Hollywood, she crucified some songs in shorts, and made another feature film, *Are You There?* But the London and New York stages claimed her again for the next eight years. If Coward had a talent to amuse, Bea Lillie had a talent for absurdity. Coward called her the only true comic genius of her generation, and she could slice through social or artistic pretentiousness with equal precision. Another film, *Dr Rhythm*, in 1938, billed her below Bing Crosby but gave her the chance to immortalise her famous 'Double Damask' sketch on celluloid. She plays Mrs Spooner, a customer who confounds and confuses everyone in the store with her requests for two dozen double damask dinner napkins, an order she has soon changed into a duzzle dubben of dabble dumusk danner nipkins and assorted variations thereof. One can imagine Lillie performing this on stage on an ad lib basis, to the consternation of her supporting cast, which in the film includes Franklin Pangborn (*qv*), usually a haughty hotelier but here an increasingly flustered store manager. She entertained Allied troops during World War Two, a period that gave her the material for her later long-running cabaret entertainment, *An Evening with Beatrice Lillie*. And she capered through another film while in Britain, the uproarious *On Approval*, as a rich American widow. With the end of the war she went back to cabaret work in Paris, London and New York. 'Each of her eyebrows is an RSVP', said one enthusiastic New York critic. The 'evenings with Beatrice Lillie' began in 1952, and continued into the late 1960s, a period in which she made her last memorable film appearance, as the white slaver Mrs Meers, the villainess of *Thoroughly Modern Millie*. A half-oriental fiend with knitting needles in her hair, Lillie scurried through the film muttering oriental imprecations through gritted teeth. Her eyebrows were never more arched, her lips never more pursed. She also seemed, perhaps for the first time, very small and slight. On stage, she was a uniquely unpredictable *Auntie Mame*, and amused sophisticated theatre audiences in her seventies with *Late Evening with Beatrice Lillie*. In 1976, however, she suffered a debilitating stroke that left her bedridden for much of her remaining years.

Beatrice Lillie married Lord Peel in 1920. He died in 1934 and her only son, John, was killed in World War Two. She engaged ex-GI John Huck as her chauffeur and bodyguard in 1948, and he became her devoted companion in later years. He died from a heart attack one day after her. Lillie was a caustic, cultured comedienne, if never really an actress. Said one writer at the time of her death: 'She played a few straight roles and left them crooked'.

*1925: * Stage Stars Off Stage. 1926: Exit Smiling. 1929: The Show of Shows. 1930: * Beatrice Lillie and Her Boy Friends. * The Roses Have Made Me Remember. Are You There? 1938: Dr Rhythm. 1943: Welcome to Britain. 1944: On Approval. 1949: Scrapbook for 1933. 1956: Around the World in 80 Days. 1967: Thoroughly Modern Millie.*

LINDER, Max
(Gabriel Maximilien Leuvielle)
1883–1925

With his foxy brown eyes matched by a like moustache, cane, elegant cutaway coat, silk cravat, kid gloves and gleaming top hat, Max Linder could have been every inch the French boulevardier who 'walked along the Bois de Boulogne with an independent air' – had not, in films, everything gone wrong for him. Max Linder was France's first great film comedian. But not for him any kind of dress that smacked of the circus clown. Max was *always* debonair, even in the face of disaster. His early films in France, of which he made scores, are cameos of catastrophe, little gems which work a variety of gags on a single situation, such as taking a bath, getting dressed, or (quite often, as the wolfish Max pursued his prey) chasing a damsel. He was enormously popular in the early 1900s. And, had not war intervened, he would perhaps have been happily entertaining continental audiences into his sixties, competing with such upstarts as Jacques Tati and Fernandel (both *qv*). Linder spent the early part of his life in America, where his father had gone to plant vineyards. When the business failed the family returned to France and Max completed his education there. He was a natural athlete (once pole-vault champion of South West France), an ability that was to stand him in good stead in the more energetic of his comedy capers on screen. Leaving high school in 1901, he studied drama for two years before beginning a stage career under his real name. But by 1905 he was playing minor film roles as Max Linder, progressing to comic leads by 1907 and international fame by 1910. His style of comedy somewhat foreshadowed that of Chaplin (one of his greatest fans) and his dapper, disaster-prone dandy would later prove a useful prototype for Charley Chase (both *qv*). These were the golden years for Linder, who directed all his own work from 1911 to 1917. But the war changed everything. Linder not only received severe shrapnel wounds but was the victim of serious gassing, which left him with moods of black melancholia in between patches of inspiration. With his work output and his popularity in France diminishing, a partially-recovered Linder accepted an offer to work in America in 1916. After three of a projected run of 12 two-reelers, however, his health broke down again. Returning to the continent after a dire battle with double pneumonia, the ailing Max entered a convalescent home in Switzerland for a year. Refusing to retire despite continued fragile health, Linder returned to America, formed his own production company there and made three feature films which contain much of his best work. The first, *Seven Years Bad Luck*, contains an extended sequence involving a mirror with no glass which predates several such scenes with other prominent American comedians, notably The Marx Brothers (*qv*) in *Duck Soup*. The last of the three, *The Three Must-Get-Theres*, a triumphant parody of Dumas's famous swashbuckler, contains sustained action tomfoolery which makes the Richard Lester version 50 years later pale by comparison. But the films were only moderately successful with American audiences and Linder found trouble getting his work distributed. Disconsolate after a deal with Samuel Goldwyn fell through, Max returned to France. There was one more film here and one in Austria but the once-confident Linder was becoming an increasingly forlorn figure. There was talk of another film but Linder and his young wife entered into a suicide pact and, a few weeks short of his 42nd birthday, were found dead together in a Paris hotel. Fortunately, in later years his daughter Maud launched a battle to bring his genius to a fresh audience, resulting in two compilation films, *Laugh with Max Linder* in 1963, and *The Man in the Silk Hat* 20 years later.

1905: La première sortie d'un collégien. 1906: Le premier cigare d'un collégien. Le poison. Le pendu. Les contrebandiers. 1907: Idée d'apache. Une mauvaise vie. La mort d'un toréador. Sganarelle. La vie de Polichinelle. Les débuts d'un patineur. 1908: La rencontre imprévue. Une conquête. La très moutarde. 1909: Un mariage à l'américaine. Le petit jeune homme. La petite rosse. En bombe. Une jeune fille romanesque. Une séance de cinématographe. La timidité vaincue. Le mariage forcé. Trop aimée. Je voudrais un enfant. Le bridge au plafond. Mes voisins me font danser. Kyrelor, bandit par amour. Une poursuite mouvementée. Une campagne electorale. L'ingénieux attendant. Un mariage au puzzle. Les débuts d'un yachtman. Cross country. N'embrassez pas votre bonne. Mon chien rapporte. La ratelier de la belle-mère. Le soulier trop petit. La chapeau-claque. Le baromètre de la fidelité. 1910: Max aéronaute. Max se trompe d'étage. Max fait de la photo. Max champion de boxe. Max joue le drame. Max prend un bain. Les débuts de Max au cinéma. Max fait du ski. Max et la belle négresse. Max célibataire. Max et l'inauguration de la statue. Max et son rival. Max et le téléphone. Max et ses trois mariages. Max et Clancy tombent d'accord. Le cauchemar de Max. Max a le feu sacré. Max maîtresse de piano. Max hypnotisé. Max cherche une fiancée. L'idiot qui se croit Max. Une bonne pour monsieur, un domestique pour madame. Max manque un ruche mariage. Max ne se mariera pas. Max fiancé. Max se marie. Max et sa belle-mère. 1911: Max dans sa famille. Max en convalescence. Max est charitable. Max est distrait. Max et son âne. Voisin ... voisine. Max a un duel. Max veut faire du théâtre. Max et les crêpes. Max victime du quinquina. Max lance la mode. Max et Jane en voyage de noces. Max reprend sa liberté. Max et son chien Dick. Max amoureux de la teinturière. 1912: Max bandit par amour. Max Linder contre Nick Winter. Que peut-il avoir? Max escamoteur. Une nuit agitée. Max professeur de tango. La malle au mariage. Max cocher de fiacre. Max et les femmes. Match de boxe entre patineurs à roulettes. Une idylle à la ferme. Un pari original. Max peintre par amour. Max et la fuite de gaz. Le mal de mer. Max boxeur par amour. La vengeance du domestique. Max collectioneur de chaussures. Max jockey par amour. Voyage de noces en Espagne. Max émule de Tartarin. Max toréador. Amour tenace. Max veut grandir. Max et l'Entente Cordiale. Un mariage au téléphone. Le roman de Max. Max pratique tous les sports. 1913: Comment Max fait le tour du monde. Les vacances de Max. Max fait des conquêtes. Max n'aime pas les chats. Max et le billet doux. Max à Monaco. Max a peur de l'eau. Un unlèvement en hydroplane. Max asthmatique. Le rendez-vous de Max. La rivalité de Max. Le duel de Max. Un mariage imprévu. Le hasard et l'amour. Qui a tué Max? Max au convent. Les escarpins de Max. La ruse de Max. Le chapeau de Max. Max virtuose. 1914: Max décoré. Max sauveteur. Max pédicure. Max et le commissaire. Max et le bâton de rouge. L'anglais tel que Max le parle. N'embrassez pas votre bonne (remake). Max illusioniste. Max et le mari jaloux. Max dans les airs. Max et la doctoresse. Max maître d'hôtel. Max médécin malgré lui. Le 2 août 1914. 1915: Max et le sac. Max devrait porter des bretelles. Max et l'espion. 1916: Max et le Main-qui-étreint. Max entre deux femmes. 1917: Max Comes Across. Max Wants a Divorce. Max in a Taxi. 1919: † Le petit café.

1920: † Le feu sacré. 1921: † Seven Years Bad Luck. † Be My Wife. 1922: † The Three Must-Get-Theres. 1923: † Au secours! 1924: † Clown aus Liebe/Le roi du cirque (GB and US: Max, King of the Circus).

All shorts except † features.

LLOYD, Christopher 1938–

It was appropriate that Lloyd, a big, shambling American actor with hollow eyes, wild hair and coathanger shoulders, should have made a belated film debut as one of the mental hospital inmates in *One Flew Over the Cuckoo's Nest*. Few of his film characters since have seemed quite in tune with this world. As Lloyd pushes on into his fifties, filmgoers can hopefully look forward to a couple of decades of elderly eccentrics. Connecticut-born, Lloyd always saw the stage as his destiny, but it kept him in off-Broadway productions for far too long in the early part of his career. After a stage debut at 16, and studies at New York's Neighborhood Play-house, he was 31 before he made his first Broadway appearance, and nearly 40 before he played there again. By this time, though, he had begun building up film credits, first catching the eye as the embryo 'News' Carver in *Butch and Sundance The Early Days*. This was followed by his running role as The Reverend Jim in the popular TV comedy series *Taxi*, which ran for five years and really triggered Lloyd's career in comedy. He was in *To Be Or Not to Be, Mr Mum* and *The Adventures of Buckaroo Banzai*, but the role that made Lloyd a name rather than a face was that of the time-travelling 'Doc' Emmett Brown in the *Back to the Future* fantasy comedies, the first of which appeared in 1985. Lloyd, as the inventor-scientist with crazed eyes and a time machine in the form of a De Lorean motor-car, stole most of the notices and, in the third of the three films, was even permitted a romance with Mary Steenburgen. Since then Lloyd, who has perfected a shuffling gait and a wonderful way of flapping his limbs around as if they are completely uncoordinated, has been billed more often than not above the title. The more extraordinary his characters have been since then, the more effective he has proved, especially heavily disguised as the fiendish Judge Doom in *Who Framed Roger Rabbit*, and, bald, bag-eyed and finding it hard to be bad as Fester, one of the few successes of *The Addams Family*.

1975: One Summer Love/Dragonfly. One Flew Over the Cuckoo's Nest. 1977: Three Warriors. 1978: Goin' South. Midnight Express. Lacy and the Mississippi Queen (TV). 1979: Stunt Seven (TV). The Lady in Red. The Onion Field. Butch and Sundance The Early Days. 1980: The Black Marble. Pilgrim, Farewell (TV). Schizoid. 1981: The Postman Always Rings Twice. The Legend of the Lone Ranger. National Lampoon Goes to the Movies (released 1983). 1982: Money on the Side (TV). 1983: To Be Or Not to Be. Mr Mom (GB: Mr Mum). September-Gun (TV). 1984: Street Hawk (TV). The Cowboy and the Ballerina (TV). Joy of Sex. Star Trek III The Search for Spock. The Adventures of Buckaroo Banzai Across the Eighth Dimension. 1985: White Dragon. Clue. Back to the Future. 1986: Miracles. Walk Like a Man. 1987: Amazing Stories. Walk Like a Man. 1988: Track 29. Eight Men Out. Who Framed Roger Rabbit. 1989: Back to the Future Part II. The Dream Team. Un plan d'enfer. Why Me? 1990: Back to the Future Part III. Duck Tales: The Movie — Treasure of the Lost Lamp (voice only). 1991: The Addams Family. Suburban Commando.

necks for laughs) it is, in this context, Lloyd we remember, hanging on to a window ledge high above ground, or dangling from the hands of a tower clock. And Lloyd rarely used a stuntman even though he lost a thumb and part of a forefinger from his right hand after a property bomb he was holding exploded in his grasp during the making of *Haunted Spooks* in 1920. By this time Lloyd was firmly established in his most fondly-recalled screen character: the hopeful trier, a sometimes brash, sometimes shy 'boob' with straw hat, bow tie, 'fresh out of high school' air and those priceless black-rimmed glasses. But it took a few years in films before Lloyd evolved the winning formula. No overnight success as a comedian, Lloyd had initial aspirations to straight acting. Smitten with the stage from an early age, he joined a stock company in his home state (Nebraska) at only 14. On leaving school Lloyd went on tour with another theatre company, ending up in Los Angeles in 1913. In between plays Lloyd did some extra work on films. A fellow extra was Hal Roach, a year older than Lloyd. Roach had ambitions to be a film maker and distributor and, coming into a legacy, invited Lloyd to join him in Hollywood. Lloyd invented a Chaplin-type character called Willie Work and played him in four comedy

shorts. In the meantime, Roach's money had run out. But he soon began again, with a new partner, forming the studio that was to rival that of the great Mack Sennett, then dethrone him as king of screen comedy in an unbroken run of success over the next 25 years. Lloyd, now well established as a comedian on screen, returned with a new character, Lonesome Luke. Luke was far from Lloyd's later screen self, being a country hobo with tight-fitting clothes and a Chaplinesque moustache. Luke proved to be popular but Lloyd was not satisfied with him as a character. His 'spectacles' character first appeared in *Over the Fence* in 1917. For a while, Luke and Specs films ran parallel until it became apparent that the latter guise was the one in which the public liked Lloyd best. Bebe Daniels (*qv*), Lloyd's co-star in the 'Luke' films, continued as his screen partner until 1920. By this time Lloyd was beginning to hit the stride that would make him America's highest-paid actor in the 1920s. The first of his escapades on high building-ledges came in 1919 with *Ask Father* and *Look Out Below!* and they were soon such a part of his appeal that one 1920 short was actually called *High and Dizzy*. By 1921 Roach was encouraging Lloyd to spread his wings by extending his two-reel comedies to three-reelers running for more

Blind to the dangers that face him, Harold Lloyd typically battles onwards and upwards in *Feet First*

LLOYD, Harold 1893–1971

With his eyes blinking myopically but ever hopefully behind horn-rimmed spectacles, fresh-faced Harold Lloyd, who portrayed young men of serious mien, used honest endeavour against overwhelming adversity and a succession of setbacks to win the girl in the end. Lloyd once summed up the whole basis of his comedies thus: 'Hard knocks will bring out a man's mettle if he has any. (My hero) triumphs only because he never loses belief in himself.' On this foundation, Lloyd's best comedies build a pyramid of precision-timed gags, scrapes and chases. Only when his (or his director's) sense of pace was less than perfect did his work fall below its usual high standard. Although Buster Keaton (*qv*) was just as much a daredevil in the cause of comedy (and many other comedians risked their

than half an hour. This produced his first classic, *Never Weaken*, in which comedy of character is combined with the inevitable 'thrill' sequence which in this case has Harold teetering precariously on top of a skyscraper. This led to a four-reeler, *A Sailor Made Man*. Two five-reelers in 1922, running at around the hour mark, confirmed that Lloyd's charm and inventiveness could carry a feature, and he never made another starring short. In 1923 Lloyd parted amicably from Hal Roach, set up his own production company and signed with Paramount. Unlike other comedians who would flounder once outside the Roach studio doors, Lloyd prospered. The next five years contain almost all of his finest screen comedy. The year began with *Safety Last* – and Harold's historic appointment with a clock. His skill at organising comedy sequences into the right formula for success was now shown to its best advantage. Suspense, an element present in most of the best visual comedy, soon combined with incident to produce laughs and thrills in the same film and make Lloyd a huge box-office draw. Disasters always came upon him, inevitably while he was trying to impress a girl. Flights up the sides of buildings would be interrupted not only by clocks, but by painters' platforms, swinging windows, awnings, nets, ropes and even mice. In *Hot Water* (1924) Harold becomes progressively more panic-stricken during a unique encounter with a live turkey, while *Girl Shy* (1924) and *For Heaven's Sake* (1926) contain breathtaking chases full of near misses and 'impossible' gags that make for brilliant climaxes to the films. But Lloyd's finest and funniest finish is the football game in *The Freshman* (1925), such a sustained draught of laughter that Preston Sturges used it as the *start* of *Mad Wednesday!*, when he ill-advisedly tempted Lloyd out of an eight-year retirement in 1946. Nothing that followed in the later film was even remotely as good. Lloyd never quite got the hang of the talkies. Although there are good moments in *Feet First*, *Movie Crazy*, *The Cat's Paw* and *The Milky Way*, Lloyd's sense of pacing too often deserted him, and he seemed unable to adapt to the different demands of sound. Perhaps becoming a millionaire had simply sapped his ambition. Maybe his bright young trier was no longer a popular image during the Depression. Lloyd married one of his silent leading ladies, Mildred Davis. She died from a heart attack in 1969, two years before Lloyd's own death from cancer. Besides the money for a film foundation, and his luxurious mansion, Lloyd left more than $5 million to his heirs.

1913: The Old Monk's Tale. † *Samson and Delilah. Algy on the Force. His Heart, His Hand, His Sword (serial). A Little Hero. Cupid in the Dental Parlor. Hide and Seek. Twixt Love and Fire. 1914: The Wizard of Oz. Willie. Willie's Haircut. From Italy's Shores. Curses! They Remarked. The Hungry Actors.*

1915: Willie at Sea. Willie Runs the Park. Once Every Ten Minutes. Soaking with Clothes. Terribly Stuck Up. Some Baby. Giving Them Fits. Tinkering with Trouble. Ragtime Snap Shots. Ruses, Rhymes, Roughnecks. A One Night Stand. Spit Ball Sadie. Pressing the Suit. A Mixup for Mazie. Fresh from the Farm. Bughouse Bell Hops. Great While It Lasted. A Foozle at a Tee Party. Peculiar Patients' Pranks. Just Nuts. Lonesome Luke. Lonesome Luke, Social Gangster. Love, Loot and Crash. Miss Fatty's Seaside Lovers. Into the Light. 1916: Lonesome Luke Lolls in Luxury. Luke Lugs Luggage. Lonesome Luke Leans to the Literary. Luke Laughs Out. Luke Foils the Villain. Luke and the Rural Roughnecks. Luke Laughs Last. Luke's Double. Luke Pipes the Pippins. Luke and the Bomb Throwers. Luke's Late Lunchers. Luke's Fatal Flivver. Luke Rides Roughshod. Luke's Washful Waiting. Luke Crystal Gazer. Luke's Lost Lamb. Luke Does the Midway. Luke and the Mermaids. Luke Joins the Navy. Luke's Society Mix-Up. Luke and the Bang-Tails. Luke's Speedy Club Life. Luke, the Chauffeur. Luke's Newsie Knockout. Luke, Gladiator. Luke's Preparedness Preparations. Luke, Patient Provider. Luke Locates the Loot. Luke's Fireworks Fizzle. Luke's Movie Muddle. Luke's Shattered Sleep. Luke the Candy Cut-Up. Lonesome Luke, Circus King. Ice. Them Was the Happy Days! Luke, Rank Impersonator. 1917: Luke's Lost Liberty. Luke's Busy Day. Luke's Trolley Troubles. Luke Wins Ye Lady Fayre. Lonesome Luke, Lawyer. Lonesome Luke's Lively Life. Lonesome Luke on Tin Can Alley. Lonesome Luke, Plumber. Lonesome Luke's Honeymoon. Stop! Luke! Listen! Lonesome Luke, Messenger. Lonesome Luke, Mechanic. Lonesome Luke's Wild Women. Over the Fence. Lonesome Luke Loses Patients. Lonesome Luke From London to Laramie. Drama's Dreadful Deal. Pinched. By the Sad Sea Waves. Bliss. Rainbow Island. Love, Laughs and Lather. The Flirt. Clubs Are Trumps. All Aboard. We Never Sleep. Move On. Bashful. The Tip. Step Lively. 1918: The Big Idea. The Lamb. Hit Him Again. Beat It. A Gasoline Wedding. Let's Go. Look Pleasant, Please. Here Come the Girls. Follow the Crowd. On the Jump. Pipe the Whiskers. It's a Wild Life. Hey There! Kicked Out. The Non-Stop Kid. Two-Gun Gussie. Fireman, Save My Child. That's Him. City Slicker. Sic 'Em Towser. Somewhere in Turkey. Bride and Gloom. Are Crooks Dishonest? An Ozark Romance. Kicking the Germ Out of Germany. Two Scrambled. Bees in His Bonnet. Swing Your Partners. Why Pick On Me? Nothing But Trouble. Hear 'Em Rave. Take a Chance. She Loves Me Not. Wanted: $5000. Going! Going! Gone! Ask Father. On the Fire. 1919: Look Out Below. The Dutiful Dub. Next Aisle Over. A Sammy in Siberia. Young Mr Jazz. Just Dropped In. Crack Your Heels. Si, Senor. Before Breakfast. The Marathon. The Rajah. Swat the Cook. Off the Trolley. Ring Up the Curtain. Back to the Woods. Pistols for Breakfast. Spring Fever. Billy Blazes Esquire. Just Neighbors. At the Old Stage Door. A Jazzed Honeymoon. Chop Suey & Co. Never Touched Me. Count Your Change. Heap Big

Chief. Don't Shove. Be My Wife. He Leads, Others Follow. Soft Money. Count the Votes. Pay Your Dues. Bumping into Broadway. From Hand to Mouth. His Royal Slyness. Captain Kidd's Kids. 1920: Haunted Spooks. An Eastern Westerner. High and Dizzy. Get Out and Get Under. Number, Please. 1921: Now or Never. Among Those Present. I Do. Never Weaken. † *A Sailor-Made Man. 1922:* † *Grandma's Boy.* † *Doctor Jack. 1923:* † *Safety Last.* † *Why Worry? Dogs of War. 1924:* † *Girl Shy.* † *Hot Water. 1925:* † *The Freshman (GB: College Days). 1926:* † *For Heaven's Sake. 1927:* † *The Kid Brother. 1928:* † *Speedy. 1929:* † *Welcome Danger. 1930:* † *Feet First. 1931: Screen Snapshots No. 8. 1932:* † *Movie Crazy. 1934:* † *The Cat's-Paw. 1936:* † *The Milky Way. 1938:* † *Professor Beware! 1946:* † *The Sin of Harold Diddlebock (later and GB: Mad Wednesday!).*

All shorts except † features.

LONG, Shelley 1949–
America's Shelley Long deserved to be a major star. And, in another era, with the benefit of studio supervision, she probably would have been. Most of the film scripts she chose after her success in television's *Cheers* would have been thrown back to the writers (or simply thrown out) in the studio days. Good comedies that don't rely on special effects, though, are tough to find today. And Long hasn't even picked the best of the ones that have been around. It's a great shame: no-one is funnier with little bits of comic business, and few have a more natural sense of comedy timing. She just needed the big one that now may never come. Tall, tawny-haired, slightly awkward, with large blue eyes and a humorous mouth, Long was a latecomer to national fame. After winning awards for humorous readings at high school in her native Indiana, she majored in drama at university and went straight into local television, eventually winning three Emmy Awards before, like many of today's star comedy performers, joining Chicago's Second City Comedy Troupe, where she became a whiz at improvisational comedy. She migrated to California in the late 1970s, but her bright,

Keep taking the tablets! Egyptologist and archaeologist Harold Lloyd seems in sore need of sustenance as he pursues his quest for an ancient tablet, in *Professor Beware!*

Josser (Ernie Lotinga, centre of three privates) endures an embarrassing moment in *Josser in the Army*. He's flanked by Jack Frost and Hal Gordon

Stanley Lupino takes it all on his shoulders in *The Love Race*. Joining his leaning tower are (top to bottom) Dorothy Boyd, Jack Hobbs and Dorothy Bartlam

chirpy personality was wasted in supporting roles in TV movies. There was a comedy film of sorts in *Caveman*, a 1981 prehistoric farce in which she and Dennis Quaid amazingly *supported* stars Ringo Starr and Barbara Bach (Mrs Ringo). But salvation was at hand. The role of Diane, the dizzy, would-be-intellectual, self-conscious, transparently pretentious barmaid in a TV comedy series, *Cheers*, came her way in 1982. Five years later, when she (possibly mistakenly) quit the role, she and Ted Danson (and a number of the supporting players) had become national figures in America, and even quite well-known elsewhere. In films, though, she continued making wrong choices. She was lost in the shuffle – and eclipsed by Michael Keaton (*qv*) – in the underrated *Night Shift*, and went straight, opposite then-starlet Tom Cruise in *Losin' It*. *Irreconcilable Differences* was saccharine romantic comedy, direly scripted. When they tried teaming her with people who had some facility with comedy, things picked up. She and Tom Hanks (*qv*) handled visual laughs very well in *The Money Pit* and she and Bette Midler made a funny team in *Outrageous Fortune*, exchanging wisecracks in fine style as they battled to find the man who has hoodwinked them both. The makers of *Outrageous Fortune*, Touchstone, gave her her own vehicle, *Hello Again*, as a housewife who literally returns from the dead – and changes her life. 'I was immediately drawn to the character', said Long. 'She's attractive, honest, fragile, and undeniably clumsy.' Long gave a marvellously-detailed comic performance and the fact that the film did well in America (though poorly elsewhere, where she was less well known) was a tribute to her. *Troop Beverly Hills* cast her delightfully as a reluctant scoutmistress. She was good again in a moderate comedy, but this time one that flopped altogether. *Don't Tell Her It's Me* was worse, a big downer on the careers of Long, Steve Guttenberg (*qv*) and Jami Gertz, and for the first time she gave a strident, overpitched performance. Just about released in America, it didn't surface in England (probably to the stars' embarrassment) until two years later. Desperate, she tried heavy drama. But she was way out of her depth in *Shattered*, and a title change to *Voices Within* made no difference. Still game, she tried another comedy, *Frozen Assets*, with *Hello Again* co-star Corbin Bernsen. The omens don't look good for the rest of Long's film career. But *Cheers* is still running happily ...

1979: The Cracker Factory (TV). 1980: A Small Circle of Friends. The Promise of Love (TV). 1981: The Princess and the Cabbie (TV). Caveman. 1982: Night Shift. 1983: Losin' It. 1984: Irreconcilable Differences. 1985: The Money Pit. 1987: Outrageous Fortune. Hello Again. 1989: Troop Beverly Hills. 1990: Don't Tell Her It's Me. Shattered/Voices Within. 1992: Frozen Assets.

LOTINGA, Ernie 1876–1951
A chipper little British north-country comedian with black, slicked-back hair, very dark brown beady eyes and a rasping voice redolent of his native Sunderland, Lotinga prospered in early sound comedies made in the bargain basements of the British cinema – though not for long. He started life as a baker. But in the evenings he began his theatrical career by singing at 'smoking concerts' for half-a-crown (12½p today) a performance. These were jolly, raucous, sometimes vulgar songs, typical of the music-hall of the day. By 1898 he was a regular variety comedian, billed as Don Roy. Later he reverted to his own name, and invented a character called Jimmy Josser, a much-put-upon little man who was to bring Lotinga fame and fortune. Henceforth, Lotinga was almost always Josser, whether in music-hall sketches or, later, in ramshackle farces on the London stage. Lotinga's army sketches were among his most popular, and it was in one of them,

The Raw Recruit, that Lotinga and Josser made their film debuts in 1928, one of the earliest British sound two-reelers. It was followed by *The Orderly Room*, based on one of Lotinga's first plays, written in 1914. Other sections of this play were filmed later the same year as *Nap* and *Joining Up*. The following year two more Lotinga plays, *Josser KC* and *The Police Force*, were raided to provide the year's quota of two-reelers for 1929. The two plays were dug up again for Lotinga's assault on the feature market in 1931. *P. C. Josser* was the most successful (indeed the best of all Lotinga's films). Made on a respectable budget by British International Pictures, it gave Lotinga fans good value by moving along like a firecracker despite a then lengthy running time of 90 minutes. Josser is fired from the police force, but redeems his reputation by bringing to book a racehorse-doping gang. The scenario gave Lotinga plenty of chances to shine in a variety of moods and disguises. And BIP kept the ball rolling with *Dr Josser KC*, a helter-skelter farce with two leading ladies, Molly Lamont and Binnie Barnes, who were shortly to go to Hollywood. The Josser films that followed were criticised for their coarseness and crudity, two qualities which had helped build Lotinga's popularity in the northern music-halls. In his late fifties, however, he was unable, and probably unwilling to change. Between films, he continued to make stage appearances, becoming an actor-manager with his production of the scatty farce *My Wife's Family*, itself filmed three times, though never with Lotinga. By 1933 Lotinga was being overtaken in popularity in the second-feature comedy market by the younger Leslie Fuller (*qv*). *Josser on the Farm*, his sole 1934 contribution, was

There isn't a dry eye in the court when Ernie Lotinga's *P. C. Josser* takes the stand. Among those quite unable to bear it are Jack Frost and Garry Marsh

less successful than previous capers. Lotinga tried a change of pace with a dual role in *Smith's Wives*, but returned to Josser (and his old co-star, Jack Frost, in *Love Up the Pole*, a long and sloppily-made farce about two waiters on the run from the police. Disillusioned with movie-making, Lotinga played out the remainder of his career on stage, mainly in revivals of his former successes.

1928: * *The Raw Recruit.* * *Nap.* * *Joining Up.* * *The Orderly Room.* 1929: * *Josser KC.* * *Doing His Duty.* * *Spirits.* * *Acci-dental Treatment.* 1931: *P. C. Josser. Dr Josser KC.* 1932: *Josser Joins the Navy. Josser on the River. Josser in the Army..* 1934: *Josser on the Farm.* 1935: *Smith's Wives.* 1936: *Love Up the Pole/Jimmy Josser in Love Up the Pole.*

received no more than the minimum of spending money. By the mid 1920s Lucan and McShane had become top-of-the-bill attractions, if mainly on the northern variety circuit. The loose-limbed Lucan was a great pantomimist and acrobat, his contortions all the funnier when he was dressed as a woman. The looks of horror, thrusting forward beady eyes and a nose that looked as if it had been made of putty, combined with inimitable wide, flapping gestures to produce a character with whom audiences could identify and sympathise, as well as laugh at. And laugh they did. By 1932 Lucan and McShane had

reached the London Palladium. Two years later they appeared at a Royal Variety Performance, presenting a relatively new routine called *Waiting for Bridget*, which was to prove the foundation stone for all their later work. Here, Lucan has already assumed the mantle of the grey-haired Irish washerwoman, waiting for an errant daughter to return in the wee small hours, amusing the audience meanwhile as he/she removes layers of underwear in preparation for bed. The return of Bridget (McShane) is the cue for a volcanic row (uncomfortably close to real life for those who knew them)

Mistaken for a spy, Old Mother Riley (Arthur Lucan) finds herself the involuntary participant in an Apache dance in *Old Mother Riley in Paris*. Her partner is George Wolkowsky

LUCAN, Arthur 1887–1954
and
McSHANE, Kitty 1898–1964

A real-life husband and wife who played mother and daughter on stage and screen. The private life of Lucan and McShane, always tempestuous, became legendary in latter days for the couple's (very public) off-stage rows. Kitty was bitchy, bossy, ambitious and promiscuous – and one of the most professional 'feeds' in the business. Her Lincolnshire-born husband was scrawny, unprepossessing and like her (though normally shy and reticent) had an explosive temper. He was also touched with comic genius.. Lucan's most famous creation, Mother Riley, was rooted in reality, the product of scores of landladies he encountered while touring in Britain and Ireland. He had started at 13, a year after leaving school, and it was on one of the Irish tours that he met a Dublin landlady's daughter called Kitty McShane, one of 18 children and anxious to escape her surroundings. She was just 15 when they married and she immediately joined Lucan's act. In post-war years, Lucan began developing and perfecting a talent for playing dame, while Kitty continued to support him on stage as well as (none too successfully) looking after the financial side of their affairs. She also saw to it that her husband

in which they destroy every item of crockery on stage – and the stars made sure there was always a lot to destroy. The sketch was filmed as part of *Stars on Parade* (1935), a cobbled-together piece of entertainment that gave Lucan and McShane their movie debut. The demand for the Irish washerwoman was such that the cut-price, northern-based Butchers distributing outfit, whose films featuring regional comics did well in the north of England, decided to put her into a film of her own. It was unfortunate in many ways that the package also included Kitty. Already rather mature for the role of the daughter (she was 39), Kitty insisted on playing it to the point of ridicule for another 15 years. She did have a certain Irish prettiness, somewhat spoilt by a strong chin and thin pencilled eyebrows. But she also insisted on wearing unsuitable clothes and singing sentimental and embarrassing Irish melodies in most of the films. Kitty's songs were definitely occasions when you went out to buy the popcorn. The Mother Riley character itself, however, was a huge success, even if the screen never seemed quite wide enough to encompass all her antics (sometimes directors and cameramen had a job simply keeping Lucan within the frame). Eager, do-gooding and never one to be put down, Mother Riley blunders into situations where she reduces everyone to her own level. The first film, *Old Mother Riley*, demonstrated Lucan's mastery of verbal comedy, accompanied of course by telling gestures. Mother Riley confounds a rich family by her earthy simplicity, and later also scores a courtroom triumph by using a mixture of blarney, native cunning and verbal counterpunch to win the audience completely over to her side. In the next film, *Old Mother Riley in Paris*, one of the best in the series, our washerwoman heroine breaks her leg, jumps from a high place, does a hilarious Apache dance and becomes involved in espionage. Through it all she remains the same lovable old conniver, concerned principally for her daughter, her corsets and her bottle of gin – not necessarily in that order. The Riley films were taken up by Rank, continuing through the war years, when Lucan and McShane decided to return to the stage. In 1949 there was an offer from Renown, which involved several of their old colleagues at Butchers, for the duo to return to films. But Kitty could no longer sustain even the appearance of youth, their marriage had fallen apart and the scripts were poor. Only Lucan was as leeringly lively as ever. By 1951 the estranged couple was even refusing to appear on the same set. *Old Mother Riley's Jungle Treasure* had to be completed shooting their scenes separately – a pity; it was the first half-way decent Riley romp in quite a while – and in the last film of all, *Mother Riley Meets the Vampire*, Lucan appeared alone. It was a dismal, dispiriting affair – about par for the course for the later career of Lucan's co-star Bela Lugosi. Lucan continued on the

Toastrack tangle. Stanley Lupino (right) and Wallace Arthur (alias Wallace Lupino) are all fingers and thumbs in this scene from *The Love Race*

variety halls without his ex-wife. He was in Hull, waiting in the wings for his cue, on 17 May 1954. The cue came and went but 'Mother Riley' never appeared on stage. They found Lucan in a crumpled heap in the wings, dead from a massive heart attack. Kitty lived on for another ten years. She died a chronic alcoholic, having squandered most of their earnings down the years – much of it in a failed beauty salon business.

1935: Stars on Parade. 1937: Kathleen Mavourneen (US: Kathleen). Old Mother Riley. 1938: Old Mother Riley in Paris. 1939: Old Mother Riley MP. Old Mother Riley Joins Up. 1940: Old Mother Riley in Society. Old Mother Riley in Business. 1941: Old Mother Riley's Ghosts. Old Mother Riley's Circus. 1942: Old Mother Riley Detective. 1943: Old Mother Riley Overseas. 1945: Old Mother Riley at Home. 1949: Old Mother Riley's New Venture. 1950: Old Mother Riley Headmistress. 1951: Old Mother Riley's Jungle Treasure. 1952: Mother Riley Meets the Vampire (US: Vampire Over London).

LUPINO, Stanley 1893–1942

Although a force in the British musical-comedy theatre for more than two decades, this small, dark, dapper, thin-mouthed, rather odd-shaped London-born entertainer never gave the impression that his stay in the cinema was more than temporary. A buoyant little man with a bright, breezy personality, Lupino came from a family that had had show business in its veins for generations. Lupino Lane (*qv*), who had some success in Hollywood, was Stanley's cousin, and the actress Ida Lupino is his daughter. Lupino first trod the boards at the age of seven as a monkey in a pantomime, and rarely left them thereafter. From being a bouncy juvenile of the immediate post-war years, he quickly developed into a fully-fledged West End star, appearing in a succession of comedy musicals through the 1920s, for many of which he had a hand in writing the scripts and/or songs. When sound films began to take a grip on Britain at the end of the decade the time was obviously ripe for Lupino to move many of his stage hits on to the screen. Still in his mid thirties, with an old/young face, Lupino could play the romantic lead as convincingly as the fool and, indeed, almost any kind of comedy or musical number was liable to crop up in his films. The first Lupino film, *Love Lies*, adapted from one of his plays, was highly successful, a brisk, no-nonsense farce that set the pattern for the rest of the Lupino films of the decade. In these he was almost always a bachelor who settled down with the right girl at the end after amorous misadventures, which often included upperclass chicks who involved our hero and his friends (usually played by fellow-comedians Will Fyffe (*qv*) and Laddie Cliff) in disastrous forays into high society. In *Sleepless Nights*, another successful Lupino offering from British International Pictures at Elstree, he settled down to showing his liking for top-hat-and-tails musical numbers (the popular one in this film was *I Don't Want to Go to Bed*) which surrounded him with glamorous showgirls who all seemed to be taller than he was. The early 1930s produced several profitable collaborations between Lupino and the writer Frank Launder, later to become more famous as the director of

the 'St Trinian's' comedies of the 1950s. Lupino called Launder 'Shakespeare' because of his ability to produce extra lines or scenes at the drop of the hat. Their first collaboration was one of Lupino's best: *Facing the Music*. Others were *You Made Me Love You* (a take-off of *The Taming of the Shrew*, opposite Hollywood's Thelma Todd (*qv*)) and *Happy*, a title that reflected the star's perennial cheerfulness on screen. Lupino's last decent film was *Cheer Up!*, in 1936, another musical mélange of mirth and mistaken identity, to (almost) quote the advertising from one of his other films. His last, *Lucky to Me*, in 1939, was probably the worst. Lupino, like other stars of the decade, returned to the medium in which he was happiest, the theatre. In his case, this return was cut tragically short when he died from cancer just a week short of his 50th birthday.

1931: Love Lies. The Love Race. 1932: Sleepless Nights. 1933: King of the Ritz. Facing the Music. You Made Me Love You. Happy. 1935: Honeymoon for Three. 1936: Cheer Up! Sporting Love. 1937: Over She Goes. 1938: Hold My Hand. 1939: Lucky to Me.

LYNN, Ralph 1881–1962 (right)
and
WALLS, Tom 1883–1949

No British duo was more successful at the box-office in the 1930s than seasoned farceurs Ralph Lynn and Tom Walls. Hit after hit was tailored to their talents by writer Ben Travers, many of them transferences to the screen of stage successes, but some film originals. Walls was the bluff, florid, moustachioed schemer, usually the black sheep of a well-to-do family. Amiable, monocled, slick-haired Lynn, with the most vacuous of idiot grins, revealing amazing teeth, was the society silly ass, wellmeaning and easy prey for gold-digging blondes. He was almost 50 when the series began and rather long in the tooth for the bungling bachelors he played, but the public accepted him anyway. Travers wrote the words, Walls produced the plays and directed the films, and Lynn and a talented company of regular supporting players provided the laughter: these would often include Robertson Hare (*qv*), Mary Brough, Winifred Shotter and Yvonne Arnaud. Lynn first appeared on the London stage at 19, but Walls was in turn steeplechase jockey and policeman before opting for an acting career. They came together at London's Aldwych Theatre in 1925, in the first of what came to be known as the Aldwych farces, *A Cuckoo in the Nest*. Its combination of confused clerics, compromising situations, high jinks at a country inn with only one room left, and falling trousers proved wildly successful with the paying public, and one farce a year followed for the next decade. Lynn and Walls also indulged in some delightful, sometimes idiotic crosstalk in many of them. The next play was *Rookery Nook*, which was the first of the farces to be filmed when the Walls-Lynn duo invaded British and Dominions studios in 1930. Walls had help with the direction from an American, Byron Haskin (who much later made a number of Hollywood films), but it was a rather stagey affair, if still very funny, complications flowing fast and furious in its 76 minutes. Walls made two excellent screen versions of comedy plays by Frederick Lonsdale, *Canaries Sometimes Sing* (as a playwright) and *On Approval* (as an

Ralph Lynn in distress in *A Cuckoo in the Nest*

Double trouble. Ralph Lynn (left) and Tom Walls played characters young and old as a diversion from their usual style of farce, in *For Valour*

Jerry (Moore Marriott) is at the wheel as The Crazy Gang, including Bud Flanagan (*qv*), in white, and Chesney Allen (*qv*), extreme right, cock a snook at Hitler in *Gasbags*

Rigby Reardon (Steve Martin) and Von Kluck (Carl Reiner) argue over who gets to reveal the plot of the film, in Reiner's *Dead Men Don't Wear Plaid*

impecunious nobleman) before re-teaming with Lynn in Travers' *Plunder*, and then directing Lynn to good effect in *Tons of Money*, a showcase for Lynn (who also co-scripted) as a penniless inventor who stages his own death to evade his creditors. He returns as his own long-lost cousin George – only for a couple of other people to turn up also claiming to be cousin George. All these were in the can before the end of 1930, and all were wildly successful. *Rookery Nook*, for example, gathered in more than ten times its cost. The Aldwych gang was now in full cry, and 1932 brought two of their best films, both from Travers plays. *A Night Like This*, first staged in 1930, handed Lynn the central spotlight again as (inevitably) a man-about-town who is black-mailed by the owner of the nightclub where Lynn has become infatuated with a dancer. Walls plays an Irish policeman who com-bines with Lynn to retrieve a missing neck-lace. The second Aldwych farce of this remarkable year remains perhaps the duo's best known. *Thark* (staged in 1927) is an archetypal spooky-house caper, in which the new owner of creepy Thark Manor (the redoubtable Mary Brough) is disturbed by eerie sounds at night. Walls and Lynn, as the people responsible for selling her the house, find themselves compelled to agree to spend a night there. Walls' spirited direc-tion was seen at its best in editing the timing of the laughs, as he and Lynn cling together in times of trial, in a very funny piece which is full of sudden side-splitting moments and far too seldom revived. As Walls was off making his own starring comedy, *Leap Year*, portly Davy Burnaby (*qv*) stood in for Lynn's third film of the year, *Just My Luck*, a somewhat less hysteri-cal farce, a sort of sideshoot of *School for Scoundrels* with Lynn as a shy, 40ish music teacher who takes a course in 'superiority and success', winning the familiar charms of Winifred Shotter in the end. Lynn had prob-ably his best solo role in *Up to the Neck*, as N. B. Good, a bank clerk who inherits a fortune and finances a disastrous show to try to make his chorus-girl friend a star. But he himself becomes a success after an uninten-tionally hilarious performance in a straight play! It was back to work in harness with Walls in *A Cuckoo in the Nest*, *Turkey Time*, *A Cup of Kindness*, *Dirty Work*, *Fighting Stock*, *Stormy Weather*, *Foreign Affaires* and *Pot Luck*. But, with the supply of source material from the stage running low in the late 1930s, the Walls-Lynn-Travers trio tried something a little different in *For Valour*. This underrated film, much longer than their average offer-ing, is a through-the-ages comedy of character, which starts with Private Doubleday (Walls) saving the life of Major Pyke (Lynn) in the Boer War, continues with their descendants trying to keep out of prison, and ends with old Doubleday wheeling old Pyke around in a bath-chair. Walls and Lynn played both sets of Double-days and Pykes. While Lynn returned to the

stage, Walls enjoyed a few more leading roles in the burgeoning British film industry of the late 1930s before reemerging as a character star of the 1940s for his last few years. He died in 1949, his old partner out-living him by 13 years.

Together. 1930: † *Rookery Nook* (US: One Embarrassing Night). † *Plunder*. † *Tons of Money* (Walls directed but did not appear). 1932: † *A Night Like This*. † *Thark*. 1933: † *Turkey Time*. † *A Cuckoo in the Nest*. 1934: † *A Cup of Kindness*. † *Dirty Work* (Walls directed but did not appear). 1935: † *Fighting Stock*. † *Stormy Weather*. † *Foreign Affaires*. 1936: † *Pot Luck*. 1937: † *For Valour*.

Lynn alone. 1929: * *Peace and Quiet*. 1931: *Chance of a Night Time*. *Mischief*. 1932: *Just My Luck*. 1933: *Summer Lightning*. *Up to the Neck*. 1936: *In the Soup*. *All In*. 1959: *The Adventures of Rex* (serial).

Walls alone. 1930: † *Canaries Sometimes Sing*. *On Approval*. 1932: † *Leap Year*. 1933: *Just Smith*. † *The Blarney Stone* (US: The Blarney Kiss). 1934: † *Lady in Danger*. 1935: *Me and Marlborough*. 1936: † *Dishonour Bright*. 1937: † *Second Best Bed*. 1938: *Strange Boarders*. † *Old Iron*. *Crackerjack* (US: Man with a Hundred Faces). 1943: *Undercover* (US: Underground Guerillas). *They Met in the Dark*. 1944: *Halfway House*. *Love Story* (US: A Lady Surrenders). 1945: *Johnny French-man*. 1946: *This Man is Mine*. 1947: *Master of Bankdam*. *While I Live*. 1948: *Spring in Park Lane*. 1949: *Maytime in Mayfair*. The *Interrupted Journey*.

† Directed by Walls

LYON, Ben
See DANIELS, Bebe

MAIN, Marjorie
(Mary Tomlinson) 1890–1975
One of the great 'reactors' of her day, Marjorie Main was an unforgettable comedy character star. One can still see her in that print frock, arms akimbo, hair scruffed high – in real life she never could do anything with it – glaring fiercely at Wallace

Beery (*qv*), Percy Kilbride, or some other miscreant. No-one, but no-one stole scenes from Marjorie Main. She was born to a minister and his wife in Indiana, became interested in drama at school and specialised in 'blood-and-thunder recitations, where my voice stepped up several gears towards the end'. This raucous squawk was to be-come her stock in trade when her film career hit its stride many years later. She became a stage actress but quit for several years in the 1920s after marrying Stanley Krebs, a lecturer and psychologist. His death in 1935 left her a widow at 45 and she threw herself full time into her acting work. Showy roles in the Broadway productions of *Dead End* and *The Women* (both of which she repeated in subsequent film versions) led to the resumption of her till-then-sporadic film career in 1937. After several good roles for MGM as housekeepers, cooks and mothers, Marjorie was put under contract by the studio and swiftly teamed with rum-bustious Wallace Beery, who had been without a female partner for his rough-and-tumble action comedies since the death of Marie Dressler (*qv*) in 1934. In their first film together, *Wyoming*, she was a lady black-smith taming Beery's outlaw. This was followed by *Barnacle Bill*, *Jackass Mail*, *Rationing*, *Bad Bascomb* and *Big Jack*. Beery died soon after the last of these, in 1949, by which time Marjorie was well established in the public eye as Ma Kettle, the character she'd created in the 1947 hit *The Egg and I*. Her homely features, shapelessly matronly figure, eagle eyes, bundle of hair and ag-gressive stance – she usually reached her prey in a few manly strides and swung a rifle from her elbows at intruders – were all perfect for Ma Kettle, haranguing her weedy, lazy husband, getting on with her homemade produce amidst the chaos of a house with seemingly dozens of children and keeping allcomers at bay. The Kettle characters, Ma and Pa, were so popular that the studio, Universal-International, spun a whole series of 80-minute comedies around them, which Main continued even after the retirement of her partner, Percy Kilbride, in 1955. The series cost around $4 million all told and grossed close to $40 million. It was responsible almost single-handed for keeping the studio solvent between 1949 and 1955. Marjorie Main was once described by a critic as being 'incredibly ferocious' but everyone knew that her characters, even Ma Kettle, had hearts of gold. She died from cancer, having never re-married.

1932: Hot Saturday. A House Divided. 1933: Take a Chance. 1934: Music in the Air. * New Deal Rhythm. Crime without Passion. 1935: Naughty Marietta. 1937: Dead End. City Girl. Boy of the Streets. Love in a Bungalow. The Shadow (GB: The Circus Shadow). The Man Who Cried Wolf. Stella Dallas. The Wrong Road. 1938: Penitentiary. Girls' School. Romance of the Limberlost. Under the Big Top (GB: The Circus Comes to Town). King of the Newsboys. Too Hot to Handle. Little Tough Guy. Three Comrades. Test Pilot. Prison Farm. There Goes My Heart. 1939: Angels Wash Their Faces. Another Thin Man. Lucky Night. They Shall Have Music (GB: Melody of Youth). The Women. Two Thoroughbreds. 1940: Women Without Names. Dark Command. Turnabout. Susan and God (GB: The Gay Mrs Trexel). Wyoming (GB: Bad Man of Wyoming). I Take This Woman. The Captain is a Lady. 1941: The Wild Man of Borneo. The Trial of Mary Dugan. Honky Tonk. A Woman's Face. The Bugle Sounds. Shepherd of the Hills. Barnacle Bill. 1942: Tish. The Affairs of Martha (GB: Once Upon A Thursday). Jackass Mail. Tennessee Johnson (GB: The Man on America's Conscience). We Were Dancing. 1943: Heaven Can Wait. Woman of the Town. Johnny Come Lately (GB: Johnny Vagabond). 1944: Rationing. Meet Me in St Louis. Gentle Annie. 1945: Murder, He Says. The Harvey Girls. 1946: The Show-off. Bad Bascomb. Undercurrent. 1947: The Egg and I. The Wistful Widow of Wagon Gap (GB: The Wistful Widow). 1948: Feudin', Fussin' and a-Fightin'. Ma and Pa Kettle. 1949: Big Jack. Ma and Pa Kettle Go to Town (GB: Going to Town). 1950: Summer Stock (GB: If You Feel Like Singing). Mrs O'Malley and Mr Malone. Mr Imperium (GB: You Belong to My Heart). 1951: It's a Big Country. The Law and the Lady. Ma and Pa Kettle Back on the Farm. 1952: Belle of New York. Ma and Pa Kettle on Vacation (GB: Ma and Pa Kettle Go to Paris). Ma and Pa Kettle at the Fair. 1953: Fast Company. 1954: Ricochet Romance. Ma and Pa Kettle at Home. The Long, Long Trailer. Rose Marie. 1955: Ma and Pa Kettle at Waikiki. 1956: The Kettles in the Ozarks. Friendly Persuasion. 1957: The Kettles on Old MacDonald's Farm.

MANN, Hank

(David Lieberman) 1888–1971

A brown-haired, sleepy-eyed American acrobatic comedian of slightly goofy good looks – reminiscent of the dancer Ray Bolger – that were soon hidden behind an enormous 'broom' moustache when he became one of Mack Sennett's Keystone Kops. Born in New York and educated in the public schools of Manhattan, the young Mann, always known as 'Hank' to his

friends, was an angelic-faced choir boy before becoming a trapeze artist in a circus, known as the Flying Mann. Later, he took his acrobatic artistry into vaudeville, and ended up in California, where he signed up with Sennett's Keystone Studio in 1913. You'd have thought that the gap between Mann's nose and mouth was too small to accommodate any kind of moustache. But somehow Hank managed to affix a giant-sized one which covered much of the lower half of his face, giving him a mournful, bloodhound expression beneath his pudding-basin haircut. After some years with Sennett, followed by a period with the L-KO company, Mann joined the American Expeditionary Force in 1917. Returning to Hollywood in 1920, he began to play character roles in films, often as bashful suitors or light comedy relief. Alternating between vaudeville and film work throughout the 1930s, Mann, still moustached but now balding, found movie roles growing scarce in the early 1940s and surprised many of his friends by becoming a film makeup artist in 1944. Towards the end of the decade he also opened a malt shop in Sierra Madre. But he was always available for Hollywood cameo roles, especially those that paired him with his old friend and Keystone colleague Chester Conklin (qv). The one-time flying aerialist who became the jolliest and most agile of the Keystone Kops was the last of them when he died at 83 – six weeks after Chester Conklin.

1913: * The Waiter's Picnic. * Barney Oldfield's Race for Life. * Old Muddington's Daughters. * Algy on the Force. * Out and In. 1914: * In the Clutches of a Gang. * The Fatal Mallet. Mabel's Strange Predicament. * Caught in a Cabaret. * The Knock-Out. * The Alarm. * Mabel's Married Life. Tillie's Punctured Romance. 1915: * His Father's Footsteps. * Shaved in Mexico. * There's Many a Fool. * The Hunt. 1916: A Modern Enoch Arden. * The Village Blacksmith (and directed). * His Bread and Butter. * Hearts and Sparks. 1917: * Domestic Hound. * Bon Bon Riot. * His Final Blow Out. 1919: * The Janitor. 1920: *Mystic Mush. 1921: The Messenger. 1922: Quincy Adams Sawyer. * Eye for Figures. *Harem

Hero. 1923: Don't Marry for Money. Hollywood. Lights Out. Tea – With a Kick. The Wanters. The Near Lady. A Noise in Newboro. 1924: The Man Who Played Square. Empty Hands. Riders Up. A Woman Who Sinned. 1925: The Arizona Romeo. The Sporting Venus. 1926: The Skyrocket. The Boob. The Flying Horseman. Wings of the Storm. 1927: The Ladybird. Paid to Love. The Patent Leather Kid. The Scorcher. Broadway After Midnight (GB: Gangsters on Broadway). When Danger Calls. Smile, Brother Smile. 1928: The Garden of Eden. * Fazil. * Should Women Drive? 1929: The Donovan Affair. Spite Marriage. * Pants at Any Price. * Nize Baby. The Fall of Eve. Morgan's Last Raid. 1930: Sinner's Holiday. The Arizona Kid. The Dawn Trail. * Their Wives' Vacation. 1931: City Lights. Annabelle's Affairs. * Stout Hearts and Willing Hands. * Easy to Get. * The Great Junction Hotel. 1932: Million Dollar Legs. The Fourth Horseman. Ridin' for Justice. The Strange Love of Molly Louvain. Scarface (The Shame of a Nation). 1933: The Big Chance. Smoky. 1934: Fugitive Road. * Men in Black. 1935: The Devil is a Woman. * Key-stone Hotel. The Big Broadcast of 1936. Barbary Coast. 1936: Modern Times. Reunion (GB: Hearts in Reunion). Call of the Prairie. The Preview Murder Mystery. 1937: * Goofs and Saddles. Saratoga. You Can't Have Everything. Ali Baba Goes to Town. 1938: Stranger from Arizona. 1939: Hollywood Cavalcade. Charlie Chan in Reno. Mr Smith Goes to Washington. 1940: * Bubbling Trouble. The Great Dictator. * Alfalfa's Double. 1941: The Man Who Came to Dinner. Nine Lives are not Enough. The Maltese Falcon. * Half Shot at Sunrise. * Love at First Fright. * Sweet Spirits of the Nighter. * So You Won't Squawk. Honolulu Lu. The Body Disappears. Kings Row. Meet John Doe. Bullets for O'Hara. 1942: Yankee Doodle Dandy. Bullet Scars. The Hard Way. The Male Animal. Always in my Heart. Larceny Inc. George Washington Slept Here. 1943: * Here Comes Mr Zerk. Two Weeks to Live. Action in the North Atlantic. The Mysterious Doctor. The Dancing Masters. Arsenic and Old Lace. 1944: Crime by Night. The Last Ride. * Gold is Where You Lose It. 1947: The Perils of Pauline. 1948: When My Baby Smiles at Me. 1949: Jackpot Jitters (GB: Jiggs and Maggie in Jackpot Jitters). The Beautiful Blonde from Bashful Bend. Look for the Silver Lining. Roseanna McCoy. 1950: Joe Palooka in Humphrey Takes a Chance (GB: Humphrey Takes a Chance). Let's Dance. 1952: Son of Paleface. 1953: The Caddy. 1954: Living It Up. 1955: Abbott and Costello Meet the Keystone Kops. Abbott and Costello Meet the Mummy. How to be Very, Very Popular. 1956: Pardners. 1957: Man of a Thousand Faces. 1958: Rock-a-Bye Baby. 1959: Daddy-O. Last Train from Gun Hill.

MARRIOTT, Moore (left)

(George Moore-Marriott) 1885–1949
and

MOFFATT, Graham 1919–1965

There couldn't have been two more dispar-

ate comic actors than the two men who made up a team with Will Hay (*qv*), then with other comic figures of the British cinema, in the 1930s and early 1940s. Moore Marriott was thin, frail, bewhiskered and seemingly ancient. Roly-poly Graham Moffatt was little more than a plump, Billy Bunter-style schoolboy, and indeed played one in some of his earlier films. Together, though, they were thorns in the side. You couldn't upset them any more than you could outwit them. Both played comedy absolutely straight, as if it were the stuff of real life. Both came from theatrical families. Moore Marriott, who once had dark, curly hair, made his first appearance on stage at five as a boy dancer. His father had his own theatre company and the young Marriott made many appearances with it as a boy. He made his first film when the British cinema was still in its infancy. Supposedly, he made many early silents for the Hepworth company, although no records exist of these appearances. But Marriott himself thought that, counting these early half- and one-reelers, he had made nearly 300 films. Certainly from 1920 he began to be billed in the credits of movies, often in sullen, bucolic roles. He had become quite popular by the late 1920s and played one or two leading roles, including the naval hero in 1927's *Carry On!* With the coming of sound, however, Marriott moved quickly into character roles, often playing garrulous, toothless, wispy-haired old codgers 20 or 30 years older than he really was. Moffatt was a call boy and clapper boy at Gaumont-British studios before winning acting roles there, gaining experience of farce in two 'Aldwych' romps, *A Cup of Kindness* and *Stormy Weather*. He first supported Hay at the age of 17 in *Where There's a Will*. Moffatt and Marriott were together in the next Hay comedy, *Windbag the Sailor*, already armed with familiar character names. Moffatt was the insolent Albert, forever taking Hay down a peg, and Marriott the cunning, eager old Jeremiah Harbottle. There was no room for Marriott in *Good Morning, Boys*, one of Hay's occasional appearances in his character of the incompetent schoolmaster (Moffatt naturally played one of the schoolboys), but

the trio was back together again in their most famous film *Oh, Mr Porter!* Hay is a stationmaster demoted to a dilapidated Irish halt for past misdemeanours. Inevitably he finds the staff consists of Moffatt and Marriott. The former treats him as if he weren't there and addresses Marriott instead. The latter, economical as ever with words, is the first person Hay meets at his new home in Buggleskelly Station, when Marriott shoots up the flap of the ticket window and announces 'Next train's gone!' Public response to the trio's subsequent misadventures was such that they were re-teamed in *Convict 99*, a film stolen by Marriott as Jerry the Mole, a prisoner forever trying to dig his way out only to end up in

the governor's office. Displeased with such scene-stealing, Hay went back to filming on his own for one film, but studio pressure resulted in Moffatt and Marriott re-joining him for *Old Bones of the River*, *Ask a Policeman?* and *Where's That Fire?*. Marriott and Moffatt excelled with their poker-faced execution of slapstick sequences with ladders, pole and other props in these films, and Hay insisted they be dropped for good. However, the public obviously wanted to see them together, and Marriott and Moffatt proved happy in harness for a while, supporting Edmund Gwenn in *Cheer Boys Cheer*, Arthur Askey (*qv*) in *The Band Waggon* (Marriott alone), *Charley's (Big-Hearted) Aunt*, *I Thank You* and *Back Room Boy*, Ben Lyon and Bebe Daniels (*qv*) in *Hi Gang!* and Tommy Handley (*qv*) in *Time Flies*. Marriott also supported the Crazy Gang around this time in *Gasbags* and *The Frozen Limits*, and he and Moffatt were reunited, along with another popular duo, Basil Radford and Naunton Wayne (both *qv*), in the appropriately titled wartime winner *Millions Like Us*. After that, the old codger and the young loafer went their separate ways, but not to long lives. Marriott was dead at 64 and Moffatt, who left show business to run a pub, succumbed to a heart attack at 46.

Together. *1936: Windbag the Sailor. 1937: Oh, Mr Porter! Owd Bob (US: To the Victor). 1938: Convict 99. Old Bones of the River.*

Whose hose is whose? Moore Marriott characteristically finds himself at the centre of a tangle that also involves Will Hay and Graham Moffatt in *Where's That Fire?*

1939: *Ask a Policeman. Where's That Fire? Cheer Boys Cheer.* 1940: *Charley's (Big-Hearted) Aunt.* 1941: *I Thank You. Hi Gang!* 1942: *Back Room Boy.* 1943: *Time Flies. Millions Like Us.*

Marriott alone. 1906: * *Dick Turpin's Ride to York.* 1912: *A Maid of the Alps.* 1914: *His Sister's Honour.* 1915: *By the Shortest of Heads.* 1920: *The Grip of Iron. Mary Latimer, Nun. The Winding Road.* 1921: *Four Men in a Van.* 1922: *The Head of the Family. The Skipper's Wedding.* 1923: *The Monkey's Paw.* * *An Odd Freak.* * *Lawyer Quince.* * *Dixon's Return.* 1924: *The Affair at the Novelty Theatre. The Conspirators.* * *The Clicking of Cuthbert.* * *The Long Hole. The Mating of Marcus.* * *Ordeal by Golf. Not for Sale.* 1925: *There's Many a Slip. King of the Castle. The Qualified Adventurer.* * *The Only Man. The Gold Cure. Every Mother's Son.* * *A Madonna of the Cells. Afraid of Love.* 1926: * *The Happy Rascals. London Love.* * *Regaining the Wind.* * *Goose and Stuffing.* * *Mined and Counter-Mined.* * *The Little Shop in Fore Street.* * *Second to None.* * *Cash on Delivery.* * *The Greater War. The Conspirators (and 1924 film).* 1927: *Passion Island. The Silver Lining. Huntingtower. Carry On!* 1928: *Victory. Widdecombe Fair.* * *The Burglar and the Girl. Toni.* * *The King's Breakfast. Kitty. Sweeney Todd.* 1929: * *Mr Smith Wakes Up. The Flying Scotsman. Lady from the Sea. Kitty (sound version).* 1930: *Kissing Cup's Race. Peace on the Western Front.* 1931: *Aroma of the South Seas. The Lyons Mail. Up for the Cup.* 1932: *Dance Pretty Lady. The Water Gipsies. Mr Bill the Conqueror (US: The Man Who Won). The Crooked Lady. Nine Till Six. Heroes of the Mine. The Little Waitress. The Wonderful Story.* 1933: *Money for Speed. A Moorland Tragedy. Dora. Lucky Blaze. A Political Party. The Crime at Blossoms. Hawleys of High Street. Love's Old Sweet Song. The House of Trent. Faces. The Song of the Plough.* 1934: * *The Black Skull.* * *The Unknown Warrior. Girls Please. The Scoop (US: A Political Scoop). Nell Gwyn. The Feathered Serpent.* 1935: *Dandy Dick. Drake of England (US: Drake the Pirate). Peg of Old Drury.* * *His Apologies.* * *The Half-Day Excursion. The Man without a Face. Gay Old Dog. Turn of the Tide.* 1936: *Strange Cargo. What the Puppy Said. The Amazing Quest of Ernest Bliss (US: Romance and Riches). Luck of the Turf. When Knights Were Bold. Wednesday's Luck. Accused. Talk of the Devil. As You Like It.* 1937: *Feather Your Nest. Fifty Shilling Boxer. The Fatal Hour. Night Ride. Victoria the Great. Intimate Relations. Dreaming Lips.* 1939: *A Girl Must Live. The Frozen Limits. The Band Waggon.* 1940: *Gasbags.* 1944: *It Happened on Sunday. The Agitator. Don't Take It to Heart.* 1945: *A Place of One's Own. I'll Be Your Sweetheart.* 1946: *Green for Danger.* 1947: *Jassy. Green Fingers. The Root of All Evil. The Hills of Donegal.* 1949: *The History of Mr Polly. High Jinks in Society.*

Moffatt alone. 1934: *A Cup of Kindness.* 1935: *Stormy Weather. The Clairvoyant.* 1936: *It's Love Again. All In. Where There's a Will. Good Morning, Boys.* 1937: *Okay for Sound. Dr Syn. Gangway.* 1938: *The Drum (US: Drums).* 1943: *Dear Octopus (US: The Randolph Family).* 1944: *Welcome Mr Washington. A Canterbury Tale.* 1945: *I Know Where I'm Going!* 1946: *The Voyage of Peter Joe (serial).* 1947: *Stage Frights.* 1948: *Woman Hater.* 1949: *Three Bags Full (serial).* 1950: *The Dragon of Pendragon Castle. The Second Mate.* 1952: *Mother Riley Meets the Vampire (US: Vampire Over London).* 1960: *Inn for Trouble.* 1963: *80,000 Suspects.*

MARTIN, Steve 1945–

The nice thing about this American stand-up comedian turned actor is that you can never be quite sure what he's going to do next. His catch-phrase – 'I'm just a wild and crazy guy' – describes the kind of tension an audience feels when he's up there on stage or screen, and almost anything might happen as Martin goes into one of his manic physical spasms. This physical comedy has been as important as the deep-thinking, single-minded execution of some zany ideas on screen. Sadly these now seem to be cooling down into character comedy.

But then, with a wild and crazy guy, you never can tell. Born in Waco, Texas, Martin found himself moved to California during childhood, and got an out-of-school job in Disneyland, as an assistant in Merlin's Magic Shop. He learned juggling, sleight-of-hand and other simple tricks, and started making a collection of jokes. After completing his drama studies at California State University, he began successfully writing comedy scripts for television (winning Emmys on the way) before launching his own act as a nightclub and TV comedian. His one-man concerts were such sellouts – in the middle of telling some supremely daft story he would launch into a juggling or banjo-playing routine – that it was surprising the film medium didn't really grab him until he was nearing his mid thirties. Even then, he didn't crack the international market until as recently as 1987. The films in between were abrasive, often rude and made a virtue of bad taste. Not so rude were the flights of fancy so idiotic as to be funny, for example the cat-juggling episode in Martin's first starring appearance, in *The Jerk*, where he plays a white boy who believes he is black because he has been raised by a family of black sharecroppers. Martin's mad-eyed good looks – his hair was well on its way to its now-premature white even then – were soon seen in a series of silly, vulgar, but endearingly absurd comedies of considerable invention. In *Dead Men Don't Wear Plaid*, made in black and white, he's a private eye investigating a case littered with old Hollywood megastars (cut in from earlier films). In *The Man with Two Brains*, he falls in love with a brain in a jar. In *All of Me*, Martin inherits the soul of a dying millionairess and becomes a split personality, giving him the opportunity to prove that he can be as funny to watch as to listen to. Though these remain Martin's funniest films to date, none of them made much

Fire chief C.D. Bales (Steve Martin) 'nose' he loves *Roxanne* (Daryl Hannah) but can't figure out how to let her know … or kiss her

Ned Nederlander (Martin Short, left), Dusty Bottoms (Chevy Chase, centre) and Lucky Day (Steve Martin) — the Three Amigos — prepare to fight oppression and injustice

As con-men working the Riviera, Steve Martin (right) and Michael Caine try to out-smart one another, here both with false identities, in *Dirty Rotten Scoundrels*

Insanity at the sanitarium. The Marx Brothers, Harpo, Groucho and Chico (in white), with Sig Rumann, Margaret Dumont and Leonard Ceeley in *A Day at the Races*

Groucho looks apprehensive and shifty. Harpo, Allan Jones and Chico remain in heavy disguise. From the famous cabin scene in *A Night at the Opera*

money, especially outside the United States. And serious roles had worked less well. It led Martin to attempt a more formalised kind of comedy, first in *Roxanne*, a modern-dress version of *Cyrano de Bergerac*, and then in *Planes, Trains and Automobiles* in which Martin more or less plays straight man to John Candy's (*qv*) country-wide pest. He had some fun with the Marlon Brando character in the *Bedtime Story* remake, *Dirty Rotten Scoundrels*, but in the semi-serious and faintly disturbing *Parenthood* he allowed himself only the odd manic moment, showing the direction in which he hopes to head. 'I have consciously been trying', he has said, 'to achieve a higher level of performance – a real character. A perfect example is a Chaplin-type film. There are some truly inventive situations and you're suckered into the character too.' It's a statement of intent that most Steve Martin fans will receive with mixed feelings. Especially as his most recent films have only taken wing when Martin allows shafts of zany humour to filter through.

*1978: Sgt Pepper's Lonely Hearts Club Band. The Kids Are Alright. 1979: The Muppet Movie. The Jerk. 1980: * The Absent-Minded Waiter. 1981: Pennies from Heaven. 1982: Dead Men Don't Wear Plaid. 1983: The Lonely Guy. The Man with Two Brains. 1984: All of Me. 1985: Movers and Shakers (Dreamers). 1986: Little Shop of Horrors. ¡Three Amigos! 1987: Roxanne. Planes, Trains and Automobiles. 1988: Dirty Rotten Scoundrels. 1989: Parenthood. 1990: My Blue Heaven. 1991: L.A. Story. Grand Canyon. Father of the Bride. 1992: The Housesitter.*

THE MARX BROTHERS

CHICO (Leonard) 1886–1961
GROUCHO (Julius) 1890–1977
HARPO (Adolph) 1888–1964
ZEPPO (Herbert) 1901–1979

Broadway had seen no faster or zanier comedy than that with which the Marx Brothers hit the stage with *I'll Say She Is* in 1924. Wild and anarchic, it reflected the title of one of their songs, *Whatever It Is, I'm Against It*. Indeed, to provide a variation on one of Groucho's most famous quotes, one couldn't see the Marxes joining any club that would have them as members. The brothers were then already veterans of show business. Together with a fifth brother, Gummo (real name: Milton), they trod the boards in varying combinations with musical acts from the early 1900s. Groucho played the guitar, Chico the piano and Gummo the mandolin. Later Harpo taught himself to play the harp. As musicians they were never a success, but the byplay that the 'Musical Mascots' slipped into the act by way of brightening it up was obviously a success with audiences. It was around 1914 that comedy took over the act almost in its entirety, much to the disapproval of their mother, Minna (Minnie) Schoenberg Marx,

who was also part of the act and the driving force behind their success. Later, looking for a similar dowager figure off whom to bounce their insults, the brothers chanced upon a light opera singer called Margaret Dumont (*qv*). She would later join them in seven of their films, but first appeared with them in their second great stage success *The Cocoanuts*, which opened in 1925. 'I was told', she later recalled, 'that they needed an actress of dignity and poise. After three weeks of acting with them, I nearly had a nervous breakdown!' By the time the brothers reached Broadway Zeppo, the youngest, had replaced Gummo, and acted as a combination straight man and juvenile lead. After the first five of their films he, too, dropped out and became their agent. Their unique brand of comedy was honed to perfection by many years on stage before they reached the cinema. Groucho was the verbal wit, master of the veiled insult, loping in stooped style after some new victim while rolling his eyes and puffing the inevitable cigar. But even Groucho's painted moustache and innate suspicion of everyone frequently failed to protect him from the wiles of the fast-talking, Italianate Chico, who would usually sell him some white elephant, in spite of Groucho's comment that he couldn't trust anyone whose head came to a point (a reference to Chico's strange headgear). Chico also acted as interpreter for the silent, red-wigged, ever-grinning, girl-chasing Harpo, whose cavernous overcoat could contain everything but the kitchen sink, but most frequently an old-fashioned motor-horn, which he sometimes used to transmit 'code' messages which Chico would excitedly translate. In between their fast and furious antics, moments of relative calm were provided by musical solos from Chico, 'firing' his finger at the piano before demonstrating his expertise, and Harpo, soulfully plucking out a tune on the harp. They made their major film debut with the film version of *The Cocoanuts* (1929), set in a hotel in Florida where, Groucho tells Margaret Dumont, 'property values have increased 1929 since 1000%'. Later he sets his cap at her: 'Did anyone ever tell you that you look like the Prince of Wales? I don't mean the present

Prince of Wales. One of the old Wales. And, believe me, when I say Wales I mean whales. I know a whale when I see one' (you have to work out the changes of spelling for yourself). This kind of dialogue set the pattern for the exchanges in all their remaining films. As ever, the brothers had to put up with a musical love interest, which had audiences shifting around on their seats waiting for the next bout of lunacy. According to the studio, however, such interludes proved a popular element in Marx films. Their next, *Animal Crackers* (1930), had also been a successful stage show and, as such, tends to run longer than it might have otherwise (their screen originals were mostly shorter). It's the film in which Harpo's pursuit of squeaking blondes reaches a peak, and Groucho has one of his most famous musical numbers, *Hurray for Captain Spaulding*. After these films in Long Island studios, the brothers became resident in Hollywood, making their next three films at the Paramount studios there. *Monkey Business* (1931) is the film in which they all give impressions of Maurice Chevalier, but it was with the next two films, *Horse Feathers* (1932) and *Duck Soup* (1933), that the Marxes fully realised their potential as film comedians. In *Horse Feathers*, Groucho, a college professor, almost defeats Chico for once in an idiotic battle of wits over the password to a speakeasy (they both end up outside), but is routed by Harpo when he tells him he can't burn the candle at both ends. Harpo inevitably reaches inside his overcoat and produces a candle lit at both ends. The plot ends up with one of the most riotous football matches ever shown on screen. Groucho also has the chance in this film to deliver one of his manic tirades that sink ever deeper into a quagmire of verbal diarrhoea. 'The blood carriers', he tells his students, 'are a hill-dwelling tribe that lives in the Alps. They feed on rice and old shoes. Then behind the Alps is more Alps and the Lord alps those who alp themselves. The blood rushes from the head to the feet, gets a look at those feet and rushes back up to the head again.' Harpo, who outwits a policeman on his dog-cart in *Horse Feathers*, has a classic encounter with a lemonade seller's cart in *Duck Soup*, in which

Groucho is fired. Chico and Harpo find the whole thing a blast. From *At the Circus*

hands of sharpster Chico in the famous tutsy-fruitsy ice-cream routine in which Groucho never does get to back the winner in the race. Groucho does, however, enjoy his most famous closing line (to Margaret Dumont, naturally): 'Marry me and I'll never look at any other horse.' After *A Day at the Races* the Marxes worked in lesser vehicles, although there are golden moments in all of them, even the last, the underrated *Love Happy* (1949), a comedy with Harpo as the central figure. And Groucho still had one of his best musical numbers to come: *Lydia the Tattooed Lady* from *At the Circus* (1939). *At the Circus* and *Go West* concentrate, at the expense of verbal exchanges, on minutely well-organised chase sequences, which displeased Marx purists, but did help to make their humour more accessible to younger filmgoers. From the 1950s onwards the brothers more or less went their separate ways, still appearing on stage, TV and film, but usually as someone else's guest star. Heart problems brought about the deaths of Chico and Harpo (both at 75), while Zeppo died from cancer and Groucho a doddery old man at 87 from pneumonia, while hangers-on fought over his assets. Their humour, however, never grew old — and neither do their films.

Groucho is president of the mythical country of Freedonia, and fights for Margaret Dumont's honour 'which is more than she ever did'. This film contains the 'mirror image' game, in which Harpo pretends to be Groucho and the latter, rather than resorting to the obvious and reaching out to see if there's a mirror between them, tries to catch Harpo out by sudden variations in his movements and gestures. *Duck Soup* performed only modestly at the box-office, causing the brothers to move across to M-G-M where the studio restored the piano and harp solos, as well as the supporting musical romance, all of which had been left out of the tightly-edited *Duck Soup*, and came up with a bumper hit in *A Night at the Opera* (1935). By way of the 'crowded cabin' sequence (which ends when Margaret Dumont opens the cabin door and everyone inside gushes out into the corridor) and the scene in which Groucho gradually tears up a contract as Chico objects to its various clauses ('Everybody knows there ain't no Sanity Claus'), the film arrives at its hilarious climax in which the Marxes completely wreck a performance at the opera. The producers rightly saw little reason to tamper with a winning formula, and *A Day the Races* again has Allan Jones singing away in brief breaks from Marx madness, as Dr Hugo Z. Hackenbush (Groucho), in reality a horse doctor, moves in to take charge of a failing sanatorium. Again there's a big finale (a horse race with Harpo as winning jockey), a charming musical number with Harpo playing pied piper to a group of black children and Groucho's complete rout at the

Chico can lead Harpo to water but can he make him drink? From *Go West*

1925: *Too Many Kisses* (H only). 1926: *Humorisk* (unreleased and possibly uncompleted. C,H,G,Z). 1929: *The Cocoanuts* (C,H,G,Z). 1930: *Animal Crackers* (C,H,G,Z). 1931: * *The House That Shadows Built* (C,H,G,Z). *Monkey Business* (C,H,G,Z). 1932: * *Hollywood on Parade No. 5* (H only). *Horse Feathers* (C,H,G,Z). 1933: * *Hollywood on Parade No. 9* (C only). *Duck Soup* (C,H,G,Z). 1935: * *La Fiesta de Santa Barbara* (H only). *A Night at the Opera* (C,H,G). 1936: *Yours for the Asking* (C,H,G). * *Hollywood – The Second Step* (C only). 1937: * *Sunday Night at the Trocadero* (G only). *A Day at the Races* (C,H,G). 1938: *Room Service* (C,H,G). 1939: *At the Circus* (C,H,G). 1940: *Go West* (GB: *The Marx Brothers Go West*. C,H,G). 1941: *The Big Store* (C,H,G). 1943: * *Screen Snapshots No. 102* (G only). *Stage Door Canteen* (H only). 1945: * *All-Star Bond Rally* (H only). 1946: *A Night in Casablanca* (C,H,G). 1947: *Copacabana* (G only). 1949: *Love Happy*/*Kleptomaniacs* (C,H,G). 1950: *Mr Music* (G only). 1951: *Double Dynamite* (G only). 1952: *A Girl in Every Port* (G only). 1957: *Will Success Spoil Rock Hunter?* (GB: *Oh! For a Man*. G only). *The Story of Mankind*. (C,H,G). 1958: *Next to No Time* (TV. C only). * *Showdown at Ulcer Gulch* (C,G). 1959: * *The Incredible Jewel Robbery* (TV C,H,G). 1968: *Skidoo* (G only).

Unsavoury proprietors of Dreamtime Escorts, Rik Mayall (right) and Adrian Edmondson fall into the clutches of the Mob, in *Mr Jolly Lives Next Door*

MAYALL, Rik 1958–

A major British comedy star of the 1980s and 1990s, with wide blue eyes, wild light-brown hair and manic grin. Unusually for a British comedian, although Tony Hancock and Wilfrid Brambell (*qv*) both had a one-character shot it, Mayall has got his laughs, and his popularity, by playing what one writer described as a 'range of deeply unlikeable characters'. TV hits have followed so hard on each other's heels that to date Mayall has had too little time for the cinema. The films he has made haven't yet offered much evidence that people who giggle at him in their living-rooms will actually pay to see the bumptious, obnoxious, often repellent characters he creates. But he himself has said that he would like to find a sustainable character in films, such as Peter Sellers' Clouseau, so that is perhaps where things

are leading. Mayall's parents were both drama teachers, and, although he has a brother who became a civil engineer, he himself always seemed set for a career as a performer. 'I was always a show-off', says Mayall, whose first notable act of 'showing-off' – pulling faces at the audience during a school carol concert, earned him a thrashing from the headmaster and hours of detention after school. So, if people who saw him when he was first coming to prominence as a comedian thought he was like a naughty boy out to shock people to get a reaction, it's a theory Mayall himself would support. 'As a kid', he remembers, 'I was too cowardly to be really naughty. I was the one who egged other people on to do the really naughty things.' After scraping into university to read drama, Mayall became involved with a local (Manchester) comedy group. At the National Student Drama Festival, he 'won' *The Guardian* newspaper's award as 'most outrageous ham'. It was all an aspiring young show-off needed. Mayall graduated and moved to London. Here he appeared for months on end at Soho's now-famous Comedy Store – 'I can proudly say that I was never gonged off stage' and then, in partnership with such friends as Adrian Edmondson and Peter Richardson, invaded television in *The Young Ones* and *The Comic Strip Presents*, doling out comedy that depended heavily on outrageous language and references to bodily functions for its impact. He had made a start in films in 1981, playing minor crazies. There were more

sweaty, foul-mouthed, out-of-hand and over-the-top characters to follow in 'Comic Strip' films and such allied ventures as *Whoops Apocalypse*. There were signs of Mayall's chew-the-scenery style being slightly tamed in another successful TV series, *The New Statesman*, in which he appeared as unctuous Tory politician Alan B'Stard. Not that he wasn't still larger than life, as other TV comedy programmes, *Catflap* and *Bottom*, showed. But they also demonstrated that Mayall's sense of comic timing had improved, and that he could now draw on visual as well as verbal humour to make an audience laugh. Some of the improvement might be attributed to Mayall's Hollywood debut in *Drop Dead Fred*, in which he plays an imaginary friend who all but wrecks the heroine's life. The film was second-rate, but Mayall, deservedly top-billed, dominated it. He says he got the role after the producers saw him in a Red Nose Day sketch, as Alan B'Stard, being whipped by Mrs Thatcher. 'They thought it was funny, seeing what they thought was a posh Englishman saying rude things and taking his trousers off', he says. In 1991-2, Mayall committed himself to a stage run with Edmondson in Samuel Beckett's *Waiting for Godot*. He drew the crowds as well as a mixed reception from critics, delaying a return to films and TV. In olden days, the manic Mayall would doubtless have been happy as a court jester. Especially as he admits that 'I don't like people to think that I'm normal.'

*1981: Eye of the Needle. An American Werewolf in London. Shock Treatment. * Couples and Robbers. 1986: Whoops Apocalypse. 1987: Eat the Rich. Mr Jolly Lives Next Door. More Bad News. 1988: The Strike. 1990: Little Noises. 1991: Drop Dead Fred. The Princess and the Goblin (voice only).*

MAYEHOFF, Eddie 1911–

An advertising man who became a band-leader and a comedian and then went back to advertising, Eddie Mayehoff enjoyed only a short time as a big wheel of Hollywood comedy. Twenty years earlier, he would probably have had a prolific career as a comedy character actor in Damon Runyon-style gangster capers. Born to a Ukrainian clothing manufacturer, Mayehoff graduated from the Yale School of Music in 1932 with a teaching certificate but for the first two years of his working life sold advertising for a magazine called *The Musician*. Later he wrote for the magazine, before leaving to form his own band. The Eddie Mayehoff Dance Band soon became popular hotel and nightspot entertainers. Eddie and his men toured for six years, and he wrote many of the lyrics to the songs sung by his vocalists. In 1939 Mayehoff threw up the band and joined the writing staff at CBS radio. He wrote comedy shows for the wireless where, by 1941, he had moved to the front of the microphone with his own show, *Eddie Mayehoff on the Town*. From the early 1940s he began making appearances on Broadway, sometimes in musicals but also in straight acting roles. It was while in dramatic vein that he was spotted by Paramount producer Hal Wallis acting in *A Season in the Sun* in 1950. Wallis thought Mayehoff had film possibilities with his gravel voice, twisted scowl, trowel chin and by now receding dark hair, and that at 39 he wasn't too young to play Jerry Lewis's (*qv*) over-demanding father in *That's My Boy*. Mayehoff's performance won him co-star billing on the marquees as the man determined to turn his nerd of a son into a reflection of himself: a sporting hero. He was again given prominent billing in support of Dean Martin and Jerry Lewis the following year in *The Stooge*. Also the same year (1952) Mayehoff starred in a

TV sitcom series called *Doc Corkle*, but it was hauled off the air after only a few weeks. Back at Paramount, Mayehoff stole scenes from Bob Hope and Mickey Rooney (both *qv*) in *Off Limits*, then tried TV again with *That's My Boy*, a spin-off from the film, but this time with Eddie star-billed as the father. He played a bull in a china shop who got on the nerves of not only his son but everyone else as well. This series managed to last a whole season before being dropped. Martin and Lewis called Mayehoff back for another role, in *Artists and Models*, and then it was back to stand-up comedy on the supper-club circuit and appearances in Broadway plays. A further TV series, *Adventures of Fenimore J. Mayehoff*, did no better than the first two. In the following decade, Mayehoff did a couple of appearances in Jack Lemmon (*qv*) comedies, and made a pilot for a proposed TV series starring himself and Terry-Thomas (*qv*) and called *See America First*. It didn't sell. By 1970 Mayehoff had left show business to become a partner in a sales promotion and advertising firm. His familiar rumpled features were still seen occasionally on TV as the firm's spokesman in beer commercials. Now in his early eighties and retired to a luxury apartment overlooking the Pacific Ocean, Mayehoff remains an avid cyclist who still uses a bike to get everywhere. He says he has finally got out of films and television not so much because of his disappointments but because of the petty jealousies among fellow funny-men. 'Advertising just isn't in the same league', he says. 'Believe me, these are the most competitive people alive.'

1951: That's My Boy. 1952: The Stooge. 1953: Off Limits (GB: Military Policemen). 1955: Artists and Models. 1956: Made in Heaven (TV). 1965: How to Murder Your Wife. 1967: Luv.

McCULLOUGH, Paul
See CLARKE, Bobby and
McCULLOUGH, Paul

MERKEL, Una 1903–1986

People remember Una Merkel, if for nothing else, for the tremendous fight her character has with Marlene Dietrich's on the saloon-room floor in the classic version of *Destry Rides Again*. By Una's standards that was quite a straight dramatic part. Always good for a laugh, the strawberry blonde from Kentucky was well worth a comedy series of her own, but she never got one. Nor, even more unexpectedly, did she become a television regular in later life – although she did once play (on TV) an 80-year-old woman who robs a bank! What she did do was play leads, or second leads, with many of Hollywood's most famous comedians, including Harold Lloyd, W. C. Fields ('a pretty grand person' she thought) and Bob Hope (all *qv*). Something of a lookalike for Lillian Gish in her teenage drama school

days, Merkel doubled for the famous star in such films as *Way Down East* wearing a dark wig. She began stage work in 1925 and had some brief experience as a vaudeville comedienne shortly afterwards. She began a film career in earnest in 1930, played her first comedy role the following year in *Don't Bet on Women*, and was quickly in demand for wisecracking secretaries (including Sam Spade's in the 1931 version of *The Maltese Falcon*), sassy showgirls, girl Fridays, heroines' friends and pixilated gossips. To all of their lines she gave her distinctive Kentucky twang. The fight with Marlene – 'I was a mess of bruises. I thought they'd never call "Cut!"' – came in 1939, and her output slowed during World War Two, when she joined Gary Cooper's Far Eastern tour to entertain US troops. One of the funniest of her post-war roles, and films, was as William Bendix's (*qv*) wife in the riotous Frank Tashlin-scripted *Kill the Umpire*. In 1961 she surprised a lot of people with a sensitive, incisive dramatic performance in the screen version of Tennessee Williams' *Summer and Smoke*, which brought her first, and only, nomination for an Academy Award. 'I was just as thrilled as if I'd won it', she said at the time. 'It's just wonderful that people think I can actually act.' Rounding off her career with some film and TV work for Walt Disney, Una Merkel retired in 1968. Her bright, happy personality had cheered many a dull picture.

*1920: Way Down East. 1923: The White Rose. 1924: † World Shadows. * Love's Old Sweet Song. The Fifth Horseman. 1930: Abraham Lincoln. The Bat Whispers. Eyes of the World. 1931: Six Cylinder Love. The Maltese Falcon. Command Performance. Wicked. Secret Witness/Terror by Night. Don't Bet on Women. Daddy Long Legs. The Bargain. Private Lives. 1932: Red-Headed Woman. She Wanted a Millionaire. Man Wanted. They Call It Sin (GB: The Way of Life). Huddle (GB: Impossible Lover). Impatient Maiden. Men Are Such Fools. 1933: Reunion in Vienna. Whistling in the Dark. Beauty for Sale (GB: Beauty). Her First Mate. Bombshell. The Women in His Life. 42nd Street. Midnight Mary. Broadway to Hollywood (GB: Ring Up the Curtain). Day of Reckoning. Clear All Wires. The Secret of*

Rik on the box. Rik Mayall, Patricia Quinn, Nell Campbell, Richard O'Brien (bottom right) and Cliff De Young (on screen) offer you some *Shock Treatment*

Max Miller was well at home as the racing tipster Educated Evans, and made two films in the character. Here he is with Hal Walters in *Thank Evans*

Here's to love. Dudley Moore plays a prominent psychiatrist who becomes obsessed with one his more beautiful patients in *Lovesick* — one of Dud's duds

Madame Blanche. 1934: Paris Interlude. This Side of Heaven. Murder in the Private Car (GB: Murder on the Runaway Train). The Cat's Paw. The Merry Widow. Bulldog Drummond Strikes Back. Have a Heart. Evelyn Prentice. 1935: Biography of a Bachelor Girl. One New York Night (GB: The Trunk Mystery). Murder in the Fleet. Baby Face Harrington. It's in the Air. Riffraff. The Night is Young. Broadway Melody of 1936. Speed. We Went to College (GB: The Old School Tie). * How to Stuff a Goose. Born to Dance. 1937: Don't Tell the Wife. Saratoga. Good Old Soak. True Confession. Checkers. 1938: Test Pilot. 1939: Four Girls in White. On Borrowed Time. Destry Rides Again. Some Like It Hot. 1940: Saturday's Children. Comin' Round the Mountain. The Bank Dick (GB: The Bank Detective). Sandy Gets Her Man. 1941: Cracked Nuts. Double Date. Road to Zanzibar. 1942: Twin Beds. The Mad Doctor of Market Street. 1943: This is the Army. * Quack Service. 1944: * To Heir is Human. * Bachelor Daze. Sweethearts of the USA (GB: Sweethearts on Parade). 1947: It's a Joke, Son. 1948: The Bride Goes Wild. The Man from Texas. 1950: Kill the Umpire. My Blue Heaven. Emergency Wedding (GB: Jealousy). 1951: Rich, Young and Pretty. Golden Girl. A Millionaire for Christy. 1952: With a Song in My Heart. The Merry Widow (remake). I Love Melvin. 1955: The Kentuckian. 1956: Bundle of Joy. The Kettles in the Ozarks. 1957: The Greer Case (TV). The Fuzzy Pink Nightgown. The Girl Most Likely. 1959: The Mating Game. 1961: Summer and Smoke. The Parent Trap. 1963: Summer Magic. A Tiger Walks. 1966: Spinout (GB: California Holiday).

† Unfinished.

MILLER, Max
(Thomas Henry 'Harry' Sargent)
1895–1963

Despite the fact that his film vehicles didn't and — censorship being what it was — couldn't capture his stage appeal, Britain's Max Miller, alias 'The Cheeky Chappie', was, fairly briefly, a popular star of his own comedy movies in the 1930s. Most of them made several times their cost in terms of box-office profit. One of the most colourful characters the British music-hall ever pro-

Phyllis Monkman looks less than wholly taken with the charms of Max Miller as Alexander the Greatest in *The Good Old Days*

duced, Miller seemed as though he had been born and bred in East London, in whose variety theatres he was usually to be found performing. In fact, he came originally from Brighton and lived there most of his life. As a comedian, he was not so much risqué as downright rude. His speciality was rhyming limericks, out of which he would leave the (dirty) last word — schoolboy smut, but with beaming panache. As one fellow performer put it, Miller could reach the punch-line and change the joke almost in the same breath. But, of course, that wouldn't do for 1930s cinema. He was one of 12 children born to a Brighton pub entertainer, and followed in his father's footsteps, in between jobs as a golf caddy, a fishmonger's boy, with a circus and as an apprentice blacksmith. On his free nights he would go to the music-hall. His hero was the blacked-up singer G. H. Elliott, who was known as the 'Chocolate-Coloured Coon' and came on singing *By the Silvery Moon*. Max committed his dance steps to memory and practised them beneath Brighton's Palace Pier. He formed a troupe called the Beachcombers and with them began to develop the hectoring comic style that was make him (in)famous. During World War One, he took a concert party to India. After the war, he married a young singer, Kitty Mash, and accepted her suggestion that, on embarking on a career as a solo stand-up comedian he should change his name from Harry Sargent to Max Miller. In real life Miller was a stingy sobersides who wore grey suits offstage, and was sentimental about women, whom he hated to see smoke, drink or swear. Once on stage he

became the exact opposite. In the 1920s he adopted his famous costume of long flowered coat and plus-fours, two-tone club-heeled shoes, rainbow kipper tie and tip-tilted white trilby that matched his flashing smile. Well, actually it was more of a confidential leer, especially when addressing those (largely female) members of the audience whom he would chide for laughing at the dirty meaning that he had just fed them. Though banned from some halls for several years (the straw that broke the camel's back was said to have been a joke about a naked blonde walking towards him on a narrow cliff path: 'I didn't know whether to toss myself off or block her passage' — actually quite clever by Miller's standards), he was a top-liner by 1930. Although not as successful on radio (naturally, much of his material was frowned on by the BBC), he began playing cameo roles in films in 1933. Surprisingly, Miller proved an engaging screen personality without the dirty jokes. Loud of voice, larger than life and quite beguiling, he succeeding in stealing scenes from those billed above him. Miller was cock-a-hoop when Warner Brothers, whose British arm produced 'quota quickies' for the native market, decided to star him in comedy films of his own. The films gave him a chance to play characters who talked fast and thought on their feet. He might be a bookmaker, a con-man or a salesman, but he was discernibly Max Miller. He played these interchangeable roles from the hip, and the lip. 'I know exactly what I'm supposed to do in each scene', he told a studio correspondent of the 1930s. 'Then I work out my own dialogue and introduce my own funny bits. In these films I'm myself, to a certain extent, but at the same time it's something of a character part.' The first of these 'character parts' was in *Get Off My Foot*,. which combined elements of a crime comedy and *The Admirable Crichton*. Max played a Smithfield meat porter who, thinking himself responsible for the death of a friend, flees London, takes odd jobs and ends up as a butler. In the end he inherits a fortune but turns down a rich girl to marry the maid. The next film was even more specifically tailored to Max Miller's genial, trickster-style personality, and proved his most successful. *Educated Evans* was a horse-racing tipster with a knack of getting in and out of tight corners and backing the wrong horse at the right time. Once again, Miller's working-class hero was allowed to run riot in high society; cheaply made, the film grossed four times its cost. There was a good sequel, *Thank Evans*, along similar lines, and some breezy, cheerful farces with daft plots and titles borrowed from Miller catchphrases: *Don't Get Me Wrong*, and *Take It From Me*. Respectability overtook (but failed to tame) the Cheeky Chappie at last when he was chosen to entertain at the Royal Variety Performance of 1937. Miller wore a suit of red, white and blue. 'I know how to dress for these occasions', he told the press. 'Nice and quiet.' His film career was still on the up, and the last two for Warners played on the top half of double-bills. *The Good Old Days* was a raucous romp set in 1840; Miller remained resolutely a man of 1939. The other, *Hoots Mon!*, was funnier, casting him as 'England's funniest comedian' constantly feuding with a Scottish male impersonator. Miller allowed himself most effectively to be a figure of fun as well as a funny figure. The war did strange things to the careers of British film comedians, it stopped some and started others. Miller was one of the unlucky ones. There was one more movie and that was it. But, as usual, Max had the last laugh. When he died at 68 he was Britain's highest-paid variety artist.

1933: The Good Companions. Friday the Thirteenth. Channel Crossing. 1934: Princess Charming. 1935: Things Are Looking Up. Get Off My Foot. 1936: Educated Evans. Don't Get Me Wrong. 1937: Take It from Me (US: Trans-atlantic Trouble). 1938: Thank Evans. Everything Happens to Me. 1939: The Good Old Days. Hoots Mon! 1943: Asking for Trouble.

MILLIGAN, Spike
(Terence Milligan) 1918–

Scriptwriter, poet and zaniest of comedians, with a maniac line in funny voices, Britain's Spike Milligan, prime mover of the innovative *Goon Show* on radio, had a twitchy mouth that always looked as if it were about to have a fit of the giggles, though it very seldom did. Born in India, Milligan was educated at places as diverse as Rangoon,

Burma, and Catford, London, and made his first appearance on a stage at the age of eight in a nativity play in a Poona convent in India. His wartime experiences would be riotously documented in *Adolf Hitler – My Part in His Downfall* (later filmed with Spike playing his own father) and his talent for comedy writing began to emerge while playing guitar in the post-war show *Stars in Battledress*. He made his first broadcast cracking jokes as a contestant in the talent show *Opportunity Knocks*. In 1951 Milligan teamed with three other enthusiasts for lunatic comedy, Peter Sellers (*qv*), Harry Secombe (*qv*) and Michael Bentine. The result was *Crazy People*, originally advertised by the BBC as the 'Junior Crazy Show', but soon to give rise to *The Goon Show*. There were films, too, at this stage, though of the rough and ready kind, such as *Penny Points to Paradise*, *Let's Go Crazy* and *Down Among the Z-Men*. Unlike *The Goon Show*, alas, these didn't have scripts by Milligan. On radio, Milligan's magic was bringing to life any number of cartoon-like characters in *The Goon Show*, among them the dim but endearing Eccles, the quavering Minnie Bannister, the unsavoury Moriarty and the wailing Little Jim. The show began in 1952 and ran until 1960. After it had ended, Milligan resumed acquaintance with the cinema. He made *Invasion Quartet*, a mild army comedy, and *Postman's Knock*, more of a solo vehicle which cast him as a village postman at large in the big city, where he becomes a hero by rounding up a gang of crooks. Goon humour never really took off on British TV, despite several attempts (*Idiot's Weekly*, *A Show Called Fred*, *Son of Fred*) and Milligan seemed happier with *The World of Beachcomber*, a picturisation of columnist Beachcomber's *By the Way*. At the cinema, towards the end of the 1960s, there was *The Bed Sitting Room*, formerly one of Milligan's forays into the theatre that also included *Oblomov*, *Son of Oblomov* and an eye-catching Ben Gunn in *Treasure Island*. Largely, films seemed content to have the middle-aged Milligan as a bearded, unpredictable cameo player in a variety of off-kilter supporting roles. These latter-day projects include some notable turkeys,

including *Rentadick*, *Alice's Adventures in Wonderland* (an all-star misfire with Spike as the Gryphon), *The Cherry Picker*, *Ghost in the Noonday Sun*, *The Hound of the Baskervilles* and *The Prisoner of Zenda*. Many of these featured Milligan's old partner Sellers, who was also the co-star (as Queen Victoria) in Spike's last starring role and most notable failure, *The Great McGonagall*. Distressingly unfunny, in spite of a screenplay co-written by Milligan, it told the story of an obscure, real-life Scottish poet. With Spike being neither pulled into line nor entirely let loose, the film made it seem as if his style of humour had been overtaken by the years. However, among the fellow lunatics of *Monty Python's Life of Brian*, Spike was at his funniest in years as a blind man who falls into a pit. He remains an amusing and unsettling guest in chat shows on TV.

*1951: Penny Points to Paradise. London Entertains. Let's Go Crazy. 1952: Down Among the Z-Men. 1953: * Super Secret Service. 1955: * The Case of the Mukkinese Battlehorn. 1960: * The Running Jumping and Standing Still Film. Suspect. Watch Your Stern. 1961: What a Whopper! Invasion Quartet. * Spike Milligan Meets Joe Brown. * Spike Milligan on Treasure Island, WC2. 1962: Postman's Knock. 1966: Fish and Milligan. 1969: The Bed Sitting Room. * The Undertakers. The Magic Christian. 1971: The Magnificent Seven Deadly Sins. 1972: Rentadick. The Adventures of Barry McKenzie. Dot and the Kangaroo (voice only). Adolf Hitler – My Part in His Downfall. Alice's Adventures in Wonderland. 1973: Digby – The Biggest Dog in the World. The Three Musketeers (The Queen's Diamonds). The Cherry Picker. 1974: The Great McGonagall. Ghost in the Noonday Sun. Man About the House. 1976: Lost in the Wild. Barney. 1977: The Hound of the Baskervilles. The Last Remake of Beau Geste. 1978: The Prisoner of Zenda. 1979: Monty Python's Life of Brian. 1981: History of the World Part I. 1983: Yellowbeard.*

MOFFATT, Graham
See **MARRIOTT, Moore**

MONKHOUSE, Bob 1928–
Dark-haired, laughing-faced, mischievous-looking British scriptwriter, comedian and, latterly, popular game-show host. Monkhouse has been as successful writing for other people as he has as a radio and television performer in his own right – and even had a go at a film career when the 'Carry On' series heralded a new, broader vein of comedy in the British cinema of the late 1950s and early 1960s. Born in Beckenham, Monkhouse was drawing strip cartoons at 12 and teamed up with fellow-student Denis Goodwin to write scripts and short stories, some of which they sold while still at school. On leaving school, he was briefly an animator, then did national service with the RAF, during which time he ran troop shows, was in charge of an RAF band and wrote for British forces radio! He began

broadcasting as a comedian in 1948 while still in the RAF then, back in civilian life, re-teamed with Goodwin, the pair becoming two of radio's most in-demand writers. In their series for Arthur Askey, *Hello Playmates*, which won the National Radio Award for 1954, they also played several of the minor characters. After successful appearances on radio and TV as performers, the team eventually broke up. Eager to get into films, Monkhouse starred in the first 'Carry On' film, *Carry On Sergeant*, in 1958. Instead of continuing with the series, however, he diverted his talents to rival comedies (two of them about dentistry) in which he sometimes had a hand in the script. From 1967, though, TV claimed Monkhouse as the bright and breezy front-man for such popular game shows as *The Golden Shot*, *Celebrity Squares*, *The $64,000 Question* and *Family Fortunes*, an occupation he still pursues today. He is also an avid collector of silent comedy films, some of which he put together for the 1956 film *All in Good Fun*, and the 1960s TV series *Mad Movies*. Monkhouse still describes himself as a stand-up comedian. And with his light but serious-sounding voice, easily adaptable to any number of distinctive male and female comic characters, there's little doubt that he was never funnier than when performing on radio.

1951: Secret People. 1956: All in Good Fun. 1958: Carry On Sergeant. 1960: Dentist in the Chair. 1961: Dentist on the Job (US: Get on with It!). A Weekend with Lulu. 1962: She'll Have to Go (US: Maid for Murder). 1968: The Bliss of Mrs Blossom. 1970: * Simon, Simon. 1983: * Out of Order.

MOORE, Dudley 1935–

Like Danny DeVito (*qv*) and many others before them, Britain's tousle-haired Dudley Moore, a master of spluttering panic, has proved that being small can be a positive advantage when it comes to comedy. He's a brilliant jazz and classical pianist and all-round musician, too, but it's for his contribution to film and TV comedy that he'll be remembered. And, like other small men of the screen, such as Mickey Rooney, the

real-life Moore has wooed and won several beautiful women much taller than himself. He came from a working-class background in Essex, but his musical talents took him to the Guildhall School of Music, and then to Oxford University. 'When I went to Oxford, I really couldn't open my mouth', he remembers, 'because everyone else was so frightfully suave.' He was also self-conscious about his height – 5 ft 2½ in. – and 'felt unworthy of anything, a little runt with a twisted foot'. All that, and the complaining mouth and pleading eyes were turned into assets when he joined fellow undergraduates Peter Cook (*qv*), Jonathan Miller and Alan Bennett in the famous series of *Beyond the Fringe* revues which made them all cel-

ebrities. On TV, Moore first made his mark in the early 1960s in a jazz programme, *Strictly for the Birds*, but soon he and Cook were striking out as a twosome, in a landmark of TV comedy called *Not Only ... But Also*, the highlight of which was almost always a duologue, conducted in mournful, common-man tones, about the state of life, but which would inevitably drift into a discussion about sex and 'busty substances'. *Not Only ... But Also* ran to a second series, but Cook and Moore were anxious to do films. They were amusing in *The Wrong Box* and *Monte Carlo or Bust* (as demon drivers), but the best scenes in *Bedazzled* all derived from the more felicitous moments in their TV shows. Almost the last of their films together, *The Hound of the Baskervilles*, was undoubtedly the worst, and Moore elected to stay in America after 1977, splitting the partnership. He got a showy role in Goldie Hawn's *Foul Play*, as a bachelor with a padful of girl-grabbing gadgets and then (after original star George Segal decamped) the lead in Blake Edwards' comedy '*10*', about a man obsessed with finding the perfect girl. Theoretically, Segal was right: it was a poor film, but one that caught the public imagination (the swimsuit-stretching Bo Derek did it no harm). Moore found himself a Hollywood star. Suddenly, he had the clout to star in a spoof on Biblical epics, *Wholly Moses!* Despite a supporting cast that included Madeline Kahn, Dom DeLuise (*qv*),

Ferocious sergeant William Hartnell tells raw recruit Bob Monkhouse just where to put his bayonet in *Carry On Sergeant*. Next in line is Gerald Campion

John Ritter and Richard Pryor (*qv*), and a director from *Saturday Night Live*, Gary Weis, the corny capers that resulted were an appalling waste of talent. Probably to the participants' relief, it was barely shown. The next was something else. Moore's impish, slightly befuddled screen personality was perfectly suited to *Arthur*, the story of a permanently tipsy millionaire who runs off with a shopgirl. The film was a massive hit and Moore found himself nominated for an Oscar. He was also in America's list of top moneymaking stars — at number three in 1981 and number four in 1982. He slid out again, though, after a series of films that were largely too sentimental and didn't rely enough on his talents for creating fun. *Unfaithfully Yours*, a remake of the Preston Sturges comedy, deserved a better reception than it got, and *Micki + Maude*, the most successful, got rather better than it deserved: Moore, living up to his real-life 'Cuddly Dudley' image, played a man who gets both wife and girlfriend pregnant. By and large, Moore's films of the early 1980s showed that, when paired with actresses who, whatever their merits, were not box-office — Nastassja Kinski, Elizabeth McGovern, Mary Steenburgen, Amy Irving, Kate Capshaw — in an average vehicle, the draw of Moore by himself was only sufficient to ensure middling returns. Understandably, he expressed himself tired of films by the mid 1980s and took a break — though he was delightfully cast as an elf in *Santa Claus*, a successful Christmas film which relied more happily on his brand of naughty-boy fun. When he did come back, it was in one of the weakest of the fashionable age-reversal comedies, *Like Father, Like Son*, and an *Arthur* sequel which, although not as bad as most critics allowed, performed only moderately at the box-office. *Crazy People* was better, and had Moore nearly back to his best as the livewire ad exec who suffers a breakdown and organises the inmates of an asylum into a profitable advertising agency. But it did little and emphasised that his days as a box-office magnet were probably over. And his was only one of three threads in the moderately amusing comedy of mistaken identity, *Blame It on the Bellboy*. Divorced from actresses Suzy Kendall and Tuesday Weld, Moore also broke up with long-time flame Susan Anton — at 5 ft 11 in. the tallest of his amours — and is currently married to actress-turned-makeup artist Brogan Lane.

1964: * The Hat (narrator only). * Flatland (voice only). 1966: The Wrong Box. 1967: 30 is a Dangerous Age, Cynthia. * Think 20th. Bedazzled. 1969: The Bed Sitting Room. Monte Carlo or Bust (US: Those Daring Young Men in Their Jaunty Jalopies). 1972: Alice's Adventures in Wonderland. 1976: Pleasure at Her Majesty's (narrator only). 1977: The Hound of the Baskervilles. 1978: Foul Play. 1979: '10'. To Russia with Elton (narrator only). 1980: Wholly Moses! Arthur. 1981: Derek and Clive Get the Horn. 1982: Six Weeks. 1983: Lovesick. Romantic Comedy! Unfaithfully Yours. 1984: Best Defense. Micki + Maude. 1985: Santa Claus. 1986: The Adventures of Milo and Otis (narrator, English-language version). 1987: Like Father, Like Son. 1988: Arthur 2 On the Rocks. 1990: Crazy People. 1991: Blame It on the Bellboy.

MOORE, Victor 1876–1962

Chunky, not-too-tall, brown-haired, solid-looking American vaudeville performer whose film credits might have run into hundreds had he not shown a preference for live entertainment. But few of those who laughed at his antics as the plumber called to remove Marilyn Monroe's toe from the bath-tap in *The Seven-Year Itch* realised that 40 years earlier he had been in demand as a silent-screen comedian who appealed to the mother instinct. Moore, who hailed from New Jersey, had already packed in 20 years' experience of making people laugh in vaudeville when he was hired by the Lasky Company to make films in 1915. At 39, his character of the diffident bumbler was well established. Podgy, but good-looking by the standards of silent film comics, Moore had beady eyes and an apologetic air, and would usually lean forward in an over-anxiety to please, especially when courting the girl in the picture. He made his debut as a character called *Chimmie Fadden*; there was a sequel, *Chimmie Fadden Out West*. The following year, Moore tried pathos with *The Clown*, the story of an entertainer devoted to his small son. It would later be revised as *The Champ* (and win Wallace Beery (*qv*) an Oscar), and filmed again several decades later under its original title by Red Skelton (also *qv*). In *Home Defense* Moore was back to basic slapstick. With straw hat and drawn-on glasses, he created a conniving rogue that was a combination of later comics Bobby Clark and W. C. Fields (both *qv*), flannelling his way through the deep South. Moore returned to vaudeville after this first flirtation with films but later made many two-reel comedies in the 1920s. Although his age disqualified him from becoming a top banana in sound films, Moore, the bush of hair now considerably thinned but the mouth as horrified, the eyes as outraged and the beetle brows as anxious as ever, came into demand as top support, often at the Paramount Studios where he had made his first films. He could still be endearing, hesitant and bumbling, but was now occasionally wily and aggressive as well. Notable repeating his Broadway triumph as compromised senator Oliver Loganberry in *Louisiana Purchase* — the film version was revamped as

David Huddleston and John Barrard look on as Patch (Dudley Moore, centre) is promoted to assist Father Christmas in *Santa Claus*

a vehicle for Bob Hope (qv) — Moore also played lovable old codgers in *Star Spangled Rhythm*, *Riding High* and *Duffy's Tavern*, three of Paramount's all-star wartime offerings. He was part of a memorable barber's shop quartet, with Fred Allen, Jack Benny (both qv) and Don Ameche in *It's in the Bag!*; repeated his *Louisiana Purchase* role for a TV production, then teamed with Allen again, as the bumbling, mumbling, stumbling Justice of the Peace in *We're Not Married*, who creates all the fuss in this multi-star movie by thinking he's licensed to marry couples a week before he is. Monroe was in that film too and, after removing her toe from the bath-tap three years later, Moore shuffled off into well-earned retirement. He was 86 when he died from a heart attack.

1915: Chimmie Fadden. Chimmie Fadden Out West. Snobs. 1916: The Race. The Best Man. The Clown. 1917: Home Defense. Invited Out. Oh! U-Boat. Faint Heart and Fair Lady. 1918: Bungalowing. Commuting. Moving. Flivering/ Flivvering. 1925: The Man Who Found Himself. 1926—28: Unidentified 'Lever' Shorts. 1930: Heads Up. Dangerous Nan McGrew. * Love in the Suburbs. 1931: * Baby Face. * Ladies not Allowed. 1932: Of Thee I Sing. 1934: Romance in the Rain. Gift of Gab. 1936: Swing Time. Gold Diggers of 1937. 1937: The Life of the Party. We're on the Jury. Meet the Missus. Make Way for Tomorrow. She's Got Everything. 1938: Radio City Revels. This Marriage Business. 1941: Louisiana Purchase. 1942: Star Spangled Rhythm. 1943: The Heat's On (GB: Tropicana). Riding High (GB: Melody Inn). True to Life. 1944: Carolina Blues. It's in the Bag! (GB: The Fifth Chair). 1945: Duffy's Tavern. 1946: Ziegfeld Follies (completed 1944). 1947: It Happened on Fifth Avenue. 1948: A Miracle Can Happen (later and GB: On Our Merry Way). 1949: A Kiss in the Dark. 1952: We're Not Married. 1955: The Seven Year Itch.

Pop (Victor Moore), a film studio gateman who has told someone that he is the head of the studio, watches anxiously as his daughter Polly (Betty Hutton), one of the studio's switchboard girls, tries to save his skin. From *Star Spangled Rhythm*

MORAN, Polly
(Pauline Moran) 1883—1952
There was a lot of Polly Moran, and most of it was funny. A big, solid American entertainer with a head that looked too small for her body and teeth that seemed crammed into too small a head, she was as rowdy and rumbustious in real life as her characters were on screen. Briefly, in harness with the immortal Marie Dressler (qv), Moran flourished as a star. The dark-haired comedienne was born in Chicago and, after appearing in school plays, set her heart on making people laugh in vaudeville. She was doing it at only 15. So it was as a veteran of the halls (with experience as far afield as Europe and South Africa) that she was signed up for two-reel comedy films by Mack Sennett in 1914. At first she was cast as harridans and husband-beaters, but won her first real popularity as a heroine — playing Nell, a rambunctious law-enforcer of the wild west. Released by Sennett in 1918, 'Polly of the Laughs', as one writer had dubbed her, spent most of the next few years back in vaudeville. It wasn't until 1926 that she returned to Hollywood on a long-term basis, playing bit comedy cameos until teamed with the formidably shapeless Dressler in 1927, as the two belligerent, beer-swilling Irish housewives of *The Callahans and the Murphys*. Thanks to opposition from the Catholic church over the portrayal of such aggressive, working-class Irish womanhood, the film was not the success it might have been. However, there were further joint Dressler-Moran appearances, nine of them in all, but most notably in *Bringing Up Father*, *The Hollywood Revue of 1929* (they sang *Strolling Through the Park One Day* together), *Dangerous Females* (a short), *Caught Short*, *Reducing*, *Politics* and *Prosperity*. The 'two heavyweight hags', as Moran once called them, were glorious foils for each other's outrageous antics, bickering, boozing and being given such lines as 'This stuff makes me see double and feel single!' which brought more than a few frowns to the ranks of the legions of decency. With Dressler destined to move on to greater things (briefly; she died in 1934), Moran returned for a while to character roles — especially a splendid Dodo in the 1933 *Alice in Wonderland* — before going back to her raucous vaudeville act. Republic Pictures, remembering the success of the Dressler—Moran comedies, paired Polly with another screen heavyweight, Alison Skipworth, in two lively programmers, *Two Wise Maids* and *Ladies in Distress*. But Skipworth was 75 and had an eye on retirement; nothing more came of the 'team'. Although she officially retired in 1944 Moran continued to be one of the community's best-loved eccentrics, holding lively parties in her Laguna Beach hideaway, at which she sometimes did an unexpected 'turn' as a waitress. She once campaigned for a seat on the local council as a pro-dog candidate (she lost). Polly's last appearance of note was as the fuddled housekeeper who gets even worse on the witness stand in court in *Adam's Rib*. She had long had heart problems and died from a heart ailment early in 1952 at 68. More subtlety in her performances might have given Polly Moran a wider-ranging Hollywood career. But that was never Polly's style. With Moran on screen, what you saw was what you got.

1914: * The Janitor. 1915: * Their Social Splash. * Ambrose's Little Hatchet. * A Favor-

Polly Moran and George Givot practise a few wrestling holds while Charles Butterworth passes by in his usual bewildered fashion, in *Hollywood Party*

Moranis has always impressed as more of a character actor, with the emphasis on character, than the majority of his fellows. In films, he has often been earnest do-gooders, nerdish but decidedly not the Woody Allen type (*qv*). Even after the world-wide success of *Honey, I Shrunk the Kids*, solo stardom seems hardly assured, and his most fruitful area may lie in close collaboration with other, but contrasting, comic talents, such as he demonstrated with Steve Martin (*qv*) in *My Blue Heaven*. In his screwed up, bug-eyed, mobile-mouthed face, and in his talent for comedy writing, Moranis has two priceless assets for carrying out his favourite occupation: making people laugh. He started performing live in his native Toronto while still in his late teens. It was there, too, that he had his first major success, in partnership with Dave Thomas, on the Second City Television Show, in which another Canadian, John Candy (*qv*), the complete physical opposite of Moranis, had already made his name. Like Candy, Moranis went into films and, also like Candy, was in his thirties before the public began to associate his name with his face. The first mainline hit with which Moranis was associated was *Ghost Busters* in 1984. After that he hung around in Hollywood, doing the odd film or two, until the perfect casting came along: the hapless Seymour in the movie version of stage musical *Little Shop of Horrors*, in which our diminutive hero becomes the slave of a blood-loving plant. No more decent comic roles were forthcoming at the time, so Moranis did *Ghostbusters II*, stealing rather more scenes than he had in the original. When this was followed by *Honey, I Shrunk the Kids*, in which he plays the inventor father who does just that, he had clearly arrived. Moranis projects a likeable character on screen. He definitely has an audience on his side, and there is none of the irritation with his ineptitude which mars some people's enjoyment of a Woody Allen comedy. He did brilliantly as the FBI agent who is tougher than he looks, protecting maverick mobster Martin in *My Blue Heaven*, and did a guest shot with that comedian as a gravedigger in Martin's *L.A. Story*. Unfortunately, there now seems to be something of a hiatus in Moranis films. *Honey, I Blew Up the Baby* was enticingly announced, but took a long time to get on to the assembly line, while he dropped out of *City Slickers* when he and co-star Billy Crystal (*qv*) seemingly couldn't get along. At 38 Moranis can't afford too many such hiccups; he needs to keep his name in the public eye.

ite Fool. * Her Painted Hero. * The Hunt. * A Rascal of Wolfish Ways, or: A Polished Villain. * Hogan Out West. * A Hash House Fraud. * Those College Girls/His Better Half. 1916: * The Village Blacksmith. * A Bath House Blunder. * By Stork Alone. * His Wild Oats. * Madcap Ambrose. * Vampire Ambrose. * Love Will Conquer. * Because He Loved Her. * Safety First Ambrose. * By Stork Delivery. 1917: * Her Fame and Shame. * Cactus Nell. * Taming Target Center. * His Naughty Thought. * Sheriff Nell. * She Needed a Doctor. * His Uncle Dudley. * Roping Her Romeo. * The Pullman Bride. 1918: * Sheriff Nell's Tussle. * The Battle Royal. * Saucy Madeline. * Two Tough Tenderfeet. * She Loved Him Plenty. 1921: Skirts. Two Weeks with Pay. The Affairs of Anatol. 1923: Luck. 1926: The Scarlet Letter. The Auction Block. The Blackbird. Twinkletoes. 1927: The Callahans and the Murphys. The Enemy. The Thirteenth Hour. Buttons. London After Midnight (GB: The Hypnotist). 1928: * Movie Chatterbox. The Divine Woman. Rose-Marie. Detectives. Bringing Up Father. Telling the World. While the City Sleeps. Beyond the Sierras. Shadows of the Night. Show People. Honeymoon. The Trail of '98. 1929: Speedway. The Hollywood Revue of 1929. * Dangerous Females. The Unholy Night. So This is College. Hot for Paris. 1930: The Girl Said No. Caught Short. Three French Girls. Chasing Rainbows. Way Out West. Way for a Sailor. Remote Control. Paid (GB: Within the Law). 1931: * Jackie Cooper's Christmas (GB: The Christmas Party). Guilty Hands. Reducing. It's a Wise Child. Politics. * The Stolen Jools (GB: The Slippery Pearls). 1932: The Passionate Plumber. Prosperity. 1933: Alice in Wonderland. 1934: Down to Their Last Yacht (GB: Hawaiian Nights). Hollywood Party. 1936: * Oh, Duchess. 1937: * Sailor Maid. Two Wise Maids. 1938: Ladies in Distress. 1939: Ambush. 1940: Meet the Missus. Tom Brown's Schooldays. 1941: Petticoat Politics. 1949: Adam's Rib. 1950: The Yellow Cab Man.

MORANIS, Rick 1954–

Snub-nosed, wide-mouthed, bespectacled, tousle-haired little character comedian from Canada. Although basically from the same stand-up comedy on late-night TV tradition as so many modern international stars,

1983: Strange Brew. 1984: The Wild Life. Hockey Night. Streets of Fire. Ghost Busters. 1985: Brewster's Millions. 1986: Head Office. Little Shop of Horrors. Club Paradise. 1987: Spaceballs. Grounded! 1988: How I Got into College. 1989: Ghostbusters II. Honey, I Shrunk the Kids. Parenthood. 1990: My Blue Heaven. 1991: L.A. Story. 1992: Golden Legs. Honey, I Blew Up the Baby.

MORECAMBE, Eric (top)
(E. Bartholomew) 1926–1984
and
WISE, Ernie
(E. Wiseman) 1925–

Britain's most popular double-act of the 1960s and 1970s were 'The tall, thin one with the glasses, and the one with the short, fat, hairy legs'. Actually Morecambe wasn't all that thin, nor Wise all that plump; it was how funny they were that counted. And Morecambe, especially, was funny, reading his punch-lines as if in sudden, surprised reaction and using his glasses as a prop. In films they were never the same force, robbed of the intimacy of a small stage and a live audience; but their popularity remained un-dimmed over a 30-year period. The tall one with the glasses was born in Morecambe, Lancashire (whence the stage name); his partner hailed from Leeds. Both were child entertainers, Wise performing with his father in northern working men's clubs. Morecambe entered talent contests in his native town in his teens as a stand-up comedian and won one for three successive years. Wise had already made his London bow in the 1939 stage production of radio's *The Band Waggon* before he first met Morecambe in the touring show *Youth Takes a Bow*. They formed a double-act almost at once, but World War Two intervened, Wise going into the Merchant Navy and Morecambe becoming a Bevin Boy in the coal-mines. Reunited in 1946, they soon became favourites on variety bills on stage and radio, becoming top-liners by the early 1950s. The breakthrough programme on radio was *You're Only Young Once*, which began in 1954 and featured them as the owners of the Morecambe and Wise Detective Agency. Each week a guest star would bring these inept sleuths a baffling case to bungle their way through. From 1955 they had their own TV series too, but it only began to take off as *The Morecambe and Wise Show* in the early 1960s. A decade later it had become *the* programme to watch each week, and by far the country's most popular comedy/variety show, with many dis-tinguished actors, singers and musicians prepared to come on the show to suffer the irreverence of the star duo. Glenda Jackson's

Cleopatra in a sketch with them was es-pecially memorable. The trio of films they made in the 1960s was popular but poor, formula comedy-thriller formats in which they no longer seemed in control of their own destinies, in spite of the fact that their TV writers, Sid Green and Dick Hills, were involved with the scripts. The last of the cinema releases, *The Magnificent Two*, had the best lines (Told by the heroine that she will always be the women behind him, Eric looks shocked: 'You'll come round the front now and again, won't you?' he asks) but is a curious sort of comedy in which dozens of people actually get killed. There might be a body waiting in a cupboard for Danny Kaye or Bob Hope (both *qv*), but you knew it wasn't real. On TV, though, the fun con-tinued unabated, until Morecambe had to ease up on his workload following a heart attack. But there were still bouts of crosstalk to savour, sometimes going off at such a tangent that you thought Eric and Ernie were ad-libbing until the punchline arrived and another subject was started. A final effort at a feature-length format, *Night Train to Murder*, a strained attempt at a spooky-house mystery with painfully mis-timed jokes, was even worse than the three films that were shown in cinemas. This went straight to TV, by which time Eric was dead, amid national mourning, from another heart attack.

Together. *1965: The Intelligence Men. 1966: That Riviera Touch. 1967: The Magnificent Two. 1970: * Simon, Simon. 1984: Night Train to Murder (TV).*
Morecambe alone. *1980. * Late Flowering Love (voice only).*

MORSE, Robert 1931–
Somewhere in the gulf between Eddie Cantor and Jerry Lewis lies the button-bright, impish-looking, crop-haired, gap-toothed talent of Robert Morse. Briefly popular in films in the 1960s, Morse was always a greater attraction on stage, where he has made the greater part of his career. A croaky-voiced comic player who could sing and dance in bright style, he has scored several major triumphs in Broadway musi-

cals. Born in Massachusetts, Morse saw service with the US Navy before enrolling in New York's American Theatre Wing. While still there, he got a small role in his first film, *The Proud and Profane*. Following work on radio, he made his Broadway debut in *The Matchmaker*, repeating his role in the subsequent film. After further Broadway success, M-G-M picked him up and put him into *Honeymoon Hotel*, where he was permitted to do a sort of Martin and Lewis act with Robert Goulet, and *Quick Before It Melts*, in which his attempts to make love to Yvonne Craig are interrupted by a call from her high-up father. 'What are you doing?' barks the VIP. Morse displays honesty in the face of adversity: 'I'm trying to seduce your daughter', he says. 'Ah yes', comes the reply. 'Had the same trouble with her mother.' These were bright and well-received comedies with Morse displaying limitless energy and an innocent look betrayed by demon eyes. Few went to see him in *The Loved One* or the direly-titled *Oh Dad, Poor Dad, Mama's Hung You in the Closet and I'm Feeling So Sad*, but he had a great success with another long title, *How to Succeed in Business without Really Trying*. This was a repeat of his Tony-winning Broadway performance as J. Pierpont Finch, the ambitious young man who rises, by a combination of nerve, luck and judgment from the bottom of his firm (literally, in the mail room) to the top. Morse's boyish glee as the youth who is, as the script puts it, 'about as protectable as a barracuda' makes him remain sympathetic in spite of his monstrous ruthlessness. But he was not to get the opportunity to dominate an enter-tainment in this way again. He was the philanderer who tried to teach devoted husband Walter Matthau the ways of a lothario in *A Guide for the Married Man* and one of several zanies bemusing Doris Day in her last really funny film, *Where Were You When the Lights Went Out?* At this juncture he tried television. *That's Life*, which ran from 1968 to 1969, was a comedy series about the courtship and subsequent married life of a young couple, told in songs, sketches, monologues and dances. Some heavyweight guest celebrities turned up during the course of the prestigious series. After its run was over, Morse went to the Disney Studio for an amiably nutty comedy called *The Boatniks*. He was cast as an accident-prone ensign, but at 39 the bright innocence of youth had all but gone. The film, though, did have one great line: 'It's the old Conrad Veidt trick!' Since then Morse has remained on stage. A few recent character roles in films have obviously prompted no desire to return to the cinema on a permanent basis.

1955: The Proud and Profane. 1958: The Matchmaker. 1963: The Cardinal. 1964: Honeymoon Hotel. 1965: Quick Before It Melts. The Loved One. 1966: Oh Dad, Poor Dad, Mama's Hung You in the Closet and I'm Feeling

So Sad. How to Succeed in Business Without Really Trying. 1967: A Guide for the Married Man. 1968: Where Were You When the Lights Went Out? 1970: The Boatniks. 1984: Calendar Girl Murders (TV). 1987: California Hunk. The Emperor's New Clothes.

MOSTEL, Zero
(Samuel Mostel) 1915–1977
Shambling, round-faced, heavyweight American comic actor with beaming smile, whose career dodged up several unexpected side turnings. Blacklisting by the Senate Committee of Un-American Activities at least returned him to musical comedy and the scene of his greatest triumphs — Broadway. In films, his characters often threatened to break out of the movie altogether. He was born in Brooklyn's Brownsville to the supervisor of a kosher slaughterhouse. The 'Zero' was a childhood nickname. He graduated with a BA degree in art but was soon making his way as an amateur entertainer and stand-up comedian. Discovered by a radio producer when doing a comedy routine at an artists' dance, he was soon himself a familiar voice on radio. After a New York debut early in 1942 with his own cabaret act, he was snapped up for the Broadway revue *Keep 'Em Laughing* and later the same year found himself under contract to MGM. But Mostel was already flirting with communism, and his studio contract was scrapped after his political attack on the MGM film *Tennessee Johnson* (GB: *The Man on America's Conscience*). His role in the one film he had completed, *DuBarry Was a Lady*, was severely trimmed. Chastened, he returned to Broadway. Here, nightclub work was followed by a brief spell in the US Army, and then more Broadway musicals. Determined to improve his abilities, Mostel enrolled at the Actors' Studio in 1950 and was rewarded with a contract from 20th Century-Fox for whom he played, strange though it now seems, a few swarthy, sweaty villains. But he was getting back into comedy roles when named as a member of the Communist Party and blacklisted. Blacklisting on Broadway followed three years later after he had been called before the Un-American Activities Committee and

declined to testify, pleading the 5th Amendment. But he played nightclubs, plus a season at London's Palladium and was back on Broadway by 1957. In the early 1960s he won three Tony awards there for his performances in *Rhinoceros*, *A Funny Thing Happened on the Way to the Forum* and *Fiddler on the Roof*. The second of these three shows, a musical farce set in ancient Rome, brought Mostel's explosive, excitable style of comedy back to the cinema when he appeared in the film version. He was very funny the following year as Bialystock in Mel Brooks' *The Producers*, but later appearances were less happy and sometimes little more than cameos. Mostel died from a heart attack during the pre-Broadway presentation of a new play. The actor Josh Mostel is his son.

*1943: DuBarry Was a Lady. 1950: Panic in the Streets. The Enforcer (GB: Murder Inc.). 1951: Sirocco. The Guy Who Came Back. Mr Belvedere Rings the Bell. The Model and the Marriage Broker. 1959: * Zero. 1966: A Funny Thing Happened on the Way to the Forum. 1967: The Producers. Great Catherine. * The Ride of the Valkyrie. 1968: Monsieur Lecoq (unfinished). 1969: The Great Bank Robbery. 1970: The Angel Levine. 1972: The Hot Rock (GB: How to Steal a Diamond in Four Uneasy Lessons). 1973: Rhinoceros. Marco (made for cinemas but shown only on TV). Once Upon a Scoundrel. 1974: Foreplay. Journey into Fear (released 1976). 1976: The Front. Mastermind (filmed 1969). Hollywood on Trial. 1978: The Little Drummer Boy (TV. Voice only). Watership Down (voice only). 1979: Best Boy.*

MOUNT, Peggy 1916–
Raucous, brown-haired, larger-than-life British actress with a homely, cheerful face and an impressive mouthful of teeth. It took her a while to impose her dominating personality on suitable material, but, once in the public eye, she enjoyed two decades of success in 'dragon' roles. Born in Southend-on-Sea, on the Essex coast, she started her working life as a secretary, but studied for the stage privately under the drama teacher Phyllis Reader before breaking into wartime concert parties from 1942. Two years later

she headed north to make her first appearance in repertory and during the next ten years built up a formidable gallery of mainly working-class roles while touring Yorkshire, Lancashire, the Midlands and Scotland. She returned south in 1954, making a minor film debut, then winning the star-making role of the fearsome Mrs Hornett in *Sailor Beware!* Mount's rampaging central performance, scaring the back of the stalls as much as her prospective sailor son-in-law, created an enormous hit. She stayed with the play for more than a thousand performances, repeating her role on film the following year. Peggy Mount made the most of her new-found stardom. There was a television series, *The Larkins* (and a film spin-off, *Inn for Trouble*) and she was well-received in the movie comedy *The Naked Truth*, holding her own against such popular funny-men as Peter Sellers and Terry-Thomas (both *qv*) as a blackmailed novelist who, like several other characters in this riotous film, decides to bump off the blackmailer. In 1960, at the Old Vic theatre, Peggy played for the first time her favourite role, the nurse in *Romeo and Juliet*. Film roles in the 1960s by and large did not justice to her talents, but there was another hit TV series, *George and the Dragon*, opposite Sidney James (also *qv*), which began in 1966 and ran for several seasons. A later TV series, *You're Only Young Twice*, was also successful, and this heartiest and most likeable of actresses has continued to be a popular attraction on stage.

1954: The Embezzler. 1956: Sailor Beware! (US: Panic in the Parlor). Dry Rot. 1957: The Naked Truth (US: Your Past is Showing). 1960: Inn for Trouble. 1963: Ladies Who Do. 1964: One Way Pendulum. 1966: Hotel Paradiso. Finders Keepers. 1968: Oliver! 1976: The Chiffy Kids (serial). 1991: The Princess and the Goblin (voice only).

MURDOCH, Richard 1907–1990
With his precise, reedy, sardonic tones, Britain's Richard Murdoch was a rare example of a straight man who was almost as funny, and as popular, as the star. As a radio comedian, he had an extraordinary run: 40 years of almost unblemished success, in-

cluding three long-running shows. As a film performer, he never quite made his mark. Straight was a good word for Murdoch in a physical sense; tall and stork-like with beaky nose, ingratiating smile and receding hairline, the dapper Murdoch began his theatrical career at 19 as a dancer in the London show *The Blue Train*. In later years, he would modestly claim that he was still a dancer before the big break came. But in truth, he had made a few uncertain steps up the ladder, before fame plucked him from relative obscurity at the age of 30. He was playing Sergeant Oliver in the long-running Stanley Lupino (*qv*) show *Over She Goes* (a role he also played in the 1937 film) when he was spotted by BBC Radio scouts as a possible 'feed-man' for up-and-coming comedian Arthur Askey (*qv*) in the first radio show to feature regular comedians, *Band Waggon*. It was originally planned as a dance-band show with innovative comic interludes, but Askey and Murdoch, who got on famously, changed all that. 'We didn't like the scripts they'd provided for us', remembered Murdoch, 'so we started writing our own.' The first *Band Waggon* stuck much to the formula envisaged, but Askey and Murdoch soon took over, creating a home for themselves in a mythical top-floor flat at Broadcasting House, and hanging out their washing on the roof. A whole myriad of supporting characters also began to appear, creating the foundations of radio comedy for the next three decades. Murdoch got his lifelong nickname – 'Stinker' – during the run of the programme, which ended when the stars were 'evicted' from their flat. A film version continued the story from this point, and a stage version of the programme was also successful. The *Band Waggon* film gave Askey and Murdoch the chance to make progress in movies. This they did with two versions of old favourites: *Charley's (Big-Hearted) Aunt* and *The Ghost Train*. A fourth film, *I Thank You* (named after one of Askey's catchphrases) was less successful, but the partnership was in any case broken by the war. Enlisting in the RAF, Flight Lieutenant Murdoch made the acquaintance of an affable, balding Wing Commander, Kenneth Horne. Together they invented the fictional RAF station *Much-Binding-in-the-Marsh*, in Laughter Command, which made its debut in January 1944 and ran virtually non-stop until the end of 1954. In this, Murdoch became a master of tongue-twisting songs sung at breakneck speed, and he and Horne always ended the programme with a song satirising events of the day ('. . . a little thing that goes something like this'). At one point in the series, Murdoch had the bright idea of 'sacking' the station's batman, moustachioed ex-singer Sam Costa, who began to wander through the BBC network, popping up in various unlikely programmes looking for work. It was a rare example of this kind of gag being carried through, and underlined Murdoch's impishly inventive

comic mind. Film ventures during this period, however, were far from successful. One, *Golden Arrow*, sat on the shelf for four years. Murdoch didn't often get solo spotlight and when he did as in 1948's *It Happened in Soho*, it proved a shoddy second-feature in which he was asked to play more or less a straight role. By the end of the 1950s he was in such bottom budget entries as *Strictly Confidential* and *Not a Hope in Hell*. Radio was again to come to the rescue. From 1962 Murdoch starred with unflappable Wilfrid Hyde White as *The Men from the Ministry*; his portrayal of a dithering Whitehall bumbler was right on the button and ensured a long run for the show even after Hyde White left, to be replaced by Deryck Guyler. It went on until 1977. In his later years, Murdoch played comic cameos in such TV series as *Rumpole of the Bailey* and *Never the Twain*, remaining active until shortly before his death from a heart attack.

1932: Looking on the Bright Side. 1934: Evergreen. 1937: Over She Goes. 1938: The Terror. 1939: Band Waggon. 1940: Charley's (Big-Hearted) Aunt. 1941: The Ghost Train. I Thank You. 1944: One Exciting Night (US: You Can't Do Without Love). 1948: It Happened in Soho. 1949: Golden Arrow (US: The Gay Adventure/Three Men and a Girl. Released 1953). 1950: Lilli Marlene. 1951: The Magic Box. 1959: Strictly Confidential. 1960: Not a Hope in Hell. 1969: Under the Table You Must Go. 1986: Whoops Apocalypse.

MURPHY, Eddie 1961–
It's clear from contemporary interviews and reviews that writers and fellow-workers alike don't care much for this hip, lithe, wisecracking American comedian turned blockbuster star. But then megastars like Murphy have rarely, down the ages, been in the business of appealing to their fellow man. Audiences adored him, even if he made too few films for their liking; but there were signs in the early 1990s that the world-record-breaking honeymoon for the catlike, contemptuous comedy star might be drawing to a close. Murphy is, in many ways, a Bob Hope (*qv*) for the modern audience, without the yellow streak, but with a whipcrack wise-

crack for every occasion. His father, a New York policeman, was an amateur comedian but died when Murphy was eight. At school, he was always 'on', jumping on desks and tables and doing his thing. Even the staff admitted that the patter was funny, although they professed to be appalled by the language. Four-letter words, though, were to be part of Murphy's appeal as a stand-up comedian. At 15 he hosted a talent show, and was making his way as a nightclub comedian a year later. He joined the popular late-night TV comedy show *Saturday Night Live* in 1980, staying with it until early in 1984. Starting in small running roles, he had become the show's star performer by the time of his departure, at the going rate of $30,000 a show. In films, his super-cool comedy cracks showed up best in an action setting: *48 Hrs*, a flashy thriller, took more than $30 million largely thanks to his presence in it. *Trading Places* took even more (it was also a much better film) and projected the Murphy image at its best. Cocking a snook at authority, turning the tables on those who think they have the upper hand and generally being the rascal you love to see come out on top. It was back to action with *Beverly Hills Cop* which, despite going through several writers, directors and stars, turned out to be one of the major box-office winners of the decade, establishing Murphy as a world star. His streetwise Detroit cop deservedly had all the best of the quickfire dialogue, beautifully scripted and delivered with a unique backstreets naturalness, so fast that you were laughing before you knew it. Paramount announced an exclusive agreement of five films for a fee of $15 million, but the megastar hype had already brought its own form of burn-out. As is often the case with stars of such magnitude, when agreement was reached on scripts, they proved to be hardly worth a two-year wait. Even so, neither *The Golden Child*, a special-effects adventure aimed more at family business, and the inevitable *Beverly Hills Cop II*, was as bad as most critics thought. Both were brisky entertaining, if down a notch from previous ventures, and brought in combined revenue of $120 million in America alone. While the wrangling over the on-off *Beverly Hills Cop III* continued, 'films' and 'videos' of Murphy's concert performances continued to keep his fans happy. So did *Coming to America*, a foul-mouthed but funny notion about an African prince working at a hamburger joint in New York while looking for a bride. Murphy played several different cameo roles as well, most notably as an elderly white Jew. If Jewish people might have seen the joke, there were several other sections of society that didn't appreciate Murphy, who was equally scathing about women and gays in his stage acts. That got him rather inglorious inclusion in the black-gay movie, *Tongues Untied*, as an example of how not to help gays integrate into society. Meanwhile, back in the mainline cinema world, Murphy bombed in a big way with *Harlem Nights*, wearing one too many hats as writer, executive producer, director and star, and giving a performance that was now much too self-aware in this story of black gangland warfare in the 1930s. Murphy played safe after that with *Another 48 Hrs* and, although there were wrangles on set and complaints about the star's timekeeping, the film doubled its $40 million cost in terms of profit. It was not, however, good. *Beverly Hills Cop III* came and went again, but Murphy and Paramount, a much-troubled partnership, were still together for *Boomerang*, another all-black venture with Grace Jones and the 'hot' Robin Givens as co-stars. And *Beverly Hills Cop III*? It will probably get made — if and when Murphy feels in need of another cast-iron hit.

1982: 48 Hrs. 1983: Trading Places. Delirious (video). 1984: Best Defense. Beverly Hills Cop. 1986: The Golden Child. 1987: Beverly Hills Cop II. 1988: Raw/Eddie Murphy Raw. Coming to America. 1989: Harlem Nights (and directed). Tongues Untied. 1990: Another 48 Hrs. 1992: Boomerang. The Distinguished Gentleman.

MURRAY, Bill
(William Doyle-Murray) 1950–

There are times when this American comedian with the amiably idiotic grin has seemed to have blown it in films. But, each time he has got 'artistic control' out of his system, and come back as part of an ensemble performance under a decent director, he has produced a funny film that audiences want to see. Unseen by cinemagoers until he was almost 30, Murray has a long, butter-wouldn't-melt-in-my-mouth face, about as much hair as Michael Keaton (*qv*) (not a lot) and ingenuous blue eyes to go with that grin. He looks like the naughty schoolboy whistling innocently with his hands behind his back as the teacher suffers under some new practical joke. Indeed, several of Murray's films have portrayed him as a man who metaphorically gets away with murder. From Chicago, he acted in college plays, became a hippie and was busted for possession of marijuana, then joined the city's famous Second City comedy

group at 21: John Belushi (*qv*) and writer-performer Harold Ramis were contemporaries there. Three years later Murray starred in *National Lampoon Radio Hour*, but it was 1977 before his laconic, laid-back humour found a spot on national television. He took over from Chevy Chase (*qv*) as anchor-man on the already-popular *Saturday Night Live*. Murray started a film career in which he was often the only point of interest in some mediocre comedies: the unconventional camp counsellor in *Meatballs*; the reluctant soldier in the occasionally funny *Stripes*; the greensman obsessed with gophers in generally execrable *Caddyshack*. What put Murray in the senior league, however, was his inheritance of the role intended for the deceased John Belushi in *Ghost Busters*. When Murray proved funnier than co-stars Dan Aykroyd (*qv*), Ramis and Rick Moranis (*qv*), he was clearly worth a vehicle of his own. What the studio got, however, were two vehicles that were worth almost nothing at the box-office: *Nothing Lasts Forever*, and Murray's one, disastrous fling at straight drama, *The Razor's Edge*, a personal project which he also co-scripted. If Tyrone Power hadn't managed to make much of the mystic central role in the 1946 film of this Maugham story, goodness knows what induced Murray to think he could do any better. He did worse. Self-seclusion followed, during which he bought several baseball teams, and studied for a year at the Sorbonne. He became a baseball commentator on Chicago radio, and did a (very funny) 'bit' in the film version of the stage musical *Little Shop of Horrors*, in the old Jack Nicholson role as the dental patient who can't wait to feel the thrill of novocaine. Since then, Murray has stuck to comedy. He returned to mainline features in 1988 with *Scrooged*, an amiable special effects-oriented update of the Dickens classic,

which did quite well at the box-office despite a critical drubbing and the enormous salary apparently demanded by the star. *Ghostbusters II* was a guaranteed success, and Murray's casual humour again the best thing in it. The downswing in takings (still sizeable) probably guaranteed, in these days of escalating budgets for sci-fi films, that there would be no *Ghostbusters III*. *Quick Change* was small change at the tills and quickly went to video. In 1991 Murray was back with a bang, mainly as a result of the perfect fusion of actor and role, in *What About Bob?* Murray plays a walking nightmare called Bob who has a phobia about touching things and going places, and thinks his bladder is about to explode. He only talks to his goldfish and, with some reluctance, to his psychiatrist (Richard Dreyfuss), whom he literally drives nuts. Murray has made something of a speciality of the man who looks like a loser but turns out a winner. Here, with more tics and hesitations than Peter Falk's Columbo, he honed it to a fine art. That's Murray all over: a charming bundle of nerves.

*1975: La honte de la jongle (GB: Jungle Burger. US: Shame of the Jungle. Voice only). 1976: * The Hat Act. 1979: Meatballs. Mr Mike's Mondo Video. 1980: Where the Buffalo Roam. Caddyshack. 1981: Stripes. Loose Shoes (completed 1977). 1982: Tootsie. 1984: Ghost Busters. The Razor's Edge. Nothing Lasts Forever. 1986: Little Shop of Horrors. 1987: Rolling in the Aisles. 1988: Scrooged. 1989: Ghostbusters II. 1990: Quick Change. 1991: What About Bob? 1992: Mad Dog and Glory. Ground Hog Day.*

MURRAY, Charlie
See SIDNEY, George
and
MURRAY, Charlie

The world can rest easy at last . . . the *Ghost Busters* are in town. Bill Murray (centre), Dan Aykroyd (left) and Harold Ramis take up stations in different sections of a room, as they prepare to entrap a demon spirit in the monstrous 1984 comedy hit.

Golden boy. Eddie Murphy played a social worker asked to rescue a holy child who can bring peace to the earth in the comedy-fantasy *The Golden Child*

Chic's-a-poppin'. Ole Olsen (left) and Chic Johnson seem to have come to a parting of the ways in this publicity still for *Hellzapoppin*

NORMAND, Mabel 1892–1930

It doesn't seem likely that any other 21-year-old girl ever directed her own films; that fact alone would make Mabel Normand unique. But there was much more to this gamine, brown-eyed, dark-haired American comedienne than that. Blessed with an attractive, expressive face, Normand instinctively knew what was right on camera. She was born to dominate scenes by actions (and reactions) rather than words, and was therefore an ideal silent film comic. Mabel's willingness to undergo any physical indignity, from a pie in the face to a fall in a muddy pool, endeared her to her fellow-workers. But when she left the Sennett studio at which she had made her name her high spirits and high living led her into a twilight world of drugs and violence that wrecked her career and her life. She came from Boston, the daughter of a pianist whose travels on the vaudeville circuit meant he was away from home more often than not. When the family moved to New York, the pretty, big-eyed, puff-cheeked, teenage Mabel was spotted by illustrator Carl Kleinschmidt, who asked her to work regularly for him as a model. This led to work with many of the top illustrators of the day, as well as some more general modelling. Through photographer friends Mabel found work in films, where her impish, uninhibited talent for comedy saw her quickly promoted from the ranks of supporting players to star

roles. At the Biograph studio, she soon met the ambitious young slapstick comedy director Mack Sennett, who was to become her mentor and her lover. In many ways Sennett was both a guiding light to her and an albatross around her comely neck. She was so popular with audiences (and, apparently, with the studio) that within a year she was making her own comedy shorts entitled *Mabel's This* or *Mabel's That*. She began directing them as well in mid 1914, sometimes co-directing with Sennett, later with Charlie Chaplin (*qv*). Normand and Sennett never did get to the altar, though their on-off personal relationship kept her in custard-pie comedies longer than was good for her career. The story of their Keystone years was told with wild inaccuracy in the 1939 film *Hollywood Cavalcade*, and hardly more truthfully in the latter-day stage musical *Mack and Mabel*. After her success in the longer-length *Tillie's Punctured Romance*, co-starring with Chaplin and Marie Dressler (*qv*), Mabel began pushing Sennett harder for features in which she could display a wider range of talents. The result (eventually) was *Mickey*. Begun in 1916, it was beset with problems and mishaps and wasn't completed for eight months. When Sennett found exhibitors less than enthusiastic about a 'new' Mabel Normand he took umbrage and refused to release the film. Finally released in 1918, the story showcased Mabel as a tomboy from the country deflating a few high-society egos in the city before donning jockey's clothes to win a crucial race at the climax. Surprisingly, the film was a huge public success. But it was too late for Sennett. After several threatened walk-outs, the fiery Mabel had finally left him to go to another studio, Goldwyn. Cut loose from Sennett, Normand continued to make successful pictures with Goldwyn. But now she also became a queen of the Hollywood social whirl of the 1920s. There were wild parties, outrageous escapades, and rumours of drug-taking and all-night orgies. Amid this atmosphere of scandal, Mabel's career was wrecked in 1922 when she was (apparently innocently) involved in two murders. The first victim was one of her lovers, director William Desmond Taylor, the second a Hollywood millionaire gunned down by Mabel's chauffeur. The effects of drugs, scandal and the effort of throwing herself back into a work routine – Sennett welcomed her back for several feature films – became clearly visible on screen, especially in her last major film, *The Extra Girl*, in 1924. She was in a flop Broadway show and then, either side of a bout of double pneumonia early in 1927, made several two-reel comedies for Hal Roach. She married an actor, Lew Cody (Louis Coté, 1884–1934), but had already contracted the tuberculosis that was to kill her. She was hospitalised in 1929 and died early the following year, just a couple of months past her 37th birthday. Charlie Chaplin once wrote of Mabel Normand that 'everyone adored her'. The

trouble was that she had too much to give in return.

1910: Over the Garden Wall. 1911: Betty Becomes a Maid. The Subduing of Mrs Nag. Troublesome Secretaries. A Victim of Circumstances. Her Awakening. Saved by Herself. The Squaw's Love. The Unveiling. The Diving Girl. 1912: The Engagement Ring. The Brave Hunter. The Furs. Help! Help! The Interrupted Elopement. A Dash thru the Clouds. The Fickle Spaniard. Helen's Marriage. Hot Stuff. Katchem Kate. † Neighbors. Oh, Those Eyes. Tomboy Bessie. The Tourists. The Tragedy of a Dress Suit. What the Doctor Ordered. The Water Nymph. The New Neighbor. Pedro's Dilemma. Stolen Glory. The Ambitious Butler. The Flirting Husband. The Grocery Clerk's Romance. Cohen at Coney Island. At It Again. Mabel's Lovers. The Deacon's Trouble. A Temperamental Husband. The Rivals. Mr Fix-It. A Desperate Lover. Brown's Seance. A Family Mix-Up. A Midnight Elopement. Mabel's Adventures. The Duel. Mabel's Stratagem. 1913: Mabel's Dad. The Cure That Failed. The Mistaken Masher. The Deacon Outwitted. Just Brown's Luck. The Battle of Who Run. Heinze's Resurrection. Mabel's Heroes. The Professor's Daughter. Red-Hot Romance. A Tangled Affair. The Sleuths at the Floral Parade. The Rural Third Degree. A Strong Revenge. Foiling Fickle Father. A Doctored Affair. The Rube and the Baron. Those Good Old Days. Father's Choice. The Ragtime Band. At 12 O'Clock. Her New Boy. A Little Hero. Mabel's Awful Mistake. Hubby's Job. The Foreman of the Jury. Barney Oldfield's Race for Life. The Hansom Driver. The Speed Queen. The Waiters' Picnic. For the Love of Mabel. The Telltale Light. A Noise from the Deep. Love and Courage. Professor Bean's Removal. The Riot. Baby Day. Mabel's New Hero. The Gypsy Queen. Mabel's Dramatic Career. The Faithful Taxicab. The Bowling Match. Speed Kings. Love Sickness at Sea. A Muddy Romance. Cohen Saves the Flag. The Gusher. Zuzu the Band Leader. The Champion. Fatty's Flirtation. 1914: A Misplaced Foot. Mabel's Stormy Love Affair. Won in a Closet. Mabel's Bear Escape. Mabel's Strange Predicament. Love and Gasoline. Mack At It Again. Mabel at the Wheel. Caught in a Cabaret. Mabel's Nerve. The Alarm. The Fatal Mallet. Her Friend the Bandit. Mabel's Busy Day. Mabel's Married Life. Mabel's New Job. Those Country Kids. Mabel's Latest Prank. Mabel's Blunder. Hello, Mabel! Gentlemen of Nerve. Lovers' Post Office. His Trysting Place. How Heroes Are Made. Fatty's Jonah Day. Fatty's Wine Party. The Sea Nymphs (GB: His Diving Beauty). Getting Acquainted. † Tillie's Punctured Romance. 1915: Mabel and Fatty's Washing Day. Mabel and Fatty's Simple Life. Fatty and Mabel at the San Diego Exposition. Mabel, Fatty and the Law (GB: Fatty's Spooning Day). Fatty and Mabel's Married Life. That Little Band of Gold (GB: For Better or Worse). Wished on Mabel. Mabel and Fatty Viewing the World's Fair at San Francisco. Their Social Splash. Mabel's Wilful Way. Mabel Lost and Won. The Little Teacher (GB: A Small Town

Bully). † My Valet. Stolen Magic. 1916: Fatty and Mabel Adrift. He Did and He Didn't (GB: Love and Lobsters). The Bright Lights (GB: The Lure of Broadway). 1917: † Mickey. † Oh! Mabel, Behave (released 1922). 1918: † Joan of Plattsburgh. † Back to the Woods. Stake Uncle Sam to Play Your Hand. † Dodging a Million. † The Floor Below. † The Venus Model. † Peck's Bad Girl. † A Perfect 36. 1919: † Sis Hopkins. † The Pest. When Doctors Disagree. † Upstairs. † Jinx. † Pinto. 1920: † The Slim Princess. † What Happened to Rosa. 1921: † The Last Chance. † Arabella Flynn. † Molly O. 1922: † Head Over Heels. 1923: † Suzanne. 1924: † The Extra Girl. 1926: Raggedy Rose. The Nickel Hopper. One Hour Married. Anything Once. 1927: Should Men Walk Home?

All shorts except † features.

NORTON, Jack
(Mortimer J. Naughton) 1889–1958
Staggering in seemingly bemused fashion from studio to studio, Jack Norton was one of the two great Hollywood enactors of comic drunks – the other was Arthur Housman (qv) – in the 1930s and 1940s. Slightly testier- and shiftier-looking than Housman, Norton had dark hair, beady eyes, pronounced cheekbones and a moustache that swept down from his nostrils before veering drunkenly up again at the end. On the whole, his characters frequented a slightly loftier prowling range than Housman's. While Housman more often than not popped up in the street, or in a bar, Norton could frequently be found in restaurants and hotel lobbies. A teetotaller in real life, Norton came from New York, and made the whole of his early career in vaudeville, perfecting his drunk impression in a double act with Lucille Haley, formerly one of the Haley Sisters, who became his wife in 1918. With Housman in heavy demand for screen roles by the early 1930s, another amiable, scene-stealing drunk was more than welcome in Hollywood's studios. Norton worked with many of the great directors there, most notably Preston Sturges, for whom he became a memorable member of the Ale and Quail Club in *The Palm Beach Story*, forever enquiring as to the whereabouts of the dogs! Norton's characters wavered and staggered,

but almost never lost their feet, either miraculously regaining balance or finding fun with the nearest solid object. Norton's services were less in demand in the more socially-concerned post-war Hollywood, where a bottle was often something to hide rather than to proffer, and he slipped off into a distinctly un-alcoholic retirement. He died from a respiratory ailment at 69.

1934: The Girl from Missouri (GB: One Hundred Per Cent Pure). * Perfectly Mismated. Cockeyed Cavaliers. * Fixing a Stew. * Super Snooper. * One Too Many. * Woman Haters. * Counsel on De Fence. Death on the Diamond. Sweet Music. Now I'll Tell (GB: When New York Sleeps). Bordertown. 1935: One Hour Late. Go into Your Dance (GB: Casino de Paree). She Gets Her Man. Calling All Cars. The Golden Lily. Dante's Inferno. Front Page Woman. Stolen Harmony. Page Miss Glory. One More Spring. Doctor Socrates. The Girl from 10th Avenue (GB: Men on Her Mind). Alibi Ike. Going Highbrow. Don't Bet on Blondes. Miss Pacific Fleet. His Night Out. Broadway Gondolier. Ship Café. Ruggles of Red Gap. 1936: The Moon's Our Home. * Down the Ribber. After the Thin Man. The Preview Murder Mystery. Gold Diggers of 1937. Too Many Parents. 1937: Marked Woman. Time Out for Romance. The Great Garrick. Pick a Star. A Day at the Races. My Dear Miss Aldrich. Married Before Breakfast. Meet the Missus. * Swing Fever. 1938: * The Awful Tooth. Man Proof. Arsene Lupin Returns. Kentucky Moonshine (GB: Four Men and a Girl). Strange Faces. Meet the Girls. Jezebel. Thanks for the Memory. King of Alcatraz (GB: King of the Alcatraz). 1939: Grand Jury Secrets. Joe and Ethel Turp Call on the President. The Roaring Twenties. Laugh It Off (GB: Lady Be Gay). Society Smugglers. The Lone Wolf Spy Hunt (GB: Lone Wolf's Daughter). It's a Wonderful World. 1940: The Farmer's Daughter. The Villain Still Pursued Her. Opened by Mistake. Let's Make Music. A Night at Earl Carroll's. The Bank Dick (GB: The Bank Detective). The Ghost Breakers. Road Show. 1941: You Belong to Me (GB: Good Morning, Doctor). Down in San Diego. No Greater Sin (GB: Social Enemy No. 1). * Crazy Like a Fox. * Ready, Willing, But Unable. The Feminine Touch. Louisiana Purchase. Ride On, Vaquero. 1942: The Spoilers. Ice-Capades Revue (GB: Rhythm Hits the Ice). Moonlight in Havana. Dr Renault's Secret. The Palm Beach Story. My Favorite Spy. Tennessee Johnson (GB: The Man on America's Conscience). The Fleet's In. Roxie Hart. Brooklyn Orchid. The McGuerins from Brooklyn. 1943: Taxi, Mister. Assignment in Brittany. It Ain't Hay (GB: Money for Jam). So's Your Uncle. Thank Your Lucky Stars. The Kansan (GB: Wagon Wheels). The Falcon Strikes Back. Gildersleeve on Broadway. Lady Bodyguard. Prairie Chickens. 1944: * His Tale is Told. Ghost Catchers. Once Upon a Time. The Story of Dr Wassell. Here Come the Waves. The Chinese Cat/Charlie Chan in The Chinese Cat. * His Hotel Sweet. * Doctor, Feel My Pulse! * Heather and Yon. The Miracle

of Morgan's Creek. Cover Girl. And the Angels Sing. Shine On Harvest Moon. Hail the Conquering Hero. Make Your Own Bed. The Big Noise. Barbary Coast Gent. Going My Way. 1945: Hold That Blonde. Her Highness and the Bellboy. Wonder Man. Fashion Model. The Naughty Nineties. The Scarlet Clue. Flame of the Barbary Coast. The Horn Blows at Midnight. Man Alive. Strange Confession. Lady on a Train. Two O'Clock Courage. Captain Tugboat Annie. A Guy, a Gal, a Pal. * Dance, Dance, Dance. Double Honeymoon. 1946: * Rhythm and Weep. The Strange Mr Gregory. No Leave, No Love. Blue Skies. Lady Luck. The Hoodlum Saint. Nocturne. The Sin of Harold Diddlebock (later and GB: Mad Wednesday!). The Kid from Brooklyn. Rendezvous 24. Shadows Over Chinatown. Bringing Up Father. 1947: Linda Be Good. Down to Earth. Variety Girl. * The Hired Husband. 1948: Variety Time. Alias a Gentleman. 1949: †† Two Knights in Brooklyn/Two Mugs from Brooklyn.
†† Combined GB version of *The McGuerins from Brooklyn/Taxi, Mister.*

OAKIE, Jack
(Lewis Offield) 1903–1978
A chubby-cheeked, brown-haired, fast-talking, plumply-built American entertainer with plain 'Honest Joe' looks. Although nimble-witted in real life, Oakie's film characters were in the main not too bright,

and had names like Slugger, Chicken, Searchlight, Elmer, Chick and Dopey. They were, however, good-natured and eager to get ahead. They quite often ended up losing the girl to the handsome co-star. Noted for his facial grimaces — his *pièce de résistance* was his famous 'triple-fade', a shocked, multi-layered reaction — this bouncy, self-assured comic performer was born in Missouri, but raised in Oklahoma whence came his stage surname. When the family moved to New York, Oakie attended business school there and became a clerk in Wall Street. A part in a charity show — his co-star was Lulu McConnell, for many years his partner on stage — resulted in his turning professional, and from 1922 he began to get Broadway roles as a 'chorus boy'. Sacked from the musical *Peggy-Ann* in 1927 for ad-libbing and upstaging the romantic lead, Oakie decided he had enough of hoofing and clowning on stage and headed for the other side of America — Hollywood. He met a director at Paramount who admired his work and was soon under contract. Oakie was flattered to be in movies but knew where his strengths lay. 'I'd have loved to have have been the guy all the girls swooned around in those college pictures', he once said. 'But some things in life are impossible and every time I shaved, the mirror told me the truth.' His chunky build got him cast as comic sporting heroes in several pictures, and he actually won Ginger Rogers in *The Sap from Syracuse*. In many ways Oakie seemed ideally fitted for sidekick roles so it was much to his credit that, for the moment, he continued to head the cast. He got a chance both to sing a double-talk song and to bandy words with W. C. Fields and Hugh Herbert (both *qv*) in the memorable *Million Dollar Legs*. Oakie played the trainer of the Olympic team from the bankrupt principality of Klopstokia. And, even though his characters seemed too dim (and too old) to be in college at all, there were some of 'those college pictures' too, notably *College Humor*, *College Rhythm* and *Collegiate*. Oakie gave a sparkling performance at the head of the cast in *Once in a Lifetime*, the funniest satire on early Hollywood this side of *Singin' in the Rain*. He was a dippy but successful Hollywood producer in the hilarious story of three conmen who take advantage of the infant industry by pretending to be vocal coaches. In the mid 1930s Oakie's standing slipped to that of co-star, and he switched from Paramount to RKO in 1936. In 1938 he went on a long European holiday and returned to find that his contract had not been renewed and no-one wanted to hire him because, since he had upped and left the film capital for several months, they believed he would be 'too difficult' to work with. In later years Oakie would be philosophical about the disasters. 'I don't blame Hollywood', he said, 'for those two black years when I couldn't get a job of any sort. Some of it was my own fault. All I had was the wife and the dogs — and I began eyeing

"Oh — I thought you were someone else~~" 1294-8

When this girl kisses you, it feels like you've been hit by a chair . . . A bewildered Jack Oakie meets an unexpected reception from Jean Arthur in *The Gang Buster*. Fortunately (or unfortunately) it's a case of mistaken identity

their meals. I hadn't been able to see how Hollywood could get along without me . . . but of course it did.' Fortunately, Oakie, always a thrifty man, had money put by even after his costly European splurge. And eventually 20th Century-Fox came to the rescue, putting him into a series of musicals, in which he is seen most often today, on late-night TV, and in which he always seemed to be losing Alice Faye or Betty Grable to John Payne or Victor Mature. And, sandwiched in between the Fox frivolities, there was one of his best roles, as Benzino Napaloni, dictator of Bacteria, in Chaplin's *The Great Dictator*. This satire on Benito Mussolini won Oakie his only Oscar nomination, although he might have added a second for his warm and wise portrait of Mac, the bartender, in his penultimate film, *The Rat Race*. By this time Oakie was severely afflicted with hearing problems but he continued to act, latterly on TV, until 1972. Oakie was always fun to have in a film, and, unlike some comic reliefs, rarely overplayed his hand.

1928: Finders Keepers. The Fleet's In. Sin Town. Road House. Someone to Love. 1929: Close Harmony. Chinatown Nights. The Man I Love. Street Girl. Sweetie. The Wild Party. The Dummy. Fast Company. Hard to Get. 1930: The Social Lion. Paramount on Parade. The Sap from Syracuse (GB: The Sap Abroad). Hit the Deck. Let's Go Native. Sea Legs. 1931: Dude Ranch. The Gang Buster. Touchdown (GB: Playing the Game). June Moon. 1932: *Hollywood on Parade. * The Stolen Jools (GB: The Slippery Pearls). * Cricket Flickers. Make Me a Star. Dancers in the Dark. Madison Square Garden. Once in a Lifetime. Sky Bride. Million Dollar Legs. If I Had a Million. Uptown New York. 1933: The Eagle and the Hawk. Too Much Harmony. From Hell to Heaven. Alice in Wonderland. Sailor Be Good. College Humor. Sitting Pretty. 1934: Shoot the Works. Looking for Trouble. Murder at the Vanities. College Rhythm. * Hollywood Rhythm. 1935: * Star Night at the Cocoanut Grove. King of Burlesque. Call of the Wild. The Big Broadcast of 1936. 1936: The Texas Rangers. Collegiate (GB: Charm School). Colleen. That Girl from Paris. Florida Special. 1937: The Toast of New York, Champagne Waltz. Hitting a New High. Super Sleuth. Fight for Your Lady. 1938: The Affairs of Annabel. Radio City Revels. Thanks for Everything. Annabel Takes a Tour. 1940: Young People. The Great Dictator. Little Men. Tin Pan Alley. 1941: The Great American Broadcast. * Screen Snapshots No. 87. Rise and Shine. Navy Blues. 1942: Song of the Islands. 1943: Wintertime. Hello, Frisco, Hello. Something to Shout About. 1944: Sweet and Low-down. It Happened Tomorrow. The Merry Monahans. Bowery to Broadway. 1945: On Stage, Everybody. That's the Spirit. 1946: She Wrote the Book. 1948: Northwest Stampede. When My Baby Smiles at Me. 1949: Thieves' Highway. 1950: Last of the Buccaneers. Tomahawk (GB: Battle of Powder River). 1956: Around the World in 80 Days. 1959: The Wonderful Country. 1960: The Rat Race. 1961: Lover Come Back.*

O'CONNOR, Donald 1925–

Jaunty, spry, pencil-slim (in his younger days) American jack-in-the-box dancer with a mane of brown hair dominating a wide mouth and cheeky face. When joking or dancing, O'Connor was irrepressibly buoyant. Asked to be serious or romantic, he became a shade earnest and dull. And his most popular hour in comedy came as straight man to a mule. Born to an Irish immigrant, O'Connor was an infant prodigy with a background of family tragedy. Three of his six brothers and sisters died in infancy. His five-year-old sister was run down by a car and his father died three months later from a heart attack. One of his two remaining brothers died in his teens from a severe attack of scarlet fever. O'Connor Senior had been a circus acrobat whose speciality was jumping off a ramp over the backs of four elephants. Abandoning circus life for vaudeville, he and his wife formed an acrobatic dancing act to which their children were added as soon as they could toddle. Donald first trod the boards at 13 months, dancing the black bottom. In spite of her numerous bereavements, Mrs O'Connor kept the family act together until 1941. Before then Donald had made his film debut with his brother Billy (the one doomed to die of scarlet fever) after being spotted at a charity concert. The boys did a speciality routine in a Warners musical, *Melody for Two*, but it was Paramount who offered Donald a permanent home after his role in their Bing Crosby musical *Sing You Sinners*. O'Connor was extremely winning, especially when singing a duet with Crosby called *Small Fry*. Subsequently, Donald had few more musical chances at the studio, often being cast as characters when young at the start of stories. When he outgrew his childhood appeal, the studio dropped him and he returned to what was left of the family act. After it disbanded, his agent got him a contract with Universal, where he would remain in double-feature fare for the next 15 years. For the moment, he became part of the studio's 'teen swing' brigade, catching the eye with his youthful enthusiasm in a string of black-and-white wartime musical comedies. He had learned how to time laughs for comic effect, and was voted Hollywood's most versatile teenage performer in 1943, when he was also named as a 'Star of Tomorrow', rather late since his name was already attracting customers. Also a dazzling dancer and a master of several musical instruments, Donald was out-doing the similarly energetic Mickey Rooney (*qv*) in popularity when he joined the USAAF Special Services unit in 1944 and disappeared to spend the next two years entertaining the troops. One or two of the several films he had completed were held over to keep his name in the public eye, but it was late 1947 before he was back at the studio. Most of the films he made there over the next nine years were bright, if lightweight, but none was as successful as the series about Francis the talking mule. Francis was certainly smarter than the average mule, and the studio realised it had a long-eared goldmine on its hands when the first film about the mule who helps its master (O'Connor) out of all kinds of scrapes grossed more than $3 million from a minimal outlay. For the next few years the *Francis* and *Ma and Pa Kettle* comedies, made in black-and-white when most Universal production was in colour, were the top-grossing films that virtually kept the studio afloat. To keep O'Connor happy as the mule's buddy, the studio gave him a series of Technicolor comedies and musicals that, while never

Short of stature but high in dynamic talent, comedian-dancer Donald O'Connor and singer Ann Blyth were two of Hollywood's fastest-rising musical talents when they made *The Merry Monahans* in 1944

great cinema, occupied the top halves of the studio's double-bills: *Yes, Sir, That's My Baby, Double Crossbones* and *Walking My Baby Back Home* were among them. Particularly funny was the unusual *Curtain Call at Cactus Creek*, a farce about a group of travelling players in the wild west, whose numbers include, besides a poker-faced O'Connor, badman Walter Brennan and ham actor Vincent Price. O'Connor never quite had the weight to carry a major film, but he was a first-class support to the stars, as he proved in his finest film, *Singin' in the Rain*. Donald's performance was wholly likeable and supportive of stars Gene Kelly and Debbie Reynolds, and his dancing devastating, especially in the *Moses Supposes* routine. MGM, the film's studio, called him and Reynolds back for *I Love Melvin*, but, though popular, the comedy-musical romance was as candyfloss light as his Universal fare. He did better at Fox with his spotlight-hogging solo number *A Boy Chases a Girl* in *There's No Business like Show Business*. Back at Universal, there was still no business like mule business, and four further crazy capers came out between 1952 and 1955, all tolerably well done. For the seventh, however, O'Connor sniffed weakening script values and both he and six-time director Arthur Lubin quit the series. 'Anyway', explained O'Connor, 'when the mule still gets more fan mail than you after six movies, it has to be time to call it a day.' He was right. The seventh film was a flop (it starred Mickey Rooney) and proved to be the last. Instead O'Connor brought his career full circle by co-starring with Bing Crosby for the first time in 18 years (they were to have appeared in *White Christmas* but O'Connor fell ill) in a new version of the old musical *Anything Goes*, which saw Donald at his liveliest for several years. The film that followed, however, *The Buster Keaton Story*, was a disaster. O'Connor had initially liked the script but, especially when the studio hired the real Keaton as adviser, realised how far from the truth it was, and lost heart in the project. His views on the flop film – 'To me it was damned dishonest' – did not endear him to Hollywood, and his 25-year career there was virtually over. Since then O'Connor has kept busy as a composer and conductor of light symphonic music, and made numerous nightclub appearances, cracking jokes about Francis the mule and going through the old dance routines. Film audiences saw him much pudgier in his last 1960s film, *That Funny Feeling*, and he eased up on his workload after a heart attack in 1971. He made an entertaining TV pilot in 1966, called *The Hoofer*, but it didn't lead to a series.

1937: Melody for Two. 1938: Men with Wings. Sing You Sinners. Tom Sawyer – Detective. Sons of the Legion. 1939: Million Dollar Legs. Unmarried (GB: Night Club Hostess). Boy Trouble. Death of a Champion. Night Work. On Your Toes. Beau Geste. 1941: What's Cookin' (GB: Wake Up and Dream). 1942:

Get Hep to Love (GB: She's My Lovely). Give Out, Sisters. It Comes Up Love (GB: A Date with an Angel). When Johnny Comes Marching Home. Private Buckaroo. 1943: Strictly in the Groove. Mister Big. Top Man. 1944: Follow the Boys. This Is the Life. The Merry Monahans. Chip Off the Old Block. Bowery to Broadway. 1945: Patrick the Great. 1947: Something in the Wind. 1948: Feudin', Fussin' and a Fightin'. Are You With It? 1949: Yes, Sir, That's My Baby. Francis. Curtain Call at Cactus Creek (GB: Take the Stage). 1950: The Milkman. Double Crossbones. 1951: Francis Goes to the Races. 1952: Singin' in the Rain. Francis Goes to West Point. I Love Melvin. 1953: Call Me Madam. Walking My Baby Back Home. Francis Covers the Big Town. 1954: There's No Business Like Show Business. Francis Joins the WACs. 1955: Francis in the Navy. 1956: Anything Goes. 1957: The Buster Keaton Story. The Jet-Propelled Couch (TV). 1961: The Wonders of Aladdin. Cry for Happy. 1965: That Funny Feeling. 1974: That's Entertainment! 1981: Ragtime. Thursday the 12th/ Pandemonium. 1984: Miracle in a Manger (released 1986 as A Time to Remember). 1992: Toys.

O'HANLON, George 1912–1989

For almost all of his career, this dark-haired, tough-looking actor from Brooklyn played minor roles, GIs, cabbies, cops, reporters, even extra work. But when he came out from behind the 8-ball in 63 short films as Joe McDoakes, O'Hanlon became the comedy star who was always welcome in a movie programme. He was the son of two professional entertainers, a comedian and a dancer who billed themselves as Sam Rice and Luly Beeson. Young Georgie combined the two talents, but not with sufficient flair to elevate him from the ranks of chorus boys and bit players at Warner Brothers in the 1930s, where he reckoned to have danced across the screen in a fistful of musicals, elegant in top hat and tails, including several choreographed or directed by Busby Berkeley. He was also part of the throng of reporters, courtroom audiences, convicts or trilbyed passers-by in the studio's many crime dramas, for which his Brooklynesque features made him ideal as a 'dress extra'. A

few lines in *Jezebel*, a Bette Davis vehicle, only led him back to more crowd work. So it was, in 1942, when a novice director-writer, Richard L. Bare, looking to break into Hollywood, wrote a one-reel script called *So You Want to Give Up Smoking*. His wife had once been O'Hanlon's girlfriend and was still in touch. O'Hanlon, still doing minor stuff in films and Broadway musicals, thought the short might lead to something better if Bare could sell it, and agreed to play the lead, Joe McDoakes, for nothing. Warners bought the film for $2,500 and optioned a second script for the same amount. At this point the war intervened, and O'Hanlon was away serving with the US Air Corps from 1942 to 1945. But a further 'So You ...' comedy, made while he was on leave, set him and Bare up for six McDoakes comedies a year when the war was over. O'Hanlon finally proved himself a splendid comic actor in this long series, basically about the misfortunes of the average man trying various professions, although sometimes the series showed real invention, as in *So You Want to Be a Detective*, a spoof of the contemporary thriller *The Lady in the Lake*, in which the detective acts as camera. In O'Hanlon's version, unseen narrator Art Gilmore, whose voice was used in many of the films, turns out to be the killer! Occasionally O'Hanlon got the chance to show his versatility and have fun too. In *So You Want to be an Heir*, he plays Joe McDoakes, his Uncle Silas, his mad half-brother Ellery, his cousin Agatha and his own grandmother. O'Hanlon managed to work himself into a fine state of frenzy in most of these little romps, which ran until 1956, with Joe's wife played variously by Jane Harker, Phyllis Coates (who was briefly married to Bare) and Jane Frazee. O'Hanlon also co-wrote many of the scripts with Bare. After the series ended O'Hanlon went back to playing supporting roles in films, though this time with a few more lines! On TV, he briefly had his own show, *Real George*, and supplied the voice of George Jetson in the cartoon series *The Jetsons*, which ran for more than a decade after its debut in 1962. In his last working years O'Hanlon returned to writing, mostly on TV situation comedy. 'The man behind the 8-ball' died from a stroke at 77, only weeks after completing the voice-over for George Jetson in a feature film version of the long-running show. His son, George O'Hanlon Jr, is also an actor.

1938: Jezebel. 1939: Hell's Kitchen. Women in the Wind. 1940: The Fighting 69th. City for Conquest. A Child is Born. Sailor's Lady. 1941: Navy Blues. New Wine. The Great Awakening. 1942: The Man from Headquarters. Ladies' Day. * So You Want to Give Up Smoking. * So You Think You Need Glasses. 1943: Nearly Eighteen. Corvette K-225 (GB: The Nelson Touch). Hers to Hold. All by Myself. 1945: * So You Think You're Allergic. 1946: * So You Want to Play the Horses. * So You Want to Keep Your Hair. * So You Think

*You're a Nervous Wreck. 1947: The Hucksters. Headin' for Heaven. Spirit of West Point. * So You're Going to be a Father. * So You Want to be in Pictures. * So You're Going on a Vacation. * So You Want to be a Salesman. * So You Want to Hold Your Wife. * So You Want an Apartment. 1948: Are You With It? June Bride. * So You Want to be a Gambler. * So You Want to Build a House. * So You Want to be a Detective. * So You Want to be in Politics. * So You Want to be on the Radio. * So You Want to be a Baby-Sitter. The Counterfeiters. 1949: Joe Palooka in The Big Fight. Zamba (GB: Zamba the Gorilla). * So You Want to be Popular. * So You Want to be a Muscleman. * So You're Having In-Law Trouble. * So You Want to Get Rich Quick. * So You Want to be an Actor. 1950: * So You Want to Throw a Party. * So You Think You're Not Guilty. * So You Want to Hold Your Husband. * So You Want to Move. * So You Want a Raise. * So You're Going to Have an Operation. * So You Want to be a Handyman. 1951: The Tanks Are Coming. Joe Palooka in The Triple Cross (GB: The Triple Cross). * So You Want to be a Cowboy. * So You Want to be a Paperhanger. * So You Want to Buy a Used Car. * So You Want to be a Bachelor. * So You Want to be a Plumber. * So You Want to Get It Wholesale. 1952: Park Row. The Lion and the Horse. Cattle Town. * So You Want to Enjoy Life. * So You're Going to a Convention. * So You Never Tell a Lie. * So You're Going to the Dentist. * So You Want to Wear the Pants. * So You Want to be a Musician. 1953: * So You Want to Learn to Dance. * So You Want a Television Set. * So You Love Your Dog. * So You Think You Can't Sleep. * So You Want to be an Heir. 1954: * So You're Having Neighbor Trouble. * So You Want to be Your Own Boss. * So You Want to Go to a Nightclub. * So You're Taking in a Roomer. * So You Want to Know Your Relatives. 1955: * So You Don't Trust Your Wife. * So You Want to be a Gladiator. * So You Want to be on a Jury. * So You Want to Build a Model Railroad. * So You Want to be a VP. * So You Want to be a Policeman. 1956: Battle Stations. * So You Think the Grass is Greener. * So You Want to be Pretty. * So You Want to Play the Piano. * So Your Wife Wants to Work. 1957: Bop Girl Goes Calypso. Kronos. 1959: † The Rookie. 1964: For Those Who Think Young. 1968: I Sailed to Tahiti with an All-Girl Crew. 1971: Million Dollar Duck. 1972: Now You See Him, Now You Don't. 1973: Charley and the Angel. The World's Greatest Athlete. 1976: Rocky. 1990: Jetsons: The Movie (voice only).*

† And directed

OLIVER, Edna May
(E. M. Nutter) 1883–1942

A brown-haired American character comedienne with a long, equine face and an amazing variety of scene-stealing tricks. She was a straight actress on stage for years and it was only after she came to Hollywood that she learned to use her long, mournful features and angular limbs and body to their full comedic effect. Edna May Oliver's

arched eyebrows, purposeful air, disapproving sniff and clickety-clack walk were guaranteed to divert attention from other stars in the film. 'I always enjoy making myself look as odd as possible', said the woman who was like a walking cartoon. 'I get great pleasure out of making people laugh. People appreciate it so much.' Under the circumstances, the title of one of her films, *Laugh and Get Rich*, could have summed up her attitudes to perfection. Born to a Boston plumber, the young Edna May was an expert pianist and mezzo-soprano. Touring New England with an open-air opera company introduced her to show business 'but ruined my voice'. Undeterred, she toured as a pianist with an all-girl orchestra before taking up acting professionally in the early 1900s. She didn't make her Broadway debut, though, until 1916, by which time she was firmly established in character roles. Films followed in 1923. She began to play comedy regularly from 1925, and was a riot the following year as the drunken hymn-book saleswoman in the film *Let's Get Married*. After playing the nagging Parthy in a Broadway production of *Show Boat*, Oliver returned to Hollywood to support hot comedy duo Wheeler and Woolsey (*qv*) in *Half Shot at Sunrise*, then upstaged them in *Cracked Nuts* as the heroine's aunt. The comedians were generous enough to invite Edna May back for a third romp, *Hold 'Em Jail*. Her studio, RKO, tried to form a new comedy team with Edna May and 'woo-woo' comic Hugh Herbert (*qv*), but the mixture didn't gell. They were much more successful casting their horsey grande dame as the spinster sleuth Hildegarde Withers in a trio of comedy-mysteries in which she would proceed to confound the exasperated Inspector Piper, beautifully played by James Gleason (*qv*). By this time the star had legally changed her name to Edna May Oliver. During this period in the 1930s Edna May also created some memorable characters in rather more depth than straight comedy allowed – notably her Aunt March in *Little Women*, Betsey Trotwood in *David Copperfield*, Miss Pross in *A Tale of Two Cities*, and the nurse in *Romeo and Juliet*. She had the happy knack of seeming perfectly cast in almost every role she played. In

lighter vein, she was the Red Queen in *Alice in Wonderland*, teamed amusingly with Edward Everett Horton (*qv*) (though the pairing of two such hardened scene-stealers wasn't as funny as it might have been) in *The Poor Rich*, and stole the laughs in all her scenes as a polo-playing grandma in *We're Rich Again*. She was another eccentric grandmother, this time a cocktail-swigging one, in *No More Ladies*. As a sturdy pioneer woman, Oliver was at last nominated for an Oscar, for *Drums Along the Mohawk* (Hattie McDaniel won it for *Gone with the Wind*). But in 1942 she fell ill with what was at first thought to be severe arthritis, but turned out to be an intestinal infection that killed her on her 59th birthday; she was much mourned by the show business community. Edna May told a writer once that, when she decided to go on the stage, her uncle ridiculed her, saying 'You've no looks and you're all bones. You'll never be successful.'

1923: Wife in Name Only. Three O'Clock in the Morning. Icebound. Restless Wives. 1924: Manhattan. 1925: Lovers in Quarantine. The Lady Who Lied. The Lucky Devil. 1926: The American Venus. Let's Get Married. 1929: The Saturday Night Kid. 1930: Half Shot at Sunrise. Hook, Line and Sinker. 1931: Fanny Foley Herself (GB: Top of the Bill). Newly Rich (GB: Forbidden Adventure). Cimarron. Cracked Nuts. Laugh and Get Rich. 1932: Hold 'em Jail. Lost Squadron. The Conquerors. Ladies of the Jury. Penguin Pool Murder (GB: The Penguin Pool Mystery). 1933: It's Great to be Alive. The Great Jasper. Only Yesterday. Little Women. Alice in Wonderland. Ann Vickers. Strawberry Roan (GB: Flying Fury). Meet the Baron. 1934: We're Rich Again. The Poor Rich. Murder on the Blackboard. The Last Gentleman. 1935: David Copperfield. A Tale of Two Cities. No More Ladies. Murder on a Honeymoon. 1936: Romeo and Juliet. 1937: My Dear Miss Aldrich. Parnell. Rosalie. 1938: Little Miss Broadway. Paradise for Three (GB: Romance for Three). 1939: The Story of Vernon and Irene Castle. Drums Along the Mohawk. Second Fiddle. Nurse Edith Cavell. 1940: Pride and Prejudice. 1941: Lydia.

OLSEN, Ole
(John Olsen) 1892–1965
and
JOHNSON, Chic
(Harold Johnson) 1891–1962

Two livewire vaudeville comedians who took their own brand of barely organised mayhem across America for 35 years. Jovial, well-rounded Chic Johnson looked a bit like Bud Flanagan (*qv*), who led a crazy gang of his own simultaneously in Britain. Slim, sad-faced Ole Olsen looked like the son of Norwegian immigrants he was. What made Olsen and Johnson top-liners was the level of their invention. Each of the shows they devised contained hundreds of gags, puns, running jokes, plus surprises for and participation by the audience. For sheer sustained

zaniness, it was matched by only two British shows — the aforementioned Crazy Gang, and the later *Goon Show* on British radio. Hollywood inevitably diluted the boys' antics. But they had enough say in their later films to leave behind some memorably funny moments. Olsen trained originally to be a classical violinist but by 1910 he was playing more modern music with two other 'fiddlers' and a pianist in restaurants and tea-rooms. Meanwhile, Johnson (he took the name Chic from Chicago, where he was born) had also trained in the classics, in piano studies. He soon diverted his attention to playing ragtime in nightclubs. That was what he was doing in 1914 when Olsen's quartet needed a replacement pianist and Johnson was hired. A colourful character who wore bright clothes and contributed bird noises and phone rings to the quartet's musical repertoire, he soon upped the comedy content of the act, and it wasn't long before Olsen — 'I knew I had to have him as a vaudeville partner' — and Johnson struck out on their own. To begin with their act remained mainly musical. But gradually stage hands and stooges were added to the act, as the gag-hungry minds of Olsen and Johnson worked overtime. They began to invade other people's acts, running riot through an entire variety bill. By 1924 they had established the formula, if it could be so dignified, of a travelling show that was supposed to run for about an hour, but which moved non-stop. A shotgun loaded with blanks was fired frequently, at which anything from a chicken to a cow could fall from the flies. People wandered in and out looking for other people. Songs hadn't a hope of being finished. There were sight gags galore in this organised chaos, which in fact needed precision timing at lightning speed. Amazingly, Olsen and Johnson also experienced some early success on radio but their greatest acclaim was (and would continue to be) in the theatre, especially in areas outside the big cities. They were grabbed for their film debuts almost as soon as sound came in. Warner Brothers snapped them up for *Oh Sailor Behave!*, billing them as 'America's funniest clowns'. World-wide audiences could now appreciate Olsen's deadpan throwaway gags, and Johnson's

lascivious grin and hyena laugh, used to good effect in *The Laughing Song*. Even when he wore smart suits, Johnson somehow still looked rumpled. Olsen, on the other hand, was always immaculately clad. The contrast was even noticeable in the similar gear they wore as American sailors. The film was quite successful but after two progressively inferior follow-ups (the first shot in dreadful colour) the team returned to vaudeville. In 1933 they made their Broadway debuts, without their usual company, in *Take a Chance*. Two years later, they had returned to the ensemble format, doing their 60-minute show as a double-bill with a film at cinemas. *Everything Goes* was the name of the show, but it was revamped and revitalised as *Hellzapoppin*. While the show was being readied for Broadway, Olsen and Johnson made two minor films for Republic, *Country Gentlemen* and *All Over Town*. *Hellzapoppin* opened and prospered, despite critical disapproval. The stars stayed with it for more than two years then went to Hollywood to make the movie version. The film duplicates some of the madness of the show, although its stars were lumbered with young romantic leads and a semblance of a story. There are still priceless moments, however, including a sequence where the film itself jumps out of frame. Olsen and Johnson's next was the only other decent film they made in this second wave. *Crazy House* is actually set in Universal Studios itself, and many guest stars are used to paint the portrait of the panic that runs through the place when it becomes known that Olsen and Johnson are coming to make a picture. Only the top

brass, it seems, are not in on the secret. 'Universal's number one comedy team is here', Chic announces. 'Ah', exclaims the studio chief. 'Abbott and Costello. Send them in.' Unfortunately, the gag rang all too true. Abbott and Costello (*qv*) *were* the studio's top comedy team, and Universal, it seemed, hadn't the patience to sustain Olsen and Johnson in 'A' budget comedies. Their next two films in which, as in the second half of *Crazy House*, they were pushed aside by far too many variety acts, concluded their tenure with the studio. The biggest mystery in Olsen and Johnson's career was their failure to conquer television. Their formula would have seemed to be the direct antecedent to the wildly successful *Rowan and Martin's Laugh-In* more than 20 years later. Their TV show, *Fireball Fun-for-All*, stuck closely to the pattern of their hour-long vaudeville shows. But, perhaps ahead of its time, it lasted only two short seasons in 1949. Olsen and Johnson went back to what they did best. There were two more Broadway shows, *Funzapoppin* and *Pardon Our French*, countrywide tours and even a dose of aqua-mania in *Hellzasplashin*. But they were semi-retired by 1960. Both men died from kidney ailments.

1930: *Oh Sailor Behave!* 1931: *Fifty Million Frenchman. Gold Dust Gertie* (GB: *Why Change Your Husband?*). 1932: * *Hollywood on Parade* (A-2). 1934: * *Hollywood on Parade* (B-13). 1937: *All Over Town. Country Gentlemen.* 1941: *Hellzapoppin.* 1943: *Crazy House.* 1944: *Ghost Catchers.* 1945: *See My Lawyer.*

He's heard of serving aces, but this is ridiculous. Chic Johnson has clearly lost interest in the game; Ole Olsen hopes to save him from hospital treatment at the hands of Mischa Auer. From *Hellzapoppin*

PALIN, Michael 1943–

It is difficult to know quite where Michael Palin stands in British film comedy. His solo vehicles have often presented him as the common man largely beset by some form of adversity or temptation. One somehow visualises him always in a pullover. A gentle, quick-witted man, he often seems to be attempting to stretch himself as an all-round writer, entertainer and guide through travels – whether the past, or the present of the TV series in which he went round the world in 80 days. Still, comedy, and his zany reputation from the Monty Python days, have pursued him like hawks. One always suspects that he will suddenly crook an everyday event into something quite absurd. He was born in Yorkshire, studied history at Oxford and made his London West End stage debut in 1964. In the mid 1960s he broke into comedy writing for television, in such programmes as *The Marty Feldman Comedy Machine* and *The Frost Report*. *Do Not Adjust Your Set*, which ran for two seasons, united him with many of the comic talents that were to make up *Monty Python's Flying Circus*, which began its run in 1969. Involved in many of the Pythons' funniest sketches, Palin was the man who sold John Cleese (*qv*) a dead parrot in perhaps the best-remembered of them all. It was transferred to the big screen in the Pythons' film debut, *And Now for Something Completely Different*. Palin's speciality in its sketches was the simple-minded soul who confuses others

with his lunatic innocence, varied with the occasional upper-class twit. While playing central characters in the Python films that followed, Palin was also working on his own TV series – *Ripping Yarns*, which proved in many ways more inventive and certainly more satirical than the original Python shows. *More Ripping Yarns* followed. Palin took solo spotlight for the first time in *The Missionary*, although he had a strong supporting cast in this spasmodically funny comedy about a cleric who opens a home for fallen women and becomes a fallen missionary. Palin's comic thunder was largely stolen by Denholm Elliott and Michael Hordern in doddering cameos. After several more Python films and videos, Palin was back in his pullover guise in *A Private Function*, very droll as a chiropodist who, in the days of wartime rationing, keeps a pig in the parlour. Palin's quirkily inventive mind continued to seek diversification. He and long-time collaborator Terry Jones, also an ex-Python, wrote a play, *Secrets*, which was turned into a film, *Consuming Passions*, which amused this writer, if not many others. Palin's profile was high after the international success of *A Fish Called Wanda* late in 1988, in which he and John Cleese (*qv*) had the brainwave of combining typically cruelly funny Pythonesque humour with Hollywood stars (Jamie Lee Curtis, Kevin Kline) in an Ealing Studio-type comedy about four unlikely bank robbers – *The Lavender Hill Mob* in new dressing. The frenetic comedy provided more of a character role for Palin, who played a stammering animal rights supporter whose stutter proves disruptive at vital times, but who is (a bit) wilier than he looks. At time of writing, the four stars are still looking for a similar comedy vehicle in which to pool their talents. In the meantime, Palin has found plenty of time for his 80-day trip around the world, which revealed more of the traveller and explorer in him. He also essayed a more serious film role (albeit with satirical undertones) in *American Friends*, a story of travel, romance and chicanery among Oxford dons (of whom Palin's script provided some wicked studies) based on a fragment from the diary of Palin's own great-great-grandfather. Asked what his hobbies were, this man of many parts once listed weaving, viniculture, tennis, ballooning, acupuncture, vibraphone construction, brass-rubbing, meteorology and fish!

1971: And Now for Something Completely Different. 1975: Monty Python and the Holy Grail. 1976: Pleasure at Her Majesty's (US: Monty Python Meets Beyond the Fringe). 1977: Jabberwocky. 1979: Monty Python's Life of Brian. The Secret Policeman's Ball. 1981: The Secret Policeman's Other Ball. Time Bandits. The Missionary. 1982: Monty Python Live at the Hollywood Bowl. 1983: Monty Python's The Meaning of Life. 1984: A Private Function. The Secret Policeman's Private Parts. Brazil. 1985: * The Dress. 1986: East of Ipswich

(TV). 1988: A Fish Called Wanda. 1991: American Friends.

PANGBORN, Franklin 1893–1958

Dark-haired, supercilious, snooty-looking, highly civilised, perpetually prissy American comic actor, one of the great character comedians of Hollywood's golden era. Whether managing a shop, a bank or a hotel, he always behaved as if even these occupations were slightly beneath him, and that guests and customers were to be tolerated, rather than treated as people who were always right. Some of his encounters with great film comedy stars still linger in the mind. The wonderful thing about Pangborn was that his precise way with dialogue – treating it as if it were wrapped in eggshell – was just as amusing in a bad film as in a good one. It was the cinema's loss that he was more often seen on television in the last decade of his career. Born in New Jersey, Pangborn was in his younger days a dramatic stage actor, often in unpleasant and penetrating roles. He played for several seasons with the great Nazimova in her stage presentation of *The Marionettes*, won praise for his performance in *Joseph and His Brethren* and was an acclaimed (and thoroughly nasty) Messala in the stage production of *Ben-Hur*. Then, after five years as a member of the Majestic Theatre company in Los Angeles, Pangborn began to make film appearances. One of his first was in *Exit Smiling*, also the first film to feature the extraordinary comic talents of Beatrice Lillie (*qv*). Years later he would act as her straight man when she committed her famous 'Double Damask' sketch to celluloid in *Dr Rhythm*. With the coming of sound, Pangborn was launched as the star of two-reel comedies, notably the 'Torchy' films, which ran for three years. At the same time he was building up a reputation as an incisive and invaluable support to the stars. In *International House* in 1933 he's the hotel manager, who, asked by Dr George Burns if he wants a different nurse to Gracie Allen (both *qv*), replies that this one is different enough. And one suspects ad-libbing when, later in the same sequence, Pangborn prefaces a feed-line to Allen with 'This one is on the house'. Other

Denholm Elliott and Michael Palin have high hopes for fallen women in their newly-opened mission. They're fulfilled all too well, in *The Missionary*

Richard Pryor seems to be threatening to strain Bill Cosby's head through a tennis racket, when they fall out in a *California Suite*

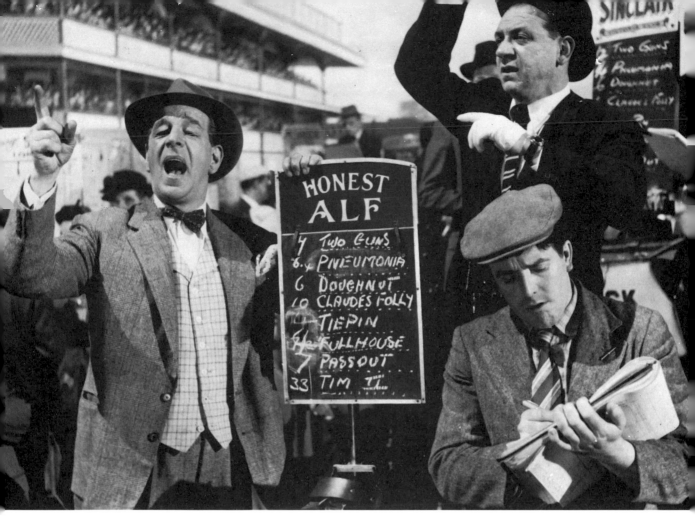

With this lot shouting the odds, what chance does the poor punter stand? Brian Rix (right, below), Ronald Shiner and Sidney James in *Dry Rot*

Mickey Rooney (right) and Buddy Hackett stare disaster in the face, in one of the cliffhanger endings at the halfway point of *It's a Mad, Mad, Mad, Mad World*

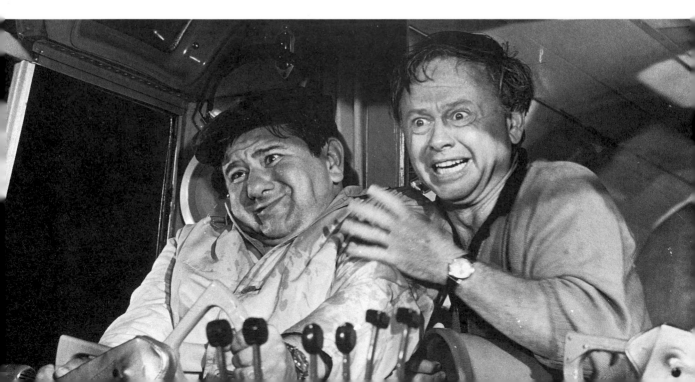

Pangborn highlights from the 1930s are the hotelier who threatens to 'dismiss, discharge and disqualify' miscreant employees in *Flying Down to Rio*, the town crier in *Cockeyed Cavaliers*, and the pointy-fingered piano tuner in the Edgar Kennedy short *Bad Housekeeping*, who ends up making every key sound the same. He supported Olsen and Johnson (both *qv*) on a number of occasions on stage and screen in the 1930s and 1940s, but the most memorable of his later appearances was as J. Pinkerton Snoopington, the short-sighted (Pangborn could do wonders with a pince-nez on screen), fussy, incorruptible bank examiner lured to his doom in the depths of the Black Pussy Cat Café by W.C. Fields (*qv*) in *The Bank Dick*. And there were happy associations with Preston Sturges in *The Palm Beach Story* and *Hail the Conquering Hero*. During his TV tenure in the 1950s, Pangborn for a while had his own series, *Myrt and Marge*.

1926: *Chasing Trouble. Exit Smiling.* 1927: *Getting Gertie's Garter. The Cradle Snatchers. My Friend from India. The Rejuvenation of Aunt Mary. The Night Bridge. The Girl in the Pullman. Fingerprints.* 1928: *On Trial. Blonde for a Night. The Rush Hour.* 1929: *The Sap. * The Crazy Nut. Watch Out. Lady of the Pavements* (GB: *Lady of the Night*). * *Who's the Boss? Masquerade.* * *Happy Birthday.* 1930: *Not So Dumb. A Lady Surrenders* (GB: *Blind Wives*). *Cheer Up and Smile. Her Man.* * *The Doctor's Wife.* * *Poor Aubrey.* * *The Chumps.* * *Reno or Bust.* 1931: * *Hollywood Halfbacks.* * *Camping Out. A Woman of Experience.* * *Against the Rules.* * *Rough House Rhythm.* * *Torchy Passes the Buck.* 1932: *A Fool's Advice.* * *Torchy Raises the Auntie.* * *Doctor's Orders.* * *Tee for Two.* * *Torchy's Two Toots.* * *Torchy's Busy Day.* * *The Giddy Age.* * *Torchy Turns the Trick.* * *Torchy's Night Cap. The Half-Naked Truth.* * *Torchy's Vocation. Over the Counter.* * *What Price, Taxi?* * *The Candid Camera.* * *Torchy Rolls His Own. Meet the Mayor* (released 1938). * *Jimmy's New Yacht.* * *Lighthouse Love.* * *The Loudmouth.* * *Station S.T.A.R.* 1932–3: *The Singing Boxer.* 1933: *Professional Sweetheart* (GB: *Imaginary Sweetheart*). *International House. Flying Down to Rio. The Important Witness. Design for Living. Headline Shooters* (GB: *Evidence in Camera*). *Only Yesterday.* * *Torchy Turns Turtle.* * *Torchy's Loud Spooker.* * *Blue of the Night.* * *Easy on the Eyes.* * *Wild Poses.* * *Dream Stuff.* * *Sweet Cookie.* * *Sing Bing Sing.* * *Art in the Raw.* * *Torchy's Kitty Coup. Bed of Roses.* 1934: *Strictly Dynamite. Manhattan Love Song. Many Happy Returns. Stand Up and Cheer. Imitation of Life. That's Gratitude.* * *Up and Down. Young and Beautiful. Unknown Blonde. King Kelly of the USA* (GB: *Irish and Proud of It*). *Cockeyed Cavaliers. College Rhythm.* 1935: *$1,000 a Minute. Headline Woman* (GB: *The Woman in the Case*). *Eight Bells. Flirtation. Tomorrow's Youth. She Couldn't Take It.* * *The Captain Hits the Ceiling.* * *Ye Old Saw Mill.* 1936: *Three Smart Girls. Mr Deeds Goes to Town. Don't Gamble with Love. To Mary — With Love. Hats Off. Doughnuts and Society* (GB: *Stepping into Society*). *The Luckiest Girl in the World. My Man Godfrey. The Mandarin Mystery. Tango.* 1937: * *Bad Housekeeping.* * *Bridal Griefs. They Wanted to Marry. Step Lively, Jeeves. She Had to Eat. It Happened in Hollywood. High Hat. Easy Living. We Have Our Moments. When Love is Young. Dangerous Number. Hotel Haywire. All Over Town. Stage Door. I'll Take Romance. The Lady Escapes. Swing High, Swing Low. Danger! Love at Work. Turn Off the Moon. Thrill of a Lifetime. A Star Is Born. She's Dangerous. Dangerous Holiday. The Life of the Party. Living on Love.* 1938: *Rebecca of Sunnybrook Farm. Vivacious Lady. Always Goodbye. Just Around the Corner. Bluebeard's Eighth Wife. Love on Toast. Topper Takes a Trip. The Girl Downstairs. She Married an Artist. It's All Yours. Three Blind Mice. Joy of Living. Carefree. Dr Rhythm. Mad About Music. Four's a Crowd.* 1939: *Fifth Avenue Girl. Broadway Serenade.* 1940: *Public Deb No. 1. The Bank Dick* (GB: *The Bank Detective*). *Turnabout. The Villain Still Pursued Her. Christmas in July. Spring Parade. Hit Parade of 1941.* 1941: *Flame of New Orleans. Where Did You Get That Girl? Bachelor Daddy. Tillie the Toiler. A Girl, a Guy and a Gob* (GB: *The Navy Steps Out*). *Never Give a Sucker an Even Break* (GB: *What a Man!*). *Week-End for Three. Mr District Attorney in the Carter Case* (GB: *The Carter Case*). *Sullivan's Travels. Obliging Young Lady. Sandy Steps Out.* 1942: *Moonlight Masquerade. George Washington Slept Here. Now, Voyager. Call Out the Marines. Strictly in the Groove. What's Cookin'?* (GB: *Wake Up and Dream*). *The Palm Beach Story.* 1943: *Reveille With Beverly. Honeymoon Lodge. His Butler's Sister. Never a Dull Moment. Stage Door Canteen. Two Weeks to Live. Crazy House. Holy Matrimony.* * *Slick Chick. The Great Moment.* 1944: *Hail the Conquering Hero. The Reckless Age. Allergic to Love. My Best Gal.* 1945: *The Horn Blows at Midnight.* * *Hollywood Victory Caravan. Hollywood and Vine* (GB: *Daisy (the Dog) Goes Hollywood*). *See My Lawyer. Tell It to a Star. You Came Along.* 1946: *Lover Come Back. Two Guys from Milwaukee* (GB: *Royal Flush*). *The Sin of Harold Diddlebock* (later and GB: *Mad Wednesday*). *I'll Be Yours.* 1947: *Calendar Girl. Addio Mimi* (GB and US: *Her Wonderful Lie*). 1948: *Romance on the High Seas* (GB: *It's Magic*). 1949: *Down Memory Lane. My Dream Is Yours.* 1957: *The Story of Mankind. Oh, Men! Oh, Women!*

PEARCE, Alice 1913–1966

A short, brown-haired, beaky, Brooklynesque comedienne who remained a popular nightclub attraction for many years, but created only one unforgettable film character — Lucy Schmeeler in *On the Town*. A radio raconteuse and club entertainer,

Alice Pearce plays gooseberry, as she usually did on screen, while waiter Free Astaire pays attention to glamorous customer Vera-Ellen in the MGM musical *Belle of New York*

Pearce's twanging tones and New York stories once broke the record at the city's Blue Angel, where she performed in stand-up routines for 67 weeks. Her chinless profile and pursed lips first made their appearance on Broadway in *New Faces of 1943*, and there were other comedies and musicals before M-G-M brought her to the screen to repeat her role of Lucy Schmeeler in their film version of *On the Town*. Sniffing, sneezing, adenoidal, toothy Lucy with her coathanger shoulders, blinky eyes and bony limbs was everybody's idea of a nightmare blind date – which was just the way Gene Kelly inherited her in the film. She did, however, have her own charm – and got a good-night kiss which touched the heart. Hollywood couldn't find a niche for Pearce but she became a popular figure in more stage musicals – *Look, Ma, I'm Dancing, Sail Away, Bells Are Ringing* – and on television, where she had her own show, *Alice Pearce*, in 1948 and 1949. Later she featured in *Jamie* (1953–4), was a brilliant panellist on *One Minute Please* (the ancestor of British radio's long-running *Just a Minute*) and created the befuddled next-door neighbour, Gladys Kravitz, in the long-running *Bewitched*, a role she was still playing at the time of her death from cancer. Films welcomed her back in 1962 for a last five years of eccentrics, ending with her role as the plaintive Mrs Fenimore in *The Glass Bottom Boat*. Unlike poor Lucy, whom one could never see netting a husband, she was twice married.

1949: On the Town. 1952: Belle of New York. 1955: How to Be Very, Very Popular. 1956: The Opposite Sex. 1962: Lad: a Dog. 1963: My Six Loves. Tammy and the Doctor. Beach Party. 1964: The Disorderly Orderly. Dear Heart. Kiss Me Stupid. 1965: Dear Brigitte . . . That Darn Cat! Bus Riley's Back in Town. 1966: The Glass Bottom Boat.

PENNER, Joe
(Josef Pinter) 1904–1941
This brash, big-smiling, babbling, dumpy, dark-haired, squeaky-voiced Hollywood comedian – a cross between Lou Costello (*qv*) and George Gobel – behaved like a demented bumble bee. Some hated his antics, most found him achingly funny – yet he is almost forgotten today, partly because his starring screen career was short, cut off by a heart attack when he was 36. Born in Hungary, Penner was brought to New York by his father (who had gone there three years earlier) at the age of nine. To pay for a college education, he sold papers, took a job as a cable messenger, sold pianos and for a while was a bellboy at a Turkish baths. On leaving college, he went to work at his father's automobile plant in Detroit. Soon, however, he became a props man in vaudeville, all the while accumulating a vast fund of jokes, delivered, once he got his start, in a breezy, amiable manner that allowed the bad jokes to get lost among the good ones. Penner could sing and dance as well – he had shown promise as a boy soprano at 12 – and his bustling style soon brought him to the fore. There were a few film shorts in the early 1930s but, like other comedians of the era, it was radio that made Penner famous nationwide. CBS gave him his own show from 1933, and Penner's catch-phrases, 'You *nasty* man' and 'Wanna buy a duck?', were soon being repeated on every street corner. The character of the duck was actually written into the show's zany proceedings. It was played by Mel Blanc, the voice of so many Warner Brothers cartoon characters, including Bugs Bunny. In 1934 Penner was voted America's outstanding radio comedian. Films soon followed, with Penner often the hapless henpeck who tries desperately to stem the tide of disaster as it threatens to overwhelm him. The films were usually only of medium budget and the quality of the scripts did not always match that of the radio scripts that had been handed to Penner. In films, he often had to rely on bumbling ad libs when funny lines were scarce. His last few films (including a big-screen version of the stage musical *The Boys from Syracuse*) were less successful and, somewhat disillusioned with his cinema career, Penner returned to revue and radio. He was starring in a stage show called *Yokel Boy* when he died from a heart attack in his sleep in January 1941.

*1930: * Stepping Out. * Seeing-Off Service. * Surface Stripes. *A Stuttering Romance. 1931: * Making Good. * Sax Appeal. 1932: * Moving In. * Gangway. * Where Men Are Men. 1934: College Rhythm. 1936: Collegiate (GB: The Charm School). 1937: New Faces of 1937. Life of the Party. 1938: I'm from the City. Mr Doodle Kicks Off. Go Chase Yourself. 1939: The Day the Bookies Wept. 1940: Millionaire Playboy (later and GB: Glamour Boy). The Boys from Syracuse.*

PERTWEE, Jon 1917–
A star on radio and TV, but confined mainly to rustics and eccentrics in films, this stork-like, long-striding British actor and comedian comes from a distinguished theatrical

family. His spluttering, stuttering, burbling funny voices were an integral part of British radio comedy for 35 years. Born with beaky features, a small mouth, strong chin and mass of red hair (later to go strikingly white), Pertwee is the son of actor-writer Roland Pertwee, and brother of screenwriter Michael Pertwee and radio comedy player Bill Pertwee. Trained at RADA for the stage, he had already had repertory experience in Jersey and Brighton before World War Two service with the Royal Navy. A chance association with Eric Barker (*qv*) – Barker needed someone to read some lines in a show and Pertwee was in the naval audience – led to a career in comedy rather than straight drama. He joined Barker aboard the fictional *HMS Waterlogged* at Sinking-in-the-Ooze in 1944 for the navy's comedy segment of *Merry-Go-Round*, a radio forces show that continued after the war, eventually becoming *Waterlogged Spa* in 1948. Many of Pertwee's characters in the show spoke gibberish of one kind or another, notably Svenson, the Norwegian stoker, Cook, the compliant solicitor, Wetherby Wett, the stammering commander, and especially the postman (who was so popular he got his own series) who always said: 'What does it matter what you do as long as you tear 'em up?' Later there were more extraordinary characters in *Up the Pole*, including Mr Burp, and, in the late 1950s, the chief petty officer of *The Navy Lark*, the longest-running radio comedy show of all time. Unfortunately, Pertwee was not part of the cast when the show was transferred to film – and the movie suffered for it. His film roles had been mostly vignettes too. He enjoyed star billing for the first time in 1953 on *Will Any Gentleman . . .?*, stood in for Danny Kaye (*qv*, to whom he bore a slight physical resemblance) for London scenes of *Knock on Wood*, and had some amusing moments as a conductor in *It's a Wonderful World*. But British film-makers never took a chance on casting Pertwee in a vehicle of his own. Elsewhere, it was different. *The Navy Lark* marched on through the 1960s, and then Pertwee was cast for five years (1970–74) as TV's *Dr Who*. He was one of the most popular interpreters of the role. There were a few more caped cameos in films before

The Navy Lark finally sank from sight in 1977. It was swiftly followed by another of Pertwee's great successes – his portrayal of *Worzel Gummidge*, the talking scarecrow, in a well-loved children's TV series. Pertwee's makeup was masterly, and his mangled Devonian tones made him perfect casting. After several years' success in the role in Britain, he took it abroad, notably to Australia. Pertwee has been married twice: his first wife was fellow TV star Jean Marsh.

1937: *A Yank at Oxford. Dinner at the Ritz.* 1939: *Young Man's Fancy. The Four Just Men (US: The Secret Four). There Ain't No Justice!* 1947: *Penny and the Pownall Case.* 1948: *William Comes to Town. Trouble in the Air. A Piece of Cake.* 1949: *Murder at the Windmill (US: Murder at the Burlesque). Helter Skelter. Stop Press Girl. Dear Mr Prohack. Miss Pilgrim's Progress.* 1950: *The Body Said No. Mr Drake's Duck.* 1953: *Will Any Gentleman . . .?* 1954: *The Gay Dog. Knock on Wood (stand-in).* 1955: *A Yank in Ermine.* 1956: *It's a Wonderful World.* 1958: *The Ugly Duckling.* 1959: *Just Joe.* 1960: *Not a Hope in Hell.* 1961: *Nearly a Nasty Accident.* 1963: *Ladies Who Do.* 1964: *Carry On Cleo.* 1965: *You Must be Joking! How to Undress in Public Without Undue Embarrassment. Carry On Cowboy. I've Gotta Horse.* 1966: *Carry On Screaming. A Funny Thing Happened on the Way to the Forum.* 1969: *Up in the Air. Under the Table You Must Go.* 1970: *The House That Dripped Blood. There's a Girl in My Soup.* 1974: *Four Against the Desert.* 1975: *One of Our Dinosaurs is Missing.* 1977: *Adventures of a Private Eye. Wombling Free (voice only). No. 1 of the Secret Service.* 1978: *The Water Babies (voice only).* 1983: *The Boys in Blue.*

PHILLIPS, Leslie 1924–
Fair-haired British actor with roguish smile, military tones and barking laugh. He made his acting debut at the age of five as a wolf in *Peter Pan*, and has been playing wolves of one kind or another ever since. Despite his long experience, Phillips was in his early thirties before leading roles came his way, and it wasn't until he played a succession of ladies' men, wolves in sheep's clothing and upper-class twits that he became a star of British comedy, seeing it through from its resurgence in the late 1950s to its decline to a new low level 15 years later. He was born in London, studied for the stage at the famous Italia Conti School and was in several films and plays as a child before his first adult West End performance was rapidly followed by four years' war service with the Durham Light Infantry. Returning to stage and films, he began to get leading roles from the early 1950s. The role of Tony in the domestic comedy *For Better, For Worse* became his favourite but although the show ran for 18 months the lead in the film version went to Dirk Bogarde. Phillips did, however, begin making inroads into films from 1955, and his foxy charm was seen to good effect in *Brothers in Law, The Smallest Show on Earth* and *The Man Who Liked Funerals*, in which he got his first star role as a man who blackmailed the bereaved in a good cause. He became a well-known radio voice from early 1959 in the hit comedy series *The Navy Lark*, as the incompetent sub-lieutenant always running the ship aground (Catchphrases: 'Left hand down a bit' and 'Everybody down!') and suddenly he was everywhere in films. There were three 'Carry On's, a film version of *The Navy Lark*, 'Doctor' films (taking over from Dirk Bogarde) and romantic farces like *No Kidding* and *In the Doghouse*. Most popular of all was a series of fast-moving comedies that teamed Phillips with Scots comedian and impressionist Stanley Baxter (1928–   ). These began with the prisoner-of-war caper *Very Important Person*, and continued with *Crooks Anonymous, The Fast Lady* (a car) and *Father Came Too*, about a disastrous honeymoon. Baxter would be the eager-beaver innocent, while Phillips played the con-man who was in fact more inept than the partner he got into so much trouble: something of a Laurel and Hardy (*qv*) relationship, with Phillips always getting his come-uppance. The films co-starred ferociously-bearded James Robertson Justice (1905–75) who also played the irascible Sir Lancelot Spratt opposite Phillips in three 'Doctor' comedies. Within the space of five years, Phillips made 18 starring comedies – while still continuing his work on *The Navy Lark* on radio. He took a break from films in 1963/64 to do the stage farce *Boeing-Boeing*, then came back to the cinema with *You Must Be Joking!*, an army farce about an initiative test. The output of comedy from British studios had suddenly become quite restricted, however, and, after making *Doctor in Clover*, Phillips made a disastrous career switch by playing the villain in *Maroc 7*, a woeful spy 'thriller'. He was confined to TV for some time after that, before embarking on his third dose of medical mayhem, *Doctor in Trouble*, in 1970. British comedy was well on the slide by this time, with even the 'Carry On's past their prime. Low-grade comedy was the order of the day, and Phillips found himself caught up in it, in such ribald lavatorial farces as *Not Now Darling, Spanish Fly, Don't Just Lie There, Say Something!* and *Not Now, Comrade*. He did better on television, especially with *Our Man at St Mark's*, and came back to films in the late 1980s in character roles. He has been twice married, latterly to the actress Angela Scoular.

1935: *A Lassie from Lancashire.* 1938: *The Citadel.* 1943: *Rhythm Serenade.* 1949: *Train of Events.* 1950: *The Woman with No Name (US: Her Paneled Door).* 1951: *Pool of London. The Galloping Major.* 1952: *The Sound Barrier (US: Breaking the Sound Barrier).* 1953: *The Fake. The Limping Man. Time Bomb (US: Terror on a Train).* 1955: *The Price of Greed. Value for Money. The Gamma People. As Long As They're Happy.* 1956: *The Big Money. Brothers in Law.* 1957: *The Barretts of Wimpole Street. The Smallest Show On Earth. Just My Luck. Les Girls. High Flight.* 1958: *I Was Monty's Double. The Man Who Liked Funerals.* 1959: *Carry On Nurse. Ferdinand of Naples. The Angry Hills. This Other Eden. Carry On Teacher. Please Turn Over. The Night We Dropped a Clanger. The Navy Lark.* 1960: *Inn for Trouble. Watch Your Stern. Carry on Constable. Doctor in Love. No Kidding (US: Beware of Children).* 1961: *Raising the Wind. A Weekend with Lulu. In the Doghouse (US: Roommates). Very Important Person.* 1962: *Crooks Anonymous. The Longest Day. The Fast Lady.* 1963: *Father Came Too.* 1965: *You Must Be Joking!* 1966: *Doctor in Clover.* * *Zabaglione. Maroc 7.* 1970: *Some Will, Some Won't. Doctor in Trouble.* 1971: *The Magnificent Seven Deadly Sins.* 1972: *Not Now Darling.* 1973: *Don't Just Lie There, Say Something!* 1975: *Spanish Fly.* 1976: *Not Now, Comrade.* 1979: *The Lion, the Witch and the Wardrobe (TV. Voice only).* 1985: *Out of Africa.* 1986: *Monte Carlo (TV).* 1987: *Empire of the Sun.* 1988: *Scandal.* 1989: *Mountains of the Moon.* 1990: *King Ralph.*

PITTS, ZaSu 1898–1963
A dark-haired, fluttering, bird-like American actress with down-turned mouth, big, care-worn eyes and long, elegant, expressive hands, ZaSu Pitts gave some of the great dramatic performances of the silent era before unexpectedly blossoming forth as a

character comedienne with the coming of sound. Named after two aunts called Eliza and Susan, she was born in Kansas but moved to California as a child, and was fired by a desire to act in films. After a hard struggle she began to get extra work in one-reel comedies and even did some work as a stunt girl. Attracting attention in *The Little Princess*, when she was 19, her darting eyes, flapping gestures and bird-like movements soon established her as an actress of individuality and some eccentricity. Pitts played some comedy in her early roles, notably *A Society Sensation* with Carmel Myers and Rudolph Valentino. But it was in intensely dramatic roles that she won most critical praise, particularly as the murderess Jennie Dunn in 1922's *For the Defense*, and the money-hoarding Trina in Von Stroheim's *Greed* two years later, in which her looks at the camera can send a shiver down the spine. Her popularity in comedy after 1930 baffled Von Stroheim, who said: 'Some people do think she is funny-looking. But I think art must weep when ZaSu plays a comedy role.' Art wept to amusing effect when ZaSu teamed with James Gleason (*qv*) in *Oh, Yeah!* and with Leon Errol (*qv*) in *Finn and Hattie*. Hal Roach poached her from features in 1931 to turn her into a two-reel comedy team with glamorous Thelma Todd (*qv*), billing them as 'the Laurel and Hardy of comediennes'. The girls worked well together, although they were more successful in situation comedy than slapstick. ZaSu is the forlorn, hapless wallflower who gets into scrapes, from which the aggressive, but sometimes embarrassed Thelma tries to extract her. After 17 of these shorts with Todd, ZaSu moved on to a series of feature comedies opposite tall, gangling Slim Summerville (*qv*). The deadpan 'comedy love team' — both were tall and stick-like — went on to make nine films together between 1932 and 1941, including *They Just Had to Get Married*, *Out All Night*, *Love, Honor and Oh, Baby!* and *Miss Polly*. More prestigiously, Pitts was Charles Laughton's love interest in the famous 1935 version of *Ruggles of Red Gap*. The following year she followed that by taking over the role of spinster sleuth Hildegarde Withers from Edna May Oliver for *The Plot Thickens*. One of ZaSu's earliest ambitions had, in fact, been to become a private detective! She tried vaudeville in 1938 — doing an impression of an impressionist doing an impression of ZaSu Pitts! — then ventured into stage work, for which she developed a liking. Her film output slowed to a trickle after 1943. Although she is best remembered from the sound era for her spinster portrayals — another outstanding one was Miss Hazy, fluttering coquettishly after W. C. Fields (*qv*) in 1934's *Mrs Wiggs of the Cabbage Patch* — Pitts was happily married, for the last 30 years of her life, to a former tennis professional (her second husband) who went into real estate. She died at 65 after a lengthy battle with

cancer, but not before taking her place alongside numerous other laughter-makers to provide a cameo for *It's a Mad, Mad, Mad, Mad World*.

1917: * *Tillie of the Nine Lives*. * *He Had 'Em Buffaloed*. * *Canning the Cannibal King*. * *The Battling Bellboy*. * *O-My the Tent-Mover*. * *Behind the Map*. * *Why They Left Home*. * *His Fatal Beauty*. * *Uneasy Money*. * *We Have the Papers*. * *Desert Dilemma*. * *Behind the Footlights*. *The Little Princess*. *A Modern Musketeer*. *Rebecca of Sunnybrook Farm*. 1918: *Talk of the Town*. *A Lady's Name*. *How Could You, Jean?* *As the Sun Went Down*. *A Society Sensation*. 1919: *Better Times*. *The Other Half*. *Men, Women and Money*. 1920: *Poor Relations*. *Bright Skies*. *Seeing It Through*. *Heart of Twenty*. 1921: *Patsy*. 1922: *Youth to Youth*. *For the Defense*. *Is Matrimony a Failure? A Daughter of Luxury*. 1923: *Poor Men's Wives*. *The Girl Who Came Back*. *Tea — With a Kick*. *West of the Water Tower*. *Mary of the Movies*. *Souls for Sale*. *Three Wise Fools*. 1924: *Triumph*. *Daughters of Today*. *The Legend of Hollywood*. *The Fast Set*. *Greed*. *The Goldfish*. *Changing Husbands*. *Wine of Youth*. 1925: *The Great Love*. *Old Shoes*. *The Business of Love*. *The Re-Creation of Brian Kent*. *Thunder Mountain*. *A Woman's Faith*. *What Happened to Jones?* *The Great Divide*. *Lazybones*. *Pretty Ladies*. *Secrets of the Night*. *Wages for Wives*. *Mannequin*. 1926: *Monte Carlo (GB: Dreams of Monte Carlo)*. *Early to Wed*. *Risky Business*. *Sunny Side Up*. *Her Big Night*. 1927: *Casey at the Bat*. 1928: † *Love (GB: Anna Karenina)*. *13 Washington Square*. *Buck Privates*. *The Wedding March*. *Wife Savers*. *Sins of the Fathers*. * *Sunlight*. *The Honeymoon/Mariage du prince*. 1929: *Her Private Life*. *The Argyle Case*. *The Dummy*. *Oh, Yeah! (GB: No Brakes)*. *The Locked Door*. *Paris*. *This Thing Called Love*. *The Squall*. *Twin Beds*. 1930: ‡ *All Quiet on the Western Front*. *Honey*. *The Lottery Bride*. *No, No, Nanette*. *River's End*. *The Squealer*. *The Devil's Holiday*. *Little Accident*. *Monte Carlo*. *Passion Flower*. *Sin Takes a Holiday*. *War Nurse*. *Free Love*. 1931: *Finn and Hattie*. *Beyond Victory*. *Their Mad Moment*. *Bad Sister*. *The Big Gamble*. *Seed*. *A Woman of Experience*. *Penrod and Sam*. *The Guardsman*. *The Secret Witness*. * *Let's Do Things*. * *Catch As Catch Can*. * *The Pajama Party*. * *War Mamas*. 1932: * *Seal Skins*. * *On the Loose*. * *Red Noses*. * *The Old Bull*. * *Strictly Unreliable*. * *Show Business*. * *Alum and Eve*. * *The Soilers*. *Shop-worn*. *Steady Company*. *The Trial of Vivienne Ware*. *Unexpected Father*. *Westward Passage*. *Blondie of the Follies*. *Make Me a Star*. *The Crooked Circle*. *Once in a Lifetime*. *Broken Lullaby (GB: The Man I Killed)*. *Destry Rides Again*. *Strangers of the Evening*. *Speak Easily*. *Is My Face Red? Roar of the Dragon*. *Vanishing Frontier*. *Madison Square Gardens*. *Back Street*. *They Just Had to Get Married*. 1933: *Hello, Sister!/Walking Down Broadway*. *Professional Sweetheart (GB: Imaginary Sweetheart)*. *Love, Honor and Oh, Baby!* * *Sneak Easily*. * *Asleep in the Fleet*. * *Maids à la Mode*. * *One Track*

Minds. * *The Bargain of the Century*. *Aggie Appleby, Maker of Men (GB: Cupid in the Rough)*. *Mr Skitch*. *Out All Night*. *Her First Mate*. *Meet the Baron*. 1934: *Two Alone*. *The Meanest Gal in Town*. *Three on a Honeymoon*. *Mrs Wiggs of the Cabbage Patch*. *Their Big Moment (GB: Afterwards)*. *Sing and Like It*. *Love Birds*. *Private Scandal*. *The Gay Bride*. *Dames*. 1935: *Hot Tip*. *Ruggles of Red Gap*. *The Affairs of Susan*. *Going Highbrow*. *She Gets Her Man*. *Spring Tonic*. 1936: *Thirteen Hours by Air*. *The Plot Thickens (GB: The Swinging Pearl Mystery)*. *Sing Me a Love Song*. *Mad Holiday*. 1937: *Forty Naughty Girls*. *52nd Street*. *Wanted*. *Merry Comes to Town*. 1939: *Naughty But Nice*. *The Lady's from Kentucky*. *Mickey the Kid*. *Nurse Edith Cavell*. *Eternally Yours*. 1940: *No, No, Nanette (remake)*. *It All Came True*. 1941: *Niagara Falls*. *Broadway Limited*. *Mexican Spitfire's Baby*. *Week-End for Three*. *Miss Polly*. 1942: *So's Your Aunt Emma/Meet the Mob*. *Tish*. *Mexican Spitfire at Sea*. *The Bashful Bachelor*. 1943: *Let's Face It*. 1946: *The Perfect Marriage*. *Breakfast in Hollywood (GB: The Mad Hatter)*. 1947: *Life with Father*. * *A Film Goes to Market*. 1949: *Francis*. 1952: *Denver and Rio Grande*. 1954: *Francis Joins the WACs*. 1956: *Mr Belvedere (TV. GB: cinemas)*. 1957: *This Could be the Night*. 1959: *The Gazebo*. 1961: *Teen-Age Millionaire*. 1963: *The Thrill of It All*. *It's a Mad, Mad, Mad, Mad World*.

† Scenes deleted from final release version.
‡ Silent version only.

POLLARD, Snub
(Harold Frazer) 1886–1962
Yet another of the many immigrants from England, Scotland and Australia who became stars of Hollywood slapstick silent comedies, Snub Pollard was a thin, jut-eared Aussie, whose long, lugubrious face and big nose gave the impression of lankiness, though he was of no more than medium height. His dark eyes matched his lank hair, and the huge drooping moustache he soon assumed for movie purposes hid any trace of expression except in eyes that became mournful when things went wrong. Pollard hailed originally from Melbourne and was a boy singer there in vaudeville. Before he was 21 he had formed a troupe called

Pollard's Lilliputians — he was the tallest member. Later he headed a group of singers under the rather grand title of the Pollard Light Opera Company. It was with this company that he first went to California, where he decided to go for a career in films as a comedian. After a few bit parts and stand-arounds in Charlie Chaplin (*qv*) films — years later, when the great days were long gone, Chaplin remembered him and cast him as the down-at-heel violinist in *Limelight* — Snub got lucky. He was taken on at the Hall Roach Studio as second banana to Harold Lloyd (*qv*), playing in scores of Lloyd comedies between 1915 and 1919. Roach rewarded him for such stalwart service by giving him his own two-reeler series from 1919. With his slight build and meek demeanour it was easy for Pollard to play henpecked husbands and downtrodden employees, but his characters often proved unexpectedly resourceful, and he was blessed with a great memory (and immaculate timing) for complex pieces of comic business. The film people seem to remember with the greatest affection from the Roach years is *It's a Gift* (1923), in which, with the help of various elaborate Heath Robinson contraptions, Snub manages to prepare and eat breakfast without even getting out of bed. As Laurel and Hardy (*qv*) would do more than a decade later, under somewhat different circumstances, Pollard decided to leave Roach in the mid 1920s and produce his own films. But the movies Pollard made did not have the same appeal for the public, and he disappeared altogether from the screen for three years at the silents-to-sound transition, returning in occasional character roles from 1930 until his death. Like other silent comedians whose star careers had faded with the coming of sound, Pollard briefly found new popularity as a 'B' western sidekick, playing the doleful Pee Wee in a series of Tex Ritter horse-operas between 1936 and 1938. But the Ritter association didn't last and Pollard spent the rest of his career in bit parts.

1915: By the Sea. His New Job. His Regeneration. Giving Them Fits. Great While It Lasted. Ragtime Snap Shots. A Foozle at the Tee Party. Ruses, Rhymes and Roughnecks. Peculiar Patients' Pranks. Lonesome Luke, Social Gangster. 1916: Lonesome Luke Leans to the Literary. Luke Lugs Luggage. Lonesome Luke Lolls in Luxury. Luke, the Candy Cut-Up. Luke Pipes the Pippins. Luke Foils the Villain. Luke and the Rural Roughnecks. Lonesome Luke, Circus King. Luke's Double. Them Was the Happy Days! Police. Luke and the Bomb Throwers. Luke's Late Lunchers. Luke Laughs Last. Luke's Fatal Flivver. Luke's Society Mix-Up. Luke's Washful Waiting. Luke Rides Roughshod. Luke — Crystal Gazer. Luke's Lost Lamb. Luke Does the Midway. Luke Joins the Navy. Luke and the Mermaids. Luke's Speedy Club Life. Luke and the Bang-Tails. Luke the Chauffeur. Luke's Preparedness Preparations. Luke the Gladiator. Luke, Patent Provider.

Luke's Newsie Knockout. Luke's Movie Muddle. Luke, Rank Impersonator. Luke Locates the Loot. Luke's Shattered Sleep. 1917: Luke's Lost Liberty. Luke's Busy Day. Luke's Trolley Troubles (GB: Luke's Tramcar Tragedy). Lonesome Luke, Lawyer. Luke Wins Ye Ladye Fayre. Lonesome Luke's Lively Life. Lonesome Luke on Tin Can Alley. Lonesome Luke's Honeymoon. Lonesome Luke — Plumber. Stop! Luke! Listen! Lonesome Luke's Wild Women. Lonesome Luke — Messenger. Lonesome Luke — Mechanic. Over the Fence. Lonesome Luke Loses Patients. Pinches. By the Sad Sea Waves. Lonesome Luke in Birds of a Feather. Rainbow Island. Bliss. Lonesome Luke from London to Laramie. The Flirt. Lonesome Luke in Love, Laughs and Lather. All Aboard. Lonesome Luke in Clubs Are Trumps. Move On. Bashful. Lonesome Luke in We Never Sleep. Step Lively. The Tip. 1918: Triple Trouble. Hello Teacher. Cleopatsy. His Busy Day. The Furniture Movers. Nipped in the Bud. An Enemy of Soap. The Great Water Peril. No Place Like Jail. Love's Young Scream. Hustling for Health. The Big Idea. The Lamb. Hit Him Again. Beat It. A Gasoline Wedding. Look Pleasant, Please. Here Come the Girls. Let's Go. On the Jump. Follow the Crowd. Pipe the Whiskers. It's a Wild Life. Hey There. Kicked Out. The Non-Stop Kid. Two-Gun Gussie. Fireman, Save My Child. The City Slicker. Sic 'Em Towser. Somewhere in Turkey. Are Crooks Dishonest? An Ozark Romance. Kicking the Germ Out of Germany. That's Him! Bride and Gloom. Two Scrambled. Bees in His Bonnet. Swing Your Partners. Why Pick on Me? Nothing But Trouble. Hear 'Em Rave. Take a Chance. She Loves Me Not. Wanted: $5,000. Going! Going! Gone! Ask Father. On the Fire (GB: The Chef). Look Out Below. Next Aisle Over. Ring Up the Curtain. 1919: I'm on My Way. The Dutiful Dub. A Sammy in Siberia. Just Dropped In. Crack Your Heels. Young Mr Jazz. Si Senor. Before Breakfast. The Marathon. Back to the Woods. Pistols for Breakfast. Swat the Cook. Off the Trolley. Spring Fever. Billy Blazes, Esq. Just Neighbors. At the Old Stage Door. Never Touched Me. A Jazzed Honeymoon. Count Your Change. Chop Suey & Co. Heap Big Chief. Don't Shove. Be My Wife. The Rajah. He Leads, Others Follow. Soft Money. Count the Votes. Pay Your Dues. His Only Father. Bumping into Broadway. Captain Kidd's Kids. From Hand to Mouth. His Royal Slyness. Start Something. All at Sea. It's a Hard Life. How Dry I Am. Looking for Trouble. Touch Luck. Call for Mr Cave Man. Giving the Bride Away. Order in Court. The Floor Below. 1920: Red Hot Hottentots. The Dippy Dentist. All Lit Up. Nearly a Maid. Getting His Goat. Don't Weaken. Trotting Through Turkey. Grab the Ghost. Any Old Port. A London Bobby. Money to Burn. Insulting the Sultan. Why Go Home? Slippery Slickers. Waltz Me Around. Raise the Rent. Find the Girl. Fresh Paint. Flat Broke. Cut the Cards. The Dinner Hour. Cracked Wedding Bells. Speed to Spare. Shoot on Sight. Drink Hearty. All Dressed Up. All in a Day. Don't Rock the Boat. The Home Stretch. Call a Taxi. Live and Learn. Run 'Em Ragged. Go As You Please.

Rock-a-Bye Baby. Doing Time. Fellow Citizens. When the Wind Blows. The Dearly Departed. Cash Customers. Park Your Car. 1921: The Morning After. His Best Girl. Fellow Romans. Big Game. Blue Sunday. The High Rollers. Law and Order. Hocus-Pocus. The Hustler. Whirl o' the West. Open Another Bottle. Make It Snappy. Rush Orders. Bubbling Over. No Children. Own Your Own Home. Save Your Money. Where's the Fire? Yes Next. The Bike Bug. At the Ringside. No Stopover. What a Whopper. Teaching the Teacher. Spot Cash. Name the Day. The Jail Bird. Late Lodgers. Gone to the Country. Fifteen Minutes. On Location. The Joy Rider. Penny-in-the-Slot. Sink or Swim. Shake 'Em Up. Corner Pocket. 1922: Call the Witness. Years to Come. Lose No Time. Blow 'Em Up. Stage Struck. Down and Out. Pardon Me. The Bow Wows. Hot Off the Press. The Anvil Chorus. Jump Your Job. Full o' Pep. Days of Old. Kill the Nerve. Light Showers. Do Me a Favor. In the Movies. Punch the Clock. Strictly Modern. Hale and Hearty. The Dumb Bell. Some Baby. Bed of Roses. The Stone Age. 365 Days. The Old Sea Dog. Hook, Line and Sinker. Nearly Rich. The Green Cat. Our Gang. 1923: A Tough Winter. California or Bust. Jack Frost. The Courtship of Miles Sandwich. The Mystery Man. It's a Gift. Dig Up. Before the Public. Where Am I? Sold at Auction. The Walk Out. Dear Ol' Pal. Join the Circus. Fully Insured. It's a Boy. Short Orders. 1924: The Big Idea. Why Marry? Get Busy. 1925: Are Husbands Human? 1926: The Doughboy. The Yokel. Do Your Duty. The Old Warhorse. The Fire. All Wet. 1927: The Bum's Rush. Thick and Thin. Once Over. Double Trouble. 1930: † Ex-Flame (GB: Mixed Doubles). 1931: † East Lynne. One Good Turn. Come to Papa. 1932: † Midnight Patrol. †Make Me a Star! † The Purchase Price. 1934: † Stingaree. † Cockeyed Cavaliers. † One More River (GB: Over the River). 1935: † The Laramie Kid. 1936: † Just My Luck. The Clutching Hand (serial). † The Crime Patrol. † The Gentleman from Louisiana. † The White Legion. † Headin' for the Rio Grande. The Black Coin (serial). 1937: † Santa Fe Rides. † Arizona Days. † Hittin' the Trail. † Sing Cowboy Sing. † Riders of the Rockies. † Tex Rides with the Boy Scouts. † Nation Aflame. 1938: † Frontier Town. † Rollin' Plains. † Utah Trail. † Starlight over Texas. † Where the Buffalo Roam. † Song of the Buckaroo. 1939: † Hollywood Cavalcade. † Lure of the Wasteland. † Mesquite Buckaroo. 1940: † Murder on the Yukon. 1941: † A Girl, a Guy and a Gob (GB: The Navy Steps Out). 1942: Bowery at Midnight. 'Neath Brooklyn Bridge. 1943: Phony Express. He Was Only Feudin'. His Wedding Scare. Quack Service. Kid Dynamite. Garden of Eatin'. † The Kid Rides Again. 1944: † Bowery to Broadway. Heather and Yon. Defective Detectives. His Tale is Told. 1945: Booby Dupes. Wife Decoy. Three Pests in a Mess. † Kitty. † San Antonio. 1946: Monkey Businessmen. † The Kid from Brooklyn. 1947: † Framed (GB: Paula). † Miracle on 34th Street (GB: The Big Heart). The Perils of Pauline. † Blackmail. † Magic Town.

† *Cheyenne*. 1948: † *Miracle of the Bells*. † *Family Honeymoon*. † *Back Trail*. † *Isn't It Romantic?* † *Johnny Belinda*. 1949: † *The Crooked Way*. † *Loaded Pistols*. † *The Beautiful Blonde from Bashful Bend*. † *Square Dance Jubilee*. 1951: † *Limelight*. 1952: † *Boots Malone*. † *Carrie*. 1954: *So You Want to be a Banker*. 1955: † *Pete Kelly's Blues*. 1956: † *Runaway Daughters*. 1957: † *Man of a Thousand Faces*. † *The Domino Kid*. † *Jeanne Eagels*. 1958: † *Rock-a-Bye Baby*. 1959: † *Who Was That Lady?* 1960: † *Studs Lonigan*. 1961: † *Pocketful of Miracles*. † *The Errand Boy*.

All shorts except † features.

PRYOR, Richard 1940–

Widely regarded as the top black comedian of his generation, and a forerunner for Eddie Murphy in that he made profane and socially relevant humour a success, the fiercely-moustached, broadly-grinning Richard Pryor has had cruel luck with his film career. Despite one star vehicle after another, few have been any good, even the ones that took money. And one or two of the better ones simply didn't catch the public's fancy. Pryor has a marvellously expressive face, a fine line in hysteria, a rasping wit, a surprising warmth (despite the explosive private life with its brushes with drugs and the law), a range of tone and colour in the voice and a dominant star presence. But he often toned down his abrasive nightclub style for the movies, which may with hindsight have been a mistake. He came originally from a ghetto district of Peoria in Illinois. He worked for his father's trucking company or in his grandfather's pool hall after leaving school at 16, but, following army service, he got a job at a local club as master of ceremonies, telling jokes he'd written himself. Inside three years, he was working at clubs in New York's Greenwich Village. Appearances further afield were often stormy and marred by controversy over Pryor's fuelling his material with his views on racial hatred and discrimination. Even so, by 1964 he had got his first TV exposure as one of the up-coming comics (Rodney Dangerfield (*qv*) was another) on Rudy Vallee's weekly show *On Broadway Tonight*. But films were calling

and it was not to Pryor's good. He supported Sid Caesar (*qv*) in his first, as an inept detective, but the film was poorly received (and attended). He was lost in the shuffle in his next few films, and it took the first of several concert films, *Richard Pryor – Live and Smokin'* – which was, as the title implied, pretty inflammatory stuff – to focus public attention on him. That led him to the highest profile of his earlier roles, as the Piano Man in *Lady Sings the Blues*, a thoroughly depressing – but big box-office – biography of Billie Holiday. Then it was back to the same old story: successful concerts but flop films. The film that began to improve Pryor's marquee rating was *The Bingo Long Traveling All-Stars and Motor Kings*, though this story of a black baseball team trying to make it to the big time in the late 1930s understandably didn't do much outside America. One that did, however, was *Silver Streak*, a fast and funny comedy-thriller set aboard a train, which co-starred Pryor for the first of several films (though this is still the best) with Gene Wilder (*qv*). And these were two opposite Bill Cosby (1938–   ), a fellow black superstar comedian whose films have been even more disappointing than Pryor's. Pryor was now given star vehicles, even if not all of them travelled well, or even travelled at all. *Greased Lightning*, about the first black racing driver, was a good film but perhaps too gentle: it did little outside the States. People seemed to want to see Pryor in films most similar to his concerts – with lots of action, wisecracks and four-letter words. There weren't many wisecracks (but lots of four-letter words) in Paul Schrader's savage *Blue Collar*, but it wasn't really a Pryor vehicle. When the only decent returns from the next batch of films

proved to be from concert movies, Pryor went back to fun and blue language with Wilder, and was proved absolutely right when *Stir Crazy* took more than $50 million world-wide – exceptionally big bucks for 1980. After this, Pryor made perhaps his best film, *Bustin' Loose*, a real heartwarmer that actually made money, with Pryor at his best as an ex-convict who not only escorts a bunch of handicapped children across country, but in one scene has Ku Klux Klan members eating out of his hands. *The Toy* wasn't as good, but made even more, a simplistic farce with Pryor as a jobless writer hired as a plaything for a rich man's son. He was now at his box-office peak, did *Superman III*, brought out more concert films, and starred in an expensive remake of *Brewster's Millions*, which took just that at the box-office, rather cloaking the fact that it was badly paced and not very good. Since then Pryor has had a series of disappointments, although a poor third film with Wilder, *See No Evil, Hear No Evil*, casting them respectively as deaf and blind witnesses to a murder, made a slight profit. His teaming with Eddie Murphy in *Harlem Nights* was, by all accounts, not a happy one (and the film lost money) and a fourth with Wilder, *Another You*, left Pryor sliding further down his losing streak. Still, there's always the videos of his concerts which prove that, as a stand-up comedian with his own material, Pryor can still be side-splittingly – and cuttingly – funny. He has been married five times.

1966: The Busy Body. 1968: ‡ *The Green Berets. Wild in the Streets. 1969: The Phynx. The Young Lawyers (TV). 1970: Carter's Army (TV). 1971: Dynamite Chicken. You'll Got to*

Richard Pryor sees the body but, being deaf, didn't hear the killing. Co-star Gene Wilder strikes a pose in the background, in *See No Evil, Hear No Evil*

Walk It Like You Talk It or You've Lose That Beat. Richard Pryor – Live and Smokin'. 1972: Lady Sings the Blues. 1973: Hit! The Mack. Wattstax. Some Call It Loving. 1974: Uptown Saturday Night. 1975: Adios Amigo. 1976: The Bingo Long Traveling All-Stars and Motor Kings. Car Wash. Silver Streak. 1977: Greased Lightning. Which Way Is Up? 1978: The Wiz. The Muppet Movie. Blue Collar. California Suite. 1979: Richard Pryor Live in Concert. In God We Trust. Richard Pryor is Back Live in Concert. 1980: Wholly Moses! Stir Crazy. 1981: Bustin' Loose. Some Kind of Hero. 1982: Richard Pryor Live on the Sunset Strip. The Toy. 1983: Superman III. [†] *Richard Pryor Here and Now. 1984: Brewster's Millions. 1985:* [†] *Jo Jo Dancer/Jo Jo Dancer, Your Life is Calling. 1986: Critical Condition. 1987: Moving. 1989: See No Evil, Hear No Evil. Harlem Nights. 1990: Look Who's Talking Too (voice only). 1991: Another You.*

[‡] As Richard 'Cactus' Pryor
[†] And directed

RADFORD, Basil 1897–1952
and
WAYNE, Naunton 1901–1970

Two affable, upper-crust British actors who so tickled the public's fancy as cricket-loving Englishmen abroad that they made several more appearances together in some very popular comedies, and provided light relief in other films. They were equally popular on radio. Although both sounded as though they came from the most affluent part of London, nothing could have been further from the truth. Wayne was actually born in Wales, and Radford just across the border in Chester. Large, bluff, hearty and moustachioed, light-haired Radford looked every inch an ex-army officer. He was on stage from 1922, made his film debut in America, but stuck mostly to the English stage until the late 1930s. Small, neat, dapper Wayne, on the other hand, with his shining black hair, concerned look and pigeon cheeks, was a compere and comedian, and a concert-party entertainer for the first eight years of his career from his 1920 debut in the Pavilion at South

Wales's Barry Island. He came to London in 1928 and was emcee and general jokester in several West End shows, also appearing in cabaret at some of the town's swishest nightspots, including the Ritz, the Dorchester and the Café de Paris. He didn't take a straight acting role until 1937, and it was only the following year that Alfred Hitchcock teamed him with Radford in *The Lady Vanishes*. They played Charters and Caldicott, names dreamed up by screenwriters Sidney Gilliat and Frank Launder, later to become famous producer-directors. As Englishmen on a train going through dangerous European territory, they were more interested in cricket scores than in bodies in the corridor or missing ladies. Both Wayne and Radford proved to have a delightfully droll way of delivering inconsequential dialogue amusingly irrelevant to the events going on around them, and they swiftly developed a marvellous rapport. The characters cropped up again in the Gilliat/ Launder-scripted *Night Train to Munich*: more trains, more Nazis. Radio showed an interest and Launder and Gilliat wrote a zippy serial for them, *Crooks' Tour*, in 1940, filmed with almost indecent haste the same year. They also popped up in wartime shorts, the multi-story *Millions Like Us* and a second radio serial, *Secret Mission 609*, bumbling their way to foiling yet another Nazi plot. Launder and Gilliat had written them into another film, *I See a Dark Stranger*, but Radford and Wayne wanted the parts built up a bit. When the writers demurred the actors declined to participate, in so doing saying goodbye to the character names. For when Radford and Wayne returned to radio, Launder and Gilliat claimed copyright on their film characters. So it was as Woolcott and Spencer that Radford and Wayne appeared in their first post-war series, *Double Bedlam*. These jolly comedy-thrillers, usually in eight parts, so pleased the nation's listeners that they proceeded at the rate of one a year: *Traveller's Joy, Crime Gentlemen Please, That's My Baby, Having a Wonderful Crime* and *May I Have the Treasure*. There was another film, too, a funny number called *It's Not Cricket*, in which, as Bright and Early, the priceless pair are private eyes dogged by a lunatic Nazi (Maurice Denham)

on cases that end, appropriately, with a cricket match – in which the ball contains a stolen diamond. They also made cameo appearances in two other late 1940s comedies, *Helter Skelter* and *Stop Press Girl*. These most popular wearers of the old school tie were half-way through their 1952 radio adventure, *Rogues' Gallery*, when Radford collapsed and died from a heart attack. He was 55. Wayne gallantly carried on to the end of the story alone. It was a gesture in keeping with two characters who always 'played up and played the game'.

Together. *1938: The Lady Vanishes. 1940: Night Train to Munich (US: Night Train). Crooks' Tour. 1942: Next of Kin.* * *Partners in Crime. 1943: Millions Like Us. 1945: Dead of Night. 1946: A Girl in a Million. 1948: Quartet. It's Not Cricket. 1949: Helter Skelter. Stop Press Girl.*

Radford alone. *1929: Barnum Was Right. 1932: There Goes the Bride. 1933: A Southern Maid. Just Smith (US: Leave It to Smith). 1936: Broken Blossoms. Dishonour Bright. 1937: Jump for Glory (US: When Thief Meets Thief). Captain's Orders. Young and Innocent (US: The Girl Was Young). 1938: Climbing High. Convict 99. 1939: Trouble Brewing. Let's Be Famous. The Four Just Men (US: The Secret Four). Spies of the Air. Jamaica Inn. Just William. She Couldn't Say No. Secret Journey (US: Among Human Wolves). The Girl Who Forgot. 1940: Room for Two. The Flying Squad. The Girl in the News. 1941:* * *Save Rubber. 1942:* * *London Scrapbook. Unpublished Story. Flying Fortress. 1943: Dear Octopus (US: The Randolph Family). 1944: Twilight Hour. 1945: The Way to the Stars (US: Johnny in the Clouds). 1946: The Captive Heart. 1948: The Winslow Boy. 1949: Whisky Galore! (US: Tight Little Island). The Blue Lamp. 1950: Chance of a Lifetime. 1951: White Corridors. The Galloping Major.*

Wayne alone. *1932: The First Mrs Fraser. 1933: Going Gay (US: Kiss Me Goodbye). For Love of You. 1939: A Girl Must Live. 1949: Passport to Pimlico. Obsession (US: The Hidden Room). 1950: Trio. Double Confession. Highly Dangerous. 1951: Circle of Danger. 1952: Tall Headlines. Treasure Hunt. The Happy Family (US: Mr Lord Says No). 1953: The Titfield Thunderbolt. You Know What Sailors Are. 1959: Operation Bullshine. 1961: Nothing Barred. Double Bunk.*

RADNER, Gilda
See **WILDER, Gene**

RANDALL, Tony
(Leonard Rosenberg) 1920–

A delightfully droll, sour-faced, wheedling-voiced American comic actor with neat, dark hair – a latecomer to films who carried some big comedies on his own and became an integral ingredient of the Doris Day/ Rock Hudson romantic romps at Universal. Born in Tulsa, Oklahoma, Randall was a Broadway and radio actor before and after US Army service between 1942 and 1946.

His first exposure to the general public came with the TV soap *One Man's Family* (1949–52), a continuation of a famous radio series. Rather more important in the formation of his career as a light comedian was a second TV show *Mr Peepers* (1952–5), as the best friend of the title character. Big Broadway success came with a leading role in *Oh, Men! Oh, Women!* and 20th Century-Fox offered him the same part in the film version of this farce about a psychiatrist and his patients. It was filmed in 1956, and released the following February. Public reaction to Randall's performance was such that the studio put him into two more films that year, the downbeat *No Down Payment*, and the wildly successful *Will Success Spoil Rock Hunter?*, which teamed him with Jayne Mansfield. That proved to be a delicious satire on TV commercials, in which timid Randall finds himself labelled as a sex symbol. Despite this success Randall found himself demoted to co-star status, although billed above the title, when he returned to Hollywood after 18 months work on Broadway and TV. But he had splendid opportunities as Rock Hudson's lugubrious best friend, helping and hindering him win Doris Day in *Pillow Talk*, *Lover Come Back* and (funniest of all) *Send Me No Flowers*. Leading roles came back to Randall after this, but the scripting was never sharp enough to make him a major star from such offerings as *Boys' Night Out*, *The Brass Bottle* (his co-star was Burl Ives as a genie), *Fluffy* (his co-star was a lion) or *Our Man in Marrakesh*. He was buried beneath mounds of makeup in *The Seven Faces of Dr Lao*, and as Agatha Christie's Hercule Poirot in *The Alphabet Murders*. Neither was exactly pushed by its studio. Randall's films since then have been a mixed bag indeed, but he has enjoyed great success on television, first in *The Odd Couple*, where he and Jack Klugman were perfectly cast in the roles played on film by Jack Lemmon (*qv*) and Walter Matthau – a fussy photographer and a sloppy sportswriter, who move in together when they're divorced. Randall, in fact, was probably even better casting than Lemmon, and revelled in the series' consistently witty scripts. *The Odd Couple* ran

for six seasons from 1970, and was replaced almost at once in Randall's world by *The Tony Randall Show*, which belied its title by being a sitcom which cast Randall as widower Judge Franklin, on the lookout for a new wife without lowering his dignity. That ran for three seasons, and Randall also had hits with *Sidney Shorr* (as a sympathetic homosexual) and *Sunday Drive*, as well as his riotous participation in the Disney telemovie *Save the Dog!* If age has made Randall's droopy features kindlier, he retains a mordant talent to amuse.

1957: *Will Success Spoil Rock Hunter? (GB: Oh! For a Man!)*. *No Down Payment*. *Oh, Men! Oh, Women! The Playroom (TV)*. 1959: *The Mating Game*. *Second Happiest Day (TV)*. *Pillow Talk*. 1960: *The Adventures of Huckleberry Finn*. *Let's Make Love*. 1961: *Lover Come Back*. 1962: *Boys' Night Out*. 1963: *Island of Love*. 1964: *The Seven Faces of Dr Lao*. *The Brass Bottle*. *Send Me No Flowers*. 1965: *Fluffy*. *The Alphabet Murders*. 1966: *Our Man in Marrakesh (US: Bang Bang You're Dead)*. 1968: *Hello Down There*. 1972: *Everything You Always Wanted to Know About Sex* * *But Were Afraid to Ask*. 1978: *Kate Bliss and the Ticker Tape Kid (TV)*. *Foolin' Around (released 1980)*. 1979: *Scavenger Hunt*. 1981: *A Girl's Best Friend/Sidney Shorr: A Girl's Best Friend (TV)*. 1982: *The King of Comedy*. 1984: *Off Sides (TV)*. 1985: *Hitler's SS: Portrait in Evil (TV. GB: cinemas)*. 1986: *That's Adequate! My Little Pony (voice only)*. *Sunday Drive (TV)*. 1987: *It Had to be You (released 1989)*. 1988: *The Man in the Brown Suit (TV)*. *Save the Dog! (TV)*. 1990: *Gremlins 2: The New Batch (voice only)*.

RANDLE, Frank
(Arthur McEvoy) 1901–1957

A big-nosed, light-haired, hard-drinking British north country comedian who specialised in toothless old codgers, barroom philosophers, workshy soldiers and ancient hikers. Randle was often difficult to work with, but convulsed northern audiences in his native Britain and delighted in a series of funny disguises, many of which involved taking out his false teeth. His jokes were

richly vulgar for their day, and revolved mostly around sex and drinking; Randle was an expert belcher who would have a 'pint of ale' at his elbow as a running gag while he rambled through his material. His few films often cast him as a private soldier, usually accompanied by a trio of fellow-grotesques, helping the hero and heroine get together for a duet at the finale, and padding out the sometimes inordinate running time with reworkings of old music-hall material: the Marx Brothers' (*qv*) formula reduced to its simplest form, with the cracks almost showing in the scenery. Randle came originally from Wigan, was a circus performer as a teenager, and a variety top-liner in his early thirties. Northern audiences flocked to see him in their thousands, even when he arrived late or drunk or both: he was still funny with his meandering monologues in which the jokes ran seamlessly one into another. Although he was a 'blue' (for his day) comedian and sexual nudger in the tradition of Max Miller and Benny Hill (both *qv*), Randle also had a fine line in wide-mouthed bafflement and outrage when anything really rude was implied, deliberately or accidentally, that could keep an audience in stitches for minutes on end. His film comedies started with the need to cheer up filmgoers in the darkest hour of wartime. The first few had him (and his cohorts Harry Korris, Dan Young and Robbie Vincent) in the army, the quartet always managing to disgrace themselves with indefatigable gusto before things came out right in the end. You could rely on Randle to burble around with the dialogue, get drunk, belch, fall downstairs, take a long time with his comedy routines, and sometimes even lose his place in the script. It was everything, in fact, guaranteed to make southern filmgoers stay away in droves, but the films actually did quite respectably outside their guaranteed Lancashire/Yorkshire market, and made decent profits on minimal budgets. Some of them even ran disgracefully close to the two-hour mark but Randle fans didn't seem to care. After the war was over Randle comedies kept on coming from their Mancunian studios; for the last one, *It's a Grand Life*, in 1953, he even imported a couple of glamour girls from the mainline British cinema, in Diana Dors and Jennifer Jayne. When not in the film studio, Randle retained his popularity in pantomime, or in his touring show, *Randle's Scandals*. His luck ran out in July of 1957 when he died, officially of gastro-enteritis, though many friends and acquaintances believed he had drunk himself to death.

1940: *Somewhere in England*. 1941: *Somewhere in Camp*. 1942: *Somewhere on Leave*. 1943: *Somewhere in Civvies*. 1945: *Home Sweet Home*. 1946: * *Randle and All That*. 1947: *When You Come Home*. 1948: *Holidays with Pay*. 1949: *Somewhere in Politics*. *School for Randle*. 1953: *It's a Grand Life*.

RAY, Ted
(Charles Olden) 1909–1977
Wildly successful as a radio comedian, Britain's dark-haired, jaunty, square-jawed, foxy-voiced, fiddle-playing Ted Ray contributed a mixture of decent straight acting performances and three-dimensional comic characters to British films without ever settling into the cinema scene. Originally from Liverpool, Ray became a top music-hall attraction in the Britain of the 1930s, with a wisecracking act billed as 'fiddling and fooling'. His dry, slightly yelping tones became familiar on British radio after 1939, but it was the post-war years that were to bring him his greatest popularity. Needing a show to replace *ITMA*, whose beloved star, Tommy Handley (*qv*) had suddenly died, the BBC dreamed up *Ray's a Laugh*. Handley had also come from Liverpool and physically the two men were not dissimilar. The show didn't have quite the same multi-character, harum-scarum format as *ITMA* however. It concentrated on Ted's domestic problems (wife Kitty was Australian comedienne Kitty Bluett) where he was always having a tiff and storming off to the Frog and Nightgown (a real-life London pub was later thus named in its honour) and encountering local characters. Ray provided some of the funny voices himself. Others came courtesy of Peter Sellers (*qv*), who was later replaced by such other British stalwarts as Kenneth Connor and Charles Hawtrey (both *qv*). As the series flourished, Ray renewed his acquaintance with the cinema. He had made his debut as a young comic of 21 in *Elstree Calling*, in which Handley, ironically, had been top of the cast. He had also been asked to do his stuff in *Radio Parade of 1935*, and was still topping film variety bills as late as 1950 with the poorly-written *A Ray of Sunshine*. His first positive contribution to British cinema was an unexpected one, as one of the feuding 'Red Peppers' in *Meet Me Tonight*, from Noël Coward's playlets *Tonight at 8.30*. He and Kay Walsh were splendid together, but Ray's only immediate follow-up was another straight part in *Escape by Night*, a vehicle for his appealing son Andrew, who had become a child star of the British cinema. When he did try comedy, it was unfortunately in *My Wife's Family*, the umpteenth screen version

of a creaky old stage farce, in which Ray succumbed to the general over-playing. He tried again with *The Crowning Touch* – four stories about a hat – and *Please Turn Over*, a tolerably funny farce about a teenager who writes a *Peyton Place*-type novel about the people she knows. These were largely ignored by the paying public, but the same year (1959) he found his most suitable film comedy role when following in the footsteps of Will Hay (*qv*) as a slightly seedy and incompetent headmaster in *Carry On Teacher*. If this hadn't been a 'Carry On' comedy, it might have led fruitfully to more school comedies – although Jimmy Edwards (*qv*) was already a rival in that field. Ironically, it was Edwards who provided Ray with more or less permanent employment for the rest of his life after *Ray's a Laugh* had finally ended its long run in 1961. Ray soon became a regular panellist on the Edwards-inspired radio panel game *Does the Team Think?*, in which a panel of comedians soon digressed from the not-too-serious questions to crack some of their favourite gags. The series started in 1957 and, with Ray joining forces with Edwards in the early 1960s, sustained its popularity right up to the last show in 1976, by which time it had become something of a (still amusing) shambles. The following year Ray died from a heart attack at 68.

1930: Elstree Calling. 1934: Radio Parade of 1935 (US: Radio Pirates). 1950: A Ray of Sunshine. 1952: Meet Me Tonight. 1953: Escape by Night. 1956: My Wife's Family. 1958: The Crowning Touch. 1959: Please Turn Over. Carry On Teacher.

RAYE, Martha
(Margaret 'Maggie' Reed) 1908–
Martha Raye would do *anything* for a laugh. She actually had quite a voluptuous figure and a tempestuous private life that included six broken marriages, but what people remember is the beer-saloon voice emanating from a vast mouth and rebounding from the back of the stalls and a wild, knockabout energy which made you sit up and take notice, even though the smile it brought to your face might wear thin after a while. She

was once described by the *New York Times* as 'a stridently funny comedienne ... a remarkable pantomimist ... who can glare in several different languages ... and sings swing music in a voice with saxophone overtones and an occasional trace of pure foghorn'. Hollywood's clangorous clown was almost literally born in a trunk – in the Montana town at which her entertainer parents were playing in the local vaudeville theatre. At three she was part of the family act, then branched out with her brother and sister (and later other partners) before hitting the vaudeville circuit as a singer with comic interludes, belting out songs in the Ethel Merman style. Rather more boisterous than A. A. Milne's Tigger, Martha simply couldn't be ignored and had hit Broadway by the late 1920s. Her first film appearance didn't come until 1934, and then it was only a short. A deal to make a series of shorts at M-G-M showcasing her as a comedienne fell through, and it was another two years before she was signed to a contract by Paramount, after studio executives had seen her at California nightclubs. 'When I opened my mouth', said Martha later, 'they thought it was another earthquake.' Anxious to parade their acquisition as a newcomer, studio publicists gave her birthdate as 1916, though she had been a dance-band vocalist since 1928. Her first film for Paramount, *Rhythm on the Range*, set the pattern for the rest of her studio tenure. She capered around the screen getting in everyone's way and being very noisy about it. She also did a funny drunk routine and sang *Mr Paganini*, a Danny Kaye-style novelty song that became her trademark. Through her 15-film Paramount stay, the Raye performance was pretty unvarying; she was the unsophisticated, man-hungry clodhopper who usually landed the comic lead at the end. Critics were, well, critical, but the public on the whole liked her. She introduced another memorable offbeat song, *Beethoven, Mendelssohn and Liszt*, in *Hideaway Girl*, and forged a useful partnership with Bob Hope (*qv*) in several comedies. The studio gave her little to do beyond exaggerated, broad comedy, so it was rather ignoble, as well as a surprise, when they dropped her in 1940. Martha Raye's film career, equally surprisingly, never really recovered, although she remained in demand as a club entertainer and showed an energy and enthusiasm entertaining the troops in various wars second only to her erstwhile partner Hope. She has been wounded three times on various USO tours, made eight trips to Vietnam and is an honorary marine colonel. In the late 1960s she played Texas Guinan, queen of 1920s nightclubs, in a stage musical *Hello Sucker*. It was a role already played on film by Martha's successor as Paramount's resident jumping jack, Betty Hutton. One critic said that Martha was 'all over the stage, singing, dancing, emoting and mugging'. In 30 years, little had changed. She was given a special Oscar in 1969 for her work entertaining the armed forces. In the TV series McMillan (1976–77), she replaced Nancy Walker as Rock Hudson's housekeeper for the last stories in the series.

1934: * A Nite in a Nite Club. 1936: Rhythm on the Range. College Holiday. The Big Broadcast of 1937. 1937: Mountain Music. Hideaway Girl. Artists and Models. Waikiki Wedding. Double or Nothing. 1938: College Swing (GB: Swing, Teacher, Swing). The Big Broadcast of 1938. Tropic Holiday. Give Me A Sailor. 1939: Never Say Die. $1,000 a Touchdown. 1940: The Farmer's Daughter. The Boys from Syracuse. 1941: Navy Blues. Hellzapoppin. Keep 'Em Flying. 1944: Pin-Up Girl. Four Jills in a Jeep. 1947: Monsieur Verdoux. 1952: * Hollywood Night at 21 Club. 1962: Billy Rose's Jumbo (GB: Jumbo). 1969: The Phynx. 1970: Pufnstuf. 1979: The Concorde – Airport '79 (GB: Airport '80 . . . the Concorde). The Gossip Columnist (TV).

REUBENS, Paul (alias **Pee-wee Herman**) (P. Rubenfeld) 1952–

Twig-thin, dark-haired, childlike American TV comedian whose painted puppet of an innocent abroad went down big with American audiences in the 1980s, but didn't travel well. Born in Peekskill, New York, Reubens grew up in Florida, where his parents ran a lamp store. While still in the sixth grade at school he won a role in an amateur production of *A Thousand Clowns*, and he continued to act while at the California Institute of the Arts. While trying to make inroads into show business as a clown Reubens worked at various odd jobs, including busboy, sandwich-maker and Fuller Brush salesman. Then he had some success with an act he formed with a former classmate, Charlotte McGinnis: they called themselves Hilarious Betty and Eddie. They did puppet shows and a stand-up sound effects routine. The duo appeared several times on TV's *The Gong Show*, where it was twice voted best act. It was as a member of the Groundlings, an improvisational comedy theatre group, that Reubens created the character of Pee-Wee Herman, a frenetic little guy in check suit and the white face makeup of a mime artist. 'I got the name from a tiny harmonica I played in one of my routines', Reubens recalled later. 'It said "Pee-Wee" on it.' By 1980 he was starring for the Groundlings in *The Pee-wee Herman Show* (the name having acquired a small 'w'). There were a couple of small roles in film comedies made by his acquaintances Cheech and Chong (*qv*) and then his acclaimed Pinocchio for TV's *Faerie Tale Theatre*, a role he might have been born to play. The success of an ensuing TV series, *Pee-wee's Playhouse*, which won six Emmys ('The most fun I've ever had was writing for five-year-olds. I wanted the five-year-olds rolling on the floor') encouraged Reubens to try films again. Luckily he found the ideal director in Tim Burton, who hadn't made a feature film before but would go on to direct such comic fantasies as *Beetlejuice*, *Batman* and *Edward Scissorhands*. In *Pee-wee's Big Adventure*, Pee-wee's toy-ridden and gadget-laden apartment, like the inside of a doll's house, is the prelude to his misadventures in trying to trace the thief who has stolen his bicycle. The character itself is that of a 12-year-old in semi-adult form, the little wooden boy sprung to life again, with ruby lips, slicked-back black hair, rosy cheeks and makeup-whitened face. The suit, with too-short arms from which emerge spindly, almost alien fingers, is a better-fitting version of others worn by comics from Stan Laurel to Norman Wisdom (both *qv*). Just like a puppet, Reubens strikes bizarre poses in the film, with joints sticking out at odd angles. The characterisation, plus the imagination of star and director, were just enough to carry the film to enormous success in its native America. A sequel, *Big Top Pee-wee*, took three years to arrive and was limp by comparison. The moral seems to be that the days are gone when an audience would accept a comic creation, and root for that same creation through film after film. Reubens continued for a while to be successful on American TV then accepted

Matador Martha . . . and no bull. Armed with only a cape, Martha Raye probably aims to keep the bull at bay by singing to it, in *Tropic Holiday*.

a cameo role in Burton's second *Batman* film.

1980: *Cheech and Chong's Next Movie* (GB: *Cheech and Chong's Close Encounters*). *The Blues Brothers*. 1981: *Cheech and Chong's Nice Dreams*. *Thursday the 12th/Pandemonium*. 1984: *Meatballs Part II*. 1985: *Pee-wee's Big Adventure*. 1986: *Flight of the Navigator* (Voice only. As Paul Mall). 1987: *Back to the Beach*. 1988: *Big Top Pee-wee*. 1992: *Batman Returns*.

RHYS JONES, Griff
See **SMITH, Mel** and **RHYS JONES, Griff**

RIANO, Renie
See **YULE, Joe** and **RIANO, Renie**

THE RITZ BROTHERS
(The Joachim Brothers)
Al (centre) 1901–1965
Jimmy (left) 1903–1985
Harry 1906–1986

Long-faced, banana-nosed, scruffy-haired American experts in lowbrow lunacy. Al and Jimmy were the two who looked like each other. Harry, who was probably the most talented of the three, had squarer, more startled-looking features. Their parents were Austrian Jews who settled in New Jersey, where all three brothers were born. There was a fourth brother, George, who like Zeppo with the Marxes (*qv*) became his famous brothers' business manager and agent. Encouraged by their father, a haberdasher, to try careers in show business, the brothers started as solo acts in local vaudeville theatres, but had teamed up by 1925, providing a typically zany nightclub act in which Jimmy Durante (*qv*) was sometimes their pianist. It would be another decade before the brothers hit Hollywood. In the meantime they continued doing very silly things in their own inimitable style, usually in Broadway revues presented by impresario Earl Carroll. Extravagant costumes and 'impossible' gags provided part of Ritz fans' staple diet. Their frenetic style was toned down a bit for their first movie, a two-reeler called *Hotel Anchovy*, in which they cause chaos as manager, house detective and bellboy. The film eventually led to a contract with 20th Century-Fox, who used the comedians in the same way that the Marx Brothers and Laurel and Hardy (*qv*) had sometimes been used in large-scale comedy musicals – as comedy relief in between romance and song. The *New York Times* thought the Ritz Brothers' occasional bursts on to the screen in these films resembled 'escapes from their keepers', an analogy the Ritzes would have appreciated. These 'escapes' varied from novelty musical numbers to ridiculous impersonations of film stars. Only the Ritzes could have done impressions of Peter Lorre, Charles Laughton

and Boris Karloff – all at once and on roller skates. The brothers made a presentable impression in their first starring roles, playing tailors who help a college win a football match in *Life Begins in College*. But the quality of their starring vehicles had begun to drop away when they suddenly made their best, *The Three Musketeers*. In this spoof of Dumas which sticks quite closely to the storyline of the original, the Ritzes play lackeys who have to masquerade as the musketeers and help out Don Ameche's D'Artagnan. The boys provided some fine modern anachronisms amid the period dialogue, and seriously threatened the dignity of patrician leading ladies Gloria Stuart, Binnie Barnes (a splendid Milady de Winter) and Pauline Moore. Just when major fame seemed to be beckoning, the Ritzes fell out with the studio over their next film, *The Gorilla*. They were both right and wrong: the film, a variation on the spooky-house comedy murder-mystery (that was being done better across at Paramount by Bob Hope (*qv*) in *The Cat and the Canary*) wasn't much good (as they suspected), but remains one of their most fondly-remembered. The result of the row (the Ritzes walked out and came back) was that the film was scaled down to a 'B' movie, as was their next, *Pack Up Your Troubles*. Amid mutual acrimony the brothers quit the studio (or were dropped, according to whose account you read). They found, like others before and after, that changing employers was a case of jumping out of the frying pan and into the fire. The studio the Ritzes moved to was Universal, a strange choice since that set-up already housed Abbott and Costello and Olsen and Johnson (both *qv*). *Argentine Nights* teamed them with the Andrews Sisters and was ramshackle, but occasionally funny, with the Ritzes in drag imitating the Andrews Sisters taking off Carmen Miranda! *Behind the Eight Ball*,

another comedy-whodunnit, was passable fun, but the remaining two in the Universal deal were terrible. One, *Hi Ya Chum*, teamed the Ritzes with Jane Frazee and Robert Paige, the straight leads from Olsen and Johnson's *Hellzapoppin*. But the comedy here was hardly on the same scale; indeed, the last three at Universal were rock-bottom 'B's, worse than the kind of film from which they'd been fleeing at Fox. The Ritzes got out of Hollywood and spent the rest of their comedy career treading the boards. They were entertaining at a large hotel complex for the Christmas season in 1965 when Al died suddenly from a heart attack. Harry and Jimmy carried on the act for another 20 years, sometimes doing a poignant comic dance routine in which a spotlight took the place of Al. It was a moment of understatement from the comic brothers for whom subtlety had never formed part of their style.

1934: * *Hotel Anchovy*. 1936: *Sing, Baby, Sing*. 1937: *Life Begins in College/Life Begins at College* (GB: *The Joy Parade*). *One in a Million*. *On the Avenue*. *You Can't Have Everything*. 1938: *Kentucky Moonshine* (GB: *Three Men and a Girl*). *The Goldwyn Follies*. *Straight, Place and Show* (GB: *They're Off*). 1939: *The Three Musketeers* (GB: *The Singing Musketeer*). *The Gorilla*. *Pack Up Your Troubles* (GB: *We're in the Army Now*). 1940: *Argentine Nights*. 1942: *Behind the Eight Ball* (GB: *Off the Beaten Track*). *Hi Ya, Chum* (GB: *Everything Happens to Us*). 1943: * *Screen Snapshots, series 2: No. 5*. * *Screen Snapshots, series 2: No. 8*. *Never a Dull Moment*.
Al alone. 1918: *The Avenging Trail*.
Harry and Jimmy. 1975: *Won Ton Ton, the Dog Who Saved Hollywood*. *Blazing Stewardesses*.
Harry alone. 1976: *Silent Movie*.

RIX, Sir Brian
(Lord Rix) 1924–

The prime mover in British farce over the past 40 years, Brian Rix was also, for a brief while, a reluctant comedy star of the British cinema. When audience interest waned he hurried back to the stage. Stocky, dark-haired and with a naturally cheerful face, Rix could relax his facial muscles to look gormless at the drop of a trouser. He came from Yorkshire, and was a stage actor at 18 for a couple of years before wartime service with the RAF intervened. After the war Rix became actor-manager with his own repertory company in Yorkshire. Attracted to a farce by Colin Morris about National Service recruits, *Reluctant Heroes*, Rix took it on tour. It was so popular that a London West End stage production followed at the Whitehall Theatre, which was to become Rix's home for the next 16 years. The play was brought to the screen as a vehicle for Ronald Shiner (*qv*), who had just scored an enormous success with *Worm's Eye View*, following years as a character actor. The film was a sort of forerunner of *Carry On Sergeant*, with Shiner as the sergeant-major, and Rix creasingly funny as the hapless Horace. After three more Whitehall years Rix supported Shiner again in *Up to His Neck*. The latter was now established as a star of the British cinema, though his material remained poor. This one was a remake of *Jack Ahoy!* Later that year (1954) Rix had one of his greatest Whitehall successes in *Dry Rot*, about three bookies trying to fix a race. The film version brought in Shiner and Sidney James (*qv*) but, under veteran director Maurice Elvey, it, too, might have been doped, and never really started running. Shiner and Rix tried again, even so, with *Not Wanted on Voyage* in which Rix, though second-billed, had the central role of the luckless purser originally played by Sydney Howard in the 1933 film *Trouble*. Rix had now overtaken Shiner in popularity, and enjoyed solo spotlight in *The Night We Dropped a Clanger*, *And the Same to You* and *Nothing Barred*, at a time when British comedies were at their most abundant. Not surprisingly, though, the material was thin. Rix elected to return to the stage for the rest of his acting days, with the exception, in

1973, of *Don't Just Lie There, Say Something*, which must have made him regret his decision to leave the boards and face the camera again. In later days, he has devoted the majority of his time to helping the mentally handicapped, working full-time in the cause for several years from 1980. He was knighted in 1986, and created Lord Rix in 1992. He has been married to the actress Elspet Gray since 1949.

1951: Reluctant Heroes. 1954: Up to His Neck. What Every Woman Wants. 1956: Dry Rot. 1957: Not Wanted on Voyage. 1959: The Night We Dropped a Clanger. 1960: The Night We Got the Bird. And the Same to You. 1961: Nothing Barred. 1973: Don't Just Lie There, Say Something!

ROBEY, Sir George
(G. Wade) 1869–1954

Perhaps Britain's most famous music-hall comedian, Robey, round of face and painted of eyebrow, turned out a surprising number of films over a staggering 53-year period. Dubbed 'the Prime Minister of Mirth', he made a number of good silent comedies and later proved himself a richly-personable character actor. Whether bowler-hatted, bescarfed and bemoaning, or romping over the boards as a truculent pantomime dame, Robey was a funny and much-loved entertainer. A Londoner, this mellowest of men began his working life in engineering, but became a music-hall comedian in his early twenties, quickly rising to the top of the bill. His character had pretentions to culture, and some things in common with Frankie Howerd (*qv*) in that he pretended to be offended at the laughter he evoked, and would instruct his audience 'Pray temper your hilarity!' He became one of the first music-hall comedians to appear on celluloid when he and two fellow-comics made *The Rats* in 1900, depicting their antics at a picnic and a subsequent dinner. With the popularity of the cinema growing apace in Britain in 1913, Robey began to make two-reel comedies with more consistency. He also recorded some of his popular music-hall songs. In many of his 'story' films, Robey was the sober soul who kicks over

traces. In *Blood Tells*, for example, he plays the Purity League chief who has a blood transfusion from a burglar and becomes a ne'er-do-well. In *The Rest Cure*, he's a businessman off to the country to take it easy, only to find life there so exhausting that he's glad to return to the town. In the early 1920s Robey committed one of his most famous pantomime dames, from *Aladdin*, to film in *One Arabian Night*; and more ambitiously essayed Sancho Panza in an adaptation of *Don Quixote*. Some of these features were described as 'George Robey Super Productions', and brought the comic new admirers. He played Herbert Jenkins' cockney antique dealer, Bindle, in a 1931 adaptation of *The Temperance Fete*, and then Sancho Panza again, in G.W. Pabst's ambitious French-made production of 1933. Now in his sixties, Robey began to mix leading roles in robust minor comedies with character work. And he was still a top attraction in variety. Robey's finest hour on film was yet to come. Many fine comedians have been admirably cast as Falstaff in *Henry V* (in the recent version Robbie Coltrane (*qv*) took on the role), but Robey had the good fortune to be cast in the classic Laurence Olivier version of 1944. At 75, it was a performance much to be admired. By now knighted, Robey came out of retirement in 1952 to play Tony Weller in a richly-characterised if not altogether successful version of Dickens' *The Pickwick Papers*. He died two years later at 85.

*1900: * The Rats. 1913: * Good Queen Bess. * And Very Nice Too. 1914: * George Robey Turns Anarchist. 1916: * £66 13s 9¾d for Every Man, Woman and Child. * Blood Tells, or: the Anti-Frivolity League. 1917: * Doing His Bit. * George Robey's Day Off. 1923: The Rest Cure. Widow Twan-Kee/One Arabian Night. Don Quixote. 1924: The Prehistoric Man. 1926: * Hints and Hobbies, No. 1. 1928: * Safety First. * The Barrister. 1929: * The Bride. * Mrs Mephistopheles. 1931: The Temperance Fete. 1932: Marry Me. 1933: Don Quixote (remake). 1934: Chu Chin Chow. 1935: Birds of a Feather. Royal Cavalcade (US: Regal Cavalcade). 1936: Men of Yesterday. Southern Roses. Calling the Tune. 1938: * Cavalcade of Stars. 1939: A Girl Must Live. 1942: Variety Jubilee. Salute John Citizen. 1943: They Met in the Dark. 1944: * Highlights of Variety No. 27. Henry V. 1945: The Trojan Brothers. Waltz Time. 1952: The Pickwick Papers. 1953: Ali Baba Nights.*

ROGERS, Will 1879–1935

Born in the same year as W. C. Fields (*qv*), this American wit and entertainer was in many ways Fields' antithesis on screen. Whereas Fields' characters were mean-spirited, conniving and under-handed, those that Rogers created were warm, wise, generous and philosophical. But although it took different forms the two men had one thing in common: sly humour. Rogers' wit

was the kind that debunks pomposity, sees things as they really are and cuts through the humbug. When somebody asks him what advertising is, in one of his most likeable films, *A Connecticut Yankee in King Arthur's Court*, Will tells him that advertising is convincing people that they must have something they've managed to do without all their lives. It's a typical Rogers remark. People laughed at such witticisms because they could see that they gleamed with truth. But it took a nimble-witted mental genius to think up so many similar maxims and pronouncements throughout his career. Born in what was then Indian territory but is now Oklahoma, Rogers became an expert rider and rope-twirler by the time he reached his teens. He entertained with amazing rope tricks – a quickness-of-the-hand talent that rivalled Fields' juggling – at country fairs, interspersing his feats with flashes of dry humour. The turn of the century found Rogers' feats of legerdemain and homespun humour touring with a wild west show in South Africa at the time of the Boer War. Eventually returning to America, he left travelling shows and joined the vaudeville circuit, becoming hugely popular on the boards before hitting Broadway in 1912. From 1917 onwards he starred in the Ziegfeld Follies, where he also expanded little-known talents for singing and doing a bewitching soft-shoe shuffle. As with Fields, films could never really make the most of Rogers until sound came along to reveal his inimitable drawling tones to a world-wide public. There were a lot of silent two-reelers but, although they began well, with the Goldwyn organisation playing up to Will's image and strengths, he felt that in too many of the early 1920s shorts he was being straitjacketed into becoming a conventional silent-screen comic. Back on stage, Will continued to consolidate his reputation of being America's most beloved humorist. Politicians, public figures and modern gadgetry were three of his favourite targets. As he said of Juliet, in a title card he wrote for the silent *Doubling for Romeo*: 'She speaketh, yet, like a politician, she sayeth nothing'. With the coming of sound, several studios chased Rogers to renew his movie career and it was Fox, for whom he hadn't pre-

viously worked, who secured his laconic services. They hit pay dirt right away with *They Had to See Paris*, a sort of comedic version of *Dodsworth*, in which a wife lets riches and society go to her head on a European tour while her feet-on-the-ground husband finds platonic consolation with a vivacious showgirl. Son and daughter also go off the rails. This being a Rogers film, the unit of the family is preserved at the end, with the action stopping dead for a full ration of Rogers philosophy. While Rogers' essential wit is still amusing today, these philosophical diatribes about the virtues of a stable existence are sometimes trying to sit through. 1930s audiences, however, swallowed them whole. Encouraged by Rogers' obvious potential as a national hero, Fox spent the next seven years catering to his every whim, including his widely-publicised dislike of retakes. Thus, slight 'fluffs' in dialogue, or hesitations as Rogers searched momentarily for the next line, can often be detected in his sound features. In those seven years, however, he built up a formidable catalogue of rural Americana, paving the way for the Frank Capra philosophy that it was still possible in America for a good man to succeed against the odds, simply by working hard and sticking to his ideals. And always, there were Will's wisecracks, thrown in to leaven the sentimentality. Extolling the virtues of the small shopkeeper in *Handy Andy*, he tells us that 'chain stores are about as friendly as chain gangs'. Obvious, but totally effective. This country boy went on outwitting the city slickers until August 1935 (a year in which he made five films – largely because his no-nonsense approach brought everything in under schedule) when he was killed in a plane crash while on holiday. The nation mourned a favourite son – voted the country's number one film box-office attraction the previous year. Will's son, Will Jr, portrayed him in an affectionate biography, *The Story of Will Rogers*, in 1952. Jane Wyman played Betty, his wife of 27 years. It is seldom revived today, perhaps because there was nothing controversial, scandalous or (apart from his death) tragic about the Rogers career. He was merely a laid-back, successful entertainer who was, to quote the title of one of his films, jes' passin' through.

*1918: Laughing Bill Hyde. 1919: Jubilo. Almost a Husband. Water, Water Everywhere. 1920: Jes' Call Me Jim. Cupid the Cowpuncher. The Strange Boarder. Scratch My Back. 1921: Boys Will Be Boys. Honest Hutch. Guile of Women. Doubling for Romeo. An Unwilling Hero. 1922: One Glorious Day. The Headless Horseman. A Poor Relation. * Hustling Hank. * The Ropin' Fool. One Day in 365. * Uncensored Movies. 1923: * Jes' Passin' Through. Fruits of Faith. Hollywood. * Gee Whiz, Genevieve. * Family Fits. * Highbrow Stuff. 1924: * Don't Park There! * The Cake Eater. * Going to Congress. * A Truthful Liar.*

*Big Moments from Little Pictures. * The Cowboy Sheik. * Our Congressman. * Two Wagons, Both Covered. 1927: Tiptoes. A Texas Steer. * Winging 'round Europe. * With Will Rogers in Dublin. * With Will Rogers in London. * With Will Rogers in Paris. * Reeling Down the Rhine. * Roaming the Emerald Isle. * Hiking Through Holland. * Hunting for Germans in Berlin. * Through Switzerland and Bavaria. * Prowling round France. * Exploring England. 1928: * Over the Bounding Blue. 1929: They Had to See Paris. 1930: So This is London. Happy Days. Lightnin'. 1931: A Connecticut Yankee (GB: The Yankee at King Arthur's Court). Ambassador Bill. Young As You Feel. 1932: Down to Earth. Too Busy to Work. Business and Pleasure. The Plutocrat. 1933: State Fair. Doctor Bull. Mr Skitch. 1934: David Harum. Handy Andy. Judge Priest. * Hollywood on Parade No. 13. 1935: The County Chairman. Life Begins at 40. Steamboat 'Round the Bend. Doubting Thomas. In Old Kentucky.*

ROONEY, Mickey

(Ninnian Joseph Yule Jr) 1920–

A human catherine-wheel. A pint-sized, blond-haired, snub-nosed American entertainer of seemingly limitless energy, Mickey Rooney has been scampering across cinema screens for close to 70 years – one of Hollywood's longest spans. Almost literally born in a trunk – actually a theatrical boarding-house – the boy, then known as Joe, was on stage with his parents' vaudeville act as soon as he could walk, banging on drums and confidently singing songs. His father, Joe Yule (qv), split from the boy's mother when he was four (he would later come to Hollywood and have a minor film career of his own) and Mrs Nellie Yule continued touring the country with her infant prodigy. She brought him to Hollywood in 1926, where he was chosen from more than two thousand applicants to play a cartoon strip character called Mickey McGuire, even though he had to dye his hair dark to get the role. The boy went on to play the mischievous Mickey in about 70 two-reel comedies made between 1927 and 1933. Legally prevented from using the name Mickey McGuire once the series had ended (the last few were released the following year), he ended up at MGM, now using the name Mickey Rooney. They employed him on a week-by-week basis until his performance as Clark Gable as a child in *Manhattan Melodrama*, whereupon he was hired at the dizzying rate of $500 a week. That rose to $750 after his loan-out to Warners to play an eye-catching Puck in their stylish version of Shakespeare's *A Midsummer Night's Dream*. After 1937 Rooney's career really began to skyrocket. Although his acting continued to be more showy than anything else, he caught the public eye with his role in Spencer Tracy's Oscar-winning *Captains Courageous*, teamed with Judy Garland for the first time in *Thoroughbreds Don't Cry*, and created all-American teenager Andy Hardy in *A Family Affair*. For the next eight years, he couldn't miss. In

1938 millions cried over his cocky, whining Whitey Marsh in *Boys' Town* (which won co-star Tracy a second consecutive Oscar), cooed over Andy Hardy through several more scrapes, and cheered when Rooney took a special Oscar 'for personifying the spirit of American youth'. By 1939 he was the nation's favourite film star. The first of the Rooney-Garland musicals was made, *Babes in Arms*. Rooney's jack-in-the-box clowning, singing and dancing and his unquenchable enthusiasm won him an Oscar nomination in a year of hot competition. And there were three more Hardy films. These flagwaving little homilies to the American way of life, almost unwatchable today, had Mickey as the troublesome teenager always in trouble over girls, money or shady company, but shown sense at the end by a few wise words from his father, the

judge (Lewis Stone). In real life he was less restrained over girls. His short-lived marriage to Ava Gardner in 1942 was the first of eight. Nellie had the measure of her son — and his bride. 'I love Ava', she said. 'She's a grand girl. I give the marriage three weeks.' She was only about five months out. On and off the screen Mickey's life continued at whirlwind pace. He captained the studio football team, the MGM lions (despite being only 5 ft 3 in), taught himself to play various musical instruments, and made two more smash musicals with Garland, *Babes on Broadway* (in which he did a wicked impersonation of Carmen Miranda) and *Girl Crazy*. By now, though, after three consecutive years at the top, he had lost his lead at the top of the nation's popularity polls to Abbott and Costello (*qv*). And war service from 1944 (he had been rejected previously because of a heart flutter) would alter the course of his career. Returning in 1946 to make the fifteenth Andy Hardy comedy, Rooney found that the public no longer wanted the series. A few years later he too was unwanted at MGM, and it took him hard work and application to win back public approval as a top-rated character star who could carry comedy or heavy drama with equal conviction. Since 1956, when his comeback was confirmed with an Oscar nomination for his gambling-crazy soldier in *The Bold and the Brave*, Rooney has continued non-stop through bankruptcy and marriages alike, entertaining in films, TV, nightclubs and theatre. One of his greatest triumphs of more recent years came in the Broadway show *Sugar Babies*, a return to his vaudeville roots in which he capered as a bald and grinning demon through a series of risqué routines. He won an Emmy for the TV movie *Bill*, as a middle-aged, mentally-retarded man, in 1981 and, having been nominated for an acting Oscar four times, was given a second special award for his services to the industry in 1983. 'It finally got through to me', said Rooney in the 1960s, 'that you learn in this business by listening. That was the trouble of being a child star. It all falls into your lap and you figure the big red balloon is going to be flying overhead forever. Then all of a sudden a hawk with a big sharp beak comes along, and there goes your balloon before you know it.' Mickey's showbiz balloon has exploded many times since that first heady success. But, unlike a real balloon, the diminutive dynamo has always managed to blow it up again.

Mickey Rooney's rebellious Whitely Marsh and Spencer Tracy's noble Father Flanagan melted all pre-war hearts in MGM's Oscar-winning *Boys' Town*

1926: * *Not to be Trusted.* 1927: †* *Mickey's Pals.* †* *Mickey's Circus.* †* *Mickey's Eleven. Orchids and Ermine.* †* *Mickey's Battle.* 1928: †* *Mickey's Parade.* †* *Mickey's Little Eva.* †* *Mickey's Nine.* †* *Fillum Frolics.* †* *Mickey's Athletes.* †* *Mickey's Rivals.* †* *Mickey's Triumph.* †* *Mickey's Movies.* †* *Mickey's Big Game Hunt.* †* *Mickey the Detective.* †* *Mickey's Babies (GB: Baby Show).* †* *Mickey's Wild West.* 1929: †* *Rattling*

Racers. †* Mickey's Surprise. †* Mickey's Big Moment. †* Mickey's Brown Derby. †* Mickey's Explorers. †* Mickey's Great Idea. †* Mickey's Initiation. †* Mickey's Last Chance. †* Mickey's Menagerie. †* Mickey's Northwest Mounted. †* Mickey's Mix-Up. †* Birthday Squeakings. †* Mickey's Midnight Follies. 1930: †* Mickey's Strategy. †* Mickey's Champs. †* Mickey's Luck. †* Mickey's Master Mind. †* Mickey's Musketeers. †* Mickey's Whirlwinds. †* Mickey's Winners. †* Mickey's Warriors. †* Mickey the Romeo. †* Mickey's Merry Men. †* Mickey's Bargain. 1931: †* Mickey's Rebellion. †* Mickey's Diplomacy. †* Mickey's Thrill Hunters. †* Mickey's Helping Hand. †* Mickey's Stampede. †* Mickey's Crusaders. †* Mickey's Sideline. †* Mickey's Big Business. †* Mickey's Wildcats. 1932: †* Mickey's Travels. †* Mickey's Holiday. †* Mickey's Golden Rule. †* Mickey's Busy Day. †* Mickey's Charity. Information Kid/Fast Companions. My Pal the King. Sin's Pay Day. Beast of the City. 1933: †* Mickey's Ape Man. †* Mickey's Race. †* Mickey's Big Broadcast. †* Mickey's Covered Wagon. †* Mickey's Disguises. †* Mickey's Touchdown. †* Mickey's Tent Show. Broadway to Hollywood (GB: Ring Up the Curtain). The Big Cage. The Chief (GB: My Old Man's a Fireman). The World Changes. The Life of Jimmy Dolan (GB: The Kid's Last Fight). The Big Chance. 1934: The Lost Jungle (serial). †* Mickey's Minstrels. †* Mickey's Rescue. †* Mickey's Medicine Men. Love Birds. Beloved. I Like It That Way. Manhattan Melodrama. Hide-Out. Half a Sinner. Death on the Diamond. Chained. Upper World. Blind Date. 1935: The County Chairman. A Midsummer Night's Dream. The Healer. Reckless. Riff Raff. Ah, Wilderness! 1936: Down the Stretch. * Pirate Party on Catalina Isle. Little Lord Fauntleroy. The Devil is a Sissy (GB: The Devil Takes the Count). 1937: The Hoosier Schoolboy (GB: Yesterday's Hero). Thoroughbreds Don't Cry. Captains Courageous. A Family Affair. Slave Ship. Live, Love and Learn. You're Only Young Once. 1938: Judge Hardy's Children. Hold That Kiss. Love is a Headache. Lord Jeff (GB: The Boy from Barnardo's). Love Finds Andy Hardy. Boys' Town. Out West with the Hardys. Stablemates. 1939: The Adventures of Huckleberry Finn. The Hardys Ride High. Babes in Arms. Judge Hardy and Son. Andy Hardy Gets Spring Fever. 1940. * Rodeo Dough. Andy Hardy Meets Debutante. Young Tom Edison. Strike Up the Band. Andy Hardy's Private Secretary. 1941: Men of Boys' Town. * Cavalcade of the Academy Awards. Life Begins for Andy Hardy. Babes on Broadway. * Meet the Stars No. 4. 1942: The Courtship of Andy Hardy. A Yank at Eton. Andy Hardy's Double Life. 1943: Girl Crazy. Thousands Cheer. The Human Comedy. 1944: National Velvet. Andy Hardy's Blonde Trouble. 1946: Love Laughs at Andy Hardy. Summer Holiday (released 1948). 1947: Killer McCoy. 1948: Words and Music. * Rough but Hopeful. 1949: The Big Wheel. 1950: He's a Cockeyed Wonder. The Fireball. 1951: My Outlaw Brother. The Strip. 1952: * Screen Snapshots No. 205. Sound Off. Off

Limits (GB: Military Policemen). 1953: A Slight Case of Larceny. * Mickey Rooney — Then and Now. 1954: Drive a Crooked Road. The Bridges at Toko-Ri. The Atomic Kid. 1955: The Twinkle in God's Eye. 1956: The Bold and the Brave. Magnificent Roughnecks. Francis in the Haunted House. 1957: The Comedian (TV). Operation Mad Ball. Baby Face Nelson. * Playtime in Hollywood. 1958: Andy Hardy Comes Home. * Glamorous Hollywood. 1959: A Nice Little Bank That Should Be Robbed. The Last Mile. The Big Operator. 1960: Platinum High School (GB: Rich, Young and Deadly). The Private Lives of Adam and Eve. 1961: King of the Roaring Twenties (GB: The Big Bankroll). Everything's Ducky. Breakfast at Tiffany's. 1962: Requiem for a Heavyweight (GB: Blood Money). 1963: It's a Mad, Mad, Mad, Mad World. 1964: The Secret Invasion. 1965: How to Stuff a Wild Bikini. The Devil in Love. 24 Hours to Kill. 1966: Ambush Bay. 1968: The Extraordinary Seaman. Skidoo. 1969: 80 Steps to Jonah. The Comic. The Cockeyed Cowboys of Calico County (GB: TV as A Woman for Charlie). 1970: Hollywood Blue. 1971: Evil Roy Slade (TV). Journey Back to Oz (voice only). B.J. Lang Presents. 1972: Pulp. Richard. 1974: That's Entertainment! Ace of Hearts. Bon Baisers de Hong Kong. 1975: Rachel's Man. 1976: The Domino Killings/The Domino Principle. Find the Lady. 1977: Pete's Dragon. 1978: The Magic of Lassie. Donovan's Kid (TV). 1979: Rudolph and Frosty's Christmas in July (voice only). Arabian Adventure. The Black Stallion. 1980: My Kidnapper, My Love (TV). Odyssey of the Pacific. 1981: Leave 'Em Laughing (TV). The Fox and the Hound (voice only). Bill (TV). Senior Trip (TV). 1983: Bill: On His Own (TV). 1984: It Came Upon the Midnight Clear (TV). 1985: The Care Bears Movie (voice only). 1986: The White Stallion. The Return of Mike Hammer (TV). Little Spies (TV). 1988: Bluegrass (TV). 1989: Erik the Viking. 1990: My Heroes Have Always Been Cowboys. Home for Christmas. 1991: Silent Night, Deadly Night 5: The Toy Maker. The Gambler Returns: The Luck of the Draw (TV). A Year Without Santa Claus (TV. Voice only). 1992: The Legend of Wolf Mountain. Maximum Force. Sweet Justice. La Vida Lactea.

† As Mickey McGuire

RUBIN, Benny 1899–1986
Dark-haired, moon-faced, pop-eyed, huge-nosed, toothy Jewish-American vaudevillian, who specialised in Yiddisher humour and was briefly popular in films at the beginning of the sound era. Unlike other such comics who disappeared when their style of humour went out of fashion, Rubin stuck around and built up a long list of credits in films and TV as a comedy cameo player. The dopey dialect humorist was born in Boston. As a boy he earned money clog dancing on street corners. At ten he ran away from home to become a boy dancer in amateur shows. Later he returned and tried his hand at boxing, having 48 fights as a teenager, which

no doubt accentuated the plumminess of the famous Rubin nose. By 15 Rubin had gained his first professional engagement as a dancer. Two years later he was to be found entertaining on riverboats with a mixture of hoofing and humour. By the early 1920s his novelty dances, flair for impersonation and mastery of dialect had made him a top-liner on the vaudeville circuit. As the decade progressed Rubin took on a number of partners; he was most happily paired with Jack Haley (qv), later to win fame as the Tin Man in the 1939 version of The Wizard of Oz. Broadway success followed in What a Widow! Impressed, MGM signed Benny for films, and he started making two-reeler comedy shorts. These have dated badly and Rubin looks more disciplined in his feature films, mostly in comic support, although in two 1930 entertainments, Hot Curves and Sunny Skies, he had the leading role. After parting company with the studio Rubin began to mix performing with writing, contributing several screenplays for other comedians, notably Wheeler and Woolsey, Joe E. Brown (both qv) and his old friend Jack Haley. Another old acquaintance, Jack Benny (qv), began to employ Rubin in character parts on his radio show — an association that would continue profitably for Rubin over many years. Accepting that his days as a Yiddisher comic were over — 'Ethnic groups were becoming hyper-sensitive in the late 1930s' — Rubin started taking on character roles in films from 1939. When these petered out he tried his hand at other things: managing a restaurant, stockbroking and even dabbling in the rag trade. With the coming of television, Benny became more involved in show business again. For a short while in 1949 he had his own show (yes, it was called The Benny Rubin Show!) and could be spotted on and off on Jack Benny's famous long-running comedy series from 1950 to 1965. The familiarity of his plump cheeks and round eyes brought him renewed character work in films, which continued up to the end of the 1960s. Frank Capra gave Rubin two of his best character roles, as Mr Diamond in A Hole in the Head, and Flyaway in Pocketful of Miracles. The fiery comedian, who admitted that his hot temper often cost him work, wrote his autobiography in 1973 and played a few odd bit parts in the 1970s before retiring to the Hollywood apartment where he lived alone until his death from a heart attack, a few weeks after a prostate operation. Embittered in later years at what he saw as a deliberate industry policy to ban ethnic comedians, Rubin once estimated that he had amassed a fortune three times over and then seen it vanish. But he lived life to the full – and women and gambling were always a weakness.

1927: * Naughty Boy. 1928: * Benny Rubin in Seven Minutes of Your Time. * Football. * Casino Gardens. * Daisies Won't Tell. * Thanksgiving. Imperfect Ladies. The Matinee Idol. 1929: Marianne. It's a Great Life. Naughty Baby. 1930: Hot Curves. Sunny Skies. Love in the Rough. Leathernecking (GB: Present Arms). Montana Moon. Lord Byron of Broadway (GB: What Price Melody?). They Learned About Women. * Talking Turkey. 1931: * Full Coverage. * Guests Wanted. * Julius Sizzer. * Messenger Boy. * The Promoter. 1935: George White's 1935 Scandals. Go Into Your Dance (GB: Casino de Paree). 1938: The Headleys at Home (GB: Among Those Present). 1939: Adventures of Jane Arden. Fighting Mad. 1940: Let's Make Music. 1941: Sunny. Here Comes Mr Jordan. Zis Boom Bah. * Double Trouble. The Bashful Bachelor. Citizen Kane. 1942: Mr Nice Guy. Broadway. 1952: * Keep It Clean. Just This Once. 1953: Tangier Incident. Torch Song. El Alamein (GB: Desert Patrol). 1954: Yankee Pasha. About Mrs Leslie. Masterson of Kansas. The Law vs Billy the Kid. 1956: Meet Me in Las Vegas (GB: Viva Las Vegas!). 1957: Up in Smoke. Will Success Spoil Rock Hunter (GB: Oh! For a Man!). Eighteen and Anxious. 1959: A Hole in the Head. 1960: Please Don't Eat the Daisies. 1961: Pocketful of Miracles. The Errand Boy. 1963: The Disorderly Orderly. 1964: The Patsy. A House is Not a Home. Looking for Love. Your Cheatin' Heart. 1965: That Funny Feeling. 1966: The Ghost in the Invisible Bikini. 1967: Thoroughly Modern Millie. 1968: The Shakiest Gun in the West. 1969: Airport. Angel in My Pocket. 1970: Which Way to the Front? (GB: Ja! Ja! Mein General. But Which Way to the Front?). 1971: How to Frame a Figg. 1975: Won Ton Ton, the Dog Who Saved Hollywood. 1976: The Shaggy DA. The Return of the World's Greatest Detective (TV). 1978: Coma.

RUGGLES, Charles (Charlie)
1886–1970

One of the many 1930s character comedians in Hollywood who were often more fun to have around than the stars they supported, Charlie Ruggles played meek and mild men to such effect that they eventually gave him a whole series in which to show off the characterisation, opposite burly, bouncy Mary Boland (qv) as his wife. They made 14 films together, but whereas Boland's career tailed away thereafter it took television to eventually rob filmgoers of Charlie Ruggles'

talent, which it did for 12 years. Huffly-snuffly, dapper, sandy-haired, moustachioed, slightly apprehensive-looking and almost always apologetic, Ruggles used every element of his round little face to steal scenes and make people laugh. But he didn't take his art lightly. Ruggles once described playing comedy as 'a very serious business'. Although his earliest sound films would be made in New York, Ruggles was born in California. Charles Sherman Ruggles Jr was expected to follow in his father's footsteps as a druggist but although he studied chemistry at college Ruggles was simultaneously active in dramatics and he made his stage debut at 19 in San Francisco. He made his Broadway bow at 30 and tried films the following year. After three movies Ruggles decided the silent cinema was not for him and went back to the stage. Here, his talent for comedy really began to flourish in 1923 with his big hit in Battling Butler, later a film vehicle for Buster Keaton (qv). Ruggles could sing as well, and some shows gave him the chance to vocalise as well as play the fool. One of these was Queen High, in 1926, in which he played a businessman who had to act as his senior partner's butler for a year after losing to him in a poker game. Ruggles repeated his role in the Paramount film of the show, and the studio signed him to a long-term contract. He set to work and quickly often got the best notices in his films. One critic spoke of 'exceptional ability and perfect delivery' and another observed that Ruggles frequently contributed the funniest bit in the film. He played a succession of drunken reporters with which he got cheesed off, but after he was cast opposite Boland in one of the episodes of 1932's If I Had a Million, there was only one role in which the public really wanted to see him. They had their own starring vehicle in Mama Loves Papa, in which Ruggles' performance set the pattern for dozens of twitchy, mild-mannered, peace-loving, henpecked husbands to come. People began to think that he and Boland were married in real life. But she was a lifetime spinster and he had been divorced in the early 1920s and wouldn't marry again until 1942. The screen's most famous 'married couple' hardly saw each other socially (which per-

haps wasn't surprising). Ruggles spent most of his spare time going to boxing matches or looking after the collection of animals (it usually included several dogs) at his Hollywood home. Meanwhile, as well as the comedies with Boland, he continued to enjoy a high profile in bigger Paramount pictures. He was a perfect March Hare in the 1933 Alice in Wonderland, the wild westerner who wins an English manservant in 1935's Ruggles of Red Gap, and crossed to RKO to play the big-game hunter Horace Applegate in Bringing Up Baby. Ruggles left Paramount in 1941 and played affable, amiable, sometimes dotty but more often wise senior citizens. But he had begun to veer away from films again. He spent much of 1942 and 1943 on USO tours, and was back on stage entertaining the troops during the Berlin airlift days of the late 1940s. In 1949, he began a TV comedy called The Ruggles, in which he played an elderly, but harassed husband with four growing children. That ran through almost 150 episodes until 1952 and it was followed by The World of Mr Sweeney. This was based on a 1934 comedy film, Friends of Mr Sweeney, a moderate movie which Ruggles regarded with affection because it had netted him excellent personal reviews. One critic noted that he had caught all the 'feverish indecision and mouselike timidity' of the character. In the TV series, Cicero Sweeney was a small-town store owner who could dispense good advice to everyone but himself. Ruggles played Sweeney through 345 live stories, during which time he became one of television's best-loved characters. The people Ruggles portrayed had undoubtedly moved from being dithering dopes to lovable eccentrics, and when he returned to film work in 1961 his remaining roles were almost always in that vein. He was still stealing scenes in his last movie, Disney's Follow Me, Boys! in 1966. One of his other 1960s films was appropriately The Pleasure of His Company. For Ruggles' genial company was always a pleasure.

1915: Peer Gynt. The Reform Candidate. The Majesty of the Law. 1923: The Heart Raider. 1928: * Wives Etc. 1929: The Lady Lies. Gentlemen of the Press. The Battle of Paris. 1930: * The Hot Air Merchants. * The Family Next Door. Queen High. Roadhouse Nights. Young Man of Manhattan. Charley's Aunt. 1931: The Girl Habit. Honor Among Lovers. Beloved Bachelor. The Smiling Lieutenant. This Is the Night. 1932: Husband's Holiday. Make Me a Star. One Hour with You. 70,000 Witnesses. Evenings for Sale. Madame Butterfly. Love Me Tonight. This Reckless Age. The Night of June 13. Trouble in Paradise. If I Had a Million. 1933: Mama Loves Papa. Murders in the Zoo. Alice in Wonderland. Melody Cruise. Girl Without a Room. Goodbye Love. Terror Aboard. 1934: Murder in the Private Car (GB: Murder on the Runaway Train). Six of a Kind. The Pursuit of Happiness. Friends of Mr Sweeney. Melody in Spring. 1935: No More

Ladies. People Will Talk. Ruggles of Red Gap. The Big Broadcast of 1936. 1936: Wives Never Know. Early to Bed. Anything Goes. Mind Your Own Business. Hearts Divided. Yours for the Asking. The Preview Murder Mystery. 1937: Exclusive. Turn off the Moon. 1938: Service De Luxe. Bringing Up Baby. His Exciting Night. Breaking the Ice. 1939: Sudden Money. Yes, My Darling Daughter. Invitation to Happiness. Boy Trouble. Balalaika. Night Work. 1940: Maryland. The Farmer's Daughter. Opened by Mistake. Public Deb No. 1. No Time for Comedy. 1941: Model Wife. The Invisible Woman. The Parson of Panamint. The Perfect Snob. Go West, Young Lady. 1942: Friendly Enemies. 1943: Dixie Dugan. 1944: Our Hearts Were Young and Gay. * The Shining Future. The Doughgirls. Three is a Family. 1945: Bedside Manner. Incendiary Blonde. 1946: The Perfect Marriage. A Stolen Life. Gallant Journey. 1947: It Happened on Fifth Avenue. Ramrod. 1948: Give My Regards to Broadway. 1949: The Loveable Cheat. Look for the Silver Lining. 1958: The Male Animal (TV). Girl on the Subway (TV. GB: cinemas). 1961: All in a Night's Work. The Pleasure of His Company. The Parent Trap. 1963: Son of Flubber. Papa's Delicate Condition. 1964: I'd Rather Be Rich. 1966: The Ugly Dachshund. Follow Me, Boys!

RUTHERFORD, Dame Margaret
1892–1972

As endearing a comic character star as the British cinema ever produced, this light-haired (later grey), fish-eyed, small-mouthed, multi-jowled, barrel-shaped woman with inimitably puffing, booming delivery left very few scenes unstolen in a 30-year career in films. Though she was universally loved, few actors could have relished sharing scripts with her, especially those British comedians of the 1950s whom she supported, but whose thunder she inevi-

tably stole. Several of her comedy creations are still memorable today, as is her interpretation of Agatha Christie's Miss Marple. And yet she did not take up acting until into her thirties. At the beginning of her working life, London-born Rutherford went into teaching. After several years' experience as a teacher of piano, speech and drama, she decided to try for a career on the stage and enrolled at the Old Vic School in 1924. She made her first stage appearance with the school company, a venerable 33-year-old among 21-year-olds, playing 'the Fairy with the Long Nose' in the Christmas pantomime, Little Jack Horner. She was happily occupied in repertory across the south of England for the next few years, but as soon as she came to London in 1933 it was apparent that hers was no ordinary talent. Even before she embarked on a memorable series of stage roles, the acquisitive cinema snapped her up as a foxy fence for forgers in the extraordinarily-titled thriller Dusty Ermine. She made several small films over the next two years, then started building up an impressive theatrical repertoire. These roles included both Miss Prism and Lady Bracknell in productions of The Importance of Being Earnest, the cycle-riding medium Madame Arcati in Blithe Spirit, the decrepit, horse-betting Aunt Bijou in Spring Meeting and – an unexpected and rare excursion into serious stuff and nastiness – Mrs Danvers in Rebecca. Several of these characterisations were repeated in Rutherford's own hearty, hilarious style in subsequent film versions. So was her headmistress, Miss Whitchurch, in The Happiest Days of Your Life, aghast at her girls' school being billeted by mistake with a boys' school, created on stage in 1948. In the riotous film version two years later she was pricelessly paired with droopfaced Alastair Sim (qv) as her opposite number. Now she was an above-the-title star, if too often in mediocre movies: nurse to a mermaid in Miranda and Mad About Men; a shoplifter with a coat more capacious than that of Harpo Marx in Trouble in Store; a criminal mastermind in The Runaway Bus; a quavering usherette in The Smallest Show on Earth. After touring in Australia with The Happiest Days of Your Life, opposite her husband Stringer Davis (they were married in 1945), she returned to make five films for M-G-M. Four of these were as a glorious Miss Marple, fighting a sword duel in the last and warning the villain that she was Roedean Ladies Fencing Champion of 1931. In between them, she won an Oscar for her grounded plane passenger in The VIPs. She was touching as Mistress Quickly to Orson Welles's Falstaff in Welles's Chimes at Midnight, but was sidelined after 1967 by hip and back injuries. She died after breaking her hip in a fall.

1936: Dusty Ermine (US: Hideout in the Alps). Troubled Waters. Talk of the Devil. 1937: Missing, Believed Married. Beauty and the Barge. Big Fella. Catch As Catch Can. 1940:

Charlie Ruggles gets the look Margaret Dumont usually reserves for Groucho Marx as he cuddles up a little closer in The Girl Habit.

Spring Meeting. 1941: Quiet Wedding. 1943: The Yellow Canary. The Demi-Paradise (US: Adventure for Two). 1944: English without Tears (US: Her Man Gilbey). 1945: Blithe Spirit. 1946: While the Sun Shines. 1947: Meet Me at Dawn. 1948: Miranda. 1949: Passport to Pimlico. 1950: The Happiest Days of Your Life. Her Favourite Husband (US: The Taming of Dorothy). 1951: The Magic Box. 1952: Curtain Up. The Importance of Being Earnest. Castle in the Air. Miss Robin Hood. 1953: Innocents in Paris. Trouble in Store. 1954: Aunt Clara. The Runaway Bus. Mad about Men. 1955: An Alligator Named Daisy. 1957: Just My Luck. The Smallest Show on Earth (US: Big Time Operators). 1959: I'm All Right, Jack. 1961: On the Double. Murder She Said. 1963: The Mouse on the Moon. Murder at the Gallop. The VIPs. 1964: Murder Most Foul. 1965: The Alphabet Murders. Murder Ahoy. 1966: Chimes at Midnight (US: Falstaff). A Countess from Hong Kong. The Wacky World of Mother Goose (voice only). 1967: Arabella.

SAKALL, S. Z. 'Cuddles'
(Eugene Gero) 1884–1955

For more than a decade in Hollywood, if you wanted to cast an actor as an easily-flustered, soft-hearted Hungarian uncle who owned a café, you just had to have S. Z. Sakall. Fair hair turning to silver during his Hollywood years, the multi-jowled, bespectacled, Hungarian-born comedy character star was a master of brow-mopping bombast. Earlier in his career Sakall had made a name for himself in drama. But when he saw that Hollywood envisioned him in comic roles he was happy to play it that way. Born in Budapest to a sculptor, he turned at an early stage of his career from writing music and lyrics to acting. He obtained his first stage name, Szöke Szakall, from the Hungarian for 'fair-haired' and 'beard', descriptive of his looks at the time. After a beginning in Hungarian films, Sakall and his second wife Bozi (his first wife died young) moved their base to Berlin. But in the early 1930s, with the advancement of Nazism, they relocated first to Vienna for a few years, then Holland, France and

England, with Szöke making a few films in various countries along the way. He arrived in America in 1939 where, at the age of 55, he found himself quickly in demand to bring his fractured English to character roles in films. He soon found that slapping his cheeks in moments of stress always gave the audience a laugh; it became one of his trademarks. Warners signed him for ten years from 1942 and he played waiters, tradesmen, uncles, agents and composers. Since his arrival in Hollywood (where he was idyllically happy) he had been billed as S. Z. Sakall. It was studio boss Jack Warner who, much to Sakall's chagrin, decided to add the 'Cuddles' to the billing. Later, Sakall got his own back when he subtitled his autobiography My Life Under the Emperor Franz Joseph, Adolf Hitler and the Warner Brothers. With the completion of his Warner Brothers contract in 1951, Sakall eased up and enjoyed the Palm Springs sunshine. He made a couple of films for M-G-M, playing variations on his familiar theme – flustered, lovable and benevolent – but then died suddenly from a heart attack, a week after his 71st birthday. His quick changes of expression and ability to get a sudden laugh from nowhere made Sakall an incorrigible stealer of scenes. There was no secret to making people laugh, he once maintained. Humour came from inside: you either had a natural talent for amusing an audience, or you didn't.

1916: † Süszterherceg. † Ujszulott Apa. 1918: † Az Onkéntes Tüzoltó. 1922: † Die Stumme von Portici/The Dumb Girl of Portici. 1926: † Wenn das Herz der Jugend spricht. 1927: † Familientag in Hause Prellstein. † Der fidele Bauer. † Der Himmel auf Erden. 1928: † Mary Lou. † Ratschbahn. 1929: † Grosstadtschmetterling. † Wer wird denn weinen, wenn man auseinandergeht. 1930: † Der Hempelmann. † Kam zu mir zum Rendezvous. † Susanne macht Ordnung. † Zweimal Hochzeit. † Zwei Herzen im 3/4 Takt. 1931: † Der unbekannte Gast. † Der Zinker. † Die Faschingsee. † Die Frau, von der man spricht. † Die schwebende Jungfrau. † Ich heirate meinen Mann. † Ihr Junge. † Ihre Majestät der Liebe (German version of Her Majesty Love). † Kopfüber ins Glück. † Meine Cousine aus Warschau.

† Walzerparadies. 1932: † Eine Stadt steht Kopf. † Glück über. Nacht. † Gräfin Mariza. † Ich will nicht wissen, wer du bist. † Kaiserwalzer. † Mädchen zum Heiraten. † Melodie der Liebe (GB: The Right to Happiness). † Muss man sich gleich scheiden lassen. 1933: † Eine Frau wie Du. † Es war einmal ein Musikus. † Gross fürstin Alexandra. † Skandal in Budapest. † Mindent a Nort. † Az Ellopot Szerda. 1934: † Frühlingstimmen. † Helvet az Oregeknek. 1935: † Harom es Fel Musketas/4½ Musketeers. † Tagebuch der Geliebten. † Baratsagos Arcot Kerek. † Smile, Please. 1936: † Mircha. † Fräulein Lilly. 1937: † The Lilac Domino. 1938: † Les affaires de Maupassant. 1940: It's a Date. Spring Parade. My Love Came Back. Florian. 1941: The Devil and Miss Jones. The Man Who Lost Himself. Ball of Fire. That Night in Rio. 1942: Seven Sweethearts. Yankee Doodle Dandy. Broadway. Casablanca. 1943: Thank Your Lucky Stars. Wintertime. The Human Comedy. 1944: Hollywood Canteen. Shine on Harvest Moon. 1945: The Dolly Sisters. Wonder Man. San Antonio. Christmas in Connecticut. 1946: Cinderella Jones. Never Say Goodbye. The Time, the Place and the Girl. Two Guys from Milwaukee (GB: Royal Flush). 1947: Cynthia (GB: The Rich, Full Life). 1948: April Showers. Whiplash. Embraceable You. Romance on the High Seas (GB: It's Magic). 1949: My Dream Is Yours. It's a Great Feeling. In the Good Old Summertime. Oh, You Beautiful Doll! Look for the Silver Lining. 1950: Tea for Two. Montana. The Daughter of Rosie O'Grady. 1951: Sugarfoot. Lullaby of Broadway. Painting the Clouds with Sunshine. It's a Big Country. 1952: * Screen Snapshots No. 205. 1953: Small Town Girl. 1954: The Student Prince.

† As Szöke Szakall.

SAWYER, William
See TRACY, William and SAWYER, Joe

SAYLE, Alexei 1952–

Big, balding, bulbous-bodied British nightclub comedian, TV star and film character actor, with contemptuous mouth and small, hostile eyes. Sayle made his name by being aggressive, offensive and funny as a stand-up comedian – a combination that proved uniquely attractive, especially to the younger viewers of his TV shows. He enjoys being self-described as 'deeply unpleasant'. As his name suggests, Sayle's origins lie in Eastern Europe. His parents were Lithuanian Jews who settled in Liverpool, where his father worked for British Rail as a guard. Talented at drawing, the younger Sayle, an only child, went to art college in Southport, and thence to do a diploma at the Chelsea School of Art in London, where his Communist beliefs propelled him to becoming vice-president of the students' union. Leaving education with no clear idea of what he wanted to do, Alexei worked as a caretaker, 'school dinner lady' and labourer on the London Underground, among other jobs. He alleges that

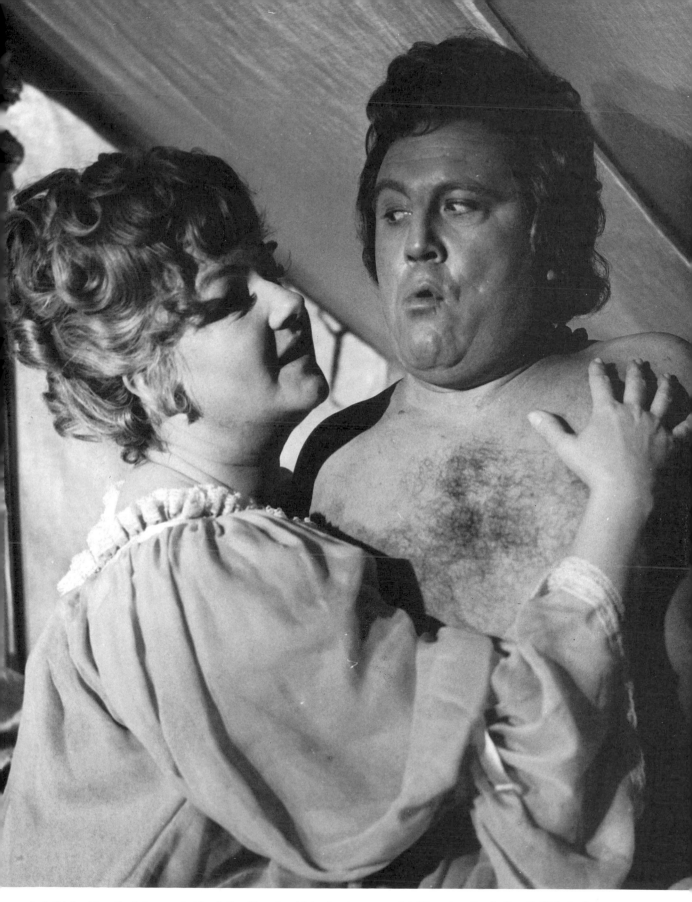

Lady Edwina (Joan Sims) discovers that Jungle Boy (Terry Scott) is her long-lost son, much to his consternation, in *Carry On Up the Jungle*

In the second of his Indian roles, Peter Sellers plays Hrundi V. Bakshi, a party guest for whom nothing goes right, in *The Party*. The onlooker is Carol Wayne

Palm court pandemonium. Alec Guinness, Peter Sellers, Danny Green, Herbert Lom and Cecil Parker are crooks pretending to be a musical quintet in *The Ladykillers*

he was sacked from every job he ever had, until he started getting work as a part-time drama lecturer, first at Chelsea then at the North London College. Teaching drama improvisation gave him the idea of doing stand-up comedy and by 1976. he was in fringe cabaret at Paddington, moving two years later to a job as compere at a new London venture called the Comedy Store. That was renamed the Comic Strip when it moved premises, and it was as part of the Strip's group of comedians that Sayle first moved to television. Dissatisfied with being a supporting player in *The Young Ones* (he played the landlord), a BBC2 comedy series that was to make several reputations, Sayle returned to stand-up comedy, as the iconoclastic, working-class funny-man of the late-night TV comedy show *OTT*, short for over-the-top, which it certainly was. Teetering at the microphone in crumpled black mohair suit and too-small pork-pie hat, Sayle deluged his audiences with phlegm, vitriol and four-letter words (and probably spit) as he slaughtered sacred cows left right and centre – and gloried in it. 'Of course', said Sayle, ever the realist, at the time, 'if England were a socialist Utopia with everyone weaving their own yoghurt, nobody would find me funny.' At around this time he began to get striking supporting parts in major films as well as those produced by stalwarts of British alternative comedy. He was the shady second-hand car dealer in *Gorky Park* – probably the best performance in a disappointing film – and the Hungarian circus owner in the equally disappointing *The Bride*. But Sayle's larger-than-life approach was patently well-suited to character roles in films and he was outstanding in a leading role in *The Strike*. Despite his own series on TV – *Alexei Sayle's Stuff* – and success with a (slightly) toned-down image, the Marxist rebel still thinks 'that I could quite easily become an actor full-time – if I were offered enough roles. Comedy was something I was good at, and it got me where I am, but I find acting easier, more attractive.' As he's now played in everything from Shakespeare (Trinculo in a stage production of *The Tempest*) to an Indiana Jones film, the bad boy of television (in reality he lives quietly with his wife of nearly 20 years

and a cat, and doesn't drive a car) has become quite sufficiently qualified.

1979: Repeater. 1982: The Secret Policeman's Other Ball. 1983: Gorky Park. Those Glory, Glory Days (TV). 1985: The Bride. The Supergrass. 1986: Whoops Apocalypse. Solar Warriors. Mr Corbett's Ghost (TV). 1987: Didn't You Kill My Brother? The Love Child. 1988: The Strike (TV). 1989: Indiana Jones and the Last Crusade. 1992: Reckless Kelly.

SCOTT, Terry 1927–

A portly, cheerful, dark-haired, large-faced British comedian with breathless, 'little boy' voice, Scott was a middle-of-the-bill variety and radio performer for years. But when he started working in collaboration with other comic actors of similar stature, Scott found a niche on television into which he would settle for more than 20 years. After war service in the Royal Navy as a teenager, Scott studied to be an accountant. But he decided that the world of figures was not for him, and instead began acting, initially in repertory with small seaside companies. When he turned to comedy, the next 10 years became a long succession of clubs, pubs, pantomimes, summer shows and funny voices in radio comedy programmes, often as indignantly spluttering schoolboys. Working at Butlin's Holiday Camp in Skegness, Scott teamed up with Bill Maynard, whose laid-back style of comedy contrasted with Scott's huff-and-puff flappability. They were so successful that the teaming soon led to a 1955 TV comedy series, *Great Scott It's Maynard*, which had them sharing a flat in a domestic sitcom that became enormously popular. Maynard's desire for straight acting eventually split the team but Scott soon found a new partner in doleful Hugh Lloyd, who had appeared on *Great Scott* as well as having his own show. The Scott-Lloyd TV series, *Hugh and I*, ran for seven successful seasons. Meanwhile, Scott had got a film career under way, mainly in comic cameos, often as perplexed policemen. When the *Hugh and I* series ended, though, he became a member of the 'Carry On' team. His juiciest role for them was as Jungle Boy in *Carry On Up the Jungle*.

On TV, Scott had found another partner in the plaintive-voiced June Whitfield, and, after 1972, he concentrated entirely on the smaller screen, with excursions into pantomime at Christmas, usually as an enthusiastic dame. Whitfield joined him on *Scott On . . .*, *Happy Ever After* and *Terry and June*, which ran comfortably on into the 1980s. Scott's continued success on TV has been achieved in spite of various health problems over the years, including the survival of a major brain operation in 1979. He also overcame cancer of the bladder and a nervous breakdown in the late 1980s. *Terry and June* finally ended its 13-year run in 1988 but Scott continued to appear in such popular stage farces as *Run for Your Wife*.

1957: Blue Murder at St Trinian's. 1958: Carry On Sergeant. Too Many Crooks. 1959: The Bridal Path. I'm All Right, Jack. And the Same to You. 1960: The Night We Got the Bird. 1961: Nothing Barred. A Pair of Briefs. Double Bunk. Nearly a Nasty Accident. No, My Darling Daughter! What a Whopper! Mary Had a Little . . . 1963: Father Came Too. 1964: Murder Most Foul. 1965: Gonks Go Beat. 1966: The Great St Trinian's Train Robbery. Doctor in Clover. 1968: A Ghost of a Chance. Carry On Up the Khyber. 1969: Carry On Camping. Carry On Up the Jungle. 1970: Carry On Henry. Carry On Loving. 1972: Carry On Matron. Bless This House. 1982: The Pantomime Dame.

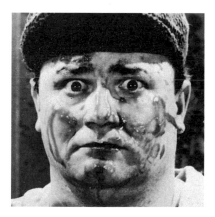

SECOMBE, Sir Harry 1925–

A tubby, cheery-looking, not-too-tall Welsh-born entertainer with dark curly hair who has always mixed bursts of operatic aria with inspired tomfoolery and, despite staunch latter-day travels for religious causes, will forever be identified with his key role as the semi-sane centre of one of British radio's most famous comedy programmes, *The Goon Show*. The singing Goon – he has written autobiographical books called *Goon to Lunch* and *Welsh Fargo* – was entertaining at church socials in his native Swansea as a child. Blessed with an angelic voice, he considered operatic training while working as a clerk in a steel mill, but wartime service in the army intervened, and his zany sense of humour got him caught up in wartime shows for the troops. After the war, he appeared in *Stars in Battledress* with his friend Spike Milligan (*qv*). Secombe was also hired to tell jokes in between girlie shows at London's Windmill Theatre, which proved a useful post-war training ground for many other British comedians, among them Peter Sellers, Tony Hancock and Graham Stark (all *qv*). Secombe had first broadcast as early as 1945, but the big breakthrough as a comedian came in a music hall-type radio show, *Variety Bandbox*, in which he became as popular for his singing as for his humour. His appearances on *Welsh Rarebit* increased his following, but undoubtedly the period of his greatest popularity coincided with the run of *The Goon Show* (initially called *Crazy People*) from 1951 to 1960. Secombe was heard as Neddie Seagoon, the disaster-prone hero of these weekly sagas, permitted only a few catchphrases ('Hello folks', 'What what-what-what?', 'Sacristi Knuckles') while Sellers and Milligan provided nearly all the other voices. The trio made a few rough-and-ready films during the show's run, but the only vehicle tailor-made for Secombe by the cinema of the 1950s was *Davy*. The film capitalised on Secombe's own dilemma of whether to concentrate on singing or clowning by casting him as a member of a knockabout comedy troupe. So as not to break up the act, he finally decides to forgo his operatic ambitions. The corny film, despite being produced by Ealing in Technicolor, found few takers at the box-office. In the theatre,

though, he was much more successful, both in shows (*Large As Life, Secombe's Here*) and musicals (*Pickwick, The Three Musketeers*). Inevitably, he played Humpty Dumpty in pantomime. Secombe had a particular affection for *Pickwick* as it was based on a book by his favourite author, Charles Dickens. So he jumped at the chance of a return to films when offered the role of the Beadle in the film version of another Dickens-based musical, *Oliver!* After that success, the cinema was willing to take him aboard for a few more lunatic comedy roles in such escapades as *The Bed Sitting Room*, *Rhubarb* and *The Magnificent Seven Deadly Sins*, and he got solo billing above the title in *Sunstruck*, a gentle Australian entertainment that featured him as a shy Welsh teacher emigrating to the Australian outback. It lit no fires at the box-office and Secombe returned to live entertainment. Knighted in 1981, and much slimmed down since a serious attack of peritonitis, Secombe continues to appear on British TV screens as host of the religion-oriented travel show, *Highway*. Jokes are few, but he does contrive to sing on every programme.

1948: *Hocus Pocus*. 1949: *Helter Skelter*. 1950: *Fake's Progress (narrator only)*. 1951: *London Entertains. Penny Points to Paradise*. 1952: *Down Among the Z Men*. 1953: *Forces' Sweetheart*. 1954: *Svengali*. 1957: *Davy*. 1959: *Jet Storm*. 1968: *Oliver!* 1969: *The Bed Sitting Room*. 1970: *Song of Norway. Rhubarb. Doctor in Trouble*. 1971: *The Magnificent Seven Deadly Sins*. 1972: *Sunstruck*. 1980: * *A Fair Way to Play*.

SELLERS, Peter
(Richard Sellers) 1925–1980

Certainly one of the funniest men of his time, Britain's Peter Sellers was possessed of an inventive comic brain that few could match. A master of disguises and extravagantly funny voices, he was one of the few comedians who could also hold centre stage as an actor, and the range of characters he created for the cinema was unique. Initially a thick-set man with plump features, bushy brows, wild dark hair and an anxious expression, Sellers was an only child whose parents ran a small seaside theatre. After wartime experience with ENSA, he was discovered by a radio scout doing impressions of film stars at the Windmill Theatre in 1948, and given a chance on *Show Time*, a radio show for new talent. His first regular spot on radio came the following year as part of the regular supporting cast of *Ray's a Laugh*, starring Ted Ray (*qv*). The Sellers gallery of comic characters began to be built from here, notably in Crystal Jollibottom with her catchphrase 'Oh, you saucebox!'. Sellers left *Ray's a Laugh* after a couple of seasons to formulate plans with three other young comedians, Spike Milligan, Harry Secombe (both *qv*) and Michael Bentine for a new kind of radio comedy show. Titled *Crazy People*, it premiered in 1951, and reappeared the following year as the landmark comedy programme *The Goon Show*. This was idiocy stirred into a highly potent potion for making you laugh, and undercurrents from it ran through all Sellers' later work. He created dozens of lunatic characters for the show, many with their own catchphrases: among the most popular were Bluebottle (the eternal fall-guy), the blustering Major Bloodnok, the scheming Hercules Grytpype-Thynne and the doddering Henry Crun. Sellers and his Goonish cohorts made a few movies, too. But none of them amounted to much. It was the type of humour impossible to translate into visuals, but when Sellers tried characterisation as full-blooded as it was clever and eccentric, he was more successful. His first hit as a movie character star was as the crêpe-soled Harry, one of *The Ladykillers*, an Ealing Studios comedy classic about a gang of shady characters making a hash of trying to

Far from Harpo Marx, Peter Sellers' Sir Guy Grand strings along with such fun as there was in *The Magic Christian*

bump off their elderly landlady. Meanwhile, Sellers stayed on with *The Goon Show*. Now (1955) at the height of its popularity, its anarchic madness would continue undiluted until 1960. There would be odd 'specials' thereafter, and a *Last Goon Show of All* in 1972. Before *The Goon Show* ended, though, Sellers had established himself as a funny-man people would pay to see at the cinema. His elderly projectionist in *The Smallest Show on Earth* had to compete with such other scene-stealers as Margaret Rutherford (*qv*) and Bernard Miles; nonetheless Sellers was on the verge of his most consistent run in films. *The Naked Truth*, which concerned the efforts of a group of people to murder the scandal-magazine publisher who threatens to expose their private lives, was the first of three films to team Sellers with Terry-Thomas (*qv*). They were astutely paired (and very funny) as the robbers in *tom thumb*, and on opposite sides of the fence in *Carlton-Browne of the FO*, with Sellers as an oily Middle Eastern premier. *Two-Way Stretch* was more of a team effort, but still explosively funny, with Sellers' trio of convicts, trying to break out to stage a robbery, being upstaged by Lionel Jeffries' (*qv*) self-opinionated warder. Sellers was again sunk heavily beneath disguise as the pernickety Scots accountant in *The Battle of the Sexes*. But the film that consolidated his standing as one of Britain's top draws was *I'm All Right, Jack*, as the militant shop steward Fred Kite, an acutely well-observed portrait that, as one

critic rightly noted, was funny because of the truth rather than in spite of it. He was himself for almost the first time as *The Mouse That Roared*, though he managed to play two other roles in the same film, including an ancient grand duchess. After the philandering Welsh librarian in *Only Two Can Play*, Sellers found the role of a lifetime in *The Pink Panther* (for which Peter Ustinov was originally intended) as the bumbling, impossibly inept Inspector Jacques Clouseau, a sort of M. Hulot of the French *Sûrêté*, who brings disaster not only upon himself but on all those around him. Sellers' mangled 'Franglais' also added to audiences' enjoyment of the role, and there was a quick (but less funny) sequel, *A Shot in the Dark*. He also played three roles in Stanley Kubrick's *Dr Strangelove*, including the title scientist, whose fake arm keeps wanting to make 'Heil Hitler' signs. Even before the acclaim for this had died down, however (it won him an Oscar nomination), Sellers had had a serious heart attack that was to prove a watershed in his career. After it, he never again achieved the same consistency of performance or material. Over the next ten years, Sellers made around 15 more films. *I Love You, Alice B. Toklas* was about the only commercial hit in the lot, although his Indian in *The Party* provoked some amusement, as well as echoes of an earlier, better performance opposite Sophia Loren in *The Millionairess*. The end of 1973 brought a merciful, if patchy, return to form.

His old busker in *The Optimists of Nine Elms* was one of his most charming portrayals, and then he was back as Clouseau in *The Return of the Pink Panther*. Further Clouseau adventures were originally planned as a TV series but all concerned were glad they changed their minds when the film was a resounding success. After the Charlie Chan role in *Murder by Death*, Sellers did another Clouseau, *The Pink Panther Strikes Again* and then another, *Revenge of the Pink Panther*. Invention was flagging, but bursts of hilarity still ran through the films, and yet another, *Romance of the Pink Panther* was planned. Meanwhile, Sellers all but won an Oscar for his simple-minded gardener in *Being There*, and his grief at not getting what he saw as a last chance for the award may have accelerated the advent of the final massive heart attack (there had been several minor ones in the intervening years) that killed him in May 1980. An autobiography, *The Mask Behind the Mask*, had been written by Peter Evans, and summed up most people's feelings about Sellers and, seemingly, even his own. 'Behind our masks', he once said, 'we clowns lead very sad lives. I've always thought I was a chap without a personality of my own. That's why I put on so many different voices and disguises. I'm sort of a plastic mock-up. The real Peter Sellers is somewhere at home doing the washing-up because he can't get any help.' Sellers was married four times, second and fourth to actresses Britt Ekland and Lynne Frederick, his widow at the time of his death. *Romance of the Pink Panther*, of course, never was made, but the makers of the series strung together a ragbag of out-takes and add-ons and called it *Trail of the Pink Panther*. It cost them more than a million dollars in compensation when his widow sued over what she considered her late husband's faked co-operation in a tawdry project.

*1951: Penny Points to Paradise. Let's Go Crazy. London Entertains. Burlesque on Carmen (sound reissue, narrator only). 1952: Down Among the Z Men. 1953: * The Super Secret Service. Our Girl Friday (US: The Adventures of Sadie: voice only). 1954: Orders Are Orders. 1955: John and Julie. The Ladykillers. * The Case of the Mukkinese Battlehorn. 1956: The Man Who Never Was (voice only). 1957: * Insomnia is Good for You. * Cold Comfort. The Smallest Show on Earth. * Dearth of a Salesman. The Naked Truth (US: Your Past is Showing!). 1958: Up the Creek. tom thumb. 1959: Carlton-Browne of the FO (US: Man in a Cocked Hat). The Battle of the Sexes. I'm All Right, Jack. The Mouse That Roared. Two-Way Stretch. 1960: Climb Up the Wall. * The Running, Jumping and Standing Still Film. Never Let Go. The Millionairess. 1961: Only Two Can Play. † Mr Topaze (US: I Like Money). Lolita. 1962: The Waltz of the Toreadors. The Road to Hong Kong. The Dock Brief (US: Trial and Error). The Wrong Arm of the Law. 1963: Heavens Above! Dr Strangelove, or: How I Learned to Stop Worrying and*

*Love the Bomb. The Pink Panther. 1964: A Shot in the Dark. A Carol for Another Christmas (TV). The World of Henry Orient. 1965: What's New, Pussycat? 1966: After the Fox. The Wrong Box. * Birds, Bees and Storks (narrator only). 1967: Woman Times Seven. The Bobo. Casino Royale. 1968: The Party. I Love You, Alice B Toklas. 1969: The Magic Christian. 1970: Hoffman. * Simon, Simon. There's a Girl in My Soup. A Day at the Beach. 1971: Where Does It Hurt? 1972: Alice's Adventures in Wonderland. 1973: Soft Beds, Hard Battles (US: Undercovers Hero). The Blockhouse. The Optimists of Nine Elms. 1974: The Return of the Pink Panther. Ghost in the Noonday Sun. The Great McGonagall. 1976: Murder by Death. The Pink Panther Strikes Again. 1978: Revenge of the Pink Panther. The Prisoner of Zenda. The Great Pram Race (voice only). 1979: Being There. 1980: The Fiendish Plot of Dr Fu Manchu. 1982: Trail of the Pink Panther.*

† Also directed

SEMON, Larry 1889–1928
Another of the silent screen's great tragic clowns, Larry Semon had much in common with Harry Langdon (*qv*). Both appeared on screen with white moon faces, from which dark eyes blinked button-like, embellished

with pencilled eyebrows and dopey grins. Both demanded charge of their own product, but financially both men lived in cloud-cuckoo-land. In each case, a break from their mentor proved the beginning of the end of their great popularity. Show business was in Semon's blood. His father was a professional magician who called himself Zera the Great. The younger Semon, however, was driven to art school rather than the stage and, by 1912, was installed as a cartoonist with the New York *Sun*. All might have been well if things had stayed that way. But Larry had already become a leading light in local amateur dramatics and a chance meeting with Vitagraph executive Frank Daniels resulted in him leaving New York to join the California-based studio in 1916 as a director and writer. The following year he branched out as a star comedian in his own vehicles. Semon wore a bowler hat, trousers that began above the waist and ended (baggily) above the ankles, boots and braces. Playing the peace-loving innocent abroad who found himself the unwilling centre of aggressive action, Semon specialised in comic chase sequences. He had a huge book of gags which enabled him to work variations on these that were to last him several years and see him soar in the popularity polls. By 1922 he had become one of Hollywood's highest-paid slapstick comics. But the danger signs were already there for those who cared to read them. He demanded total loyalty and long hours from his units while the films themselves, sometimes unnecessarily made on location, were running more and more over budget and over schedule. Semon was always worried that a certain scene would never be perfect and constantly lived in fear of being upstaged by other comedians. This involved longer and longer hours, and constant cast changes: Stan Laurel (*qv*) was one comedian who soon refused to work with Semon, although Laurel's future partner Oliver Hardy (*qv*) remained with Semon as a comic heavy for several years, eventually playing the Tin Man to Semon's Scarecrow in the 1925 feature version of *The Wizard of Oz*. Semon's long-expected break with Vitagraph came mid-way through 1924 and his fortunes went into a steady decline from that point. He made only 13 more starring films after the split, eight of them shorts. Few were well received and Semon, who had been footing the bills as his own producer, declared bankruptcy in 1928, just as Langdon would do three years later. The same year there was a short-lived attempt to start a career in vaudeville but Semon, beset by his own personal ghosts, suffered a nervous breakdown and never worked again. He died from pneumonia in October 1928. Some said he had just worried himself to death. His gag book, just like himself, was exhausted. One's abiding memory of is of him fleeing, like some demented pierrot, from log cabin to log cabin as trees come down and smash them up in *The Sawmill*.

Conspicuous, moi? Cato (Birt Kwouk) helps Clouseau (Peter Sellers) with his latest unobtrusive disguise in *The Pink Panther Strikes Again.*

Finally, in real life, there was just one tree too many for filmland's frenzied fool. His second wife was actress Dorothy Dwan, Dorothy in his version of *The Wizard of Oz*.

(Semon directed or co-directed all the following unless indicated.) *1917: Boasts and Boldness. Worries and Wobbles. Champs and Chances. Shells and Shivers. Slips and Slackers. Gall and Golf. Risks and Roughnecks. Plans and Pajamas. Sports and Splashes. Plagues and Puppy Love. Tough Luck and Tin Lizzies. Rough Toughs and Roof Tops. Noisy Naggers and Nosey Neighbors. Spooks and Spasms. 1918: Guns and Greasers. Babes and Boobs. Rooms and Rumors. Stripes and Stumbles. Meddlers and Moonshine. Rummies and Razors. Whistles and Windows. Spies and Spills. Romans and Rascals. Boodle and Bandits. Skids and Scalawags. Hindoos and Hazards. Bathing Beauties and Big Boobs. Dunces and Danger. Mutts and Motors. Huns and Hyphens. Bears and Bad Men. Frauds and Frenzies. Pluck and Plotters. Humbugs and Husbands. 1919: Traps and Tangles. Scamps and Scandals. Scars and Stripes. Soapsuds and Sapheads. Well, I'll Be . . . Passing the Buck. The Star Boarder. His Home Sweet Home. The Simple Life. Between the Acts. Dull Care. Dew Drop Inn. The Headwaiter. 1920: The Grocery Clerk. The Fly Cop. School Days. Solid Concrete. The Stagehand. The Suitor. 1921: The Sportsman. The Hick. The Rent Collector. The Bakery. The Fall Guy. The Bell Hop. 1922: The Sawmill. The Show. A Pair of Kings. Golf. The Sleuth. The Counter Jumper. 1923: No Wedding Bells. The Barnyard. Midnight Cabaret. The Gown Shop. Lightning Love. Horseshoes. 1924: Trouble Brewing. Her Boy Friend. Kid Speed.* [†] *The Girl in the Limousine. 1925:* [†] *The Perfect Clown. The Dome Doctor. The Cloud Hopper.* [†] *The Wizard of Oz. 1926:* [†] *Stop, Look and Listen. 1927: The Stuntman. Oh, What a Man!* [†] *Spuds.* [†‡] *Underworld. 1928: Dummies. A Simple Sap.*
Also as director. *1916: The Man from Egypt. A Villainous Villain. Love and Loot. 1917: Footlights and Fakers.*

All shorts except [†] features. [‡] Did not direct.

SHINER, Ronald 1903–1966

As English as a cup of strong tea with three sugars, Shiner was an aggressive, haranguing cockney actor with slicked-down black hair, a truculent cockney voice that sounded as though he was shouting when he wasn't, beadily suspicious eyes and a thrusting nose that, at the height of his fame, he insured for amounts variously estimated at between £10,000 and £30,000. 'It's me beak what makes 'em laugh', Shiner once told an interviewer, but he was much more complex a comic than that. A colourful early life and years of experience behind and before the scenery on stage, mixed in with dozens of mostly furtive character roles in films, built up a comic personality that fed on the unique combination of ebullience, quick-wittedness, bravado, self-reliance, cunning and desperate improvisation in the face of

disaster. Shiner wasn't born a cockney at all, but was initially raised in a salubrious north London suburb, the son of a technical artist (who advised architectural firms on interior decoration) and a singer. But the family fell on hard times, and Shiner was sent to a much rougher school where he became the leader of the pack. Leaving school, he became a 'screw bluer' (he heated up screws for some unknown purpose) and a clerk with an insurance broker, before enlisting in the Canadian Mounties at 17 by lying about his age. He bought himself out after two years in Canada, but a prospective civilian job helping to manage a rubber plantation in Malaya fell through. Out of work, he enlisted

in the Royal Corps of Signals, where he and a friend founded a concert party called The Breezes. Three years later, he was back in London with only a dog called Kitbag to show for his life to date. He tried farming, and jobs as a fishmonger, greengrocer and milkman. For extra money he appeared at local halls and church bazaars 'singing songs and doing turns'. He got a few more customers for the milk round, but his performing talents continued to elude show business. A family friend suggested he push himself in that direction, and the nearly 25-year-old Shiner began a long round of agents before actor-manager Russell Thorndike gave him a job at the bottom − as an assistant stage manager on tour. Three years later, Shiner was stage manager at London's Whitehall Theatre, which was to be the scene of his greatest stage triumph 15 years on. For the moment, however, he played a long succession of minor roles. He entered films in 1934 and sidled shiftily through nearly 60 of them in the next decade. Most of his characters were tough and shady or cocky comic cockneys − a personality he assumed in several films with burly Wally Patch (Walter Vinnicombe. 1888−1970). One writer rather optimistically described them in the early 1940s as 'the Abbott and Costello of Britain', but Shiner and Patch were not the same types, nor even in the same league, though doubt-

However else you might criticize Ronald Shiner, you could never say he was expressionless. Here he adopts a typically trenchant pose to deal with over-age schoolboys Ronnie Corbett and Alfie Bass (right) in *Top of the Form*

less they envied the Hollywood stars their money. Shiner served as a special constable from 1940 to 1943, but kept his show-business career going in film roles, as well as broadcasting weekly in a programme for forces overseas. In 1944, he discovered *Worm's Eye View*, a stage farce about workshy RAF 'erks' billeted on a suburban family, and determined to bring it to the West End of London with himself in the lead. 'I was convinced that if only I could get to London,' he said later, 'we'd all be made.' He was right – but it was a struggle. There were months of touring before the play opened at a fringe London theatre in 1945, then transferring to the Whitehall in December of that year. After limping through its first few weeks, the play caught on – and ran until 1947. Shiner stayed with the play, at various theatres, until 1950. Then he found himself in another comedy hit, *Seagulls Over Sorrento*. He was a crafty naval rating in this one, in comparison to his *Worm's Eye View* role of a malingering spiv always on the make. Meanwhile, Shiner had relaunched his cinema career, as a star. The rough-edged screen version of *Worm's Eye View* made an obvious beginning, and the follow-up, *Reluctant Heroes*, a sort of earlier version of *Carry On Sergeant*, hit the box-office bullseye. In Britain, Shiner was now a top attraction, his head hugely dominating caricatured bodies above the title of his latest comedy. These early 1950s canters were all pretty makeshift stuff, sometimes based on film comedies from earlier decades. *Little Big Shot* (as an inept crook) was followed by *Top of the Form*, with Shiner as a racing tipster posing as the hectoring head of a boys' school. It was a remake of Will Hay's (*qv*) *Good Morning Boys*, tailored to Shiner's broad, scenery-crashing style. By the end of 1952, Shiner was Britain's favourite home-grown star, ahead of Alastair Sim, Alec Guinness (both *qv*) and Anna Neagle. Shiner said he was so embarrassed by it all that he could never look Neagle in the face again. 'Personally', he added, candidly, 'the kind of farcical slapstick I'm so popular in just gives me a pain. If I had to see one of my own starring films, I'd need half a dozen gins before I could face up to it.' Unfortunately, there were signs that the public was beginning to share his view. His film personality was insufficiently sympathetic to compensate for script deficiencies and the lack of polish in his vehicles, the best of which, from the next few years, was a happy collaboration with Margaret Rutherford (*qv*) in the seldom-revived *Aunt Clara*. There was another film for Britain's biggest studio, Rank: *Up to His Neck*, a remake of Jack Hulbert's (*qv*) *Jack Ahoy!* It was quite popular, if laboured stuff, but Shiner had been overtaken in popularity at the studio by Norman Wisdom (*qv*), who would reign supreme there for the next decade. After audiences stayed away from the independently (and cheaply) made *Keep It Clean*, Shiner was paired off with other comedians

– Brian Rix (*qv*) in *Dry Rot* and *Not Wanted on Voyage*, Ted Ray (*qv*) in *My Wife's Family*, David Tomlinson (*qv*) in *Carry On Admiral* and Leslie Phillips (*qv*) in *The Navy Lark*. Given the low standards of many of these, and, indeed, Shiner's other films from his star period, it was surprising that his admirers remained faithful for as long as they did. But he was in featured roles by the end of the 1950s and played second-fiddle to Rix in his last film, *The Night We Got the Bird*. He accepted it philosophically. 'It's true that I had luck', he said, 'But what I've always held is that you've got to make the most of that luck when it comes, for as long as you can. You've got to get your teeth in, and hang on. Tenacity of purpose – that's the thing.' Shiner never did get to play his famous role of Charlie Badger in the film version of *Seagulls Over Sorrento* (Sidney James (*qv*) did) and was forced to retire in 1963 after a narrow shave with a bout of bronchial pneumonia that left him in an oxygen tent for several days. He went to live by the sea, but three years later Britain's craftiest cockney was dead, from heart problems brought on by chronic bronchitis.

1934: *My Old Dutch. Doctor's Orders.* 1935: *Gentleman's Agreement. It's a Bet. Limelight* (US: *Backstage*). *Squibs. Royal Cavalcade* (US: *Regal Cavalcade*). *Once a Thief. Line Engaged.* 1936: *Excuse My Glove. King of Hearts.* 1937: *Silver Blaze/Murder at the Baskervilles. Dreaming Lips. The Black Tulip. Farewell Again* (US: *Troopship*). *Dinner at the Ritz. Beauty and the Barge. A Yank at Oxford.* 1938: *Prison Without Bars. They Drive By Night. St Martin's Lane* (US: *Sidewalks of London*). 1939: *The Spider. Flying Fifty Five. The Mind of Mr Reeder* (US: *The Mysterious Mr Reeder*). *I Killed the Count* (US: *Who is Guilty?*). *Discoveries. The Middle Watch. Trouble Brewing. The Missing People. The Gang's All Here* (US: *The Amazing Mr Forrest*). *The Lion Has Wings. Come On George.* 1940: *'Bulldog' Sees It Through. *Salvage with a Smile. Spare a Copper. Let George Do It. The Case of the Frightened Lady* (US: *The Frightened Lady*). *Old Bill and Son.* 1941: *The Black Sheep of Whitehall. South American George. The Seventh Survivor. Major Barbara. The Big Blockade. They Flew Alone* (US: *Wings and the Woman*). 1942: *The Young Mr Pitt. Sabotage at Sea. The Balloon Goes Up. Those Kids from Town. King Arthur Was a Gentleman. The Night Invader. Unpublished Story. Squadron Leader X.* 1943: *The Gentle Sex. Get Cracking. Thursday's Child. Miss London Ltd. My Learned Friend. The Butler's Dilemma.* 1944: *Bees in Paradise.* 1945: *I Live in Grosvenor Square* (US: *A Yank in London*). *Caesar and Cleopatra. The Way to the Stars* (US: *Johnny in the Clouds*). 1946: *George in Civvy Street.* 1947: *Dusty Bates* (serial). *The Man Within* (US: *The Smugglers*). *The Ghosts of Berkeley Square. Brighton Rock* (US: *Young Scarface*). 1948: *Forbidden. Rise and Shiner.* 1951: *The Magic Box. Worm's Eye View. Reluctant Heroes.* 1952: *Little Big Shot. Top of the Form.* 1953:

Innocents in Paris. Laughing Anne. 1954: *Aunt Clara. Up to His Neck.* 1955: *See How They Run.* 1956: *Keep It Clean. Dry Rot. My Wife's Family.* 1957: *Carry On Admiral* (US: *The Ship Was Loaded*). *Not Wanted on Voyage.* 1958: *Girls at Sea.* 1959: *Operation Bullshine. The Navy Lark.* 1960: *The Night We Got the Bird.*

SHORT, Martin 1951–
Short by name and short by nature is this little Canadian humorist with the clown's smile. Tremendously successful as a writer and as a television and stage performer, he has been in some big film successes too but hasn't been able to attract movie audiences under his own steam. Although he's a young-looking fortysomething, time for movie stardom is, if he'll pardon the expression, short. After taking a degree in social work and writing at the McMaster University in his native Hamilton, Ontario, Short, like his brother Michael, settled down to a career in comedy writing. But, while Michael remained largely behind the scenes, Martin was soon taking his zany brand of fun up on to the stage of Toronto's Second City comedy troupe, where he met fellow Canadian comics John Candy (*qv*; the troupe's founder) and Dan Aykroyd (also *qv*). While Candy started building up a prolific film career, Short continued expanding his range of comic characters. It was the early 1980s before he moved to America, where, in 1984, he became a regular on the popular TV show *Saturday Night Live*. Steve Martin and Chevy Chase (both *qv*) brought Short to international attention in 1986 when they hired him to join them in *¡Three Amigos!*, a spoof western about three silent-film cowboy heroes who have a real adventure. As Ned Nederlander, Short was the nearest thing audiences had seen to Harpo Marx for 40 years. He had a smash hit with *InnerSpace*, which featured him as a hypochondriac accidentally injected with a man who has been miniaturised. Short's excitable personality was perfectly suited to the role, and he was well cast too as the mega-highly-strung bank robber in *Three Fugitives*, a remake of a French comedy hit. Without the comforting bulwark of a Steve Martin, a

Dennis Quaid or a Nick Nolte, Short struck out when heading the cast of the romantic comedy *Cross My Heart*, opposite never-quite-made-it Annette O'Toole. Other projects are awaited with interest.

1979: The Outsider. Lost and Found. 1983: Sunset Limousine (TV). 1985: The Canadian Conspiracy. 1986: ¡Three Amigos! 1987: Inner-Space. Really Weird Tales (TV). 1988: Cross My Heart. The Big Picture. 1989: Three Fugitives. 1991: Father of the Bride. 1992: Clifford. Pure Luck. We're Back (voice only). The Pebble and the Penguin (voice only)

SIDNEY, George
(Samuel Greenfield) (left) 1876–1945
and
MURRAY, Charlie 1872–1941
Ethnic comedians were popular for a while in early Hollywood sound films. Prominent among the Jewish jokers was the short, barrel-like, frog-faced George Sidney. Sidney was a star in his own right but, in their 20 films together, he met his perfect match in tall, wizened, slit-mouthed, twinkle-eyed 'Irish' comedian Charlie Murray, a veteran of Sennett days. The son of a Hungarian shoemaker who had emigrated to New York, Sidney won his first amateur talent contest as a stand-up comic at the age of 12, and became a full-time entertainer while still in his teens. He devised cross-talking burlesque routines with various partners, and went solo after inventing a character called Busy Izzy Marks, a bearded Jewish tramp he portrayed in a number of roughly-crafted touring shows in the earliest years of the twentieth century. By 1914 the character had become so well known that it was featured in a couple of two-reel silents, one of which, coincidentally, also featured Charlie Murray. At the same time Sidney began to make a name for himself as a comedy character actor after his first Broadway success in 1914's *The Show Shop*. His greatest personal stage hit was in *Welcome Stranger* as a Jewish newcomer to a community who finds himself regarded with suspicion. The play ran for several years but when a film version came to be made in 1924 Sidney was, ironically, unavailable,

being occupied making his feature-film debut for another company. This was also a Jewish subject, the second screen comedy about the comic Jewish clothes manufacturers Potash and Perlmutter. The original 'Potash' had died, and Sidney was an instant success in the role. He had a rich range of facial expressions from slyness though fake joviality to outrage, and was quickly taken into the Hollywood community. Sidney's next film, *The Cohens and the Kellys*, was the first of a series. He was storekeeper Jacob Cohen and his Irish neighbour, policeman Patrick Kelly, was played by Charlie Murray. The son of circus performers (he had had circus experience himself as a boy), Charlie was another ex-vaudevillian who had enjoyed great success as one half of a comedy team called Murray and Mack. By 1912 he had begun making the odd film, and signed for Mack Sennett's Keystone outfit in 1914. A popular member of the Sennett troupe, Murray played hayseeds and cops (and the hero of the 'Hogan' comedies) and was often contrasted amusingly with some of the famous Sennett bathing beauties. Gangling and seemingly toothless from the start of his film career, Murray graduated easily to avuncular character roles, enjoying one of his greatest successes in the title role of the 1925 version of *The Wizard of Oz* (Larry Semon (*qv*) was the Scarecrow and Oliver Hardy (*qv*) the Tin Man). As Cohen and Kelly, Sidney and Murray ranted, raved and reconciled through half-a-dozen reels of rough-hewn humour. Both very visual comedians, their comic capers were often heightened by their physical disparity. Studios quickly put them into other films together, and for Universal they made a series of two-reel comedies in 1930. Murray was unavailable for the next two Cohen and Kelly comedies (which are often erroneously credited to him) but appeared in all the rest, ending with *The Cohens and Kellys in Trouble* in 1933. The title was appropriate for the series had run its course and was beginning to seem outdated against the zanier antics of such 'new' film comedians as the Marx Brothers (*qv*). Neither man made much of a go of character roles, appearing in just four films apiece after the Cohens and Kellys had bitten the dust. Strangely, both died at 69 years and one month old, Murray from pneumonia and Sidney after a long bout with cancer. Despite the broadness of the strokes with which they painted the Jew and the Irish Catholic, both created fully rounded characters, highlighting both their strengths and weaknesses. They made other films together, but it was always as the friendly rivals of contrasting religions and physiques that the public loved them best. When Sidney and Murray made their stage debut together in 1932, it was in a Christmas holiday production of *Abie's Irish Rose*, the old chestnut about the children of warring families falling in love. Sidney played Solomon Levy, Murray was Patrick Murphy, and the orchestra struck up *The*

Cohens and the Kellys as the performance began.

Together. *1914: * The Passing of Izzy. 1926: Classified. 1926: The Cohens and the Kellys. Sweet Daddies. 1927: Lost at the Front. Clancy's Kosher Wedding. The Life of Riley. 1928: Flying Romeos. 1930: The Cohens and Kellys in Scotland. * The Big Butter and Yegg Man. The King of Jazz. Around the Corner. The Cohens and Kellys in Africa. * Discontented Cowboys. * Go to Blazes. * Divorce à la Carte. * In Old Mazuma. * The Love Punch. 1931: Caught Cheating. 1932: The Cohens and Kellys in Hollywood. 1933: The Cohens and Kellys in Trouble.*
Sidney alone. *1915: * Busy Izzy. 1924: In Hollywood with Potash and Perlmutter (GB: So This is Hollywood). 1926: Partners Again – Potash and Perlmutter (GB: Partners Again). The Prince of Pilsen. The Millionaires. 1927: The Auctioneer. For the Love of Mike. 1928: The Cohens and Kellys in Paris. We Americans (GB: Heart of a Nation). The Latest from Paris. Give and Take. 1929: The Cohens and Kellys in Atlantic City. 1932: High Pressure. The Heart of New York. 1934: Rafter Romance. Manhattan Melodrama. 1935: Diamond Jim. 1937: Good Old Soak.*
Murray alone. *1912: * A Disappointed Mama. 1913: * All Hail to the King. * Almost a Wild Man. 1914: Tillie's Punctured Romance. * A Fatal Flirtation. * Her Friend the Bandit. * The Trouble Mender/Love and Bullets. * The Great Toe Mystery. * Soldiers of Misfortune. * The Bungling Burglars/She's a Cook. * The Masquerader. * Stout Heart but Weak Knees. * The Anglers. * Cursed by His Beauty. * His Talented Wife. * His Halted Career. * The Noise of Bombs. * The Plumber. * Hogan's Annual Spree. * His Second Childhood. * The Fatal Bumping. * Mabel's Married Life. * A Missing Bride. 1915: * A Gambling Rube. 1915: * Hogan's Wild Oats. * From Patches to Plenty. * Hogan's Mussy Job. * The Beauty Bunglers. * Hogan the Porter. * Their Social Splash. * Hogan's Romance Upset. * Those College Girls. * A Game Old Knight. * Her Painted Hero. * Hogan's Aristocratic Dream. * The Great Vacuum Robbery. * Hogan Out West. * Only a Farmer's Daughter. 1916: * His Hereafter. * Fido's Fate. * A Love Riot. * The Judge. * Pills of Peril. * Her Marble Heart. * Bombs. * Maid Mad. * The Feathered Nest/ The Girl Guardian. 1917: * Her Fame and Shame. * A Bedroom Blunder. * That Night. * Maggie's First False Step. * His Precious Life. * The Betrayal of Maggie. 1918: * Watch Your Neighbor. * His Wife's Friend. 1919: * Yankee Doodle in Berlin. 1920: Gee Whiz. By Golly (and directed). Married Life. 1921: Home Talent. * A Small Town Idol. 1922: The Crossroads of New York. 1923: Bright Lights of Broadway. Luck. 1924: Lilies of the Field. Empty Hearts. Sundown. Painted People. The Girl in the Limousine. The Fire Patrol. The Mine with the Iron Door. Fool's Highway. 1925: White Fang. Percy. Fighting the Flames. The Wizard of Oz. Sea Women/Why Women Love. My Son.*

Paint and Powder. 1926: Subway Sadie. Irene. The Boob. Mismates. * Her Second Chance. Mike. The Reckless Lady. Steel Preferred. Paradise. The Silent Lover. 1927: The Gorilla. McFadden's Flats. The Poor Nut. The Masked Woman. 1928: The Head Man. Do Your Duty. Vamping Venus. 1930: Clancy in Wall Street. The Duke of Dublin. His Honor the Mayor. 1932: Hypnotized. 1936: Dangerous Waters. 1937: Circus Girl. 1938: Breaking the Ice. The Road to Reno. 1939: *A Small Town Idol (revised version for sound).

SILVERS, Phil
(P. Silversmith) 1911–1985

Mention Phil Silvers and everyone, but everyone, remembers You'll Never Get Rich, alias The Phil Silvers Show, alias Bilko, which ran for four riotous seasons on TV, and would have gone on much longer had not Silvers had to quit with exhaustion. Silvers, in real life a serious man with a rather bleak view of the world, threw everything into the comic art that made his name, and often had to rest on doctors' orders after overwork. A far cry from the non-stop fast-talking, ever-conniving, deliberately-misunderstanding Master Sergeant Ernest Bilko, the terror of Fort Baxter. Perhaps it was working non-stop in so many branches of his profession for so long that weakened Silvers' health. A boy singer, he was entertaining at 11 (born in Brooklyn, he was the eighth and last child of Russian immigrant Jews) and left school at 13 to sing in a revue. When his voice broke Silvers found himself out of a job but, determined to stay in show business, he took work as a stooge to a vaudeville double-act, then branched out on his own from 1934 as a bespectacled down-the-bill comic at burlesque theatres. Five years later he made the leap from burlesque to Broadway in a show called Yokel Boy, and was signed up for films by MGM. His career here was disappointing; if they weren't giving him unsuitable parts, it seemed that they were cutting him out of the film altogether. Other studios, though, did see him as an eye-catching funny-man. There was Tom, Dick and Harry for RKO (as the balefully awful ice-cream seller) and a minor but popular army comedy with Jimmy Durante

(qv) at Warners, before he quit MGM and signed on with 20th Century-Fox. Here he quickly settled in to third or fourth billing as the comedy relief who was the hero's friend, adored the heroine from afar, danced a little and sometimes got a chance to shine in a novelty number. Silvers once recalled that these characters all seemed to be called Blinky and managed to get the hero and heroine back together in the last reel. He even played a variation on the role on loan-out to Columbia for his most successful wartime musical, Cover Girl. It was back on stage, though, that Silvers really became a top star. First there was High Button Shoes, and in it he played just the sort of semi-lovable conniver from which Bilko would eventually develop. He tried Hollywood again, but they gave him another hero's friend role, this time with Judy Garland and Gene Kelly in Summer Stock. So it was back to Broadway and Top Banana, more of a revue than a play, which cast Silvers as a self-centred TV comedian. Half-way through the 350-show run, Silvers collapsed. He declined the six weeks' rest advised by the doctor and was soon back, to rapturous praise, and several awards, including a Tony. The show was filmed after a fashion (the movie was cut to ribbons outside America), and Silvers fared little better with Lucky Me, not one of Doris Day's brighter musicals. And so to Bilko. First conceived in the autumn of 1954, the show began a year later, with Silvers delivering in machine-gun style some masterly comic dialogue by Nat Hiken. Rather than actually working, Bilko spent much of his time browbeating the men of the motor-pool, gambling (a passion the real-life Silvers shared), outmanoeuvring and out-talking his superiors, and hatching strictly illegal money-making schemes. Silvers was perpetual motion in the role. Small wonder that he was worn out when he called a halt to the series in September 1959. It is still revived on television stations all over the world today. Nothing could match up to Bilko and the rest of Silvers' career was a mixture of film and TV guest spots and a few broad comedy film leads in the Bilko manner. He came to Britain to make Follow That Camel with the 'Carry On' team and was one of a team of ageing farceurs in the film version of A Funny Thing Happened on the Way to the Forum, having ill-advisedly turned down the lead in the original stage hit. He did get to lead the cast in a revival of Funny Thing in 1971. It played successfully on Broadway from March 1972, but in August of that year Silvers suffered a severe stroke. He was never the same force again, although returning to occasional cameo roles in films from 1975 to 1980. He was in poor health for much of his last five years before his death following another stroke. Something of a manic depressive in private life, Silvers once said: 'I only smile in public.' But when he did it as Ernie Bilko, millions smiled with him.

1940: Hit Parade of 1941. † Strike Up the Band. † Pride and Prejudice. 1941: † Ball of Fire. The Penalty. The Wild Man of Borneo. Ice-Capades. Tom, Dick and Harry. Lady Be Good. You're in the Army Now. 1942: Roxie Hart. All Through the Night. † Tales of Manhattan. My Gal Sal. Footlight Serenade. Just Off Broadway. 1943: Coney Island. A Lady Takes a Chance. 1944: Cover Girl. Four Jills in a Jeep. Something for the Boys. Take It Or Leave It. 1945: Billy Rose's Diamond Horseshoe (GB: Diamond Horseshoe). A Thousand and One Nights. 1946: If I'm Lucky. 1950: Summer Stock (GB: If You Feel Like Singing). 1952: Top Banana. 1954: Lucky Me. 1962: 40 Pounds of Trouble. 1963: It's a Mad, Mad, Mad, Mad World. 1966: A Funny Thing Happened on the Way to the Forum. 1967: Follow That Camel (later Carry On Follow That Camel). 1968: Buona Sera, Mrs Campbell. 1970: The Boatniks. 1975: The Deadly Tide (TV). The Strongest Man in the World. Won Ton Ton, the Dog Who Saved Hollywood. All Trails Lead to Las Vegas (TV). 1976: † Murder by Death. 1977: The Chicken Chronicles. The New Love Boat (TV). 1978: Racquet. The Night They Took Miss Beautiful (TV). The Cheap Detective. 1979: 'Hey Abbott!' (TV). Goldie and the Boxer (TV). 1980: The Happy Hooker Goes to Hollywood. Hollywood Blue.

† Scenes deleted from final release print.

SIM, Alastair 1900–1976

One of the British actors who made us laugh the loudest in post-war times wasn't really a comedian at all. Alastair Sim's expressions, diction and demeanour, though, were all unique. He was a pleasure to be savoured (even on your way to the cinema) in any role. His balding head, ghoulish eyes, twitching cheeks, drooping lower lip and open-mouthed dismay, as well as secret, uncontrollable schoolboy chuckles, made him a British eccentric of a highly relishable kind. He began life as the academic he was often to play on screen. Briefly in the family business of tailoring, he was soon involved in teaching poetic drama, later teaching elocution in his native Edinburgh. In his late twenties he came to London, and friends, seeing him perform in amateur productions, urged him to turn professional. So it was that

Ronald Shiner's famous nose is well to the fore as he and fellow policeman George Merritt inspect the evidence of a strangler at work in *The Case of the Frightened Lady*

Flash Harry (George Cole) anticipates a job for the undertaker when Miss Fritton (Alastair Sim) brandishes her cane in *The Belles of St Trinians*

An enthusiastic tennis player in real life, Jacques Tati reworks a routine from one of his early shorts in this scene from *Monsieur Hulot's Holiday*

Pipe dreams. Monsieur Hulot's mind is definitely not on the disasters that will befall him on his vacations. Jacques Tati in *Monsieur Hulot's Holiday*

he made his London West End stage debut at 29. Films eventually grabbed him after seeing him in a 1934 Christmas production of *Alice in Wonderland* as the Mad Hatter (a delicious prospect cinemagoers were denied) and he began appearing in movies at an unguessably right stage in his career. The first was *The Riverside Murder*, third-billed as one of several police-sergeants he would play in films, though Sim always seemed Inspector material. His first brush with broad comedy came later the same year, as one of two shyster lawyers called Cutte and Shuffle (he was Cutte) in the Flanagan and Allen (*qv*) film *A Fire Has Been Arranged*. Top billing came along in a minor sort of way in 1936 with *The Big Noise* as a gullible employee jacked up the ladder to carry the can for his bosses' dishonesty; but the film was neither big enough, nor funny enough to be a star-making vehicle. He was back with Flanagan, Allen and the Crazy Gang in *Alf's Button Afloat*, wickedly funny as the genie who takes the exclamation 'Strike me pink' as a command to *stripe* everything pink. Sim was coming to the fore, and the three popular Inspector Hornleigh comedy thrillers made between 1938 and 1941 (he was the sergeant again) gave him an even higher profile. They also marked the first major association between himself and the filmmaking partnership of Frank Launder and Sidney Gilliat, later to give him several of his best roles. In 1941 Sim gave the first of his numerous performances in one of his favourite roles, Captain Hook (and Mr Darling) in stage productions of *Peter Pan*. He was still dashing around in the role as late as 1965. Launder and Gilliat were responsible for making Sim an actor the post-war British public would pay to see when, though fourth-billed, he stole all the notices in their scary comedy-thriller *Green for Danger*, with his highly individual interpretation of the police investigator trying to discover the perpetrator of deadly goings-on at a wartime hospital. The role brought his quirky, edgy sense of humour to the fore, and gave him one of his most-quoted lines. Told that it's impurities in laughing gas that cause the laughter, Sim replies: 'Ah, yes. Much the same as in our English music-halls.' Now billed above the title, Sim was the bescarfed author of blood-and-thunder comics in Ealing's *Hue and Cry*, and the fake medium in the Launder/Gilliat *London Belongs to Me*. Next occupied with bringing a successful stage farce, *The Happiest Days of Your Life*, to the screen, the latter filmmakers rightly preserved Margaret Rutherford (*qv*) from the original production, but executed a master-stroke in bringing in Sim as her opposite number, head teachers both. The confrontations between the two, as her girls' school has to share premises (through a ministerial blunder) with his boys' school, are the stuff that hysteria is made of, she all truculence and determination, he all stiff-necked protest leading to dismayed whining and wheed-

In one of Alastair Sim's rare appearances in female disguise, he played both the headmistress and her rascally bookmaker brother in *The Belles of St Trinian's*

ling and a trip to the bathroom where he has to bed down for the night. The film was rightfully a roaring success all over Britain and even did respectably in America. When it came to making a new version of Charles Dickens' *A Christmas Carol* the following year (1951), there was really only one candidate for the lead. Sim remains an imperishable *Scrooge* (as the film was eventually called), convincing whether rattily shouting 'Bah!' or 'Humbug!' to companions, clerks and charities, in a state of quavering, gurgling panic over the visitation of ghosts, or expressing childlike glee when converted to the joys of the season. It remains as much the perfect blend of part and player as was Robert Newton a year earlier as Long John Silver in *Treasure Island*. Sim frequently had audiences eating out of his hand for the next decade. He guested as a movie mogul in

Lady Godiva Rides Again, played a novelist trying to commit a jailworthy offence to inherit money in *Laughter in Paradise*, doubled as the headmistress and her bookie brother in *The Belles of St Trinian's*, dominated *An Inspector Calls* as the mysterious title character and was brilliant as one of the world's least likely assassins in *The Green Man*. Sim was to have co-directed the last one, too, but dropped out after disagreement in casting. He has, however, directed numerous stage productions. And the stage was where he was now heading, as the flourishing of films in post-war Britain faltered. There were no Sim appearances in 1957 and 1958 for filmgoers to savour, apart from the briefest of guest spots as the now-imprisoned headmistress in the first St Trinian's sequel. At the end of the decade, he supported Ian Carmichael in a couple, *Left, Right and Centre* and *School for Scoundrels*. He was the head-master of the title school in the latter, the last film example of Sim's own brand of devious cunning, doomed usually (though not in this case) to failure. He was more genuinely benevolent in his few remaining film roles, but was much missed amid the coarser comedy surging through British film-making of the 1960s and 1970s. He died from cancer a few weeks short of his 76th birthday.

1935: *The Riverside Murder. The Case of Gabriel Perry/Wild Justice. A Fire Has Been Arranged. The Private Secretary. Late Extra.* 1936: *Wedding Group (US: Wrath of Jealousy). Troubled Waters. Keep Your Seats Please. The Mysterious Mr Davis (US: My Partner Mr Davis). The Big Noise. The Man in the Mirror. She Knew What She Wanted. Strange Experiment.* 1937: *The Squeaker (US: Murder on Diamond Row). Clothes and the Woman. Melody and Romance. Gangway. A Romance in Flanders (US: Lost on the Western Front).* 1938: *Alf's Button Afloat. Sailing Along. The Terror. Climbing High. This Man is News. Inspector Hornleigh.* 1939: *This Man in Paris. Inspector Hornleigh on Holiday.* 1940: *Law and Disorder. Her Father's Daughter.* 1941: *Cottage to Let (US: Bombsite Stolen). Inspector Hornleigh Goes to It (US: Mail Train).* 1942: *Let the People Sing.* 1943: * *Fiddling Fuel.* 1944: *Waterloo Road.* 1945: *Journey Together.* 1946: *Green for Danger.* 1947: *Hue and Cry. Captain Boycott.* 1948: *London Belongs to Me (US: Dulcimer Street).* 1950: *The Happiest Days of Your Life. Stage Fright.* 1951: *Laughter in Paradise. Lady Godiva Rides Again. Scrooge (US: A Christmas Carol).* 1952: *Folly to be Wise.* 1953: *Innocents in Paris.* 1954: *The Belles of St Trinian's. An Inspector Calls.* 1955: *Escapade.* * *Festival in Edinburgh (narrator only). Geordie (US: Wee Geordie).* 1956: *The Green Man.* 1957: *Blue Murder at St Trinian's.* 1959: *The Doctor's Dilemma. Left, Right and Centre. School for Scoundrels.* 1960: *The Millionairess.* 1961: *The Anatomist.* 1971: *The Ruling Class.* 1975: *Royal Flash.* 1976: *Rogue Male (TV). Escape from the Dark (US: The Littlest Horse Thieves).*

SIMS, Joan
(Irene J. Sims) 1930–
Pleasantly-plump, jolly, fair-haired British comedy actress described by one latter-day interviewer as 'a sweet woman and a good laugh'. After honing her impish comedy skills in stage revue she played supporting roles in nearly 30 films before becoming a regular member of the 'Carry On' comedies, moving from twittering, man-hungry cockneys to nagging, dragon-like wives as the series progressed. The only child of a railway stationmaster, Joan was always 'on'. 'I'd dress up and do an act for passengers, or the signalman. I was a weird child.' The weird child went to RADA, in spite of her parents' misgivings, and made her debut in repertory in 1950. By 1952 her talent had already got her into a West End revue, *Intimacy at Eight*.

There were several more such shows before she really made her name in *Intimacy at 8.30* two years later, becoming much written about for her routine as a girl who puts sex appeal into station loudspeaker announcements – an idea which doubtless had its roots in her own childhood. She had already made her film debut (in 1953) in *Will Any Gentleman? . . .*, and was soon at home in film farce, playing a teacher in *The Belles of St Trinian's* and saucy roles in 'Doctor' comedies. The cinema was to dominate her life for the next 20 years, a period when she returned to the stage only four times. She became a favourite foil of such TV comedians as Dick Emery (*qv*) and Stanley Baxter, and made her first appearance in a 'Carry On' comedy film with *Carry On Nurse* in 1959. Twenty-three more 'Carry Ons', plus three more 'Doctors' and several other ensemble comedies were to follow. Joan has never married and the 'Carry On' team became something of a surrogate family for her. 'We would work together twice a year', she once recalled, 'and it was always a very happy time. There were pranks and jokes, but it was hard work. Of course, they were all the same – variations on a theme and the familiar tired jokes. It was saucy post-card humour, but never got beyond family entertainment. If you were old enough to understand the innuendoes and remember the jokes, you were old enough. As for it being glamorous, the furthest I ever got on location for a 'Carry On' was Snowdonia for *Carry On Abroad*, which was supposed to be set in Spain. The prop man was holding a palm tree to stop it blowing over and I was under a lamp because my nose was turning blue with the cold.' She admits that she found the going tough after the series ended but, since the mid 1980s, has been busy again on TV. In comedy of course, although there was one occasion when she played a murderess in the 1979 true-life series *Lady-killers*. 'Making people laugh', she said, 'is a front you put on, a barrier you erect. A lot of comics are inwardly quite serious. In *Lady-killers*, I was thrilled to be able to make people churn in their stomachs, and make people feel sorry for me – much more difficult than just coming on and seeing people laugh.'

1953: *Will Any Gentleman? . . . The Square Ring. Colonel March Investigates. Trouble in Store. Meet Mr Lucifer.* 1954: *Doctor in the House. What Every Woman Wants. The Young Lovers (US: Chance Meeting). The Belles of St Trinian's. To Dorothy a Son (US: Cash on Delivery). The Sea Shall Not Have Them.* 1955: *As Long As They're Happy. Doctor at Sea. Lost (US: Tears for Simon).* 1956: *Keep It Clean. The Silken Affair. Stars in Your Eyes. Dry Rot.* 1957: *Just My Luck. Davy. Carry On Admiral (US: The Ship Was Loaded). No Time for Tears. The Naked Truth (US: Your Past is Showing).* 1958: *The Captain's Table.* 1959: *Passport to Shame (US: Room 43). Carry On Nurse. Life in Emergency Ward 10. Carry On Teacher. Upstairs and Downstairs. Please Turn Over.* 1960: *Carry On Constable. Doctor in Love. Watch Your Stern. His and Hers.* 1961: *Carry On Regardless. Mr Topaze (US: I Like Money). No, My Darling Daughter! A Pair of Briefs.* 1962: *Twice Round the Daffodils. The Iron Maiden (US: The Swingin' Maiden). Nurse on Wheels.* 1963: *Strictly for the Birds.* 1964: *Carry On Cleo.* 1965: *The Big Job. San Ferry Ann. Carry On Cowboy. Doctor in Clover.* 1966: *Carry On Screaming. Don't Lose Your Head.* 1967: *Follow That Camel. Carry On Doctor.* 1968: *Carry On Up the Khyber.* 1969: *Carry On Camping. Carry On Again, Doctor. Carry On Up the Jungle.* 1970: *Doctor in Trouble. Carry On Loving. Carry on Henry.* 1971: *The Magnificent Seven Deadly Sins. Carry On at Your Convenience.* 1972: *Carry On Matron. The Alf Garnett Saga. Carry On Abroad. Not Now Darling.* 1973: *Carry On Girls. Don't Just Lie There, Say Something.* 1974: *Carry On Dick. Love Among the Ruins (TV).* 1975: *Carry On Behind. One of Our Dinosaurs is Missing.* 1976: *Carry on England.* 1978: *Carry On Emmannuelle.* 1990: *The Fool.*

SINGLETON, Penny
(Mariana Dorothy McNulty) 1908–
It's strange that a career-making role as a scatterbrained blonde should have gone to one of the brightest (and originally brunette!) people in the acting business. For a later role in the career of newspaperman's daughter Penny Singleton was as spokesman

for the American Guild of Variety Artists, some of whom dubbed her 'the brains of the Union'. Yet it was as half of a union that had no brains, the infamous Blondie and Dagwood of strip cartoon fame, that Penny Singleton achieved a lifelong niche in film history. In this capacity she showed she could almost have been a rival for Judy Holliday (qv) in post-war years had not the Blondie series so typecast her in people's minds. But the early Penny Singleton, or Dorothy McNulty as she was known in her first Hollywood years, was tall, dark, gawky, thin-mouthed and sharp-witted. Even at six years old, Dorothy was singing and dancing at a show business school. One of her fellow-pupils was Milton Berle (qv). At 18 she was playing straight girl for Jack Benny (qv) in revue, but it was her musical talents that got her into Hollywood, in the first (1930) screen version of the college musical *Good News*, although not in the same role she had played on stage. It took six more years of stage work before Dorothy decided to try again. In 1938 she changed her name to Penny Singleton and, among many other roles in a hectic year, appeared opposite Humphrey Bogart in *Swing Your Lady*. The film was bad but the new Penny (still dark-haired) was good, as a sort of harebrained Eve Arden (qv). The performance caught the eye of Columbia, who had just parted company with the actress who was to have played Blondie, and they called Penny across from Warners for a test. It proved positive; Penny went blonde to play Blondie and stayed that way thereafter. Under her skilled interpretation, the Blondie character was just about believable – and an instant success, the first film grossing nine times its cost and spawning 27 sequels. Up to the end of 1943, the films, all directed by Frank R. Strayer, maintained a generally excellent standard. After a gap of two years, the series returned without Strayer and, even with Singleton's peppy performances, the decline in standards was soon apparent. In the series, Blondie and Dagwood would generally work to cross-purposes, leaving Dagwood in a fine mess which Blondie somehow contrived to sort out before the end. They were greatly aided in their audience appeal by a cute kid called Larry Simms who appeared (and grew up with the series) as Baby Dumpling and a talented dog called Daisy. In one film, *Blondie Goes Latin*, Singleton even got a chance to show that she could sing and dance. When the series ended in 1950 Singleton returned to stage musical work. Union business followed in the 1960s and she soon proved that she had a talent for organisation and negotiation as well as screen comedy. She helped win better working conditions for showgirls in the famous Radio City Rockettes strike of 1966, and remained active in union business until the late 1970s, at one time ousting the entire board of the AGVA (in 1974) when she felt they were not adequately serving their members. Some going for a dizzy dame!

1929: *† *Belle of the Night*. 1930: † *Good News*. † *Love in the Rough*. 1936. † *After the Thin Man*. 1937: † *Vogues of 1938/Vogues*. † *Sea Racketeers*. 1938: *Men Are Such Fools*. *Outside of Paradise*. *Mr Chump*. *Garden of the Moon*. *Hard to Get*. *Swing Your Lady*. * *Campus Cinderella*. *The Mad Miss Manton*. *Boy Meets Girl*. *Secrets of an Actress*. *Blondie*. *Racket Busters*. 1939: *Blondie Meets the Boss*. *Blondie Brings Up Baby*. *Blondie Takes a Vacation*. 1940: *Blondie on a Budget*. *Blondie Has Servant Trouble*. *Blondie Plays Cupid*. 1941: *Blondie Goes Latin (GB: Conga Swing)*. *Blondie in Society (GB: Henpecked)*. *Go West, Young Lady*. 1942: *Blondie for Victory (GB: Troubles Through Billets)*. *Blondie Goes to College (GB: The Boss Said 'No')*. *Blondie's Blessed Event (GB: A Bundle of Trouble)*. 1943: *Footlight Glamour*. *It's a Great Life*. 1945: *Leave It to Blondie*. *Life with Blondie*. 1946: *Blondie's Lucky Day*. *Blondie Knows Best*. *Young Widow*. *Blondie's Big Moment*. 1947: *Blondie's Holiday*. *Blondie in the Dough*. *Blondie's Anniversary*. 1948: *Blondie's Secret*. *Blondie's Reward*. 1949: *Blondie Hits the Jackpot (GB: Hitting the Jackpot)*. *Blondie's Big Deal (GB: The Big Deal)*. 1950: *Beware of Blondie*. *Blondie's Hero*. 1964: *The Best Man*. 1990: *Jetsons the Movie (voice only)*.

† As Dorothy McNulty.

SKELTON, Red
(Richard Skelton) 1910–

Why is it that 1940s comedy (especially in Hollywood) has worn less well than comedy from any other decade? Perhaps because American screen comedians had less control over their material in this period (and into the first half of the 1950s) than at any other time. Few comedians of the time directed their own material, or were even given time to try it out in live performance. Thus the decline of Laurel and Hardy and the Marx Brothers (both qv). The work of Red Skelton, Abbott and Costello, Danny Kaye and even some Bob Hope (all qv) comedies from the period today look rushed and ill-paced, while lesser comedians are simply forgotten men. Never was comedy more popular than at this time, and never were audiences prepared to accept fun fare at such a low standard. Skelton, a funny man on radio and (to a slightly lesser extent) on

television, was good enough to stay popular in films for a decade without ever becoming a major money-spinner. He had a funny, india-rubber face, with a pencil-line mouth that could split open into the most extraordinary shapes, and expressive limbs beneath clothes that frequently looked a shade too big. If he often seemed brash and over-the-top, who could blame him at MGM, where he was never quite allowed to develop a relaxed style of his own? Still, you couldn't help but like the man on screen, even if he sometimes outstayed his welcome. But the more low-key he played it, the more pleasure he gave, especially in comedies similar in style to those that had shot Hope to stardom, even though Skelton's gag-writers at the time couldn't quite compare with Hope's. The son of a circus clown who died before he was born, Red had an impoverished childhood, the beginning of a traumatic private life that remained carefully guarded until the inevitable latter-day biographies revealed all. After busking on the streets of his home town in Indiana as a child, Skelton left home at ten to join a medicine show, where he sang in blackface. A veteran of circuses, showboats and minstrel shows at 15, he moved into burlesque and eventually developed routines of his own that had audiences in stitches. These poked fun at the way people did various things. The one that got the most laughs was a skit that showed how someone's personality would show up in the way he dunked his doughnut in coffee. The 'dunkin' doughnuts' routine became Skelton's trademark, and an ever-popular part of his repertoire. He made his debut on radio and clicked right away with audiences. Film fame, though, remained elusive until Metro signed Skelton in 1940. Billed as Richard 'Red' Skelton in his earlier films (he had flaming red hair), he dropped the Richard once at MGM, where he was rather mysteriously 'nursed along' with a variety of straight and comic supporting roles in other people's pictures. At the end of 1941 the studio gave him his first starring vehicle, *Whistling in the Dark*, casting him as a chicken-hearted radio detective known as 'The Fox', who proves far less adept at solving the real-life mysteries he finds himself mixed up in, than at the ones he tackles on the air. Although the film sired two successful sequels, the studio seemed more interested in Red as comedy relief in splashy (sometimes literally when they starred Esther Williams) musicals. Later, when Skelton came under the influence of writer Frank Tashlin and former comedy star Buster Keaton (qv), he made some fast-moving slapstick comedies in which he seemed entirely at home, and which comprised his last wholly successful vehicles: *The Fuller Brush Man* (in Britain, *That Mad Mr Jones*), *A Southern Yankee* (in Britain, *My Hero*) and *The Yellow Cab Man*. Attempts at pathos were predictably less successful, and Skelton saw out his MGM contract with a couple of fairly minor 'B' films in 1953. That year he began a wildly successful TV comedy show which ran for the next two decades. During that time, his son Richard Jr died from leukaemia at only nine, and his second wife shot herself. She later recovered, although the couple divorced in 1971. Once described as 'that greatest of contradictions, a mime artist who was most successful on radio', Skelton proved on TV that he could be visually funny when given the spotlight all to himself. Not that he didn't agonise over those performances as well as all of those on film. His first wife once said that 'He just couldn't see how funny he sometimes was. It was a wonder to him that he'd ever gotten this far.'

1938: *Having Wonderful Time.* 1939: * *Seein' Red.* * *Broadway Buckaroo.* 1940: *Flight Command.* 1941: *The People vs. Dr Kildare* (GB: *My Life is Yours*). *Dr Kildare's Wedding Day* (GB: *Mary Names the Day*). *Lady Be Good. Whistling in the Dark.* 1942: *Maisie Gets Her Man* (GB: *She Got Her Man*). *Panama Hattie. Ship Ahoy. Whistling in Dixie.* 1943: *DuBarry Was a Lady. I Dood It* (GB: *By Hook or By Crook*). *Thousands Cheer. Whistling in Brooklyn.* 1944: *Bathing Beauty. Ziegfeld Follies* (released 1946). * *Radio Bugs* (voice only). 1946: *The Show-Off.* * *Luckiest Guy in the World* (voice only). 1947: *Merton of the Movies.* 1948: *A Southern Yankee* (GB: *My Hero*). *The Fuller Brush Man* (GB: *That Mad Mr Jones*). 1949: *Neptune's Daughter.* 1950: *The Yellow Cab Man. The Fuller Brush Girl* (GB: *The Affairs of Sally*). *Three Little Words. Duchess of Idaho. Watch the Birdie.* 1951: *Texas Carnival. Excuse My Dust.* 1952: *Lovely to Look At. The Clown.* 1953: *Half a Hero. The Great Diamond Robbery.* 1954: *Susan Slept Here.* 1956: *The Big Slide* (TV). *Around the World in 80 Days.* 1957: *Public Pigeon No. 1.* 1960: *Ocean's Eleven.* 1965: *Those Magnificent Men in Their Flying Machines.*

Well might Red Skelton look flustered at getting such a powerful partner as Eleanor Powell in the MGM comedy-musical *I Dood It*, a remake of the Buster Keaton classic *Spite Marriage*

SMITH, Joe
(Joseph Seltzer) (left) 1884–1980
and
DALE, Charlie
(Charles Marks) 1881–1971

Remarkably long-lived Jewish vaudevillians who worked together for 70 years. Irascible cross-talkers, they made only a handful of films but will go down in history as the originals of the grouchy old comedians portrayed by Walter Matthau and George Burns (qv) in Neil Simon's *The Sunshine Boys*. Smith was the more manic of the two, a tall, dark-haired man with a frenzied gleam in his eye, his nose and chin both shaped like arrows. Dale was his smaller, quieter partner, though he was often given the better of their verbal exchanges, notably in their famous Dr Kronkhite sketch which would later be reprised almost intact in *The Sunshine Boys*. Smith and Dale would insist in later years that they met as teenagers on New York's Delancey Street in 1898 when their bicycles collided. Both interested in getting a foothold in show business, they thought up a comic dancing act which they hawked with varying success around the saloons and halls of the city's Lower East Side. Becoming part of an act called the Avon Four (in which Dr Kronkhite made his debut), Smith and Dale finally hit Broadway in 1916. The Avons broke up into two double acts three years later, and Smith and Dale became part of the Broadway revue scene for more than 30 years. There were a few film shorts from time to time, and cameo appearances in larger films, but Smith and Dale always seemed content to take their own particular brand of escalating insanity back to the stage. They appeared on TV in the late 1950s in a show called *Life Begins at Eighty* (even though they hadn't quite got there) and as late as 1970 were still entertaining nightly at a club in New York. The team was finally broken by Charlie Dale's death a year later at the age of 90. In later days, Smith would tell Dale (and the audience): 'You should go to the mountains for your rheumatism'. 'Is mountains good for rheumatism?' Dale would ask. 'Sure', Smith replied. 'That's where I got mine.'

1929: * *Knights in Venice.* * *The False Alarm*

Fire Campany. 1930: * Schnapps Inc. * The S.S. Malaria. * Accidents Will Happen. * The Great Pants Mystery. 1931: Manhattan Parade. * What Price Pants? * The Arabian Shrieks. 1932: The Heart of New York. 1938: * A Nag in the Bag. 1939: * Mutiny on the Body. 1951: Two Tickets to Broadway.

SMITH, Mel (right) 1952–
and
RHYS JONES, Griff 1953–

Once revered for their rudeness as they ascended to fame on TV in the ingeniously-titled Alas Smith and Jones, these two British comedians were soon overtaken as the bad boys of TV, as is the nature of things, by even ruder comics. Now their shows remain middle-brow half-hours to treasure, just as Morecambe and Wise and the Two Ronnies were looked forward to by British TV viewers in their day. The funniest things that Smith and Jones did – and still do – in these programmes are their head-to-heads; dressed in white sweaters or shirts against a black background, they indulge in delightfully-structured cross-talk, poker-faced in a sea of deliberate misunderstandings. The failure to transfer this kind of comedy, a descendant of the Peter Cook/Dudley Moore (both qv) 'raincoat' discussions on sex and the world, to the screen, goes some way to explaining their flops in films so far. It's Smith who has had the greatest success to date here, by diversifying more in solo appearances, though Jones has proved himself a solo attraction in farces and festive shows on stage. They come from quite different backgrounds. Jones, long-jawed and lugubrious, with dark curly hair, is a doctor's son, Welsh by descent, but brought up in Essex and educated at Cambridge University. Smith, plump and piggy, with small eyes, a drooping lower lip and disappearing fair hair, is the son of a Durham miner who came to London and became a bookmaker. Mel's brightness at school got him to Oxford University to study experimental psychology, but he never completed the course despite becoming president of the Oxford Union Debating Society. Instead, he became an assistant director at London's Royal Court Theatre, and then moved to the Young Vic,

from where he 'stormed out in high dudgeon after a row'. Jones performed with the famous Cambridge Footlights Society then, on leaving university, joined the BBC as a producer. Smith had gone north as associate director at Sheffield's Crucible Theatre but he, too, ended up at the BBC, where he and Jones were two of the writers for the BBC2 comedy programme Not the Nine O'Clock News in the late 1970s. They also performed on camera in support of stars Rowan Atkinson and Pamela Stephenson, and decided to stay together as a team. Alas Smith and Jones began in 1981 and has continued every year since, with a break between 1990 and 1992 when both found their schedules too hectic to fit a series in. During the run, they have had a couple of attempts at making films together. They clearly learned something from Morons from Outer Space, a disgusting mess, as their next, Wilt, four years later, though disappointing,

was a clear improvement. Things may still go their way in the cinema, though Smith has proved more effective in the few tough, straight, hard-cursing, blue-collar roles he has tackled in dramatic films. 'I'd love to do more serious stuff', he has said, 'but no-one approaches me.' So he went off and indulged in his other passion – directing. His feature film debut came, after several TV commercials, with the erotic offbeat comedy The Tall Guy, which drew a mixed critical reception but was certainly popular by the recent standards of star Jeff Goldblum. Smith also made a cameo appearance, rather inevitably as a belching drunk. He and Jones have both admitted to alcohol problems that now seem to be behind them. In recent times Jones, too, has branched out on his own, in a TV film and as Toad in Toad of Toad Hall. He described that as 'my equivalent of playing Hamlet', although the following year (1992) he really was trying Shakespeare, in

Wilt thou have this woman? Griff Rhys Jones wants to get rid of the inflatable Angelique. Mel Smith would like to find her, in Wilt.

a film version of *As You Like It*. There are no plans for a permanent split, though, and the team continues to look for suitable films to do together. 'We make a good team', says Mel. 'I'm laid back and relaxed, Griff is edgy and tense but has a brilliant mind. It's a bit like a marriage – you go on with it as long as you're having fun.'

Together. *1985: Morons from Outer Space. 1989: Wilt.*
Smith alone. *1980: Babylon. 1983: Bullshot. 1984: Number One. 1985: Restless Natives. National Lampoon's European Vacation. 1987: The Princess Bride. 1988: The Wolves of Willoughby Chase. 1989: The Tall Guy (and directed). 1991: Father Christmas (voice only). Lame Ducks.*
Jones alone. *1982: The Secret Policeman's Other Ball. 1991: Ex (TV). 1992: As You Like It.*

STARK, Graham 1922–
This short, stocky, scurrying, mischievous-looking, Mr Punch-faced British comic character has done almost everything in a 55-year show business career except become a major star. Boy actor, scriptwriter, director, photographer, radio actor and friend of the famous, Stark has almost never stopped shuffling across our radio, television and cinema lives, often in disguise and usually looking as if he's about to double up with laughter. Born in London, Stark got into acting before World War Two, then joined up and found himself in comedy, as part of the RAF Gang Show. Among his fellow-performers were Dick Emery, Peter Sellers and Tony Hancock (all *qv*). In post-war years, there were four years of struggle in repertory companies and he was on the breadline until Hancock got him a job on a variety show called *Happy Go Lucky*. The star of the show was comedian Derek Roy, but it was stolen each week by a troop of boy scouts comprised of Hancock, Stark, Peter Butterworth (*qv*) and Bill Kerr. That set Hancock on the road to stardom, and Stark on to a treadmill of funny voices in such radio comedy hits as *Ray's a Laugh, Educating Archie* and *The Goon Show*, for which he also contributed script material. Stark appeared with the Goons in their early films *Down*

Among the Z Men, The Super Secret Service and *Forces' Sweetheart*, as well as their television series *A Show Called Fred* and *Son of Fred*. And from 1959 he began appearing more regularly in films, in character roles. His association with arch-Goon Peter Sellers continued with parts in all of the 'Pink Panther' films, once in two roles. 'I kept turning up in those films like a bad penny', he remembers. 'But I couldn't resist doing them, because we had such a hilarious time making them.' In the meantime, BBC-TV had attempted to make the little man a star in his own right with *The Graham Stark Show* in 1965. But it flopped in the ratings. Stark blamed sketches that were 'too cruelly satirical'. He also attempted to break into direction but it was a short-lived experiment. With photography, he has had more luck, having had exhibitions of his work. In the cinema, he continued to crop up in increasingly broad comic vignettes. He became reconciled to being a familiar face that made you smile, but not the name above the title. 'I'm very happy where I am' he said in the 1980s. 'I'm simply hired to do a job of work,

and that's what I enjoy doing best. It's like running a marathon. One way or another I never seem to have stopped working.'

1939: The Spy in Black (US: U-Boat 29). 1952: Emergency Call (US: Hundred Hour Hunt). Down Among the Z Men. 1953: * The Super Secret Service. Forces' Sweetheart. Flannelfoot. 1954: Johnny on the Spot. The Sea Shall Not Have Them. 1955: * Song of Norway. 1956: They Never Learn. 1959: Inn for Trouble. Sink the Bismarck! 1960: * The Running, Jumping and Standing Still Film. The Millionairess. 1961: Dentist on the Job (US: Get On With It!). Watch It Sailor! She'll Have to Go (US: Maid for Murder). A Weekend with Lulu. Double Bunk. Only Two Can Play. On the Fiddle (US: Operation Snafu). Village of Daughters. A Pair of Briefs. 1962: Operation Snatch. The Wrong Arm of the Law. Lancelot and Guinevere (US: Sword of Lancelot). 1963: The Mouse on the Moon. Ladies Who Do. Strictly for the Birds. The Pink Panther. Becket. 1964: Guns at Batasi. A Shot in the Dark. Go Kart Go! 1965: Runaway Railway. San Ferry Ann. Those Magnificent Men in Their Flying

Graham Stark puts on his famous perturbed expression when disturbed in the undergrowth with a close friend during *Rhubarb*

Machines. You Must Be Joking! 1966: Alfie. Finders Keepers. The Wrong Box. 1967: Casino Royale. The Plank. Jules Verne's Rocket to the Moon (US: Those Fantastic Flying Fools). Ghost of a Chance. 1968: Salt and Pepper. 1969: The Picasso Summer. Start the Revolution Without Me. The Magic Christian. 1970: * Simon Simon. Scramble. Doctor in Trouble. Rhubarb. 1972: Hide and Seek. 1973: * The Laughing Girl Murder. * Le Pétomane (released 1979). Secrets of a Door-to-Door Salesman. 1974: Where's Johnny? Return of the Pink Panther. 1975: I'm Not Feeling Myself Tonight. The Remarkable Rocket (voice only). 1976: Gulliver's Travels (voice only). The Pink Panther Strikes Again. Virginity/Come una rosa al naso. 1977: The Prince and the Pauper (US: Crossed Swords). Hardcore (US: Fiona). What's Up Nurse? Chimpmates (second series). Let's Get Laid. 1978: Revenge of the Pink Panther. 1979: There Goes the Bride. The Prisoner of Zenda. 1980: Hawk the Slayer. The Sea Wolves. 1982: Trail of the Pink Panther. Victor/Victoria. 1983: Superman III. Curse of the Pink Panther. Bloodbath at the House of Death. 1986: Neat and Tidy (TV). 1987: Jane and the Lost City. Blind Date.

As director. 1970: * Simon Simon. 1971: The Magnificent Seven Deadly Sins.

STERLING, Ford
(George F. Stitch) 1880–1939
Dark-haired, scowling, arm-waving American silent comedian whose solid, handsome features were usually concealed by a goatee beard and a frenzied variety of facial grimaces. Until the arrival of Charlie Chaplin (qv), Sterling was the top star at Mack Sennett's Keystone Studio, often co-starring with Sennett's other great attraction, Mabel Normand (qv). Born in Wisconsin, Sterling ran away from home at 14 to join a circus. Billed as Keno the Boy Clown, he soon proved a major attraction, and stayed with the circus for five years, later gaining acrobatic experience with the Flying Leos. After touring in vaudeville, Sterling entered the growing motion picture industry with Biograph in 1911. He met comedy actor-director Mack Sennett there, and went with him when Sennett formed his own studio, Keystone, the following year. Soon, he was

making one- and two-reel comedies there at a phenomenal rate — more than one a week in 1913. Following Chaplin's arrival early in 1914, Sterling was switched to villains and leading character roles. He became the apoplectic Chief Teeheezal of the Keystone Kops in many films, perhaps most notably opposite Fatty Arbuckle in In the Clutches of a Gang. Later Sennett gave Sterling his own comedy series again, plus a little experience in directing, but his exaggerated style of comedy dated quickly, and he left Sennett in 1921 to take on character roles in feature films for the rest of the decade. With the coming of sound, Sterling found that his broad mugging often stood out like a sore thumb in film comedy, rather like that of Edgar Kennedy (qv) who was a king in two-reel comedy but often an embarrassment in longer films. Kennedy was able to prolong his career in film shorts, but Sterling's chances of doing the same, after a few starring shorts in the early sound years, were irreparably damaged when he lost a leg in an accident. It was a great blow to a man accustomed to using body language and wild stunts to get his comedy across. There were a few more roles for him in the early 1930s, but he had been out of films for almost three years when he died from a coronary thrombosis at 58. His wife, former actress Teddy Sampson, outlived him by 31 years.

1911: * Abe Gets Even with Father. 1912: * The Flirting Husband. * Cohen Collects a Debt. * The Beating He Needed. * A Bear Escape. * The Deacon's Troubles. * The Water Nymph. * Riley and Schultz. * The New Neighbor. * Pedro's Dilemma. * Stolen Glory. * The Ambitious Butler. * The Flirting Husband. * The Grocery Clerk's Romance. * At It Again. * Pat's Day Off. * The Deacon's Troubles. * At Coney Island. * A Temperamental Husband. * The Rivals. * Mr Fix-It. * A Midnight Elopement. * Mabel's Adventures. * Hoffmeyer's Legacy. 1913: * On His Wedding Day. * The New Conductor. * That Rag Time Band. * Hide and Seek. * Safe in Jail. * The Firebugs. * The Gusher. * A Double Wedding. * The Cure That Failed. * How Hiram Won Out. * The Mistaken Masher. * The Elite Ball. * Just Brown's Luck. * The Battle of Who Run. * The Stolen Purse. * Heinze's Resurrection. * The Professor's Daughter. * The Sleuths at the Floral P-Rade. * The Two Widows. * A Strong Revenge. * The Rube and the Baron. * The Man Next Door. * On His Wedding Day. * Murphy's IOU. * A Poker Game. * His Ups and Downs. * A Fishy Affair. * Barney Oldfield's Race for Life. * The Speed Queen. * The Hansom Driver. * Out and In. * The Waiters' Picnic. * Peeping Pete. * Love and Rubbish. * His Crooked Career. * The Peddler. * Professor Bean's Removal. * A Game of Pool. * Cohen's Outing. * The Firebugs. * Baby Day. * The Bowling Match. * Mabel's Dramatic Career. * Schnitz the Tailor. * A Healthy Neighborhood. * Love Sickness at Sea. * The Speed Kings. * Cohen Saves the Flag. * A

Landlord's Trouble. * The Deacon Outwitted. * The Land Salesman. * A Red Hot Romance. * A Life in the Balance. * Father's Choice. * The Faithful Taxicab. * When Dreams Come True. * A Small Time Act. * Teddy Telzlaff and Earl Cooper — Speed Kings. * A Muddy Romance. * A Bad Game. * Some Nerve. * The Bangville Police. * Rastus and the Game Cock. * For Lizzie's Sake. * Toplitsky and Company. * Wine Making. * Zuzu, the Band Leader. 1914: * Between Showers. * Tango Tangles. * Love and Dynamite. Raffles — Gentleman Burglar. * A Dramatic Mistake. * Too Many Brides. * A Robust Romeo. * Double Crossed. * A False Beauty. * The Minstrel Man. * In the Clutches of a Gang. 1915: * That Little Band of Gold. * Our Dare Devil Chief. * Only a Messenger Boy. * Court House Crooks. *‡ His Father's Footsteps. *‡ The Hunt. * Ambrose's Little Hatchet. * He Wouldn't Stay Down. * Dirty Work in a Laundry. 1916: * Fatty and the Broadway Stars. *‡ His Pride and Shame. *‡ His Wild Oats. * The Snow Cure. *‡ His Lying Heart. *† The Manicurist. 1917: *† Stars and Bars. * A Maiden's Trust. * Her Torpedoed Love. * Pinched in the Finish. 1918: * Beware of Boarders. * Her Screen Idol. * Moonshine. 1919: * Trying to Get Along. * Hearts and Flowers. * His Last False Step. * Yankee Doodle in Berlin/The Kaiser's Last Squeal. 1920: * His Youthful Fancy. * Married Life. * Don't Weaken. * Love, Honor and Behave. 1921: * A Ladies' Tailor. * Among Those Present. * Uncle Tom Without the Cabin. * An Unhappy Finish. 1922: *‡ Oh! Mabel Behave (completed in 1917). * The Stranger's Banquet. Quincy Adams Sawyer. 1923: The Brass Bottle. The Day of Faith. The Spoilers. Hollywood. The Destroying Angel. Guardian Angel. 1924: Wild Oranges. Galloping Fish. Love and Glory. He Who Gets Slapped. The Woman on the Jury. So Big. 1925: The Trouble with Wives. Daddy's Gone a-Hunting. Stage Struck. Steppin' Out. My Lady's Lips. 1926: The Road to Glory. Good and Naughty. Miss Brewster's Millions. The American Venus. Everybody's Acting. Stranded in Paris. The Show-Off. Mike. 1927: Casey at the Bat. Drums of the Desert. For the Love of Mike. Hearts and Flowers (and 1919 film). The Trunk Mystery. The Little Widow. 1928: Sporting Goods. Wife Savers. Gentlemen Prefer Blondes. Oh, Kay! Chicken a la King. Mr Romeo. That's My Daddy. 1929: * The Fatal Forceps. The Fall of Eve. Sally. Figures Don't Lie. 1930: * Our Nagging Wives. Bride of the Regiment (GB: Lady of the Rose). Kismet. Show Girl in Hollywood. Spring is Here. Girl in the Show. 1931: * Come to Papa. * The Foolish Forties. * It Ought to Be a Crime. * Trouble from Abroad. * Stars of Yesterday. * Auto Intoxication. 1932: * Pretty Puppies. * Twenty Horses. 1933: Alice in Wonderland. 1935: The Headline Woman (GB: The Woman in the Case). Behind the Green Lights. Black Sheep. * All Business. * A Returned Engagement. * Keystone Hotel. 1936: * Framing Father. * Bridle Grease. 1937: * Many Unhappy Returns.

† Also directed
‡ Also co-directed

ST JOHN, Al 'Fuzzy' 1893–1963

A plump-nosed, stringy, smiley, sandy-haired, pale-eyed, funny-to-look-at American comedian, the nephew of Fatty Arbuckle (*qv*). A vaudevillian from boyhood, St John began his career as a trick cyclist at 14. Five years later he had found his way into films via the Keystone studio, where he occasionally played a Keystone cop, as well as stooging for the company's roster of comedians, including Arbuckle, Charlie Chaplin and Mabel Normand (all *qv*). In these he typically played a hayseed character in too-short trousers, too-tight jacket, plaid shirt and vacuous expression. If his comedy had more energy than invention, his skilful manipulation of his gangling limbs – he often worked his bicycling and acrobatic talents into his roles – made him an amusing supporting foil. In the 1920s St John had a few starring comedies of his own, often writing, producing and directing as well, activities which led him to spend a greater part of the decade behind the camera. With the 1930s, though, came his best-known persona – as the bewhiskered, yarn-spinning, pop-eyed comic sidekick of numerous western heroes, including Buster Crabbe, Bob Steele, Fred Scott and Lash La Rue. It was in one of his films with Scott that he first created the character of 'Fuzzy Q. Jones', which gave him his nickname, and which he played in dozens of other 'B' oaters. In these low-budget horse-operas, St John's antics were often the focus of attention and in one, *Fuzzy Settles Down*, he even got his character into the title. His last westerns were with Al 'Lash' La Rue, but with the demise of the genre St John retired from films at 60, to a house he had acquired in Georgia. Only nine years later, however, he died there from a heart attack.

1913: * *Algy on the Force.* * *The Waiters' Picnic.* * *The Gangsters.* 1914: * *All at Sea.* * *Lover's Luck.* * *He Loved The Ladies.* * *The Knockout.* * *Bombs and Bangs.* * *In the Clutches of a Gang.* * *Our Country Cousin.* * *The Rounders.* * *The New Janitor (GB: The New Porter).* *Tillie's Punctured Romance.* * *Mabel's New Job.* * *The Sky Pirate.* 1915: * *Mabel, Fatty and the Law.* * *Mabel's Wilful*

Way. * *Dirty Work in a Laundry.* * *Our Dare Devil Chief.* * *A Village Scandal.* * *Fickle Fatty's Fall.* * *Crossed Love and Swords.* * *Fatty and the Broadway Stars.* * *Fatty's Magic Party.* 1916: * *Fatty and Mabel Adrift.* * *Bright Lights.* * *He Did and He Didn't.* * *His Wife's Mistakes.* * *The Waiters' Ball.* * *The Other Man.* * *The Stone Age.* * *The Moonshiners.* * *A Creampuff Romance.* * *Rebecca's Wedding Day.* * *A Movie Star.* 1917: * *The Butcher Boy.* * *Fatty at Coney Island.* * *A Country Hero.* * *A Reckless Romeo.* * *Rough House.* * *His Wedding Night.* * *Out West.* * *Oh Doctor!* 1918: * *The Bell Boy.* * *Moonshine.* * *Goodnight Nurse.* * *The Cook.* * *Camping Out.* 1919: * *The Hayseed.* * *The Pullman Porter.* * *Love.* * *The Bank Clerk.* * *A Desert Hero.* * *Backstage.* * *The Garage.* 1920: * *The Scarecrow.* * *Life of the Party.* * *The Round-Up.* * *The Traveling Salesman.* * *Brewster's Millions.* * *Crazy to Marry.* *† *Speed.* 1921: * *The High Sign.* *† *The Slicker.* * *Fast and Furious.* 1922: * *All Wet.* *† *The City Chap.* *† *The Village Sheik.* 1923: † *Young and Dumb.* † *The Salesman.* 1924: † *Love Mania.* *The Garden of Weeds.* *† *Stupid, But Brave.* 1925: * *The Iron Mule.* * *Dynamite Doggie.* * *Curses.* 1926: * *Pink Elephants.* 1927: *American Beauty, Casey Jones.* 1928: *Hello Cheyenne. Painted Post.* 1929: *The Dance of Life. She Goes to War.* 1930: *Land of Missing Men. Hell Harbor. Oklahoma Cyclone. Western Knights. Two Fresh Eggs.* * *Voice of Hollywood No. 10.* 1931: *The Painted Desert. Son of the Plains (GB: Vultures of The Law). Aloha.* * *Marriage Rows.* * *That's My Meat.* * *Harem Scarem.* * *The Door Knocker.* * *Mlle. Irene the Great.* * *All Sealed Up.* * *Honeymoon Trio.* 1932: *Fame Street. Law of the North.* * *Bridge Wives. Police Court. Riders of the Desert.* 1933: * *Buzzin' Around. His Private Secretary. Public Stenographer (GB: Private Affairs).* 1935: *Trigger Tom (GB: Dangerous Mission). Law of the 45's (GB: The Mysterious Mr Sheffield). The Wanderer of the Wasteland. Bar 20 Rides Again.* 1936: *Pinto Rustlers. West of Nevada. The Millionaire Kid. Hopalong Cassidy Returns. Trail Dust.* 1937: *Melody of the Plains. Sing, Cowboy, Sing. A Lawman is Born. The Fighting Deputy. Moonlight on the Range. Roaming Cowboy.* * *Love Nest on Wheels. The Outcasts of Poker Flat. Saturday's Heroes.* 1938: *Rangers' Roundup. Knight of the Plains. Songs and Bullets. Frontier Scout. Gunsmoke Trail. Call of the Yukon.* 1939: *Oklahoma Terror. Trigger Pals.* 1940: *Billy the Kid Outlawed. Billy the Kid in Texas. Billy the Kid's Gun Justice. Texas Terrors. Friendly Neighbors. Murder on the Yukon. Marked Man.* 1941: *Billy the Kid's Range War. Billy the Kid in Santa Fe. Billy the Kid's Fighting Pals. The Apache Kid. Missouri Outlaw. The Lone Rider Rides On. The Lone Rider Crosses the Rio. The Lone Rider in Ghost Town. The Lone Rider in Frontier Fury (GB: Frontier Fury). The Lone Rider Ambushed. The Lone Rider Fights Back. Billy the Kid Wanted. Billy the Kid's Roundup.* 1942: *Law and Order (GB: Double Alibi). Arizona Terrors. Stagecoach Express. Jesse James Jr. The Lone Rider*

and the Bandit. The Lone Rider in Cheyenne. The Lone Rider in Texas Justice (GB: The Lone Rider). The Lone Rider in Border Roundup (GB: Border Roundup). Outlaws of Boulder Pass. Overland Stagecoach. Billy the Kid Trapped. Billy the Kid's Smoking Guns (GB: Smoking Guns). Sheriff of Sage Valley. The Mysterious Rider.* 1943: *Wild Horse Rustlers. Death Rides the Plains. Wolves of the Range. Law of the Saddle. Raiders of Red Gap. Western Cyclone. The Kid Rides Again. Fugitive of the Plains. Cattle Stampede. The Renegade. Blazing Frontier. Devil Riders. Frontier Outlaws. My Son, the Hero.* 1944: *Thundering Gunslingers. The Drifter. Valley of Vengeance. Fuzzy Settles Down. Rustlers' Hideout. Wild Horse Phantom. Oath of Vengeance. I'm from Arkansas.* 1945: *His Brother's Ghost. Gangsters' Den. Stagecoach Outlaws. Border Badmen. Fighting Bill Carson. Prairie Rustlers.* 1946: *Lightnin' Raiders. Gentlemen with Guns. Terrors on Horseback. Ghost of Hidden Valley. Prairie Badmen. Overland Raiders. Outlaw of the Plains. My Dog Shep. Colorado Serenade.* 1947: *Law of the Lash. Border Feud. Pioneer Justice. Ghost Town Renegades. Stage to Mesa City. Return of the Lash. Fighting Vigilantes. Cheyenne Takes Over. Code of the Plains. Raiders of Red Rock. Frontier Fighters.* 1948: *Panhandle Trail. Dead Man's Gold. Mark of the Lash. Frontier Revenge.* 1949: *Outlaw Country. Son of a Badman. Son of Billy the Kid.* 1950: *The Daltons' Women.* 1951: *King of the Bullwhip. The Thundering Trail.* 1952: *The Black Lash. Frontier Phantom.*

† Also directed.

THE THREE STOOGES

FINE, Larry
(Lawrence Feinburg) (bottom) 1902–1974
HOWARD, Curly
(Jerome Horowitz) (top) 1903–1952
HOWARD, Moe
(Moses Horowitz) 1895–1975
HOWARD, Shemp
(Samuel Horowitz) 1891–1955

Whether or not the Three Stooges make you laugh, you have to admit that you only need to see one of their films to find out what they are all about. Short, aggrieved, aggressive and moronic, they are the blind led by the blind. Their comedy is entirely physical, that is to say not skilful but the comedy of crude contact – the blow on the head, the finger in the eye, the whack on the knee, the punch in the stomach, the slap in the face. The throwing of inanimate objects to create chaos, notably custard pies, was also a favourite Stooges' pastime. The soundtracks of their films are grating, harsh and noisy. But they had a knack of hitting the funnybones – an analogy that would have pleased them – of children, and sustained a long series of two-reel comedies over 25 years. The Stooges took the idea that physical violence and subsequent damage makes you laugh to the ultimate degree. Though totally unfunny to the kind of audience that laughs at the respectively visual

and verbal subtleties of Buster Keaton and Woody Allen (both *qv*), the Stooges are the great primitives of screen comedy. The leader Moe (the one with the pudding basin haircut and very short temper) and his brothers Curly and Shemp were key members of their personnel through the decades. Like a number of other star comedians of the early twentieth century, Moe ran away from home while still a boy and joined a Mississippi riverboat show. He was nine years old. After shorebound experience with travelling stock companies, Moe teamed up with his older brother Shemp to do a black-face act in minstrel shows and on vaudeville. In the early 1920s the Howards agreed to act as stooges to Ted Healy, an up-and-coming comedian who reckoned he was going places. Around 1928 the act was joined by 25-year-old Larry Fine (the one with the wild hair) and Fred Sanborn, and the whole troupe hit Hollywood sound films in 1930 as Ted Healy and His Racketeers. Larry, too, had been on stage as a boy, and had developed an act in which he clowned, sang and played the violin (not that he ever had much chance to demonstrate the last two talents in Stooges comedies). He fitted in well with Healy and the Howards and, as

Shemp (who gradually forged a career as a comic character actor in films) and Sanborn (1899–1961) returned to vaudeville, Larry stayed with the Racketeers, joined by Moe's younger brother Curly. After a handful of feature film comedies in support of Healy the Stooges decided to break out on their own and, under the wing of Columbia Studios, quickly settled into the long line of violent farces that made them famous. In these the child-like Curly and perpetually panicking Larry are led by the grouchy intolerance of Moe (in whom we can see, as Oliver Hardy (*qv*) declared, that there's nothing so dumb as the dumb guy who thinks he's smarter than the others) into a long series of situations that they never come anywhere near handling. Although the comedies, whatever their subjects, seem relentlessly similar, one of the early ones, *Men in Black*, was nominated for an Academy Award, and 90 of them were made between 1934 and 1946 before Curly was forced to leave the team after suffering a stroke at only 43. He was replaced by a somewhat reluctant Shemp, who had become a prolific 'familiar face' in Hollywood features. And, truth to tell, Shemp was never as effective as Curly as a member of the trio. Both visually and in attitudes he was too similar to Moe. When Shemp died from a coronary occlusion in 1955, he was replaced by Joe Besser (1916–   ), who was physically much more in the Curly mould. When the shorts series finally came to an end (the last was released early in 1959) TV exposure of their work brought the Stooges back into the limelight, and Moe and Larry had a go at a few features with another new Stooge, Joe De Rita (1918–   ). In the early 1970s Larry suffered a debilitating stroke; at 72 he was dead. Even then, Moe, the old warhorse, was poised for one last try, a star-size cameo, with Joe De Rita and Emil Sitka (long a straight man in Stooges shorts) in *Blazing Stewardesses*. But Moe fell ill during rehearsals, and the new team was replaced by the two surviving Ritz Brothers (*qv*). Moe died from cancer later that year.

1930: *‡ *Hollywood on Parade*. ‡ *Soup to Nuts*. 1933: ‡ *Dancing Lady*. ‡ *Turn Back the Clock*. ‡ *Meet the Baron*. ‡ *Fugitive Lovers*. ‡ *Myrt and Marge* (GB: *Laughter in the Air*). 1934: ‡ *Hollywood Party*. ‡ *The Captain Hates the Sea*. ‡ *Gift of Gab*. *Hello Pop*. *Plane Nuts*. *The Big Idea*. *Beer and Pretzels*. *Woman Haters*. *Punch Drunks*. *Men in Black*. *Three Little Pigskins*. 1935: *Pop Goes the Easel*. *Horses' Collars*. *Restless Knights*. *Hoi Polloi*. *Uncivil Warriors*. *Screen Snapshots No. 6*. *Pardon My Scotch*. *Three Little Beers*. 1936: *Half-Shot Shooters*. *A Pain in the Pullman*. *Whoops I'm an Indian*. *Ants in the Pantry*. *Movie Maniacs*. *Disorder in the Court*. *False Alarms*. *Slippery Silks*. 1937: *Three Dumb Clucks*. *Grips, Grunts and Groans*. *Back to the Woods*. *Playing the Ponies*. *Dizzy Doctors*. *Goofs and Saddles*. *Cash and Carry*. *The Sitter-Downers*. 1938: ‡ *Start Cheering*. *Termites of 1938*. *Tassels in the Air*.

Three Missing Links. *Mutts to You*. *Wee Wee Monsieur*. *Healthy, Wealthy and Dumb*. *Violent is the Word for Curly*. *Flat Foot Stooges*. 1939: *A Ducking They Did Go*. *Three Little Sew and Sews*. *Saved by the Belle*. *Oily to Bed, Oily to Rise*. *We Want Our Mummy*. *Yes We Have No Bonanza*. *Calling All Curs*. *Three Sappy People*. 1940: *A-Plumbing We Will Go*. *You Natzy Spy!* *Nutty But Nice*. *No Census No Feeling*. *Boobs in Arms*. *How High is Up?* *Cuckoo Cavaliers*. *Rockin' Through the Rockies*. 1941: ‡ *Time Out for Rhythm*. *All the World's a Stooge*. *So Long, Mr Chumps*. *An Ache in Every Stake*. *Some More of Samoa*. *In the Sweet Pie and Pie*. *Dutiful But Dumb*. *I'll Never Heil Again! Loco Boy Makes Good*. 1942: ‡ *My Sister Eileen*. *Matri-Phony*. *Cactus Makes Perfect*. *Even as IOU*. *Sock-a-Bye Baby*. *What's the Matador?* *Three Smart Saps*. 1943: *Spook Louder*. *They Came to Conga*. *Three Little Twerps*. *I Can Hardly Wait*. *Phony Express*. *Dizzy Detectives*. *Back from the Front*. *Higher Than a Kite*. *Dizzy Pilots*. *A Gem of a Jam*. 1944: *The Yoke's on Me*. *Crash Goes the Hash*. *Gents without Cents*. *Busy Buddies*. *Idle Roomers*. *No Dough, Boys*. 1945: ‡ *Rockin' in the Rockies* (and 1940 short with similar title). *Idiots Deluxe*. *Three Pests in a Mess*. *Micro Phonies*. *If a Body Meets a Body*. *Booby Dupes*. 1946: ‡ *Swing Parade of 1946*. *Uncivil Warbirds*. *Beer Barrel Polecats*. *Monkey Businessmen*. *G. I. Wanna Go Home*. *Three Little Pirates*. *A Bird in the Head*. *The Three Troubledoers*. *Three Loan Wolves*. *Rhythm and Weep*. 1947: *Out West*. *Half Wits' Holiday*. *Brideless Groom*. *All Gummed Up*. *Fright Night*. *Hold That Lion*. *Sing Me a Song of Six Pants*. 1948: *Squareheads of the Round Table*. *Shivering Sherlocks*. *Heavenly Daze*. *I'm a Monkey's Uncle*. *Crime on Their Hands*. *Pardon My Clutch*. *Fiddlers Three*. *Hot Scots*. *Mummy's Dummies*. 1949: *The Ghost Talks*. *Hocus Pokus*. *Who Done It?* *Fuelin' Around*. *Vagabond Loafers*. *Malice in the Palace*. *Dunked in the Deep*. 1950: *Dopey Dicks*. *Punchy Cowpunchers*. *Love at First Bite*. *Three Hams on Rye*. *Slap Happy Sleuths*. *Hugs and Mugs*. *Self Made Maids*. *Studio Stoops*. *A Snitch in Time*. 1951: ‡ *Gold Raiders* (GB: *Stooges Go West*). *Don't Throw That Knife*. *Three Arabian Nuts*. *Merry Mavericks*. *Hula La-La*. *Baby Sitters' Jitters*. *Scrambled Brains*. *The Tooth Will Out*. *The Pest Man Wins*. 1952: *Corny Casanovas*. *Gents in a Jam*. *Cuckoo on a Choo-Choo*. *Three Dark Horses*. *He Cooked His Goose*. *Listen, Judge*. *A Missed Fortune*. 1953: *Loose Loot*. *Up in Daisy's Penthouse*. *Spooks*. *Rip, Sew and Stitch*. *Goof on the Roof*. *Booty and the Beast*. *Tricky Dicks*. *Pardon My Backfire*. *Bubble Trouble*. 1954: *Pals and Gals*. *Income Tax Sappy*. *Shot in the Frontier*. *Knutzy Knights*. *Scotched in Scotland*. *Musty Musketeers*. 1955: *Gypped in the Penthouse*. *Fling in the Ring*. *Stone Age Romeos*. *Hot Ice*. *Of Cash and Hash*. *Bedlam in Paradise*. *Wham-Bam-Slam*. *Blunder Boys*. 1956: *Flagpole Sitters*. *Husbands Beware*. *Rumpus in the Harem*. *Scheming Schemers*. *Creeps*. *For Crimin' Out Loud*. *Hot Stuff*. *Commotion on the Ocean*. 1957: *A Merry Mix-Up*. *Hoofs and Goofs*. *Space Ship Sappy*.

Horsing Around. Outer Space Jitters. Muscle Up a Little Closer. Gun a-Poppin'. Rusty Romeos. 1958: *Pies and Guys. Quiz Whiz. Flying Saucer Daffy. Fifi Blows Her Top. Sweet and Hot. Oil's Well That Ends Well.* 1959: † *Have Rocket, Will Travel. Triple Crossed. Sappy Bullfighters.* 1960: † *Three Stooges Scrapbook.* † *Stop! Look! And Laugh!* 1961: † *Snow White and the Three Stooges (GB: Snow White and the Three Clowns).* 1962: † *The Three Stooges in Orbit.* † *The Three Stooges Meet Hercules.* 1963: † *It's a Mad, Mad,.Mad, Mad World.* † *The Three Stooges Go Around the World in a Daze.* † *Four for Texas.* 1964: † *The Outlaws is. Coming.*

Moe and Curly. 1934: † *Jail Birds of Paradise.*

Moe alone. 1958: † *Space Master X-7.* 1966: † *Don't Worry, We'll Think of a Title.* 1973: † *Dr Death — Seeker of Souls.*

Shemp alone. 1933: † *In the Dough.* 1934: † *Convention Girl (GB: Atlantic City Romance). Art Trouble.* 1936: † *Three of a Kind. For the Love of Pete.* 1937: † *Headin' East.* † *Hollywood Round-Up.* 1938: *Home on the Range. Not Guilty Enough.* 1939: *Glove Slingers.* † *Another Thin Man.* 1940: † *Road Show. Pleased to Mitt You. Boobs in the Woods. Money Squawks.* † *Millionaires in Prison.* † *Give Us Wings.* † *The Bank Dick (GB: The Bank Detective).* † *Buck Privates (GB: Rookies).* † *The Leather Pushers.* † *Murder over New York.* 1941: † *The Invisible Woman.* † *Meet the Chump.* † *Mr Dynamite.* † *Tight Shoes.* † *Hold That Ghost.* † *Too Many Blondes.* † *Hellzapoppin.* † *The Flame of New Orleans.* † *Six Lessons from Madame La Zonga.* † *In the Navy.* † *San Antonio Rose.* † *Hit the Road.* 1942: † *Mississippi Gambler.* † *The Strange Case of Dr RX.* † *Private Buckaroo.* † *Arabian Nights.* † *Butch Minds the Baby.* † *Pittsburgh.* 1943: † *It Ain't Hay (GB: Money for Jam). Farmer for a Day.* † *How's About It?* † *Crazy House. Strictly in the Groove.* † *Keep 'Em Slugging.* 1944: † *Three of a Kind.* † *Strange Affair.* † *Moonlight and Cactus. Pick a Peck of Plumbers. Open Season for Saps.* 1945: *Off Again, On Again. Where the Pest Begins. A Hit with a Miss.* 1946: † *The Gentleman Misbehaves.* † *Blondie Knows Best.* † *Swing Parade of 1946.* † *Dangerous Business.* † *One Exciting Week. Mr Noisy. Jiggers, My Wife. Society Mugs.* 1947: *Bride and Gloom.* 1949: † *Africa Screams.*

All shorts except † features. ‡ As the Racketeers.

SUMMERVILLE, Slim

(George Summerville) 1892–1946

A very tall (6 ft 2½ in) and gangling, light-haired, big-nosed Hollywood comedian with a wide, clamp-lipped smile that expressed homeliness and toothlessness in one motion, Summerville played 'countrified' characters who had solid, reassuring presence. Very popular in his early days at Mack Sennett's studios, he was even for a brief while one of the famous Keystone Kops. Much later, he was to become one of America's favourite comedy character actors. Born either in

Calgary, Canada, or Albuquerque, New Mexico (not much difference) according to which version you read, Summerville was certainly raised in Canada but, like so many of the silent clowns, ran away from home as a teenager. In the years that followed, he earned his living in all sorts of manual jobs, ending up in California in 1913, where, with his distinctive looks, he found a fruitful living playing (mostly comedy) extra roles in films. Fellow comedian Edgar Kennedy (qv) spotted him on one such assignment, and suggested he try his luck with the Keystone studios as a featured player. Unmistakeable in aspect, with skinny legs and jug ears, Summerville was soon in demand for rustic roles, something in which he would be typecast for the rest of his career. He stayed with Sennett until 1918 and, after a period in vaudeville, joined the Fox studio as a director, turning out dozens of two-reel comedies throughout the 1920s, a decade during which he was hardly seen on screen. With sound films, though, Summerville started a gradual return to acting, a comeback that was crowned with his notable performance in *All Quiet on the Western Front*. He starred in two-reel comedies, was a natural for any film with a rural setting, and began a series of very successful low-budget comedies — there were nine of them in all — opposite twittering, pinch-lipped ZaSu Pitts (qv). These included *Out All Night, Her First Mate, The Love Birds* and *They Just Had to Get Married*. The stars appeared in the last of these as a butler and maid who come into money. Summerville also supported Shirley Temple in a couple of the moppet's most popular films, including (naturally) *Rebecca of Sunnybrook Farm*. He would doubtless have continued as increasingly emaciated old-timers up to the end of the studio years in the late 1950s, had he not had a stroke at only 53, from which he did not recover.

1914: * *A Rowboat Romance.* * *Gentlemen of Nerve.* * *The Knock-Out.* * *Mabel's Busy Day.* * *Laughing Gas.* * *Cursed by His Beauty.* * *Dough and Dynamite.* * *Ambrose's First Falsehood. Tillie's Punctured Romance.* 1915: *Caught in the Act.* * *Her Winning Punch.* * *Other People's Wives/The Home Breakers.*

* *Their Social Splash.* * *Gussie's Day of Rest.* * *The Great Vacuum Robbery.* * *His Bitter Half.* * *Her Painted Hero.* * *A Game Old Knight.* * *Beating Hearts and Carpets.* * *Those College Girls.* * *Those Bitter Sweets.* 1916: * *Bucking Society.* * *His Bread and Butter.* * *Her Busted Trust.* * *The Three Slims. Cinders of Love.* 1917: * *A Dog Catcher's Love. The Winning Punch.* * *Villa of the Movies.* * *Are Witnesses Safe?* * *Her Fame and Shame.* * *His Precious Life.* * *A Pullman Bride.* * *Mary's Little Lobster.* * *Roping Her Romeo.* * *Hold That Line.* * *It Pays to Exercise.* * *High Diver's Last Kiss.* * *Ten Nights without a Barroom.* 1918: * *The Kitchen Lady. The Beloved Rogue.* 1921: *Skirts.* 1926: *The Texas Steer. The Texas Streak.* 1927: *The Beloved Rogue (remake). The Denver Dude. Hey Hey Cowboy. Painted Ponies. The Chinese Parrot. The Wreck of the Hesperus.* 1928: *Riding for Fame.* 1929: *King of the Rodeo. The Shannons of Broadway. The Last Warning. Strong Boy. Tiger Rose.* 1930: *One Hysterical Night. Under Montana Skies. Troopers Three.* * *Voice of Hollywood No. 2. The King of Jazz. Her Man. See America Thirst. All Quiet on the Western Front. Little Accident. The Spoilers. Free Love.* * *Parlez-Vous.* * *Hello Russia! * We! We! Marie.* 1931: *Reckless Living. Heaven on Earth. Many a Slip. Bad Sister. The Front Page. Lasca of the Rio Grande.* * *Arabian Nights.* * *Bless the Ladies.* * *First to Fight.* * *Hotter Than Haiti.* * *Let's Play.* * *Royal Bluff.* * *Here's Luck.* * *Parisian Gaieties.* * *Sarge's Playmates.* 1932: *Tom Brown of Culver. They Just Had to Get Married. Unexpected Father. Airmail. Racing Youth.* * *Eyes Have It.* * *In the Bag.* * *Kid Glove Kisses.* 1933: *Love, Honor and Oh! Baby. Her First Mate. Out All Night.* * *Early to Bed. Meet the Princess.* * *See Soldier's Sweeties.* 1934: *Their Big Moment (GB: Afterwards). The Love Birds.* * *Horse Play.* 1935: *Way Down East. Life Begins at 40. The Farmer Takes a Wife.* 1936: *The Country Doctor. Captain January. Pepper. Reunion (GB: Hearts in Reunion). Can This Be Dixie? White Fang.* 1937: *The Road Back/Return of the Hero. Off to the Races. Fifty Roads to Town. Love is News.* 1938: *Up the River. Kentucky Moonshine (GB: Three Men and a Girl). Five of a Kind. Rebecca of Sunnybrook Farm. Submarine Patrol.* 1939: *Charlie Chan in Reno. Jesse James. Winner Take All. Henry Goes Arizona (GB: Spats to Spurs).* 1940: *Anne of Windy Poplars (GB: Anne of Windy Willows). Gold Rush Maisie.* 1941: *Miss Polly. Puddin' Head (GB: Judy Goes to Town). Niagara Falls. Highway West. Tobacco Road. Western Union.* 1942: *The Valley of Vanishing Man (serial).* * *Garden of Eatin'.* 1944: *I'm from Arkansas. Bride by Mistake. Swing in the Saddle (GB: Swing and Sway).* * *Bachelor Daze.* 1945: *Sing Me a Song of Texas (GB: Fortune Hunter).* 1946: *The Hoodlum Saint.*

As director (all shorts). 1920: † *Hold Me Tight.* 1921: *Pardon Me. One Moment Please.* 1922: *Hold the Line. Ranch Romeos. The Eskimo. High and Dry. The Barnstormer.* 1923: *The Cyclist. The Five Fifteen. The Artist. The Riding Master. Rough Sailing.* 1924: *Why*

Wait? The Green Grocers. Hello, 'Frisco! Her Ball and Chain. Keep Healthy. The Orphan. The Pinhead. Ship Ahoy! The Very Bad Man. Case Dismissed. 1925: When Dumb Bells Ring. Absent Minded. All Out. All Tied Up. Back to Nature. Faint Heart. Happy Go Lucky. Kick Me Again. 1926: The Village Cut Up. Wanted, a Bride. Badly Broke. A Bedtime Story. Business Women. Don't Be a Dummy. A Dumb Friend. Hearts for Rent. The Honeymoon Quickstep. Oprey House Tonight. Papa's Mamas. A Perfect Lie. A Swell Affair. Switching Sleepers. Tune Up! Too Much Sleep. 1927: Hop Along. Jailhouse Blues. In Again, Out Again. Meet the Husband. The Midnight Bum. A Run for His Money. 1929: Don't Say Ain't. Who's the Boss?

† Co-directed

SUTTON, Grady 1908–

A comedy specialist in slightly overweight suitors who didn't get the girl, America's dark-haired, plump-jowled, piggy-eyed, apprehensive-looking Grady Sutton was so ineffectual that you could almost feel the damp handshake. Tall and diffident, Sutton usually played bashful types undone by their own inadequacies or, occasionally, bumptious hotel managers whose small features could explode into an impressive variety of outraged or anguished expressions. For a born scene-stealer, he was popular with the stars and directors with whom he worked, and in later years he remembered with gratitude those who gave him regular employment. Not that Grady Sutton was out of work for long, from his arrival in California as a pasty-faced kid of 16 who had just left school. Vacationing at the home of director William Seiter, with whose younger brother he had gone to school, Sutton was invited over to Universal Studios and immediately given a bit part in Seiter's latest picture, The Mad Whirl. After some stock company experience in the late 1920s, Sutton returned to Hollywood with the coming of sound and was almost immediately pitched into 'The Boy Friends' two-reeler comedies, which ran through 15 shorts from 1930 to 1932. Their casts included several former members of the 'Our Gang' group, as well as Grady as the naive,

faintly backward southerner Alabam (he himself was born in Tennessee). Several of these little comedies were directed by the later famous George Stevens, who employed Sutton in a number of his feature films. Another benefactor was W. C. Fields (qv) – 'One of the nicest people I've ever met' said Sutton once – who, after Sutton appeared with him in the classic short The Pharmacist, in 1933, made room for him in several of his classic comedies. Most notable of these was The Bank Dick, in which Sutton enjoyed one of his fattest (!) roles, as the dithering Og Oggleby who is persuaded by prospective father-in-law Fields to purchase shares in worthless Beefsteak Mines. In wartime, Sutton, unfit for active service, worked at the Lockheed plant making aircraft parts. At the same his career as a comic bit-parter continued apace, up to 1949, when he shifted to television. Even though he appeared in scores of TV programmes, Sutton, ironically for such a distinctive player, had to wait until 1966 for his first regular role in a comedy series, when he played the butler in Phyllis Diller's (qv) The Pruitts of Southampton. Although he had an expressive face and used it at the right moment, the beauty of Grady Sutton was that he could look alarmed, or offended, without moving a muscle. And he got a laugh at the same time.

1925: The Mad Whirl. Skinner's Dress Suit. The Freshman. 1926: The Boy Friend. 1928: The Sophomore. 1929: Tanned Legs. 1930: * Doctor's Orders. Bigger and Better. Wild Company. Let's Go Native. Hit the Deck.

* Blood and Thunder. * Ladies Last. 1931: * Love Fever. * Air Tight. * High Gear. * Call a Cop! * The Kick-Off! * Mama Loves Papa. 1932: * Boys Will Be Boys. * You're Telling Me. * Family Troubles. * Who, Me? Movie Crazy. * Love Pains. The Knockout. * Too Many Women. * Wild Babies. This Reckless Age. Are These Our Children?/Age of Consent. Hot Saturday. Pack Up Your Troubles. 1933: The Story of Temple Drake. College Humor. * The Big Fibber. * Don't Play Bridge with your Wife. * See you Tonight. * Husbands' Reunion. * Uncle Jack. * The Pharmacist. Ace of Aces. * Flirting in the Park. * Walking Back Home. The Sweetheart of Sigma Chi (GB: Girl of My Dreams). Only Yesterday. 1934: * The Undie-World. * Rough Necking. * Contented Calves. * Hunger Pains. Bachelor Bait. Gridiron Flash (GB: Luck of the Game). 1935: Stone of Silver Creek. Laddie. * A Night at the Biltmore Bowl. * Pickled Peppers. Alice Adams. The Man on the Flying Trapeze (GB: The Memory Expert). Dr Socrates. 1936: Palm Springs (GB: Palm Springs Affair). King of the Royal Mounted. She's Dangerous. The Singing Kid. Valiant is the Word for Carrie. Pigskin Parade (GB: The Harmony Parade). My Man Godfrey. 1937: Waikiki Wedding. Stage Door. We Have Our Moments. Dangerous Holiday. Love Takes Flight. Turn Off the Moon. Behind the Mike. Two Minutes to Play. 1938: Vivacious Lady. Having Wonderful Time. Alexander's Ragtime Band. Joy of Living. Hard to Get. Three Loves Has Nancy. The Mad Miss Manton. 1939: You Can't Cheat an Honest Man. It's a Wonderful World. In Name Only. Naughty But Nice. Blind Alley. Blondie Meets the Boss. They Made Her a Spy. Angels Wash Their Faces.

In spite of their height and bulk, Grady Sutton's film characters disliked taking chances, and were always ready to turn and run. This is from Doctors Don't Tell, and Grady's the one in the light suit

Three Sons. Three Smart Girls Grow Up. The Flying Irishman. 1940: Anne of Windy Poplars (GB: Anne of Windy Willows). Lucky Partners. Sky Murder. Torrid Zone. Too Many Girls. The Bank Dick (GB: The Bank Detective). City of Chance. We Who Are Young. Millionaire Playboy. He Stayed for Breakfast. Millionaires in Prison. 1942: Whispering Ghosts. Dudes Are Pretty People. The Affairs of Martha (GB: Once Upon a Thursday). The Bashful Bachelor. Somewhere I'll Find You. 1943: The More the Merrier. A Lady Takes a Chance. What a Woman! (GB: The Beautiful Cheat). The Great Moment. 1944: Johnny Doesn't Live Here Anymore. Week-End Pass. Nine Girls. Allergic to Love. Goin' to Town. Since You Went Away. Hi, Beautiful (GB: Pass to Romance). Casanova Brown. Guest Wife. 1945: Grissly's Millions. A Royal Scandal (GB: Czarina). Three's a Crowd. On Stage, Everybody. Her Lucky Night. Captain Eddie. The Stork Club. She Went to the Races. A Bell for Adano. Anchors Aweigh. Pillow to Post. Brewster's Millions. 1946: Ziegfeld Follies (completed 1944). The Fabulous Suzanne. My Dog Shep. Hit the Hay. It's Great to be Young. Nobody Lives Forever. Idea Girl. The Plainsman and the Lady. The Magnificent Rogue. Partners in Time. The Show Off. Susie Steps Out. Dragonwyck. Two Sisters from Boston. No Leave, No Love. Dead Reckoning. 1947: Beat the Band. Philo Vance's Gamble. Love and Learn. My Wild Irish Rose. Always Together. 1948: Romance on the High Seas (GB: It's Magic). Jiggs and Maggie in Court. Last of the Wild Horses. My Dear Secretary. 1949: Grand Canyon. Air Hostess. 1954: Living It Up. A Star is Born. White Christmas. 1961: Madison Avenue. The Chapman Report. 1962: Jumbo/Billy Rose's Jumbo. 1963: Come Blow Your Horn. 1964: My Fair Lady. 1965: Tickle Me. The Chase. The Bounty Killer. Paradise, Hawaiian Style. 1968: I Love You, Alice B. Toklas. Something for a Lonely Man (TV). 1969: The Great Bank Robbery. 1970: Suppose They Gave a War and Nobody Came. Myra Breckinridge. Dirty Dingus Magee. 1971: Support Your Local Gunfighter. 1979: Rock 'n' Roll High School.

SWAIN, Mack 1876–1935

Big Mack Swain was a 300-pound bundle of fun. With light-brown hair, bulbous grey-green eyes, thick lips and thicker double-chin and a fearsome painted moustache, Swain was one of the funniest – and certainly heaviest – comedians of Hollywood's silent era. Though he made many early films at the Mack Sennett fun factory, including a series of his own, it is Swain's films with Charlie Chaplin (*qv*) over a 12-year period that have assured him a place in film history. He was born in Salt Lake City, Utah, and left home at 14 to sing and clown in a minstrel show. Roly-poly even then, he soon grew to 6 ft 2 in and made a good living out of glowering villains, both comic and serious.

In this way he spent 23 years in vaudeville, on riverboats, in musical-comedy and finally on the Broadway stage (a big hit in *Brown's in Town*) before coming to Hollywood late in 1913. At Sennett's Keystone studios, it wasn't long before Swain was supporting Chaplin and Mabel Normand (*qv*), the studio's top comedy stars. The contrast between the slight Chaplin and enormous Swain meant surefire audience laughter. The two men became firm friends off the set too. In those days, Swain would claim, he was a mere stripling at 280 pounds. The extra 20 came with affluent living! While the David and Goliath antics with Chaplin continued, Swain found another opponent half his size in weedy Chester Conklin (*qv*), a one-time Keystone Kop who now joined with Swain in the 'Ambrose and Walrus' series, little essays in manic mayhem in which the crafty Walrus (Conklin) usually managed to get the better of his opponent in their human Tom-and-Jerry antics. After a few years Swain's painted moustache was replaced by a fake one and later still by a real one. But the exaggerated gestures and outraged expressions remained the same. Although he was still playing the leering, bull-in-a-china-shop Ambrose after several years, his films were becoming fewer and dried up altogether in 1920. Chaplin came to the rescue by giving Swain roles in his early 1920s films *The Idle Class*, *Pay Day* and *The Pilgrim*. But it was Swain's performance as Big Jim McKay in Chaplin's 1925 masterpiece *The Gold Rush* that really revived his career. He and Chaplin are prospectors in the Klondike, so hard up for food that Chaplin has to boil his own boot, which they tuck into with many a meaningful glance. Later Swain, even hungrier, sees Charlie as a giant chicken and chases him with a chopper. All's well that end well when Big Jim loses his memory of these events, promises his partner a 50–50 split and eventually finds his lost gold. The success of this film brought Swain back into demand as a character player. He played in a remake of *Tillie's Punctured Romance* (he was also part of the star-studded cast in Chaplin's original 1914 version), and had leading roles in *The Shamrock and the Rose* and *Finnegan's Ball.*

Having played a featured part in *The Cohens and the Kellys* in 1926, the beginning of a profitable comedy series starring George Sidney and Charlie Murray (both *qv*), Swain was upped to co-star with Sidney for one adventure when Murray proved unavailable for *The Cohens and Kellys in Atlantic City*. He took off his moustache for the occasion! And he and Slim Summerville (*qv*) were well received as John Barrymore's cronies in the François Villon biopic *The Beloved Rogue*. Work grew scarcer again for a now ageing Swain with the coming of sound, although he made a few comedy shorts in the early 1930s. He died from an intestinal haemorrhage at 59.

*1914: *A Busy Day. *A Gambling Rube. *A Rowboat Romance. *Caught in a Cabaret. *Caught in the Rain. *The Fatal Mallet. *Mabel's Married Life. *The Knockout. *Laughing Gas. *Getting Acquainted. *Ambrose's First Falsehood. *His Prehistoric Past. *Gentlemen of Nerve. *His Musical Career. *His Trysting Place. *Sea Nymphs. *Among the Mourners. *Leading Lizzie Astray. *Other People's Business. *A Dark Lover's Play. Tillie's Punctured Romance. 1915: *Wilful Ambrose. *Ambrose's Fury. *Ambrose's Lofty Perch. *Love, Speed and Thrills. *The Home Breakers. *Ambrose's Sour Grapes. *Our Dare Devil Chief. *The Battle of Ambrose and Walrus. *Gussie, The Golfer. *From Patches to Plenty. *That Little Band of Gold. *Ambrose's Nasty Temper. *A Human Hound's Triumph. *Mabel Lost and Won. *When Ambrose Dared Walrus. *Saved by Wireless. *The Best of Enemies. *Ye Olden Grafter. *Ambrose's Little Hatchet. 1916: A Movie Star. A Modern Enoch Arden. *By Stork Delivery. *His Bitter Pill. *Vampire Ambrose. *The Danger Girl. *Love Will Conquer. *His Wild Oats. *Madcap Ambrose. *Safety First Ambrose. *Ambrose's Cup of Woe. *Ambrose's Rapid Rise. *His Auto-Ruination. *Sheriff Ambrose. 1917: *His Naughty Thought. *The Pullman Bride. *Danger Girl. *Lost – A Cook. *Thirst. 1918: *Poppy. 1919: *Ambrose's Day Off. *Ambrose and the Lion-Hearted. *The Schemers. 1921: *The Idle Class. 1922: *Pay Day. 1923: The Pilgrim. 1925: The Gold Rush. 1926: The Cohens and the Kellys. Hands Up! The Torrent. Whispering Wires. Sea Horses. Footloose Widows. Kiki. *The Nervous Wreck. *Honesty – The Best Policy. *Her Big Night. 1927: My Best Girl. The Beloved Rogue. The Shamrock and the Rose. Finnegan's Ball. Mockery. See You in Jail. Becky. The Girl from Everywhere. The Tired Business Man. 1928: Tillie's Punctured Romance (GB: Marie's Millions). Caught in the Fog. Gentlemen Prefer Blondes. A Texas Steer. The Last Warning. 1929: The Cohens and Kellys in Atlantic City. Marianne. 1930: The Sea Bat. Redemption. *Cleaning Up. The Locked Door. 1931: *Stout Hearts and Willing Hands. Finn and Hattie. 1932: Midnight Patrol. *The Engineer's Daughter. *Lighthouse Love.*

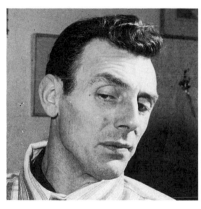

SYKES, Eric 1923–

Tall, long-headed, sparely-built, dark-haired, scarecrow-like British writer and comedian with doleful, Eeyore-like tones and slightly untidy hair. After years writing scripts for other comedians, he came before the camera to steal scenes in many a film, sometimes in unusual roles. Leading parts in film comedy were sparse and somewhat less successful, and he returned to the comfort of his long-running, affectionately-viewed TV series with Hattie Jacques, only ended by her early death in 1980. He is one of the few comedy writers who prefers to work alone rather than in collaboration. Born in Lancashire, the son of a cotton-mill labourer, Sykes' early ambitions to be a comedian were thwarted by war service, during which he made the acquaintance of many of the young comedians who were to be in the forefront of post-war British comedy, including Peter Sellers, Tony Hancock, Spike Milligan and Harry Secombe (all *qv*). He supplied them with gags for such post-war shows as *Stars in Battledress*. The BBC took him on and he wrote for *Variety Bandbox* and other all-star programmes, graduating to the immensely successful *Educating Archie* from 1950 to 1954. He made a low-key film debut (alongside Hancock, Sellers and Sidney James, *qv*) as a lanky private soldier in *Orders Are Orders*. Although he continued much in demand as a scriptwriter, things started happening for him as a performer after he got his own radio series at the end of the 1950s. His TV series *Sykes* began in 1960, an unpolished but likeable series of domestic disasters which paired him with Hattie Jacques (*qv*) as his sister, 'Hat'. He also started making more appearances in films. His first good notices were for *Very Important Person*, as Willoughby, the Mole, forever trying to tunnel his way out of POW camp and ending up in the most unlikely places, rather like Moore Marriott (*qv*) in *Convict 99*. He was a World War Two band conductor (and very funny) in *Invasion Quartet*, successfully essayed a comedy lead, surrounded by pretty girls in the *Village of Daughters*, then helped Terry-Thomas (in the first of three fruitful collaborations) solve murders at a health club in *Kill or Cure*. He brought off an unusual piece of casting

as the expressionless assassin in *The Liquidator*, though the film was poor. With Terry-Thomas (*qv*) again, he was the chief delight of the 'travel' comedies, *Those Magnificent Men in Their Flying Machines* and *Monte Carlo or Bust!*, with T-T as the nobleman determined to win the races by foul means rather than fair, and Sykes as his much put-upon manservant. He was very good (and second-billed) in the disappointing *Rotten to the Core* as the bumbling detective who is jack of all disguises but master of none.

And, at much the same time, he became interested in wordless comedies that he also directed, such as *The Plank* (which he later remade for TV) and *Rhubarb*. These were only mildly funny compared to his best work. After 1973 Sykes devoted his time to television and the last seven years of *Sykes*. There were also a number of riotous, fiercely ad-libbed stage tours with Jimmy Edwards (*qv*) in the play *Big Bad Mouse*. These were finally ended by Edwards' death in 1988. Sykes himself continues to make appear-

Eric Sykes (right) and Tommy Cooper appear somewhat bemused by their day's work as removal men in *It's Your Move*

ances, looking like the senior citizen of comedy. One suspects that a series about an elderly caretaker may be only just around the corner. 'I've never bothered with messages', he says. 'I'm just in it to make 'em laugh.'

1954: *Orders Are Orders.* 1956: *Charley Moon.* 1959: *Tommy the Toreador.* 1960: *Watch Your Stern.* 1961: *Very Important Person (US: A Coming Out Party). Invasion Quartet. Village of Daughters.* 1962: *Kill or Cure.* 1963: *Heavens Above!* 1964: *One Way Pendulum. The Bargee.* 1964: *Those Magnificent Men in Their Flying Machines. Rotten to the Core. The Liquidator.* 1966: *The Spy with a Cold Nose.* 1967: [†]* *The Plank.* 1968: *Shalako.* 1969: *Monte Carlo or Bust! (US: Those Daring Young Men in Their Jaunty Jalopies).* 1970: [†] *Rhubarb.* 1972: *The Alf Garnett Saga.* 1973: *Theatre of Blood.* 1982: * *It's Your Move.* 1983: *The Boys in Blue.* 1984: *Gabrielle and the Doodleman.* 1986: *Absolute Beginners.* 1988: *Mr H is Late (TV).*

[†] Also directed

There's confusion in the constabulary when Eric Sykes (left) and Jimmy Edwards whistle up the force in *Rhubarb*.

TALMADGE, Constance 1898–1973

In the list of Hollywood's adorable female silent clowns, second only to Mabel Normand (*qv*) was brown-haired, strong-chinned, flat-chested, big-eyed, irrepressible Constance Talmadge. She could angle her plain, almost plaintive features to hilarious comic effect, but could, when she cared to, look ethereally attractive as well. Whereas Mabel was a slapstick specialist and often appeared in tomboy roles, Constance — although she did play one or two hoydens — was more usually the screwball sophisticate. Hers was comedy played in Paris fashions. A natural mimic who could do wicked send-ups of other stars, Constance would often take attention away from other players by sheer variation of facial expression. But she was unlucky in love. That, and the approach of sound, spelled an early end to her dazzling career. One of a trio of acting sisters from New York, Constance, nicknamed 'Dutch' from childhood, was always the most extrovert of the three. Her impromptu impersonations brought her to the attention of

executives at the studio, Vitagraph, where sister Norma had soared to stardom, and the teenager was put into comic supporting roles in two-reelers. She became a star at 18 with her interpretation of the Mountain Girl in D. W. Griffith's *Intolerance*. Constance learned to drive a chariot, scorning a double in the action sequences. Directors loved her because of her willingness to do anything, and because she made them laugh on and off the set. Even the staid Griffith was seen to smile when Constance walked on to the set in her Mountain Girl costume wearing only one half of the bosom padding designed to give her a shapelier figure. Constance's comedies thereafter were mainly frothy frolics with risqué situations, which gave her the soubriquet of the Virtuous Vamp. The title, said to have originally been coined for her by Irving Berlin, later became the name of one of her more successful films. Her happy attitudes and zest for life certainly came across on screen, and she was soon jostling her sister Norma in terms of popularity. In 1925 she scored a major success in a dual role opposite Ronald Colman in *Her Sister from Paris*, playing both a dowdy wife and her dashing, man-hungry sister. But at the beginning of 1926 she married for the second time and announced her retirement from the screen. Eighteen months later, she had filed for divorce. But her career in screen comedy never really got going again. There was more life in the costumes of her last few movies than in the scenarios. Constance married for the third time in 1929 (that too would end in divorce), by which time she had already decided, like her sister Norma, that her voice was unlikely to survive a transition to sound films. Years later the harum-scarum Constance did eventually marry happily, staying wed for 25 years until

her husband's death. She herself died from pneumonia at 75. Few more versatile comediennes graced the screen, and it was a pity she didn't at least try sound films. One critic got it about right when he said he found her 'gay and charming, funny and elegant, affectionate and coy'.

1914: * *Buddy's First Call.* * *Buddy's Downfall.* * *The Maid from Sweden.* * *Our Fairy Play.* * *Father's Timepiece.* * *The Mysterious Lodger.* * *The Peacemaker.* * *In The Latin Quarter.* * *In Bridal Attire.* * *The Egyptian Mummy.* * *The Moonstone of Fez.* 1915: * *Beached and Bleached.* * *You Can't Beat It.* * *The Little Puritan.* * *Billy, the Bear Tamer.* * *The Green Cat.* * *Billy's Wager.* * *The Lady of Shalott.* * *The Vanishing Vault.* * *Spades Are Trump (GB: Spades Are Trumps). The Missing Links. Captivating Mary Carstairs.* 1916: *The Matrimaniac. Intolerance. The Microscope Mystery. The She-Devil.* 1917: *The Girl of the Timber Claims. Scandal. Betsy's Burglar. The Lesson. The Honeymoon.* 1918: *Up the Road with Sally. A Pair of Silk Stock-*

Sporting an amazingly glossy wig, Terry-Thomas (as shifty Alfred Green) discusses the case with barristers Richard Attenborough (left) and Ian Carmichael (right) in *Brothers in Law*

Dirty work afoot. George Banks (David Tomlinson) arrives home after work to find his house full of dancing chimney sweeps in *Mary Poppins*

On the run? All the essential ingredients of Tommy Trinder are in this 'mug shot': the narrowed eyes, the pursed lips, the jutted jaw — and the trilby hat

ings. *Goodnight, Paul. The Shuttle. The Studio Girl. Sauce for the Goose. Mrs Leffingwell's Boots. A Lady's Name.* 1919: *The Veiled Adventure. The Fall of Babylon* (expanded footage from *Intolerance*). *Who Cares? Romance and Arabella. Experimental Marriage. Happiness à la Mode. A Temperamental Wife. A Virtuous Vamp.* 1920: *Two Weeks. In Search of a Sinner. The Perfect Woman. A Good Reference. The Love Expert. A Dangerous Business.* 1921: *Mama's Affair. Lessons in Love. Wedding Bells.* 1922: *Polly of the Follies. The Divorcé. Woman's Place. The Primitive Lover. East is West.* 1923: *Dulcy. The Dangerous Maid.* 1924: *The Goldfish. Her Night of Romance. In Hollywood with Potash and Perlmutter* (GB: *So This is Hollywood*). 1925: *Her Sister from Paris. Learning to Love.* 1926: *The Duchess of Buffalo.* 1927: *Venus of Venice. Breakfast at Sunrise.* 1929: *Venus.*

TATI, Jacques
(J. Tatischeff) 1908–1982
Reading various critical assessments of the work and achievements of this tall, mournful French mime and comedian, it is obvious that opinion is sharply divided as to his merits. Yet many comedians descend into the only occasionally amusing after early career highlights of hilarity. It's just that Tati spent rather more time doing it than most other people. He was born in Paris of Russian origin, the grandson of a one-time Russian ambassador to France of Tsarist days. Intended for a career in his father's art restoration business, Jacques turned instead to sport, becoming a professional rugby player on the verge of the national team. He was also an excellent tennis player. He used his love of sport and knowledge of its leading figures of the day to produce a cabaret act in which he impersonated many of them in mime. The resultant hilarity set him off on a professional career and one of his routines was turned into a short film, his first: *Oscar, champion de tennis.* There were other shorts but Tati remained an attraction mainly on the club circuit. It wasn't until after World War Two that he became really fascinated by the possibilities of cinema. It was almost a fatal fascination, as Tati's battles with artistic and financial problems became in-

creasingly agonised towards the end of his life. When it first arrived, however, Tati's initial short comedy as both director and star, *L'école des facteurs*, proved to be like a breath of fresh air in the then-stagnating field of world comedy. In the event, it proved to be something of a dry run for his first feature, *Jour de fête*, in that both films revolved around postmen. Tati discarded his character of François the postman for his next film, opting instead for the persona that would gain him immortality – the gangling, raincoated Monsieur Hulot, whose shapeless hat, too-short trousers, boat-like feet, ridiculously long stride, perennial pipe, umbrella with a will of its own and general absent-minded air, all served to create the unwitting perpetrator of comic chaos. There are some wondrously extended pieces of comedy in *Hulot*, where the star acts as the catalyst to a series of disasters which continue long after he has left the scene. And there are the short, sharp visual gags – Hulot being thrown out to sea after stepping on a taut rope, a rocket from a fireworks display blazing through a newly-opened window, a canoe folding up around Hulot like a collapsible bed. The film was a world-wide success, and Tati paused for five years before coming up with the next one, *Mon oncle*, again as Hulot but this time lost in an urban world of gadgets and contrivances, themes that would increasingly occupy Tati and suck the humanity from his film character. By the time the next film, *Playtime*, arrived international audiences seemed to have lost interest in a comedian who hardly ever made films. It had some wonderful moments but both it and the film that followed it, *Traffic*, lost money. *Parade*, made for television, was a celebration of Tati's earlier days of pantomime skills. He an-

nounced another film in the Hulot character, to be called *Confusion*. Alas, the title was all too appropriate as far as financing and setting the film up was concerned, and it was never made. A few years later Tati died from a pulmonary embolism. Had Tati been a little less of a worrier and a perfectionist, there might have been a whole legacy of Hulot comedies for us to drool and cackle over. But there is still enough for succeeding generations to relish.

1932: * *Oscar, champion de tennis.* 1934: * *On demande une brute.* 1935: * *Gai dimanche.* 1936: *Soigne ton gauche.* 1938: *Retour à la terre.* 1945: *Sylvie et la fantôme* (US: *Sylvia and the Ghost*). 1946: *Le diable au corps* (GB and US: *Devil in the Flesh*). 1947: [†]* *L'école des facteurs.* 1949: [†] *Jour de fête.* 1951: [†] *Monsieur Hulot's Holiday.* 1956: *Mon oncle/ My Uncle.* 1967: [†] *Playtime.* * *Cours du soir.* 1970: *Domicile conjugal* (GB: *Bed and Board*). 1971: [†] *Trafic/Traffic.* 1974: [†] *Parade* (TV).

[†] Also directed

TERRY-THOMAS
(Thomas Terry Hoar-Stevens)
1911–1990
Beaming, dark-haired, moustachioed ultra-British comedian and star comic actor with wolfish smile and remarkable gap in the centre of his front teeth in which he would often prop a long cigarette holder. He was at his best as cads and con-men. Born in London, his upper-class background was reflected in his cultured tones, which he later exaggerated for comic effect. His second cousin is the radio, TV and theatre comedy player Richard Briers. Terry-Thomas first gravitated towards show business through his prowess as an exhibition

Tired of the regimentation of modern living, Monsieur Hulot (Jacques Tati) opts for his own idea of a rest, to the consternation of his hosts in *Mon oncle*

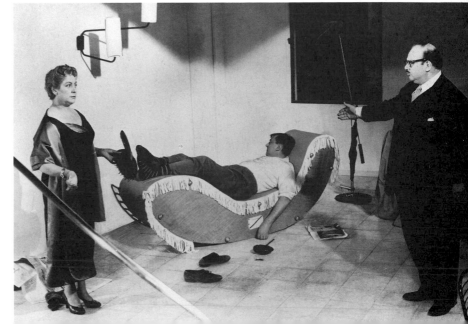

ballroom dancer (they called them adagio dancers in the 1930s), but he had already begun a career as a radio comedian before war service with the Royal Corps of Signals. After the war Terry-Thomas quickly came to the fore as one of Britain's best-liked stand-up comedians. striding to the microphone with his opening catchphrases: 'How do you *do*? Are you *frightfully* well?' (Pause) 'Good *show*!' He had his own series (*To Town with Terry*) by 1948, and there were a few early films, but solo comedians were not in vogue in post-war British cinema (until the advent of Norman Wisdom (*qv*) in 1953) and 'T-T' continued on radio with *Top of the Town* and on TV with *Strictly T-T*. In 1955, though, films reached out and grabbed him for what would prove to be more than 20 years. He was ideally cast as the bristling army CO in *Private's Progress*, got the chance to call his men 'an absolute shower' and proved no mean actor. The Boulting Brothers, who achieved great box-office success with the film, used him on most of their subsequent films. His darting eyes and tightly-controlled range of facial expressions made him a splendid comic villain who would stoop to any depths, whether it were in costume, in *tom thumb*, or as the ultimate 'swine' in *School for Scoundrels*. He was also quite effective in a few 'harassed hero' roles and in the early 1960s went to Hollywood, where he was in the habit of running the Union Jack up outside his home and going to work in a Rolls-Royce. Pickings for T-T were leaner after the mid 1960s and he often looked to international vehicles to continue his film career. However, he was very funny as the dastardly Ware-Armitages, attempting to sabotage *all* their rivals, in *Those Magnificent Men in Their Flying Machines* and *Monte Carlo or Bust*. In the late 1970s Terry-Thomas learned that he had Parkinson's Disease, which cut short his career and had completely immobilised him ten years on. A sad twilight for Britain's brightest bounder.

*1936: This'll Make You Whistle. It's Love Again. Rhythm in the Air. 1937: Rhythm Racketeer. 1940: For Freedom. Under Your Hat. 1947: The Brass Monkey/Lucky Mascot. 1948: A Date with a Dream. 1949: Helter Skelter. Melody Club. 1951: * Cookery Nook. * The Queen Steps Out. 1955: Private's Progress. 1956: The Green Man. Brothers in Law. 1957: Blue Murder at St Trinian's. Lucky Jim. The Naked Truth (US: Your Past is Showing!). 1958: Happy is the Bride! tom thumb. 1959: Too Many Crooks. Carlton-Browne of the F. O. (US: Man in a Cocked Hat). I'm All Right, Jack. School for Scoundrels. 1960: Make Mine Mink. His and Hers. 1961: A Matter of WHO. 1962: Operation Snatch. Kill or Cure. Bachelor Flat. The Wonderful World of the Brothers Grimm. 1963: It's a Mad, Mad, Mad, Mad World. Mouse on the Moon. 1964: The Wild Affair. 1965: Strange Bedfellows. Those Magnificent Men in Their Flying Machines. How to Murder Your Wife. You Must Be Joking! 1966: The Daydreamer (voice only). Our Man in Marrakesh (US: Bang Bang You're Dead). Operation Paradise. The Sandwich Man. Munster Go Home! Kiss The Girls and Make Them Die. La grande vadrouille (GB: Don't Look Now, We're Being Shot At). 1967: Rocket to the Moon (US: Those Fantastic Flying Fools). Arabella. Bandidos. I Love a Mystery (TV). The Karate Killers (TV. GB: cinemas). The Perils of Pauline. A Guide for the Married Man. Top Crack. Diabolik (GB: Danger: Diabolik). 1968: Don't Raise the Bridge, Lower the River. Uno scacco tutto matto (US: Mad Checkmate). Sette volte sette/Seven Times Seven. How Sweet It Is! Where Were You When the Lights Went Out? 1969: † Arthur, Arthur. 2,000 Years Later. Monte Carlo or Bust (US: Those Daring Young Men in Their Jaunty Jalopies). Twelve Plus One/Una su Zradici. 1970: Le mur de l'Atlantique. The Abominable Dr Phibes. 1972: The Cherry-picker. The Heroes. Dr Phibes Rises Again. 1973: Vault of Horror. Robin Hood (voice only). 1974: Who Stole the Shah's Jewels? 1975: Side by Side. The Bawdy Adventures of Tom Jones. Spanish Fly. 1977: The Hound of the Baskervilles. The Last Remake of Beau Geste. 1981: Happy Birthday Harry!*

† Unreleased.

TODD, Thelma 1905–1935

There can't be many blonde American beauty queens who became character comediennes in films. Indeed, Thelma Todd was a well-liked performer and almost a star. She just lacked that extra some- thing – like the dangerous bite of a Carole Lombard – that would have put her at the top of the tree. She might still have reached stardom, even so, if her career had not been cut short by her sudden, dramatic and mysterious death at the age of 30. Thelma did have a vivacious sense of humour, as reflected in her happy, open, expressive features, and was a willing stooge for some of the great comedians of the era, such as Laurel and Hardy and the Marx Brothers (both *qv*). And, in a long series of two-reelers, she did enjoy a stardom of her own. She was born far away from Hollywood, in the opposite corner of America – Boston, Massachusetts. Although winner of the 1924 Miss Massachusetts contest, she started her working life as a schoolteacher, until enrolling at 20 in a six-month crash course for screen acting run by Paramount at its East Coast Astoria Studios. The top 16 students won one-year contracts with the studio, and Thelma was one (of the 16, she and Charles 'Buddy' Rogers were the only two to become major names). She got some leading roles, including a co-starring assignment with Ed Wynn (*qv*), in his film debut *Rubber Heels*. But the studio didn't renew her one-year contract when it expired. Undeterred, Thelma stuck around, learning from another great comedienne, Louise Fazenda (*qv*) in *Heart to Heart* (Thelma played her daughter), making a bit of a name for herself as a singer, and then signing on with Hal Roach's fun factory early in 1929. Here she was soon set to work learning the tricks of the trade in comedy two-reelers, quickly making the acquaintance of Laurel and Hardy in their first sound short, *Unaccustomed As We Are*. In the next few years she kept a straight face, and her dignity, while stooging for Harry Langdon, Charley Chase, the Marx Brothers, Buster Keaton and Wheeler and Woolsey (all *qv*). Most of her later appearances opposite these comedians were in features, as the Roach Studio had given her a short-film series of her own from 1931, at first in harness with pinched ZaSu Pitts (*qv*), then with peppy Patsy Kelly (also *qv*). Although they ran for five years, these two-reelers, like so many from the Roach Studio (with the exception of those from Laurel and Hardy) never achieved a sense of overall momentum, of building-up of characters. On the whole, the shorts Thelma made with Patsy Kelly are superior, better-plotted and more fun, with Thelma as usual providing the grace and glamour but taking the pratfalls (mindful, no doubt of her beauty queen figure, Roach always seemed to have her falling in water), while Patsy provided the physical zaniness that had been ZaSu Pitts' forte. One of the best of their shorts together, *Top Flat*, with Thelma as a poet who poses as a French maid to a wealthy society couple (don't ask) was their penultimate together. Shortly after its release, Thelma was found dead in her garaged car. Despite blood on her face and dishevelled clothing, the subsequent inquiry was unable to decide whether it was murder or suicide and returned a verdict of accidental death. It was half a century later that facts emerged that seemed to indicate she had been killed by a gangster boyfriend frightened she would reveal his activities to the law. Although level-headed in many ways — a non-smoker and light drinker who never touched drugs — Thelma was extremely fond of men (not for nothing was she known as Hot Toddy). It seemed to have been her misfortune that she discovered the wrong sort of lover at the wrong time. Had it not been for that, Thelma's bright, lively, wisecracking personality would surely have been employed in films for many years to follow.

*1926: Fascinating Youth. God Gave Me Twenty Cents. The Popular Sin. 1927: Rubber Heels. Nevada. The Shield of Honor. Fireman, Save My Child. The Gay Defender. 1928: The Haunted House. Vamping Venus. Seven Footprints to Satan. Hell's Angels (silent version only; never publicly shown). The Crash. Heart to Heart. The Noose. Naughty Baby (GB: Reckless Rosie). 1929: Trial Marriage. Bachelor Girl. Careers. House of Horror. Her Private Life. * Look Out Below. * Snappy Sneezer. * Crazy Feet. * Stepping Out. * Unaccustomed As We Are. * Hurdy Gurdy. * Hotter Than Hot. * Shy Boy. * The Head Guy. * The Real McCoy. 1930: Command Performance. Follow Thru (GB: Follow Through). Swanee River. No Limit. Her Man. * Whispering Whoopee. * Another Fine Mess. * All Teed Up. * Dollar Dizzy. * Looser Than Loose. * High Cs. * The Fighting Parson. * The Shrimp. * The King. 1931: Aloha (GB: No Greater Love). The Hot Heiress. Broad Minded. † Corsair. Monkey Business. The Maltese Falcon. Beyond Victory. * Catch As Catch Can. * Love Fever. * Let's Do Things. * Chickens Come Home/Chicken Come Home. * Rough Seas. * The Pip from Pittsburgh. * Voice of Hollywood. * The Pajama Party (GB: The Pyjama Party). * War Mamas. This is the Night. 1932: Klondike. Speak Easily. Call Her Savage. Horse Feathers. Big Timer. No Greater Love. * The Nickel Nurser. * Seal Skins. * On the Loose. * Cauliflower Alley. * Strictly Unreliable. * Red Noses. * Alum and Eve. * The Old Bull. * Show Business. * The Soilers. 1933: The Devil's Brother (GB: Fra Diavolo). Air Hostess. Mary Stevens M.D. Sitting Pretty. Deception. Cheating Blondes (GB: House of Chance). Counsellor-at-Law. Son of a Sailor. * Maids a la Mode. * Sneak Easily. * One Track Minds. * Asleep in the Fleet. * Bargain of the Century. * Beauty and the Bus. * Air Fright. * Backs to Nature. You Made Me Love You. 1934: Palooka (GB: The Great Schnozzle). Bottoms Up. Hips, Hips, Hooray! Cockeyed Cavaliers. The Poor Rich. Take the Stand. * Maid in Hollywood. * Babes in the Goods. * Three Chumps Ahead. * Opened by Mistake. * Bum Voyage. * Soup and Fish. * I'll Be Suing You. * One Horse Farmers. * Done in Oil. 1935: Two for Tonight. Lightning Strikes Twice. After the Dance. * The Tin Man. * Treasure Blues. * Slightly Static. * Twin Triplets. * Sing,*

*Sister, Sing. * The Misses Stooge. * Hot Money. * Top Flat. * All American Toothache. 1936: The Bohemian Girl.*

† As Alison Loyd.

TOMLIN, Lily
(Mary Tomlin) 1939–
Slim, indiarubber American comedy star with dark hair and goofy grin. Tomlin's wide range of characters and extensive repertoire of satirical situations made her one-woman shows major attractions. As a film star she never established the same drawing-power, even though she proved herself a good enough actress to win an Academy Award nomination. Born in Detroit, Tomlin was always an inventive writer with a cartoon-like mind. While still in college, she started inventing characters for comedy sketches and performing them for classmates. After dropping out of university, she used the material she had stored up to make a living as a comedienne on café and nightclub dates. At the same time, she studied acting under Peggy Fleury. Tomlin found a writing partner in Jane Wagner, a Tennessee-born writer-producer-director who has remained her collaborator ever since. Tomlin's comedy, often bitingly satirical, sometimes just simply fun that stemmed from character, began to assume a higher profile, and she gained national attention when joining the cast of the hot TV show *Rowan and Martin's Laugh-In* in 1969. Her star turn on *Laugh-In* was Ernestine, the zany switchboard girl with the nasal voice who came on at the beginning of the show; also highly amusing was a demon child called Edith Ann. Tomlin stayed with the show until 1973 by which time her reputation as a stand-up funny-girl was firmly established. She made her film debut

Pairs at the Plaza. It's hotel hilarity when Lily Tomlin (left in both pairings) and Bette Midler meet their lookalikes in *Big Business*

as the gullible gospel singer Linnea in Robert Altman's *Nashville* in 1975. Tomlin not only took an Oscar nomination for her performance but sang two songs, one of which she co-wrote. Before establishing further footholds in films, however, she returned to TV as a member of the cast of the innovative *Saturday Night Live*, a comedy show that proved as popular and star-making as *Laugh-In* had been a few years earlier. Among Tomlin's fellow-performers were Steve Martin, Chevy Chase, John Belushi, Dan Aykroyd, Bill Murray (all *qv*), Gilda Radner, Jane Curtin and Albert Brooks. Films still wanted her and she made *The Late Show* as the client whose incessant yammering nearly drives elderly detective Art Carney round the bend. Wagner wrote and directed *Moment by Moment* for her but the film was a notable misfire and the last time she tried anything but comedy. Much more successful was *Nine to Five*, about three secretaries who take revenge on their chauvinist boss. Dolly Parton and Jane Fonda were the other two, in a film full of felicitous moments, and one that gave full rein to Tomlin's comedy style for perhaps

the first time. She played three roles, but principally the title one, in the underrated *The Incredible Shrinking Woman*. That did less well than it should have done, and she was paired with box-office pets for the next two. *All of Me* was a silly but quite endearing farce about a man forced to share his body with the soul of a dead woman: Steve Martin and Tomlin were the reluctant partners. *Big Business* offered two Tomlins and two Bette Midlers in the story of twins mixed up at birth. The size of Midler's personality tended to overwhelm Tomlin's two contributions as forthright union organiser and dippy, nature-loving misfit. Since then Tomlin has concentrated on stage shows and television specials. Surely, though, there must be room for *one* of her weirdo characters in the upcoming film of *The Munsters*?

1975: Nashville. 1977: The Late Show. 1978: Moment by Moment. 1980: Nine to Five. 1981: The Incredible Shrinking Woman. 1984: All of Me. 1986: Lily Tomlin. 1988: Big Business. 1991: The Search for Signs of Intelligent Life in the Universe. Shadows and Fog. 1992: The Player.

TOMLINSON, David 1917–

Squashed of face, reedy of voice and squinty of eye, this dark-haired British comedy actor tried a great variety of roles before developing, in the 1950s, into an attractive 'silly ass' in the finest Ralph Lynn (*qv*) tradition. For a few years he reigned supreme in the field until overtaken in popularity by Ian Carmichael (*qv*). But Tomlinson had the last laugh, prolonging his career with some excellent comic character roles in Hollywood for the Disney studio. At first he considered a military career and left Tonbridge School at 16 to join the Grenadier Guards. But acting in amateur productions decided him on a career turnabout and he left the Guards and joined a repertory company in 1936, assisting the stage manager and playing small roles. He had already made a film or two when director Anthony Asquith saw him in a tour of *Quiet Wedding*, as the bridegroom, and put him in his film version of the play – as the best man. Two minor films roles later and Tomlinson was back in the forces, training then serving as a pilot instructor during World War Two. He quickly picked up his film career again in 1946. At first he essayed mainly serious roles, but began to play more comedy after appearing in *Miranda* and *Warning to Wantons* in 1948. The film that set him up as a leading comedian in the post-war British cinema was *The Chiltern Hundreds*, a very popular farce in which Tomlinson was a young viscount trying to get out of army service by standing for Parliament, winning and then resigning. He was the light relief in the POW classic *The Wooden Horse* but, after *Hotel Sahara*, another popular romp, and *Calling Bulldog Drummond* (perfectly cast as the asinine but plucky Algy), Tomlinson was top-billed in his next nine films, all comedies. Unfortunately these were not on the whole of a high standard, the funniest being *Up the Creek*, although the amusing effects of Tomlinson's own brand of petulant or indignant outrage never wavered. He was almost inevitably one of Jerome K. Jerome's *Three Men in a Boat*, but the seemingly surefire film (not helped by the casting of the humourless Laurence Harvey as one of the other two) was a flop. There was a gap of three years after *Follow That Horse!* in 1960 before Tomlinson re-

Fire and brimstone! David Tomlinson's Professor Emelius Browne delivers the goods in the Walt Disney fantasy-musical *Bedknobs and Broomsticks*

appeared, looking somewhat older, in a supporting role in *Tom Jones*, ironically the most successful comedy he had made to that date. A year later, the Disney studio in Hollywood invited him to play probably the best role of his career — tyrannical bank employee George Banks in *Mary Poppins*. As the man who likes his household to run like clockwork, Tomlinson was allowed to run the full gamut of comic moods, from joy to despair, and got to sing as well. He was exceptionally unlucky that year not to have been nominated for a Best Supporting Actor Oscar. He was now accepting top character roles and Disney called for him again as the dastardly villain who tries to sabotage his race rival in *The Love Bug*, a skilful and funny performance. And he was star-billed for the studio three years later as Erasmus in *Bedknobs and Broomsticks*, singing, dancing and clowning to a high order in another high-grossing entertainment. Tomlinson, who married late in life but now has four sons, hasn't made a film since 1980. 'I am sure', he says, 'that there must be some people who think I've died off. But it doesn't bother me when I'm not working, because I'm on the go all the time. I'm the most relaxed actor you'll ever meet. Mind you, I loved working in America, and it would be nice to do another film there. I'm all packed and ready to go!'

1940: * Name, Rank and Number. Garrison Follies. 1941: Quiet Wedding. My Wife's Family. Pimpernel Smith (US: Mister V). 1945: The Way to the Stars (US: Johnny in the Clouds). Journey Together. 1946: I See a Dark Stranger (US: The Adventuress). School for Secrets (US: Secret Flight). 1947: Master of Bankdam. Easy Money. Fame is the Spur. Broken Journey. 1948: Love in Waiting. Here Come the Hugnetts. My Brother's Keeper. Sleeping Car to Trieste. Miranda. Warning to Wantons. 1949: Helter Skelter. Vote for Huggett. Landfall. Marry Me. The Chiltern Hundreds (US: The Amazing Mr Beecham). 1950: So Long at the Fair. The Wooden Horse. 1951: The Magic Box. Hotel Sahara. Calling Bulldog Drummond. 1952: Castle in the Air. Made in Heaven. 1953: Is Your Honeymoon Really Necessary? 1955: All for Mary. 1956: Three Men in a Boat. 1957: Carry On Admiral (US: The Ship Was Loaded). 1958: Up the Creek. Further Up the Creek. 1960: Follow That Horse! 1963: Tom Jones. 1964: Mary Poppins. The Truth About Spring. 1965: City Under the Sea (US: War Gods of the Deep). The Liquidator. 1968: The Love Bug. 1971: Bedknobs and Broomsticks. 1974: Bon baisers de Hong Kong. 1977: Wombling Free. 1978: Dominique. The Water Babies. 1980: The Fiendish Plot of Dr Fu Manchu.

TRACY, William (top) 1917–1967
and
SAWYER, Joe
(Joseph Sauers) 1901–1982
Slightly-built, boyish, moon-faced, dark-haired William Tracy, and big, beefy, blond

Joe Sawyer, were an unlikely combination for comedy. Tracy was a failed juvenile lead and Sawyer a popular tough-guy character actor. But producer Hal Roach had them both under contract at the beginning of the 1940s, and used their physical contrast and complementary styles of acting to re-create on film the popular strip-cartoon army sergeants Doubleday and Ames. Tracy had trained for the stage while still a teenager, and had several Broadway plays and musicals under his belt before he reached 21. He came to Hollywood in 1938 to recreate his role in the comedy hit *Brother Rat*. Most of his other film roles, though, were minor, apart from his Dude Lester in *Tobacco Road*, and the lead in a lively serial *Terry and the Pirates*, for which he dyed his hair blond. Joe Sawyer had been around a lot longer than Tracy, and had made more than 100 films before they appeared together. Typically he played gangsters, car drivers, sergeants in the police or army, or bodyguards. He was noteworthy as the aggressive sergeant on whom Humphrey Bogart eventually exacts revenge in *The Roaring Twenties*. The saturnine Tracy and the flour-faced Sawyer were brought together at the Roach fun factory for the first time in 1941 in *Tanks a Million*. Tracy was Doubleday, the brains with the photographic memory. Sawyer was Ames, the brawn with the strong right arm. Tracy is a private soldier in the first film, his promotion to sergeant beginning the long-standing feud with his rival. The second film, *Hay Foot*, revealed that Doubleday

was secretly afraid of guns. True to Roach fashion, as begun in the early silents of Laurel and Hardy (*qv*) and their contemporaries, the Doubleday and Ames comedies usually contained some fracas in which, by the end, pretty well the whole cast seemed to have joined. In *About Face*, there's a car-wrecking scene that harks all the way back to *Two Tars*, and memories of Laurel and Hardy free-for-alls in *The Battle of Century* and *You're Darn Tootin'* were stirred by the massive brawl at the end of *Fall In*, with half the US servicemen in town grappling with a whole nest of enemy agents. The comedies would probably have continued apace had it not been for Tracy's own World War Two service. In post-war years, there was one more for Roach, *Here Comes Trouble* (made in colour!) which had Doubleday and Ames as a reporter and a detective. But they were back in the army for the appropriately-titled *As You Were*, and served in Korea for the last of the series, *Mr Walkie Talkie*, a funny piece about Doubleday adopting a duck as the platoon mascot. Neither Tracy nor Sawyer made many more films after the release of *Mr Walkie Talkie* in November 1952. Tracy worked in a TV series, ironically a weekly version of *Terry and the Pirates*, now no longer playing the eager-beaver lead, but in a character role as Hotshot Charlie. Sawyer enjoyed six years as flinty but warmhearted Sgt. Biff O'Hara in the animal action series *The Adventures of Rin Tin Tin*. Ironically, Sawyer outlived his younger partner by 15 years, before his death from cancer of the liver in 1982.

Together. 1941: Tanks a Million. 1942: Hay Foot. About Face. 1943: Fall In. Yanks Ahoy. 1948: Here Comes Trouble. 1951: As You Were. 1952: Mr Walkie Talkie.
Tracy alone. 1938: Brother Rat. Angels With Dirty Faces. 1939: The Jones Family in Hollywood. Million Dollar Legs. 1940: Terry and the Pirates (serial). The Amazing Mr Williams. Strike Up the Band. The Shop Around the Corner. Gallant Sons. 1941: Tillie the Toiler. Mr and Mrs Smith. She Knew All the Answers. Tobacco Road. Her First Beau. 1942: Young America. George Washington Slept Here. 1948: The Walls of Jericho. 1949: Henry, the Rainmaker. 1950: One Too Many. 1951: Sunny Side of the Street. 1957: The Wings of Eagles.

Sawyer alone. 1929: †* Campus Sweethearts. 1931: † Surrender. 1932: † Arsene Lupin. † Huddle (GB: Impossible Lover). † Forgotten Commandments. 1933: † College Humor. † Saturday's Millions. † Three-Cornered Moon. † College Coach (GB: Football Coach). † Blood Money. † The Stranger's Return. † Ace of Aces. † Son of a Sailor. 1934: † Death on the Diamond. † Looking for Trouble. † Behold My Wife! † College Rhythm. † The Case of the Howling Dog. † The Prescott Kid. † The Band Plays On. † Stamboul Quest. † Jimmy the Gent. † The Notorious Sophie Lang. † The Westerner. † The Whole Town's Talking (GB: Passport to Fame). 1935: † Broadway Gondolier. † Car 99. † Special Agent. † The Arizonian. The In-

former. *I Found Stella Parish. Little Big Shot. Man of Iron. Frisco Kid. Moonlight on the Prairie. The Man on the Flying Trapeze* (GB: *The Memory Expert*). *The Revenge Rider. The Petrified Forest.* 1936: *Big Brown Eyes. And Sudden Death. Murder with Pictures. Crash Donovan. The Leathernecks Have Landed* (GB: *The Marines Have Landed*). *Two in a Crowd. Freshman Love* (GB: *Rhythm on the River*). *The Country Doctor. The Last Outlaw. The Walking Dead. High Tension. Special Investigator. Pride of the Marines. Black Legion.* 1937: *Great Guy* (GB: *Pluck of the Irish*). *A Dangerous Adventure. Slim. Midnight Madonna.* * *Behind the Criminal. The Lady Fights Back. They Gave Him a Gun. Navy Blues. Reported Missing. Motor Madness. San Quentin.* 1938: *Always in Trouble. Tarzan's Revenge. Stolen Heaven. Gambling Ship. Heart of the North. The Storm. Passport Husband.* 1939: *You Can't Get Away with Murder. The Lady and the Mob. I Stole a Million. Union Pacific. Sabotage* (GB: *Spies at Work*). *Inside Information. Confessions of a Nazi Spy. Frontier Marshal. The Roaring Twenties.* 1940: *The Man from Montreal. The Grapes of Wrath. King of the Lumberjacks. Women Without Names. The Long Voyage Home. Border Legion. Santa Fe Trail. The House Across the Bay. Dark Command. Lucky Cisco Kid. Melody Ranch. Wildcat Bus.* 1941: *The Lady from Cheyenne. Last of the Duanes. Down in San Diego. Swamp Water* (GB: *The Man Who Came Back*). *You're in the Army Now. Sergeant York. Belle Starr. Down Mexico Way. They Died with Their Boots On.* 1942: *The McGuerins from Brooklyn.* * *A Letter from Bataan. Wrecking Crew. Sundown Jim. Brooklyn Orchid.* 1943: *Buckskin Frontier* (GB: *The Iron Road*). *Prairie Chickens. Taxi, Mister. Let's Face It. Tarzan's Desert Mystery. The Outlaw. Cowboy in Manhattan. Hit the Ice. Tornado. Alaska Highway. Sleepy Lagoon.* 1944: *Moon Over Las Vegas. Hey, Rookie. Raiders of Ghost City* (serial). *The Singing Sheriff. South of Dixie.* 1945: *The Naughty Nineties. High Powered. Brewster's Millions.* 1946: *Joe Palooka — Champ. Deadline at Dawn. GI War Brides. The Runaround. Gilda. Inside Job.* 1947: *Big Town After Dark. Christmas Eve. A Double Life. Roses Are Red.* 1948: *Half Past Midnight. If You Knew Susie. Fighting Back. Coroner Creek. The Untamed Breed. Fighting Father Dunne.* 1949: *The Gay Amigo. Deputy Marshal. And Baby Makes Three. Curtain Call at Cactus Creek* (GB: *Take the Stage*). *Kazan. The Lucky Stiff. The Stagecoach Kid.* ‡ *Two Knights in Brooklyn/Two Mugs from Brooklyn.* 1950: *Blondie's Hero. Operation Haylift. The Traveling Saleswoman. The Flying Missile.* 1951: *Pride of Maryland. Comin' Round the Mountain.* 1952: *Red Skies of Montana. Indian Uprising. Deadline USA* (GB: *Deadline*). 1953: *It Came from Outer Space.* 1954: *Taza, Son of Cochise. Johnny Dark. Riding Shotgun.* 1955: *The Kettles in the Ozarks.* 1956: *The Killing.* 1960: *North to Alaska.* 1962: *How the West Was Won.* 1973: *Harry in Your Pocket* (GB: *Harry Never Holds*).

† As Joseph Sauer
‡ Combined GB version of *The McGuerins from Brooklyn/Taxi, Mister*

Tommy Trinder thrust his chin into a fairly straight acting role in *The Bells Go Down*. Among the assembled company are William Hartnell, Campbell Singer, Sydney Tafler, Mervyn Johns and Beatrice Varley

TRINDER, Tommy 1909–1989
Long-chinned, toothily-smiling, aggressive-seeming, dark-haired British music-hall comedian who unexpectedly became a film star too — a working-class equivalent of Jack Hulbert (*qv*), whom he matched in popularity from 1938 on. His catchphrase — 'You lucky people!' became famous nationwide. Trinder's opening words to his music-hall act were 'If it's laughter you're after, Trinder's the name' and it was, too, from the age of 12 when, an early school leaver, he threw up his job as an errand boy and went on the stage to make people smile, touring South Africa with a revue company in 1921 and appearing as a boy vocalist at Collins' Music-Hall the following year. The son of a London tram driver, Tommy always possessed a quick wit. It was to make him one of the finest ad-libbers in the business, and he rarely needed a script to be funny. One suspects some of his film appearances are less than riotous simply because he has to stick to the script! Trinder spent years touring Britain on variety bills as a stand-up comic before nationwide success found him. It began to come in 1937 with the revues *Tune In* and *In Town To-Night*, by which time music-hall audiences had become familiar with the leering smile, the pork-pie hat and the wagging finger. The British cinema, regaining confidence after its mid-1930s slump, drew him in, but *Almost a Honeymoon*, *Save a Little Sunshine* and *She Couldn't Say No* straitjacketed him into roles that most light comedians could have played. *Laugh It Off*, an army farce, was more likely material but the script was poor. His standing was boosted by *Sailors Three*, a genuinely funny war comedy that harnessed him with Claude Hulbert (*qv*) and Michael Wilding as three matelots who capture a German pocket battleship. Trinder's robust performance brought him further roles with the film's makers, Ealing Studios, with whom he was to do his best film work. Meanwhile, he had virtually taken up residence at the London Palladium. First appearing there in *Band Waggon* in 1939, he supported Flanagan and Allen (*qv*) in *Top of the World* (1940) and Bebe Daniels (*qv*) and Ben Lyon in *Gangway*, before starring in his own shows, *Best Bib and Tucker*, *Happy and Glorious* and

Here, There and Everywhere, which between them ran at the Palladium until 1947. Back at Ealing, he successfully played two fairly straight roles laced with his own engaging brand of humour and native London wit. *The Foreman Went to France* was the story of a true wartime exploit, and *The Bells Go Down* a smoke-grimed tribute to the work of London's firemen in the Blitz. Trinder's character died at the end of the film trying to save another fireman. There was a follow-up to *Sailor's Three*, *Fiddlers Three*, a sort of cross between *Roman Scandals* and *A Yankee at King Arthur's Court*. But Ealing had not really found its feet in comedy (it was to do so spectacularly a few years later) and *Fiddlers* lacked the sparkle of the earlier film. There was no lack of sparkle, though, about *Champagne Charlie*, with Trinder swaggering, top-hatted and well in character as the belligerent George Leybourne, a music-hall entertainer of the 1860s not unlike himself. The comedy-musical was swinging, invigorating stuff, but before Ealing could find further films for the Trinder personality he was off (between further Palladium appearances) on worldwide appearances, covering countries as far apart as America, South Africa and Australia. He was, ironically, taken back to Australia by his final Ealing venture, *Bitter Springs*, another salt-of-the-earth role in this story of a family fighting to make a new life in Aborigine country. In between appearing in pantomime, and becoming a favourite of the British Royal Family, Trinder was off on his travels again, taking in Canada, Australia, South Africa and New Zealand, before returning to Britain in 1954. He also found time to indulge in his favourite pastime, soccer, becoming chairman of Fulham Football Club, and its guiding light for many years to come. With the arrival of independent television in the London area in 1955, a big variety show was mounted called *Sunday Night at the London Palladium*. Trinder was the obvious choice as compere, and he did his old stamping-ground proud, becoming the top British TV star of the time, and even making another movie, a rusty old army farce called *You Lucky People*. The Palladium show – with Trinder displaying frantic energy and wit, especially in its 'Beat the Clock' fun-and-games section – was the last real highlight of his career. He continued to appear in pantomimes and cabaret, but further film appearances were only cameos. Radio audiences welcomed him through the 1960s and 1970s in such displays of ready wit as *My Wildest Dream* and *Does the Team Think?* He celebrated his 80th birthday shortly before his death from heart problems.

1938: Almost a Honeymoon. Save a Little Sunshine. 1939: She Couldn't Say No. Laugh It Off. 1940: Sailors Three (US: Three Cock-eyed Sailors). 1941: * Eating Out with Tommy. 1942: The Foreman Went to France (US: Somewhere in France). 1943: The Bells Go Down. 1944: Fiddlers Three. Champagne Charlie. 1946: * Staggered Holidays. 1947: * Family Guide. 1950: Bitter Springs. 1955: You Lucky People. 1959: Make Mine A Million. 1961: The Damned (US: These Are the Damned). 1964: The Beauty Jungle (US: Contest Girl). 1969: Under the Table You Must Go. 1974: Barry McKenzie Holds His Own.

TURPIN, Ben
(Bernard Turpin) 1868–1940

It seems that, after the accepted 'greats', Ben Turpin, with his diminutive build, swan's neck, virtually no chin, energetic Adam's apple, brush moustache, mere scrag of dark hair and above all, heroically crossed eyes, is the figure most people remember from the halcyon days of Hollywood silent comedy. A genuine, 22-carat eccentric (he would often introduce himself to people as 'Ben Turpin – three thousand dollars a week'), Turpin took his comedies, whose themes were more ludicrous than most, dead seriously. He was also well aware of his good fortune in starting a star comedy career in his late forties, and saved or invested most of his money. Proud of his acrobatic abilities, the 5 ft 4 in Turpin could do some quite amazing stuntwork well into his fifties. He was also a pernickety man who could be difficult to work with. Those he didn't get along with described him variously as boastful, mean, superstitious or, at best, temperamental. Ben was, however, a devout Catholic, and the story is told that Hollywood directors spread the word that, if Ben played up, the thing to do was threaten to go home and pray to St Joseph that his eyes would uncross. After that, Ben would be as good as gold. Furthermore, he insured his crossed eyes with Lloyds of London for $50,000. Born in New Orleans, Turpin, whose grandparents were French, took up acting after his parents (his father ran a sweet shop) moved to New York. He worked in burlesque for many years, most popularly as a character called Happy Hooligan. His efforts to get a foothold in films, though, were unsuccessful until 1914, when he was taken on as a foil in Wallace Beery's (*qv*) Sweedie comedies, which involved the star appearing in drag. It wasn't until 1917 that he was starred, and quickly became so popular that he must have been baffled as to why the breakthrough took so long. He was most successful with a series of parodies of big films, his theatrical and heroic melodramatics raising many a chuckle thanks to his small stature and a pair of eyes whose owner couldn't possibly be taken seriously. Thanks to revivals and compilations, the Turpin film people recall most vividly is probably *Yukon Jake*, in which he drives a dog team including a whelp whose feet never touch the snow, tangles both with a bear and with the eponymous villain, becomes a human snowball after losing his footing and dreams about the Sennett Bathing Beauties in igloos after being knocked out in an accident. Throughout it all, Turpin maintained the same beatific, slightly bemused look. Turpin's wife Carrie died in 1925 following a series of strokes. She was only 43. After his remarriage late the following year, Turpin's interest in movies began to wane. Sound was looming, and he was too old (and wealthy) to really meet the challenge. After a further half-dozen comedies for Sennett in 1927, he moved into a comfy semi-retirement, only emerging for cameo roles when the producers were willing to pay his asking price of $1,000 a week. One such producer who thought it worthwhile was Hal Roach. He needed someone to play a plumber in the last Roach comedy with Laurel and Hardy (*qv*) in 1940, *Saps at Sea*. Their apartment – the plumbing, electricals etc – is all mixed-up. But when cross-eyed Ben comes to call, he's soon on the phone to his employer, remarking that it looks all right to him. Turpin looked nothing like his 71 years in *Saps at Sea*, but his heart had for some time been failing and a few weeks after the film's completion he was dead. In his heyday, one of his favourite games was misdirecting people round the Mack Sennett lot. If they complained, Turpin would counter with: 'Well, you wouldn't go where I was looking!'

1907: Ben Gets a Duck and is Ducked. 1909: Midnight Disturbance. The New Cop. Hurray! Hurray! The Wife's Away. Mr Flip. 1914: Sweedie and the Lord. Sweedie and the Double Exposure. Sweedie's Skate. Sweedie Springs a Surprise. The Fickleness of Sweedie. Sweedie Learns to Swim. She Landed a Big One. Sweedie and the Trouble Maker. Sweedie at the Fair. Madame Double X. Chick Evans Links with Sweedie. Sweedie's Suicide. Two Hearts That Beat as Ten. 1915: Sweedie and Her Dog. Sweedie's Hopeless Love. Sweedie Goes to College. Love and Trouble. Sweedie Learns to Ride. Sweedie's Hero. The Clubman's Wager. Countess Bloggie. Bloggie's Vacation. Curiosity. A Coat Tale. Others Started But Sophie Finished. A Quiet Little Game. The Merry Models. Sophie and the Fakir. Snakeville's Hen Medic. Snakeville's Champion. Snakeville's Debutantes. Snakeville's Twins. It Happened in Snakeville. How Slippery Slim Saw the Show. Two Bold Bad Men. The Undertaker's Wife. A

Bunch of Matches. The Bell Hop. Versus Sledge Hammers. Too Much Turkey. By the Sea. His New Job. A Night Out. A Christmas Revenge. The Champion. † Carmen/Charlie Chaplin's Burlesque on Carmen. 1916: Some Bravery. A Waiting Game. Taking the Count. National Nuts. Nailing on the Lid. Just for a Kid. Lost and Found. Bungling Bill's Dress. When Papa Died. The Plumber/His Blowout. The Delinquent Bridegrooms. The Iron Mitt. Hired and Fired. A Deep Sea Liar. For Ten Thousand Bucks. Some Liars. The Stolen Booking. Doctoring a Leak. Poultry à la Mode. Ducking a Discord. He Did and He Didn't. Picture Pirates. Shot in the Fracas. Jealous Jolts. The Wicked City. A Safe Proposition. 1917: A Circus Cyclone. The Musical Marvels. The Butcher's Nightmare. His Bogus Boast. A Studio Stampede. Frightened Flirts. Why Ben Bolted. Masked Mirth. Bucking the Tiger. Caught in the End. Sole Mates. Oriental Love. A Clever Dummy. Lost − a Cook. A Pawnbroker's Heart. Roping Her Romeo. Are Waitresses Safe? Taming Target Center. 1918: Sheriff Nell's Tussle. Saucy Madeline. The Battle Royal. Two Tough Tenderfeet. She Loved Him Plenty. Hide and Seek. Detectives. 1919: Cupid's Day Off. East Lynne with Variations. When Love is Blind. No Mother to Guide Him. † Yankee Doodle in Berlin. Uncle Tom without a Cabin. Sleuths. Whose Little Wife Are You? Salome versus Shenandoah. 1920: The Star Boarder. † Down on the Farm. † Married Life. You Wouldn't Believe It. 1921: A Small Town Idol. Love's Outcast. Love and Doughnuts. † Home Talent. 1922: Bright Eyes. Step Forward. Home-Made Movies. 1923: † Hollywood. † The Shriek of Araby. Where's My Wandering Boy Tonight? Pitfalls of a Big City. Asleep at the Switch. The Daredevil. 1924: Ten Dollars or Ten Days. The Hollywood Kid. Yukon Jake. Romeo and Juliet. Three Foolish Weeks. The Reel Virginian. 1925: Wild Goose Chaser. Raspberry Romance. † Hogan's Alley. The Marriage Circus. 1926: † Steel Preferred. A Harem Knight. When a Man's a Prince. A Prodigal Bridegroom. A Blonde's Revenge. 1927: † A College Hero. A Hollywood Hero. The Jolly Jilter. Broke in China. Pride of Pikeville. Love's Languid Lure. Daddy Boy. † A Woman's Way. 1928: † The Wife's Relations. The Eyes Have it. She Said No. 1929: † The Show of Shows. † The Love Parade. 1930: † Swing High. 1931: † Cracked Nuts. Our Wife. 1932: † Hypnotized. † Million Dollar Legs. † Make Me a Star. Lighthouse Love. Chase Me, Charlie. 1933: Hollywood on Parade. Techno-Crazy. 1934: The Law of the Wild (serial). 1935: Keystone Hotel. Bring 'Em Back a Lie. 1939: † Hollywood Cavalcade. A Small Town Idol (revised version for sound). 1940: † Saps at Sea.

All shorts except † features.

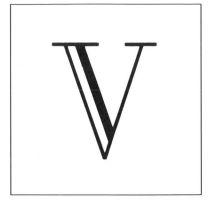

VAGUE, Vera
(Barbara Jo Allen) 1904−1974

A tall, dark-haired radio actress, Barbara Jo Allen had made no movies until she happened on the character called Vera Vague as a party piece she had thought up for a radio staff get-together. She was encouraged to turn the dizzy spinster with the high-pitched voice into a radio personality, and soon found herself with her own show, as well as 'gag' guest spots on shows of other comedians. Even British radio got a taste of Vera. She started appearing in films as well from 1940, although producers were a little perturbed to find an elegant, attractive woman who hardly matched the physical appearance most audiences had conjured up in their minds for Vera Vague. So the Vague of movies (she was usually billed as Vera Vague, although occasionally, especially in later days, under her real name) was more often than not the scatterbrained friend of the heroine, stealing all the scenes and pinching all the best laughs with her dry delivery. She was given her own series of two-reeler comedies in 1943. Unfortunately, it was at Columbia, home of the Three Stooges, (qv) where slapstick reigned over characterisation. Vera found herself swapping blows, taking pies in the face, having fights with water-hoses and wrestling with a gangster. Had the unit allowed her to develop her own film character, possibly along the lines of an interfering busybody, she might have become an even better-known name. A couple of the shorts did allow her room to stamp her individual brand of humour on them. In Doctor, Feel My Pulse she's a hypochondriac who mistakes a lunatic for a trained doctor. And in The Jury Goes Round 'n' Round, she's the juror who gets in everyone's hair because she alone believes that the defendant is innocent. This was one of two Vera Vague shorts nominated for an Academy Award. At her best, she proved with her mobile face and excellent timing that she could command attention in a solo spotlight. Alas, it was back to custard pies. In 1952 she gave up on a film comedy career. Barbara Jo Allen went back to what she did best − putting the real Vera Vague across on American radio.

1940: Sing, Dance, Plenty Hot (GB: Melody Girl). Melody and Moonlight. Village Barn Dance. Melody Ranch. The Mad Doctor (GB: A Date with Destiny). 1941: Buy Me That Town. Kiss the Boys Goodbye. Ice-Capades. 1942: Larceny Inc. Hi Neighbor. Design for Scandal. Mrs Wiggs of the Cabbage Patch. Priorities on Parade. 1943: Swing Your Partner. Get Going. Henry Aldrich Plays Cupid (GB: Henry Plays Cupid). * You Dear Boy. * Doctor, Feel My Pulse. 1944: Rosie the Riveter (GB: In Rosie's Room). Moon Over Las Vegas. Lake Placid Serenade. Girl Rush. Cowboy Canteen (GB: Close Harmony). * Strife of the Party. * She Snoops to Conquer. * The Jury Goes Round 'n' Round. 1945: Snafu (GB: Welcome Home). * Calling All Fibbers. 1946: Earl Carroll Sketchbook (GB: Hats Off to Rhythm). * Hiss and Yell. * Headin' for a Weddin'. * Reno-Vated. 1947: * Cupid Goes Nuts. 1948: * A Miss in a Mess. 1949: * Clunked in the Clink. * Wha' Happen? 1950: Square Dance Katy. * Nursie Behave. 1951: * She Took a Powder. 1952: * Happy Go Wacky. 1956: The Opposite Sex. Mohawk. 1958: Sleeping Beauty (voice only). 1959: Born to Be Loved.

VAN DYKE, Dick 1925−

Although people still know his name today, America's Dick Van Dyke has had a strange career whose years of prime fame and acclaim were all crammed into one decade, the 1960s. After that a succession of poor career decisions cost him his place at the top. That's a shame, because at his peak Van Dyke was undoubtedly a major comic talent, and one of the cheeriest personalities on the entertainment scene. Long-faced, long-chinned and duck-nosed ('As a boy I looked just like Stan Laurel'), with giraffe-like joints, Van Dyke could use body language to create a laugh out of some quite ordinary situation. He could also sing pleasantly and dance with acrobatic abandon. Born in Missouri 12 days before Christmas, Van Dyke was briefly in advertising after service in the wartime US Air Force. After experience as a radio announcer, he took to the boards for six years as half of a variety act called the Merry Mutes, a comedy-mime duo. During the

1950s Van Dyke was busy on television, but couldn't get a breakthrough to the top. 'People kept telling me', he once recalled, 'that I ought to have an evening comedy show and when I said "Yes", they told me it was a bad time for comedy.' Things began to happen for Van Dyke after he returned to the stage. He had the leading role in *Bye Bye Birdie*, as the promoter involved in the nationwide search to find a girl to give a megastar his last kiss before he goes in the army. The show opened in April 1960 and was an immense hit. Eighteen months later, the 'evening comedy show' on prime-time TV happened at last. *The Dick Van Dyke Show*, co-starring Dick with Mary Tyler Moore, soon became a national favourite. Van Dyke was a writer for a big-headed TV comic. He and Tyler Moore played perfectly off one another and the series made national figures of them both. The programme won an Emmy in 1962. A year later, the film version of *Bye Bye Birdie* came along, and launched Van Dyke on his cinema career. That really took off with his casting as Bert the chimney sweep in *Mary Poppins*. His playing had vigour, freshness, breeziness and charm. Although it was Julie Andrews who won the Oscar as Mary, Van Dyke undoubtedly played a large part in the film's success. He stole the show in *The Art of Love*, especially when running to the rescue like a hamstrung antelope. A solo starring vehicle for the Disney studio, *Lt Robin Crusoe USN*, was flaccid stuff but made lots of money. At this point, the star closed the door on *The Dick Van Dyke Show* at the height of its success to concentrate on the movies. It was a sad misjudgment. Van Dyke's only remaining film hit was *Chitty Chitty Bang Bang*, and even that was slaughtered by the critics. The only good film he did make, *The Comic*, a tragi-comedy about a silent comedian vaguely based on Stan Laurel (*qv*), was mishandled by its studio, and flopped. His last cinema feature for nearly a decade, *Cold Turkey*, was appropriately titled. Belatedly, Van Dyke returned to TV, but it was too late. *The New Dick Van Dyke Show* lasted three seasons, beginning in 1971, but never repeated the success of the original. Around 1973, Van Dyke made public (rather too public) the alcoholism of

himself and his wife, and the 'Days of Wine and Roses' life they had lived because of pressures brought on by his struggling career. He was very good in a TV movie about the subject, *The Morning After*, but the public really didn't want to know about a Van Dyke that wasn't being funny. Nor did they want to know about him playing a priest who falls in love with a nun in *The Runner Stumbles*, in 1979. That ill-judged role is his last starring assignment in films to date. He returned to comedy (and TV) in *Van Dyke and Company*, which concentrated on his abilities as a mime. It lasted scarcely three months. The best of Dick's more recent ventures has been the TV movie *Found Money*, which co-starred him with Sid Caesar (*qv*), and cast him as a bank executive who, forced into unwanted retirement, uses the bank's new computer to donate funds to the needy. A pilot for a TV series *Ghost of a*

Chance failed to take. Van Dyke is philosophial about it all. 'You have to take one day at a time', he says. 'And never try to figure out why comedy works. It can feel good for no apparent reason. You'll only make yourself miserable trying to work it out.'

1963: *Bye Bye Birdie*. 1964: *What a Way to Go! Mary Poppins*. 1965: *The Art of Love*. 1966: *Lt Robin Crusoe USN*. 1967: *Divorce American Style*. *Fitzwilly (GB: Fitzwilly Strikes Back)*. *Never a Dull Moment*. 1968: *Chitty Chitty Bang Bang*. 1969: *The Comic*. 1971: *Cold Turkey*. 1974: *The Morning After (TV)*. 1977: *Tubby the Tuba (TV, voice only)*. 1979: *The Runner Stumbles*. 1982: *Drop-out Father (TV)*. 1983: *Found Money (TV)*. 1987: *Ghost of a Chance (TV)*. 1990: *Dick Tracy*. 1992: *Freddie Goes to Washington (voice only)*.

When he's not busy being a chimney sweep, Bert (Dick Van Dyke) keeps busy entertaining people in the park as a one-man band, in Walt Disney's *Mary Poppins*

VARNEY, Reg 1916–

Puckish, solidly-built, always cheerful, versatile British comedian with a shock of dark hair not always quite kept in check by masses of grease. Facially very much like the American Joe E. Brown (qv), Varney had a tough climb to the top, reaching starring roles in films at perhaps a later stage in life than any other comic except America's Rodney Dangerfield (qv). For many years Varney was a middling entertainer out of the limelight. He was born in London, the son of a working man whose chief enjoyment in leisure hours was playing the piano at pubs and clubs. Varney Jr could play by ear when he was seven. 'For a seven-year-old kid', he says, 'I was damn good.' At 13 his parents forked out for piano lessons; they also bought him an accordion, which he taught himself to play by looking in a mirror. At 14 he began his career by singing and playing in pubs for 8s 6d (42½p) a night; every encore meant another 1s 6d (7½p). For several months he played piano and accordion at a nightclub in London's Soho, then worked as a pianist at a club for film extras, played piano at cinemas and finally took his act to Collins' Music-Hall. By 1938 he was pianist for London's Windmill Theatre's girlie revues, but during war service – most of the time he was a sheet-metal worker with the Royal Electrical and Mechanical Engineers – he organised concert parties and cracked jokes while playing the accordion. He found, too, that his cheery countenance amused people just by itself. 'You can work up a good line of patter', he said, 'and once it goes over well, you'll find half a dozen other chaps doing the same thing. But no-one can pinch your face.' After a tour of the Far East with the *Stars in Battledress* Varney quickly won popularity back in England on variety bills. By late 1947 he was being hailed as a new comic discovery; producer Sydney Box talked of starring him in a film, but somehow the momentum never carried through and it was Varney's 'gormless' stooge, a cheeky young comic called Benny Hill (qv) who made it to stardom first. It was 1961, after years of pantomime, music-hall, troop shows and guest spots in TV shows, that Varney first got a taste of the TV big-time when he appeared

as the foreman forever producing his tape-measure in the union satire *The Rag Trade*. Three seasons of this hit show were followed by his own series, *The Valiant Varneys*, in which he played various of his ancestors, including a schoolboy pitched half-way between Joe E. Brown and Norman Wisdom (qv). The next series, *Beggar My Neighbour*, was a mild success for Varney, now firmly established as a British TV star. The one that followed it in 1968, *On the Buses*, with Varney as a bus conductor at the centre of a warring working-class family, was an immense hit. Tellingly scripted to take constant advantage of the foibles in its characters, it also produced some inspired visual moments. *On the Buses* ran until 1975 and spawned three rather ramshackle feature films. Varney, who had appeared in co-starring roles in two 1960s film comedies, suddenly found himself an attraction in British films. He made *Go for a Take*, which allowed him to run amok in a film studio and play lots of film stereotypes, from vampires to Vikings, while on the run from gangsters. He also made *The Best Pair of Legs in the Business*, a genuine try at mixing comedy with pathos, as an ageing drag artist at a holiday camp, but it was understandably less popular than his *Buses* films. Since *On the Buses* finished, Varney has toured Australia and New Zealand with the series, made a less successful TV series called *Down the Gate*, and floated an idea to go

Back on the Buses which never came to anything. Comfortably off as he advances towards old age, he spends much time on his favourite occupation – painting landscapes.

1952: Miss Robin Hood. 1965: Joey Boy. 1966: The Great St Trinian's Train Robbery. 1971: On the Buses. 1972: Mutiny on the Buses. Go for a Take. The Best Pair of Legs in the Business. 1973: Holiday on the Buses.

VELEZ, Lupe

(Guadalupe V. de Villalobos) 1908–1944
Lupe Velez was a very hot tamale. Every bit as tempestuous off the screen as she looked

Mexican chatterbox Lupe Velez for once finds herself outgunned in the vocal department by the warring Victor McLaglen and Edmund Lowe in *Hot Pepper*

on it, this Mexican firecracker took Hollywood by storm twice — once as an exotic hoyden heroine, and the next as a fractured-English screen-hogging comedienne. Dark-haired, flashing-eyed and curvaceous, she was a fraction over five feet of diminutive dynamite. Her mother was an opera singer (Lupe could sing, too, though not with the same range) and her father a colonel in the army who was killed in an insurrection when she was 14. After his death, Lupe (pronounced Loopy) left her Texas boarding school and returned home, initially as a salesgirl, but soon, at 15, as a dancer in a Mexico City stage show. Descending on Hollywood in 1926, she got a featured dancing spot in *Music Box Revue* at a local theatre, and came to the attention of producer Hal Roach, who signed her up for his comedy factory and put her in a few two-reelers, including one with Laurel and Hardy (*qv*) called *Sailors, Beware!* Her explosive vivacity impressed legendary swashbuckling star Douglas Fairbanks so much that he gave her the plum role of the Mountain Girl in his silent feature *The Gaucho*. Lupe's success in that film set her up for a series of exotic, spirited, strong-willed characters. Like her, these girls were usually about as volatile as TNT. To her chiselled Latin-American looks, Lupe added an ability to express various wild emotions with complete conviction, an energy that grabbed the attention in any scene and a seemingly natural sense of comedy timing that would soon stand her in good stead. Her real-life love affairs were equally intense. A three-year fling with Gary Cooper ended in 1933 when she married the screen's Tarzan, Johnny Weissmuller, the beginning of a storm-tossed on-off union that ended in the divorce courts six years later. Meanwhile, after such films as *Tiger Rose*, *East is West* and *Cuban Love Song*, Lupe took to the stage, starring in a Ziegfeld revue called *Hot-Cha!* (after that, she was often known as the Hot-Cha Girl), in which she sang Carmen Miranda-type songs and sharpened up her comedy techniques. One critic described her as 'enticing and frenzied'! Freelancing with various studios, Lupe returned to films playing more comedy and trading on her own image. If this corresponded all too accurately with her role in 1932's *The Half-Naked Truth* as a temperamental celebrity who's her own best publicist, Lupe was quite happy. Her broken English and endless energy quite stole the show from series stars Edmund Lowe and Victor McLaglen in the Flagg and Quirt comedy *Hot Pepper* (they must have meant Lupe). After co-starring with *Hot-Cha!* partner Bert Lahr (*qv*) in *Mr Broadway*, Lupe had a memorable run-in with Laurel and Hardy (*qv*) in the all-star *Hollywood Party*. Jimmy Durante (*qv*) was in that too, and he and Lupe, the Schnozzle and the dazzle, were teamed in two more, *Palooka* and *Strictly Dynamite*. In between filing for divorces from Weissmuller and then withdrawing the suits,

Lupe managed to find time for a few films in England. She plagued RKO's comedy team Wheeler and Woolsey (*qv*) in what would turn out to be their last film, *High Flyers*. Despite a great comedy cast that included Lupe, Jack Carson and Margaret Dumont (both *qv*), the film was a disappointment. Lupe's standing in Hollywood had gradually slipped as the 1930s passed. To add to her woes, she finally went through with one of her divorce suits against Weissmuller and the marriage ended in 1939. A temporary salvation, however, was at hand, in the shape of the famous 'Mexican Spitfire' comedy series, which co-starred Lupe with the equally explosive Leon Errol (*qv*). Inspired by the unexpected success of *The Girl from Mexico* (in the face of critical indifference), the studio rushed out another comedy about Carmelita, the graceless senorita who embarrasses everyone and sticks out like a sore thumb in high society. *Mexican Spitfire* was ready for the 1939/40 holiday season and heralded a further six Spitfire comedies over the next four years. In between them, the irrepressible, now red-headed, Lupe made such other low-budget capers as *Six Lessons from Madame La Zonga* (she was Madame), *Honolulu Lu* and *Redhead from Manhattan*. Lupe was noisier and more dominant than ever, and in *Lu* did imitations of Gloria Swanson and Katharine Hepburn. Suddenly, in December 1944, it was all over. Lupe, rejected by a new lover and pregnant by him, dressed herself in her finest blue silk pyjamas and committed suicide with sleeping pills. She left a note for her housekeeper that said. 'Don't think bad of me. I love you many . . . say goodbye to all my friends, and the American press that were always so nice to me.' Lupe never did quite master the English language. It was part of her enduring appeal.

*1927: * What Women Did for Me. * Sailors, Beware! The Gaucho. 1928: Stand and Deliver. 1929: Lady of the Pavements (GB: Lady of the Night). Wolf Song. Tiger Rose. Where East is East. 1930: † East is West. Hell Harbor. * Voice of Hollywood No. 1. The Storm. 1931: † Resurrection. Cuban Love Song. The Squaw Man (GB: The White Man). Hombres en mi Vida. 1932: The Half-Naked Truth. The Broken Wing. Kongo. 1933: Hot Pepper. Mr Broadway. 1934: Palooka (GB: The Great Schnozzle). Hollywood Party. Strictly Dynamite. 1935: The Morals of Marcus. 1936: Gypsy Melody (US: Under Your Spell). 1937: High Flyers. La Zandunga. Mad About Money (US: He Loved an Actress). 1939: The Girl from Mexico. Mexican Spitfire. 1940: Mexican Spitfire Out West. 1941: Six Lessons from Madame La Zonga. Honolulu Lu. Mexican Spitfire's Baby. Playmates. 1942: Mexican Spitfire at Sea. Mexican Spitfire Sees a Ghost. Mexican Spitfire's Elephant. 1943: Ladies' Day. Mexican Spitfire's Blessed Event. Redhead from Manhattan. 1944: Nana.*

† And Spanish version

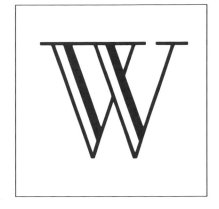

WALLS, Tom
See LYNN, Ralph and WALLS, Tom

WARRISS, Ben
See JEWEL, Jimmy and WARRISS, Ben

WAYNE, Naunton
See RADFORD, Basil and WAYNE, Naunton

WEST, Mae 1892–1980
Many actress/singer/comediennes have reminded one of Mae West over the years, notably Hollywood's Bette Midler in recent times. But they have all, in one way or another, tried to diversify their talent, so that none has had the concentrated impact of the original Mae West, who found her image and stayed within it. Blonde, blue-eyed and buxom, with a curl of the lips, Mae as an adult had a habit of speaking from somewhere near the side of her mouth in a throaty drawl, and of looking sideways at her 'victims'. The character of the aggressive, vampish, voluptuous, always-in-control, never fazed female was one unique in show business history. Her best ripostes were always immaculately timed to cause the most damage, usually coming after a brief pause to take the measure of her adversary. On stage, she was scandalously smutty for her day, and often fell foul of the law. Cinema tamed her just enough to make her twice as funny, and twice as entertaining. The eldest

daughter of a Brooklyn boxer who tried various jobs after retirement until settling for a career in real estate, Mae had made her stage debut at five, singing and dancing in a concert put on by her dancing school. She did a song-and-dance number, already a solo attraction. Her mother began taking her to vaudeville shows, in the meantime allowing Mae to perform with local stock companies until she was 11. At 14, she began appearing in burlesque, vaudeville and, soon, Broadway revues, initially billed as 'The Baby Vamp'. She became part of a song-and-dance act with Frank Wallace, and married him in 1911. That was the year of her first Broadway show, *A La Broadway*, in which the *New York Times* critic confessed himself 'pleased by her grotesquerie and snappy way of singing and dancing'. She followed up with another show the same year, *Vera Violetta*, appearing with Al Jolson and Gaby Deslys. Her fellow-performers in *A Winsome Widow* the following year included Leon Errol (*qv*) and the Dolly Sis-

ters. Mae had clearly arrived. For a while she concentrated on developing her solo vaudeville act, incorporating comic monologues from 1913. Briefly, she toured in a double-act with her younger sister, but Beverly West never managed to become a show business star. Mae also signed to make films for Universal in 1915 but, apparently nothing came of it. On her own again, Mae went back to the stage and her song-and-patter act, now well in charge of her audience. *Variety* approved, although it sniffily qualified its praise in 1916 by observing that 'she occasionally oversteps the line between facetiousness and freshness'. The line would soon be well crossed and often. In 1918, critics howled with outrage when she did the Shimmy. 'After a show in Chicago', Mae later recalled, 'I went to this coloureds' cabaret downtown. I see them dancing the bump and the jelly-roll and all that, and then a girl starts doin' a funny sort of dance and I asked "What's that?". And the waiter, he says: "Oh lady that's shakin' the Shimmy"'.

Next night I put it in my act and it like to tore the house down. The audience went wild. I took ten bows. The manager came backstage and asked me what caused the riot. When I showed him he was afraid to let me do it again.' Confident that she could write her own show, Mae had left vaudeville by 1923, and was busy researching sex, and the underworld of America's big cities. The resultant play, *Sex*, opened in 1926 and was an instant New York smash. After 385 performances it was raided by the police, and Mae was jailed for ten days. In 1927 she presented her homosexual comedy *The Drag* and the short-lived *The Wicked Age*, both reviled by the critics. But 1928 brought the enormously successful *Diamond Lil*, which ran and ran. It also saw the première of Mae's *Pleasure Man* (in which she didn't take part), a farrago of drugs, murder and emasculation, which was raided at the first and third performances, at which stage the entire cast was arrested. Mae indisputably had a way with comic dialogue; her stumbling-block was she couldn't see when risqué material became sheer smut — hence the unevenness of her successes. But Hollywood and the movies were to solve the problem for her. She had made a debut of sorts singing two of her songs in a 'Screen Snapshots' short for Columbia Pictures. But nothing came of it, and it was another two years before Paramount came through with a positive offer. She was fourth-billed on her debut feature, *Night After Night*, and proved even more of a scene-stealer in this George Raft vehicle than the veteran Alison Skipworth. She had only a few of the carefully-worded wisecracks that would become her trademark, but among them was the moment when the hat-check girl says: 'Oh goodness, what beautiful diamonds' and Mae replies 'Goodness had nothing to do with it, dearie.' Although Paramount could see it had a hot potato on its hands, it put Mae into the starring role of *She Done Him Wrong*, a slightly watered-down and revamped (by herself) version of Mae's own stage success *Diamond Lil*, Costing only $200,000, the film made more than $3 million world-wide. As Lady Lou, Mae had a formidable supporting cast including Cary Grant, Gilbert Roland, Noah Beery and Owen Moore, but she wiped the floor with all of them. Self-described as 'one of the finest women who ever walked the streets', Lady Lou is a star of Bowery saloon entertainment in the 1890s. Mae's other gems from the star-making movie include 'When women go wrong, men go right after 'em', 'Why doncha come up some time, see me?', and the loaded dialogue with Grant about hands not being everything when he threatens to handcuff her. She also sings *I Wonder Where My Easy Rider's Gone*. The censorial crackdown of the Hays Code was still a few months away, so Mae had similar freedom with dialogue on *I'm No Angel*, which also realised more than ten times its production costs. As a sideshow vamp, she tames lions

Mae West, playing 'one of the finest women who ever walked the streets', sizes up Cary Grant in a second in *She Done him Wrong*

Shooting star. A rare shot of Tom Walls the director setting up a shot before dashing round to the front of the camera to become 'a Don Juan and a barnacle on society' in *Dishonour Bright*

When gambling gal Ruby (Mae West) tells Brooks (John Mack Brown) to make his play, he knows she is talking about more than roulette. From *Belle of the Nineties*

Clad unusually in sartorial splendour, Bert Wheeler (left) and Robert Woolsey had some lavish production numbers for a change in their musical comedy *Hips Hips Hooray*

Bert Wheeler gives the cameraman the full range of the legendary Wheeler teeth in this pose for the World War One comedy *Half Shot at Sunrise*. Co-star, as she so often was, is the lively Dorothy Lee

(somehow Mae managed to persuade Paramount to let her actually go into the cage) as well as men. The man-in-chief is again Cary Grant. 'If only I could trust you', he says to her. 'Hundreds have', she replies. *I'm No Angel* also has the famous instruction to her black maid to 'Peel me a grape, Beulah', as well as the exchange between Tira and Grant's younger brother (Kent Taylor) in which she tells him she likes sophisticated men to take her out. 'I'm not really sophisticated', he apologises. She looks him up and down. 'You're not really out yet, either' she replies (brilliantly). Towards the end comes another of her most famous lines. 'Why did you admit to knowing so many men?' coos a reporter. Mae has no doubts. 'It's not the men in my life', she tells her, 'but the life in my men.' No-one ever wrote dialogue quite like Mae West, or delivered it as she did. It was a black day for filmgoers when the Hays Code took the sting out of the best of her badinage. Hollywood had already toned it down but now it was to become commonplace. In later films the outrageousness of her costumes caused more comment than that of her dialogue. 'You're a dangerous woman' Paul Cavanagh tells her in *Goin' to Town*, one of the best of her subsequent vehicles. 'Thanks', says Mae laconically, but she was becoming less of a danger at the box-office. Her scenes as Delilah ('a female barber that made good') in the mock-opera within this film, though, are splendid. There was a union with that other slayer of sacred cows, W. C. Fields (*qv*), a few years later in *My Little Chickadee*, but it was relishable more in anticipation than in the execution. Mae wrote the lioness's share of the screenplay, and was gracious enough to hand Fields one of its best lines. On being asked to tell him about herself, she says there's nothing good to tell him. 'I can see what's good', he rumbles. 'Tell me the rest.' After the moderate *The Heat's On* in 1943, Mae left the Hollywood scene. The greatest triumph of her later years was a revival of *Diamond Lil*. Although Mae was 56 when it opened in 1948, she never looked lovelier, and wowed the customers each night with a few of her most famous songs towards the end of the evening. Only a broken ankle robbed her of a long Broadway run. There were more stage shows until the early 1960s, some TV appearances, an autobiography, and two ill-advised starring films in the 1970s. Fans preferred to remember her in her prime, when it wasn't Mae's life they worried about, but the life in Mae. She was 88 when she died from complications following a stroke.

1930: * Unidentified 'Screen Snapshots' short. 1932: Night After Night. 1933: She Done Him Wrong. I'm No Angel. 1934: Belle of the Nineties. 1935: Goin' to Town. 1936: Klondike Annie. Go West, Young Man. 1938: Every Day's a Holiday. 1940: My Little Chickadee. [....] The Heat's On (GB: Tropicana). 1970: [....] 1977: Sextette.

WHEELER, Bert (top) 1895–1968
and
WOOLSEY, Robert 1889–1938
American vaudeville and film comedy team of the late 1920s and early to mid 1930s. Bert (born Albert) Wheeler was small, round-faced and crinkle-haired and often looked mournful. His partner Robert Woolsey was a (bit) taller, George Burns-style, wisecracking figure with glasses, centre-parted hair and perennial cigar. Their brash, fast, cross-talking style hit the bullseye with American audiences in their heyday of the early 1930s, although few critics were ever converted. Ironically, the sections of the Wheeler and Woolsey films that survive best when viewed today are the well-staged chase-and-movement scenes rather than the less-than-sparkling chit-chat. In later years Wheeler would say that the films 'were all pretty indifferent compared to our Broadway stuff. But they all made money, so we kept on making 'em.' They kept on making them, indeed, until Woolsey's affliction with kidney disease – he was seriously ill for a year before his death – broke the team's run in full flight. They had been together less than ten years. Bert Wheeler was a vaudeville top-of-the-bill man in his early twenties, sharing a successful double-act with his wife Betty. The act, and the marriage, broke up and Wheeler went solo, becoming a star comedian with the Ziegfeld Follies in 1924, before he was 30. Robert Woolsey started his career in a very different sphere – as a jockey. After three years' racing, his career was ended by an injury resulting from a fall. He tried a number of other jobs before drifting into acting, followed by light opera, and eventually a solo comedy turn. He became a star comedian on Broadway in 1921's *The Right Girl*, and first teamed with Bert Wheeler in Ziegfeld's show *Rio Rita* in 1927. Wheeler and Woolsey were still part of the cast when the show was filmed two years later, and the public clearly liked them as a team. They were reunited with *Rio Rita* co-star Dorothy Lee (a sort of prettier poor-man's Ruby Keeler, not too talented but charming and with a strong sense of the ridiculous: she was to appear in most of their films until 1936) in *The Cuckoos* the following year. In these films and in *Dixiana* (also 1930), Wheeler and Woolsey, like the Marx Brothers (*qv*) in many of their movies, were constricted within a music-comedy format, providing light relief while the romantic leads sang and spooned. Then the team was given a straight solo vehicle, *Half-Shot at Sunrise*, the first of many to follow. Some of the dialogue in these early efforts by the team is almost worthy of the Marxes themselves. 'Hah', says Wheeler in *Hook, Line and Sinker*, 'I'm not as big a fool as I used to be!' Woolsey arches an eyebrow. 'Oh', he replies, 'did you diet?' The standards of the Wheeler and Woolsey comedies, however, remained inconsistent, and they were less successful at interpolating musical numbers than almost any of their top contemporaries. Thus a film like *Hips! Hips! Hooray!* is pretty painful today, whereas a straight farce such as *Kentucky Kernels* (both films are from 1934) still looks quite funny throughout, especially in its climactic sequences. The two films that followed, *Cockeyed Cavaliers* and *The Nitwits*, contain the team's last good work. Although Robert Woolsey continued to work for as long as his illness permitted, the team's last few films made it hardly worth the effort. After Woolsey's death, Wheeler displayed his seemingly endless teeth in a couple of second-rate features (and, much later, two shorts) as well as working in nightclubs, on Broadway and on TV. He died from emphysema. Had Woolsey lived, the partnership would doubtless have proved profitable for RKO, or some other studio, until the end of the war years. As Bert Wheeler might have said, in a world where Abbott and Costello (*qv*) were box-office kings, how could Wheeler and Woolsey have made a loss?

Together. 1929: Rio Rita. 1930: The Cuckoos. Half-Shot at Sunrise. Dixiana. Hook, Line and Sinker. 1931: * Oh! Oh! Cleopatra. Cracked Nuts. Caught Plastered. Peach o' Reno. 1932: * The Stolen Jools (GB: The Slippery Pearls). * Hollywood on Parade B-3. Girl Crazy. Hold 'Em Jail. 1933: So This is Africa. Diplomaniacs. 1934: Hips! Hips! Hooray! Cockeyed Cavaliers. Kentucky Kernels (GB: Triple Trouble). 1935: The Nitwits. The Rainmakers. 1936: Silly Billies. Mummy's Boy. 1937: On Again, Off Again. High Flyers.

Bert Wheeler, (left), Dorothy Lee and Robert Woolsey strike various poses in the face of danger in *Hook, Line and Sinker*

Wheeler alone. *1922: Captain Fly-By-Night. 1929: * Small Timers. * The Voice of Hollywood. 1931: Too Many Cooks. 1932: * Hollywood Handicap. 1935: * A Night at the Biltmore Bowl. 1939: Cowboy Quarterback. 1941: Las Vegas Nights (GB: The Gay City). 1950: * Innocently Guilty. 1951: * The Awful Sleuth.*

Woolsey alone. *1930: * The Voice of Hollywood (second series). 1931: Everything's Rosie. 1933: * Hollywood on Parade (B-7).*

WICKES, Mary

(M. Wickenhauser) 1912–

Hawk-eyed, chestnut-haired, tall (5 ft 9 in), hook-nosed and gawky, Mary Wickes' domestics, landladies, nurses and busybodies all had an aggressive air. A reluctant immigrant from the Broadway stage to Hollywood, she was once described as 'one of the world's most hilarious wonders'. The daughter of a banker, she attended high school and university in her native St Louis, graduating in 1932 and tackling a summer school of journalism. While at college, though, she had already played small parts with a St Louis stock company and with a musical comedy troupe, where she learned singing and acrobatic dancing (what an Olive Oyl she might have made). Discarding the idea of journalism, she worked in summer stock, then went to New York and understudied Margaret Hamilton (later to be the wicked witch in *The Wizard of Oz*) in *The Farmer Takes a Wife*. That led to three seasons with Orson Welles's famous Mercury Theatre; she was in their unreleased film *Too Much*

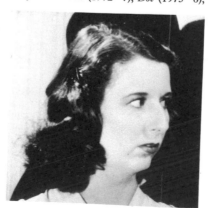

Johnson but, by the time *Citizen Kane* was made, had left the company to play the nurse described as 'Miss Bedpan' in the smash Broadway production of *The Man Who Came to Dinner*. Coming to Hollywood to re-create the role, Wickes found herself staying for other work, her caustic way of delivering a funny line stealing scenes from many an unwary star. Cinema never quite made the most of her, although it and television between them kept her well employed from 1950 onwards. Besides the films listed below, and one-off TV appearances, she was popular in numerous TV series, including *The Peter and Mary Show* (1950–1), as a housekeeper, *Bonino* (1953), as Martha the maid – another housekeeper in *The Halls of Ivy* (1954–5) and then *Mrs G. Goes to College* (1961–2), as a woman running a boarding-house. More recent TV series include *Sanford and Son* (1972–7), *Doc* (1975–6),

and *The Father Dowling Mysteries* (1987–90), still playing a housekeeper! The original *Mary Poppins* in a TV production of 1949, Mary Wickes' characters would stand no nonsense from anyone, whether it was Abbott and Costello (*qv*) or Doris Day. Arms on hips, lips pressed firmly together, she would always get the better of the situation. She had Hayley Mills to deal with when she played a nun in *The Trouble with Angels*, and was still in habit for the sequel, *Where Angels Go ... Trouble Follows*. Still acting into her eighties, she played yet another nun in the 1992 Whoopi Goldberg (*qv*) comedy *Sister Act*. Wickes, who has never married, spends much of her spare time these days working for charitable causes. Scorn her collection box at your peril!

*1938: Too Much Johnson (unreleased). 1939: * Seeing Red. 1941: The Man Who Came to Dinner. Andy Hardy's Private Secretary. 1942: Private Buckaroo. Now, Voyager. Blondie's Blessed Event (GB: A Bundle of Trouble). Who Done It? The Mayor of 44th Street. 1943: My Kingdom for a Cook. Rhythm of the Islands. Happy Land. Higher and Higher. 1948: The Decision of Christopher Blake. June Bride. 1949: Anna Lucasta. 1950: The Petty Girl (GB: Girl of the Year). Ma and Pa Kettle At Home. 1951: I'll See You in My Dreams. On Moonlight Bay. 1952: The Will Rogers Story (GB: The Story of Will Rogers). Young Man with Ideas. Bloodhounds of Broadway. 1953: By the Light of the Silvery Moon. Half a Hero. The Actress. 1954: Destry. White Christmas. 1955: Good Morning, Miss Dove. 1956: Dance with Me, Henry. 1957: Don't Go Near the Water. 1959: It Happened to Jane/That Jane from Maine. 1960: Cimarron. 1961: The Sins of Rachel Cade. 101 Dalmatians (voice only). The Music Man. 1964: Fate is the Hunter. Dear Heart. 1965: How to Murder Your Wife. The Trouble with Angels. 1966: The Spirit is Willing. 1967: Where Angels Go ... Trouble Follows. 1969: The Monk (TV). 1971: Napoleon and Samantha. 1973: Snowball Express. 1979: Willa (TV). 1980: Touched by Love. 1987: Fatal Confession (TV). 1989: The Missing Body Mystery (TV). 1992: Sister Act.*

THE WIERE BROTHERS

Harry (left) 1908–
Herbert (centre) 1909–
Sylvester 1910–1970

Most people who have seen the Wiere Brothers think that they had a screamingly funny act. But one had to sympathise with a Hollywood that didn't know what to do with them. It was hard to see how the grinning idiots the trio portrayed could ever be anything more than an extra added attraction in the movies. On stage, however, it was another matter. They all played musical instruments, could dance, juggle and do acrobatics, were masters of the silly sight gag and amusing sleight-of-hand routines. They also used every opportunity to get t most out of their fractured English. For the Wieres were Europeans, the offspring of a touring theatrical family whose ancestors came from East Prussia. Harry was born in Germany, Herbert in Austria and the angelic-looking Sylvester in Czechoslovakia. When the health of their father, himself a comedian, began to fail, the brothers put together their own act and became the family breadwinners. They made their first trip to America in 1935 and settled there for good two years later. Their subsequent film appearances together are peripheral, although everyone remembers them in Bob Hope (qv) and Bing Crosby's *Road to Rio*, in which they play the smiling, stripe-blazered Brazilian musicians hired to impersonate American members of a band on the strength of learning a few American phrases — including Herbert's immortal 'Solid, Jackson'. They were last seen, as disruptive as ever, as defective detectives in the 1967 Elvis Presley comedy, *Double Trouble*. Impish and irrepressible, the Wieres did have a successful TV series called *Oh! Those Bells* in 1962, but the partnership was broken eight years later by Sylvester's early death from a kidney ailment.

1937: † *Vogues of 1938.* 1941: *The Great American Broadcast.* 1943: *Hands Across the Border. Swing Shift Maisie* (GB: *The Girl in Overalls*). 1947: *Road to Rio.* 1967: *Double Trouble.*

WILDER, Gene
(Jerry Silberman) 1934–

A quizzical, sometimes even loopy American comedian with fuzzy, sandy-gingery hair and a slightly bemused expression which he can use to confuse adversaries. Alternately gentle and zany, Wilder has a beguiling (sometimes faintly annoying) personality, and a fine line in babbling, windmilling panic. His writing and directing talents, however, have not always been up to his abilities on-camera and this has resulted in an uneven and, on the whole, disappointing movie output. The son of a Russian immigrant who made money out of manufacturing miniature bottles for liqueurs, Wilder was a bright student who became interested

in drama while at the University of Iowa. After graduation he went to England and studied at the Old Vic Theatre School in Bristol. He also became interested in fencing and won the school championship. On returning to America, he studied at the Actors' Studio and worked as a chauffeur, toy salesman and fencing instructor before beginning to make a reputation off-Broadway in the early 1960s. Director Arthur Penn gave him his film debut as the frightened undertaker literally taken for a ride in *Bonnie and Clyde*. Then he struck up a working relationship with Mel Brooks (qv)

that brought him the role of the frenetic Leo Bloom in *The Producers*. It also brought him an Oscar nomination and a reputation as a man who could make people laugh. He certainly did that in *Start the Revolution Without Me*, a sort of comic sideshoot of *The Corsican Brothers*, with himself and Donald Sutherland as two sets of twins, and some richly funny dialogue. He was perfectly cast as the eponymous master of the chocolate factory in *Willy Wonka and the Chocolate Factory*, a smile always playing around the edges of his mouth as he triggers some new and often devilish scheme; and a scream as the man caught in bed with a sheep in Woody Allen's *Everything You Always Wanted to Know About Sex*. Wilder seemed on top of the world after 1974, first in *Blazing Saddles* as the alcoholic Waco Kid, opposite Cleavon Little's black sheriff, a role originally intended for himself by dialogue contributor Richard Pryor (qv), with whom Wilder would catch up later. Then he played Frederick Frankenstein, forever insisting on the correct pronunciation of his name, in *Young Frankenstein*; though in truth the pleasures of this second Brooks ragbag of good and bad belonged more to Peter Boyle, Marty Feldman (qv) and guest Gene Hackman as the blind hermit. Nonetheless, Wilder was now a name the public would

Gene Wilder with Gilda Radner, soon to become his real-life wife, in *Hanky Panky*. Tragically she died a few years later

pay to see. He wrote, directed and starred in *The Adventure of Sherlock Holmes' Smarter Brother*, a well-dressed spoof in which the action came off better than the comedy. Rather more cash, though, was generated by his next (though he didn't direct it), *Silver Streak*. A train-set comedy-thriller with lots of funny *and* suspenseful moments, it teamed Wilder at last with Richard Pryor, had several good characters, twisty plot developments and a sensational finale. He went back to directing himself: if *The World's Greatest Lover* wasn't the world's greatest comedy, its light satire on Hollywood's silent era had its moments, with Wilder wild-eyed as the man following in Valentino's footsteps. Wilder was quite amiable as a Polish rabbi in the wild west in *The Frisco Kid*, but he and Harrison Ford didn't gell and not many went to see it. He re-teamed with Pryor. And, despite *Stir Crazy* being raucous, vulgar and devoid of real wit, the $60 million it took in America alone suggested that the public now liked its comedy this way. In the early 1980s Wilder had become the regular off-screen companion of feisty TV comedienne Gilda Radner (b. 1946). They made three films together, *Hanky Panky*, *The Woman in Red* and, last and very much least, *Haunted Honeymoon*. The second of these was easily the most successful, partly thanks to a zippy advertising campaign and a No. 1 hit song, *I Just Called to Say I Loved You*. In truth, though, it was an inferior remake of a much lighter French film, *Pardon mon affaire*. Wilder and Radner married in 1984 but after only five years she died from cancer. Wilder, who hadn't appeared in a film since 1987, came back after her death with another romp opposite Pryor, *See No Evil, Hear No Evil*. An abysmal comedy about a blind man and a deaf man who 'witness' a murder, it still managed to show a small profit. That was more than could be said for the Wilder-Pryor vehicle *Another You*, a third-rate farce that sank without trace and seemed to prove that public patience with the pairing was at an end.

1967: Bonnie and Clyde. 1968: The Producers (shown 1967). 1969: Start the Revolution Without Me. 1970: Quackser Fortune Has a Cousin in the Bronx. 1971: Willy Wonka and the Chocolate Factory. 1972: The Scarecrow (TV). The Trouble with People (TV). Everything You Always Wanted to Know About Sex** But Were Afraid to Ask. 1973: Rhinoceros. 1974: The Little Prince. Thursday's Game (TV. Originally for cinemas). Blazing Saddles. Young Frankenstein. 1975: [†] The Adventure of Sherlock Holmes' Smarter Brother. 1976: Silver Streak. 1977: [†] The World's Greatest Lover. 1979: The Frisco Kid. 1980: Stir Crazy. Les seducteurs/Sunday Lovers. 1982: Hanky Panky. 1984: [†] The Woman in Red. 1986: [†]Haunted Honeymoon. 1987: Grandpère. Hello Actors Studio. 1989: See No Evil, Hear No Evil. 1990: Funny About Love. 1991: Another You.

[†] Also directed

WILLIAMS, Kenneth 1926–1988
The creator of as many comic characters as any other British funny-man, brown-haired, twisty-mouthed, outraged-looking Kenneth Williams was a man of many voices who became the main stalwart of the 'Carry On' films, whose pre-occupation with camp comments and double-entendres he epitomised. With the Williams voice wrapped

around them, however, these remarks were never offensive – just very funny. Born in London, Williams left school at 14. Slight and not very tall, he had avoided bullying by bigger boys by becoming the class clown. 'The toughs liked my jokes and especially my impressions of the teachers, so I was all right.' He became an apprentice cartographer, the job forging a passion for maps, manuscripts and calligraphy that never left him even after he decided to make the stage his career. Before that, though, there was World War Two. Williams joined the army and served with the Royal Engineers survey section as a map-maker. With the end of hostilities, he managed to get himself transferred to the Combined Services Entertainmènt Unit touring Malaya, Burma and Singapore. Demobbed from the army, Williams returned to a job as a draughtsman, but the comedian Stanley Baxter, whom he had met during his time with the CSEU, urged him to make a try for the stage and, after several failures, Williams was finally taken on by a provincial repertory company in Cornwall in 1948. After four years of

W.C. Boggs (Kenneth Williams) is the worse for drink when he emerges from Brighton's Pier Bar in company with Joan Sims (rear), Sidney James and Patsy Rowlands in *Carry On at Your Convenience*

Just a wilder kind of girl. Perhaps one of the screen's least likely female impersonators, Gene Wilder, to Gilda Radner's disbelief, tries to get away with it in *Hanky Panky*

Block-heads. Kenneth Williams and Terry Scott prepare for the axe to fall in *Carry on Henry*

Hello sailor. This one is 'strong to the finish 'cos he eats his spinach'. Yes it's *Popeye* the sailor man, and this was Robin Williams' impression of him in 1980

repertory work, he reached London (inauspiciously: he got bad reviews in his first play) and at the same time began to pick up small roles in films. As yet, however, he had not been discovered as a comic talent, and anyone who has seen his performance in, for example, *The Seekers*, could have forecast that drama was not to be his forte. His ability to make people laugh just by using a variety of funny voices first came to the fore with the radio comedy series *Hancock's Half-Hour*. When it began in 1954, Williams used his haughtiest, upper-crust voice as Lord Dockyard. It was in the following year's series, though, that Williams really became a scene-stealer. His appearances as insufferable pests, often prefaced by 'Good evening!' or 'Stop messin' about!' were invariably greeted with shrieks of laughter. Tony Hancock (*qv*) not only resented it but disliked Williams' use of what he termed 'cartoon characters'. Hancock was restless for more reality. Williams was heard no more in the show after 1956. By the following year, however, Williams had overridden this disappointment, and was beginning to make a name for himself in West End revue, sharpening his incisive, split-second timing in such shows as *Share My Lettuce*, *Pieces of Eight* and *One Over the Eight*. The years of Williams' greatest popularity began in 1958. The first of the 'Carry On' films, *Carry On Sergeant*, appeared in that year. So did *Beyond Our Ken*, a 'sort of radio show' that proved the most successful British radio comedy series since *Take It from Here*, even, ironically, outstripping *Hancock's Half-Hour*. The 'Ken' of the title wasn't Williams, but avuncular Kenneth Horne. But it was Williams who provided most of the show's biggest laughs with a series of outrageous characters. These included rural philosopher Arthur Fallowfield (for whom the answer always 'lay in the soil'), the seedy J. Peasemould Gruntfuttock, and the madrigal singer Rambling Syd Rumpo. The show ran for ten years and was only ended by Horne's untimely death. Williams made 'Carry On' films for another ten years, and also became a rowdy and undisciplined panellist on radio's *Just a Minute*. A few weeks before he was due to go into hospital for an operation, Williams was found dead from an overdose of sleeping pills. He once said: 'The shorter your life is, the better. I think to go at 65 or 70 is fine. Why hang about?'

1952: Trent's Last Case. 1953: Innocents in Paris. Valley of Song (US: Men Are Children Twice). The Beggar's Opera. 1954: The Seekers (US: Land of Fury). 1958: Carry On Sergeant. 1959: Carry On Nurse. Carry On Teacher. Tommy the Toreador. 1960: Make Mine Mink. Carry On Constable. His and Hers. 1961: Carry On Regardless. Raising the Wind (US: Roommates). 1962: Carry On Cruising. * Love Me, Love Me, Love Me (narrator only). Twice Round the Daffodils. 1963: Carry On Jack (US: Carry On Venus). 1964: Carry On Spying. Carry On Cleo. 1965: Carry On

Cowboy. 1966: Don't Lose Your Head. Carry On Screaming. 1967: Follow That Camel. Carry On Doctor. 1968: Carry On Up the Khyber. 1969: Carry On Camping. Carry On Again, Doctor. 1970: Carry On Loving. Carry On Henry. 1971: Carry On at Your Convenience. 1972: Carry On Matron. Carry On Abroad. 1974: Carry On Dick. 1975: Carry On Behind. 1977: The Hound of the Baskervilles. That's Carry On. 1978: Carry On Emmannuelle.

WILLIAMS, Robin 1952–
This American comedian is at his best, several of his directors have said, when you simply wind him up and let him go. But when Williams isn't giving an impersonation of a clockwork cockroach, he has been able also to offer one or two considered and impressive demonstrations of serious, underplayed acting. All this suggests a major talent at work – given the right role, in which, comic or serio-comic, he can dominate a film. Chestnut-haired, square-faced, widemouthed and narrow-eyed, with a natural twinkle, he was born in Chicago (or, if you believe some accounts, Edinburgh in Scotland) where his father was a big wheel in the automobile business. Soon the class clown – 'I was a little fat guy. And I was picked on. They didn't want so much to beat me up as see me roll. So I got funny' – he was voted both 'most humorous student' and 'student most likely to succeed' by fellow-students in California, where his father had retired. He studied drama for three years at the Juilliard Academy in New York, then headed back west, where he joined a comedy workshop in San Francisco, then moved to Los Angeles, where it didn't take him long to get bookings at the famous Comedy Store. One thing Williams has never been lost for is words, and his nonstop, all-systems-go style of humour, adlibbing ad infinitum, soon made him a big favourite there. He might have become famous in his early twenties if the 1976 revival of *Rowan and Martin's Laugh-In* had been a success, but it wasn't. He had to wait another two years until a guest appearance on the hit series *Happy Days*, as a spaced-out alien called Mork, led to a

series of his own called *Mork and Mindy*. Mork was an excessively excitable creature, a characterization that suited Williams' seemingly limitless supply of nervous energy. The huge audiences that the programme attracted made Robert Altman think of Williams when casting his live-action film of *Popeye*. Though underrated, the film was a considerable flop; it would certainly have been unbearably worse without the perfect casting of Williams as Popeye and Shelley Duvall as Olive Oyl. It didn't do much for Williams' film career and neither, despite some critical praise, did *The World According to Garp*. Williams was still, in fact, looking for a film that would showcase his own personality. It certainly wasn't *The Survivors*, but *Moscow on the Hudson* was nearer the mark, in which he played a bewildered Russian musician defecting to America in the middle of Bloomingdales. Williams was fond of the film and still talks of doing a sequel. By this time he had shaken off drink and drugs problems and his raunchy stage shows were becoming major attractions, as Williams' stream-of-consciousness comic patter took satirical swipes at anything that might bring a laugh. He took the show on a 23-city tour of America, with a routine essentially preserved in the video *Robin Williams Live at the Met*. But there were few laughs for Williams on the movie front, where *The Best of Times*, *Club Paradise* and *Seize the Day* all lost money and scarcely emerged even on the video market outside America. The big one, though, was just around the corner. He finally got to play 'someone like myself' as the rebel disc jockey in *Good Morning, Vietnam*. 'I developed the script', he admitted. 'The film character is 90 per cent me.' Irreverent, headstrong, sensitive and outrageously over-the-top: these adjectives, then, might apply both to role and actor, who undoubtedly ad-libbed much of the DJ's constant haranguing chatter on screen. Whatever the truth, it won Williams his first Oscar nomination. He followed it with another, in very different style, as the free-thinking, character-forming teacher in *Dead Poets Society* who tells his pupils to 'Seize the day. Make your lives extraordinary.' Williams' aggressive yet compassionate performance is his best to date. He brazenly took centre stage again as the cocksure car salesman in *Cadillac Man*. He was more quietly good in *Awakenings* (as the doctor who 'awakens' patients from a catatonic state) and *The Fisher King*, but made one of the silly guest appearances he sometimes does in *Dead Again*. That was a mistake and so was *Hook*. Williams wasn't right for the Peter Pan role but few would have been under Steven Spielberg's heavy direction of this musical without songs. Shrugging this off, Williams kept working hard, jumping on board the seemingly failproof Barry Levinson's fantasy-comedy *Toys*, as a whimsical toy maker out to save his father's toy factory from the clutches of his demented uncle. 'Comedy', he philosophises, 'is something that you can get under the radar with. It lets you talk about serious matters to people who wouldn't listen if you talked to them in any other way.'

1977: Can I Do it ... 'Til I Need Glasses? 1980: Popeye. 1982: The World According to Garp. 1983: The Survivors. 1984: Moscow on the Hudson. 1985: The Best of Times. Club Paradise. 1986: Seize the Day (originally for TV). Robin Williams Live at the Met (video). 1987: Dear America (voice only). Good Morning, Vietnam. 1988: The Adventures of Baron Munchausen. 1989: Dead Poets Society. 1990: Awakenings. Cadillac Man. 1991: The Fisher King. Dead Again. Hook. Shakes the Clown. 1992: Toys.

WINDSOR, Barbara
(B. Deeks) 1937–

A tiny British blonde sex symbol with apple cheeks and friendly grin who has played little else but comedy in a crowded career. In particular, she willingly lost both dignity and clothes (but never the smile) in ten films in the 'Carry On' series, to which she brought an only slightly knowing sex appeal. She was rarely given the chance to play 'straighter' comedy but proved in such films as Crooks in Cloisters that she could handle that just as well. She was also a success in TV's The Rag Trade. Born in London, she went to dancing school – Madame Behenna's Juvenile Jollities – at an early age, and then to the Aida Foster School, getting her first stage part at 12 as one of the Aida Foster Babes in a London panto. In 1952, she got a job in the chorus of the musical Love from Judy – 'they wanted eight small teenage girls with loud voices' – and stayed with the show for two years. She grew no higher than 4 ft 11 in and was lost in a crowd of busty sixth-formers in her first film, The Belles of St Trinian's. There followed a period singing in revue and a few more film bits, but the famous squeaky voice was barely heard on screen until 1962 when she had featured roles in an Edgar Wallace thriller, Death Trap, and, more importantly, in Sparrows Can't Sing. The latter role resulted from an association with theatre director Joan Littlewood, who had given

Windsor her first real break in the West End musical Fings Ain't Wot They Used T'Be, after spotting her singing, clowning and doing impressions in a nightclub. When Littlewood came to transfer another stage hit, Sparrows (originally Sparrers) from stage to screen, she plumped for Windsor in the leading role. After Carry on Spying, British comedies relied more on her abilities to stretch a sweater than stretching her talents, culminating in the (in)famous bra-bursting scene in Carry On Camping. Still Windsor, like all the cast, was clearly having a good time, and stayed with the series until the last decent one, Carry On Dick, in 1974. A plan to revive the series with Carry On Texas, a spoof of Dallas, in 1988, was nipped in the bud by the deaths that year of cast stalwarts Kenneth Williams and Charles Hawtrey (both qv). Meanwhile, Barbara's personal life was less of a laugh. Her husband of many years, nightclub owner Ronnie Knight, was constantly in trouble with the police, and finally fled to Spain, seemingly to avoid being questioned about a massive robbery. She divorced him, and later married a man 19 years her junior, with whom, from the late 1980s, she ran a pub. The hour-glass figure and the cheerful smile are still intact.

1954: The Belles of St Trinian's. 1955: Lost (US: Tears for Simon). 1960: Too Hot to Handle (US: Playgirl After Dark). 1961: On the Fiddle (US: Operation Snafu). Flame in the Streets. Hair of the Dog. 1962: Death Trap. Sparrows Can't Sing. 1963: Crooks in Cloisters. 1964: Carry on Spying. 1965: San Ferry Ann. A Study in Terror (US: Fog). 1967: Carry on Doctor. 1968: Chitty Chitty Bang Bang. 1969: Carry On Camping. Carry On Again, Doctor. 1970: Carry On Henry. 1971: The Boy Friend. 1972: Carry On Matron. Carry On Abroad. Not Now Darling. 1973: Carry On Girls. 1974: Carry On Dick. 1977: That's Carry On. 1986: Comrades. 1987: It Couldn't Happen Here.

WISDOM, Norman 1915–
'Don't laugh at me 'cos I'm a fool' warbled Britain's Norman Wisdom, in the most famous of his self-penned popular songs. That, of course, was exactly what the diminutive, dark-haired Londoner wanted people to do, and, thanks to his willingness to appear totally foolish, he found no lack of admirers. For, following phenomenal success in variety and TV, he was taken up by Britain's largest film distributor, and enjoyed one of the longest unbroken runs of cinema success ever recorded by a British comic.

Sidney James admires Barbara Windsor's bottles of stout as they plan their holiday in Spain in Carry On Abroad.

The films he made between 1953 and 1966 were in some ways British equivalents of the solo work of Jerry Lewis (*qv*) in America. Wisdom played the willing, gormless trier, in whose hands everything, but everything, fell apart. But there was a greater sentimental side to Wisdom than to his Hollywood contemporary. Another line of the song ran 'I'd give it all to share my life with someone who really loves me' and, indeed, he was almost always seen to get the girl in the final fadeout. It was a tough early life for the boy from Paddington. His mother left home when he was nine, and he and his brother were left in the charge of a father who was more often drunk than sober. Wisdom ran away from home when he was 11, but returned to become an errand boy with a grocery store on leaving school at 13. Later he was a coal-miner, a waiter, a pageboy and a cabin-boy, before joining the army as a band boy, seeing service in India, and becoming unit boxing champion at his weight. That was with the 10th Hussars, but Wisdom had transferred to the Royal Corps of Signals by the time war broke out in 1939. Leaving them in 1946, he made his debut as an entertainer at the advanced age of 31 – but his rise to the top was phenomenally fast after that. A West End star within two years, he made his TV debut the same year (1948), and was soon commanding enormous audiences. By this time, he had adopted the 'gump' suit that would remain his 'uniform' – tweed cap askew with peak turned up, too-tight jacket, barely-better trousers, crumpled collar and tie awry. This outfit was put together with an idiot grin, and an appealing upward look at those Wisdom hoped would forgive him for another fine mess. There was also his provocative shyness – described by one critic as 'bashfulness verging on mental deficiency' – and little-boy naughtiness, which occasionally led him to gleefully enjoy his own acts of destruction. On stage, at least, Wisdom was also master of the pratfall – anything from tumbles down flights of stairs to crashes into the orchestra. He could also play several musical instruments and often used to cram bursts of instrumental dexterity into his performance. Encouraged by the viewing figures, Rank signed him up and set him loose in a department store in *Trouble in Store* in 1953. They hedged their bets by throwing in Wisdom's regular stooge, the supercilious Jerry Desmonde (who would be on hand for all his best films), the incomparable Margaret Rutherford (*qv*) as a shoplifter, and a pretty (but necessarily short) leading lady in Lana Morris. The results were amazing. *Trouble in Store*, opening to moderately enthusiastic reviews, had queues snaking through (sometimes outside and round the block) cinemas wherever it played. It set house records in 51 of its 67 London cinemas. Rank clearly had a goldmine on its hands. Thereafter Wisdom was able to turn out comedies at the rate of one a year. Most are fairly painful now, but some show com-

Norman Wisdom faces a wartime execution squad as *The Square Peg*, 'the story of an individualist, roadmender and soldier extraordinaire'

mendable originality, notably *Man of the Moment* and, later, *On the Beat* and *A Stitch in Time*. *Man of the Moment*, directed by John Paddy Carstairs (who helmed a number of other vehicles for British comics of the time) has one of the few original plots in this kind of post-war comedy. The story casts Norman as a junior filing clerk at the Foreign Office who, through a series of mishaps and misunderstandings, becomes a figure of international prominence, and the only man trusted by the natives of Tawaki to decide if their island should become a strategic base and, if so, whose. Triumphant and knighted, Norman sets sail for the island, only to see it sink into the sea, a victim of volcanic eruption. Wisdom clung to black and white film as long as he dared, and the eventual switch to colour in 1965 only proved how right he'd been. It robbed his comedy of some of its simplicity and, battling against poor

scripts, Wisdom was out of films by the end of the decade. Meanwhile he had some success on Broadway, especially in the show *Walking Happy*, then returned to television where he had a disappointing 1970 series, *Norman*, and the rather more profitable *A Little Bit of Wisdom*, which ran for four seasons from 1973 to 1976. Appearances have been sporadic since then, although there's always pantomime and, like most comedians, he has tried straight acting, most successfully as a dying cancer patient in the 1981 BBC play *Going Gently*. In 1987 he announced his screen return in a 'horror comedy' called *Adam and Eve*, but it was never made. But, with videos of his old material, panto and commercials, the little man keeps busy. 'Looking back', he says, 'I know I had a hell of a lot of luck. What followed was harder work than it must have looked, but lots of fun.'

1948: *A Date with a Dream.* 1953: *Meet Mr Lucifer. Trouble in Store.* 1954: *One Good Turn.* 1955: *As Long As They're Happy. Man of the Moment.* 1956: *Up in the World.* 1957: *Just My Luck.* 1958: *The Square Peg.* 1959: *Follow a Star.* 1960: *There Was a Crooked Man. The Bulldog Breed. The Girl on the Boat.* 1962: *On the Beat.* 1963: *A Stitch in Time.* 1965: *The Early Bird.* 1966 : *Press for Time. The Sandwich Man.* 1968: *The Night They Raided Minsky's.* 1969: *What's Good for the Goose.* 1992: *Double X: The Name of the Game.*

WOOLSEY, Robert
See **WHEELER, Bert** and **WOOLSTY, Robert**

WYNN, Ed
(Isaiah Edwin Leopold, later legally changed) 1886–1966

A beaming, bespectacled, dumpy little American comic with gurgling voice and beguiling giggle, Ed Wynn was probably the most successful stage comedian never to make it in films – until his latter-day career as a versatile character star. His relaxed delivery, non-stop merriment and collection of outlandish costumes and even wilder hats led to him being nicknamed after the title of one of his best shows – *The Perfect Fool.* The baggy-panted, arch-eyebrowed comedian was born to an immigrant hat-maker and seemed destined to work in the family business. At 15, however, he ran away from home to join a travelling theatre company. It folded after five months and Wynn endured a few months selling hats before embarking on a show business career in earnest. Ed played vaudeville circuits, did some legitimate stage work and formed a double-act with another funny-man, Jack Louis, (it was called the Rah Rah Rah Boys) before branching out with his own shows. The first of these was *The King's Jester* in 1913. A 'jester' was exactly what Ed Wynn was, rather than a stand-up comic, his antics taking him all over the stage. By this time, he had perfected the tricks of his trade. Besides the vocal gymnastics, there was the widening of the bright blue eyes behind the assortment of weird-shaped glasses, the flapping of the hands, an apologetic hiccup

and a forehead that seemed to rise and fall at will. As well as perpetual motion, Ed's legions of fans also knew they could expect the unexpected. He wasn't averse to muscling in on other people's acts (a famous running feud with W. C. Fields (*qv*) resulted from Ed's sudden appearances among his props) and popping up here, there and everywhere during a show. The Fields encounters stemmed from Ed's two engagements with the Ziegfeld Follies (1914 and 1915). The run of Broadway successes that followed was only briefly interrupted when Wynn was boycotted following his leadership of the victorious actors' strike of 1919. His response was to write and stage his own show, *Ed Wynn's Carnival.* Films were another matter. There was a silent, *Rubber Heels* (Ed played an amateur detective), an early 'soundie', *Follow the Leader* (as an amateur kidnapper), and a disaster called *The Chief.* They only proved that Ed Wynn couldn't be straitjacketed into a conventional plot. In the early 1930s Wynn enjoyed radio success in the character of a panicking fire chief, but the years 1936–1939 were the lowpoint of his private and professional lives. His first dramatic show as producer folded within a week, his wife of 22 years filed for divorce, a radio chain that he had backed collapsed. A second marriage in 1937 ended in divorce two years later, and he even turned down the role of the Wizard in M-G-M's classic *The Wizard of Oz.* He enjoyed some success back on Broadway in the war years but television was to bring him his next acclaim. A year after being voted by fellow comedians as 'the greatest visual comedian of our day', Ed began *The Ed Wynn Show* on TV in 1949. During its run, it won an Emmy as best live show, and Ed himself won the same award as most outstanding live personality. Ed's career had slowed again, though, when his son Keenan Wynn, a well-known Hollywood character player, persuaded his father to enter the final phase of his career, as an actor. From 1956 a series of sometimes funny, sometimes dramatic film assignments in featured roles was enriched by Ed's humour and natural warmth. He was nominated for an Academy Award for his portrayal of Mr Dussell in *The Diary of Anne Frank* in 1959, but the role for which most people remember him came five years later. This was Uncle Albert in Disney's phenomenally successful *Mary Poppins.* Albert was a jovial individual who liked having tea-parties. But once you made him laugh, he couldn't stop, and floated clear up to the ceiling. Ed's big scene gave him the chance to sing one of the film's many hits, *I Love to Laugh.* His last film role was also for Disney, as the 1,100-year-old Gnome King in *The Gnome-Mobile.* In real life 'The Perfect Fool' had not quite reached 80 when he died from a combination of Parkinson's Disease and the effects of an operation for the removal of a tumour. His benign inanity and famous lisp were much missed on the entertainment scene.

1927: *Rubber Heels.* 1930: *Follow the Leader.* 1933: *The Chief.* 1943: *Stage Door Canteen.* 1951: *Alice in Wonderland* (voice only). 1956: *The Great Man. Requiem for a Heavyweight* (TV). 1957: *The Great American Hoax* (TV). 1958: *Marjorie Morningstar.* 1959: *The Diary of Anne Frank. Miracle on 34th Street* (TV). 1960: *The Absent-Minded Professor. Cinderfella.* 1961: *Babes in Toyland.* 1962: *The Golden Horseshoe Revue.* 1963: *Son of Flubber.* 1964: *Those Calloways. Mary Poppins. The Patsy.* 1965: *Dear Brigitte . . . That Darn Cat! The Greatest Story Ever Told.* 1966: *The Daydreamer* (voice only). 1967: *Warning Shot. The Gnome-Mobile.*

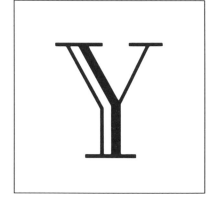

YOUNG, Roland 1887–1953
Low-browed – though the left one was frequently raised in incredulity, close-mouthed, faintly sly-looking British comedy character star in Hollywood, with just a wisp of brown hair, a worried frown and a tooth-brush moustache that went just too far towards the thin top lip to be considered suave. In some ways similar to the slightly later Wilfrid Hyde White, with similarly confidential, aristocratic tones, Young had a much wider range as an actor. But it was in light comedy that he excelled. As early as 1933 one writer described him as 'a unique character comedian' and must have been pleased to see Young justify that judgement over the next 20 years, especially as the

Words of wisdom. 'Don't laugh at me 'cos I'm a fool', pleaded Norman Wisdom in *Trouble in Store*. But he wanted audiences to do just the opposite — and they did

Norman (Norman Wisdom) and Grimsdyke (Edward Chapman) manage to see the funny side of things despite a series of disasters at the end of *A Stitch in Time*

The world at his fingertips. George Fotheringay McWhirter (Roland Young) finds that he has the ability to move inanimate objects in *The Man Who Could Work Miracles*

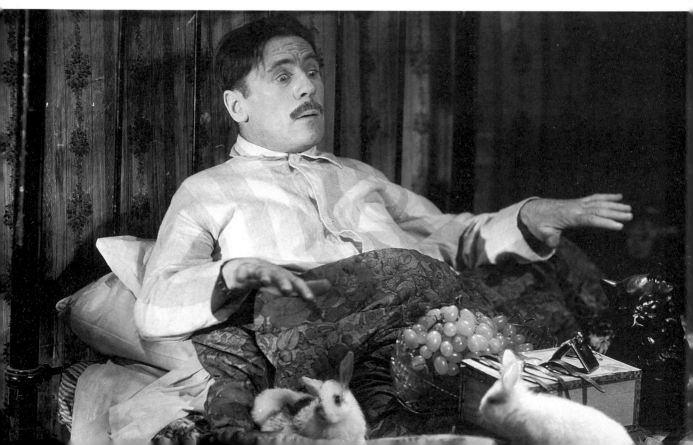

ghost-beset banker Cosmo Topper. He was born in London and impeccably educated at Sherborne in Dorset and University College, London. He expressed no desire to follow his father's footsteps as an architect, instead going straight to RADA from University College and making his stage debut as early as 1908. Four years later he went to America to appear on Broadway and stayed, though he never lost his English accent. He served in the US Army during World War One, and must have looked almost as out of place as when he played a sultan many years later in Eddie Cantor's comedy *Ali Baba Goes to Town*. Afterwards he returned to the States, built up a reputation on Broadway, and made a few silent films, including playing Dr Watson to John Barrymore's Sherlock Holmes in 1922. Up to the early 1930s Young played mainly affable rogues and confirmed bachelors. He returned to Britain in 1932 (the first of several such trips to film there) in the latter capacity to make *Wedding Rehearsal*, as the marquis who finds something wrong with every 'suitable' girl. 'Such a long nose', he comments on one, to be told by his mother that that nose has come straight down from the Normans. 'Yes', he complains, 'but does it have to come down so far?' Even after he became typed as a beautifully bewildered businessman later in the 1930s, Young sought a vivid variety of roles. He was unexpectedly unctuous as Uriah Heep – a role even his friends didn't think he could bring off – and hilariously in character as the baffled aristocrat in *Ruggles of Red Gap*. The year was 1935 and the two films made Young an accepted name on movie billboards at the age of 48. He returned to Britain to play *The Man Who Could Work Miracles*. He was not too happily cast in this title role, although he dropped his aitches with a will as the tweedy George Fotheringay who finds that his power to create miracles even extends to commanding the earth to stand still. The fantasy was rather more successful in America, where Young's stock was high, than in its native Britain, where H. G. Wells's tale was a little too high-flown (and indigestible) for the average filmgoer. A more successful British venture came in 1937, with his spirited and un-stuffy Commander John Good in *King Solomon's Mines*, still the best available version of H. Rider Haggard's classic adventure. The same year in Hollywood, Young excelled as the *very* stuffy *Topper*, a meek-and-mild banker tugged into racy misadventures by a couple of ghosts. Young, who was stoutly supported by Billie Burke as fluttery Mrs Topper, was nominated for an Oscar. He reappeared in the role in the slightly less amusing *Topper Takes a Trip* and, two years later, still with Burke, in *Topper Returns* which, although less skilful, proved the best of the three in terms of speed of pace and outright hilarity. Young and Burke were also felicitously teamed in *The Young in Heart* – a splendid demonstration of his whole range of gestures

and comedy techniques as a roguishly charming confidence trickster, *Irene* and *They All Kissed the Bride*. He was one of the longer survivors in René Clair's *Ten Little Niggers* – with Billy Wilder's *Witness for the Prosecution*, the best Agatha Christie adaptation ever put on screen. In postwar years he returned to Britain to play the wily father in the portmanteau *Bond Street*, and enjoyed his last really juicy role as the duplicitous cardsharp who lands Bob Hope in another nice mess in *The Great Lover*. Young died in his sleep in New York at 64, shortly after completing his last film, a thriller unworthy of his talents. In almost any film in which he was properly cast, Roland Young ensured that the pleasure of his company was all ours.

1922: Sherlock Holmes (GB: Moriarty). 1923: Fog Bound. Grit. 1929: The Unholy Night. Her Private Life. 1930: Madame Satan. Wise Girl. New Moon. The Bishop Murder Case. 1931: The Squaw Man (GB: The White Man). The Prodigal. The Sin of Madelon Claudet (GB: The Lullaby). The Guardsman. Don't Bet on Women. Annabelle's Affairs. Pagan Lady. This is the Night. 1932: Wedding Rehearsal. A Woman Commands. Street of Women. Lovers Courageous. One Hour with You. 1933: Pleasure Cruise. They Just Had to Get Married. His Double Life. A Lady's Profession. Blind Adventure. 1934: Here is My Heart. 1935: David Copperfield. Ruggles of Red Gap. 1936: The Man Who Could Work Miracles. Gypsy. The Unguarded Hour. One Rainy Afternoon. Give Me Your Heart (GB: Sweet Aloes). 1937: King Solomon's Mines. Call It a Day. Ali Baba Goes to Town. Topper. 1938: Sailing Along. The Young in Heart. 1939: The Night of Nights.

Topper Takes a Trip. Here I Am, a Stranger. Yes, My Darling Daughter. 1940: Star Dust. He Married His Wife. Dulcy. The Philadelphia Story. Irene. Private Affairs. No, No, Nanette. 1941: Two Faced Woman. Topper Returns. The Flame of New Orleans. 1942: Tales of Manhattan. The Lady Has Plans. They All Kissed the Bride. 1943: Forever and a Day. 1944: Standing Room Only. 1945: And Then There Were None (GB: Ten Little Niggers). 1948: Bond Street. You Gotta Stay Happy. 1949: The Great Lover. 1950: Let's Dance. 1951: St Benny the Dip (GB: Escape If You Can). 1953: That Man from Tangier.

YULE, Joe
(Ninnian J. Yule Jr) 1888–1950
and
RIANO, Renie 1899–1971
Two vaudevillian veterans who came together at a time when they must have thought that star roles in films had avoided

An unusually amorous Roland Young (centre) joined Ralph Forbes and Genevieve Tobin on a *Pleasure Cruise* in 1933

them. As it happened, they were only to make a handful of movie comedies before death split the team. The rudimentary films they did make were understandably more popular in rural areas of America than in the cities. Joe Yule was a stocky, sandy-haired Scotsman who, ironically, ended up playing Irishmen in Hollywood films. A music-hall comic, he emigrated to America where he married a dancer, Nell Carter. They became well-known as a team on the burlesque circuit, especially in the New York area. In 1920 the Yules had a son, Ninnian Joseph Yule III, who would win world fame two decades later as Mickey Rooney. At little more than a year old, the toddler was appearing in his parents' act, but they separated when he was four and later divorced. Joe Yule continued his career as a burlesque comic on his own. When Rooney became a world star, he brought his father to Hollywood as a comic character actor, working for the same studio, M-G-M. Yule stayed with the studio from 1938 until 1946 when the opportunity came to make a starring comedy with Renie Riano. Sharp-faced, beaky, bony, dark-haired, inquisitive-looking Riano had been making people smile since she was a child. Born in Chicago, she made her stage debut in that city at the age of seven, billed as 'Little Baby Renie'. Renie's mother, the stage actress Irene Riano, sent her daughter to acting lessons, and saw her make a Broadway debut at 18 in the show *Honey Girl*. Later she did nightclub work and scored Broadway hits in Irving Berlin's *Music Box Revue*, and in *The Man Who Came to Dinner*, in the role played by another beaky funny-lady Mary Wickes (*qv*) in the subsequent film. Coming to Hollywood in 1937 with a vivid reputation as a comedienne, Riano found herself assigned to a treadmill of bright but small character roles from which it seemed impossible to escape, including a running role in the popular Nancy Drew mysteries. The offer of starring roles for Riano and Yule came from Monogram, the minor studio that were also making the Bowery Boys (*qv*) comedies. The film they were to make, *Bringing Up Father*, was based on a long-running comic strip by George McManus. The first version had been made as early as 1928, with J. Farrell MacDonald and Marie Dressler (*qv*). Yule played Jiggs, a short-fused henpecked, nouveau-riche Irish-American. Riano was his wife Maggie, determined to climb up the social ladder. They were sort of distant Brooklyn relations of the Flouds of *Ruggles of Red Gap*. Critics commented that the antics were distinguished only by good casting of the main characters. The film's reception was good enough to warrant a sequel, *Jiggs and Maggie in Society*. Three more slices of raucous fun followed that and more were planned. Three weeks before the release of the last, *Jiggs and Maggie Out West*, however, Joe Yule collapsed and died from a heart attack. He was only 61. Renie Riano stayed in show business until her late six-

ties, acting in a Bowery Boys comedy, a couple of Jerry Lewis (*qv*) films and three of American-International's 'beach' comedies for teenagers. Had Yule lived, the Jiggs and Maggie comedies would have probably gone on happily, as did those of the Bowery Boys, well into the 1950s.

Together. *1946: Bringing Up Father. 1947: Jiggs and Maggie in Society. 1948: Jiggs and Maggie in Court. 1949: Jackpot Jitters/Jiggs and Maggie in Jackpot Jitters. 1950: Jiggs and Maggie Out West.*
Yule alone. *1938: Idiot's Delight. 1939: Judge Hardy and Son. Sudden Money. Fast and Furious. They All Come Out. The Secret of Dr Kildare. 1940: Florian. Broadway Melody of 1940. New Moon. Go West/Marx Brothers Go West. Third Finger, Left Hand. Boom Town. 1941: Billy the Kid. I'll Wait for You. Babes on Broadway. Maisie Was a Lady. The Trial of Mary Dugan. Wild Man of Borneo. Woman of the Year. Kathleen. The Big Store. 1942: Jackass Mail. Born to Sing. Nazi Agent. Panama Hattie. 1943: Air Raid Wardens. Three Hearts for Julia. 1944: Two Girls and a Sailor. Nothing but Trouble. Kismet. Lost Angel. The Thin Man Goes Home. 1945: The Picture of Dorian Gray. 1946: The Mighty McGurk. Murder in the Music Hall.*
Riano alone. *1937: Tovarich. You're a Sweetheart. 1938: Thanks for Everything. Strange*

Faces. Outside of Paradise. Spring Madness. Four's a Crowd. Nancy Drew, Detective. Men Are Such Fools. The Road to Reno. 1939: Wife, Husband and Friend. The Honeymoon's Over. Disputed Passage. The Women. Nancy Drew and the Hidden Staircase. Mr Moto in Danger Island (GB: Mr Moto on Danger Island). Honeymoon in Bali (GB: Husbands or Lovers). Tell No Tales. Wings of the Navy. Nancy Drew, Trouble Shooter. Daytime Wife. 1940: Kit Carson. The Man Who Wouldn't Talk. The Ghost Comes Home. Remedy for Riches. The Shop Around the Corner. Oh Johnny, How You Can Love. 1941: Unfinished Business. You're the One. Adam Had Four Sons. Ziegfeld Girl. Ice-Capades. Affectionately Yours. You Belong to Me (GB: Good Morning, Doctor). 1942: Whispering Ghosts. Blondie for Victory (GB: Troubles Through Billets). There's One Born Every Minute. 1943: The Man from Music Mountain. 1944: None But the Lonely Heart. Take It Or Leave It. Jam Session. Three is a Family. 1945: Club Havana. A Song for Miss Julie. Anchors Aweigh. 1946: Bad Bascomb. So Goes My Love (GB: A Genius in the Family). 1947: Winter Wonderland. 1948: The Time of Your Life. 1951: As Young As You Feel. The Barefoot Mailman. 1953: Clipped Wings. 1964: Bikini Beach. Pajama Party. 1965: The Family Jewels. 1966: Three on a Couch. Fireball 500.

Joe Yule (looking every diminutive inch Mickey Rooney's dad) prepares to give Renie Riano the brush-off in *Jiggs and Maggie in Jackpot Jitters*

Selected bibliography

Many books on individual comedy stars were consulted in the compilation of this book, as well as hundreds of feature articles in magazines and newspapers and more general books on film comedy. Those that proved particularly useful, and might be of interest to the researcher, are listed below.

BARBOUR, Alan G. *Cliffhanger, a Pictorial History of the Motion Picture Serial*. A & W Publishers/BCW Publishing, 1977.

CURTHOYS, Alan (and others, reds). *Who's Who in Television* (Five editions). ITV Books/Michael Joseph, 1980 through 1990.

GIFFORD, Denis. *The Golden Age of Radio*. B.T. Batsford, 1985.

HALLIWELL, Leslie. *Double Take and Fade Away*. Grafton, 1987.

HERBERT, Ian (and others, eds). *Who's Who in the Theatre* (17 editions). Pitman Publishing, various dates: 1929 through 1984.

HULBERT, Jack. *The Little Woman's Always Right*. W.H. Allen, 1975.

JONES, Ken D., MCCLURE, Arthur F. and TWOMEY, Alfred E. *Character People*. Citadel Press, 1976.

JONES, Ken D., MCCLURE, Arthur F. and TWOMEY, Alfred E. *More Character People*. Citadel Press, 1985.

BROOKER, John. *Movie Memories*. Patrick Stephens, 1982.

KATZ, Ephraim. *The International Film Encyclopedia*. Macmillan, 1980.

LAMPARSKI, Richard. *Whatever Became Of?...* (11 volumes). Crown Publishing, various dates, 1967 through 1989.

LOW, Rachael. *Film Making in 1930s Britain*. George Allen and Unwin, 1985.

MALTIN, Leonard. *The Great Movie Comedians*. 1975.

MALTIN, Leonard. *The Great Movie Shorts*. Bonanza Books, 1972.

MALTIN, Leonard. *Movie Comedy Teams*. Signet, 1970.

MALTIN, Leonard, (and others). *The Real Stars*. Two volumes, Signet Books, 1969 and 1972.

MONACO, James (and others). *The Encyclopedia of Film*. Baseline, 1991.

PARISH, James Robert. *The Slapstick Queens*. Arlington House, 1972.

PARISH, James Robert. *The Funsters*. Arlington House, 1979.

PARISH, James Robert, and BOWERS, Ronald L. *The MGM Stock Company*. Ian Allan, 1973.

ROBINSON, David. *The Great Funnies*. Studio Vista, 1969.

SHIPMAN, David. *The Great Movie Stars: the Golden Years*. Angus and Robertson, 1970, 1979.

SHIPMAN, David. *The Great Movie Stars: the International Years*. Angus and Robertson, 1972, 1980, 1989.

SHIPMAN, David. *The Great Movie Stars: the Independent Years*. Macdonald, 1991.

YOUNG, Jordan R. *Reel Characters*. Moonstone Press, 1986.

(Overleaf) Beaming for the camera before they started *Great Guns*, their first film away from the Hal Roach studio, Laurel and Hardy would soon be at odds with their new masters